THE EASTERN MYSTERIES

THE SECRET POWER OF THE EAST

From the time the first major trade routes were established and explorers returned with an array of wonderful goods and stories of amazing sights, the Western seeker has been drawn to the mysteries of the ancient Eastern civilizations. However, the vast differences between the two systems of thought—and particularly the differences in the form and import of the languages—has put a nearly insurmountable barrier in the way.

That is, until the publication of *The Eastern Mysteries*. In this comprehensive yet very accessible work, the magickal basis behind each of the major Eastern alphabets, number systems, and esoteric symbolisms is laid bare. Inside, you will find the occult keys to:

- Cuneiform
- Hebrew
- Arabic
- Sanskrit
- Tibetan
- Chinese

Although each section is self-contained and can be read as a separate work, each secret tradition parallels the rest. A complete index and annotated bibliography round out this essential guide to understanding the real power of magickal language.

About the Author

David Allen Hulse was born in the capital of America's 31st state when Sol was in the Rainbow, at 9:45 P.M. on the 346th day of the Old Year in Anno 44 of the New Year. From an early age, he diligently studied the alphabets of the ancient world. As a child, David possessed a great affinity for the alphabets of Egypt, Phoenicia, and Greece.

In college, a reading of MacGregor Mathers' *Kabbalah Unveiled* opened up the Hebrew alphabet-number technique of Qabalistic research. After Hebrew, many other ancient languages were decoded and studied, including Sanskrit and Tibetan. In 1979, a discovery led to the need to capture the extent of all prior Qabalistic research into one great reference work. Research is still being carried out to discover new definitions for the number series as well as new magickal systems.

To Write to the Author

If you wish to contact the author or would like more information about this book, please write to the author in care of Llewellyn Worldwide and we will forward your request. Both the author and publisher appreciate hearing from you and learning of your enjoyment of this book and how it has helped you. Llewellyn Worldwide cannot guarantee that every letter written to the author can be answered, but all will be forwarded. Please write to:

David Allen Hulse
c/o Llewellyn Worldwide
P.O. Box 64383, Dept. K429–4
St. Paul, MN 55164-0383, U.S.A.

Please enclose a self-addressed, stamped envelope for reply, or $1.00 to cover costs.
If outside U.S.A., enclose international postal reply coupon.

DAVID ALLEN HULSE

THE EASTERN MYSTERIES

AN ENCYCLOPEDIC GUIDE TO THE SACRED LANGUAGES & MAGICKAL SYSTEMS OF THE WORLD: THE KEY OF IT ALL, BOOK I

2004
LLEWELLYN PUBLICATIONS
ST. PAUL, MINNESOTA 55164-0383, U.S.A

Second Edition, 2000
Second printing, 2004
(Previously titled *The Key of It All—Book I: The Eastern Mysteries*)

Cover design: Anne Marie Garrison
Editing, design, and layout: David Godwin
Editing for second edition: Matthew Segaard

Library of Congress Cataloging-in-Publication Data

Hulse, David Allen, 1948-
    The key of it all: an encyclopedic guide to the sacred languages & magickal systems of
the world / David Allen Hulse. -- 2nd ed.
        p. cm. -- (Llewellyn's sourcebook series)
    Includes bibliographical references and index.
    Contents: -- bk. 1. The eastern mysteries.
ISBN 1-56718–428-6
    1. Magic 2. Symbolism of numbers. 3. Alphabet--Miscellanea. 4. Language and
languages--Miscellanea. 5. Divination. I. Title. II. Series

BF1623.P9 H85 2000
133.3'3--dc21

                                                                99-04518

Llewellyn Publications
A Division of Llewellyn Worldwide, Ltd.
P.O. Box 64383, St. Paul, MN 55164-0383
www.llewellyn.com

DEDICATED TO

my
secret guide

the Moon
Goddess
whose name
numbers
to
480

M[80]	t	l	a	G[20]	l	r
a	u	o	m	o	i	d
h	T[62]	o	d	n	n	l
a	t	a	h	i	a	a
n	n	t	z	m	d	n
e	o	r	a	r	o	n
P[12]	i	p	a	d	a	n
M[73]	a	n	o	n	a	p
T[34]	s	c	a	c	r	i
V[32]	c	m	o	a	z	C[61]
O[1]	o	t	c	o	l	r
C[29]	o	u	D[91]	a	i	p
T[60]	C[46]	t	n	h	s	a

The 13 Enochian Angels Which Correspond to the 13 Magickal Languages and Their Provinces in the Angelic World

KEY TO THE THIRTEEN ENOCHIAN ANGELS WHICH CORRESPOND TO THE THIRTEEN MAGICKAL LANGUAGES AND THEIR PROVINCES IN THE ANGELIC WORLDS

The previous page contains a magick square of 7 x 13 Enochian letters. These 91 letters compose 13 seven-letter names for 13 selected angelic Governors of this world. These 13 Governors rule over the 13 countries described in the 13 keys of this two-volume work.

The angelic names should be read starting with the upper left corner of the rectangle, starting with M^{80}. The successive letters should be read on a diagonal line starting at the left and moving diagonally to the top of the rectangle.

Thus the first angelic name is *Mathula,* generated from the following squares:

M^{80}	t	l
a	u	
h		
a		

Each of the 13 capital letters in this rectangle corresponds with the first letter of one of the 13 angelic names. The number at the upper right corner of the letter refers to the order of the angelic Governor name.

The 13 angelic Governors, their seals, numbers, countries, and corresponding keys in this book are given on the facing page.

Key for the Thirteen Enochian Angels

Divine Name	Sigil	Order	Country Governed	Corresponding Key
				Book One:
Mathula		80	Babylon	1. Cuneiform
Toantom		62	Phenices (Phœnicia)	2. Hebrew
Genadol		20	Arabia	3. Arabic
Pothnir		12	India	4. Sanskrit
Mirzind		73	Serici Populi (Tibet)	5. Tibetan
Tapamal		34	Onigap (China/ Japan)	6. Chinese
				Book Two:
Vsnarda		32	Græcia (Greece)	7. Greek
Occodon		1	Ægyptus (Egypt)	8. Coptic
Comanan		29	Germania (Germany)	9. Runes
Totocan		60	Italia (Italy)	10. Latin
Cucarpt		46	Sauromatica (Poland)	11. Enochian
Dozinal		91	Mauritania (Morocco)	12. Tarot
Chirspa		61	Brytania (Great Britain)	13. English

All of the above attributes are drawn from John Dee's Enochian table, *The Book of Earthly Knowledge, Aid, and Victory.*

ACKNOWLEDGEMENTS

I would like to thank the following people for their help, support, and feedback over the last twenty-five years during the creation of this work: Gene Black, Bill Caruthers, Greg DiRicco, Grace, Bill Heidrick, Bari Kennedy, Denise King, John Mitchell, Barbara Naiditch, Hans Nintzel, Courtney Page, Lee Page, Israel Regardie, Karen Ronning, Patricia Ryan, Linda Sandidge, Gene Shusko, Carlos Suares, Bob Ward, Tom White, Bob Wright. Special thanks to my parents David and Bernyce and my brother Thomas; the staff of Beers Book Center; Carl, Nancy, and David of Llewellyn Publications; Chuck, Lee, and Allison of LeVel Press; Joe Metz, Liz Osborne, Lyle Giffin, Nancy Doran, and Christine Pavalasky, my inner core Tarot students; and to all my lovers, friends, students, and teachers who have helped me throughout my life work.

MAGICK

The spelling of the word "magic" as "magick" throughout *The Key of It All*, is in accordance with the variant spelling first adopted in the writings of Aleister Crowley. Crowley used the term *magick* to distinguish the tradition of Western ritual magick from the stage magic of illusion popularized by Harry Houdini.

The term "magick" is used throughout this book to denote the Western magickal tradition, which includes Hermetic, Alchemical, and Qabalistic dogma and ritual. It is also used to denote the parallel tradition of magick found in the East.

GENDER

The alphabet number traditions presented in this book came about in the patriarchal age (magickally referred to as the Aeon of Osiris). Therefore, many cosmological schemes use the gender-specific term "Man" to denote humanity, male and female. No effort has been made to mask or modify this identification. Rather, every attempt has been made to preserve the original meanings of every ancient alphabet symbol set decoded in *The Key of It All*.

Table of Contents

List of Tables

Key 6—Chinese (cont'd.)

Key 6—Chinese (cont'd.)

Magickal Figures

Introduction

*"When God called the world into existence,
he worked as a mathematician."*

"Numbers contain the secret of all things."

"Number rules everything; it is a weaving, living essence."

—Teachings attributed to Pythagoras

Prologue

To the mind of the ancient world, the universe came into being through the even-measured compass and square held in the hands of God, the Grand Architect of the Universe. In the secret teachings of the Greek mathematician-philosopher Pythagoras, the pattern behind the universe could be apprehended only through the agency of number. For the concept of number was seen as one step closer to God than the concept of word, as the formula:

GOD
|
Thought (Idea) of GOD
|
Expressed as NUMBER
|
Revealed as WORD

Yet to the ancient world view, number and word were intimately commingled. For every word was identified as a specific number, by the letters which compose that word. By imparting a number value to every word, the words composing a religious chant, magickal invocation, or epic poem would each possess its own number value. When combined as phrases, sentences, and verses these words would generate a higher number equal to the sum of their individual values.

Therefore, to the ancient mind, in order to get to the root essence of any word, that word must first be reduced to its essential number value. Thus number was concealed in every word, just as number is closer to the mind of God than word. The system which the Greeks used to ascribe a number value to their language was possibly derived from the Phoenician-Semitic languages, which also possess number value. In this ancient mathematical-philosophical system:

- Every letter of the alphabet is given a unique number value.
- These number values grade the letters of the alphabet in three ranges of
  a. 1–10
  b. 10–100
  c. 100–1000.
- Since every letter of the alphabet is a number, any word is equal to the sum of the number values of its component letters.
- Just as every word can be given a number value, so can every phrase, verse, sentence, page, or complete text.
- This is accomplished by adding together the number values of every word.

Therefore a hierarchy of number-word metaphors build in meaning as:

Number
|
Letter
|
Word
|
Phrase
|
Verse
|
Paragraph
|
Page
|
Chapter
|
Text

Now by equating word to number, the cold, sterile range of infinite numbers, which by their very abstractness are remote in meaning, become infused with poetical-magickal meanings. For every number is defined in character, meaning, and dimension by all words and phrases which fall to that specific number value. The most popular term for this philosophical art is *Gematria*, a term lettered in Hebrew but based phonetically on Greek. *Gematria*, is a play upon *Geometria* and *Grammametria*. For as

Geometry is the measurement *(metria)* of the earth *(geo)*, Gematria is the measurement *(metria)* of the letters of the alphabet *(gramma)*. However, Gematria is a term specifically coined within the Jewish Qabalistic school of number philosophy. For the Greek number philosophers, the term to describe this numbering of words is "Isopsephic." This little-known technical term is defined in the *Oxford English Dictionary* as "of equal numerical value, said of words in which the numerical values of the letters (according to the ancient Greek notation) made up the same amount." "Isopsephic verses" are two words (or phrases) which equal the same number. This equality between two different words or phrases is referred to as an "isopsephic relation," while the use of words as numbers can be seen as an "isopsephism."

An example of this Greek method of isopsephism is the well known linking of the two Greek terms of "Love" and "Will" by the 20th century magician and Qabalist, Aleister Crowley. These two terms of "Love" and "Will" in Greek are *Agape* (ἀγάπη) and *Thelema* (θέλημα). By the ancient number values ascribed to Greek, the numbering of each term is as follows:

ἀγάπη = α + γ + α + π + η = 1 + 3 + 1 + 80 + 8 = 93

θέλημα = θ + ε + λ + η + μ + α = 9 + 5 + 30 + 8 + 40 + 1 = 93

Thus the isopsephic relation

ἀγάπη = 93 = θέλημα

Love, Love Feast, Celebration = 93 = Magickal Will, Intention, Enchantment

By this process two basic metaphors are established:

1. That Love and Will, as 93, are equal to each other, and

2. That the number 93 can now be defined as two known concepts valued at 93: Love and Will.

Now, the term "isopsephic" conceals the actual method which the ancient Greeks first used to calculate the number value of any given word. For isopsephic in the original Greek is written ἰσόψηφος, which can be defined as

ισο (equal)
and
ψηφος (pebble, counter)

One of the first calculators invented by the ancients was the use of pebbles as counters. In the term "isopsephic," words of equal number value are equated to two piles of pebbles, composed of equal numbers of counters. In order to calculate the number value of any word, pebbles were counted out, letter by letter, to form one pile of counters. This pile was then tallied to obtain the grand total for the word. In order to prove that one word was the same number value as another, the pile of stones for the first word would be recounted in light of the letters of the second name. If the second count matched the first (i.e., there were no stones remaining, and no additional stones needed to count the second word) then the two words were deemed to be of equal value.

You may want to experiment with this method in order to appreciate this ancient Greek method of alphabet computation. In essence, this is a proto-form of our own alphanumeric computers. You will need a pile of pebbles or counters (for the example below, around 100) and the values of the Greek alphabet according to the Pythagorean number tradition (found in the seventh key of this work, in Book Two). For our example let's use the Greek terms of Love and Will.

GREEK ISOPSEPHIC ALPHANUMERIC PEBBLE CALCULATOR

First count out the letters for the word Love, ἀγάπη:

Five piles of pebbles would first be counted out, one for each letter.

The first pile, equaling α, would contain 1 pebble.

The second pile, equaling γ, would contain 3 pebbles.

The third pile, equaling α, would contain 1 pebble.

The fourth pile, equaling π, would contain 80 pebbles.

The fifth pile, equaling η, would contain 8 pebbles.

After forming these five separate piles, combine them all into one pile, and count out all the pebbles. The resultant number should be 93. Now to demonstrate that the word Will, θέλημα, also equals 93, take the existing pile of stones (for the word ἀγάπη) and count the pebbles as the individual letters of θέλημα:

Six piles of pebbles would next be counted out, one for each letter.

The first pile, equaling θ, would contain 9 pebbles.

The second pile, equaling ε, would contain 5 pebbles.

The third pile, equaling λ, would contain 30 pebbles.

The fourth pile, equaling η, would contain 8 pebbles.

The fifth pile, equaling μ, would contain 40 pebbles.

The sixth pile, equaling α, would contain 1 pebble.

If done correctly, every pebble used to count ἀγάπη would be used in the counting of the word θέλημα, leaving no missing or extra counters.

This method can be applied to Hebrew (as well as any other addition-based language). That this method is so laborious may be the reason for the invention of the Qabalistic rule *Colel*. By the rule of Colel, any word can be equal to any other word by plus or minus one. Therefore a word valued at 887 is equal to 886 and 888 as well. This may have come about to justify that two words were really equal if, after counting out two stone piles, one fell short of the other by one pebble.

In order to calculate the number of many Greek words, the counters required would number beyond a thousand. For instance, in order to calculate the number value of the three-lettered word for light, φῶς, no less than 1,500 counters would be required. For φῶς is composed of the three values of 500, 800, and 200, which would require three piles of stones counted out as 500, 800, and 200 and then recombined into one great pile of 1,500 counters.

My own research into the number has revealed at least nine key Greek phrases or words valued at 1,500. In order to prove that these nine verses were each equal to Light (φῶς), the pile of 1,500 counters would have to be recounted as follows:

Isopsephic Calculation of Light

Pebbles	Word	Meaning
500+800+200	φῶς	Light, luminary; the Light of Spirit
800+700	ὤψ	Eye; face, countenance
70+500+9+1+30+40+800+50	ὀφθαλμων	The eyes
300+400+500+30+70+200	τυφλός	Blindness
(300+8) + (200+20+70+300+10+1) + (80+5+100+10+80+1+300+5+10)	τῇ σκοτία περιπᾰτέι	to walk in darkness
(40+5+100+70+200) + (300+10) + (200+20+70+300+5+10+50+70+50)	μέρος τι σκοτεινόν	dark part (darkness)
(7+8+300+5+10) + (5+80+10+40+5+30+800+200)	ζήτει ἐπιμέλως	search carefully
4+400+50+1+40+5+800+200	δυναμεως	Power, source of power
(20+1+9+1+100+200+10+200) + (20+1+10) + (300+5+30+5+10+70+300+8+200)	κᾰθάρσις καί τελειότης	Purification and perfection

The manipulation of 1,500 counters to prove the above isopsephic relations would take well over an hour because of the high number values of certain Greek letters. As pointed out before, the values assigned to the Greek alphabet span the triple range of 1–10, 10–100, and 100–1,000. Possibly at one point of development, the counters for this isopsephic calculator were made into three different shapes, sizes, or colors to denote the values of 1, 10, and 100.

This method of calculation is also a perfect example to reveal the way the ancient mind perceived number, for the true esoteric meaning for any number was always determined by the words or phrases which equaled that specific number. Thus the ancient Greek number philosopher would immediately associate to 1,500 the major concept of Light. Then to further flesh out the esoteric meaning for the number, the association of both the eyes and the face would be added to that of light. Here immediately the vivid image of light entering or extending from the eyes of the face is conjured and would be the mnemonic image which the ancient mind would associate with the number 1,500. Moreover, this definition for 1,500 is further refined by the continual references to blindness, or darkness, and the process of searching or seeking the light through darkness, which leads to purification, perfection, and the source of all power.

What a marvelous, complex poem which would be continually rediscovered by the rearrangement of the philosopher's pebble counters! And this poetical numerical calculation was accomplished for every conceivable number, limited only by the words, phrases, or verses which fell to each number.

This esoteric language which associates word to number, and number to word, has been given many names, such as the Angelic Language, the Language of the Gods, the Divine Language, and the Magickal Language. The term which I have chosen to use throughout this book is the Magickal Language. The logic of this magickal language, which is an artificial hybrid of many ancient languages, can be summed up in nine basic statements:

What Is the Magickal Language?

1. It is the assumption that language evolved in a multidimensional manner on both a numerical basis and a phonetic basis.

2. That every number possesses a nature and character which is distinct and unique from every other number and is infinite unto itself in nuance and meaning.

3. Yet in their numerical interrelationships, each individual number develops a further set of characteristics and correspondences which is brought out and reinforced by every individual number's position in the infinite range of numbers.

4. That the very letters of the alphabet of every esoteric language are numbers in themselves imbuing a sense of beauty and poetry into motion, number, and measure.

5. That every letter, word, phrase, verse, sentence, paragraph, chapter, even every book, contains a precise number described by the numerical values of the original language in which the words appear.

6. That every language, in its original format in accordance with the correct esoteric numeration of its alphabet, generates a set of poetic metaphors for the range of the number series zero to infinity, which is consistent, correct, and ever expanding in content and meaning.

7. That the essence of the numerical metaphors for all languages must be combined to completely flesh out and clearly define the number series.

8. In this sense no language leads or is the primary metaphor for the language of numbers, but each in its own unique alphabet, grammar, and numeration bestows a special set of definitions for certain numbers in the infinite number series which are sympathetic to that specific language.

9. So that all languages of the world from all previous times unite at the ever-present moment as one gargantuan poetic series of word images, for every number conceivable to the mind of Man.

Scope of This Book

This text is a primer, or grammar, describing the esoteric traditions for 13 distinct languages—six languages in the current volume and seven in Book Two. These secret teachings ascribe a magickal character to the letters of each sacred alphabet. The alphabet letters are seen as:

- Number values

- Hieroglyphic characters by their own unique shapes

- A cosmological division of the universe (such as the elements, planets, or zodiac)

- A set of correspondences which parallels each particular alphabet letter to such diverse sets of meanings as the parts of the human body, the colors of the rainbow, musical notes of the scale, or the divisions of time.

This book attempts to chart out every surviving system of correspondences for every sacred alphabet, whose letters are correlated to numbers (which determine the number value of any given word). This book is the first volume of a three-volume series. As the first two books lay out the rules for numbering 13 separate esoteric languages, the third volume will be a dictionary detailing the key word metaphors for the number series, as generated from the languages described in the first two volumes.

This number dictionary of magickal languages is a reconstruction of a fabled text described in the original Rosicrucian manifesto of the 17th century. The Rosicrucian movement was a Qabalistic-magickal system which united an esoteric Christian mysticism with the exotic, esoteric schools of the East (especially that of the Hebrew Qabalah). In the founding document of this secret European brotherhood, a certain cryptic dictionary or thesaurus is referred to in the following quotes from *The Fame and Confession of the Fraternity of R.C., commonly of the Rosie Cross:*

> After this manner began the Fraternity of the Rosie Cross; first by
> four persons only, and by them was made the Magickal Language
> and writing, with a large Dictionary, which we yet daily use to

> God's praise and glory, and do find great wisdom therein ...
> For as this is the whole sum and content of our Rule, That every Letter or Character which is in the World ought to be learned and regarded well ...
>
> From the which Characters or Letters we have borrowed our Magick writing, and have found out, and made a new Language for ourselves, in the which with all is expressed and declared the Nature of all Things.

These quotes confirm the following:

- That the knowledge of this order was based on a large dictionary cataloging the Magickal Language (by the respective numerical values of the component sacred languages),

- That this Magickal Language was based on every letter or character of every sacred language of the world, and

- That the hybrid combination of every sacred language, reduced to its number metaphors, engendered a completely new language which intimately connected word metaphors with number values.

It has been my driving ambition for the last 20 years to reconstruct this dictionary by recreating this synthetic Magickal Language. This introductory book, *The Key of It All*, has distilled the results of my research into a series of interrelated tables, illustrations, and commentaries detailing every symbolic nuance of each of these sacred languages. Armed with the information provided in this book, you will be able to explore firsthand any of the esoteric number languages, even though you may have had no previous exposure to the language.

The Key of It All relies heavily upon the late 19th- and early 20th-century Western occult tradition. The writings of key figures in this occult revival have been fully incorporated into the body of this book.

There are four major personalities which have served as my most reliable guideposts into this unchartered territory of the Magickal Language:

Madame Helena Petrovna Blavatsky. This one writer is responsible for the bridging of Eastern mysticism and Western occultism. Blavatsky was instrumental in the foundation of the Theosophical Society in 1875. The formation of an Esoteric Section (or School) of Theosophy was intimately connected with another influential force of the 19th century, the Hermetic Order of the Golden Dawn.

Blavatsky wrote many volumes on every conceivable subject of Eastern and Western occultism. The term "occult" as we know it today is, by and large, a product of Theosophy. Terms such as "karma," "yoga," and "swami" (or master, mahatma) first gained popularity in the West through Theosophical literature. As such, any student of occultism should thoroughly study the body of Theosophical literature to understand the roots of modern occultism.

Unfortunately, Blavatsky's writing style is very difficult for today's average reader. Don't let that stop you from persevering through at least the two hallmarks of her writings, *Isis Unveiled* (1879) and *The Secret Doctrine* (1889). For a complete understanding of the Theosophical system, you should obtain *The Collected Writings of H. P. Blavatsky* (which spans 14 volumes and covers the period 1874–1891).

S. L. MacGregor Mathers. If there is one genius responsible for the creation of the 19th-century Qabalistic-Masonic tradition known as the Golden Dawn, it must be S. L. MacGregor Mathers. Mathers, by his own forceful personality and trained will, dedicated countless years in the stacks of the British Museum and other European libraries, synthesizing the essential symbolic correspondences for the tradition of Western ritual magick.

I have in my possession a copy of Mathers' 14th volume of notes on magickal alphabets (both Eastern and Western). This volume alone contains hundreds of beautifully executed tables in his own hand, betraying a deep regime of self-initiated study with which many modern Golden Dawn scholars do not credit him. I have exclusively used Mathers' own secret correspondences for the Hebrew alphabet in all of the tables appearing in this book which utilize Western Qabalistic symbolism.

Unique to this text are two proofs I have devised to demonstrate that Mathers alone created the essential Golden Dawn system of magickal correspondences:

- In the 11th chapter of this book (in Book Two), on Enochian, there is a detailed analysis of Mathers' scheme of connecting Enochian to Hebrew via geomantic astrology.

- In the 12th chapter of this book, on the Tarot, there is a detailed analysis of how Mathers rediscovered the secret Qabalistic order for the Tarot.

Any student of modern magick should own *The Golden Dawn* by Israel Regardie (Llewellyn Publications, 1970) and *The Kabbalah Unveiled* by MacGregor Mathers (Arkana) (which contains one of the best introductions to the Qabalistic system). In addition, the Falcon Press revision of the Golden Dawn material is a good adjunct (although the Tarot court card symbolism is in error).

Aleister (Edward) Crowley. The most important exponent of the Golden Dawn system of magick must surely be Aleister Crowley. His extensive writings on magick and mysticism clarified, extended, and supplemented the core correspondences found in the Golden Dawn system.

Crowley's accomplishments in light of the Golden Dawn system include:

- The first publication of Mathers' esoteric Tarot correspondences (in *Liber 777*)

- The extension of Eastern correspondences for the Golden Dawn into Chinese mysticism by linking the Taoist I Ching with the Qabalistic Tree of Life (in *Liber 777* and *The Book of Thoth*)

- The creation of one of the most influential modern Tarot decks based on the Golden Dawn system in his *Book of Thoth*

- The extensive, exhaustive research into the esoteric meanings of numbers by the art of Hebraic, Greek, Coptic, and Arabic Qabalahs. Crowley realized Blavatsky's mythic Chaldaen *Book of Numbers* by publishing an extended number language dictionary known as *Sepher Sephiroth* (Hebrew for "Book of Numbers"). This is the most extensive analysis to date of any number language. It is based largely on a dictionary started by the Golden Dawn member Allan Bennett and can be seen in vol. 1, no. 8 of Crowley's *Equinox*

- The copious revised and new magickal rituals, practices, and instructions based on Golden Dawn theory as published in his monumental *Equinox* series as well as in such classics as *Magick in Theory and Practice*

- The trance reception of *The Book of The Law* in 1904, which among other things contains the key to the Golden Dawn rituals as the formula Aleph = 1 = 111 = 0 = The Fool (found in the 57th verse of the first chapter)

Paul Foster Case. Possibly the most underrated of all 20th-century Qabalistic magicians, this American genius created some of the most refined work on the teachings of the secret Western mystery schools, including Alchemy, astrology, Eastern Hatha, Kundalini, and Tantrik (right-hand) yogic practices, Greek gnostic and Pythagorean number mysticism, Masonic ritual and symbolism, Western and Eastern Qabalistic philosophy, Rosicrucian symbolism, Hermetic Tarot, Theosophical Tattva system, and sound and color coordinated for healing, attunement, and alignment.

Where the genius of Case really shines through is in his agile ability to interpret the dense language of number symbolism. His forte was the Hebrew Qabalah as interpreted through Mathers' reconstructed Qabalistic Tarot. Case was involved with the Chicago Temple of the Golden Dawn in the early 1920s. He became editor of the obscure American occult digest *Azoth,* and within this periodical can be found his first thoughts on the Tarot.

The most readily accessible book for Case's final word on the Tarot is *The Tarot: A Key to the Wisdom of the Ages* (Macoy Publishing Co., 1947). This book is still in print and presents the most pristine development of the Golden Dawn Tarot system, applying the correct mystical attributes for the Hebrew alphabet to the 22 keys of the Tarot known as the Major Arcana.

The problem with understanding Case is the inaccessibility into the heart of his own Qabalistic research. He founded a Golden Dawn-Masonic offshoot in the 1930s known as the order of the Builders of the Adytum (B.O.T.A.). Most of his writings can only be obtained as correspondence lessons, and the prevailing attitude within the present organization is a departure from the rigid study demanded in Case's original writings. In light of today's revived interest in the Hermetic tradition, all of Case's original writings should be made available in print to the general public, before they are lost to time.

Beyond these four major players, my research has been greatly influenced by the following lesser writers:

W. Wynn Westcott, cofounder of the Golden Dawn. All of his Hermetic studies are worth studying. Westcott possessed a deep knowledge of both the Hebrew Qabalah in general and specifically the Qabalistic art of Gematria. His own research was combined with that of Mathers to form the majority of practices referred to as the Golden Dawn system of magick. Westcott's interest in the ancient Indian version of chess, Chatarangi, must have led to the suggestion of creating a Rosicrucian form using the Enochian cosmology.

Manly P. Hall must be paired with Case as an unsung American genius of the early 20th-century occult movement. The one monumental work worth owning from Hall is *An Encyclopedia Outline of Masonic, Hermetic, Qabbalistic and Rosicrucian Symbolical Philosophy* (also known as *The Secret Teachings of All Ages*). However, this work is marred by Hall's misunderstanding of the significance of the Golden Dawn Tarot system. Hall worked with equating The Magician, rather than the The Fool, to Aleph. In this sense, he pursued the French school of Tarot symbolism. So, when approaching any of Hall's many writings, this Tarot variation should be kept in mind.

Arthur Edward Waite is one of the leading proponents of the Golden Dawn system. He has left copious published writings to posterity, documenting the many aspects of Western mysticism and magick. The single, most important work accomplished by Waite is his own published version of the Golden Dawn Tarot deck, executed by the artist Pamela Colman Smith. The Waite Tarot deck, first printed in 1910, has greatly influenced every successive Tarot deck, for Waite, in designing the 40 numbered pips of the Minor Arcana, created an innovation which has been copied by almost all successive Tarot artists (including Salvador Dali). This innovation in symbolism is the creation of a pictorial symbolic scene for each of the 40 cards of the Minor Arcana. Until Waite's time, every existing European Tarot deck designed these cards with only the emblems of Wands, Cups, Swords, and Pentacles. Occasionally, additional embellishments, such as flowers or leaves, were added to these designs. But when Waite designed his own Tarot deck he drew a symbolic picture for each of these cards, based on their divinatory meanings as recorded in the Golden Dawn document, "Book T." Since that time, almost every other Tarot designer has copied Waite's innovation, without realizing that its true source is in the symbolism of Mathers' "Book T." Crowley's Tarot is the only major deck uninfluenced by Waite's design. Case, on the other hand, in the creation of his Tarot deck, although he copied Waite's Major Arcana almost exactly, restored the Minor Arcana symbolism back to the design prevalent before Waite, which involved only the emblems of each suit. The reason Waite's method of depicting these cards is so popular is that their symbols afford the uninitiated some sense of what the cards truly represent. I have written a detailed analysis of every symbol used by Waite in his Tarot deck and their true connection back to the Golden Dawn source. I plan to incorporate this material into a much larger text on the Tarot in the near future.

Eliphas Levi was the greatest French occult writer of the 19th century. His *Dogma and Ritual of Magick* (also translated as *Transcendental Magic*) is the single most important work to show what Mathers already had at his disposal, when creating his own system of Golden Dawn magick. Other French occultists worth studying are Paul Christian, Oswald Wirth, and Papus (Gérard Encausse). Their major writings have all been recently translated into English.

Francis Barrett represents the magickal viewpoint in England at the end of the 18th century. His classic work, *The Magus*, is well worth studying to discover what was open knowledge within the English circle of occultism before the Golden Dawn came into being. Barrett's discussion of Qabalistic number symbolism, the planetary magick squares, and the hierarchy of angels and demons were cannibalized into Mathers' system without sourcing them back to Barrett.

Beyond this source material there now exist a few important historical sketches of the late 19th- and early 20th-century occult movement that anyone attempting to study this path should diligently read. Israel Regardie recommended that all beginning students of the occult undergo psychoanalysis to maintain the proper mental balance necessary for all novices. Whereas I cannot recommend this practice, I do strongly urge any student to critically read the following studies in order to better understand the historical foundations of modern magick. Certain writers have caused great consternation in many occult circles in their attempt to debunk such movements as the Golden Dawn. Don't let this prejudice your view of the material offered. I have found, in my own case, that a continual challenging of my basic assumptions in my studies has permitted me to discover new material, and new ways of approaching established material, which I would have otherwise missed. The following books can be read in any order:

Colquhoun, Ithell, *Sword of Wisdom* (G.P. Putnam Sons, 1975)

Harper, George Mills, *Yeats' Golden Dawn* (Aquarian Press, 1987)

Howe, Ellic, *The Magicians of the Golden Dawn* (Samuel Weiser, 1978)

King, Francis, *The Rites of Modern Occult Magic* (MacMillan Co., 1970)

Symonds, John, *The Lady with the Magic Eyes* (Thomas Yoseloff, 1960)

Webb, James, *The Occult Underground* and *The Occult Establishment* (Open Court 1974, 1976).

LAYOUT OF THIS BOOK

The book is divided into 13 basic chapters: six chapters (Book One) are dedicated to the Eastern tradition, six to the Western (Book Two), and one to English (seen as a bridge between East and West—also in Book Two). Each chapter is a key to a temple or house enshrining the essence of that esoteric tradition. The layout of these 13 symbolic keys is as follows:

The 13 Keys of the One Magickal Language

The Six Golden Keys of the Eastern Temple (Book One)

1st Key	Cuneiform
2nd Key	Hebrew
3rd Key	Arabic
4th Key	Sanskrit
5th Key	Tibetan
6th Key	Chinese

The Six Silver Keys of the Western Temple (Book Two)*

7th Key	Greek
8th Key	Coptic
9th Key	Runes
10th Key	Latin
11th Key	Enochian
12th Key	Tarot

The One Mercurial Key not from the East, nor from the West (also Book Two)

13th Key	English

Certain keys end with an addendum. These addenda contain the following additional information:

Book One:

- *Sepher Yetzirah* (the Jewish Qabalistic textbook on alphabet magick)
- Gurdjieff's number philosophy (both the Enneagram and the Ladder of Numbers)
- The East Indian Chakra system
- The Tattva system

---

*Forthcoming in May 1994.

Book Two:

- The Pythagorean number philosophy

- The Egyptian hieroglyphs
- The Irish Ogham and Beth-Luis-Nion alphabets

- The Renaissance cosmological model of Three Worlds

- The Golden Dawn Enochian system of correspondences

- Mathers' own method for deciphering the Tarot

Within the 13 keys themselves, other languages and traditions are also deciphered, including:

- Persian

- Georgian

- Japanese

- Chinese I Ching system

- Qabalistic Tree of Life

- Raymond Lull's philosophical machine and Latin Qabalah

- Magickal Calendar systems of Chinese 60-year cycle, Greek 168-hour planetary week cycle, Egyptian God-Form year cycle, Norse calendrical cryptography (365-day Rune cycle), and Tattvic Tide Tables (for the 24-hour day)

As stated earlier, this book serves as a primer, or foundation, for the third volume, the actual Magickal Language dictionary, which is the result of many years of research. Every code detailed in this first two volumes will be incorporated into the body of the third volume. However, the first two books are intended to give the reader every tool necessary to decipher any existing alphanumeric language. From the tables provided, a personal number dictionary can be developed by any diligent reader.

How This Book Came About

It was in 1969, while attending school in San Francisco, that I first pulled from the shelves of a library, S. L. MacGregor Mathers' *Kabbalah Unveiled*. Viewing this one work set my feet firmly upon the path of Qabalistic study. But in those beginning days of research, I never imagined that the one mysterious book containing the key to every magickal-numerical alphabet code, the book I would frantically search for in the years to come, would ultimately be written by myself.

It was in the introductory pages of Mathers' book that I first discovered the numerical correspondences for the Hebrew alphabet. Upon viewing this chart, a key opened up a deep recess hidden inside me, a lost memory of magickal correspondences between word and number. From that day on, the letters of the Hebrew alphabet would exert a special force of attraction to my inner self. I found myself consumed by hundreds of hours of studying key words and phrases in Hebrew, converting them to their proper number values, and then cataloging them in the draft of the first of my many "number" dictionaries.

As my studies with Qabalistic Hebrew developed, I began to sense that this sacred tradition of ascribing mystical, magickal, and numerical values to Hebrew extended beyond Hebrew. I began to devour every work in English I could find concerning the magickal nature of ancient alphabets, but for such Eastern sacred languages as Sanskrit, Tibetan, and Chinese, I could discover next to nothing concerning their secret numerical values. Through many years of deep, self-directed study, an inner intuitional guiding voice was cultivated which greatly accelerated the required insights necessary to uncover the hidden tradition surrounding the most recondite Eastern languages. Slowly, but surely, through clues scattered in translations of ancient texts, esoteric diagrams, and symbol sets, and by my own inner conviction that such Eastern languages possessed a numerical key not unlike Hebrew, I was able to decipher first Sanskrit, then Tibetan, and finally at the end of my research, Chinese. Thus I ultimately came to craft the magickal book I had so desperately searched for, the book containing the magickal and numerical keys to every ancient alphabet.

I have appended to this work an extensive annotated bibliography which clearly delineates all sources consulted in composing this work. However, this book is the result of both detailed "occult" archaeology and intuitional reconstructions of material which has been lost, obscured, or misunderstood. Therefore, the work is greater than the sum of its parts, for most of what is recorded here is recorded in its complete rectified form for the first time.

Many times late at night, exhausted from the day's work, a flash of intuition, couched in the right word, phrase, or sentence, would descend through my inner intuitional voice, and that which I could not solve before would now be clear. I believe that this is the same technique Mathers was able to tap into, when creating the majority of the magickal teachings of the Golden Dawn. Mathers labored for years in the stacks of the British Museum, but it was not just the material he was studying, but rather his own intuitional insight which slowly developed, that allowed him to correct, rectify, and restore the secret Western magickal tradition. In a similar vein, the work which you have before you is the result of the same combination of deep study and intuitional insight. And this work is a definite continuation of the Golden Dawn tradition established by the occult genius of S. L. Macgregor Mathers, extending the Western traditions far into the realm of the Eastern traditions.

How to Use This Book

The Key of It All is first and foremost a reference work. You will be able to return to this book again and again, each time finding new levels of meaning.It has been crafted so that the chapters themselves may be read in any given order. Because of the sheer scope and size of the work, the subject which most interests you may not occur for hundreds of pages. Therefore, when first reading this book, you may peruse the table of contents and decide which chapter most appeals to your present interests. Read that chapter first, and then progress at your leisure to any other point of the text that may interest you. I have linked every system presented to every other system. Thus, for example, in reading the Runes section in Book Two, the references to the Greek alphabet may stimulate you to read the Greek section next. However, reading the text in its established order may be the preferred approach, since the layout of the text progresses from East to West, and ancient to modern. You will also find that some of the chapters contain an addendum. This device is used so that when you return to the text at a later time, searching out a specific set of tables, they can be easily found for ready reference.

When reading, don't be intimidated by the use of foreign scripts. I have kept their use to a minimum, and after first detailing an alphabet in its original format I will always subsequently use English transliterations in place of the foreign script. However, the original alphabet script has been included in every case, so that any word encountered in its original language at a future time can be successfully deciphered and numbered with the use of the tables found in this text.

This book contains the most detailed, comprehensive material yet to appear in print concerning the occult nature of ancient alphabets. Because of its comprehensive nature, it may seem overwhelming, not only to the novice, but to the advanced reader as well. At times the text is hard going by the simple nature of the fact that it deals with the most recondite of "lost" or "secret" knowledge. However, I have tried to be as straightforward as possible, distilling as much as I could into reference tables, which can be studied again and again. To help you progress through this spiritual mountain of occult knowledge, the beginning of each chapter consists of a detailed overview of its contents. You may wish to read these overviews chapter by chapter as you proceed through the text, or you may wish to read all the overviews in turn before tackling the main body of the text.

CREATING YOUR OWN
NUMBER-LANGUAGE DICTIONARY

Every student of the Qabalah should have a set of note cards listing various terms reduced to their specific number values and filed in numerical order. Such a file is an invaluable reference tool. If you have not started one yet, with such a rich set of entries at your disposal in this book, now may be the time. All of the Hebrew key terms included in the addendum to chapter 2 (Hebrew) can be entered separately on note cards and serve as the beginnings of your own number-language dictionary file.

In fact every relevant term in its original language appearing in every chapter of this book should be entered onto a separate note card, numbered by its own intrinsic code, and added to your Qabalistic number dictionary file. The format that I have found most workable for these cards is shown below, but obviously this system can be easily adapted to various computer software filing systems as well.

Format for Number-Language Dictionary

Number Value:

Entry in Original Script:

Transliteration:

Meaning:

Additional Comments:

Language: Method of Numbering Used:

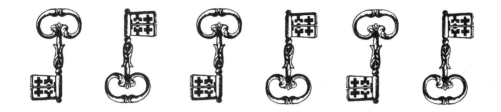

THE SIX GOLDEN KEYS OF
THE EASTERN TEMPLE

FIRST KEY

CUNEIFORM

OVERVIEW

This chapter deals with the oldest example of number value being given to the alphabetical components of a language. However, it is incomplete in that the entire language cannot be numbered, but only a portion of the words composing the language. It has been included in the text to show the source for all subsequent numerical alphabets. This is also true of both the Egyptian and Mayan alphabets, which cannot be given a number value for the complete language.

This first chapter is one of the shortest because it describes the source for the more elaborate alphanumeric values of subsequent systems. The basic composite strokes are first given. This is followed by a comparison of Sumerian, Egyptian, and Mayan numerical notations. As pointed out earlier, all three of these languages exist outside the tradition of languages which can be numbered in their entirety (such as Hebrew and Greek).

Next, the seven basic Cuneiform numerals are detailed, followed by a table showing the few extant word signs for names of gods and goddesses possessing number value.

This is followed by the Babylonian tradition of Cuneiform, which is detailed in charts showing basic number values, place values and fractions, and the four Indian Yugas (ages) as Cuneiform numbers. The Yuga chart shows the ease with which Cuneiform numerals can express high values of number (a trait we will discover in Sanskrit as well).

The section ends with two surviving historical examples of Cuneiform words used as numbers. As pointed out before, this chapter should be used for theoretical rather than practical knowledge, since Cuneiform cannot be numbered in its entirety.

3

ORIGIN

3300 BCE—Appearance of Sumerian numerals in base 60

3100 BCE—Appearance of Sumerian picture glyphs

2700 BCE—Appearance of wedge-shaped Cuneiform both as word images and numerals

2000 BCE—Assyrian-Babylonian Cuneiform both as word images and numerals

1700 BCE—Babylonian Cuneiform numerals evolve into a place value base 60 system

1500–300 BCE—Further sophistication of Babylonian place-value system with the introduction of zero as a place value.

ALPHABET CODE

Cuneiform, which first emerged in the East out of Sumer 5,000 years ago, is our first magickal language, heading the 13 keys. Yet it is not the first language whose alphabet characters are also numbers, but the prototype language that would influence the development of such an alphanumeric code.

The Sumerian language first represented word concepts as picture signs. Numbers and words were independent symbols, and historical evidence shows that the creation of number signs preceded the creation of word signs. With the emergence of Cuneiform script, these picture glyphs were transformed into abstract representations, losing their apparent hieroglyphic shapes. The tally system for numbers which was independent of the picture glyphs in earlier Sumerian was also transformed into the abstract strokes of Cuneiform. As such, word and number merged in this new script, both being created by the two basic strokes which form all Cuneiform.

The characters of Cuneiform were formed by a stylus making impressions on a clay tablet. Two essential shapes were made with this stylus: a straight line and a wedge. This straight line could be positioned vertically, horizontally, or at a 45-degree angle.

The vertical straight line and the wedge possess a number value, but the horizontal and the angled straight line (which is a composite stroke in most Cuneiform word ideograms) possess no number value. Therefore the strokes composing most words in Cuneiform cannot be equated to a number.

The isolated ideograms composed of vertical straight lines and wedges were numbers distinct from words. The vertical stroke (𒁹) symbolized the finger of the hand and represented the unit (or one), while the wedge shape (‹) symbolized two hands held in prayer and represented the number ten. These two basic shapes were combined to represent the number range of 1 through 59, while 60 initiated a new cycle and was represented by an enlarged vertical stroke (the units place).

By the position of these two basic strokes, the mathematical function of addition or multiplication occurs. If a large number is placed in front of a smaller number, addition occurs. Thus ‹⫪ represents 12 as 10 + 2. If a smaller number is placed in front of a larger number, multiplication occurs. Thus ⫪‹ represents 20 as 2 x 10.

Like Sumerian Cuneiform, the Egyptian and the Mayan hieroglyphs could not be numbered in their entirety. Only a select few signs were used for numbers. Unfortunately, neither of these two ancient languages can be seen as an isopsephic magickal language.

All three languages used a basic tally system to serve as the model for their numeral hieroglyphs. The following table will show the number series of 1 through 10 in these languages.

Hieroglyphic Tally of One Through Ten

Number	Sumerian Cuneiform	Egyptian Hieroglyphs	Mayan Hieroglyphs
1	⫪	|	•
2	⫪⫪	||	• •
3	⫪⫪⫪	|||	• • •
4	▽	||||	• • • •
5	▽	||| ||	▬
6	▽	||| |||	⎯•⎯
7	▽	|||| |||	• • over ▬
8	▽	|||| ||||	• • • over ▬
9	▽	||| ||| |||	• • • • over ▬
10	‹	∩	▬ over ▬

By 2600 BCE, Sumerian Cuneiform possessed seven basic symbols for the number series of 1, 10, 60, 60 x 10, 60^2, 60^2 x 10, 60^3. (Note that this range is base 60 multiplied by 10.)

Seven Sumerian Cuneiform Numerals

Cuneiform	Number
⟘ (the unit)	1
⟨ (ten 1s as two 5s)	10
⟘ (1 enlarged to 60)	60
⟘⟨ (60 touches 10)	60 x 10 (600)
◇ (60 is repeated four times)	60^2 (3600)
◇⟨ (square of 60 encloses 10)	60^2 x 10 (36,000)
◇⟘ (square of 60 encloses 60)	60^3 (216,000)

Cuneiform possessed a limited cryptographic code for certain God-names. In many surviving astrological and magickal Sumerian texts a select number sign would be used in lieu of a specific God-name.

Sumerian God Names

God Name	Cuneiform	Number Value
Ishtar Goddess of the Moon	⟨♛	15 (alluding to the day of the Full Moon)
Shamash The One Eyed Sun God	⟨⟨	20 (note that Kaph in Hebrew is the Sun by the *Sepher Yetzirah*, and the number 20)
Sin The Moon God	⟨⟨⟨	30 (alluding to the lunar month)
Ea The Water God	⟨⟨⟨ ⟨	40 (note that Mem in Hebrew is Water, and the number 40)
Enlil The Storm God	⟨⟨⟨ ⟨⟨	50

God Name	Cuneiform	Number Value
Anu God of the Heavens	⊤	60 (note that Anu's counterpart, Adad, The Earth is numbered both as 6 and 10, counterpoint to 60)

From these sparse surviving relics of Cuneiform number lore it can be seen as a source for the Hebrew alphabet number symbolism based in part upon astrological measurements.

The infusion of Babylonian culture into the development of Cuneiform created three further sophistications of place value, fractions, and the zero symbol.

The concept of place value in Babylonian Cuneiform numeral notation has its beginnings in 1800 BCE with a place value system in base 60, and culminates in 300 BCE with the invention of a zero symbol with place value.

As to base 60, the Babylonian notation system in its evolution combined base 60 with base 10.

The basic Babylonian numerals in base 60 are

⊤   1 = (as the basic unit)

⊤   60 = (enlarged or separated by a space)

⧣   600 = (as 10x60), or

⊤⌐   (as 100 raised to 600)

The basic Babylonian numerals in base 10 are:

⊤   1 = (1 finger)

⟨   10 = (10 fingers in two hands)

⊤⌐   100 = (1 raised 100 times)

⟨⊤⌐   1,000 = (10 x 100)

This Babylonian convergence of base 10 and base 60 was memorialized in two of King Ezra's Flame Hebrew Letters of Vav and Samekh. For *Vav* (ו) is the straight vertical stroke valued at 6 (equating 1 with 6), while *Samekh* (ס) is the full circle valued at 60, showing one complete cycle of 60 (equating 0 with 60).

As to place value, the Babylonian system was devised strictly on base 60. The place of any given Cuneiform numeral in a series of numbers determines its number value. The place value to the farthest right is always the units place, followed by 60^1, 60^2, 60^3, 60^4. The numerals for each place value were separated by spaces or double slashing lines and were always multiplied times the place value of its particular position in any given sequence of numbers:

Position of Babylonian Place Value

60^4 (12,960,000)	60^3 (216,000)	60^2 (3,600)	60^1 (60)	Units Place
X (Numeral farthest left is always the highest power of 60)	X	X	X	X (Numeral farthest right is always the units place)

The following Thelemic numbers of 93, 330, 418, 666, and 888 will illustrate the Babylonian place value notation system.

93:

$$(1 \times 60) + (33 \times 1) = 93$$

330:

$$(5 \times 60) + (30 \times 1) = 330$$

418:

$$(6 \times 60) + (58 \times 1) = 418$$

666:

$$(11 \times 60) + (6 \times 1) = 666$$

888:

⟨👑   ⟨⟨⟨⟨👑

(14 x 60) + (48 x 1) = 888

In addition to the sophistication of place value, a limited set of four symbols for fractions was added to the seven basic Cuneiform numerals. These four signs are all made with the straight stroke.

Babylonian Cuneiform Fractions

Cuneiform		Number
	1 (or 60)	2/6
𒐞	divided twice	
𒑉	1 divided in half	3/6
𒑊	4 strokes	4/6
𒑋	5 strokes	5/6

The number secret for the concept of "God" in Cuneiform is based on the symbolic use of fractions. God as

𒐊𒑉

is the number 1.5 (1 + 1/2), while the Pantheon of the Gods as

𒐊𒑉⟨

is the number 15 (1.5 x 10), ten times the fractional value of 1.5 for God.

The ultimate sophistication for the Babylonian Cuneiform numeral system is the development of zero as a place value, which occurred by 300 BCE. As early as 1500 BCE, two slanting lines (𒑊) in Babylonian numerals designated the blank spaces separating the powers of 60 in place value. By 300 BCE, these two slanting strokes became the positional zero symbol.

In addition to the place value notation in powers of base 60, the introduction of a zero symbol streamlined the use of Cuneiform as numbers. This zero symbol could occur as a terminal as well as a medial cipher.

Zero at the end of a number:

𒐊𒑊 = (1 x 60) + (0 x 1) = 60

Zero at the middle of a number:

⟨↙⟨ = (10 x 60²) + (0 x 60) + (10 x 1) = 36,010

The Hindu tradition of four cosmic ages measuring the age of Man can be easily numbered by the use of this Cuneiform cipher.

The Four Yugas (Ages)

Age	Sanskrit Name of Yuga	Length in Years	As Cuneiform Numerals	Power of 60
Gold	Dvapara	864,000	♡↙↙↙	(4 x 60³) + (0 x 60²) + (0 x 60¹) + (0 x 60⁰)
Silver	Treta	1,296,000	₩↙↙↙	(6 x 60³) + (0 x 60²) + (0 x 60¹) + (0 x 60⁰)
Bronze	Krita	1,728,000	♡↙↙↙	(8 x 60³) + (0 x 60²) + (0 x 60¹) + (0 x 60⁰)
Iron	Kali	432,000	∏↙↙↙	(2 x 60³) + (0 x 60²) + (0 x 60¹) + (0 x 60⁰)
Total Ages (Maha Yuga)		4,320,000	⟨⟨↙↙↙	(20 x 60³) + (0 x 60²) + (0 x 60¹) + (0 x 60⁰)

With the development of the Babylonian zero symbol, Hebrew, Greek, and Arabic cultures developed a similar cipher (⚊) to be combined with the alphanumeric symbols of their own languages. Before turning to Hebrew for the first example of a truly isopsephic language in which every word concept can be numbered, two historical examples from the 7th century BCE of symbolic meaning imbued into Cuneiform numerals should be examined.

The first example is an inscription on the wall surrounding the fortress of King Sargon II in Khorsabad, Iraq. This inscription states that the wall has been built to correspond to the number value of the name, King Sargon II. That number value is 16,280; the exact measure of the wall of 16,280 cubits. The numeral notation for the cubit measure is not in the sophisticated base 60 positional, or base 10, but rather in older Babylonian numerals which must be added together (in base 60). The symbolic numeral name for King Sargon II is as follows:

◇ ◇ ◇ ◇ 𝕂 𝕂 𝕂 𝕀 𝕞 ∏
(3600 + 3600 + 3600 + 3600) + (600 + 600 + 600) + (60) + (3 x 6) + (2)
(14,400 cubits) + (1,800 cubits) + (60 cubits) + (18 cubits) + (2 cubits)

The second historical example from this same period demonstrates how politics, mythology, and numerology can converge to explain a significant historical event. In 689 BCE, Sennacherib conquered Babylon. Through oracle, the God Marduk decreed to the Babylonians that Babylon should remain desolate for 70 years, which would be notated as 60 + 10 (𝕀⟨).

But after 11 years of desolation, Sennacherib's son initiated Babylon's restoration. Through oracle again, the God Marduk allowed his numerical omen to become reversed, and 70, as 60 + 10 (𒐕𒌋), became 11, as 10 + 1 (𒌋𒐕), the wedge replacing the vertical stroke.

THE TOWER OF BABEL

One last historical example of Babylonian number symbolism is the Tower of Babel. The true Tower of Babel is the ziggurat at Borsippa dedicated to the god Nebo (Mercury). This step pyramid was composed of seven levels of differently colored bricks, each level dedicated to one of the seven planetary divinities, each divinity having a corresponding Cuneiform numeral-name. The following table shows these attributes.

Tower of Babel Planetary Numeral Names

Ziggurat Level	Color	Planet	God Name	Cuneiform Numeral	Number Value
7th (top)	Silver plated	Moon	Sin	𒌍	30
6th	Azure glazed	Mercury	Nebo	𒌋𒐕𒐕	12
5th	Pale yellow	Venus	Ishtar	𒌋𒐚	15
4th	Gold plated	Sun	Shammash	𒌋𒌋	20
3rd	Red clay	Mars	Nergal	𒐚	8
2nd	Burnt orange	Jupiter	Marduk	𒌋	10
1st (base)	Bitumen black	Saturn	Adar	𒐉	4

The Cuneiform planetary numeral names contain certain number harmonies: Saturn + Mars = 12 = Mercury; Mars + Mercury = 20 = Sun; Jupiter + Sun = 30 = Moon; Saturn + Jupiter + Mars + Sun = 42 = Mercury + Moon; Saturn (4) is one-half of Mars (8); Jupiter (10) is one-half of the Sun (20); Venus (15) is one-half of the Moon (30). All seven numeral names total to 99, bringing to mind the 99 Arabic names of God as well as the number value of the Greek term, *amen* (ἀμήν, A = 1 + M = 40 + H = 8 + N = 50).

The height of the tower was 156 feet, which included 3 feet (platform base) + 26 feet (first level) + 26 feet (second level) + 26 feet (third level) + 15 feet (fourth level) + 15 feet (fifth level) + 15 feet (sixth level) + 15 feet (seventh level) + 15 feet (shrine at top). This is significant in that Aleister Crowley's own reconstruction of the name "Babylon" in Hebrew also totals to 156: BABALON (באבאלען) = 156 = (B = 2 + A = 1 + B = 2 + A = 1 + L = 30 +O = 70 + N = 50).

However, as intricate as Cuneiform became in developing a poetical-oracular vocabulary for number, it is the Sinai Semites of 1700 BCE who created the all-encompassing number language. By combining the phonetic sounds of Sumerian Cuneiform, with 22 select Egyptian Hieroglyphs, in a base 10 numeration of their own invention, the angelic numerical alphabet of the Hebrew Qabalah was brought down to the world of Man.

SECOND KEY

HEBREW

OVERVIEW

This is the second largest chapter in the text (Chinese being the largest). Although the basic number values ascribed to Hebrew have already been detailed in many other texts, I have found that the secret alphabet tradition for Hebrew requires much clarification and rectification. The language which started my work ended up requiring the most clarification in light of the variety of texts already available to the student. Whether you possess a basic or an advanced knowledge of Hebrew Qabalistic symbolism, you will find that the abundance of new information available in this chapter is well worth the effort necessary to read and understand its contents.

I can recommend no better overview to the magickal and mystical aspect of Hebrew than this chapter, for every element of both the historic and modern Qabalah is clearly tabled out for easy reference. This chapter should also be read in conjunction with chapter 12, the Tarot, because the commentary on the Tarot is based on the symbolism of the Hebrew Qabalah. Also, the Eastern traditions of the chakra system, the Tattvas, and the Chinese elemental and I Ching systems are all directly connected back to the Hebrew alphabet system. In essence, almost every chapter is related back to the basic Qabalistic symbolism of the Hebrew alphabet.

Upon being initiated into the Hermetic Order of the Golden Dawn, Aleister Crowley was surprised to find that the only secrets entrusted to him were the occult order and virtues of the Hebrew alphabet. And yet these simple secrets are the most profound and important set of correspondences to be found in the whole history of alphabet magick. In essence, what was imparted to Crowley, in the context of the basic Golden Dawn magickal curriculum, was the allocation of each letter of the Hebrew alphabet to a number value, an astrological characteristic, and a Tarot card. These correspondences are as shown in the below table.

Key Golden Dawn Hebrew Correspondences
(Yetziratic Attributes)

Alphabet		Number Value	Astrological Nature	Tarot Key
א	A	1	Air (Spirit)	0—The Fool
ב	B	2	Mercury	I—The Magician
ג	G	3	Moon	II—The High Priestess
ד	D	4	Venus	III—The Empress
ה	H	5	Aries	IV—The Emperor
ו	V	6	Taurus	V—The Hierophant
ז	Z	7	Gemini	VI—The Lovers
ח	Ch	8	Cancer	VII—The Chariot
ט	T	9	Leo	VIII—Strength
י	I	10	Virgo	IX—The Hermit
כ	K	20	Jupiter	X—The Wheel of Fortune
ל	L	30	Libra	XI—Justice
מ	M	40	Water	XII—The Hanged Man
נ	N	50	Scorpio	XIII—Death
ס	S	60	Sagittarius	XIV—Temperance
ע	O	70	Capricorn	XV—The Devil
פ	P	80	Mars	XVI—The Tower
צ	Tz	90	Aquarius	XVII—The Star
ק	Q	100	Pisces	XVIII—The Moon
ר	R	200	Sun	XIX—The Sun
ש	Sh	300	Fire (Spirit)	XX—Judgement
ת	Th	400	Saturn (Earth)	XXI—The World

Crowley would work with these basic building blocks for the rest of his life. The complete contents of *The Equinox*, the symbolism of *The Book of the Law*, the tables comprising *777*, the formulas described in *Magick*, the very Tarot cards of the Book of Thoth, all depend upon the simple Hebrew correspondences in the table. This can be said as well for all the dogma and rituals of the Golden Dawn.

The Hebrew section begins with a description of the technical term "gematria," followed by a description of the basic Qabalistic methods for analyzing the Hebrew alphabet. This is followed by a very detailed discussion of the essential attributes of the Hebrew alphabet laid out in narrative, tables, and examples.

The first table shows the basic Hebrew alphabet number code. Next the hieroglyphic meanings for each of the 22 letters of the Hebrew alphabet are given. This is followed by the basic astrological characteristics of Hebrew (derived from *The Book of Formation*). Lastly, the most detailed, to date, listing of every number value assigned to each letter of the Hebrew alphabet is given in no less than 19 separate sets of number values.

The text then details the origin and symbolism of the Qabalistic Tree of Life. First a basic timeline establishes the evolution of this key Western mandala from 1500 BCE. to 1909 CE. Then two prototype systems of the Tree of Life are given, the Binary Qabalah and the Tree of Four Directions. The detailing of these two systems can only be found in this work, as they are a result of my own original analysis of the Qabalistic text, *The Zohar*.

The Binary Qabalah is the basic division of the Tree of Life into Right and Left, Above and Below, and Front and Behind, where two basic correspondences are brought out:

ZOHARIC BINARY CORRESPONDENCES

Right = Above = Front = Positive = 1
Left = Below = Behind = Negative = 0

From these two basic divisions the complete Universe can be classified, which in essence is the basis for the ten basic divisions of the Tree of Life (referred to as *Sephiroth*, circles, or numbers). This Qabalistic system is strangely reminiscent of the Taoist classification system known as Yin and Yang.

The Directional system found in *The Zohar* is a sophistication of the Binary Qabalah. In the Directional system the Tree of Life is seen as a five-fold system of East, West, South, North, and Center. Again this system parallels the Chinese five-elemental system, which allocates the five elements of the East to the four cardinal directions and center.

Next follows an elaboration and extension of an existing work, Aleister Crowley's *Liber 777*. Crowley, in 1909, first published *777*, which cataloged the 32 component parts of the Tree of Life (10 numbers and 22 letters). Crowley based his research on a Golden Dawn document which allocated symbols to each component part of the Tree of Life. To this document Crowley added an enormous amount of Eastern symbol sets not used in the Golden Dawn tradition.

In constructing my own version of this work I focused my attention to only the first ten Sephiroth (or numbers) composing the Tree of Life. Based on those ten basic categories for the Tree of Life, 149 tables were developed, the majority of which do not appear in *777*. However, certain symbol sets unique to Crowley's *777* have been included here. In each case, they are sourced back to the appropriate table in *777*, . These 149 tables are grouped into 21 topics for easy reference:

    I. Sephirotic Names (Tables 1-6)

    II. Number (Tables 7-14)

    III. Letter (Tables 15-18)

    IV. Color (Tables 19-22)

Again, this portion of the text was developed to supplement and extend, but not to replace. the contents of Aleister Crowley's ground-breaking 777.

This extended commentary on the ten Sephiroth of the Tree of Life is followed by a discussion of the 22 Paths that connect these ten Sephiroth. The 22 Paths of the Tree of Life are shown in two forms, the Proto-Tree of Life (which is the classic Jewish Qabalistic pattern) and the Revised Tree of Life (which is the Western magickal Qabalistic pattern).

In terms of the first diagram, the Proto-Tree of Life, I have rectified the extant Qabalistic diagrams, which all betray a blind in attributes when concerning the allocation of the Hebrew letters governing the two Paths which cross a symbolic abyss and connect the numbers 2 to 5 and 3 to 4. The correct attributes are as follows.

Secret Abyss Alphabet Correspondences

Hebrew Letter	Path Number	Connected Sephiroth
Zain (ז)	17	2 to 5
Cheth (ח)	18	3 to 4

The symbolism for the 22 Paths of the Tree of Life is then detailed as follows.

1. Path Number
2. Hebrew Letter
3. Connecting Sephiroth (Proto-Tree)
4. Connecting Sephiroth (Revised Tree)
5. Kircher's Allocations for the Paths as Gods
6. Levi's Allocations for the Paths as Magickal Powers
7. Human Body (Crowley)
8. Animal (Crowley)
9. Plant (Crowley)
10. Perfume (Crowley)
11. Magickal Weapon (Crowley)
12. Magickal Power (Crowley)
13. Initial Letter of Divine Name of God (Rabbi Akiba)
14. Astrology (Sepher Yetzirah)
15. Number Value (of Hebrew Letter)
16. Tarot: Exoteric Order (Levi)
17. Tarot: Esoteric Order (Golden Dawn)
18. Four Color Scale: Atziloth
19. Four Color Scale: Briah
20. Four Color Scale: Yetzirah
21. Four Color Scale: Assiah

These 21 tables for the Paths are followed by a detailed description of the 33rd secret Path of the Tree of Life, the Sephirah Daath.

This discussion of the Tree of Life ends with a description of the Qabalistic number concept of zero, the number out of which emanate the 32 Paths of Wisdom.

Appended to this Hebrew key is the first addendum of the book. This addendum is a reconstruction and distillation of the oldest surviving key to the sacred construction of the Hebrew alphabet: the *Sepher Yetzirah* (Book of Formation). Possibly as old as 200 BCE, the *Book of Formation* gives every key attribute for the ten numbered stations and 22 lettered Paths composing the Tree of Life. Many versions of this text survive, which results in a disagreement upon certain symbolic allocations for the Hebrew alphabet. The distilled version offered in this addendum has corrected every uncertain attribution found in the text. The *Book of Formation* is the most important text that any student of Qabalah should understand. It is the most accurate record detailing the original Qabalistic symbolism for both the first ten numbers and the 22 letters of the Hebrew alphabet.

In crafting this addendum, I purposely retained all of the original key Hebrew terms. These terms appear in brackets following all major concepts and are written as transliterated English and Hebrew. If entered on note cards, these terms can form the basis of your own number-language dictionary file as described in the introduction.

As to the contents of the addendum, first a historical overview of the development of the *Sepher Yetzirah* is offered. Next, the contents of the text itself are presented in a diagrammatic and tabled format. The ten Sephiroth (or numbers) are first discussed. The text of the *Sepher Yetzirah* itself divides these ten numbers into two groups of 1 through 4 and 5 through 10. The tables conform to this division.

The numbers 1 through 4 are categorized as:

- A number

- A number value

- A main attribute

- An element

- A symbol of the world

- A combination of the three mother (elemental) letters

The numbers 5 through 10 are categorized as:

- A number

- A number name

- A direction in space

- A counterchange of the divine name IHV

- A double (planetary) letter as well as a counterchange of the three mother letters

- A planet

Following the discussion of the first ten numbers, the *Sepher Yetzirah* then details the heart of its symbolism for the 22 letters of the Hebrew alphabet. First a table shows the division of all 22 letters into five pronunciation positions within the mouth. Next the text discusses the Hebrew alphabet as 3 mother letters, 7 double letters, and 12 simple letters.

The three mother letters, assigned to the three elements of Air, Water, and Fire, are categorized first by:

1. Root element

2 Element in the world

3. Scale (balance)

4. Human body

5. Six rings (3 male, 3 female)

6. Temperature

7. Time of year

8. Direction in space

9. Direction in body

10. Family trigram

The seven double letters, assigned to the seven planets, are analyzed next. This symbol set is the most blinded of all attributes in the *Sepher Yetzirah*. Mathers felt that the Tarot offered the pictorial key to clarify which planet should be governed by each of the seven double letters. (Refer to the addendum to the Tarot section for a discussion of this Qabalistic decipherment.) Six separate tables clarify the secret planetary symbolism for these seven double letters.

The first table gives the symbolic values obtained by the double pronunciation values for each of the seven planetary letters. One value is positive, the other negative. They are governed by the pronunciation known as the Dagesh value (a pronunciation mark occurring as a dot within the letter).

The second table gives four disparate traditional sets of planetary attributes for the double letters. Most modern Jewish Qabalistic interpretations of these attributions adopt the Ptolemaic Order, which ascribes Saturn to the first letter and the Moon to the last.

The third table details the true esoteric order, that which S. L. Macgregor Mathers pioneered in the Qabalistic correspondences used by the Golden Dawn. This secret order can be justified by the pictorial imagery of the Tarot. Again, this table is worked out in great detail in the addendum to the 12th Key (The Tarot).

The fourth table shows three cosmological sets of correspondences for the seven double letters based on the secret planetary order.

The fifth table gives the seven directions in space, which form the six faces of a cube and its center, based again on the secret planetary order.

The sixth, and last, table uses the metaphor of a cube to solve the puzzle posed in the *Sepher Yetzirah* of "3 set against 3 with one in balance."

The next section of the addendum lays out the symbolism for the 12 simple letters, which rule the 12 signs of the zodiac. The basic attributes for these 12 zodiacal letters are described in a table which categorizes the simple letters as follows:

• Zodiac

• Month

• Time of year

- The 12 tribes

- Direction (as one of the 12 edges of a cube)

- Banners of God (Yahweh)

- Human activity

- Human body according to the *Sepher Yetzirah*

- Human body according to classical astrology

- Alternate direction (found in Isidore Kalisch's 1877 translation)

This table of correspondences is followed by three different symbolic groupings of the 12 letters as suggested (but not detailed) in the *Sepher Yetzirah*. The first grouping is the 12 letters as six couples or pairs. The second grouping is four sets of triads. Both of these groupings are based on the *Sepher Yetzirah*'s division of the human body by these 12 letters. The third grouping mixes a select group of mother, double, and simple letters to give an alternate solution to the puzzle. Finally all 22 letters are combined to form 22 divisions of the human body as described in the *Sepher Yetzirah*.

The above tables detailing the rich Qabalistic symbolism for the Hebrew alphabet can be seen as the prototype text for Crowley's *Liber 777*. Indeed, it is the *Sepher Yetzirah* that Mathers used not only to unlock the secrets of the Tarot but also to discover the very pattern to qualify all Qabalistic-Masonic symbolism.

The remaining part of this section of the addendum deals with two aspects not directly covered in the original *Sepher Yetzirah*. The first elaboration is the description of all 32 components of the Tree of Life as "The Thirty-Two Paths of Wisdom." These additional attributes were appended to Renaissance translations of the text. Two tables give these additional attributes. The first shows the names of the stations on the Tree of Life, as well as the 32 key intelligences for each of these Paths of Wisdom. The second table shows the rainbow color scheme devised by Mathers to correspond to these 32 Paths.

The second elaboration is the symbolic correspondences for the five final letter forms, invented by King Ezra around 400 BCE. The fact that the *Sepher Yetzirah* does not give any attributes for these five final forms may be proof that the *Sepher Yetzirah* was composed before the invention of the five finals, and therefore predates 400 BCE.

The symbolism for the five finals is divided into two tables. The first categorizes the five final letters as follows:

- Type of letter (Mother, Double, or Simple)

- Number value (final and simple)

- Initial letter denoting five types of transmitted knowledge

- Five points of the pentagram

- Five elements

- Five parts of the Qabalistic soul

- Five additional directional components of the cube

The second table is derived from Athanasius Kircher and divides the Universe into 27 (rather than 22) categories to encompass the five additional final letters.

This addendum concludes with a final major table not found in any text or commentary on the *Sepher Yetzirah*. This important table, spanning many pages, details the 231 gates, or possible pairings, of the 22 letters of the Hebrew alphabet. This is the most important Qabalistic exercise to establish a symbolic meaning for every possible pairing, or interaction, of the 22 Hebrew alphabet letters. Likewise, this meditation can be the means to give real meaning to every possible pairing of the 22 major arcana Tarot cards.

Each of the 231 gates is given nine separate sets of meanings derived from the numerical values of the Hebrew letters (and corresponding Tarot keys), as well as select key symbols from the *Sepher Yetzirah*. These attributes can be expanded by referring back to the elaborate tables given in the discussion of the *Sepher Yetzirah*. They can also be supplemented by any other set of tables, found in the text at large, which is keyed to the Hebrew alphabet in some fashion. The nine categories used in the analysis of the 231 gates are as follows:

1. Serial order of Gate

2. Hebrew letters composing Gate

3. Total value of Hebrew letters based on simple number value (i.e., Aleph = 1)

4. Total value of Hebrew letters based on letter name values (i.e., Aleph = 111, 831)

5. Total value of Hebrew letters based on corresponding Tarot Key (i.e., Aleph=0)

6. Corresponding Tarot cards to Hebrew letters

7. Astrological correspondences for Hebrew letters derived from the *Sepher Yetzirah*

8. Directions in space from the *Sepher Yetzirah*

9. Divisions of the human body from the *Sepher Yetzirah*.

Thus ends the very detailed section governing the Hebrew Qabalah. You can progress directly to the next key, Arabic, or skip to the 12th key, the Tarot: the Tarot section depends and further elaborates upon the symbolism of the Tree of Life and the Qabalistic Hebrew alphabet.

ORIGIN

1500 BCE—Adaption of Phoenician alphabet into the 22 characters of Rock Hebrew

450 BCE—King Ezra and Nehemiah compiled the Pentateuch (the first five books of the Bible). At this point the versification of the Holy Scriptures as we know them was firmly established. This in turn created the number-letter codes which all later Qabalistic work would decipher.

400 BCE—Addition of five final letters in the formation of King Ezra's Flame Alphabet

300 CE—Establishment in print of astrological pattern to the 22 letters of the Hebrew alphabet)

ALPHABET CODE

If the Divine Language of the Angels is of this earth, then that language must surely be Hebrew. Of all the number codes of the world Hebrew may be the most holy, the most sanctified of all sacred alphabets. Its number lore extends back to the times of the Patriarchs, when such codes were the most concealed of secrets.

Every passage of the Torah was guided in its construction by these marvelous number secrets, allowing every sentence to contain a book of numerical nuances and interpretations. As a number code covering the range of 1 through 1000, both Hebrew and Greek form the basic skeleton of numerical interpretation for all other sacred languages constructed on this number range.

Gematria (גמטריא—GMTRIA) is the Hebrew technical term for the substitution of number values for alphabet letters as a means of interpreting scripture. It is first found in print in a collation of 32 rabbinical rules called the *Bariatha of R. Eliezer ben R. Jose, the Galiean.* This canon appeared around 200 CE, and in its 29th rule gematria (or letter-number substitution) is defined as a legitimate Rabbinical method of biblical exegesis.

The root for this Qabalistic term "gematria" is found in Greek rather than in Hebrew. Gematria is a play on both *geo-metria* and *gramma-metria.* As *geometria* is the measure *(metria)* of the earth *(geo),* therefore *gramma-metria* (or gematria) is the measure of the letters of the alphabet *(gramma).*

In later Qabalistic literature there is distinction made between three Qabalistic methods of interpretation: Gematria, Temurah, and Notariqon. In essence, Temurah and Notariqon are extensions of Gematria.

Temurah is the rearranging of the letters of a word to spell another word. In this case, both words would be of the same number value because they are both composed of the same letters. A further development of Temurah is the Substitute Alphabet Tables. These tables swap one letter of the alphabet with another in a systematic format, to form a cryptogram or cipher substitute alphabet. The two classic substitute alphabet tables are AThBSh (אתבש) and ALBM (אלבמ). AThBSh exchanges the first letter with the last, while ALBM exchanges the first with the 12th. The number values for these cipher substitutions are detailed in the eighth section of the rules tabulated below, under the 13th and 14th columns of number values for Hebrew.

Notariqon (from the Latin *notarius,* shorthand) is the reduction of a word to one of its component letters. Usually the reduction, or initialization, involves the initial letter of the word, but sometimes the final or medial letter is used as well. After the initials are produced by Notariqon, the letters are then totaled to give a variant number. This method is usually employed to analyze a verse. Thus the initials of the first seven words of Genesis are BBAAHVH (בבאאהוה). When numbered by gematria these seven letters add up to 22. Thus the 22 letters of the Hebrew alphabet are contained in the initials (or Notariqon) of the first seven words of Genesis. The inverse to the above rule of Notariqon holds true as well, for any word can be seen as a series of initials. Thus Adam (אדם—ADM) can be seen as the initials of **Abraham, David, Moses.**

The Hebrew alphabet number code is as follows:

The Hebrew alphabet reads from right to left. The number base is 10, as opposed to the Babylonian base 60. The alphabet is divided into the number values of 1–10, 10–100, and 100–1000, a pattern which exists as well in Coptic, Arabic, Greek, and Enochian. The letters composing a word are added together to form the number value of that word. Thus the name Adam in Hebrew, אדם, is composed of the 3 letters א, ד, ם, valued at 1, 4, and 40. Together these three letters total to 45, the number value of the name Adam.

The original Hebrew alphabet of 22 letters spanned the number range 1 through 400. This alphabet was remodeled by King Ezra in 400 BCE to contain 27 letters that could span the number range 1–900. These five additional letters are called "finals," for they are five alternate final forms for five of the 22 Hebrew letters. These five letters are Kaph, Mem, Nun, Peh, and Tzaddi. When these five letters appear as the last letter of a word they possess an alternate value, from 500 to 900. Any word ending in a final letter would therefore possess two number values. Thus the Hebrew word Adam, which ends with the final letter Mem, has two number values

    אדם = 1 + 4 + 40 = 45 (Mem as 40)
    אדם = 1 + 4 + 600 = 605 (Mem as 600)

If a letter of the Hebrew alphabet is written in an enlarged script, the value of that letter is 1,000 times its normal value. Thus Beth written in this enlarged script would be valued at 2,000 (Beth is normally valued at 2; 2 x 1,000=2,000). This enlarged Beth is the first letter of the Torah. An alternate method of indicating this 1,000-fold value is by placing one (or sometimes two) dots directly over the letter.

The alphabet code is as follows:

The Hebrew Alphabet Code

Hebrew Letter	Trans- literation	Letter Name	Number Value	Positional Value
א	A	Aleph	1	1
ב	B	Beth	2	2
ג	G	Gimel	3	3
ד	D	Daleth	4	4
ה	H	Heh	5	5
ו	V	Vav	6	6
ז	Z	Zain	7	7
ח	Ch	Cheth	8	8
ט	T	Teth	9	9
י	I	Yod	10	10
כ	K	Kaph	20	11
ל	L	Lamed	30	12
מ	M	Mem	40	13
נ	N	Nun	50	14
ס	S	Samekh	60	15
ע	O	Ayin	70	16
פ	P	Peh	80	17
צ	Tz	Tzaddi	90	18
ק	Q	Qoph	100	19
ר	R	Resh	200	20
ש	Sh	Shin	300	21
ת	Th	Tav	400	22
ך	Kf	Kaph Final	500	23
ם	Mf	Mem Final	600	24
ן	Nf	Nun Final	700	25
ף	Pf	Peh Final	800	26
ץ	Tzf	Tzaddi Final	900	27
א	A	Aleph enlarged	1000	28

The original symbolic meanings for each Hebrew letter have been retained in the literal meanings for each of the alphabetical nominal names. This alphabet is hieroglyphic in nature, and undoubtedly was based on 22 selected Egyptian hieroglyphs, which were given Sumerian phonetic, and numerical equivalents.

Thus the original Hebrew alphabet of 22 numbered-hieroglyphic letters is a magickal blend of Egyptian hieroglyphs and Sumerian Cuneiform.

The following tables delineate the 22 letter names, their number values, and their original hieroglyphic meanings:

The 22 Hebraic Hieroglyphs

Letter	Letter Name	Number Value of Letter Name	Hieroglyphic Meaning of Letter Name
A (א)	ALPf (אלף)	111 (831)	Ox, plow the ox pulls, the horns of an ox; clan, one, first, one thousand, one million; to learn, to train oneself, tame, train (animals), to become used to, to teach, to study
B (ב)	BITh (בית)	412	House, walled enclosure, the temple, the temple as a metaphor for the great universe, house of God, palace, fortress, storehouse, town, city, sepulcre, congregation, tent as as a tabernacle, school, college, lodge; household, family, daughter, wife, pudenda, marital intercourse; body, limb, organ; cup, purse, sheath, receptacle, thorn; the inner part, what is inside, to go within, to pass the night, go inside, lodge
G (ג)	GML (גמל)	73	Camel (carrier of loads), dromedary, camel's tracks, camel's hump, camel's throat, neck (crescent Moon, talisman around camel's neck), camel driver, couple, teaming arrangement, caravan; walking forward and backward, a small bridge; to load (good or evil) on, to deal with, do good, be kind, repay, charitable

The 22 Hebraic Hieroglyphs (cont'd.)

Letter	Letter Name	Number Value of Letter Name	Hieroglyphic Meaning of Letter Name
D (ד)	DLTh (דלת)	434	Door, leaf, folding door, two-leveled door, a shut door, doorway, tent flap, porch, roof, gate, portico; womb, vagina (delta), the doorway (muscles) of the womb; tablet, page of a manuscript, scroll, column of a book, half of the ten commandments, first half of a verse
H (ה)	HH (הה) (also HA [הא], HAH [האה], HVH [הוה], HIH [היה])	10 (6) (11) (16) (20)	Window, lattice, opening, aperture, sighting of a star (hence astrology); desire, to be, exist, to long, to breathe, to become, happen; is it that?, here, here it is, this, the, of the; lo, behold, ah, aha, ha, woe, alas, oh; a name of a worm in the pomegranate
V (ו)	VV (וו) (also VAV [ואו], VIV [(ויו])	12 (13) (22)	And (that which joins), but, is it indeed so?; oh, woe; ah; hook, nail, penis, peg which holds the door curtain before the Ark of the Law
Z (ז)	ZINf (זין)	67 (717)	Sword, blade, hilt of a sword, any implement of war; to equip, arming, putting on armor; the decoration or crownlets on Rabbinical Hebrew letters
Ch (ח)	ChITh (חית)	418	Hedge, fence, wall, ladder, partition, divider; animal, beast, life-force; living, alive, distinct
T (ט)	TITh (טית)	419	Serpent, coiled serpent; something rolled up or twisted together; cross within the circle; crossroads
I (י)	IVD (יוד)	20	Hand, right hand, fist, pointing index finger, handle; the hand as a symbol of God, power and activity; seed, semen, penis

The 22 Hebraic Hieroglyphs (cont'd.)

Letter	Letter Name	Number Value of Letter Name	Hieroglyphic Meaning of Letter Name
K (כ)	KPf (כף)	100 (820)	Left hand, the palm or hollow of the hand, glove, to raise the hand in benediction or prayer; something arched or hollow; cave, cavity, vault; scalepan of balance; hub of a wheel; top of a palm tree; bundle, sheaf; pan, censer; mason's trowel; the crest of flesh over the genitalia
L (ל)	LMD (למד)	74	Ox goad, prod, staff, erect serpent, serpent-rod; to tame, lead, train, chastise, discipline; to be joined, affixed to, to learn, educate, accustom oneself; student, scholar, teacher; studies, deduced, defined, to argue in favor of, plead, throw light on, hint; even, to, until, towards, into, against, on account of, because
M (מ)	MIMf (מים) (MMf (ממ))	90 (650) (80 [640])	The waves of the ocean, water, river, rainwater, spring, ocean, sea, fluid, secretion (blood, semen, urine), juice of fruits (especailly wine), any liquid, running water, to cleanse with washing; from, of, since; what? (with the letter "H"), why? (with the letter "T")
N (נ)	NVNf (נון)	106 (756)	Fish, tadpole, sea creature, the body of the fish (with head and tail cut away); fish of the genus *Anthias,* called by some "gravefish"; the prolific nature of fish, to sprout, generate, put forth, flourish, seed (hence regenerate); to waste away, deteriorate
S (ס)	SMKf (סמך)	120 (600)	Serpent biting its tail, circle of the sky (vault of heaven); one cycle, circuit, orbit; the vagina, womb (as opposed to "V," the penis); prop, tent peg, foundation, base, support; to pack,

The 22 Hebraic Hieroglyphs (cont'd.)

Letter	Letter Name	Number Value of Letter Name	Hieroglyphic Meaning of Letter Name
S (ס) (cont'd.)			make close, bring close, join, make a thick mass, stamp; to lean on, support, uphold, aid, sustain, help, rely on; authority, ordination, laying of hands, to lay hands on the head of a teacher (scholar)
O (ע)	OINf (עין)	130 (780)	Eye, face, self, perception, sight, aspect, appearance, reflection; look, to look at (with anger, hate); to ponder, weigh, contemplate, discern; bewitchment, evil-eye; abstraction; guidepost, ring, hole, anus, collar, spring, well, fountain, source; to flow, flow out (secretion, water, tears); enjoyment, pleasure, delight and its counterpart pain, affliction, poverty
P (פ)	PH (פה) (PA (פא))	85 (81)	Mouth and tongue, opening, opening of a bag, orifice; by word of mouth; to speak, breathe, vibrate, blow, blast, blow away, scatter, disperse, divide, split; part, partition, a fourth of the heaven; curl, lock, spiral lock of hair, whiskers; edge of a sword, cutting edge, teeth
Tz (צ)	TzDI (צדי)	104	Fishhook, to cast, ensnare, angle for, hunt, capture, buzzing of a cricket's wings; to be bent, prostrate, kneeling posture; to aim, fix the eyes on anything, lying in wait, deliberate purpose (hence meditation); precious stone, crystal-shaped (for focus of eyes in meditation); the upright, the just; the side of a mountain, border; the left side (Lilith), to turn sideways, to turn to the left; to cast out, pour out, excrement;

The 22 Hebraic Hieroglyphs (cont'd.)

Letter	Letter Name	Number Value of Letter Name	Hieroglyphic Meaning of Letter Name
Tz (צ) (cont'd.)			advesary; design, purpose; confounded, astounded, desolation, confusion, despair; the hunter and the hunted
Q (ק)	QVPf (קוף)	186 (906)	The face turned away, the face concealed, the face turned towards the right; back of head, skull, skull as hollow vessel, cup, basket, tub, box, money-bag, pouch, anus, vulva; eye (of a needle), hole (in an ax handle); lance, pole, hatchet, mushroom; to surround, go around, encircle; heap, pile, parapet, arch, doorway; cast forth, spew, vomit; ape, monkey, the tail (of a monkey), the ape as a demon
R (ר)	RISh (ריש) (RASh [ראש])	510 (501)	Face, to see, perceive, brain, head, countenance, the face turned to the left; top, apex, summit, crown; the sum, head, or amount of anything; highest, supreme, first, chief, foremost, beginning, point, main thing, principle; embryo; capstone; drug, intoxicant, poisonous plant (wormwood, head of poppy plant, flower tops of hemp); to be moved, tremble, be in awe; crossbeam, triangle, wedge, ox head; one after the other, succession; poverty, poor; dwellers of the North (Russia)
Sh (ש)	ShINf (שין)	360 (1010)	Tooth, fang, ivory, triple fang (of a serpent), to sharpen, pierce, penetrate; cliff, mountain; midnight, year, duration; sleep, urine; hated, enemy, foe, different, transformation, angel; second, two, duality; who, which, that, because

The 22 Hebraic Hieroglyphs (cont'd.)

Letter	Letter Name	Number Value of Letter Name	Hieroglyphic Meaning of Letter Name
Th (ת)	ThV (תו)	406	Cross, brand, mark, Tau, musical note, letter of alphabet, sign, symbol, cross within a circle; cross branded on camels and horses; wild ox; twin, desire, longing, lust, cohabitation, delight; bed chamber, cell, holy of holies; come ye, again, furthermore

With the writing of the Qabalistic text, *The Book of Formation (Sepher Yetzirah)*, an astrological equivalent for each letter of the Hebrew alphabet was established. Thus the letters of any word can be written as astrological symbols. "Adam" by this script, known as the Yetziratic script, becomes Air + Venus + Water. By such information, "Adam" (humanity) can be seen as: (1) Air (the life breath), (2) Venus (the mother, the source of living), and (3) Water (the water of the womb and the human body).

Astrological Attributes from the *Sepher Yetzirah*

Hebrew Letter	Astrological Attribute	Hebrew Letter	Astrological Attribute
A (א)	Air (Spirit)	L (ל)	Libra
B (ב)	Mercury	M (מ)	Water
G (ג)	Moon	N (נ)	Scorpio
D (ד)	Venus	S (ס)	Sagittarius
H (ה)	Aries	O (ע)	Capricorn
V (ו)	Taurus	P (פ)	Mars
Z (ז)	Gemini	Tz (צ)	Aquarius
Ch (ח)	Cancer	Q (ק)	Pisces
T (ט)	Leo	R (ר)	Sun
I (י)	Virgo	Sh (ש)	Fire
K (כ)	Jupiter	Th (ת)	Saturn (Earth)

The development of the Hebrew Qabalah in the Middle Ages produced a variety of minor numerical values for the 22 basic Hebrew alphabet letters. There are 19 basic numeral variations for the Hebrew alphabet. The table on the opposite page details these variations:

Hebrew Number Variations

Hebrew Alphabet	1 Normal Value	2 Minor Value	3 Serial Order	4 Square Value of Serial Order	5 Cube Value of Serial Order	6 Square of Normal Value	7 Cube of Normal Value	Inclusive Value 8 Serial	9 Normal
A (א)	1	1	1	1	1	1	1	1	1
B (ב)	2	2	2	4	8	4	8	3	3
G (ג)	3	3	3	9	27	9	27	6	6
D (ד)	4	4	4	16	64	16	64	10	10
H (ה)	5	5	5	25	125	25	125	15	15
V (ו)	6	6	6	36	216	36	216	21	21
Z (ז)	7	7	7	49	343	49	343	28	28
Ch (ח)	8	8	8	64	512	64	512	36	36
T (ט)	9	9	9	81	729	81	729	45	45
I (י)	10	1	10	100	1,000	100	1,000	55	55
K (כ)	20	2	11	121	1,331	400	8,000	66	75
L (ל)	30	3	12	144	1,728	900	27,000	78	105
M (מ)	40	4	13	169	2,197	1,600	64,000	91	145
N (נ)	50	5	14	196	2,744	2,500	125,000	105	195
S (ס)	60	6	15	225	3,375	3,600	216,000	120	255
O (ע)	70	7	16	256	4,096	4,900	343,000	136	325
P (פ)	80	8	17	289	4,913	6,400	512,000	153	405
Tz (צ)	90	9	18	324	5,832	8,100	729,000	171	495
Q (ק)	100	1	19	361	6,859	10,000	1,000,000	190	595
R (ר)	200	2	20	400	8,000	40,000	8,000,000	210	795
Sh (ש)	300	3	21	441	9,261	90,000	27,000,000	231	1,095
Th (ת)	400	4	22	484	10,648	160,000	64,000,000	253	1,495

Hebrew Number Variations (cont'd.)

Hebrew Alphabet	10 Nominal Value	11 Numeral Value	12 Double Integrated Nominal Value	13 Value by Permutation AThBSh	14 ALBM	15 Final (Great) Value	16 Tarot—Exoteric	17 Tarot—Esoteric	18 Paths on Tree of Life	19 Enlarged Letter
A (א)	111 (831)	13	270	400	30		1	0	11	1,000
B (ב)	412	400	838	300	40		2	1	12	2,000
G (ג)	73	335	237	200	50		3	2	13	3,000
D (ד)	434	278	914	100	60		4	3	14	4,000
H (ה)	10	350	20	90	70		5	4	15	5,000
V (ו)	12	605	24	80	80		6	5	16	6,000
Z (ז)	67 (717)	377	193	70	90		7	6	17	7,000
Ch (ח)	418	395	844	60	100		8	7	18	8,000
T (ט)	419	775	845	50	200		9	8	19	9,000
I (י)	20	575	466	40	300		10	9	20	10,000
K (כ)	100 (820)	620	185	30	400	500 (ך)	11	10	21	20,000
L (ל)	74	680	595	20	1		12	11	22	30,000
M (מ)	90 (650)	323	200	10	2	600 (ם)	13	12	23	40,000
N (נ)	106 (756)	398	224	9	3	700 (ן)	14	13	24	50,000
S (ס)	120 (600)	650	310	8	4		15	14	25	60,000
O (ע)	130 (780)	422	256	7	5		16	15	26	70,000
P (פ)	85	440	95	6	6	800 (ף)	17	16	27	80,000
Tz (צ)	104	820	558	5	7	900 (ץ)	18	17	28	90,000
Q (ק)	186 (906)	455	283	4	8		19	18	29	100,000
R (ר)	510	1,157	890	3	9		20	19	30	200,000
Sh (ש)	360 (1,010)	1,077	486	2	10		0	20	31	300,000
Th (ת)	400	720	418	1	20		21	21	32	400,000

To serve as an illustration, these 19 variations will be used to number the Hebrew word for humanity, as well as Adam: ADM (אדם).

1. **Normal Value:** The well-known range of 1 through 400 for Aleph through Tav.
   ADM = (A = 1) + (D = 4) + (M = 40) = 45

2. **Minor Value:** The normal value minus any zeroes. Two values are created by adding the letters of a word, or valuing each letter of a word as a digit of a number.
   ADM = (A = 1) + (D = 4) + (M = 4)
   Two values are formed: 1 + 4 + 4 = 9 and 1 + 4 + 4 = 144

3. **Serial Order:** The order of the 22 alphabet letters.
   ADM = (A = 1) + (D = 4) + (M = 13) = 18

4. **Square Value of Serial Order:** The value of the serial order multiplied by itself (squared). Thus $A = 1^2 = 1$, $B = 2^2 = 4$, $G = 3^2 = 9$, etc.
   ADM = (A = 1) + (D = 16) + (M = 169) = 186

5. **Cube Value of Serial Order:** The value of the serial order cubed (the serial value times the squared serial value). Thus $A = 1^3 = 1$, $B = 2^3 = 8$, $G = 3^3 = 27$, etc.
   ADM = (A = 1) + (D = 64) + (M = 2197) = 2,262

6. **Square of Normal Value:** The normal value multiplied by itself (squared). Thus $R = 200^2 = 4,000$, $Sh = 300^2 = 9,000$, $Th = 400^2 = 16,000$, etc.
   ADM = (A = 1) + (D = 16) + (M = 1,600) = 1,617

7. **Cube of Normal Value:** The normal value cubed (the normal value multiplied by the squared normal value). Thus $R = 200^3 = 8,000,000$, $Sh = 300^3 = 27,000,000$, $Th = 400^3 = 64,000,000$, etc.
   ADM = (A = 1) + (D = 64) + (M = 64,000) = 64,065

8. **Inclusive Value, Serial:** The summation of the serial order of the alphabet. Thus A = 1, B = 1 + 2 = 3, G = 1 + 2 + 3 = 6, etc.
   ADM = (A = 1) + (D = 10) + (M = 91) = 102

9. **Inclusive Value, Normal:** The summation of the normal values of the alphabet in sequential order. Thus K = 1 + 2 + 3 + 4 + 5 + 6 + 7 + 8 + 9 + 10 + 20 = 75 (rather than 66, the inclusive value, serial).
   ADM = (A = 1) + (D = 10) + (M = 145) = 156

10. **Nominal Value:** The value of the letter name for each specific alphabet letter. Thus A = ALP = 1 + 30 + 80 = 111.
    ADM = (A = 111) + (D = 434) + (M = 90) = 635

11. **Numeral Value:** The value of the numeral name corresponding to the normal value for each alphabet letter. Thus A = 1 = AChD (One) = 1 + 8 + 4 = 13.
    ADM = (A = 13) + (D = 278) + (M = 323) = 614

12. **Double Integrated Nominal Value:** The value of the letter name expanded so that each letter is represented by a letter name. Thus

A = ALP = ALP LMD PH = (1 + 30 + 80) + (30 + 40 + 4) + (80 + 5) = 270.
ADM = (A = 270) + (D = 914) + (M = 200) = 1,384

13. **Value by Permutation, AThBSh:** The value of the substitution letter
    when the first letter of the alphabet is exchanged with the last. Thus
    A = Th = 400, while B = Sh = 300.
    ADM = (A = 400) + (D = 100) + (M = 10) = 510

14. **Value by Permutation, ALBM:** The value of the substitution letter
    when the first letter of the alphabet is exchanged with the 12th, the
    second with the 13th, etc. Thus A = L = 30, while B = M = 40.
    ADM = (A = 30) + (D = 60) + (M = 2) = 92

15. **Final (Great) Value:** The alternate value of the five select letters, K,
    M, N, P, and Tz (ך, ם, ן, ף, ץ) when these five letters appear at the
    end of a word. These five alternate values span the range of 500–900
    beyond the normal value of 1–400 for Hebrew.
    ADM = (A = 1) + (D = 4) + (M = 600) = 605

16. **Tarot, Exoteric:** Though not strictly Rabbinical, these 22 Tarot num-
    bers are allocated to the Hebrew alphabet according to Eliphas
    Levi. This is the same value as the serial value except that Sh (ש) =
    0 and Th (ת) = 21.
    ADM = (A = 1) + (D = 4) + (M = 13) = 18

17. **Tarot, Esoteric:** The Hebrew-Tarot attributions of S. L. MacGregor
    Mathers. These number values are one less than the serial order of
    the alphabet.
    ADM = (A = 0) + (D = 3) + (M = 12) = 15

18. **Paths on Tree of Life:** The 22 connecting Paths for the 10 Sephiroth
    valued at 11 through 32.
    ADM = (A = 11) + (D = 14) + (M = 23) = 48

19. **Enlarged Letter:** The normal value times 1,000, when the alphabet is
    written in an enlarged script. The classic example is the first letter
    of Genesis, which is Beth written in an enlarged script (and valued
    at 2,000).
    ADM = (A = 1,000) + (D = 4,000) + (M = 40,000) = 45,000

By these 19 basic values for Hebrew, 19 distinct number values are
computed for "Adam": 9, 15, 18, 45, 48, 92, 102, 144, 156, 186, 270, 510, 605,
614, 635, 1,617, 2,262, 45,000, and 64,065.

One final number variant for Hebrew should be mentioned. With the
refinement of the pronunciation and writing of Hebrew, vowel-point marks
were created apart from the 22 basic alphabet characters. These vowel
points are combinations of dots and lines. Each can be given a number
based on its apparent shape. The dot equals 10, based on "Yod" valued at
10, while the line equals 6, based on "Vav" valued at 6. The table on the following page delineates the specific number values of each vowel point.

The Vowel Points
Number Composition

Sign	Name	Transliteration	Value	of Yod and Vav
ָ	Qames (Chatup)	ā (o)	16	(IV—וֹי)
־	Patah	a	6	(V—ו)
ֵ	Sere	ē	20	(II—יי)
ֶ	Segol	e	30	(III—ייי)
ִ	Chireq	i	10	(I—י)
ֹ	Cholem	ō	10	(I—י)
ֻ	Qibos	u	30	(III—ייי)

THE ORIGIN AND SYMBOLISM OF THE TREE OF LIFE

A unique symbol for the number series 1 through 10 was developed out of the Jewish Qabalah from the symbolism in Genesis. The Tree of Life that grew in the center of Eden became the mandala or symbolic pattern used to describe the mysticism behind the first ten numbers.

This symbolic Tree appears in a variety of forms throughout the literature of the Qabalah. It is typically composed of ten circles (known as Sephiroth) connected by a series of straight lines (known as Paths).

The Babylonian-Assyrian Tree of Life (usually composed of 13 fruits joined by bent and straight Paths) can be seen as the prototype for this Jewish Tree of Life. The Greek tetractys, a four-tiered pyramid of ten dots, can also be seen as a source of the Qabalistic Tree of Life.

Ultimately, the shape of the Tree of Life developed into a circle surmounting a cross, resembling both the Egyptian Ankh and the medeival astrological symbol for Venus (both symbolic of life).

The following timeline details the evolution of the Tree of Life.

EVOLUTION OF TREE OF LIFE

1500 BCE—Babylonian Tree of Life utilizing 13 fruits connected by interlaced path work

800–400 BCE—Recording of the Torah and the Holy Scriptures which contain the Hebrew names for the Sephiroth, the concept of the "Tree of Life," and a variety of symbolism based on the decad.

150 CE—The period of the historical Simeon Ben Yohai, who is credited with the doctrines contained in the key Qabalistic work, the *Zohar*.

200 CE—The Bariatha Rabbinical Rules of Interpretation are recorded, which contain the Qabalistic formula for gematria as a means of interpreting scripture.

200–900 CE—The *Sepher Yetzirah* is written, capturing what had previously only been communicated orally concerning the cosmology of the Hebrew alphabet.

900-1100 CE—The Qabalistic school of thought develops out of the writings of the *Sepher Yetzirah*.

1200 CE—The *Zohar* is written by Moses de Leon and contains the most detailed description of the ten Sephiroth that compose the Tree of Life. This text will become the classic reference for all future speculation concerning the Tree of Life.

1200–1400 CE—The complete development of the Sephirothic system takes place. Its greatest Jewish exponent in this period is Abraham Abulafia, who was able to successfully combine the Sephirothic doctrine with that of letter-number mysticism.

1300 CE—The Christian Raymond Lull, inspired by the Jewish Qabalah, creates his own version of a Latinized Qabalah using nine select Latin letters for both a Sephirothic system and a letter-number mysticism. In Lull's system, an attempt was made to combine the mystical doctrines of Judaism, Islam, and Christianity into one great system which can be demonstrated by mathematical proofs.

1400–1600 CE—Later Jewish development of the Qabalistic Sephirothic doctrine. In this period the *Zohar* is first published in 1558 in Cremona. Isaac Luria's Sephirothic doctrines are also published in 1572 (by his pupil Chiam Vital) as *The Tree of Life*.

1513 CE—The first definitive work in Latin on the Jewish Qabalah is published by Johann Reuchlin, *On the Qabalistic Art*.

1557 CE—Pistorius translates the *Sepher Yetzirah* into Latin in his Qabalistic Collection.

1652 CE—Athanasius Kircher, with his publication of *Oedipus Aegypticus*, establishes the shape of the Tree of Life for all later Qabalists.

1500–1700 CE—The infusion of the Qabalah into the Western magickal tradition transforms the Qabalah from a purely Jewish doctrine into the universal magickal tradition that it has become in the 20th century. Of especial interest is the Angelic-Enochian work of John Dee around 1580, the birth of the Rosicrucian movement around 1600, and Knorr Von Rosenroth's translation into Latin of the *Zohar* published in 1677.

1877–1888 CE—The Theosophical works of Madame Blavatsky in both *Isis Unveiled* and *The Secret Doctrine* bridge the doctrines of East Indian and Tibetan thought with that of the Jewish Qabalah.

1887 CE—The founding of the Hermetic Order of the Golden Dawn in England brings into being the most coherent Masonic-Qabalistic system known to Man.

1909 CE—The combination of the Chinese divination system of the *I Ching* with that of the Sephirothic system is accomplished by Aleister Crowley and recorded in his classic text, *Liber 777*, which unites the symbols of every great religion with those of the 32 Paths of the Tree of Life.

The shaping of the Tree of Life can be first sourced to the Qabalistic text, the *Sepher Yetzirah,* which may date back to 200 CE. This cosmological text describes the matrix of our universe as the first ten numbers—known in Hebrew as *Sephiroth* (singular *Sephirah),* from the Greek word for spheres— and the 22 letters of the Hebrew alphabet, collectively known as the 32 Paths of Wisdom of the Tree of Life. It has been argued that the proto-text of the *Sepher Yetzirah* only concerned itself with the symbolism of the first decad of numbers (akin to the philosophical number school of the Pythagoreans). Subsequent revisions of the text added the alphabet symbolism.

This may be the case for the classic Jewish texts on the Qabalistic symbolism of the Tree of Life such as the *Bahir* (The Book of Clear Light), the *Zohar* (The Book of Splendorous Light), and Luria's classic, *The Tree of Life.* All these detail in depth the symbolism of the basic ten numbers that compose the Tree of Life but are not as systematic when approaching the actual symbolism of the 22 additional letters (known as Paths, as opposed to the ten basic Sephiroth).

The infusion of this exclusively Jewish cosmogony into Western Renaissance magick opened the Tree of Life to a variety of esoteric symbols that were not intended in its original construction. Yet the further evolution of the Western magickal tradition in the late 19th and early 20th centuries brought the Tree of Life into the realm of such exotic systems as the Tibetan-Indian Tattvas and the Chinese *I Ching.*

Thus the Tree of Life became for both the work of the Golden Dawn and for Aleister Crowley the one indispensible classification system for interpreting all magickal visions, symbols, and configurations.

The Tree of Life as discussed in the Qabalistic text, the *Zohar,* is measured in two categories other than the ten Sephiroth:

- By the pair or polarity of male and female, resembling the Yin-Yang doctrine of Taoism

- By the four directions of the earth as East, South, North, and West (as well as the center or middle of these four directions)

Like the Yin-Yang system of Taoism, the Qabalah in the writings of the *Zohar* contains an esoteric binary system based on the Tree of Life. In this system, the Tree of Life is divided into two basic Sephiroth: Chesed and Geburah, the fourth and fifth on the Tree of Life, governing Jupiter and Mars respectively.

As a parallel to the Taoist system, Chesed is basically Yang and Geburah basically Yin (yet each are counterchanged by the other, reminiscent of the Taoist two fishes, or Yin-Yang symbol).

One paramount symbol for the interaction of Chesed and Geburah is Chesed as the Blue (or White) Man and Geburah as the Red Woman. The immediate parallel in Eastern Philosophy to this association of blue to male, red to female is the Hindu-Tantrik image of the divine couple Krishna and Radha. Krishna is the Blue Man and Radha is the Red Woman (as the alternate color of red and white Sakti is the red woman, Siva the white man). This image of a blue/red couple is central to all Tibetan and Indian Yab-Yum (sexual union) symbols.

Therefore like the Yin-Yang system, the Qabalah contains a classification system based on two, using the right and left sides of the Tree of Life: Chesed and Geburah.

The following list catalogs the *Zohar's* binary Qabalah based on Chesed and Geburah.

The Binary Qabalah

Geburah	Chesed
1. Left	Right
2. Left hand	Right hand
3. Below	Above
4. Behind	Front
5. Severity	Mercy
6. Punishment	Kindness
7. Poverty (the Hebrew letter Daleth)	Beneficence (the Hebrew letter Gimel)
8. Forgetfulness	Remembrance
9. Push Away	Draw Close
10. Keep	Bless
11 Preserve, Constitute (שׁית—the last three letters of *Berashith*)	Create (ברא—the first three letters of *Berashith*)
12. End	Beginning
13. Utterance	Thought
14. Beth (the second letter of the alphabet)	Aleph (the first letter of the alphabet)
15. Malkuth (the tenth Sephirah, Kingom)	Kether (the first Sephirah, Crown)
16. Tav (the last letter of the alphabet)	Aleph (the first letter of the alphabet)
17. Dim (Opaque) Glass	Clear Glass
18. Darkness (Black)	Light (White)
19. Fire	Water
20. Fire	Ice
21. Red	Blue
22. Red	White
23. Menstrual Blood	Semen
24. Honey	Milk
25. Rose	Lily
26. Female	Male
27. The warrior as angry, threatening, thrusting, penetrating	The mother as open, receptive, enveloping
28. Sun	Moon
29. Night	Day
30. Midnight	Noon

The Binary Qabalah (cont'd.)

Geburah	Chesed
31. Gold	Silver
32. Adam as the Red Man	Lilith as the White Moon
33. Lilith	Yahweh
34. Eve	Adam
35. Serpent (Samael)	Eve
36. The pain of child-birth (Eve)	Foreskin (of Adam) circumcised
37. Samael, Serpent	Lilith
38. Qain (sacrificer)	Abel
39. Herder of Animals (Abel's occupation)	Tender of Crops (Qain's occupation)
40. Isaac (Sacrifice)	Abraham
41. Northwest	Southwest
42. West	East
43. North	South
44. The potter's wheel turned to the left, the evil impulse	The potter's wheel turned to the right, the good impulse
45. Evil	Good
46. Sunset	Sunrise
47. The wheel of God, the bottom revealed	The wheel of God, the top concealed
48. Prayer, supplication must be made from below	For blessing to descend from above
49. Impulse from Below (Malkuth)	Influence from Above (Kether)
50. Midnight studying, chanting	Prayer, meditation, supplication
51. Left Hand-attractive force of woman to man	Right Hand-attractive force of man to woman
52. Prayer standing	Prayer sitting
53. Tephelim (talismans for prayer) marking the head	Tephelim marking the arm and hand
54. Asleep	Awake
55. Earth	Heaven
56. The serpent on earth	The celestial dragon TALI in the sky
57. Tool of iron (prohibited in the Temple of Solomon)	Shamir (magickal worm which could cut stone)
58. Through the hand of the artisan	Inspiration descending
59. Six months in fire (Hell)	Six months in snow, ice (Hell)

The Binary Qabalah (cont'd.)

Geburah	Chesed
60. Bitter herb	Salt
61. The serpent which entwines the Tree of Life	The Paths of the Tree of Life
62. The hollow abyss of the North	The mountain peak of the South
63. Intake	Outpour
64. Wine (Earth)	Bread (Heaven)
65. Blood	Tissue
66. Heart	Brain
67. Muscles	Skeleton
68. Egypt	Israel
69. Ham	Shem
70. Black Pillar, Pillar of Severity, Pillar of Boaz	White Pillar, Pillar of Mercy, Pillar of Jachin
71. Pomegranate	Palm Tree
72. Wine	Oil
73. Seeds within fruit	Constellations in the sky
74. Sea	Sky
75. The Great Whale	Jonah
76. Head of the serpent	Heel of Eve
77. Abram	Sarai
78. Sarah	Abraham
79. Mount Ebal (Curse)	Mount Gerizim (Blessing)
80. Left hand as this world	Right hand as next world
81. The languages of man confounded on earth	One angelic language after death
82. He-goat (Scapegoat)	Lamb
83. Lion	Lamb
84. Fire descending from heaven	Hailstones descending from heaven
85. Desire	Wisdom
86. Lightning at midnight	Morning star at dawn
87. Unclean spirit	Steadfast spirit
88. Wine	Milk
89. Ash (Sterile)	Dust (Fertile)
90. Elohim (ALHIM—אלהים) The Gods	Yahweh (IHVH—יהוה) God
91. Beginnings are rough	Subsequent course is smooth
92. Pillar of Fire by night	Pillar of Smoke by day

The Binary Qabalah (cont'd.)

Geburah	Chesed
93. Shekinah	Yahweh
94. King (Evil impulse)	Child (Good impulse)
95. Evil prompter (witness of one's soul's action from 13 years onward, being Samael, or Satan)	Good prompter (witness of one's soul's action from birth being Metatron)
96. Weak body	Strong spirit
97. God breaks the body	To liberate the spirit
98. Full Moon (white) to dark Moon (red)	New Moon (green) to Full Moon (white)
99. Wife (body)	Husband (soul)
100. Vision while asleep— dream (transmitted by Gabriel)	Vision while awake— prophecy (transmitted by the holy living creatures)
101. BINH (בינה)—Binah, the third Sephirah, Understanding	ChKMH (חכמה),Chockmah, the second Sephirah, Wisdom
102. Death	Life
103. Visitation	Remembrance
104. Lower world	Upper world
105. Rachael (open and realized)	Leah (veiled and undisclosed)
106. Judgment	Forgiveness
107. Cold winds of the North freezing water into ice	Sun in the South melting ice into water
108. As rods for divination, the almond tree, peeled revealing red	As rods for divination, the poplar tree with its white branch
109. The fir tree that is her nest	The white stork
110. The Lion's den	Daniel
111. Samson (of the Sun, Sunflower)	Delilah (of the night)
112. Orbit of Sun to the North (left) for fall/winter	Orbit of Sun to the South (right) for spring/summer
113. Sun turns to the North to illumine the Moon at night	Sun goes towards the South for day
114. Moon is obscured through the heel of Esau	Sun is illuminated through the head of Jacob

The Binary Qabalah (cont'd.)

Geburah	Chesed
115. Seduction by the serpent	Sacrifice of the scapegoat
116. Defiled	Holy
117. AThH (אתה)—Thou	HVA (הוא)—He
118 End of all flesh	End of all spirit
119. QL (קל)—Inaudible voice	QVL (קול)—Audible voice
120. Meditation	Chanting
121. Afternoon prayer	Morning prayer
122. North concealed	South revealed
123. West goes out	East goes in
124. At death, two birds depart from the Tree of Life The black bird goes to the North at dusk	The white bird goes to the South at dawn
125. The black cock at midnight	The white dove of Noah's Ark
126. Wisdom of Egypt	Wisdom of Solomon
127. Fire	Gold
128. Song	Faith
129. West as the Moon	East as the Sun
130. Flaming Sword East of Eden	Tree of Life in the center of Eden
131. The numeral five	The numeral four
132. Masturbation	Circumcision
133. Invisible Path of "Hell" (Gehinnon) on Tree of Life from 2nd to 5th Sephirah	Invisible Path of "the Garden of Eden" on Tree of Life from 3rd to 4th Sephirah

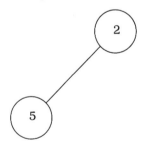

134. Flood (the destroyer)	Ark (the preserver)
135. Ocean below	Formed by rain from above
136. Beasts	God
137. Clouds on a rainy day	Rainbow after a rainstorm

The Binary Qabalah (cont'd.)

Geburah	Chesed
138. The blue end of the rainbow spectrum	The red end of the rainbow spectrum

139. Four couples buried together at the cave of Machpelah, representing the Tetragrammaton)

Eve (Yod—')	Adam (Yod—')
Sarah (Heh—ה)	Abraham (Heh—ה)
Rebecca (Vav—ו)	Issac (Vav—ו)
Leah (Final Heh—ה)	Jacob (Final Heh—ה)
140. Mother	Father
141. Four Matriarchs	Three Patriarchs
142. Shekinah	Yahweh
143. Torah	Yahweh
144. Humanity	Torah
145. Shaitan	Yahweh

The second category found in the *Zohar* is the Tree of Life as a directional map. Here the ten Sephiroth of the Tree of Life are reduced to Above, Below, Right, Left, and Center. The Tree can thus be applied to the four directions of space as follows.

Zohar Directional Tree of Life

Direction	Position on Tree	Sephirah
East	Above	1st—Kether
South	Right	4th—Chesed
North	Left	5th—Geburah
Center	Center	6th—Tiphereth
West	Below	10th—Malkuth

By use of this directional Tree of Life, the *Zohar* categorizes the Qabalistic symbolism found in the Torah as groups of four, resolved in a central fifth symbol. The following two tables delineate this directional symbolism of the four directions found in the Torah (the second table shows the attributes for the center of these four directions).

The Symbolism of the Four Directions as the Tree of Life

Symbols	East	West	South	North
	(MZRCh)	(MORB)	(DRVM)	(TzPVNf)
	(מזרח)	(מערב)	(דרום)	(צפון)
Sephiroth of Tree of Life	KThR (כתר) Kether (Crown)	MLKVTh (מלכות) Malkuth (Kingdom)	ChSD (חסד) Chesed (Mercy)	GBVRH (גבורה) Geburah (Severity)
Position in Space	MOLH (מעלה) Above	MTH (מטה) Below	IMINf (ימין) Right	ShMAL (שמאל) Left
Part of Day	BQR (בקר) Morning	ORB (ערב) Evening	IVMf (יום) Day	LILH (לילה) Night
Sun Cycle	ZRCh (זרח) Sunrise	BA (בא) Sunset	TzHRIMf (צהרים) Noon	ChTzVTh (חצות) Midnight
Location in Universe	ShMIMf (שמים) Sky (Heaven)	ARTzf (ארץ) World(Earth)	LBNH (לבנה) Moon	ShMSh (שמש) Sun
Location in World	IShRAL (ישראל) Israel (Freedom)	MTzRIMf (מצרים) Egypt (Bondage)	HR GZRIMf (הר גזרים) Mt. Gerizim (Blessing)	HR OIBL (הר עיבל) Mt. Ebal (Curse)
Location in Man	RASh (ראש) Head	GVPf (גוף) Body	ID IMINf (יד ימין) Right Hand	ID ShMAL (יד שמאל) Left Hand
Element	RVCh (רוח) Air	ADMH (אדמה) Earth	MIMf (מים) Water	ASh (אש) Fire
Alchemical Metal	NChShA (נחשא) Brass	PRZLA (פרזלא) Iron	KSPA (כספא) Silver	DHBA (דהבא) Gold
Color	SPIR (ספיר) Sapphire (Clear)	IRVQ (ירוק) Green	ChVVR (חוור) White	SVMQ (סומק) Red
Degree of Vision	NBVAH (נבואה) Prophesy	OVR (עור) Awake	MRAH (מראה) Vision (Mirror)	ChLVMf (חלום) Dream

The Symbolism of the Four Directions as the Tree of Life (cont'd.)

Symbols	East	West	South	North
Good-Evil Polarity	TVB MKRIO RO (טוב מכריע רע) Good and Evil in balance	TVB LOMVTh RO (טוב לעמות רע) Good and Evil at War	ITzR TVB (יצר טוב) Good Impulse	ITzR RO (יצר רע) Evil Impulse
Embodiment of Good-Evil Polarity	ShLMH (שלמה) Solomon	AIVB (איוב) Job	MTTRVNf (מטטרון) Metatron	SMAL (סמאל) Samael
Patriarchs (World of Assiah)	DVD (דוד) David	IOQB (יעקב) Jacob	ABRHMf (אברהם) Abraham	ITzChQ (יצחק) Isaac
Holy Living Creatures (World of Yetzirah)	ADMf (אדם) Man	NShR (נשר) Eagle	ARIH (אריה) Lion	ShVR (שור) Ox
Archangels (World of Briah)	RPAL (רפאל) Raphael	AVRIAL (אוריאל) (N) Uriel	MIKAL (מיכאל) Michael	GBRIAL (גבריאל) Gabriel
Tetragrammaton (World of Atziloth)	I (׳)—Yod (Father	V (ו)—Vav (Son)	H (ה)—Heh (Mother)	H (ה)—Heh final (Daughter)

The Symbolism of the Center, Which Equalizes and Synthesizes the Four Directions

Symbol	Hebrew	Translation
Position in Space	ThVKf (תוך)	Center, Midst, Middle
Sephiroth	ThPARTh (תפארת)	Tiphereth—Beauty of Proportion—The sixth Sephirah
Color	ARGMNf (ארגמן)	Purple, violet, admixture of scarlet and royal blue
Location in Universe	TzIVNf (ציון)	Zion, the center of the universe
Location in World	IRVShLIMf (ירושלים)	Jerusalem, the center of the world
Location in Man	LB (לב)	The heart, the center of the body
Creation	GNf ODNf (גן עדן)	The Garden of Delight, Gan Eden, the center of the first creation
Degree of Vision	QNf TzPVR (קן צפור)	The bird's nest, the location of the soul in deep meditation, the center of the brain
Patriarch	ADMf (אדם)	Adam, the first creation
Penta-grammaton	Sh (ש)	The fifth point of the pentagram, IHShVH (יהשוה), spirit descending in the midst of the four elements

The ultimate evolution of the Tree of Life expanded the binary and fourfold systems just described to a tenfold system composed of the first ten numbers.

As the Pythagoreans venerated the first ten whole integers as the four-layered pyramid known as the Tetractys, the Qabalists venerated this number series in the form of the Tree of Life as ten emanations or Sephiroth.

The following 149 tables detail the rich symbolism for each of the first ten numbers which the Tree of Life offers in light of the developments of the Western Qabalistic magickal traditions.

The Sephirotic Tables

I. Sephirotic Names (Tables 1-6)

This section details the Hebrew names for the ten Sephiroth.

Table 1. The Hebrew name, transliteration, and translation according to the Golden Dawn system of magick, 1887

Table 2. The Latinized names of the Sephiroth as found in the *Magical Calendar* attributed to Tycho Brahe, dated 1582, published 1620

Table 3. Robert Fludd's translation of the Hebrew Sephiroth names, found in his *Collectio operum*, 1617

	1. Hebrew Golden Dawn Sephirotic Titles			2. Magical Calendar's Sephiroth Names	3. Fludd's Translation of the Sephiroth
	Hebrew	Transliteration	Meaning		
1	KThR (כתר)	Kether	Crown	Kether	Crown
2	ChKMH (חכמה)	Chokhmah	Wisdom	Hocma	Wisdom
3	BINH (בינה)	Binah	Understanding	Binach	Prudence
4	ChSD (חסד) (GDVLH גדולה)	Chesed Gedulah	Mercy (Greatness)	Heseth	Clemency
5	GBVRH (גבורה) (PChD פחד)	Geburah Pachad	Strength (Fear)	Geburah	Punishment
6	ThPARTh (תפארת)	Tiphereth	Beauty	Tipheret	Grace
7	NTzCh (נצח)	Netzach	Victory	Nezah	Triumph
8	HVD (הוד)	Hod	Splendor	Hod	Praise
9	ISVD (יסוד)	Yesod	Foundation	Iesod	Redemption
10	MLKVTh (מלכות)	Malkuth	Kingdom	Malchuth	Kingdom

I. Sephirotic Names (cont'd.)

Table 4. Eliphas Levi's translation of Hebrew Sephirotic titles in light of his exoteric Tarot order, from *Transcendental Magic*, 1856

Table 5. Masonic translation of the Sephirothic names from the 19th century (Pike, *Morals and Dogma*, 1871)

Table 6. Esoteric translation of the Sephiroth from the French Qabalistic circle of Papus (Papus, *The Qabalah*, 1892)

	4. Levi's Sephirotic Titles	5. Masonic Translation of Sephirotic Names (Pike)	6. Papus' Esoteric Names or the Sephiroth
1	The Equilibrating Power as the Crown of All	The supreme crown, corona, circlet	Equilibrating Providence
2	Wisdom equilibrated by intelligence	To be wise, wisdom	Divine Wisdom
3	Active intelligence equilibrated by wisdom	Understanding, intelligent, conceiver	Ever Active Intelligence
4	Mercy ever benevolent because it is strong	Great, magnificence, benignity	Infinite Mercy
5	Severity necessitated by wisdom itself and goodwill	Austerity, rigor, severity	Absolute Justice
6	Beauty as the mediating principle between Creator and Creation	Beauty, beautiful	Ineffable Beauty
7	Eternal triumph of intelligence and justice	Victory, overcoming	Victory of Life over Death
8	Eternity achieved by mind over matter	Glory, glorious	Eternity of Being
9	The basis of all belief and all truth	Foundation, basis, just	Generation, cornerstone of stability
10	The work and mirror of God	Rule, reign, royalty, dominion, power, king	Principle of Forms

II. Number (Tables 7-14)

The various associations of number values to each of the ten Sephiroth

Table 7. Two values are given in this table. The first value is the square of the number of each Sephirah. Thus the first Sephirah is 1 x 1, or 1; the second 2 x 2, or 4, etc. The second number value is the gematria equivalent for the Hebrew name of the Sephirah found in table 1. For the invisible Sephirah, Daath, the square value is 121 (as the 11th Sephirah) and 1089 (as the 33rd Sephirah). The gematria value for Daath is 406 (as DAATh, דעת) and 474 (as DOTh, דעות). (Refer to the end of this essay for more on Daath).

Table 8. The mystic number value given for each Sephirah is the summation of the number for each of the ten Sephiroth. Thus 1 is 1, 2 is 1 + 2 = 3, 3 is 1 + 2 + 3 = 6, etc. The Hebrew name associated with each one is given in the Golden Dawn rituals as a password for that particular grade on the Tree of Life. For the Golden Dawn grade structure, refer to table 144.

Table 9. The traditional Qabalistic number values given here refer to the position on the Tree of Life covered by both the number values of the Hebrew Alphabet and *gematriots* (words and phrases totaling to particular number values).

	7. Square of Sephirotic Number and NumberValue of Sephirotic Name	8. Mystic Number and Hebrew Password (Golden Dawn)	9. Traditional Qabalah Alphanumeric range
1	1 : 620	1 = Silence	Beyond Thousands
2	4 : 73	3 = AB (אב) (Father)	Thousands
3	9 : 67	6 = DB (דב) (Bear)	Hundreds
4	16 : 72	10 = AT (אט) (Enchanter)	Tens
5	25 : 216	15 = IH (יה) (Monogram of the Eternal)	Tens
6	36 : 1081	21 = AHIH (אהיה) (I am)	Tens
7	49 : 148	28 = KCh (כח) (Power)	Tens
8	64 : 15	36 = ALH (אלה) (God)	Tens
9	81 : 80	45 = MH (מה) (What)	Tens
10	100 : 496	55 = NH (נה) (Ornament)	Units

II. Number (cont'd.)

Table 10. The geometrical shapes derived from the number values of the Sephiroth as listed in this table are based on the number of points circumscribed by each geometrical shape. These are taken from the Golden Dawn tradition.

Table 11. The abstract Qabalistic number concept as expressed by the number series 1 through 10. These attributes were received in a visionary glimpse by Aleister Crowley while vacationing in Naples, thus the title "The Naples Arrangement" (from *The Book of Thoth*, 1944).

Table 12. The ten Pythagorean pairs describing each of the ten points of the Tetractys, applied to the ten Sephiroth.

	10. Geometrical Shape (Golden Dawn)	11. Crowley's Naples Arrangement	12. Ten Pythagorean Principia
1	Point	The Point: positive yet indefinable	Finite and Infinite
2	Straight Line	The Point: distinguished from one other	Odd and Even
3	Triangle	The Point: defined by relation to two others	One and Many
4	Square	The Point: defined by three coordinates: Matter	Right and Left
5	Pentagon, pentagram	Motion (Time): the womb	Male and Female
6	Hexagon, hexagram, unicursal hexagram	The Point: now self-conscious, able to define itself (in terms of 1 through 5)	Rest and Motion
7	Heptangle, heptagon, heptagram	The Point's Idea of Bliss (Ananda)	Right Angle and Curve
8	Octagon, octagram octangle	The Point's Idea of Thought (Chit)	Light and Darkness
9	Enneangle, enneagram enneagon	The Point's Idea of Being (Sat)	Good and Evil
10	Dekagon, dekagram, dekangle	The Point's Idea of itself (in terms of 7, 8, 9)	Square and Oblong

II. Number (cont'd.)

Table 13. G.I. Gurdjieff's number ladder as applied to the ten Sephiroth is listed in this table. There is an 11th rung to this number ladder of Gurdjieff which is valued at 1536 or –1 and is assigned to Absolute Inert Matter (being metaphorically the Devil, as +1 is God). This 11th rung can be assigned to the Qlippoth or inverted Tree of Life (symbolized in the black fourth quadrant of Malkuth), and as Daath, the 11th invisible Sephirah.

Table 14. G. I. Gurdjieff's Enneagram, the quintessential symbol for "work on oneself," is allocated to the ten Sephiroth in regards to the motion of dance of the nine points of the enneagram.

13. Gurdjieff Number Ladder

1	1 (+1) Absolute
2	3 (+3) Eternal Unchanging (All Worlds)
3	6 (+6) Archangel (All Suns)
4	12 (+12) Angels (Our Sun)
5	24 (+24) Man (All planets)
6	48 (±0) Vertebrates (The Earth)
7	96 (–24) Invertebrates (The Moon)
8	192 (–12) Plants (Air)
9	384 (–6) Minerals (Water)
10	768 (–3) Metals (Food)

14. Gurdjieff's Enneagram

Enneagram Point 9
Enneagram Point 6

Enneagram Point 3
Enneagram Point 7
Enneagram Point 5
Enneagram Point 8
Enneagram Point 2
Enneagram Point 4
Enneagram Point 1
The Enneagram as a whole
    at rest; approach to Point 1

III. Letter (Tables 15–18)

The alphabet correlations of the ten Sephiroth are listed in this section.

Table 15. The Hebrew Alphabet as laid out on the Qabalistic cipher grid (known as AIQ BKR, אי״ק בכ״ר) is correlated to each of the ten Sephirothic numbers.

Table 16. The letter-Paths emanating out of the ten Sephiroth of the Tree of Life, as allocated in the Golden Dawn tradition, are listed. These are allocated according to the Tree of the later Qabalists.

Table 17. The ten Qabalistic gradations of the vowel points are shown according to traditional Qabalah. The number by each vowel- point name is the number value allocated to each mark.

Table 18. The three traditional ten-lettered names of God are allocated letter by letter to each of the ten Sephiroth, as tabled by Francis Barrett in his work, *The Magus*, 1801. The first name is the Tetragrammaton as the tetractys, in the progression I, IH, IHV, and IHVH (י, יה, יהו, and יהוה). The second name is the Yetziratic, or Third World, letter-name spelling for the Tetragrammaton, valued at 45. The formula is IVD HA VAV HA (יוד הא ואו הא)—The third name, ALHIM TzBAVTh (אלהים צבאות—Elohim Tzabaoth, Lord of the Hosts), is the ten-lettered Divine Name assigned to the eighth Sephirah, Hod (see table 35).

	15. Hebrew Alphabet (AIQ BKR)	16. Hebrew Alphabet (G.D.) (Paths emanating from Sephiroth)	17. Traditional Qabalah: Vowel Points (and their number value)		18. Barrett's Three God Names Totaling 10 letters		
1	A (1)	A, B, G	Kametz (16) ⊤ (Bottom of letter)	I	I	A
2	B(2), K(20), R(200)	D, H, V	Patach (6) — (Bottom)	I	V	L
3	G(3), L(30), Sh(300)	D, Z, Ch	Tzerey (20) ･･ (Bottom)	H	D	H
4	D(4), M(40), Th(400)	V, T, I, K	Segol (30) ∴ (Bottom)	I	H	I
5	H(5), N(50), Kf(500)	Ch, T, L, M	Shva (20) ⁚ (Bottom)	H	A	M
6	V(6), S(60), Mf(600)	G, H, Z, I, L, N, S, O	Cholem (10) · (Upper Left)	V	V	Tz
7	Z(7), O(70), Nf(700)	K, N, P, Tz, Q	Chirek (10) · (Bottom)	I	A	B
8	Ch(8), P(80), Pf(800)	M, O, P, R, Sh	Kibutz (30) ∴ (Bottom)	H	V	A
9	T(9), Tz(90), Tzf(900)	S, Tz, Q, R, Sh, Th	Shurek (10) ֻ (Center Left)	V	H	V
10	I(10), Q(100), A(1000)	Q, Sh, Th	No vowel mark	H	A	Th

IV. Color (Tables 19–22)

This section details the esoteric colors allocated to the ten Sephiroth.

Table 19. This color scale for the ten Sephiroth (the Golden Dawn Queen Scale) resembles Goethe's hexagonal color wheel. The first Sephirah is white light as the source of all colors. The second Sephirah is gray as the admixture of all colors, while the third Sephirah is black as the absence of all color (and light). Sephiroth one and three mix to form two. Daath (the invisible 11th Sephirah) is positioned between the first supernal three and the seven infernal Sephiroth. Daath by this color scheme is seen as a prism whose crystal shape refracts the white light of Kether into the seven planetary shades of the rainbow of the seven infernal Sephiroth. The three primary colors (blue, red, yellow) correspond to the fourth, fifth, and sixth Sephiroth. The three secondary colors (green, orange, violet) correspond to the seventh, eighth, and ninth Sephiroth. Thus the blue of four is mirrored in the orange of eight, the red of five is mirrored in the green of seven, while the yellow of six is mirrored in the violet of nine. The tenth Sephirah becomes blue-violet, the sixth Saturnian band of the rainbow, and in an alternate scheme the three tertiary colors—russet, olive, and citrine—and black. Both of these color schemes suggest a further admixture of the primary colors with the secondary colors to produce the tertiary colors.

Table 20. The Qabalistic color scheme of Azriel (12th century) for the ten Sephiroth, one of the earliest set of recorded color attributes, is given in this table. It is both Alchemical and Tantrik in nature by its use of white as male and red as female, mixing to form the lesser gradations of the Tree. The three supernal Sephiroth are seen as the heavens, concealed light being God (the light behind the Sun), yellow being the Sun of the Heavens, and sky blue being the heavens themselves. Malkuth occupies the position of Daath, as light reflecting all colors through the prism, or rainbow.

Table 21. Aleister Crowley's variant to Azriel's scheme, derived from the Westernized Qabalistic writings of Dr. Jellinek, is listed in this table. The second and third Sephiroth are swapped (taken from Crowley's *Liber 777*).

	19. Classic Rainbow Color Scale	20. Azriel's Color Scheme (1160–1238)	21. Crowley's Sephirotic Colors (Dr. Jellinek)
1	White	Concealed Light	Concealed Light
2	Gray	Yellow	Sky Blue
3	Black	Sky Blue	Yellow
4	Blue	White	White
5	Red	Red	Red
6	Yellow	White and Red or Pink	White-Red
7	Green	Whitish-Red	Whitish-Red
8	Orange	Reddish-White	Reddish-White
9	Violet	Whitish-Red and Reddish-White	White-Red, Whitish-Red, Reddish-White
10	Blue-Violet	Light reflecting all colors	The Light reflecting all colors

IV. Color (cont'd.)

Table 22. The intricate Golden Dawn color scheme for each of the four worlds. Atziloth is the highest, or first, world, translated as "Archetypal." Briah is the second world, translated as "Creative." Yetzirah is the third world, translated as "Formative." Assiah is the fourth or last world (corresponding to our world as Malkuth) and is translated as "Action." Each of these four world color scales is referred to in the Golden Dawn by the name of the corresponding Tarot Court Card. The table on the following page shows these correspondences.

22. Four-Color Scale—Golden Dawn

	Atziloth	Briah	Yetzirah	Assiah
1	Brilliance	White Brilliance	White Brilliance	White flecked Gold
2	Soft Sky Blue	Gray	Bluish-Gray (Mother of Pearl)	White flecked Red, Blue, Yellow
3	Crimson	Black	Dark Brown	Gray flecked Pink
4	Deep Violet	Blue	Deep Purple	Deep Azure flecked Yellow
5	Orange	Scarlet Red	Bright Scarlet	Red flecked Black
6	Clear Pink Rose	Yellow (Gold)	Rich Salmon	Gold Amber
7	Amber	Emerald	Bright Yellow-Green	Olive flecked Gold
8	Violet	Orange	Red Russet	Yellow-Brown flecked White
9	Indigo	Violet	Very Dark Purple	Citrine flecked Azure
10	Yellow	Citrine, Russet, Olive, Black	Citrine, Russet, Olive, Black flecked Gold	Black rayed Yellow

22A. Golden Dawn Color Scale

Number	Qabalistic World of Color Scale	Golden Dawn Court Card	Crowley's Variant	Traditional Court Card
1	Atziloth	King Scale	Knight	Knight
2	Briah	Queen Scale	Queen	Queen
3	Yetzirah	Prince Scale	Prince	King
4	Assiah	Princess Scale	Princess	Page

V. Sound (Tables 23–24)

This section deals with the much neglected esoteric correlation of sound to the Sephiroth.

Table 23. The Golden Dawn correlation of sound to each of the ten Sephiroth, based on the Queen Color Scale. These attributes are recorded in Paul Foster Case's *Highlights of the Tarot* (1934) and are supposedly also found in the Golden Dawn notebooks of Allan Bennett. The color-sound correspondences are based on the flashing (or opposite) colors of the rainbow scale of seven planetary rays. They are premised on the color seen projected upon the closed eyelids after meditating on the tattvas (for approximately five minutes). The correlations are shown in Table 23A on the opposite page.

Table 24. The *Magical Calendar* (1620) of Tycho Brahe divides the religious music of its time into each of the ten Sephiroth, as listed here.

23. Musical Scale (Golden Dawn)

1	Sound of Creation (the lost chord); also E (A = א)
2	Echo, Resonance; also A (O = ע)
3	Silence; also G# (M = מ)
4	G#
5	C
6	E
7	F#
8	D
9	A#
10	A

24. Tycho's Gradations of Music

1	Odes
2	Organums
3	Psalms
4	Canticles
5	Orations
6	Benedictions
7	Praises
8	Gratitudes
9	Felicities
10	Hallelujahs

23A. Golden Dawn Color-Sound Correlations

Infernal Sephiroth	Sound	Color	Flashing Color	Planet	Tattva
4	G#	Blue	Orange	Jupiter	Vayu
5	C	Red	Green	Mars	Tejas
6	E	Yellow	Violet	Sun	Prithivi
7	F#	Green	Red	Venus	Tejas
8	D	Orange	Blue	Mercury	Vayu
9	A#	Violet	Yellow	Moon	Prithivi (and Apas)
10	A	Blue-Violet	Yellow-Orange	Saturn	Akasha

However, the mathematical correlation between color and sound as frequency relationships does not completely support these allocations. The following table shows the mathematical correspondences between color and sound in cycles per second. The relationships between the two are approximate.

23B. Color-Sound Frequency Relationships

Gradations of 12 Prismatic Colors	Frequency (x 10^{12})	Traditional Astrological Color Correspondences	Corresponding Sound	Frequency (Pitch)
Red	430–470	Aries, Mars	G	392
Red-Orange	480	Taurus	G#	415
Orange	490–500	Gemini, Mercury	A	440
Yellow-Orange	510	Cancer	A#	466
Yellow	520	Leo, Sun	B	494
Yellow-Green	530–550	Virgo	C	523
Green	560–590	Libra, Venus	C#	553
Blue-Green	600–610	Scorpio	D	587
Blue	620–630	Sagittarius, Jupiter	D#	622
Blue-Violet	640–680	Capricorn, Saturn	E	659
Violet	690–710	Aquarius, Moon	F	698
Red-Violet (Dark Violet)	720–750	Pisces	F#	740

VI. Symbol (Tables 25-34)

This section lists the symbolic images for each of the ten Sephiroth.

Table 25. The Qabalistic image for each of the ten Sephiroth, derived from the Golden Dawn system of magick and tabled by Aleister Crowley in *Liber 777* is shown here. This image is to be visualized during meditation on each of the ten Sephiroth.

Table 26. The Qabalistic Tetragrammaton family as four levels of the Tree of Life, with the corresponding Court Cards for the family, are listed according to Golden Dawn tradition.

Table 27. The correspondence between the Minor Arcana of the Tarot and the ten Sephiroth are listed here. These attributes were first listed by Eliphas Levi in his *Trancendental Magic* (1856) and were later incorporated into the Tarot traditions of the Golden Dawn and Aleister Crowley.

	25. Crowley's Magickal Archetypes (Golden Dawn)	26. Fourfold Qabalistic Family (Golden Dawn)	27. Minor Arcana of Tarot (Levi-Golden Dawn)
1	Ancient bearded king seen in profile	Yod (Father)	4 Aces
2	Almost any male image	Heh (Mother); Knight as Father	4 Twos
3	Almost any female image	Heh (Mother); Queen as Mother	4 Threes
4	A mighty crowned, enthroned King	Vav (Son)	4 Fours
5	A mighty warrior in his chariot armed and crowned	Vav (Son)	4 Fives
6	A majestic King, a child, a crucified god	Vav (Son); King as Son	4 Sixes
7	A beautiful naked woman	Vav (Son)	4 Sevens
8	A hermaphrodite	Vav (Son)	4 Eights
9	A beautiful naked man, very strong	Vav (Son)	4 Nines
10	A young woman, crowned and veiled	Final Heh (Daughter); Page as Daughter	4 Tens

VI. Symbol (cont'd.)

Table. 28. The Major Arcana of the Tarot applied to Oswald Wirth, is listed here, from his *Tarot of the Magicians* (1927).

Table. 29. Ten select Major Arcana cards corresponding to the three mother letters and seven double letters of Hebrew are paralleled to the ten Sephiroth according to the Golden Dawn allocations (where Aleph = 0, The Fool).

28. Tarot Card Allocations of Wirth

1 1. The Magician—the source of activity and thought

2 2. The Priestess—the creative thought

3 3. The Empress—conception and generation of ideas

4 4. The Emperor—power which gives and spreads life

5 5. The Pope—willpower which holds in check and governs life given

6 6. The Lovers—heart (affections) which determines the will

7 7. The Chariot—the coordinating principle which governs the world

8 8. Justice—the order which nature brings into her work

9 9. The Hermit—the divine plan

10 10. Wheel of Fortune—that which synthesizes the actions of thinking, of willing, and of acting

29. Tarot Cards (Major Arcana) Three Mothers and Seven Doubles

0 The Fool (Air)

XX Judgement (Fire)
XII The Hanged Man (Water)

X The Wheel of Fortune (Jupiter)

XVI The Tower (Mars)

XIX The Sun (Sun)

III. The Empress (Venus)

I. The Magician (Mercury)

II The High Priestess (Moon)
XXI The World (Earth-Saturn)

VI. Symbol (cont'd.)

Table. 30. The alternate Major Arcana order to table 27 (where Kether = Aleph = 0, The Fool) is listed here, based on the Golden Dawn Tarot rather than the Tarot of Eliphas Levi.

Table 31. The 16 geomantic figures as applied to the Sephiroth, according to the Golden Dawn system. Here, the planetary rulers of the geomantic shapes determine the Sephirothic order.

Table 32. The seven esoteric Tattvas of the Theosophical Society are paralleled to the Tree of Life in accordance with the systems of Aleister Crowley and Israel Regardie.

	30. Secret Major Arcana Tarot Order (Golden Dawn)	31. Golden Dawn Geomancy	32. Theosophical Tattvas (based on seven levels of tree)
1	0 The Fool (The Divine Self)	Carcer and Tristitia	Adi Tattva
2	I The Magician (The All-Father)	Carcer and Tristitia	Anupapadaka Tattva
3	II The High Priestess (The All Mother)	Carcer and Tristitia	Anupapadaka Tattva
4	III The Empress (The Mercy of a Mother)	Acquisitio and Laetitia	Akasha Tattva
5	IV The Emperor (The Severity of the Warrior)	Puer and Rubeus	Akasha Tattva
6	V The Hierophant (The Inner Teacher)	Fortuna Minor and Fortuna Major	Vayu Tattva
7	VI The Lovers (Venusian Love)	Amissio and Puella	Tejas Tattva
8	VII The Chariot (Language as Hermetic Art)	Albus and Conjunctio	Tejas Tattva
9	VIII Strength (Secret Force of all spiritual activity)	Populus and Via	Apas Tattva
10	IX The Hermit (The isolated self in the world of illusion)	Caput Draconis and Cauda Draconis	Prithivi Tattva

VI. Symbol (cont'd.)

Table 33. The eight trigrams of the *I Ching* are allocated to the directions of the Tree of Life, based on Fu-Hsi's order of the trigrams. Here Kether is East, Malkuth is West, Geburah is North, and Chesed is South. This is in accordance with the Golden Dawn directional attributes shown in table 75. A second set of trigram attributes is also given in brackets; these represent Aleister Crowley's Chinese cosmology as found in his *Book of Thoth* (1944).

Table 34. The magickal symbolic images for each of the ten Sephiroth according to the Golden Dawn Western magickal tradition as found in the writings of Aleister Crowley, Dion Fortune, and Gareth Knight.

33. Eight Trigrams (Fu-Hsi Directions) and Crowley's Chinese cosmology

1. Li (Tao-Teh)
2. Tui (Yang)
3. Chen (Yin and Ch'ien)
4. Ch'ien (Tui)
5. K'un (Chen)
6. All eight trigrams (Li)
7. Sun (Ken)
8. Ken (Sun)
9. All eight trigrams as Center and K'an as West (K'an)
10. K'an (K'un)

34. Magickal Images (Crowley, Fortune, Knight)

Point; Point within a circle; Crown; Swastika

Straight line; Phallus; Wand

Vesica piscis; Kteis; Cup

Tetrahedron; Pyramid; Equal-armed cross; Orb and scepter; Crook

Sword; Spear; Chain; Scourge; Pentagon; five-petaled rose

Cube; Rosy and calvary cross; Truncated pyramid; Lamen

Rose; Lamp; Girdle

Names; Versicles; Apron

Perfumes; Sandals

Double cube altar; Magical circle and triangle; Equal-armed cross

VII. Theology (Atziloth) (Tables 35-38)

The Divine Names which correspond to the highest world of Atziloth on the Tree of Life are shown in this section.

Table 35. The original Hebrew transliteration and translation of the Divine Names of God, according to the Golden Dawn, as listed in MacGregor Mathers' *The Kabbalah Unveiled* (1887), are tabled for each of the ten Sephiroth. These ten names correspond to the Highest of the Four Worlds, Atziloth. Each name of the deity is found in the Torah and the Holy Writings.

Table 36. The variants to the Divine Names of God, as found in Tycho Brahe's *Magical Calendar* (1620), are listed here. These ten variants are in essence the same order as that found in the Golden Dawn.

35. Golden Dawn Names of God (Divine Names)—World of Atziloth

	Hebrew	Transliteration	Meaning	36. Tycho's Names of God
1	AHIH (אהיה)	Eheih	I am	Eheie
2	IH (יה)	Jah	Power	Iod Tetragrammaton
3	IHVH ALHIMf (יהוה אלהים)	Jehovah Elohim	The One God and the Gods	Tetragrammaton Elohim
4	AL (אל)	El	The Law, Power, Might	El
5	ALHIMf GBVR (אלהים גבור)	Elohim Gibor	The God of Strength, The Gods of War	Elohim Gibor
6	IHVH ALVH VDOTh (יהוה אלוה ודעת)	Jehovah Eloah Vadaath	The God of Gods and Knowledge The All Knowing God of Gods	Eloha
7	IHVH TzBAVTh (יהוה צבאות)	Jehovah Tzabaoth	The One God of the Celestial Army (Hosts)	Tetragrammaton Sabaoth
8	ALHIMf TzBAVTh (אלהים צבאות)	Elohim Tzabaoth	The Gods of the Celestial Army (Hosts)	Elohim Sabaoth
9	ShDI AL ChI (שדי אל חי)	Shaddai El Chai	The Almighty Living God	Sadai
10	ADNI HARTzf (אדני הארץ)	Adonai Ha-Aretz	Lord of the Earth	Adonai Melech

VII. Theology (Atziloth) (cont'd.)

Table 37. The ten Divine Names as attributed by Robert Fludd in his *Collectio operum* (1617) are listed for each of the ten Sephiroth. In these attributes, the main variant can be found in the name of Elohim (rather than Jehova. Elohim) listed for Binah.

Table 38. The Divine Names and their definitions as attributed by Athanasius Kircher in his *Oedipus Ægyptiacus* (1623) are listed in this table. Kircher's main variants are the attributution of Jah to Chockmah, Jehova to Binah, and Elohim to Tiphereth.

37. Fludd's God-Names

1   Ehieh
2   Iah: Jehova
3   Elohim
4   El
5   Elohim Gibor
6   Eloah
7   Jehovah Sabaoth
8   Elohim Sabaoth
9   Sadai
10 Adonai

38. Traditional Renaissance God Names in Hebrew with number value and translation (Kircher)

AHIH (אהיה) (21)—I am that I am

IH (יה) (15)—Essentializing Essence

IHVH (יהוה) (26)—God of Gods

AL (אל) (31)—God, Creator

ALVH (אלוה) (42)—God, Powerful

ALHIM (אלהים) (86)—God, Strong

IHVH TzBAVTh (יהוה צבאות) (525)—God of Armies

ALHIM TzBAVTh (אלהים צבאות) (585)—Lord of Armies

ShDI (שדי) (314)—All Powerful

ADNI (אדני) (65)—Lord

VIII. Archangelology (Briah) (Tables 39-43)

This section lists the archangels who rule the ten Sephiroth in the World of Briah.

39. The Hebrew transliteration, and translation of the archangels (who rule the World of Briah) according to the Golden Dawn system are listed in this table. Note that Michael and Raphael are interchangeable (as Sun and Mercury), while Auriel (AVRIAL, אוריאל, Light of God) can be substituted for Haniel.

40. A listing of the Sephirotic archangels as found in Tycho Brahe's *Magical Calendar* (1620) is given. Note that Iophiel is attributed to Chockmah, instead of Raziel, and Raphael, rather than Michael, is Tiphereth.

41. The archangels of Robert Fludd's Qabalistic hierarchy are listed. Fludd attributes Samael rather than Kamael to Geburah and uses the preferred Golden Dawn allocation of Michael to Tiphereth.

	39. Golden Dawn Archangels—World of Briah	40. Tycho's Archangelic Hierarchy	41. Fludd's Archangelic Hierarchy
1	MTTRVNf (מטטרון): Metatron—World Prince, Measurer, Angel of the Presence	Metatron	Metattron
2	RZIAL (רזיאל): Raziel—Secrets of God, Herald of God	Iophiel	Iophiel
3	TzPQIAL (צפקיאל): Tzaphqiel—Concern (Worry) of God, Spiritual strife against evil	Zaphkiel	Zephkiel
4	TzDQIAL (צדקיאל): Tzadqiel—Justice (Mercy) of God	Zadkiel	Zadkiel
5	KMAL (כמאל): Kamael—Heat, Fire, Severity of God	Camael	Samael
6	MIKAL (מיכאל): Michael—Angel of God, Like unto God, Who is like God (also RPAL, רפאל)	Raphael	Michael
7	HNIAL (הניאל): Haniel—Pleasure (Enjoyment) of God	Haniel	Hanael
8	RPAL (רפאל); Raphael—Healer of God; Divine Physician (also MIKAL, מיכאל)	Michael	Raphael
9	GBRIAL (גבריאל): Gabriel—Strength of God, Hero of God	Gabriel	Gabriel
10	SNDLPVNf (סנדלפון): Sandalphon—The Messiah, World Prince on Earth, the setting (on Earth) of the sandals of God	Soul of the Messiah	Soul of the Messiah

VIII. Archangelolology (Briah) (cont'd.)

Table 42. Francis Barrett's archangelic hierarchy is shown here; it is derived from Tycho's *Magical Calendar* rather than the work of Kircher, Fludd, or Khunrath.

Table 43. The archangels and the prophets of old whom they guarded are listed in accordance with the Qabalah of Papus (*The Qabalah*, 1892). These attributes can be found in an incomplete form as table 91 of Crowley's *Liber 777*.

42. Barrett's Angelic Hierarchy (Intelligible World)	**43. Angelic Intelligence (Papus)**
1	Merattron	Mithraton (Prince of the Faces)—through his ministry the Lord spoke to Moses
2	Jophiel	Raziel—celestial tutor of Adam
3	Zaphkiel	Zafohiel—protector of Noah; Jofiel—protector of Shem
4	Zadkiel	Zadkiel—guardian of Abraham
5	Camael	Kamael—guardian of Samson
6	Raphael	Raphael—protector of Isaac and Tobias; Feliel—guardian of Jacob
7	Haniel	Haniel (or Cerirel)—guardian of David
8	Michael	Michael—protector of Solomon
9	Gabriel	Gabriel—guardian of Joseph, Joshua, and Daniel
10	The Soul of the Messiah	Metalhin—protector and guide of Moses

IX. Angelology (Yetzirah) (Tables 44-47)

This section lists the angels who rule the ten Sephiroth in the World of Yetzirah.

Table 44. The Hebrew transliteration and translation of the angels, which correspond to the ten Sephiroth in the World of Yetzirah, are listed in accordance with the Golden Dawn system.

Table 45. The angels listed in Tycho Brahe's *Magical Calendar* (1620) are shown here; they can be seen to be exactly the same attributes used in the Golden Dawn.

Table 46. The angelic Hierarchy of Robert Fludd, which is based on the nine angelic hierarchies of the Christian school of Dionysius, is listed. Note that this listing is different in every attribute.

Table 47. Francis Barrett's angelic hierarchy found in his work *The Magus* (1801) is tabled here. It corresponds to Tycho's *Magical Calendar*, the basis of the Golden Dawn attributes.

	44. Golden Dawn Angels—World of Yetzirah	45. Tycho's Angelic Hierarchy	46. Fludd's Angelic Hierarchy	47. Barrett's Angelic Hierarchy—Intelligible World
1	ChIVTh HQDSh (שדקה תויח): Chaioth Ha-Qadesh—Holy Living Creatures, All Living Things are Holy	Haioth haca	Seraphim	Hajoth ha Kados
2	AVPNIMf (םינפוא): Auphanim—Wheels within wheels	Ophanim	Cherubim	Orphanim
3	ARALIMf (םילארא): Aralim—Mighty Ones	Aralim	Thrones	Aralim
4	ChShMLIMf (םילמשח): Chashmalim—Brilliant Ones	Hasmalim	Dominations	Hasmallim
5	ShRPIMf (םיפרש): Seraphim—Flaming Serpents	Seraphim	Powers	Seraphim
6	MLKIMf (םיכלמ): Melekim—Kings	Malachim	Virtues	Malachim
7	ALHIMf (םיהלא): Elohim—Gods and Goddesses	Elohim	Principalities	Elohim
8	BNI ALHIMf (םיהלא ינב): Beni Elohim—Children of the Gods	Bene Elohim	Archangels	Ben Elohim
9	KRVBIMf (םיבורכ): Kerubim—Cherub, Face of a Child, The Four Holy Creatures: Leo, Scorpio, Aquarius, Taurus	Cherubim	Angels	Cherubim
10	AShIMf (םישא): Ashim—Heavenly Men, Heroes among men	Issim	Souls	Issim

X. Astrology (Assiah) (Tables 48-55)

This section contains the divine attributes of the World of Assiah (the Heavenly Spheres), as well as astrological variations for the ten Sephiroth.

Table 48. The Hebrew transliteration and translation of the heavenly spheres of the World of Assiah are listed in accordance with the Golden Dawn system. These attributes are the primary planetary allocations for the Sephiroth and are based on the Platonic order of the seven planets, with Saturn as the highest planetary orbit closest to God and the Moon as the lowest planetary orbit closest to Man.

Table 49. The Heavenly Spheres found in Tycho Brahe's *Magical Calendar* are listed here, which are in accordance with the Golden Dawn system.

48. Golden Dawn Hebrew for The Heavens (Planets)—World of Assiah

1 RAShITh HGLGLIMf (מַזָּלוֹת הַגַּלְגַלִים): Rashith Ha-Galgalim—The Beginning of Whirlings: Primum Mobile

2 MZLVTh (מַזָּלוֹת): Masloth—Auspicious, Good Luck: Zodiac

3 ShBThAI (שַׁבְּתַאי): Shabbathai—Rest; Saturn

4 TzDQ (צֶדֶק): Tzedeq—Righteousness: Jupiter

5 MADIMf (מַאְדִים): Madim—Vehement Force: Mars

6 ShMSh (שֶׁמֶשׁ): Shemesh—Solar Light: Sun

7 NVGH (נֹגַהּ): Nogah—Glittering Splendor: Venus

8 KVKB (כּוֹכָב): Kokab—Stellar Light: Mercury

9 LBNH (לְבָנָה): Levanah—Lunar Flame: Moon

10 ChLMf ISVDVTh (חֹלַם יְסוֹדוֹת): Cholom Yesodoth—Breaker (Dreamer) of Foundations: The Four Elements

49. Tycho's Heavenly Spheres

Primum Mobile

Zodiacal Sphere

Sphere of Saturn

Sphere of Jupiter

Sphere of Mars

Sphere of Sun

Sphere of Venus

Sphere of Mercury

Sphere of the Moon

Sphere of the Elements

X. Astrology (Assiah) (cont'd.)

Table 50. Robert Fludd's astrological hierarchy is listed, as well as the essential energy and function of each of these ten astrological levels.

Table 51. The Zodiac as the ten Sephiroth is listed in light of the planetary rulership of each Sephirah. This table is based on the seven ancient planets.

Table 52. The ten modern planets (including Uranus, Pluto, and Neptune) as the ten Sephiroth, where Saturn is Malkuth, are listed.

	50. Fludd's Astrological Hierarchy	51. Zodiac (Seven Ancient Planets)	52. Ten Modern Planets
1	Primum Mobile—Material Essence	Beyond Zodiacal Qualities	Uranus (root of Air)
2	Stellar Heavens—Essence of Form	All 12 signs of the Zodiac	Pluto (root of Fire)
3	Sphere of Saturn—Junction of Matter with Form	Capricorn and Aquarius	Neptune (root of Water)
4	Sphere of Jupiter—Nature's Energy	Sagittarius and Pisces	Jupiter
5	Sphere of Mars—Impulsive Energy	Aries and Scorpio	Mars
6	Sphere of Sun—Vital Energy	Leo	Sun
7	Sphere of Venus—Power of Desire	Taurus and Libra	Venus
8	Sphere of Mercury—Power of Fancy	Gemini and Virgo	Mercury
9	Sphere of The Moon—Vegetative Energy	Cancer	Moon
10	Elements—Corruptive Energy	Elemental Personalities (Fire, Water, Air, Earth)	Saturn

X. Astrology (Assiah) (cont'd.)

Table 53. The Zodiac, in light of table 52, is allocated to the ten Sephiroth in accordance with planetary rulership.

Table 54. The seven horizontal planes of the Tree of Life as the seven ancient planets are listed here in accordance with Golden Dawn symbolism.

Table 55. The seven Qabalistic palaces of the King (God) are listed in accordance with Golden Dawn symbolism. Each palace is a planet as shown in table 54.

	53. Zodiac (Modern Planets)	54. Seven Planetary Planes (Golden Dawn)	55. Seven Palaces of the King (Golden Dawn)
1	Aquarius	Saturn	First Palace (Highest) (Saturn)
2	Scorpio	Jupiter	First Palace (Highest) (Saturn)
3	Pisces	Jupiter	First Palace (Highest) (Saturn)
4	Sagittarius	Mars	Second Palace (Jupiter)
5	Aries	Mars	Third Palace (Mars)
6	Leo	Sun	Fourth Palace (Sun)
7	Taurus and Libra	Venus	Fifth Palace (Venus)
8	Gemini and Virgo	Venus	Sixth Palace (Mercury)
9	Cancer	Mercury	Seventh Palace (Lowest) (Moon)
10	Capricorn	Moon	Seventh Palace (Lowest) (Moon)

XI. Demonology (Assiah) (Tables 56-59)

The hierarchy of demons as reflected both in the World of Assiah and the inverted (or evil) Tree of Life are listed in this section.

Table 56. The Hebrew transliteration and translation of the archdemons who rule the World of Assiah (or matter) are listed in accordance with the Golden Dawn system.

Table 57. The Hebrew transliteration and translation of the devils who rule the inverted Tree of Life reflected in the fourth (black) quadrant of Malkuth, known as the Qlippoth (or Shells), are given in accordance with the Golden Dawn system.

56. Golden Dawn Hebrew for Archdemons—World of Assiah

1 ShTNf VMLKf (שֶׂטֶן וּמֶלֶךְ): Satan and Moloch—Accuser and King
2 BOLZBVB (בַּעַלְזְבוּב): Beelzebub—Lord of the Flies
3 AILThA D ShChRA (אִילְתָא דְ שַׁחְרָא or אֵילְתָא): Lucifuge (Lucifer)—The Morning Star
4 OShThRTh (עַשְׁתָּרֶת): Ashtaroth—Goddess of Fertility
5 AShMDAI (אַשְׁמְדָאִ): Asmodeus—King of Men
6 BOLPGR (בַּעַלְפְּגָר): Belphegor—Lord of Death (Opium)
7 BOL (also BAAL) (בַּעַל; also בַּעֲל): Baal—Lord, Master
8 ADRMLKf (אֲדַרְמֶּלֶךְ): Adrammelech—Magnificence (swelling) of the King
9 LILITh (לִילִית): Lilith—Queen of the Night
10 NHMH (נַחֲמָה): Nahema—Groaning of the Afflicted

57. Golden Dawn Hebrew for Qlippoth (inverted Tree of Life)

ThAVMIAL (תַּאוּמִיאֵל): Thaumiel—Two Heads (contending forces)
OVGIAL (עוּגִיאֵל): Ghogiel—Hinderers
SThRIAL (or SAThRIAL) (סְתְרִיאֵל or סַתְרִיאֵל): Satariel—Concealers
GVG ShKLH (גּוֹג שְׁכֶלָה): Gog Shekeloh—Breakers in Pieces
GVLChB (גָּלָחָב): Golohab—Coal burners
ThGRIRVN (תַּגְרִירוֹן): Tagiriron—Disputers
ORB ZRQ (also ORB ShRQ) (עֹרֵב זְרַק; also עֹרֵב שְׁרַק): Harab Tzerek—Ravens of Death
SMAL (סַמָאֵל): Samael—Liar (Poison) of God
GMLIAL (גַּמָלִיאֵל): Gamaliel—Obscene Ones
LILITh (לִילִית): Lilith—Queen of Night and Demons

XI. Demonology (Assiah) (cont'.d.)

Table 58. Francis Barrett's Infernal World of the Damned is given as found in his work, *The Magus* (1801).

Table 59. The ten false idols of the ten Sephiroth are listed as found in Eliphas Levi's *The Mysteries of the Qabalah* (1861).

58. Barrett's Order of the Damned

1	False Gods
2	Lying Spirits
3	Vessels of Iniquity
4	Revengers of Wickedness
5	Jugglers
6	Airy Powers
7	Furies, the Seminaries of Evil
8	Sifters, or Triers
9	Tempters, or Ensnarers
10	Wicked Souls Bearing Rule

59. Ten False Idols (Infernal World) (Eliphas Levi)

Remphan—The Reverse Star of Despotism (fatality)

Nibbas—The Dog (blind faith and fanaticism)

Thartac—The Ass (limited stupidity, stubborn fatality)

Azima—The Goat (obscure love)

Marcolis—The Stone (inflexible rigor, fatality)

Anamelech—The Horse (triumph of the beast)

Nergal—The Cock (foolish pride)

Succoth Benoth—The Hen (fatal maternity)

Nisroch—The Lingam (impure marriage)

Adramelech—The Peacock (the proud world)

XII. Cosmology (Tables 60-77)

The various descriptions of the hierarchies of the Universe as relating to the ten Sephiroth are given in this section.

Table 60. The Four Worlds and Adam Qadmon (the archetypal form of Man) are allocated to the ten Sephiroth in accordance with the orthodox Jewish Qabalah.

Table 61. The seven days of creation are paralleled with the ten Sephiroth as found in the *Zohar* (13th century CE). Note that the three Supernals existed before the creation of this world, while the seven infernals are the actual seven days of creation, God resting in Malkuth. By analogy, the eighth day of creation, when Eve was formed, can be allocated to Daath, the 11th invisible Sephirah.

60. Traditional Qabalah: The Four Worlds and Man

1	Adam Qadmon—Divine Man
2	World of Atziloth (Archetype)—1st World (אצילה)
3	World of Briah (Creation)—2nd World (בריאה)
4	World of Yetzirah (Formation)—3rd World (יצירה)
5	World of Yetzirah (Formation)—3rd World (יצירה)
6	World of Yetzirah (Formation)—3rd World (יצירה)
7	World of Yetzirah (Formation)—3rd World (יצירה)
8	World of Yetzirah (Formation)—3rd World (יצירה)
9	World of Yetzirah (Formation)—3rd World (יצירה)
10	World of Asiah (Action)—4th World (עשיה)

61. Seven Days of Creation (*Zohar*)

Before Creation

Before Creation

Before Creation

1st Day (Sunday)

2nd Day (Monday)

3rd Day (Tuesday)

4th Day (Wednesday)

5th Day (Thursday)

6th Day (Friday)

7th Day (Saturday)

XII. Cosmology (cont'd.)

Tables 62 through 64 show Francisco Giorgi's threefold division of the Universe.

Table 62. Description of the Highest or Angelic World of the ten Sephiroth. These correspondences are found in *Celestial Harmonies of the World* (1525). In this first table, God is Kether while the angels are Malkuth.

Table 63. This table details the Middle or Celestial World of Giorgi's threefold universe. Here the planetary order found in tables 48–50 is displaced by one with the allocation of the Celestial Government as Kether.

Table 64. This table details the Lowest or Corruptible World of Giorgi's threefold universe. Here, Man is allocated to Kether of the Third World as God is Kether of the First World. The elemental order of Fire, Water, Air, and Earth is the same elemental order found in the Golden Dawn Tetragrammaton order of the Minor Arcana (Wands, Cups, Swords, and Pentacles).

	62. Giorgi's Threefold World (Highest Angelic World)	63. Giorgi's Threefold World (Middle—Celestial World)	64. Giorgi's Threefold World (Lowest—Corruptible World)
1	God	Celestial Government	Man
2	Seraphim	First Cause	Animals
3	Cherubim	Zodiac	Reptiles, Birds, Fish, Insects
4	Thrones	Saturn	Plants
5	Dominions	Jupiter	Metals
6	Virtues	Mars	Ether
7	Powers	Sun	Fire
8	Principalities	Venus	Water
9	Archangels	Mercury	Air
10	Angels	Moon	Earth

XII. Cosmology (cont'd.)

Tables 65 through 69 show Athanasius Kircher's 50 Gates of Light, which reside in the Sephirah of Binah and the Hebrew letter *Nun*. These 50 gates are the ten Sephiroth as a fivefold cosmos of 5 x 10, or 50 gradations of matter from chaos, the first gate, to God, the 50th gate. These 50 gates are allocated to the Sephiroth, where the first gate is the tenth Sephirah of the first order and the 50th and last gate is the first Sephirah of the fifth order. These 50 gates are found in Kircher's *Oedipus Ægyptiacus* (1623).

Table 65. This table shows the first ten gates of the first order, corresponding to the Elementary World. Here the elemental order is male first and female last as Fire, Air, Water, and Earth.

Table 66. This table details the second ten gates of the second order, corresponding to the Evolutionary World. This order is composed of gates 11 through 20, 11 being Malkuth and 20 being Kether. Here the inanimate kingdom evolves into the world of invertebrates and vertebrates.

65. Kircher's 50 Gates of Understanding (First Order: Elementary)

1   Gate 10—Mixture and Combination
2   Gate 9—Differentiation of Qualities
3   Gate 8—Fire
4   Gate 7—Air
5   Gate 6—Water
6   Gate 5—Earth (no seed germs)
7   Gate 4—Origin of Elements
8   Gate 3—Abyss
9   Gate 2—Formless, Void, Lifeless
10   Gate 1—Chaos, Hyle, First Matter

66. Kircher's 50 Gates of Understanding (Second Order: Evolution)

Gate 20—Quadrupeds, Vertebrate Earth Animals
Gate 19—Birds, Vertebrate Life in the Air
Gate 18—Fishes, Vertebrate Life in Water
Gate 17—Insects and Reptiles appear
Gate 16—Origin of Law forms of animal life
Gate 15—Fructification in vegetable life
Gate 14—Herbs and Trees
Gate 13—Seeds germinate in moisture
Gate 12—Vegetable principles appear
Gate 11—Minerals differentiate

XII. Cosmology (cont'd.)

Table 67. This table details the third order of the 50 gates, corresponding to the Human World. This order is composed of gates 21 through 30, 21 being Malkuth and 30 being Kether. Here the appearance of Man in the evolutionary scale is Malkuth, while Kether is Man in the image of God (reminiscent of Giorgi's attributing of both God and Man to Kether in his 30 gradations of the Universe).

Table 68. This table details the fourth order of the 50 gates, corresponding to the Heavenly World (or World of the Spheres). Here the astrological correspondences are reminiscent of Francisco Giorgi's planetary order, in which Saturn is Chesed rather than Binah and the Moon is Malkuth rather than Yesod. The Empyrean Heaven takes the place of Giorgi's Celestial Government as Kether.

67. Kircher's 50 Gates of Understanding (Third Order: Humanity)

1	Gate 30—Man in the Image of God
2	Gate 29—Angelic Beings
3	Gate 28—Adam Kadmon, The Heavenly Man
4	Gate 27—Gift of five powers to the soul
5	Gate 26—Gift of five human faces acting exteriorly
6	Gate 25—Complete man as the microcosm
7	Gate 24—Mystery of Adam and Eve
8	Gate 23—Human soul conferred
9	Gate 22—Material Human Body
10	Gate 21—Appearance of Man

68. Kirchers's 50 Gates of Understanding (Fourth Order: Heavenly)

Gate 40—The Empyrean Heaven

Gate 39—The Primum Mobile

Gate 38—The Firmament

Gate 37—The Heaven of Saturn

Gate 36—The Heaven of Jupiter

Gate 35—The Heaven of Mars

Gate 34—The Heaven of Sun

Gate 33—The Heaven of Venus

Gate 32—The Heaven of Mercury

Gate 31—The Heaven of Moon

XII. Cosmology (cont'd.)

Table 69. This table shows gates 41 through 50. Here two worlds are shown, making the gates in reality a sixfold universe. Gates 41 through 49, corresponding to Malkuth through Chockmah, form the fifth order, being the Angelic World. The angelic order is similar to the angelic order of the *Magical Calendar* of Tycho Brahe, but is permutated, swapping the lead angel of the Cherubim with the Auphanim. The 50th gate, corresponding to the only gate of the sixth order, the Archetypal World, is attributed to God, whom no mortal eye, save that of Moses, has beheld. Here God is allocated to the *Ain Soph*, the concept of zero which precedes and is the source of the ten Sephiroth.

69. Kircher's 50 Gates of Understanding (Angelic and Archetype; Fifth and Sixth Order)

1	Gate 50—God, Ain Soph (6th Order)
2	Gate 49—Cherubim, Archangels
3	Gate 48—Ben Elohim, Angels
4	Gate 47—Elohim, Principalities
5	Gate 46—Melachim, Powers
6	Gate 45—Seraphim, Virtues
7	Gate 44—Chashmalim, Dominions
8	Gate 43—Aralim, Thrones
9	Gate 42—Ophanim, Cherubim
10	Gate 41—Ishim, Sons of Fire

XII. Cosmology (cont'd.)

Tables 70 through 72 outline the sevenfold system of the Theosophical cosmology. The threefold set of seven worlds is paralleled to the seven horizontal planes of the Tree of Life.

Table 70. This table shows the chain of seven globes corresponding to the Theosophical order of the seven planets which comprise the Kosmos. The highest world is Jupiter and the lowest world is the Sun.

Table 71. This table details the seven Higher Theosophical Worlds known as Lokas. These seven Lokas range from the blindness of Earth to the enlightenment of Nirvana, Bhur to Satya.

Table 72. This table details the Theosophical seven Lower Worlds known as Talas. These seven talas range from the gross body (Patala) to death and rebirth (Atala).

	70. Seven Theosophical Worlds (Globes, Kosmos)	71. Seven Theosophical Higher Worlds (Lokas)	72. Seven Theosophical Lower Worlds (Talas)
1	Auric (or Prakritic) World (Jupiter)	Satya (Nirvana)	Atala (Death and Rebirth)
2	Alayic World (Mercury)	Tapar (Of The Gods and Goddesses)	Vitala (Separation of Higher from Lower)
3	Alayic World (Mercury)	Tapar (Of The Gods and Goddesses)	Vitala (Separation of Higher from Lower)
4	Mahatic World (Saturn)	Janar (Of The Masters Beyond the Physical Plane)	Sutala (Mind struggling with desire)
5	Mahatic World (Saturn)	Janar (Of The Masters Beyond the Physical Plane)	Sutala (Mind struggling with desire)
6	Fohatic World (Venus)	Mahar (Between Earth and Utmost limits of Universe)	Talatala (Lower Mind, Objective Life)
7	Jivic World (Mars)	Svar (Between Pole Star and Sun —of the yogis)	Rasatala (Desire)
8	Jivic World (Mars)	Svar (Between Pole Star and Sun —of the yogis)	Rasatala (Desire)
9	Astral World (Moon)	Bhuvar (Between Earth and Sun —of the Wiseman)	Mahatala (Astral shadow or double body)
10	Objective World (Sun)	Bhur (Earth)	Patala (Gross Body)

XII. Cosmology (cont'd.)

Table 73. Paul Foster Case, in his *Book of Tokens* (1934), divides the Tree of Life into seven horizontal planes of the Universe. These seven planes are Hermetic modifications of the Theosophical sevenfold universe, in light of the teachings of the Golden Dawn.

73. Seven Planets of the Universe (Case, Golden Dawn)

1 Spiritual Plane
2 Causal Plane
3 Causal Plane
4 Higher Mental Plane
5 Higher Mental Plane
6 Egoic Plane
7 Lower Mental Plane
8 Lower Mental Plane
9 Astral Plane
10 Physical Plane

XII. Cosmology (cont'd.)

Table 74. The double-cube altar used in the ritual furniture of the Golden Dawn is composed of two perfect cubes joined together to form ten square faces. Each face is a direction in space, a color, and one of ten Sephiroth, as shown in this table. The elemental order used is Enochian in origin, allowing each of the ten Sephiroth to be aligned by the directions of the four Enochian Watchtowers. The Enochian-Sephirotic directional symbolism system is shown in the table on the opposite page.

Table 75. This table gives the directions in space for the ten Sephiroth based on the Golden Dawn arrangement of the Tree of Life (where Kether is East, Malkuth is West, Chesed South, Geburah North, and Tiphereth center). The diagonal directions of SE, NE, SW, and NW are extrapolated from the above directions. This table is the basis for the first set of trigram allocations found in table 33 and serves as a variant to the directional Sephiroth found in the double-cubic altar of table 74.

74. Ten Faces of Double Cube Altar (Golden Dawn)

1	Above (White)
2	Below (Gray)
3	North Above (Black)
4	West Above (Blue)
5	South Above (Red)
6	East Above (Yellow)
7	South Below (Green)
8	West Below (Orange)
9	East Below (Violet)
10	North Below (Citrine, Russet, Olive, Black)

75. Direction in Space (Golden Dawn)

	East
	Southeast
	Northeast
	South
	North
	Center
	Southwest
	Northwest
	Center (W)
	West

74A. Enochian-Sephirotic Directions

Enochian Watchtower	Element	Direction in Space	Sephirah
Tablet of Union	Spirit	Above (Center)	Kether
Tablet of Union	Spirit	Below (Center)	Chockmah
Tablet of Air	Air	East	Tiphereth
Tablet of Air	Air	East	Yesod
Tablet of Fire	Fire	South	Geburah
Tablet of Fire	Fire	South	Netzach
Tablet of Water	Water	West	Chesed
Tablet of Water	Water	West	Hod
Tablet of Earth	Earth	North	Binah
Tablet of Earth	Earth	North	Malkuth

XII. Cosmology (cont'd.)

Table 76. The Enochian universe of John Dee is allocated to the ten Sephiroth. The allocations for the first, seventh, eighth, ninth, and tenth Sephiroth are from the Golden Dawn. The second through sixth Sephiroth are extrapolated from the ritual working tools used by John Dee and Edward Kelley in their skrying sessions.

Table 77. The nine worlds of the Nordic Tree of Life (the Yggdrasil Tree) are allocated to the Tree of Life according to the elemental allocations of the Golden Dawn. Here the second world of Light, Spirits, and Fairies occupies both Chockmah and Binah in the scheme of ten Sephiroth.

	76. Enochian Universe (Dee and Golden Dawn)	**77. Yggdrasil Tree (Nine Caverns of Odin)**
1	Tablet of Union (Spirit)	1st World: Asgard—highest point of the universe, Heaven of the Gods
2	21 letters of Enochian alphabet	2nd World: Alfheim—World of Light, Spirits and Fairies
3	48 Calls of 30 Aethyrs	2nd World: Alfheim—World of Light, Spirits and Fairies
4	Skrying Table	6th World: Vanaheim—Watery World of the Vanes, Sea-Gods (West)
5	Pantacles supporting legs of Skrying Table	7th World: Muspellsheim—Fiery World of Flame Gods (South)
6	Skrying Crystal	5th World: Midgard—Middle Place between Asgard and Hel, World of Humans
7	Watchtower of South (Fire)	4th World: Jotunheim—World of Earth's First Inhabitants of Giants (East)
8	Watchtower of West (Water)	3rd World: Niflheim—World of Fog, Mist, or Ice; Doorway to Netherworld (North)
9	Watchtower of East (Air)	8th World: Svartalfaheim—Dark World Under the Earth of Treacherous Elves
10	Watchtower of North (Earth)	9th World: Helheim—Lowest point of the Universe, World of Cold, Abode of Dead

XIII. Pantheons (Tables 78-87)

This section deals with the various hierarchies of Gods and Goddesses as allocated to the ten Sephiroth. This technique of symbolism met its fruition in the Qabalistic circles of the Golden Dawn and was recorded in Aleister Crowley's *Liber 777*.

Table 78. The *Zohar* allocated seven traditional couples as seven successive incarnations of the Divine Male Soul (Adam) and the Divine Female Soul (Eve). These allocations fall to the ten Sephiroth, where Kether is God, Chockmah is Adam, and Binah is Eve, while the seven infernal Sephiroth are the seven transmigrations of the souls of Adam and Eve.

Table 79 The hierarchy of the Egyptian Gods as compiled in Crowley's *Liber 777* is listed (derived from the Egyptian symbolism of the Golden Dawn rituals).

Table 80. The hierarchy of the Greek Gods is extrapolated by Crowley (from 777) in accordance with the traditional planetary allocations of the Sephiroth.

Table 81 The parallel Roman Gods and Goddesses to the Greek Gods and Goddesses of table 80 are listed (from Crowley's 777).

	78. Hebrew Divine Couples (Zohar)	79. Crowley's Egyptian Gods	80. Crowley's Greek Gods	81. Crowley's Roman Gods
1	Beyond Male or Female (Yahweh)	Ptah	Zeus	Jupiter
2	Adam	Isis	Athena	Janus
3	Eve	Nephthys	Demeter	Saturn
4	Abraham and Miriam	Amoun	Poseidon	Jupiter
5	Isaac and Leah	Horus	Hades	Mars
6	Jacob and Hannah	Ra	Apollo	Apollo
7	Moses and Rebeccah	Hathoor	Aphrodite	Venus
8	Aaron and Sarah	Thoth	Hermes	Mercury
9	Joseph and Tamar	Shu	Diana	Diana
10	David and Rachael	Osiris	Persephone	Ceres

XIII. Pantheons (cont'd.)

Table 82. The Pythagorean mythic symbolic images of the ten numbers of the tetractys is paralleled to the ten Sephiroth.

Table 83. The Nordic pantheon of Odinic myths is rectified from the clues found in Israel Regardie's *Garden of Pomegranates* (1932).

82. Pythagorean Pantheon

1	Apollo, Jupiter, Axis
2	Diana, Isis, Erato
3	Saturnia, Hecate, Harmonia
4	Hercules, Mercury, Bacchus
5	Androgynia, Gamelia, Nemesis
6	Venus, Thalia, Panaceia
7	Minerva, Mars, Osiris
8	Rhea, Themis, Neptune
9	Juno, Vulcan, Prometheus
10	Atlas, Phanes, Urania

83. Nordic Pantheon of Odin

Odin—the one-eyed God, Creator of the Universe

Vili—⎱
Ve—⎰ brothers who helped Odin form the Universe

Aegir—God of the Stormy Seas (also the primordial First Giants)

Thor—God of the Hammer and Forge (also the primordial Flame Giant)

Balder—the beautiful, son of Odin

Freyja—sister of Freyr, Goddess of Love

Hothr—blind God of Fate, slayer of Balder with an arrow of mistletoe

Loki—evil murderer of Balder

Ymir—the hoarfrost giant from whose body the Universe was fashioned

XIII. Pantheons (cont'd.)

Table 84. The Theosophical Hindu cosmology as found in Madame Blavatshy's *Isis Unveiled*, vol.2 (1877), is paralleled to the Tree of Life.

Table 85. This table lists the Theosophical Hindu pantheon as allocated to the ten Sephiroth by Papus in his work, *The Qabalah* (1892).

Table 86. This table lists the Hindu pantheon allocated to the ten Sephiroth as compiled by Crowley in his 777.

Table 87. This table lists the Theosophical Hindu pantheon allocated to the ten Sephiroth by Regardie in his *Garden of Pomegranates* (1932).

	84. Hindu Cosmology as Tree of Life (Theosophy-Blavatsky)	85. Papus' Theosophical Indian Sephiroth	86. Crowley's Hindu Deities	87. Hindu-Theosophical Concepts (Regardie)
1	Aditi (That which is beyond Name) A	Brahma	Parabrahm	Adi-Buddha (Ultimate Consciousness)
2	Brahma (Father Ray) U	Vishnu	Shiva	Mahat (Cosmic Ideation)
3	Vach (Sea of Wisdom) (Mother Ray) M	Shiva	Bhavani	Mulaprakriti (Cosmic Root Substance)
4	Vishnu	Maya	Indra	Indra (Lord of Fire and Lightning)
5	Sarasvati	Aum	Vishnu	Sakti (Martial)
6	Inner Shrine (The World within the Universe)	Harangherbeha	Krishna	Hari (Shri Krishna)
7	Parvati	Purusha	Lalita	Bhavani (Venusian)
8	Siva	Pradiapata	Hanuman	Hanuman (Ape or Monkey)
9	Lakshmi	Prakriti	Ganesha	Ganesha (Elephant God)
10	Maya	Prana	Lakshmi	Lakshmi

XIV. Gradations of the Soul (Tables 88–96)

This section details the ten Sephiroth as a measure of the soul, or essence, found within Man as the Microcosm, or Little World.

Table 88. The traditional orthodox Qabalah divides the soul of man into five states, each appearing in the Torah and the Holy Writings. These five states of the soul correspond to five levels of the Tree of Life as detailed in this table.

Table 89. Robert Fludd, in his *Collected Works* (1617), divides the soul of man into the ten Sephiroth, where the supernal Sephiroth comprise the triad of Spirit, Soul, and Body, while the seven infernal Sephiroth are seven elemental gradations of the soul. These ten Sephirotic attributes are listed in this table.

Table 90. Aleister Crowley's tenfold division of the soul, as tabulated in his 777, is listed in this table.

	88. Traditional Qabalah: Five Divisions of the Soul	89. Fludd's Division of the Soul	90. Crowley's Division of the Soul
1	Yechidah (יהידה)—Uniqueness, quintessential principle, Divine Self	Spirit	The Self—The Divine Ego, Divine Repose
2	Chiah (היה)—Vital Life Energy, Creative impulse, Will	Soul	The Ego—That which thinks "I," Divine Will
3	Neshamah (נשמה)—Breath of Life, Intuition, Aspiration, Intelligence	Body	The Soul, Divine Intelligence
4	Ruach (רוח)—Wind-Spirit; The Intellect, Reason	Internal Spirit	Memory, Intellectual Self, Divine Repose
5	Ruach (רוח)—Wind Spirit; The Intellect, Reason	Fiery Realm	Will, Divine Will interplaying with Matter
6	Ruach (רוח)—Wind Spirit; The Intellect, Reason	Vivifying Realm	Imagination—Conscious Self, Mind
7	Ruach (רוח)—Wind Spirit; The Intellect, Reason	Spermatic Realm	Desire, Animal Emotion
8	Ruach (רוח)—Wind Spirit; The Intellect, Reason	Windy Realm	Reason, Intellect, Change in stability
9	Ruach (רוח)—Wind Spirit; The Intellect, Reason	Watery Realm	Animal Being—Unconscious Self, Stability in change
10	Nephesh (נפש)—Soul, Animal Soul, Senses, Emotion	Earthy Realm	Illusory physical envelope, Divine End

XIV. Gradations of the Soul (cont'd.)

Table 91. Paul Foster Case's tenfold division of the soul found in his *Book of Tokens* (1934) is listed in this table. Note that Case used Crowley's allocations (table 90) as the basis for his own system.

Table 92. The Theosophical divisions of the soul as allocated by Crowley to the ten Sephiroth is shown in this table (from *Liber 777*).

Table 93. The seven chakras of the Hindu Tantrik School are tabulated in light of Crowley's allocations (*777*).

	91. Divisions of the Soul (Case—Golden Dawn)	92. Theosophical Division of the Soul (Crowley)	93. Crowley's Chakras
1	Divine Self (Cosmic Self)	Atma	Sahasara
2	Divine Life (Life Force)	Buddhi	Ajna
3	Divine Mind (Intuition)	Higher Manas	Visuddhi
4	Memory	Lower Manas	Anahata
5	Volition	Lower Manas	Anahata
6	Central Self (The Ego)	Lower Manas	Anahata
7	Desire	Kama	Manipura
8	Intellect	Prana	Svadistthana
9	Vital Soul (Automatic Consciousness)	Linga Sharira	Muladhara
10	Body (Sensation)	Sthula Sharira	Muladhara

XIV. Gradations of the Soul (cont'd.)

Table 94. A variant to Crowley's Sephirotic chakras is shown in this table, based on the seven horizontal planes of the Tree of Life. This allocation allows the five lower chakras (ruled by the five gross Tattvas) to correspond to the seven infernal Sephiroth, and the two higher chakras (ruled by the two esoteric chakras) to correspond to the three supernal Sephiroth.

Table 95. The tenfold Egyptian soul as outlined by Florence Farr in her book *Egyptian Magic* (1896) is paralleled to the ten Sephiroth of the Tree of Life.

Table 96. The Egyptian division of the soul as allocated by Crowley (in his *777*) and revised by Regardie (in his *Garden of Pomegranates*).

	94. Chakras (based on 7 horizontal levels of the Tree of Life)	95. Tenfold Egyptian Soul (S.S.D.D.-Golden Dawn)	96. Egyptian Parts of the Soul (Crowley-Regardie)
1	Sahasara (7th) Crown of Head (Mercury)	Hammemit (Unborn Soul)	Khabs (Individuality)
2	Ajna (6th) Third Eye (Moon)	Khu (Magickal Powers)	Khu (Magickal Power)
3	Ajna (6th) Third Eye (Moon)	Ba (Penetrating Mind)	Ba (Penetrating Mind)
4	Visuddha (5th) Throat (Venus)	Ka (Human Ego)	Ab (The heart as Human Will)
5	Visuddha (5th) Throat (Venus)	Aib (The Will)	Ab (The heart as Human Will)
6	Anahata (4th) Heart (Sun)	Hati (Human Heredity)	Ab (The heart as Human Will)
7	Manipura (3rd) Navel (Jupiter)	Khaibt (Aura)	Ab (The heart as Human Will)
8	Manipura (3rd) Navel (Jupiter)	Tet (Spiritual Body)	Ab (The heart as Human Will)
9	Svadhisthana (2nd) Genitals (Mars)	Sahu (Astral Body)	Hati (Instinct)
10	Muladhara (1st) Anus (Saturn)	Khat (Body)	Khat (Body)

XV. Gradations of the Mental Body (Tables 97-103)

This section deals with the human mind and its allocation to the Tree of Life.

Tables 97 through 100 detail the tenfold division of the mind found in Henry Khunrath's work, *The Amphitheatre of Eternal Wisdom* (1609).

Table 97. This table details the ten faculties of the mind in Latin with English translation.

Table 98. This table shows Khunrath's tenfold division of the modes which engage the human mind.

Table 99. This table shows Khunrath's ten virtues of the mind, through which man can ascend to God.

97. Khunrath's Faculties

1	Mens (Mind)
2	Intellectus (Intellect)
3	Ratio (Reason)
4	Judicium Superius (superior discernment)
5	Judicium Inferius (inferior discernment)
6	Phantasia (Image-making)
7	Sensus Interior (Internal Senses)
8	Sensus Exterior (External Senses)
9	Medium (Middle)
10	Objectum (Obstacle)

98. Khunrath's Modes

Fides (Faith)
Meditatio (Contemplation)
Cognito (Study)
Amor (Love)

Spes (Hope)

Oratio (Speech)
Conjunctio (Union)

Frequentia (Populace)

Familarities (Friends)
Similtudo (Likeness)

99. Khunrath's Ascending Virtues of Man

Castitas (Chastity)
Benignitas (Benignity)
Prudentia (Prudence)
Misericordia (Mercy)

Fortitudo (Strength)

Patientia (Patience)
Justica (Justice)

Humilitas (Humility)

Temperantia (Temperance)
Timor Dei (Fear of God)

XV. Gradations of the Mental Body (cont'd.)

Table 100. This table shows Khunrath's ten descending aspects, through which God can commune with the mind of man.

Table 101. This table shows Eliphas Levi's division of society as perceived by the mind of man into the hierarchy of the ten Sephiroth.

100. Khunrath's Descending Aspects of God

1	Optimus Omnia Videns (The Optimum Good for All)
2	Multus Benignitate (Great Benignity)
3	Solus Sapiens (Solitary Wisdom)
4	Misericors (Compassionate)
5	Fortis (Powerful)
6	Longanimis (Longest)
7	Justus (Equal)
8	Maximus (Greatest)
9	Verax Zelotes (Envied Spoken Truth)
10	Terribilis (Dreadful)

101. Society as Ten Sephiroth (Levi)

	Authority
	Wisdom
	Intelligence
	Devotion
	Justice
	Honour
	Progress
	Order
	Social Truth
	Humanity

XV. Gradations of the Mental Body (cont'd.)

Table 102. The Masonic teachings as found in Albert Pike's *Morals and Dogma* (1871) allocate to each Sephirah a different gradation of God as perceived by the mind of man, as shown in this table.

Table 103. This table shows the various states of consciousness open to man through the ten channels of the Sephiroth.

102. Aspects of God and Man (Masonry-Pike)

1	Will, Determination to act
2	Intellectual power, Wisdom to create, To will and act
3	Intellectual action, Faculty; Intelligence
4	Equity, Mercy, Divine, Infinite, Good, Light, Male, Free Will
5	Law, Justice, Human, Finite, Evil, Dark, Female, Necessity
6	Perfect equilibrium, Intimate union, Mutually tempering
7	Perfect success, Reconciliation, Harmonious issue
8	Successful result, Glory and laudation
9	Foundation, Basis, Stability, Permanency of things
10	Dominion, Rule, Supremacy, Absolute control

103. States of Consciousness

1	Enlightenment (Vision of God)
2	Vision of the true structure of the Universe
3	Vision of Universal Sorrow
4	Forgiveness
5	Sterness, Control
6	Compassion
7	Devotion
8	Insight, Intuition
9	Visionary dreaming
10	Awareness of the Body

XVI. Gradations of the Physical (Gross) Body (Tables 104–117)

This section deals with the parallel between the human body and the 10 Sephiroth.

Table 104. Traditional Qabalistic symbolism ascribes each of the ten Sephiroth to a division of the human body. The three Supernals control the head, while Yesod and Malkuth are the genitals of male and female.

Table 105. Tycho Brahe's *Magical Calendar* (1620) divides the human body into nine divisions from Chockmah to Malkuth, with Kether assigned to the intangible spirit.

Table 106. Athanasius Kircher's Qabalistic division of the human body is a variant to the attributes of Tycho's *Magical Calendar*. Spirit is not used in this system, while the stomach is added as an extra body division. Kircher assigns the three major organs of the human body—brain, lungs, and heart—to the three Supernals.

Table 107. Francis Barrett's Qabalistic division of the human body is duplicated from the attributes of Tycho's *Magical Calendar*.

	104. Traditional Qabalistic Division of the Body	105. Tycho's Division of Man	106. Kircher's Division of the Body	107. Barrett's Division of Man (Lesser World)
1	Crown of Head	Spirit	Brain	Spirit
2	Right side of brain (right eye)	Brain	Lung	Brain
3	Left side of brain (left eye)	Spleen	Heart	Spleen
4	Right Arm	Liver	Stomach	Liver
5	Left Arm	Gall	Liver	Gall
6	Heart, Trunk of body	Heart	Gall	Heart
7	Right Leg (Right testicle, kidney, ovary)	Kidneys	Spleen	Kidneys
8	Left Leg (Left testicle, kidney, ovary)	Lungs	Kidneys	Lungs
9	Tongue, Genitals (male)	Genitals	Genitals	Genitals
10	Mouth, Genitals (female)	Womb	Womb	Matrix

XVI. Gradations of the Physical (Gross) Body (cont'd.)

The Masonic use of the Tree of Life as a source of ritual symbolism is well known. Tables 108 and 109 give two Masonic variants to the Sephirotic division of the human body.

Table 108. This table is taken from Albert Mackey's *Lexicon of Masonry* (1852). Here Kircher's attribution of the heart to Binah is combined with the traditional orthodox Qabalistic attributes. Note that in this scheme Malkuth is assigned to the feet (an alternate attribute found in Orthodox Jewish Qabalism).

Table 109. This table shows the alternate Masonic division of the human body, taken from Albert Pike's *Morals and Dogma* (1871). This is an exact duplication of the traditional Qabalistic division found in table 104.

Table 110. Tycho Brahe's *Magical Calendar* offers two additional Sephirotic divisions, or gradations, of the human body. This table divides the body into ten substances of which it is composed. Kether is the skeleton structure while Malkuth is the skin.

Table 111. This table shows the gradations of blood according to the ten Sephiroth as detailed in Tycho Brahe's *Magical Calendar*. Here the first five Sephiroth are obvious divisions of blood, while the lower five Sephiroth are abstract concepts supposedly carried within the circulation of blood in the human body.

	108. Masonic-Qabalistic Division of the Human Body (Mackenzie, Mackey)	109. Adam Kadmon's Sephirothic Division of the Body (Masonic-Pike)	110. Tycho's Substances of the Body	111. Tycho's Gradations of Blood
1	Head	Cranium	Bone	Menstruum
2	Brain	Two lobes of brain (Right)	Cartilage	Sperma
3	Heart	Two lobes of brain (Left)	Nerves	Plasma
4	Right Arm	Two arms (Right)	Gut	Clot
5	Left Arm	Two arms (Left)	Ligament	Humors
6	Chest	Trunk	Arteries	Organic Body
7	Right Leg	Two thighs (Right)	Veins	Life Force
8	Left Leg	Two thighs (Left)	Membrane	Sensation
9	Privates	Male organ of generation	Flesh	Reason
10	Feet (or Body as a Whole)	Female organ of generation	Skin	Mind

XVI. Gradations of the Physical (Gross) Body (cont'd.)

Table 112. Robert Fludd gives an additional Sephirotic gradation of breath (or prana). Here breath as the food of life is assigned to Kether, while Malkuth is dense fumes found exuding out of the earth.

Tables 113 through 117 illustrate five separate esoteric systems of allocating the ten fingers of the human body to the ten Sephiroth. These allocations can also be applied to the ten toes, for the *Sepher Yetzirah* informs us that the ten fingers of the right and left hands parallel the ten toes of the right and left feet.

Table 113. This table shows the traditional Qabalistic allocation of the Tetragrammaton to the ten fingers and the ten Sephiroth when the two hands are held in the triangular Qabalistic mudra known as the Kiddush, or blessing of the cup, in imitation of the supernal Sephiroth. Here the five fingers of the right hand are the five upper Sephiroth, while the five fingers of the left hand are the five lower Sephiroth. Kether is the right middle finger while Malkuth is the left index finger.

Table 114. The Golden Dawn allocation of the ten fingers is based on the pentagram placed over each hand. The right thumb represents Kether (and Spirit) while the left middle finger is Malkuth (and Earth). Here the two thumbs are Kether and Chockmah, while the eight remaining fingers are the eight remaining Sephiroth.

	112. Fludd's Gradations of Breath (Prana)	**113. 10 Fingers as Tetragrammaton (Traditional) Valued at 45**	**114. Golden Dawn Order of 10 Fingers**
1	Food of Life	I (Right Middle Finger)	Right Thumb (Spirit)
2	Impulse of Life	V (Right Ring Finger)	Left Thumb (Spirit)
3	Terrestrial Fume	D (Right Little Finger)	Right Middle (Earth)
4	Vapor of Life	H (Right Thumb)	Right Index (Water)
5	Warm Exhalations	A (Right Index Finger)	Right Ring (Fire)
6	Humid Exhaltations	V (Left Middle Finger)	Right Little (Air)
7	Life Vapor Greater Humidity	A (Left Ring Finger)	Left Ring (Fire)
8	Medium Exhaltations	V (Left Little Finger)	Left Index (Water)
9	Dense Vapor	H (Left Thumb)	Left Little (Air)
10	Dense Fumes	A (Left Index Finger)	Left Middle (Earth)

XVI. Gradations of the Physical (Gross) Body (cont'd.)

Table 115. The Golden Dawn attributes given in Table 114 may be blinded. In light of the symbolic hand positions found in the Major Arcana of the Tarot, this table offers a rectification of the attributes of table 114. Table 115A compares both elemental allocations.

115. Secret Elemental-Planetary Order of the Ten Fingers

1 Right Thumb (Spirit—1st Cause)
2 Left Thumb (Spirit—Zodiac)
3 Right Little Finger (Earth—Saturn)
4 Right Index Finger (Water—Jupiter)
5 Right Middle Finger (Fire—Mars)
6 Right Ring Finger (Air—Sun)
7 Left Middle Finger (Fire—Venus)
8 Left Index Finger (Water—Mercury)
9 Left Ring Finger (Air—Moon)
10 Left Little Finger (Earth—The Four Elements)

115A. Elemental Finger Order

Finger	G.D. Exoteric Order	Secret Order
Thumb	Spirit	Spirit
Index	Water	Water
Middle	Earth	Fire
Ring	Fire	Air
Little	Air	Earth

XVI. Gradations of the Physical (Gross) Body (cont'd.)

Table 116. Esoteric Buddhism allocates the five fingers of each hand to the cycle of five Tattvas. The natural order of the Tattvas is allocated to five fingers of each hand, with the thumb as Akasha and the little finger as Prithivi.

Table 117. The Chinese symbolism of the *I Ching* allocates the eight trigrams to the eight lesser fingers of the hands while Yin and Yang are allocated to the two thumbs. Yang is assigned to the left hand, while Yin is assigned to the right hand. The left little finger is Ch'ien, the trigram composed of all Yang lines, while the right little finger is K'un, the trigram composed of all Yin lines. The actual allocation of the trigrams to the Sephiroth is based on Crowley's Chinese cosmology (see the bracketed information in table 33).

	116. Ten Fingers as Tattvas (Esoteric Buddhism)	117. Ten Fingers as Trigrams (Crowley Sephirotic order)
1	Right Thumb (Akasha)	Left Thumb (Yang)
2	Left Thumb (Akasha)	Right Thumb (Yin)
3	Right Little Finger (Prithivi)	Left Little Finger (Ch'ien)
4	Right Ring Finger (Apas)	Left Ring Finger (Tui)
5	Right Middle Finger (Tejas)	Left Index Finger (Chen)
6	Right Index Finger (Vayu)	Left Middle Finger (Li)
7	Left Middle Finger (Tejas)	Right Ring Finger (Ken)
8	Left Ring Finger (Apas)	Right Index Finger (Sun)
9	Left Index Finger (Vayu)	Right Middle Finger (K'an)
10	Left Little Finger (Prithivi)	Right Little Finger (K'un)

XVII. Animals (Tables 119-120)

This section deals with the assignment of animals (both real and mythic) to the ten Sephiroth.

Table 118. Tycho Brahe's *Magical Calendar* lists ten animals in light of the astrological attributes of the Sephiroth. Tycho combines Christian and alchemical animal symbolism. The dove is the descent of Spirit as Kether, while the lamb is the embodiment of Spirit in flesh as Malkuth. The spots of the leopard represent the fixed stars of the night sky, while the remaining seven animals pertain to the seven ancient planets.

Table 119. Barrett's Sephirotic animals are copied from Tycho's *Magical Calendar*, with a few variants. Barrett substitutes a lizard for the leopard of Chockmah, and changes the Mercurial snake of Hod to a fox. For Yesod, the cow is changed to a bull, the cow being more lunar in nature than the bull.

Table 120. Aleister Crowley's listing of animals (mythic and real) to the ten Sephiroth assigns the Supernals to God, Man, and Woman, while the seven infernals are mostly mythic animals.

	118. Tycho's Sacred Animals	119. Barrett's Animals Consecrated to God (Elementary World)	120. Crowley's Animals (Real and Imaginary)
1	Dove	Dove	God
2	Leopard	Lizard	Man
3	Dragon	Dragon	Woman
4	Eagle	Eagle	Unicorn
5	Horse	Horse	Basilisk
6	Lion	Lion	Phoenix
7	Man	Man	Lynx
8	Snake	Fox	Jackal
9	Cow	Bull	Elephant
10	Lamb	Lamb	Sphinx

XVIII. Plants, Perfumes, Drugs, and Stones (Tables 121-124)

This section deals with the Sephirotic attributes of the vegetable and mineral kingdoms. The four tables of this section are all extracted from Aleister Crowley's *Liber 777*, since such Qabalistic classifications are not detailed in most other sources.

Table 121. This table categorizes ten select plants for the ten Sephiroth, based on their Qabalistic-astrological attributes.

Table 122. This table details ten gradations of magickal perfumes which correspond to the ten Sephiroth.

Table 123. This table details ten vegetable drugs which serve as doorways to the ten Sephiroth.

Table 124. This table lists ten precious stones corresponding to the ten Sephiroth as envisioned by Crowley.

	121. Crowley's Plants	122. Crowley's Perfumes	123. Crowley's Vegetable Drugs	124. Crowley's Precious Stones
1	Almond in Flower	Ambergris	Elixir Vitae	Diamond
2	Amaranth	Musk	Hashish	Turquoise
3	Cypress	Myrrh	Belladonna	Pearl
4	Olive	Cedar	Opium	Sapphire
5	Oak	Dragon's Blood	Nux Vomica	Ruby
6	Acacia	Frankincense	Jimson Weed	Topaz
7	Rose	Rose	Damiana	Emerald
8	Moly	White Sandalwood	Mescaline	Opal
9	Mandrake	Jasmine	Orchid Root	Quartz
10	Lily	Dittany of Crete	Alcohol	Rock Crystal

XIX. Alchemy (Tables 125-136)

XIX. —This section details both the alchemical and elemental associations for the ten Sephiroth. The Hebrew Qabalistic text, *The Fire of the Alchemist* (*Aesch Mezareph*), found as an addenda to the *Zohar*), was translated by Wynn Westcott and utilized in the teachings of the Golden Dawn. Tables 125 through 128 detail four Sephirotic gradations of alchemical metals found in the *Aesch Mezareph*.

Table 125. This table shows the ten types of lead which occur in the Holy Scriptures and their correspondences to the ten Sephiroth. Lead is assigned to the Sephirah Chockmah.

125. Ten Grades of Lead for Chokmah (*Aesch Mezareph*)

1 KKR OPRTh NShATh (שָׂאת עוֹפֶרֶת כִּכַּר)—A lead cover was lifted up (Zech. 5:7)

2 ABN HOVPRTh AL PIH (פִּיהָ אֶל הַעוֹפֶרֶת אָבֶן)—Lead stone on its mouth (Zech. 5:8)

3 OVPRTh NThNV OZBVNIKf (עִזְבוֹנָיִךְ נָתְנוּ עוֹפֶרֶת)—Lead they gave for your wares (Ezek. 27:12)

4 VBIDV ANKf (אֲנָךְ וּבְיָדוֹ)—And in his hand a lead plumbline (Amos 7:7)

5 VATh HOPRTh KL DBR AShR BA BASh (בָּאֵשׁ בָּא אֲשֶׁר דָּבָר כָּל הָעוֹפֶרֶת וְאֵת)—And the lead, everything that goes through the fire (Num. 31:22, 23)

6 BOT BRZL VOPRTh (וְעוֹפֶרֶת בַּרְזֶל בְּעֵט)—With an iron and lead pen (Job 19:24)

7 VOVPRTh BThVKf KVR SIGIMf KSPf HIV (הָיוּ כֶסֶף סִיגִים כּוּר בְּתוֹךְ וְעוֹפֶרֶת)—And lead in the middle of the furnace, they are the dross of silver (Ezek. 22:18)

8 VOVPRTh AL ThVKf KVR LPChTh OLIV ASh LHNThIKf (לְהַנְתִּיךְ אֵשׁ עָלָיו לָפַחַת כּוּר תּוֹךְ אֶל וְעוֹפֶרֶת)—And lead into the middle of the furnace to blow the fire on it to melt it (Ezek. 22:20)

9 MAShThMf OPRTh (עוֹפֶרֶת מְאַשְׁתַם)—The lead comes whole from the fire (Jer. 6:29)

10 TzLLV KOVPRTh BMIMf ADIRIMf (אַדִּירִים בְּמַיִם כָעוֹפֶרֶת צָלְלוּ)—They sank like lead in mighty waters (Exod. 15:10)

XIX. Alchemy (cont'd.)

Table 126. This table details the ten Sephirotic gradations for Alchemical Silver. Silver is assigned to the Sephirah Gedulah (Chesed).

126. Ten Grades of Silver for Gedulah (Aesch Mezareph)

1. RAShIHMf KSPf (כסף ראשׁיהם)—The capitals (of the pillars were) silver (Exod. 38:16)

2. AS TBQShNH KKSPf (כסף אם תבקשׁנה)—If you seek her as silver (Prov. 2:4)

3. BINH NBChR MKSPf (מכסף נבחר בינה)—Binah (understanding) to be chosen above silver (Prov. 16:16)

4. KBD BKSPf (בכסף כבד)—(Abram) was (very) rich in silver (Gen. 13:2)

5. MTzRPf LKSPf (לכסף מצרף)—The alchemist's furnace for silver (Prov. 17:3)

6. ChDVHI VDROVHI DI KSPf (כסף די וׁדרעוׁהי וחדוׁהי)—Its breasts and its arms (were) of silver (Dan. 2:32)

7. LKSPf MVTzA (מוׁצא לכסף)—A mine for silver (Job 28:1)

8. ShThI HTzVTzRTh KSPf (כסף חצוׁצרת שׁתי)—Two trumpets of silver (Num. 10:2)

9. KSPf NBChR (נבחר כסף)—Choice silver (Prov. 10:20)

10. KSPf TzRVPf BOLIL LARTzf (כסף צרוׁף בעליל לארץ)—Silver refined in an earthen furnace (Ps. 12:6)

XIX. Alchemy (cont'd.)

Table 127. This table details the ten Sephirotic gradations for Alchemical Gold. Gold is assigned to the Sephirah Geburah.

Table 128. This table shows the ten Sephirotic gradations for Alchemical Brass as symbolized in the Altar of Incense. Brass is assigned to the Sephirah Hod. This set of ten attributes appears as a pyramidal diagram in the rituals of the Golden Dawn.

127. 10 Grades of Gold for Geburah (*Aesch Mezareph*)

1 KThMf PZ (פז כתם)—Pure gold of the head (Song of Sol. 5:11)

2 OPR BTzR (בצר עפר)—Gold dust (white gold) (Job 22:24)

3 ChRVTzf NBChR (נבחר חרוץ)—Choice gold (black) (Prov. 8:10)

4 ZHB ShChVT (שחוט זהב)—Beaten (fine and drawn) gold (II Chron. 9:15)

5 MTzPVNf ZHB (זהב מצפון)—Gold out of the North (Job 37:22)

6 ZHB MVPZ (מופז זהב)—Refined gold (I Kings 10:18)

7 SGVR (סגור)—Pure gold (gold which is shut up in the earth) (Job 28:15)

8 ZHB PRVIMf (פרוים זהב)—Red-orange gold from Parvaim (II Chron. 3:6)

9 ZHB TVB (טוב זהב)—Good gold (silver-colored) (Gen. 2:12)

10 ZHB AVPIR (אופיר זהב)—Arabic gold, gold of Ophir (for coins) (color of ashes) (I Chron. 29:4)

128. The Altar of Incense (Golden Dawn) (From *Aesch Mezareph*: Grades of Brass for Hod)

The Burnt Offering

The Receptacle for The Offering

The Base

The Right Bay

The Left Bay

The Body of the Altar

Two Rings at Right

Two Rings at Left

The Network or Grille

The Foundation

XIX. Alchemy (cont'd.)

Table 129. The Alchemical text, *The Golden Chain of Homer*, describes the alchemical process as a chain of ten circular emblems. This table shows these ten alchemical realms as applied to the Tree of Life. This book formed the basis of much Golden Dawn alchemical symbolism.

Table 130. Robert Fludd's alchemical and elemental hierarchy is listed here in its Sephirotic order. Fludd establishes the Supernals as Kether = Mercury, Chockmah = Sulfur, and Binah = Salt.

129. The Golden Chain of Homer (Alchemical) (Golden Dawn)

1	A perfect consummation, The quintessential; Vapor and humidity changing to earth and dry, Red blood
2	Sperm of the world fixed converting vapor and water into earth
3	Mineral Kingdom
4	Vegetable Kingdom
5	Animal Kingdom
6	Male and female meeting, engendering a perfect fruit
7	Common Salt, Alkali
8	Nitre, the father of all things
9	Dew, Hail, Rain, Snow; Volatile sperm
10	Chaos divided

130. Fludd's Alchemical Hierarchy

Mercury—Water

Sulfur—Fire

Salt—Earth

Mercury of Life—Lower Air

Sulfur—Fire

Salt—Region of the Upper or Fiery Air

Mercurial Virtue—Fresh Water

Mercury with Sulfur—Windy Air

Salt with Mercury—Sea of Dense Water

Salt—Earth

XIX. Alchemy (cont'd.)

Table 131. The Alchemical attributes for each of the ten Sephiroth as found in the Holy Scriptures are presented in this table (from the Qabalistic text, *Aesch Mezareph).*

Table 132. The alternate alchemical attributes found in *Aesch Mezareph* for the ten Sephiroth, based on the three primal elements of Mercury, Salt, and Sulfur, are listed in this table as a variant to table 131. Note that Robert Fludd's assignment of Chockmah to Sulfur and Salt to Binah is switched in these attributes.

Table 133. The traditional alchemical metals, as allocated to the seven ancient planets, are compiled in this table (derived from the Golden Dawn tradition).

	131. Golden Dawn Alchemical (*Aesch Mezareph:* Biblical)	132. Golden Dawn Alchemical (*Aesch Mezareph:* 3 Elements)	133. Golden Dawn Alchemical (Planetary)
1	Metallic Root	Mercury	Root of all Metals
2	Lead	Salt	Electrum (blend of all seven metals)
3	Tin	Sulfur	Lead
4	Silver	Silver	Tin
5	Gold	Gold	Iron
6	Iron	Iron	Gold
7	Hermaphroditical Brass	Copper	Copper
8	Brass	Tin	Quicksilver
9	Mercury	Lead	Silver
10	Medicina Metallorum	Mercury Philosophorum	Ore-bearing metals

XIX. Alchemy (cont'd.)

Table 134. The elemental allocations for each of the ten Sephiroth as designated in the Golden Dawn system, are listed in this table. Note that, for the three Supernals, Kether is the root of Air, Chockmah the root of Fire, and Binah the root of Water.

Table 135. The Golden Dawn elemental associations are listed here, based on four levels of the Tree corresponding to the Tetragrammaton.

Table 136. This table, derived from Flying Roll #7 of the Golden Dawn, updates the alchemical-Sephirotic attributes in light of "modern" chemistry.

134. Golden Dawn Elemental Allocations	135. The Four Elemental Levels and the Tetragrammaton	136. Modern Chemistry (Golden Dawn)
1 Root of Air	Fire (Yod)	Hydrogen
2 Root of Fire	Water (Heh)	Oxygen
3 Root of Water	Water (Heh)	Nitrogen
4 First Reflection of Water	Air (Vav)	Flourine
5 First Reflection of Fire	Air (Vav)	Chlorine
6 First Reflection of Air	Air (Vav)	Carbon
7 Second Reflection of Fire	Air (Vav)	Bromine
8 Second Reflection of Water	Air (Vav)	Iodine
9 Second Reflection of Air	Air (Vav)	Phosphorus
10 Root of Earth	Earth (Heh Final)	Sulfur

XX. Magick (Tables 137-143)

This section deals with the application of Western magickal symbolism to the ten Sephiroth.

Table 137. Henry Khunrath in his *Amphitheatre of Eternal Wisdom* (1609) detailed ten magickal states of consciousness. This table applies these ten states to the ten Sephiroth.

Table 138. Eliphas Levi, in the first book of his *Transcendental Magic* (1856), secretly allocates the ten Sephiroth to the chapter headings of the first ten chapters. These ten magickal grades are detailed in this table.

Table 139. Secret Latin titles for the ten Sephiroth were affixed to the first ten chapter headings of Eliphas Levi's *Transcendental Magic* (1856). This table translates these secret Latin appellations for the Sephiroth.

	137. Magickal Powers (Khunrath)	138. Magickal Division of Sephiroth (Levi)	139. Secret Latin Names for Sephiroth (Levi)
1	Wakefulness	The Candidate	*Disciplina* (instruction, training)
2	Ecstasy	The Pillars of the Temple	*Domus* (house, temple); *gnosis* (secret widsom)
3	Lethargy	The Triangle of Solomon	*Plenitudo* (plenitude, full, complete); *vocis* (voice, word); *physis* (science)
4	Exaltation	The Tetragram	*Porta* (gate); *librarum* (book); *elementa* (four elements)
5	Sleep	Pentagram	*Ecce* (behold, lo)
6	Dream	Magical Equilibrium	*Uncus* (a hook, peg)
7	Epilepsy	The Fiery Sword	*Gladius* (a sword)
8	Catalepsy	Realization	*Vivens* (living, alive)
9	Somnambulism	Initiation	*Bonum* (good, useful, virtuous)
10	Thaumaturgy	The Kabalah	*Principium* (groundwork); *phallus* (penis)

XX. Magick (cont'd.)

Table 140. Crowley, in his work *Liber 777*, classified ten magickal virtues as ten gradations of the Sephiroth. These ten magickal virtues are listed in this table.

Table 141. Crowley, in addition to ten magickal virtues, described ten magickal powers (similar to Henry Khunrath's descriptions found in table 137) in light of the ten Sephiroth. These ten powers, found in *777*, are listed in this table.

140. Crowley's Magickal Virtues

1	Accomplishment of Great Work
2	Devotion
3	Silence
4	Obedience
5	Energy
6	Devotion of Great Work
7	Unselfishness
8	Truthfulness
9	Independence
10	Scepticism

141. Crowley's Magickal Powers

	Union with God
	Vision of God face to face
	Vision of Sorrow
	Vision of Love
	Vision of Power
	Vision of the Harmony of Things
	Vision of Beauty Triumphant
	Vision of Splendor
	Vision of the Machinery of the Universe
	Vision of the Holy Guardian Angel

XX. Magick (cont'd.)

Table 142. The magickal weapons and paraphernalia of modern Western magick have been equated to the ten Sephiroth by Crowley in *Liber 777* and are listed in this table.

Table 143. Israel Regardie, in his *Garden of Pomegranates* (1932), elaborated on Crowley's allocation of the magickal paraphenalia to the Tree of Life. This table shows Regardie's correspondences and explanations.

142. Crowley's Magickal Weapons

1. Crown
2. Inner Robe of Glory
3. Outer Robe of Concealment
4. Wand and Scepter
5. Sword and Scourge
6. Lamen and Rose Cross
7. Lamp and Girdle
8. Names and Aprons
9. Perfumes and Sandals
10. Magickal Circle and Triangle

143. Ritual Magick and Its Symbolic Meaning (Regardie)

Lamp—Spiritual Light and Real Self

Wand—Magickal Will and Divine Wisdom

Cup—Intuition

Scepter and Crown—Lordship and Divinity

Sword—Reason, capacity to disperse alien thoughts

Lamen—Intention to perform the Great Work

Robe—Splendor and Glory

Book of Invocations—Karmic Record, Magickal Memory

Altar and Perfumes—Fixed Will and Aspiration

Temple, Circle, Pantacle—The Temple of the Holy Ghost

XXI. Ritual (Tables 144-149)

This section deals with the Sephirotic grade structure of certain magickal societies.

Table 144. The Order of the Golden Dawn developed an elaborate set of Masonic grades and rituals based on the structure of the Tree of Life. The grades and their numerical equivalents are listed in this table. The pair of numbers assigned to each grade designated the position of the candidate on the Tree of Life. The first number represents the number of grade advancements, while the second number is the actual number of the Sephiroth to which the grade is assigned.

Table 145. Crowley, in establishing his own occult order of the A∴A∴ (Silver Star) in 1907, modeled his grades on those of the Golden Dawn. This table lists Crowley's variants.

Table 146. Crowley was initiated by 1912 into the German Ordo Templi Orientis (O.T.O.). Its grade structure, as of 1917, can be paralleled to the Tree of Life as shown in this table. Crowley subsequently introduced an XIth degree, which can correspond to the invisible Sephirah, Daath.

144. Golden Dawn Grade Structure (1887)	**145. Crowley's A.A. Grade Structure (1907)**	**146. Grades of O.T.O. Linear Order (1917)**
1 Ipsissimus (10=1)	Ipsissimus (10=1)	X° Supreme and Most Holy King
2 Magus (9=2)	Magus (9=2)	IX° Illuminatus Perfectus
3 Magister Templi (8=3)	Magister Templi (8=3)	VIII° Oriental Templar
4 Adeptus Exemptus (7=4)	Adeptus Exemptus (7=4)	VII° Mystic Templar
5 Adeptus Major (6=5)	Adeptus Major (6=5)	VI° Historical Templar
6 Adeptus Minor (5=6)	Adeptus Minor (5=6)	V° Rose-Croix
7 Philosophus (4=7)	Philosophus (4=7)	IV° Scotch Masonry
8 Practicus (3=8)	Practicus (3=8)	III° Craft of Masonry
9 Theoricus (2=9)	Zelator (2=9)	II° Minerval
10 Zelator (1=10)	Neophyte (1=10) (and Probationer 0=0)	I° Probationer (Neophyte I0=0I)

XXI. Ritual (Tables 144-149)

Table 147. Crowley, in becoming the head of the revised German O.T.O., believed that the grade structure approximated the chakra scheme more closely than the Tree of Life. This table compares the chakras as both the Tree of Life and the lower grades of the O.T.O., as Crowley perceived the two to be interrelated.

Table 148. The officers of a Masonic Lodge were paralled to the ten Sephiroth by Aleister Crowley in *Liber 777*. This table reflects these Masonic correspondences.

Table 149. The Officers of a Golden Dawn Temple relate to the ten Sephiroth, with the Secret Chiefs occupying the position of the Supernals. This table details the Sephirotic symbolism, derived from the actual rituals of the Golden Dawn.

	147. Grades of O.T.O. (Crowley-Chakra Order)	148. Crowley's Masonic Officers	149. Golden Dawn Temple Officers
1	IV° Prince of Jerusalem	P.M. (Past Master)	The Secret Chiefs
2	IV° Companions of the Royal Arch of Enoch (and 0° Minerval)	P.M. (Past Master)	The Secret Chiefs
3	I° Man and Brother	P.M. (Past Master)	The Secret Chiefs
4	II° Magician	W.M. (Worshipful Master)	Praemonstrator
5	II° Magician	S.W. (Senior Warden)	Imperator
6	II° Magician	J.W. (Junior Warden)	Cancellarius, Hierophant
7	IV° Companions of the Royal Arch of Enoch	S.D. (Senior Deacon)	Hegemon, Dadouchos
8	III° Master Magician	J.D. (Junior Deacon)	Hegemon, Stolistes
9	0° Minerval	I.G. (Inner Guard)	Kerux
10	0° Minerval	T. (Tyler) and Candidate	Hiereus, Candidate

THE 22 PATHS

Each of the ten Sephirotic numbers is linked to the others by certain connecting Paths, each Path allocated to a Hebrew letter. These additional 22 Paths combine with the first ten Sephiroth to form the 32 Paths of Wisdom, as outlined in the *Sepher Yetzirah* (refer to the Addendum of this Key for an analysis of the *Sepher Yetzirah)*. These Paths have been drawn in many manners throughout the evolution of the Tree of Life. Ultimately, two prominent designs evolved. One was exclusively used in orthodox Qabalistic circles while the other was used in both the orthodox tradition and the Western Magickal tradition.

The first Tree of Life (shown on opposite page), which is the prototype for the Western Magickal Tradition, has only one Path linking the tenth Sephirah to the rest of the Tree. Further, two Paths, connecting the third to the fourth Sephirah and the second to the fifth Sephirah, are not connected in the revised Tree of Life.

Note that the diagonal Paths are usually blinded in most printed illustrations of this Tree of Life. The correct logic for allocating these Paths is in the order of above to below, right first, then left.

This tree ultimately lost the two Paths crossing the abyss from Sephirah three to four and two to five. These two Paths dropped to the bottom of the Tree of Life to support Malkuth (the tenth) as the three letters which form the word "rainbow" in Hebrew (QShTh, קשׁת).

This second tree (shown on page 112) was introduced to the West in Athanasius Kircher's *Oedipus Ægyptiacus*. Though previously appearing as an appendix in Jewish printings of the *Zohar,* this Tree of Life would ultimately serve as a Rainbow Bridge of Paths traversed, in all the magickal workings, by members of both Mathers' Golden Dawn and Crowley's A.˙.A.˙. and O.T.O.

The layout of this second Tree of Life does not take into consideration the threefold division of the Hebrew alphabet, but it is allocated in the same fashion as the first in the ordering of above to below, right first, then left. However, this is complicated by a further cycle of right, left, and middle, changing to right middle and left.

The Paths themselves for both systems can be interpreted in light of the two specific Sephiroth they connect. Using the allocations found in the 149 Sephirotic Tables, each Path can be viewed as no less than 149 pairs of symbolic attributes.

In addition to this method, each of the 22 Paths has been given symbolism of its own, refined through the Western Qabalistic systems (especially the Golden Dawn). Apart from the symbolism of the *Sepher Yetzirah* (given in detail as an addendum to this Key), the tables beginning on page 113 delineate the additional Path symbols.

Twenty-Two Paths Connecting the Ten Sephiroth of the Tree of Life

Path Number	Hebrew Letter	Connecting Sephiroth Proto-Tree	Revised Tree	Kircher's Allocations for the Paths as Gods	Levi's Allocations for the Paths as Magickal Powers
11	A (א)	4 to 5	1 to 2	Infinity	To behold God face to face without dying
12	B (ב)	2 to 4	1 to 3	Wisdom	To be above all grief and fear
13	G (ג)	3 to 5	1 to 6	Retribution	To reign with heaven and be served by hell
14	D (ד)	1 to 6	2 to 3	The Gates of Light	To control the health of oneself and others
15	H (ה)	1 to 2	2 to 6	God of God	To be protected from diasters, misfortunes, and enemies
16	V (ו)	1 to 3	2 to 4	The Founder	To know the past, present, and future
17	Z (ז)	2 to 5	3 to 6	Thunder and Lightning	To possess the key of immortality
18	Ch (ח)	3 to 4	3 to 5	Mercy	To find the Philosophical Stone
19	T (ט)	2 to 6	4 to 5	Goodness	To possess the universal medicine
20	I (י)	3 to 6	4 to 6	Principle	To know perpetual motion and the quadrature of the circle
21	K (כ)	4 to 7	4 to 7	Immutable	To change into gold all metals, earth and the refuse of the earth
22	L (ל)	4 to 6	5 to 6	30 (and 2) Paths of Wisdom	To paralyse and charm serpents with words
23	M (מ)	7 to 8	5 to 8	The Arcane	To have the *ars notaria*, the Universal Science
24	N (נ)	5 to 6	6 to 7	The 50 Gates of Light	To speak learnedly on all subjects without study
25	S (ס)	6 to 7	6 to 9	The Destroyer	To know the deep mysteries of the souls of men and the hearts of women

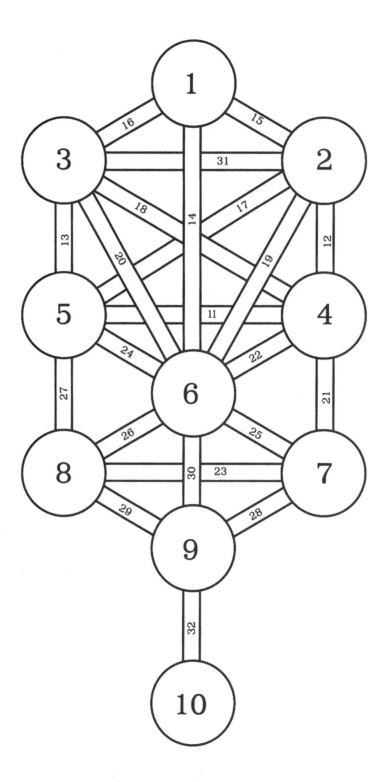

The Proto-Tree of Life

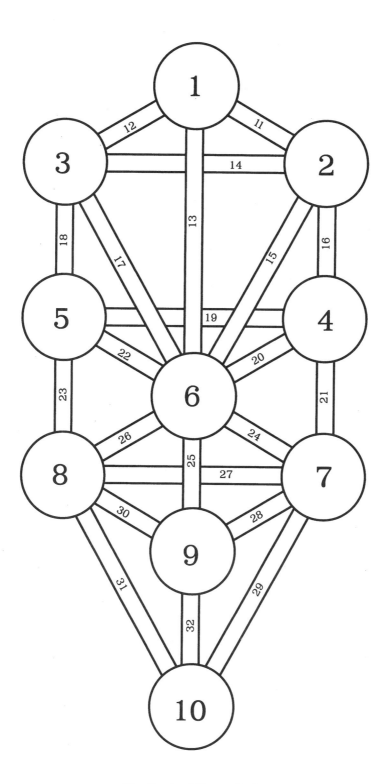

The Revised Tree of Life

Twenty-Two Paths Connecting the Ten Sephiroth of the Tree of Life (cont'd.)

Path Number	Hebrew Letter	Connecting Sephiroth Proto-Tree	Connecting Sephiroth Revised Tree	Kircher's Allocations for the Paths as Gods	Levi's Allocations for the Paths as Magickal Powers
26	O (ע)	6 to 8	6 to 8	Adjuration	To force nature to make oneself free
27	P (פ)	5 to 8	7 to 8	Discourse	To foresee all future events not affected by free will
28	Tz (צ)	7 to 9	7 to 9	Justice	To give to all the most wholesome counsels
29	Q (ק)	8 to 9	7 to 10	Rectitude	To triumph over adversaries
30	R (ר)	6 to 9	8 to 9	The Head	To conquer Love and Hate
31	Sh (ש)	2 to 3	8 to 10	The Saviour	To have the secret of wealth
32	Th (ת)	9 to 10	9 to 10	The End of All	To rule the elements, still tempests, cure diseases, and raise the dead

Crowley's Attributions to the Paths (*Liber 777*)

Path Number	Hebrew Letter	Human Body	Animal	Plant	Perfume	Magickal Weapon	Magickal Power
11	A (א)	Respiratory Organs	Man	Aspen	Galbanum	Dagger	Divination
12	B (ב)	Cerebral and Nervous System	Ibis	Palm	White Sandal	Caduceus	Knowledge of Science
13	G (ג)	Lymphatic System	Dog	Almond	Camphor	Bow	Divination by Dreams
14	D (ד)	Genital System	Dove	Rose	Red Sandal	Girdle	Love-philtres
15	H (ה)	Head and Face	Ram	Geranium	Dragon's Blood	Burin	Consecration
16	V (ו)	Shoulders and Arms	Bull	Mallow	Storax	Labor of Preparation	Secret of Physical Strength
17	Z (ז)	Lungs	Magpie	Orchid	Wormwood	Tripod	Prophecy
18	Ch (ח)	Stomach	Crab	Lotus	Onycha	Furnace	Casting Enchantments
19	T (ט)	Heart	Lion	Sunflower	Frank-incense	The Discipline	Training Wild Beasts
20	I (י)	The Back	Virgin	Lily	Narcissus	Bread	Invisibility
21	K (כ)	Digestive System	Eagle	Oak	Saffron	Scepter	Acquiring Political Power
22	L (ל)	Liver	Elephant	Aloe	Galbanum	Cross of Equilibrium	Works of Equilibrium
23	M (מ)	Organs of Nutrition	Snake	All Water Plants	Myrrh	Cup	Talismans
24	N (נ)	Intestines	Scorpion	Cactus	Siamese Benzoin	Pain of Obligation	Necromancy

Crowley's Attributions to the Paths (*Liber 777*) (cont'd.)

Path Number	Hebrew Letter	Human Body	Animal	Plant	Perfume	Magickal Weapon	Magickal Power
25	S (ס)	Hips and Thighs	Centaur	Rush	Lign-aloes	Arrow	Transmutations
26	O (ע)	Genital System	Goat	Indian Hemp	Musk	The Secret Force	Witches' Sabbath
27	P (פ)	Muscular System	Bear	Absinthe	Pepper	Sword	Work of Vengeance
28	Tz (צ)	Kidneys, Bladder	Peacock	Olive	Galbanum	Censer	Astrology
29	Q (ק)	Legs and Feet	Dolphin	Opium	Ambergris	Magic Mirror	Bewitchments
30	R (ר)	Circulatory System	Sparrow-Hawk	Heliotrope	Cinnamon	Lamen	Power of Acquiring Wealth
31	Sh (ש)	Organs of Circulation	Sphinx (Sworded and Crowned)	Red Poppy	Frank-incense	Lamp	Evocation
32	Th (ת)	Execretory Organs and Skelton	Bull	Yew	Assafoetida	Sickle	Alchemy

The construction of the proto-tree is derived from the *Sepher Yetzirah's* division of the alphabet into three mother, seven double, and twelve simple letters: the three horizontal Paths of the Tree of Life are the three mother letters, the seven vertical Paths of the Tree are the seven double letters, while the 12 simple letters are the 12 slanting Paths of the Tree.

The 32 Paths of Wisdom laid upon this Tree result in the following allocations.

The Thirty-Two Paths of Wisdom

Path Number	Hebrew Letter	Initial Letter of Divine Name of God (Rabbi Akiba)	Astrology (Sepher Yetzirah)	Number Value
11	A (א)	AHIH (אהיה) (I am)	Air and Spirit	1
12	B (ב)	BHVR (בהור) (Clarity)`	Mercury	2
13	G (ג)	GDVL (גדול) (Great)	Moon	3
14	D (ד)	DGVL (דגול) (Flag, Insignia)	Venus	4
15	H (ה)	HDVNf (הדון) (Beautifully formed)	Aries	5
16	V (ו)	VZIV (וזיו) (With splendor)	Taurus	6
17	Z (ז)	ZKAI (זכאי) (The righteous)	Gemini	7
18	Ch (ח)	ChSID (חסיד) The merciful)	Cancer	8
19	T (ט)	THVR (טהור) (The Purified)	Leo	9
20	I (י)	IH (יה) (God, the powerful)	Virgo	10
21	K (כ)	KBID (כביד) (Weighty, influential)	Jupiter	20
22	L (ל)	LMD (למד) (Learned)	Libra	30
23	M (מ)	MBRKf (מברך) (Consecrated)	Water	40
24	N (נ)	NVRA (נורא) (Fiery)	Scorpio	50
25	S (ס)	SVMKf (סומך) (Supporting)	Sagittarius	60
26	O (ע)	OZZ (עזז) (Strength)	Capricorn	70
27	P (פ)	PDVTh (פדות) (Redemption)	Mars	80
28	Tz (צ)	TzDQ (צדק) (Just)	Aquarius	90
29	Q (ק)	QDSh (קדש) (Sacred)	Pisces	100
30	R (ר)	RDH (רדה) (To Rule)	Sun	200
31	Sh (ש)	ShDI (שדי) (All-forceful)	Fire	300
32	Th (ת)	ThChNH (תחנה) (Prayers)	Saturn and Earth	400

The Thirty-Two Paths of Wisdom (cont'd.)

Path Number	Hebrew Letter	Tarot (Major Arcana) Exoteric (Levi)	Esoteric (Golden Dawn)
11	A (א)	I. The Magician	0. The Fool
12	B (ב)	II. The High Priestess	I. The Magician
13	G (ג)	III. The Empress	II. The High Priestess
14	D (ד)	IV. The Emperor	III. The Empress
15	H (ה)	V. The Hierophant	IV. The Emperor
16	V (ו)	VI. The Lovers	V. The Hierophant
17	Z (ז)	VII. The Chariot	VI. The Lovers
18	Ch (ח)	VIII. Justice	VII. The Chariot
19	T (ט)	IX. The Hermit	VIII. Strength
20	I (י)	X. The Wheel of Fortune	IX. The Hermit
21	K (כ)	XI. Force	X. The Wheel of Fortune
22	L (ל)	XII. The Hanged Man	XI. Justice
23	M (מ)	XIII. Death	XII. The Hanged Man
24	N (נ)	XIV. Temperance	XIII. Death
25	S (ס)	XV. The Devil	XIV. Temperance
26	O (ע)	XVI. The Tower	XV. The Devil
27	P (פ)	XVII. The Star	XVI. The Tower
28	Tz (צ)	XVIII. The Moon	XVII. The Star
29	Q (ק)	XIX. The Sun	XVIII. The Moon
30	R (ר)	XX. Judgement	XIX. The Sun
31	Sh (ש)	0. The Fool	XX. Judgement
32	Th (ת)	XXI. The World	XXI. The World

The Thirty-Two Paths of Wisdom—Color Scales

Path Number	Hebrew Letter	Atziloth	Briah	Four-Color Scale Yetzirah	Assiah
11	A (א)	Pale Yellow	Sky Blue	Blue Green	Emerald flecked Gold
12	B (ב)	Yellow	Purple	Gray	Indigo rayed Violet
13	G (ג)	Blue	Silver	Cold Pale Blue	Silver rayed Sky Blue
14	D (ד)	Emerald Green	Sky Blue	Spring Green	Bright Rose rayed Pale Yellow
15	H (ה)	Scarlet	Red	Brilliant Flame	Glowing Red
16	V (ו)	Red-Orange	Deep Indigo	Deep Olive	Rich Brown
17	Z (ז)	Orange	Pale Mauve	New Yellow	Reddish Gray inclined to Mauve
18	Ch (ח)	Amber	Maroon	Bright Russet	Dark Greenish-Brown
19	T (ט)	Yellow	Deep Purple	Gray	Reddish Amber
20	I (י)	Yellow Green	Slate Gray	Green Gray	Plum
21	K (כ)	Violet	Blue	Rich Purple	Bright Blue rayed Yellow
22	L (ל)	Emerald Green	Blue	Deep Blue Green	Pale Green
23	M (מ)	Deep Blue	Sea Green	Deep Olive Green	White flecked Purple
24	N (נ)	Blue Green	Dull Brown	Very Dark Brown	Livid Indigo Brown
25	S (ס)	Blue	Yellow	Green	Dark Vivid Blue
26	O (ע)	Blue-Violet	Black	Blue Black	Cold Dark Gray near Black
27	P (פ)	Scarlet	Red	Venetian Red	Bright Red rayed Emerald
28	Tz (צ)	Violet	Sky Blue	Bluish Mauve	White tinged Purple
29	Q (ק)	Red Violet	Buff flecked Silver-White	Translucent Pink-Brown	Stone Gray
30	R (ר)	Orange	Gold Yellow	Rich Amber	Amber rayed Red
31	Sh (ש)	Scarlet Orange	Vermillion	Scarlet flecked Gold	Vermillion flecked Crimson and Emerald
32	Th (ת)	Blue-Violet	Black	Blue Black	Black rayed Blue

Beyond these 32 Paths, one further Path was configured through the Western Qabalistic Tradition known as the 33rd invisible Path on the Tree of Life. This 33rd Path is titled Daath (Hebrew: DOTh, דעת, or DAATh, דאאת), meaning knowledge, and is a pendant to Chockmah (Wisdom) and Binah (Understanding).

Daath is positioned midway between Kether and Tiphereth, at the center of the 13th Path (Gimel), and represents the position Malkuth once occupied on the Tree of Life before the fall of Adam and Eve.

This 33rd Path is sometimes numbered 11 when only the ten Sephiroth are being discussed. As 11, Daath represents the dissolution of the ego every adept must face when crossing the trackless Abyss of the Tree of Life from Chesed (the fourth Sephirah) to Binah (the third Sephirah).

As the 33rd Path on the Tree of Life, Daath represents the quintessential Path which describes all the other 32 Paths. As such, Daath is a crystal prism placed between the white light of Kether and the prismatic colors of the lower seven Sephiroth.

The Golden Dawn color scale for Daath as the 33rd Path of the Tree of Life assigns the following four colors:

Four Colors of Daath as Thirty-Third Path

World	Color	Symbolic Meaning
Atziloth	Pale Lavender	White (Kether) mixed with Violet (Yesod), end of spectrum on a spiritual plane
Briah	Gray-White	The merging of Kether with Chockmah, light filtering through all colors
Yetzirah	Pure Violet	Yesod to which Daath is counterpoised around Tiphereth, the end of the spectrum
Assiah	Gray flecked Gold	Chockmah merging with Tiphereth, light breaking through all colors

As to specific Tarot or astrological allocations, no one symbol can describe Daath, for it is rather the combination of all symbols and possibilities at once.

Behind, and situated as a source to all 33 Paths of the Tree of Life is the Qabalistic concept of Zero.

Before the number One is Zero, and this Zero has two basic formulae in Hebrew.

The first concept of Zero is that which Frater Achad rediscovered when deciphering the Qabalistic puzzles of *The Book of the Law*: the word for "No," or "Nought," which can be construed as the cipher Zero, when written backwards, becomes "GOD" as the power of the Universe. This Qabalistic formula is as follows:

The Cipher of God

LA (לא) (Heb.) = no, nought, the cipher or zero which precedes all numbers.

AL (אל) (Heb.) = is LA written backwards, becoming the root word for Elohim (אלהים) and Allah (الله), meaning the power (of God).

Thus all that is beyond our conception, that thought which escapes our conceptualization, is the end of Man and the beginning of God. For No God means God who is beyond the conception of Man.

The second concept of Zero premises that behind the corona of Kether on the Tree of Life exist 18 veils (resembling clouds) of negativity, each bearing one Hebrew letter of an 18-letter formula describing the manifest action of All out of Nothing.

This second formula depends on the Hebrew word AIN (אין), which means "nothing" or "not" in a literal sense, and "the void from which all evolves out of and returns to" in a Qabalistic sense.

This Qabalistic formula is as follows:

The Eighteen Veils of Ain

Out of AIN (nothing) evolved the one known as KThR (כתר, Kether), the Crown, through the agency of 18 veils of negativity.

These 18 veils are the letters in the 18 lettered formula:

AIN (אין)
AIN SVP (אין סוף)
AIN SVP AVR (אין סוף אור)

This 18-lettered formula forms three basic statements, each a stage of Zero developing into One. These three stages are defined as follows:

The Three Stages of Zero Becoming One

Formula	Mathers' *Kabbalah Unveiled*	Crowley's *Liber 777*	Crowley's Naples Arrangement
AIN	Negative Existence	Nothing	Zero
AIN SVP	The Limitless	No Limit	Undefined Space
AIN SVP AVR	The Limitless Light	Limitless L.V.X.	Basis of Possible Vibration

This formula then shows that Nothing, which is beyond definition, being limitless and boundless, concentrates itself through the agency of light into one point, becoming the corona around Kether on the Tree of Life.

This 18-lettered formula also contains a peculiar number harmony: AIN (אין) plus SVP (סוף), "nothing" plus "limit," is equal to AVR (אור), "light." The complete numbering of the AIN formula is as follows:

The Eighteen-Lettered Ain Formula

Formula	Number Value	Gematriots
AIN (אין) (no, nought, nothing, infinite, nonexistent, the primal form of negativity)	61 (Note: 61 is the 18th prime)	ANI (אני)—I, myself (a rearrangement of AIN, אין, as ANI, אני) AMK (אמך)—Thy mother, Thy source BTN (בטן)—Bowels, belly, womb, womb, the inmost part
AIN SVP (אין סוף) (boundless, without limit, no-limit)	207	AVR (אור)—Light, Illumination GDR (גדר)—To enclose, Boundary, Limit, Wall ZR (זר)—Crown, Wreath, Rim (alternate of Kether)
AIN SVP AVR (אין סוף אור) (the limitless light, light without limitation or diminishment)	414	MShVTTIM (משוטטים)—A going forth, Emanation MQVR ChIIM (מקור חיים)—The fountain of Life HGVTh (הגות)—Deep Meditation
AIN AIN SVP AIN SVP AVR (אין אין סוף אין סוף אור) (nought without limit light without limit)	672	VLADMf LA (ולאדם לא)—But for Adam there was NOT IHVH ALHIMf (יהוה אלהים)—Jehovah Elohim (God name of Binah and Tiphereth) QVP BITh LMD (קוף בית למד)—The word QBL (קבל), to receive illumination, written in full

The mystery of the order of the Tarot (refer to Addendum of Key 12 for further information) and the correct placement of the card "The Fool" as the number Zero and the Hebrew letter Aleph (א, initial of AIN, אין) all depend upon this Qabalistic formula of Zero as AIN. If one Tarot card could describe the AIN formula, it would be the Fool.

Crowley's *Book of the Law*, echoing the secrets of the Golden Dawn's Book T allocation of the Fool to Aleph and Zero, states:

> My prophet is a fool with his one, one, one; are not they the Ox, and none by the Book?. (AL, I:48)

ADDENDUM

THE 32 PATHS OF WISDOM
SECRETS OF THE *SEPHER YETZIRAH*

> In thirty-two wonderful Paths of Wisdom did Jah, Jehovah Tzabaoth, the God of Israel, the Elohim of the living, the King of ages, the merciful and gracious God, the exalted One, the Dweller in eternity, most high and holy—engrave his name by the three Sepharim—Numbers, Letters, and Sounds.

The *Sepher Yetzirah* (Book of formation) is the one fundamental Qabalistic text which gives the cosmological correspondences for the Hebrew alphabet.

A scale of 32, the framework for the Hebrew Qabalistic Tree of Life, is outlined for the first time in written format with the writing of the *Sepher Yetzirah*. This cosmological scale is divided into four categories of ten, three, seven, and twelve. Though this text employs a rigid division of universe into number, it does not directly give the number value of the Hebrew alphabet, or the qabalistic methods of gematria, notariqon, and temurah. Rather the *Sepher Yetzirah* defines the Hebrew alphabet in terms of symbolic equivalents involving man, time, and space. The mystical angelic hiearchies of Ibn al-Arabi, Raymond Lull, Francisco Giorgi, John Dee, and Robert Fludd were influenced by this alphabet cosmology.

The authorship of the *Sepher Yetzirah* is unknown, but the text itself refers to its author as the patriarch Abraham, which would put the *Sepher Yetzirah* before the Torah.

As to its origin, the writing itself occurred between 200 BCE and 600 CE. However, the origins of this alphabet code are probably of the same period as the recording of the Torah (around 800 BCE).

There are two versions of the *Sepher Yetzirah:* a shorter version which deals only with the mysticism of the number range one through ten, and an extended version which adds the attributes of the Hebrew alphabet divided into three categories of three, seven, and twelve letters. Though many commentators stress the correctness of the shorter version and the fradulent content of the additional Hebrew-alphabet attributes, these additional alphabet attributes are the heart of the *Sepher Yetzirah*.

The following tables are an attempt to reduce the attributes of the Hebrew alphabet to their essential correspondences as outlined in the *Sepher Yetzirah*. No two editions of the *Sepher Yetzirah* agree on the order of these attributes. As such, the corrections are in light of the Golden Dawn Qabalistic tradition epitomized in the writings of S. L. MacGregor Mathers, W. Wynn Westcott, Aleister Crowley, A. E. Waite, and Paul Foster Case. Columns in the following tables which are extrapolations, additions, or corrections to the original text are starred with an asterisk.

The Sephiroth One Through Four

Number	Number Name	Main Attribute	Element	In The World	Mother/Double Letter
1	One (AChTh, אחת)	Beginning (RAShITh, ראשׁית)	The Spirit of the Living Gods (RVCh ALHIM ChIIM, רוח אלהים חיים)	Sound, Breath, Word (QVL, RVCh, DBVR, קול, רוח, דבור)	AMSh (אמשׁ)
2	Two (ShThIM, שׁתים)	End (AChRITh, אחרית)	Air from Spirit (RVCh MRVCh, רוח מרוח)	The 22 Letters of the Alphabet (OShRIM VShThIM AVThIVTh, עשׂרים ושׁתים אותיות)	A (א)
3	Three (ShLSh, שׁלשׁ)	Good (TVB, טוב)	Water from Air (MIM MRVCh, מים מרוח)	Unstructured Matter, Mud and Clay (ThHV VBHV, RPSh VTIT, תהו ובהו, רפשׁ וטיט)	M (מ)
4	Four (ARBO, ארבע)	Evil (RO, רע)	Fire from Water (ASh MMIM, אשׁ ממים)	Throne of Glory, Seraphim, Auphanim, Holy Living Creatures, the Angels and His Great Name (KSA HKBVD, ShRPIM, AVPNIM, ChIVTh HQVDSh, MLAKI, ShMV HGDVL, כסא הכבוד, שׂרפים, אופנים, חיות הקודשׁ, מלאכי, שׁמו הגדול)	Sh/Th (שׁ/ת)

The Sephiroth Five Through Ten

Number	Number Name	Direction In Space	Divine Name Counterchange	Double Letter Mothers	Planet by Direction in Space*
5	Five (ChMSh) (חמש)	Height (RVM) (רום)	IHV (יהו)	B, AMSh (ב, אמש)	Mercury (KVKB) (כוכב)
6	Six (ShSh) (שש)	Depth (ThChTh) (תחת)	IVH (יוה)	G, AShM (ג, אשם)	Moon (LBNH) (לבנה)
7	Seven (ShBO) (שבע)	East (MZRCh) (מזרח)	HIV (היו)	D, MASh (ד, מאש)	Venus (NGH) (נגה)
8	Eight (ShMVNH) (שמונה)	West (MORB) (מערב)	HVI (הוי)	K, MShA (כ, משא)	Jupiter (TzDQ) (צדק)
9	Nine (ThShO) (תשע)	South (DRVM) (דרום)	VIH (ויה)	R, ShAM (ר, שאם)	Sun (ChMH) (חמה)
10	Ten (OShR) (עשר)	North (TzPVN) (צפון)	VHI (והי)	P, ShMA (פ, שמא)	Mars (MADIM) (מאדים)

THE TEN SEPHIROTH

The first section of the *Sepher Yetzirah* makes a distinction between the first ten numbers (one through ten) and the Hebrew alphabet. This is indeed a departure from gematria, for the first ten letters of the Hebrew alphabet are those first ten numbers. Yet the *Sepher Yetzirah* calls these first ten numbers Sephiroth, to denote number apart from letter. These first ten numbers are the basis for the ten circles or stations comprising the medieval Qabalistic diagram known as the Tree of Life. Of these ten Sephiroth or numbers, the first four produce the next six, in accordance with the formula $1 + 2 + 3 + 4 = 10$. The tables on pages 124 and 125 detail the attributes of one through four and five through ten.

THE 22 HEBREW LETTERS

The 22 mystical categories of the Hebrew alphabet are treated in the extended version of the *Sepher Yetzirah*. They are given attributes apart from the first ten numbers, and in medieval Qabalism they represent the 22 channels which connect these 10 numbers in the diagram known as the Tree of Life.

The mystical attributes for these 22 letters are based on one key concept, astrology, upon which all other attributes depend for their symbolism. However, no two editions of the *Sepher Yetzirah* seem to agree on the correlation of the astrological attributes to the letters of the alphabet, especially in regards to the seven double letters which rule the seven planets.

These 22 letters are divided into two distinct categories. The first division is into five categories to denote the position in the mouth which each letter takes when properly pronounced. These five phonetic categories are as follows:

The Five Phonetic Categories

Letters	Position in Mouth	Name of Position in Hebrew	Element*
A H Ch O (א ה ח ע)	Throat (Gutturals)	GRVN (גרין)	Air
G I K Q (ק כ י ג)	Palate (Palatals)	ChK (חך)	Earth
B T L N Th (ת נ ל ט ב)	Tongue (Linguals)	LShVN (לשון)	Spirit
Z S Tz R Sh (ש ר צ ס ז)	Teeth (Dentals)	ShNIM (שנים)	Fire
D V M P (פ מ ו ד)	Lips (Labials)	GRVN (גרין)	Water

Phonetic Key Divided to Mother, Double, and Simple

	Mother	Double	Simple
Throat	A (א)		H Ch O (ה ח ע)
Palate		G K (ג כ)	I Q (י ק)
Tongue		B Th (ב ת)	T L N (ט ל נ)
Teeth	Sh (ש)	R (ר)	Z S Tz (ז ס צ)
Lips	M (מ)	D P (ד פ)	V (ו)

The above phonetic division appears in writing for the first time in the *Sepher Yetzirah*. The *Sepher Yetzirah* thereby combines a grammar with a grimoire. A phonetic order rather than a numerical order conditions the categorization of the universe by the alphabet, both in the above division of five and the tripartite division of the alphabet into mother, double, and simple letters.

The *Sepher Yetzirah* is not a numerical treatise, but a treatise that makes a magickal distinction between letter and number and treats both as astrology based on angelology. The second division of the 22 letters of the alphabet is into three basic divisions of three mother letters, seven double letters, and twelve simple letters. The three mother letters form the first section of the alphabet treatise. These three letters are Aleph (A, א), Mem (M, מ) and Shin (Sh, ש). The table on the opposite page describes the basic symbols for these three mother or matrix letters, which represent the range of the alphabet's phonetic sound; the breath of Aleph, the mute of Mem, and the hissing of Shin.

The Three Mother Letters

Hebrew Letters

Attributes	Sh (Shin, ש)	A (Aleph, א)	M (Mem, מ)
Element (Root)	Fire (ASh, אש)	Life Breath (RVCh, רוח)	Water (MIM, מים)
Element (In the World)	Heaven (ShMIM, שמים)	Sky (Air between Heaven and Earth) (AVIR, אויר)	Oceans and the Earth (MIM ARTz, מים ארץ)
Balance	Scale Pan of Guilt (KP ChVBH, כף חובה)	Tongue which balances the two pans (LShVN ChQ MKRIO, לשון חק מכריע)	Scale Pan of Merit (KP ZQVTh, כף זכות)
Human Body	Head, Brain (RASh, ראש)	Chest, Body, Spine (GVIH, גויה)	Belly, Womb, Bowels, Gentials (BTN, בטן)
Six Rings: Male	ShAM (שאם)	AMSh (אמש)	MASh (מאש)
Female	ShMA (שמא)	AShM (אשם)	MShA (משא)
Temperature	Heat (ChVM, חום)	Moistness (RVIH, רויה)	Coldness (QVR, קור)
Time of Year by Temperature	Aries, Taurus, Gemini, Cancer (NISN AIIR SIVN ThMVZ, ניסן אייר סיון תמוז)	Leo, Virgo, Libra Scorpio (AB ALVL ThShRI MRChShVN, אב אלול תשרי מרחשון)	Sagittarius, Capricorn, Aquarius, Pisces (KSLV TBTh ShBT ADR, כסלו טבת שבט אדר)
Direction in Space*	South to North (DRVM LTzPVN, דרום לצפון)	Above to Below (MOLH LMTH, מעלה למטה)	East to West (MZRCh LMORB, מזרח למערב)
Direction (In Body)	Left (ShMAL, שמאל)	Center (AMTzO, אמצע)	Right (IMIN, ימין)
Trigrammaton	Father (I, י)	Child (V, ו)	Mother (H, ה)

THE SEVEN DOUBLE LETTERS

The seven double letters are B, G, D, K, P, R, and Th (ב, ג, ד, כ, פ, ר, and ת). These seven double letters represent seven letters within the alphabet which possess two distinct pronunciations, one hard and one soft. When marked in the center with a dot, known as a *dagesh,* they are hard (בּ, גּ, דּ, כּ, פּ, רּ, and תּ); without the dagesh they are soft.

The *Sepher Yetzirah* gives seven pairs of attributes to signify these seven letters with and without the dagesh mark. When marked with the dagesh, the attribute is positive; without the dagesh, the attribute is negative.

The Dagesh Values

Double Letter	Positive Attribute (with Dagesh)	Phonetic Value	Negative Attribute (without Dagesh)	Phonetic Value
B (ב)	Life (ChIIM, חיים)	B	Death (MVTh, מות)	V
G (ג)	Peace (ShLVM, שלום)	G	War (MLChMH, מלחמה)	Gh
D (ד)	Wisdom (ChKMH, חכמה)	D	Folly (AVLTh, אולת)	Dh
K (כ)	Wealth (OShR, עשר)	K	Poverty (OVNI, עוני)	Kh
P (פ)	Grace (ChN, חן)	P	Hideousness (KIOVR, כיעור)	F
R (ר)	Fruitfulness (ZRO, זרע)	R	Desolation (ShMMH, שממה)	Rh
Th (ת)	Dominion (MMShLH, ממשלה)	T	Slavery (OBDVTh, עבדות)	Th

The greatest discrepency between different editions of the *Sepher Yet-zirah* is in the allocation of the seven ancient planets to these seven double letters. The order of the seven planets was the greatest secret concerning the Qabalistic alphabet, and no printed edition of the *Sepher Yetzirah* possesses the correct attributes. These attributes could only be communicated by someone who "knew" the correct order, or by intense study. The most popular attributes are as follows.

The Planetary Double Letters

Double Letter	Ptolemaic Order	Kircher and Meyer	Stenring and Week Order	East Indian Planetary Order (Chakras)
B (ב)	Saturn	Sun	Sun	Mercury
G (ג)	Jupiter	Venus	Moon	Moon
D (ד)	Mars	Mercury	Mars	Venus
K (כ)	Sun	Moon	Mercury	Sun
P (פ)	Venus	Saturn	Jupiter	Jupiter
R (ר)	Mercury	Jupiter	Venus	Mars
Th (ת)	Moon	Mars	Saturn	Saturn

The order used in the following tables was devised by S. L. MacGregor Mathers (and rediscovered by Paul Foster Case with the aid of Crowley's *Liber 777*). This order may indeed be the secret order of the planets for the Hebrew alphabet. The order is based on the Tarot for the images to qualify the astrological value of each double letter.

The Secret Order of the Double Letters

Hebrew Letter	Planet	Corresponding Tarot Card	Qualifying Image
B (ב)	Mercury	Key I. The Magician	Thoth-Hermes (Mercury) as the God of Magick
G (ג)	Moon	Key II. The High Priestess	The Moon Goddess Isis as the veiled High Priestess
D (ד)	Venus	Key III. The Empress	Venus as the Luxuriant Queen
K (כ)	Jupiter	Key X. Wheel of Fortune	Jupiter as the Sky God (Heaven as interlocking wheels)
P (פ)	Mars	Key XVI. The Tower Struck by Lightning	Mars as the Solar disc striking the Tower
R (ר)	Sun	Key XIX. The Sun	The Sun itself centrally portrayed as the chief image of this card
Th (ת)	Saturn	Key XXI. The World	The central figure as Aima, the Saturnian mother of Binah, as well as the night sky

Based on these seven planets the *Sepher Yetzirah* places the seven double letters in the universe, in the human body, in the days of the week, and as seven heavens, seven earths, seven houses, and seven angels. The following table, based on MacGregor Mathers' secret planetary order, details these attributes.

The Seven Double Letters

Double Letter	Universe	Day of Creation*	Human Body
B (ב)	Mercury (KVKB, כוכב)	Fourth Day (Wednesday) (IVM RBIOI, יום רביעי)	Mouth (PH, פה)
G (ג)	Moon (LBNH, לבנה)	Second Day (Monday) (IVM ShNI, יום שני)	Left Eye (OIN ShMAL, עין שמאל)
D (ד)	Venus (NVGH, נוגה)	Sixth Day (Friday) (IVM ShShI, יום ששי)	Left Nostril (NChIR ShMAL, נחיר שמאל)
K (כ)	Jupiter (TzDQ, צדק)	Fifth Day (Thursday) (IVM ChMIShI, יום חמישי)	Right Ear (AZN IMIN, אזן ימין)
P (פ)	Mars (MADIM, מאדים)	Third Day (Tuesday) (IVM ShLIShI, יום שלישי)	Right Nostril (NChIR IMIN) נחיר ימין
R (ר)	Sun (ChMH, חמה)	First Day (Sunday) (IVM RAShVN, יום ראשון)	Right Eye (OIN IMIN, עין ימין)
Th (ת)	Saturn (ShBThI, שבתי)	Seventh Day Day of Rest (Saturday) (IVM ShBTh, יום שבת)	Left Ear (AZN ShMAL, אזן שמאל)

Beyond the above attributes the *Sepher Yetzirah* assigns a direction in space (as an ever expanding cube) for each of these seven double letters. The directional coordinates are as follows:

Directional Coordinates of the Seven Double Letters

Letter	Direction	Hebrew
B (ב)	Above (Height)	MOLH, מעלה
G (ג)	Below (Depth)	MTH, מטה
D (ד)	East (Before)	MZRCh, מזרח
K (כ)	West (Behind)	MORB, מערב
P (פ)	North (Left)	TzPVN, צפון
R (ר)	South (Right)	DRVM, דרום
Th (ת)	Center (Midst)	AMTzO, אמצע

These seven coordinates can define the symbology of the orientation of any temple or religious edifice. All 22 letters are used in this directional symbolism, for the three mother letters are the three inner coordinates of the cube, while the 12 simple letters are the 12 edges of the cube.

In the *Sepher Yetzirah,* as a comment on these seven directional letters, the seven double letters are described as "three which are against three and one which places them in equilibrium."

The three set against three are the three faces of this directional cube that are in the light (above, East, and South) set against the three faces that are in the dark (below, West, and North). The one reconciling all is the center of the cube.

The Three Set Against Three

Three Faces in Light	Three Faces in Dark
B, ב (Above)	G, ג (Below)
D, ד (East)	K, כ (West)
R, ר (South)	P, פ (North)

The Reconciling Middle
Th, ת (Center)

The Twelve Simple Letters

The 12 remaining letters possess one basic pronunciation each, and as such are the 12 simple letters. Since they are 12 in number, they are obviously the range of the Zodiac (and the 12 tribes). As the zodiac is the border of the heavens, and the 12 tribes the border of this world, so the 12 simple letters are the border or edges of the directional cube.

Unlike the seven double letters, almost all editions of the *Sepher Yetzirah* agree as to the allocation of the 12 signs to the 12 simple letters. However, the attributes that depend on these 12 Zodiacal signs differ in order from edition to edition of the *Sepher Yetzirah* and are here rectified in light of the esoteric Qabalistic system of the Golden Dawn.

Twelve Simple Letters

Simple Letter	Zodiac	Month	Time of Year	Tribe*
H (ה)	Aries—The Ram (TLH, טלה)	Nisan (NISN, ניסן)	Mar. 21-Apr. 19	Gad (GD, גד)
V (ו)	Taurus—The Bull (ShVR, שור)	Iyar (AIIR, אייר)	Apr. 19-May 20	Ephraim (APRAIM, אפרים)
Z (ז)	Gemini—The Twins (ThAVMIM, תאומים)	Sivan (SIVN, סיון)	May 20-June 21	Manasseh (MNShH, מנשה)
Ch (ח)	Cancer—The Crab (SRTN, סרטן)	Tamus (ThMVZ, תמוז)	June 21-July 22	Issachar (IShShKR, יששכר)
T (ט)	Leo—The Lion (ARIH, אריה)	Ab (AB, אב)	July 22-Aug. 22	Judah (IHVDH, יהודה)
I (י)	Virgo—The Virgin (BThVLH, בתולה)	Elul (ALVL, אלול)	Aug. 22-Sept. 23	Naphtali (NPThLI, נפתלי)
L (ל)	Libra—The Scales (MAZNIM, מאזנים)	Tishri (ThShRI, תשרי)	Sept. 23-Oct. 23	Asher (AShR, אשר)
N (נ)	Scorpio—The Scorpion (OQRB, עקרב)	Marcheshvan (MRChShVN, מרחשון)	Oct. 23-Nov. 22	Dan (DN, דן)
S (ס)	Sagittarius—The Bow (QShTh, קשת)	Kislev (KSLV, כסלו)	Nov. 22-Dec. 21	Benjamin (BNIMN, בנימן)
O (ע)	Capricorn—The Goat (GDI, גדי)	Tevet (TBTh, טבת)	Dec. 21-Jan. 20	Zebulon (ZBVLN, זבולן)
Tz (צ)	Aquarius—The Water Pail (DLI, דלי)	Schwat (ShBT, שבט)	Jan. 20-Feb. 19	Reuben (RAVBN, ראובן)
Q (ק)	Pisces—The Fishes (DGIM, דגים)	Adar (ADR, אדר)	Feb. 19-Mar. 21	Simeon (ShMOVN, שמעון)

Twelve Simple Letters (cont'd.)

Simple Letters	Direction (Stenring)	Banners of Yahweh	Human Activity	Human Body	Human Body According to Astrology*	Alternate Direction (Kalisch)
H (ה)	Northeast (MZRChITh TzPVNITh, מזרחית צפונית)	IHVH (יהוה)	Seeing (RAIH, ראיה)	Right Hand (ID IMIN, יד ימין)	Head (RASh, ראש)	East Above
V (ו)	Southeast (DRVMITh MZRChITh, דרומית מזרחית)	IHHV (יההו)	Hearing (ShMIOH, שמיעה)	Left Hand (ID ShMAL, יד שמאל)	Throat (GRVN, גרון)	Northeast
Z (ז)	East Above (MZRChITh RVMITh, מזרחית רומית)	IVHH (יוהה)	Smelling (RICh, ריח)	Right Foot (RGL IMIN, רגל ימין)	Hands (IDIM, ידים)	East Below
Ch (ח)	East Below (MZRChITh ThChThITh, מזרחית תחתית)	HVHI (הוהי)	Speaking (ShIChH, שיחה)	Left Foot (RGL ShMAL, רגל שמאל)	Chest (ChZH, חזה)	South Above
T (ט)	North Above (TzPVNITh RVMITh, צפונית רומית)	HVIH (הויה)	Tasting (Swallowing) (LOITCh, לעיטה)	Right Kidney (Testicle) (KVLIA IMIN, כוליא ימין)	Heart (LB, לב)	Southeast
I (י)	North Below (TzPVNITh ThChThITh, צפונית תחתית)	HHVI (ההוי)	Coition (ThShMISh, תשמיש)	Left Kidney (Testicle) (KVLIA ShMAL, כוליא שמאל)	Intestines (QIBH, קיבה)	South Below

Twelve Simple Letters (cont'd.)

Simple Letters	Direction (Stenring)	Banners of Yahweh	Human Activity	Human Body	Human Body According to Astrology*	Alternate Direction (Kalisch)
L (ל)	Northwest (TzPVNITh MORBITh, צפונית מרבית)	VHIH (והיה)	Working (MOShH, מעשה)	Liver (KBD, כבד)	Kidneys (KLIVTh, כליות)	West Above
N (נ)	Southwest (MORBITh DRVMITh, מרבית דרומית)	VHHI (והיי)	Walking (HLVK, הלוך)	Spleen (TChL, טחל)	Genitals (ORIH, ערוה)	Southwest
S (ס)	West Above (MORBITh RVMITh, מרבית רומית)	VIHH (ויהה)	Anger (RVGZ, רוגז)	Gall (MRH, מרה)	Thighs (IRKIM, ירכים)	West Below
O (ע)	West Below (MORBITh ThChThITh, מרבית תחתית)	HIHV (היהו)	Laughter (ShChVQ, שחוק)	Stomach, Colon (QIBH, קיבה)	Knees (BRKIM, ברכים)	North Above
Tz (צ)	South Above (DRVMITh RVMITh, דרומית רומית)	HIVH (היוה)	Contemplation (HRHVR, הרהור)	Bladder, Genitals (HMSS, המסס)	Ankles (APSIM, אפסים)	Northwest
Q (ק)	South Below (DRVMITh ThChThITh, דרומית תחתית)	HHIV (ההיו)	Sleep (ShNH, שנה)	Rectum, Bowels (QVRQBN, קורקבן)	Feet (RGLIM, רגלים)	North Below

The *Sepher Yetzirah* divides the 12 simple letters into two main group-ings. The first involves six pairs of letters, while the second involves four sets of three letters. Both depend on the allocation of the human body to the 12 simple letters.

THE SIX PAIRINGS OR COUPLES OF SIMPLES

Two Discontented
L ל (Liver)
S ס (Gall)

Two Laughing
O ע (Stomach)
N נ (Spleen)

Two Advising
T, I ט, י (Kidneys)

Two Taking Advice
Tz צ (Bladder)
Q ק (Rectum)

Two Robbing
H,V ה, ו (Hands)

Two Hunting
Z, Ch ז, ח (Feet)

THE FOUR TRIADS OF SIMPLES

Three Friends
H ה Right Hand
Z ז Right Foot
T ט Right Kidney

Three Enemies
V ו Left Hand
Ch ח Left Foot
I י Left Kidney

Three That Give Life
L ל Liver
N נ Spleen
S ס Gall

Three that Destroyeth
O ע Stomach
Tz צ Bladder
Q ק Rectum

As to the foregoing four triads, tradition gives a second set of 12 which involves 12 select mother, double, and simple letters:

ALTERNATE FOUR TRIADS

Three Friends
K, Th כ, ת Two Ears
A א Heart

Three Enemies
L ל Liver
S ס Gall
Sh ש Tongue

Three Life Givers
D, P ד, פ Two Nostrils
N נ Spleen

Three Destroyers
Tz, Q צ, ק Two lower Apertures (Bladder, Rectum)
B ב Mouth

As to one grand symbol set involving the complete alphabet and the human body, the *Sepher Yetzirah* in the second section of the first chapter draws the parallel between ten fingers, ten toes, and the tongue and genitals. These 22 components of the human body as the alphabet are as follows:

The Twenty-Two Components of the Human Body

A (א)—Tongue (upper covenant between ten fingers)

B (ב) (Thumb)
G (ג) (Index Finger)   Five Fingers
D (ד) (Middle Finger)   of
H (ה) (Ring Finger)   Right Hand
V (ו) (Little Finger)

Z (ז) (Thumb)
Ch (ח) (Index Finger)   Five Fingers
T (ט) (Middle Finger)   of
I (י) (Ring Finger)   Left Hand
K (כ) (Little Finger)

L (ל) Genitals (Lower covenant between 10 toes)

M (מ)
N (נ)   Five Toes
S (ס)   of
O (ע)   Right Foot
P (פ)

Tz (צ)
Q (ק)   Five Toes
R (ר)   of
Sh (ש)   Left Foot
Th (ת)

This symbol set involves both the division of 10 and 22, for 10 and 22 combine to form the 32 Paths of Wisdom which form the framework of the Tree of Life.

The later editions of the *Sepher Yetzirah* end with a list of 32 intelligences for the 32 Paths. The following table shows these 32 Paths and the parts of the Tree of Life they form.

The Thirty-Two Paths of Wisdom

Number/ Letter	Number of Path	Tree of Life	Intelligence
1	1	Kether	Mystical (MVPLA, מופלא)
2	2	Chockmah	Illuminating (MZHIR, מזהיר)
3	3	Binah	Sanctifying (MQVDSh, מקודש)
4	4	Chesed	Measuring (QBVO, קבוע)
5	5	Geburah	Root (NShRSh, נשרש)
6	6	Tiphereth	Mediating (ShPO NBDL, שפע נבדל)
7	7	Netzach	Secret (NSThR, נסתר)
8	8	Hod	Perfect (ShLMf, שלם)
9	9	Yesod	Pure (THVR, טהור)
10	10	Malkuth	Resplendent (MThNVTzO, מתנוצע)
A (א)	11	Aleph	Scintillating (MTzVChTzCh, מצוחצח)
B (ב)	12	Beth	Transparency (BHIR, בהיר)
G (ג)	13	Gimel	Uniting (HAChDVTh, האחדות)
D (ד)	14	Daleth	Illuminating (MAIR, מאיר)
H (ה)	15	Heh	Constituting (MOMID, מעמיד)
V (ו)	16	Vav	Triumphant (NTzChI, נצחי)
Z (ז)	17	Zain	Disposing (HHRGSh, ההרגש)
Ch (ח)	18	Cheth	House of Influence (BITh HShPO, בית השפע)
T (ט)	19	Teth	Secret of All Spiritual Activity (SVD HPOVLVTh, סוד הפעולות)
I (י)	20	Yod	Will (HRTzVNf, הרצון)
K (כ)	21	Kaph	Rewarding (HChPTzf, החפץ)
L (ל)	22	Lamed	Faithful (NAMNf, נאמן)
M (מ)	23	Mem	Stable (QIIMf, קיים)
N (נ)	24	Nun	Imaginative (DMIVNI, דמיוני)
S (ס)	25	Samekh	Temptation (NSIVNI, נסיוני)
O (ע)	26	Ayin	Renewing (MChDSh, מחדש)
P (פ)	27	Peh	Exciting (MVRGSh, מורגש)
Tz (צ)	28	Tzaddi	Natural (MVTBO, מוטבע)
Q (ק)	29	Qoph	Corporeal (MVGShM, מוגשם)
R (ר)	30	Resh	Collective (KLLI, כללי)
Sh (ש)	31	Shin	Perpetual (ThMIDI, תמידי)
Th (ת)	32	Tav	Administrative (NOBD, נעבד)

COLOR

Although the *Sepher Yetzirah* does not give concrete color symbolism for
the 32 Paths of Wisdom, a very beautiful system based on the rainbow was
developed by MacGregor Mathers, who created 16 separate combinations
of colors for the 32 Paths. The following table, combining the two scales
known as Queen and King, is the basis for all 16 combinations.

Mathers' Thirty-Two Path Color Scale
(King/Letters, Queen/Numbers)

Color	Sephiroth	Simple	Double	Mother
White	1			
Gray	2			
Red	5	H (ה)	P (פ)	Sh (ש)
Red-Orange		V (ו)		
Orange	8	Z (ז)	R (ר)	
Yellow-Orange		Ch (ח)		
Yellow	6	T (ט)	B (ב)	A (א)
Yellow-Green		I (י)		
Green	7	L (ל)	D (ד)	
Blue-Green		N (נ)		
Blue	4	S (ס)	G (ג)	M (מ)
Blue-Violet		O (ע)	Th (ת)	
Violet	9	Tz (צ)	K (כ)	
Red-Violet		Q (ק)		
Russet	10			
Olive	10			
Citrine	10			
Black	3/10			

THE FIVE FINALS

The *Sepher Yetzirah* gives no special attributes for the five final letters.
Since these five final letters were created by 400 BCE, this may be evidence
to show that the origin of the *Sepher Yetzirah* predates the creation of the
five final letters. These five final letters (K, M, N, P, Tz—ך, ם, ן, ף, ץ), however, possess a symbolic set of attributes. Moreover, with the addition of
five final letters to the 22 original Hebrew letters, a scale of 27 was ultimately developed by the Renaissance Christian Qabalist Athanasius
Kircher to resemble the cosmology of both the *Sepher Yetzirah* and the
mystical work of Raymond Lull.

The Five Finals

Letter	Type of Letter	Number Value	Five Transmissions of Knowledge	Five Points of Pentagram	Five Elements	Five Parts of Soul	Directional Cube of 22 Components
K (ך)	Double	500 (20)	KP (כף)—Hand to Hand	Lower Left	Earth (ARTz, ארץ)	Animal Soul (NPSh, נפש)	Southeast lower corner to upper Northwest corner
M (ם)	Mother	600 (40)	MAMR (מאמר)—Saying to Saying	Apex Point	Spirit (RVCh, רוח)	True Self (IChIDH, יחידה)	Center of Cube
N (ן)	Simple	700 (50)	NAMN (נאמן)—The Faithful to the Faithful	Upper Right	Water (MIM, מים)	Intuitive (NShMH, נשמה)	Northeast lower corner to upper Southwest corner
P (ף)	Double	800 (80)	PH (פה)—Mouth to Mouth	Lower Right	Fire (ASh, אש)	Life Force (ChIH, חיה)	Southwest lower corner to upper Northeast corner
Tz (ץ)	Simple	900 (90)	TzDQ (צדק)—The Righteous to the Righteous	Upper Left	Air (AVIR, אויר)	Intellect (RVCh, רוח)	Northwest lower corner to upper Southeast corner

Hebrew—Final
Kircher's Cosmological Scale of Twenty-Seven

Number	Hebrew Letter	Division of Universe
1	A (א)	Seraphim (God)
2	B (ב)	Ophanim
3	G (ג)	Thrones
4	D (ד)	Dominations
5	H (ה)	Powers
6	V (ו)	Virtues
7	Z (ז)	Principalities
8	Ch (ח)	Archangels
9	T (ט)	Angels
10	I (י)	Celestial Government
11	K (כ)	Primum Mobile
12	Kf (ך)	Zodiac
13	L (ל)	Saturn
14	M (מ)	Jupiter
15	Mf (ם)	Mars
16	N (נ)	Sun
17	Nf (ן)	Venus
18	S (ס)	Mercury
19	O (ע)	Moon
20	P (פ)	Fire
21	Pf (ף)	Air
22	Tz (צ)	Water
23	Tzf (ץ)	Earth
24	Q (ק)	Minerals
25	R (ר)	Plants
26	Sh (ש)	Animals
27	Th (ת)	Man

THE 231 GATES OF THE SEPHER YETZIRAH

ShMf AChD = 913 = BRAShITh

(בראשית = 913 = שם אחד)

"The Name of Unity"

"The One Name All Creation Emanated From"

The *Sepher Yetzirah* describes a process of pairing every letter of the alphabet with each other. In chapter 2, verse 4, in describing the creation of the Universe, the following description occurs:

> He fixed the twenty-two letters, stamina, on the sphere like
> a wall with two hundred and thirty-one gates, and turned
> the spheres forward and backward.

This passage is an obvious source for the alphabet wheels of Raymond Lull. It describes the combining of every letter of the alphabet with every other letter without duplication, forming 231 pairs of numbers known as the 231 Gates.

The first gate is "Aleph Beth," while the last (or 231st) is "Shin Tav."

These 231 pairs form building blocks from which all words in Hebrew can be extracted.

In terms of Qabalistic tradition, in creating the "golem," these 231 gates are chanted from "Aleph Beth" to "Shin Tav." In order to uncreate the golem, these gates must be chanted backwards from "Tav Shin" to "Beth Aleph."

Thus, moving forward through the 231 gates is the creative process, while going backward through the gates is the dissolution process

Each of the 231 gates possesses a rich set of symbols, allowing each of the gates to be a specific meditation. The Qabalistic symbolism of each of the 231 gates appears in the following tables.

Number of Gate	Hebrew Alphabet Pair	Simple Number Value	Letter Name Value	Tarot Numeral Value	Tarot Card Pair	Astrological Conjunction	Directions in Space	Human Body
1	AB (אב)	3	523 (1243)	1	The Fool, The Magician	Air, Mercury	Above to Below, Above	Heart, Mouth
	Meaning: Father, Teacher, Master, Source, Ancestor, Originator, the Zodiacal month Leo; initials of ALP BITh (אלף בית), "alphabet"							
2	AG (אג)	4	184 (904)	2	The Fool, The High Priestess	Air, Moon	Above to Below, Below	Heart, Left Eye
	Meaning: Initials of ALHIM GBVR (אלהים גבור)—God of Strength; God name for fifth Sephirah, Geburah; to spell letters, curse, swear							
3	AD (אד)	5	545 (1265)	3	The Fool, The Empress	Air, Venus	Above to Below, East	Heart, Left Nostril
	Meaning: Vapor, mist, ether							
4	AH (אה)	6	121 (841)	4	The Fool, The Emperor	Air, Aries	Above to Below, Northeast	Heart, Right Hand
	Meaning: Initials of ADM HARTz (אדם הארץ)—Man of Earth, a title for tenth Sephirah, Malkuth; Ah!							
5	AV (או)	7	123 (843)	5	The Fool, The Hierophant	Air, Taurus	Above to Below, Southeast	Heart, Left Hand
	Meaning: Desire, will; he, that, this; either … or							
6	AZ (אז)	8	720 (1548)	6	The Fool, The Lovers	Air, Gemini	Above to Below, East-Above	Heart, Right Foot
	Meaning: Then, at that time, before, because of that (Alpha and Omega of Latin Alphabet)							
7	ACh (אח)	9	529 (1249)	7	The Fool, The Chariot	Air, Cancer	Above to Below, East-Below	Heart, Left Foot
	Meaning: Ah! Alas!, brother, equal, kin, family, howlings, the howl of the screech-owl, owl (Lilith); initials of ADM ChVH (אדם חוה)—Adam and Eve							

Number of Gate	Hebrew Alphabet Pair	Simple Number Value	Letter Name Value	Tarot Numeral Value	Tarot Card Pair	Astrological Conjunction	Directions in Space	Human Body
8	AT (אט)	10	530 (1250)	8	The Fool, Strength	Air, Leo	Above to Below, North-Above	Heart, Right Kidney (testicle)
	Meaning: Fortuneteller, soothsayer, diviner, enchanter							
9	AI (אי)	11	131 (851)	9	The Fool, The Hermit	Air, Virgo	Above to Below, North-Below,	Heart, Left Kidney (testicle)
	Meaning: Island; jackal; impossible, the numbers for first Sephirah (Kether) and tenth Sephirah (Malkuth)							
10	AK (אכ)	21	211 (1651)	10	The Fool, The Wheel of Fortune	Air, Jupiter	Above to Below, West	Heart, Right Ear
	Meaning: Certainly, only, but, together, affliction, calamity							
11	AL (אל)	31	185 (905)	11	The Fool, Justice	Air, Libra	Above to Below, Northwest	Heart, Liver
	Meaning: Power, strength; God, deity; God name of fourth Sephirah (Chesed); absolutely, certainly, nothing							
12	AM (אמ)	41	201 (1481)	12	The Fool, The Hanged Man	Air, Water	Above to Below, East to West	Heart, Genitals
	Meaning: Mother, source, womb, beginning, origin, crossroads							
13	AN (אנ)	51	217 (1587)	13	The Fool, Death	Air, Scorpio	Above to Below, Southwest	Heart, Spleen
	Meaning: Pain; sorrow; Heliopolis, a city in lower Egypt; where? whither?							
14	AS (אס)	61	231 (1431)	14	The Fool, Temperance	Air, Sagittarius	Above to Below, West-Above	Heart, Gall
	Meaning: Rim, edge; initials of AIN SVP (אין סוף)—infinity, without end, the second veil of the Void							

Number of Gate	Hebrew Alphabet Pair	Simple Number Value	Letter Name Value	Tarot Numeral Value	Tarot Card Pair	Astrological Conjunction	Directions in Space	Human Body
15	AO (אע)	71	241 (1611)	15	The Fool, The Devil	Air, Capricorn	Above to Below, West-Below	Heart, Stomach (colon)

Meaning: Wood, woods, forest; any wooden object, initials of AVR OGVL (אור עגול)—circular light which descends through the ten Sephiroth

16	AP (אפ)	81	196 (916)	16	The Fool, The Tower	Air, Mars	Above to Below, North	Heart, Right Nostril

Meaning: The nose; anger; initials of AVR PShVT (אור פשוט)—light which concentrates to a simple point

17	ATz (אצ)	91	215 (935)	17	The Fool, The Star	Air, Aquarius	Above to Below, South-Above	Heart, Bladder

Meaning: To hasten, urge, press, hurry

18	AQ (אק)	101	297 (1737)	18	The Fool, The Moon	Air, Pisces	Above to Below, South-Below	Heart, Rectum

Meaning: She goat; initials of ADM QDMVN (אדם קדמון)—the first man, the body of the Tree of Life as the divine body of man

19	AR (אר)	201	621 (1341)	19	The Fool, The Sun	Air, Sun	Above to Below, South	Heart, Right Eye

Meaning: Light (of the Sun)

20	ASh (אש)	301	471 (1841)	20	The Fool, Judgement	Air, Fire	Above to Below, North to South	Heart, Brain

Meaning: Fire; fever; heat

21	ATh (את)	401	517 (1237)	21	The Fool, The World	Air, Saturn	Above to Below, Center	Heart, Left Ear

Meaning: Essence; the thing itself; alpha and omega of Hebrew alphabet; letter, sign, mark; plowshare, spade

Number of Gate	Hebrew Alphabet Pair	Simple Number Value	Letter Name Value	Tarot Numeral Value	Tarot Card Pair	Astrological Conjunction	Directions in Space	Human Body
22	BG (בג)	5	485	3	The Magician, The High Priestess	Mercury, Moon	Above, Below	Mouth, Left Eye
	Meaning: Delicacy, food, bread							
23	BD (בד)	6	846	4	The Magician, The Empress	Mercury, Venus	Above, East	Mouth, Left Nostril
	Meaning: Bar, limb, arm							
24	BH (בה)	7	422	5	The Magician, The Emperor	Mercury, Aries	Above, Northeast	Mouth, Right Hand
	Meaning: To be broken into, confounded, confused, to burst forth, to be stirred up							
25	BV (בו)	8	424	6	The Magician, The Hierophant	Mercury, Taurus	Above, Southeast	Mouth, Left Hand
	Meaning: To come in, within, enter into, split, insert, sexual union							
26	BZ (בז)	9	479 (1129)	7	The Magician, The Lovers	Mercury, Gemini	Above, East-Above	Mouth, Right Foot
	Meaning: Plunder, conquer, shutter, tread upon; give away, squander, treat lightly; cut into pieces; prey, spoil							
27	BCh (בח)	10	830	8	The Magician, The Chariot	Mercury, Cancer	Above, East-Below	Mouth, Left Foot
	Meaning: To look out, be cautious							
28	BT (בט)	11	831	9	The Magician, Strength	Mercury, Leo	Above, North-Above	Mouth, Right Kidney (testicle)
	Meaning: To swell, burst forth, shine; to tread, to dash to pieces							

Number of Gate	Hebrew Alphabet Pair	Simple Number Value	Letter Name Value	Tarot Numeral Value	Tarot Card Pair	Astrological Conjunction	Directions in Space	Human Body
29	BI (בי)	12	432	10	The Magician, The Hermit	Mercury, Virgo	Above, North-Below	Mouth, Left Kidney (testicle)
Meaning: To dwell within; in me, at me, with me, by me; to pray, to please; the temple's innermost sanctuary							
30	BK (בכ)	22	512 (1232)	11	The Magician, The Wheel of Fortune	Mercury, Jupiter	Above, West	Mouth, Right Ear
Meaning: The first and last letter of the *Sepher Yetzirah*—implying the 22 letters of the Hebrew alphabet; to cause to weep, make cry, lament							
31	BL (בל)	32	486	12	The Magician, Justice	Mercury, Libra	Above, Northwest	Mouth, Liver
Meaning: The first and last letters of the Torah, implying the 32 Paths of the Tree of Life; mind, heart, center; no, not; care, anxiety; Babylonian deity Bel (the planet Jupiter); Greater Fortune (astrology)							
32	BM (בם)	42	502 (1062)	13	The Magician, The Hanged Man	Mercury, Water	Above, East to West	Mouth, Genitals
Meaning: Entrance, gathering place, ascent							
33	BN (בן)	52	518 (1168)	14	The Magician, Death	Mercury, Scorpio	Above, Southwest	Mouth, Spleen
Meaning: The son, child, the first and last letter of the New Testament in Greek							
34	BS (בס)	62	532 (1012)	15	The Magician, Temperance	Mercury, Sagittarius	Above, West-Above	Mouth, Gall
Meaning: To trample, step, pile up; to establish firmly, to rest safely							
35	BO (בע)	72	542 (1192)	16	The Magician, The Devil	Mercury, Capricorn	Above, West-Below	Mouth, Stomach (colon)
Meaning: To seek, request, petition, pray							

Number of Gate	Hebrew Alphabet Pair	Simple Number Value	Letter Name Value	Tarot Numeral Value	Tarot Card Pair	Astrological Conjunction	Directions in Space	Human Body
36	BP (בפ)	82	497	17	The Magician, The Tower	Mercury, Mars	Above, North	Mouth, Right Nostril
Meaning: Ball, stone, lump, hailstone, resin								
37	BTz (בצ)	92	516	18	The Magician, The Star	Mercury, Aquarius	Above, South-Above	Mouth, Bladder
Meaning: Bubbles; bubble forth, burst forth, swamp, pond, puddle								
38	BQ (בק)	102	598 (1318)	19	The Magician, The Moon	Mercury, Pisces	Above, South-Below	Mouth, Rectum
Meaning: Initials of BITh QVL (בית קול)—Daughter of the Voice, Muse, Echo; gnat, to enter into, search, investigate, examine, find out								
39	BR (בר)	202	922	20	The Magician, The Sun	Mercury, Sun	Above, South	Mouth, Right Eye
Meaning: First two letters of the Torah (Gen 1:1); purity, cleanliness, innocence; grain, corn, field; forest, prarie; exterior, outside, clear; son, offspring								
40	BSh (בש)	302	772 (1422)	21	The Magician, Judgement	Mercury, Fire	Above, North to South	Mouth, Brain
Meaning: Initials of BITh ShMSh (בית שמש)—House of the Sun; troubled mind; to be ashamed; to act shamefully								
41	BTh (בת)	402	818	22	The Magician, The World	Mercury, Saturn	Above, Center	Mouth, Left Ear
Meaning: Child, girl, daughter (a title of the tenth Sephirah, Malkuth): initials of BITh ThBL (בית תבל)—House of the World								
42	GD (גד)	7	507	5	The High Priestess, The Empress	Moon, Venus	Below, East	Left Eye, Left Nostril
Meaning: Divinity of Fortune, luck, good fortune; Gad (a tribe of Israel); thunder; coriander seed; genius, God-head; initials for God as G-D.; initials of the Magickal Lodge, the Golden Dawn								

Number of Gate	Hebrew Alphabet Pair	Simple Number Value	Letter Name Value	Tarot Numeral Value	Tarot Card Pair	Astrological Conjunction	Directions in Space	Human Body
43	GH (הג)	8	83	6	The High Priestess, The Emperor	Moon, Aries	Below, Northeast	Left Eye, Right Hand
	Meaning: Removal of bandages, healing; to thrust away, remove; bending over one, protecting							
44	GV (וג)	9	85	7	The High Priestess, The Hierophant	Moon, Taurus	Below, Southeast	Left Eye, Left Hand
	Meaning: Interior of the body, back of the body, middle, hump, belly, innermost							
45	GZ (זג)	10	140 (790)	8	The High Priestess, The Lovers	Moon, Gemini	Below, East-Above	Left Eye, Right Foot
	Meaning: To pass, to change							
46	GCh (חג)	11	491	9	The High Priestess, The Chariot	Moon, Cancer	Below, East-Below	Left Eye, Left Foot
	Meaning: Break out, break forth, burst, issue forth							
47	GT (טג)	12	492	10	The High Priestess, Strength	Moon, Leo	Below, North-Above	Left Eye Right Kidney (testicle)
	Meaning: Pamphlet, legal document, letter; tool							
48	GI (יג)	13	93	11	The High Priestess, The Hermit	Moon, Virgo	Below, North-Below	Left Eye, Left Kidney (testicle)
	Meaning: Valley; valley (of death)							
49	GK (כג)	23	173 (893)	12	The High Priestess, The Wheel of Fortune	Moon, Jupiter	Below, West	Left Eye, Right Ear
	Meaning: Thy altar							

Number of Gate	Hebrew Alphabet Pair	Simple Number Value	Letter Name Value	Tarot Numeral Value	Tarot Card Pair	Astrological Conjunction	Directions in Space	Human Body
50	GL (גל)	33	147	13	The High Priestess, Justice	Moon, Libra	Below, Northwest	Left Eye, Liver
	Meaning: Heap of stones, ruin of bones; fountain, spring; bowl, oil lamp; wave, circle, wheel							
51	GM (גמ)	43	163 (723)	14	The High Priestess, The Hanged Man	Moon, Water	Below, East to West	Left Eye, Genitals
	Meaning: Addition, accumulation; yea, indeed, truly; absorb, drink up, swallow							
52	GN (גנ)	53	179 (829)	15	The High Priestess, Death	Moon, Scorpio	Below, Southwest	Left Eye, Spleen
	Meaning: Garden; garden of trees, arbor; enclosed garden; fenced in place							
53	GS (גס)	63	193 (673)	16	The High Priestess, Temperance	Moon, Sagittarius	Below, West-Above	Left Eye, Gall
	Meaning: Bulky, crude, coarse							
54	GO (גע)	73	203 (853)	17	The High Priestess, The Devil	Moon, Capricorn	Below, West-Below	Left Eye, Stomach (colon)
	Meaning: Longing, homesickness, wallowing, the lowing of an ox; initials of GN ODN (גן עדן)—Garden of Delight, Paradise, Garden of Eden; Eye in the Triangle, where Eye = O (ע) and Triangle = G (ג) as 3							
55	GP (גפ)	83	158	18	The High Priestess, The Tower	Moon, Mars	Below, North	Left Eye, Right Nostril
	Meaning: Wing (of a bird, angel), arm; back, body; person, self; to bend, join, press, clasp, close, surround, embrace							
56	GTz (גצ)	93	247	19	The High Priestess, The Star	Moon, Aquarius	Below, South-Above	Left Eye, Bladder
	Meaning: Spark from the forger's hammer; the soul as a divine spark of God; white earth, chalk							

Number of Gate	Hebrew Alphabet Pair	Simple Number Value	Letter Name Value	Tarot Numeral Value	Tarot Card Pair	Astrological Conjunction	Directions in Space	Human Body
57	GQ (גק)	103	249 (979)	20	The High Priestess, The Moon	Moon, Pisces	Below, South-Below	Left Eye, Rectum
	Meaning: Initials of GN QBLH (גן קבלה)—the enclosed garden of the Qabalah, the mystery school							
58	GR (גר)	203	583	21	The High Priestess, The Sun	Moon, Sun	Below, South	Left Eye, Right Eye
	Meaning: Wanderer, stranger, dweller, nomad; a lion's whelp; a lime; proselyte, convert to Judaism							
59	GSh (גש)	303	433 (1083)	22	The High Priestess, Judgement	Moon, Fire	Below, North to South	Left Eye, Brain
	Meaning: Framework of a ship, sounding pole, to beat, ring; to feel, touch, wrestle, fight							
60	GTh (גת)	403	479	23	The High Priestess, The World	Moon, Saturn	Below, Center	Left Eye, Left Ear
	Meaning: A marked off space; wine-press							
61	DH (דה)	9	444	7	The Empress, The Emperor	Venus, Aries	East, Northeast	Left Nostril, Right Hand
	Meaning: To go slowly, to languish; to fly, float; to walk, pull, hop, trip							
62	DV (דו)	10	446	8	The Empress, The Hierophant	Venus, Taurus	East, Southeast	Left Nostril, Left Hand
	Meaning: Two, bi-; love, friendship							
63	DZ (דז)	11	501 (1151)	9	The Empress, The Lovers	Venus, Gemini	East, East-Above	Left Nostril, Right Foot
	Meaning: Initials of DI ZHB (די זהב)—a place abounding with gold							

Number of Gate	Hebrew Alphabet Pair	Simple Number Value	Letter Name Value	Tarot Numeral Value	Tarot Card Pair	Astrological Conjunction	Directions in Space	Human Body
64	DCh (חד)	12	852	10	The Empress, The Chariot	Venus, Cancer	East, East-Below	Left Nostril, Left Foot
Meaning: To push, to throw down, to thrust; a concubine								
65	DT (טד)	13	853	11	The Empress, Strength	Venus, Leo	East, North-Above	Left Nostril, Right Kidney (testicle)
Meaning: Upper chamber; nethermost room; compartment								
66	DI (יד)	14	454	12	The Empress, The Hermit	Venus, Virgo	East, North-Below	Left Nostril, Left Kidney (testicle)
Meaning: Sufficient, enough, plenty, two, twice; longing for								
67	DK (כד)	24	534 (1254)	13	The Empress, The Wheel of Fortune	Venus, Jupiter	East, West	Left Nostril, Right Ear
Meaning: Crushed, broken, afflicted, humbled; to be cleansed of sin, to be restored to purity								
68	DL (לד)	34	508	14	The Empress, Justice	Venus, Libra	East, Northwest	Left Nostril, Liver
Meaning: Something hanging, swinging; the hinge of a door, the door of the lips, the tent flap (a metaphor for womb and vagina), that which draws water; thin, weak, feeble, lesser, low, ignoble								
69	DM (מד)	44	524 (1084)	15	The Empress, The Hanged Man	Venus, Water	East, East to West	Left Nostril, Genitals
Meaning: Blood, life, bloodshed, blood of the grape; liquid; likeness, image								
70	DN (נד)	54	540 (1190)	16	The Empress, Death	Venus, Scorpio	East, Southwest	Left Nostril, Spleen
Meaning: Dan (a tribe of Israel): to judge, weigh; this, this one								

Number of Gate	Hebrew Alphabet Pair	Simple Number Value	Letter Name Value	Tarot Numeral Value	Tarot Card Pair	Astrological Conjunction	Directions in Space	Human Body
71	DS (ס ד)	64	554 (1034)	17	The Empress, Temperance	Venus, Sagittarius	East, West-Above	Left Nostril, Gall
	Meaning: Dish, plate, disc, graal							
72	DO (ע ד)	74	564 (1214)	18	The Empress, The Devil	Venus, Capricorn	East, West-Below	Left Nostril, Stomach (colon)
	Meaning: Knowledge; knowing; what one knows							
73	DP (פ ד)	84	519	19	The Empress, The Tower	Venus, Mars	East, North	Left Nostril, Right Nostril
	Meaning: Board, plank, tablet, column; to hammer, join							
74	DTz (צ ד)	94	538	20	The Empress, The Star	Venus, Aquarius	East, South-Above	Left Nostril, Bladder
	Meaning: To prick, stick, squeeze; to skip, dance, rejoice							
75	DQ (ק ד)	104	620 (1340)	21	The Empress, The Moon	Venus, Pisces	East, South-Below	Left Nostril, Rectum
	Meaning: Thin, fine, tender, a veiled spot; crushing, humilation, sufferings; to investigate, to be strict; to crush; pound, powder							
76	DR (ר ד)	204	944	22	The Empress, The Sun	Venus, Sun	East, South	Left Nostril, Right Eye
	Meaning: Row, range, order; period, generation; row of wood as funeral pyre; to form a circle or enclosure; to lodge							
77	DSh (ש ד)	304	794 (1444)	23	The Empress, Judgement	Venus, Fire	East, North to South	Left Nostril, Brain
	Meaning: Herb, tender grass, herbage; entrance, doorway, door							

Number of Gate	Hebrew Alphabet Pair	Simple Number Value	Letter Name Value	Tarot Numeral Value	Tarot Card Pair	Astrological Conjunction	Directions in Space	Human Body
78	DTh (דת)	404	840	24	The Empress, The World	Venus, Saturn	East, Center	Left Nostril, Left Ear
Meaning: Custom, law; as thou sayest, judgment, punishment								
79	HV (הו)	11	22	9	The Emperor, The Hierophant	Aries, Taurus	Northeast, Southeast	Right Hand, Left Hand
Meaning: The second and third letter of the Tetragrammaton; mother and son; he, myself, thyself								
80	HZ (הז)	12	77 (727)	10	The Emperor, The Lovers	Aries, Gemini	Northeast, East-Above	Right Hand, Right Foot
Meaning: Sprinkling of the blood of sacrifices, of the water of purification upon the unclean								
81	HCh (הח)	13	428	11	The Emperor, The Chariot	Aries, Cancer	Northeast, East-Below	Right Hand, Left Foot
Meaning: The last and first letter of the word for the life-force: ChIH								
82	HT (הט)	14	429	12	The Emperor, Strength	Aries, Leo	Northeast, North-Above	Right Hand, Right Kidney (testicle)
Meaning: Inclination, sliding; perversion of justice; performing coition with a virgin without causing bleeding								
83	HI (הי)	15	30	13	The Emperor, The Hermit	Aries, Virgo	Northeast, North-Below	Right Hand, Left Kidney (testicle)
Meaning: The second and first letter of both Jah and the Tetragrammaton: IH + IHVH (יה + יהוה); behold, here is; she; woe! oh!								
84	HK (הך)	25	110 (830)	14	The Emperor, The Wheel of Fortune	Aries, Jupiter	Northeast, West	Right Hand, Right Ear
Meaning: To go; this, that; here, hither								

Number of Gate	Hebrew Alphabet Pair	Simple Number Value	Letter Name Value	Tarot Numeral Value	Tarot Card Pair	Astrological Conjunction	Directions in Space	Human Body
85	HL (חל)	35	84	15	The Emperor, Justice	Aries, Libra	Northeast Northwest	Right Hand, Kidney
Meaning: To be bright, shine; praise (God)								
86	HM (חם)	45	100 (660)	16	The Emperor, The Hanged Man	Aries, Water	Northeast, East to West	Right Hand Genitals
Meaning: To be noisy, excited; to rush after, be greedy, envious								
87	HN (חן)	55	116 (766)	17	The Emperor, Death	Aries, Scorpio	Northeast, Southwest	Right Hand Spleen
Meaning: They; he who; here is; behold; enjoyment, pleasure; initials of Had and Nu: HAD + NU (הד + נו)								
88	HS (חס)	65	130 (610)	18	The Emperor, Temperance	Aries, Sagittarius	Northeast, West-Above	Right Hand Gall
Meaning: To be silent; hush								
89	HO (חע)	75	140 (790)	19	The Emperor, The Devil	Aries, Capricorn	Northeast, West-Below	Right Hand Stomach (colon)
Meaning: Sexual contact, the first stage of sexual connection								
90	HP (חפ)	85	95	20	The Emperor, The Tower	Aries, Mars	Northeast, North	Right Hand Right Nostril
Meaning: The letter name Peh (meaning mouth) written backwards: PH=HP (פה=הפ); the foam of the sea, froth, what is blown off								
91	HTz (חצ)	95	114	21	The Emperor, The Star	Aries, Aquarius	Northeast, South-Above	Right Hand Bladder
Meaning: The two Tarot cards which Crowley exchanged in accordance with AL I:57; palm branch; hedge work								

Number of Gate	Hebrew Alphabet Pair	Simple Number Value	Letter Name Value	Tarot Numeral Value	Tarot Card Pair	Astrological Conjunction	Directions in Space	Human Body
92	HQ (קה)	105	196 (916)	22	The Emperor, The Moon	Aries, Pisces	Northeast, South-Below	Right Hand, Rectum
	Meaning: Initials of Abel and Qain: HBL + QIN (הבל + קין)							
93	HR (רה)	205	520	23	The Emperor, The Sun	Aries, Sun	Northeast, South	Right Hand, Right Eye
	Meaning: Mountain; hill; pyramid							
94	HSh (שה)	305	370 (1020)	24	The Emperor, Judgement	Aries, Fire	Northeast, North to South	Right Hand, Brain
	Meaning: Relief, delivery; help, I pray; welfare, salvation							
95	HTh (תה)	405	416	25	The Emperor, The World	Aries, Saturn	Northeast, Center	Right Hand, Left Ear
	Meaning: To break in upon, rush in upon; to melt							
96	VZ (זו)	13	79 (729)	11	The Hierophant, The Lovers	Taurus, Gemini	Southeast South-Above	Left Hand, Right Foot
	Meaning: To carry, burden, laden with guilt, sin							
97	VCh (חו)	14	430	12	The Hierophant, The Chariot	Taurus, Cancer	Southeast South-Below	Left Hand, Left Foot
	Meaning: Last, outmost							
98	VT (טו)	15	431	13	The Hierophant, Strength	Taurus, Leo	Southeast North-Above	Left Hand, Left Kidney (testicle)
	Meaning: The last and first substitute numeral letters for Jah = IH (יה) = 15 = TV (טו); penis, phallus							

Number of Gate	Hebrew Alphabet Pair	Simple Number Value	Letter Name Value	Tarot Numeral Value	Tarot Card Pair	Astrological Conjunction	Directions in Space	Human Body
99	VI (וי)	16	32	14	The Hierophant, The Hermit	Taurus, Virgo	Southeast, North-Below	Left Hand, Left Kidney (testicle)
Meaning: The third and first letters of the Tetragrammaton: son + father: IHVH (יְהֹוָה); woe! oh!; (V וי =penis + I וי =hand)								
100	VK (וכ)	26	112 (832)	15	The Hierophant, The Wheel of Fortune	Taurus, Jupiter	Southeast, West	Left Hand, Right Ear
Meaning: To be firm, stand, be right; the numeral letters for Jehovah:KV (כו) = 26 = VK (וכ)								
101	VL (ול)	36	86	16	The Hierophant, Justice	Taurus, Libra	Southeast, Northwest	Left Hand, Liver
Meaning: Child; the numeral 36 denotes the 36 rightous souls who support the world, LV (לו) = 36 = VL (ול)								
102	VM (ומ)	46	102 (662)	17	The Hierophant, The Hanged Man	Taurus, Water	Southeast, East to West	Left Hand, Genitals
Meaning: Initials for the Rose of Heaven; VRD MOLH (וֶרֶד מַעְלָה)								
103	VN (ונ)	56	118 (768)	18	The Hierophant, Death	Taurus, Scorpio	Southeast, Southwest	Left Hand, Spleen
Meaning: To be torpid, weak, meek; the numbers six + fifty referred to in AL I:24 as Nuit's name, VN (ונ) = 6 + 50 = 56 = NV (נו)								
104	VS (וס)	66	132 (612)	19	The Hierophant, Temperance	Taurus, Sagittarius	Southeast, West-Above	Left Hand, Gall
Meaning: The penis (V, ו) as a straight line + the vagina (S, ס) as a circle; the menstrual cycle; to color, stain, soil								
105	VO (וָע)	76	142 (792)	20	The Hierophant, The Devil	Taurus, Capricorn	Southeast, West-Below	Left Hand, Stomach (colon)
Meaning: Addition, increase, large measure								

Number of Gate	Hebrew Alphabet Pair	Simple Number Value	Letter Name Value	Tarot Numeral Value	Tarot Card Pair	Astrological Conjunction	Directions in Space	Human Body
106	VP (פו)	86	97	21	The Hierophant, The Tower	Taurus, Mars	Southeast, North	Left Hand, Right Nostril
	Meaning: Addition							
107	VTz (צו)	96	116	22	The Hierophant, The Star	Taurus, Aquarius	Southeast, South-Above	Left Hand, Bladder
	Meaning: Dove							
108	VQ (קו)	106	198 (918)	23	The Hierophant, The Moon	Taurus, Pisces	Southeast, South-Below	Left Hand, Rectum
	Meaning: Sting, goad							
109	VR (רו)	206	522	24	The Hierophant, The Sun	Taurus, Sun	Southeast, South	Left Hand, Right Eye
	Meaning: Rose; heart; jugular vein							
110	VSh (שו)	306	372 (1022)	25	The Hierophant, Judgement	Taurus, Fire	Southeast, North to South	Left Hand, Brain
	Meaning: Gullet, esophagus							
111	VTh (תו)	406	418	26	The Hierophant, The World	Taurus, Saturn	Southeast, Center	Left Hand, Left Ear
	Meaning: The last letter of the Hebrew alphabet written backwards, ThV (תו), as 111 is the value of the first letter ALP (אלף); and thou; stork							
112	ZCh (חז)	15	485 (1135)	13	The Lovers, The Chariot	Gemini, Cancer	East-Above, East-Below	Right Foot, Left Foot
	Meaning: To be elated, cheerful, overbearing; to cause to move, force, remove; to cause to tremble							

Number of Gate	Hebrew Alphabet Pair	Simple Number Value	Letter Name Value	Tarot Numeral Value	Tarot Card Pair	Astrological Conjunction	Directions in Space	Human Body
113	ZT (זט)	16	486 (1136)	14	The Lovers, Strength	Gemini, Leo	East-Above, North-Above	Right Foot, Right Kidney (testicle)
	Meaning: Young man, youth, student							
114	ZI (זי)	17	87 (670)	15	The Lovers, The Hermit	Gemini, Virgo	East-Above, North-Below	Right Foot, Left Kidney (testicle)
	Meaning: Spider; fabulous bird ziza, frame of a door, window							
115	ZK (זכ)	27	167 (1537)	16	The Lovers, The Wheel of Fortune	Gemini, Jupiter	East-Above, West	Right Foot, Right Ear
	Meaning: Clear, transparent, pure, guiltless, sinless							
116	ZL (זל)	37	141 (791)	17	The Lovers, Justice	Gemini, Libra	East-Above, Northwest	Right Foot, Liver
	Meaning: To be light, slender; to be treated lightly, neglected, despised, to be of little value							
117	ZM (זמ)	47	157 (1367)	18	The Lovers, The Hanged Man	Gemini, Water	East-Above, East to West	Right Foot, Genitals
	Meaning: To think, to meditate, the tinkling of a stringed instrument; the ring in the nose of a camel which serves as a goad and muzzle							
118	ZN (זנ)	57	173 (1473)	19	The Lovers, Death	Gemini, Scorpio	East-Above, Southwest	Right Foot, Spleen
	Meaning: Voluptuousness, to be unchaste; prostitution, to glisten, stroke, dress; to be unclean, greasy, foul							
119	ZS (זס)	67	187 (1317)	20	The Lovers, Temperance	Gemini, Sagittarius	East-Above, West-Above	Right Foot, Gall
	Meaning: Apron							

Number of Gate	Hebrew Alphabet Pair	Simple Number Value	Letter Name Value	Tarot Numeral Value	Tarot Card Pair	Astrological Conjunction	Directions in Space	Human Body
120	ZO (זֹו)	77	197 (1497)	21	The Lovers, The Devil	Gemini, Capricorn	East-Above, West-Below	Right Foot, Stomach (colon)
	Meaning: To tremble, shake, be agitated; shock; fright							
121	ZP (זֹפ)	87	152 (802)	22	The Lovers, The Tower	Gemini, Mars	East-Above, North	Right Foot, Right Nostril
	Meaning: Pitch, black; pitch-coating							
122	ZTz (זֹצ)	97	171 (821)	23	The Lovers, The Star	Gemini, Aquarius	East-Above, South-Above	Right Foot, Bladder
	Meaning: Initials of ZMR TzDQ (זמר צדק)—Song of the Righteous							
123	ZQ (זֹק)	107	253 (1623)	24	The Lovers, The Moon	Gemini, Pisces	East-Above, South-Below	Right Foot, Rectum
	Meaning: To rivet, forge, chain, join, bind, obligate							
124	ZR (זֹר)	207	577 (1227)	25	The Lovers, The Sun	Gemini, Sun	East-Above, South	Right Foot, Right Eye
	Meaning: stranger; oppressor, enemy; burden, edge, wreathwork for a crown							
125	ZSh (זֹש)	307	427 (1077)	26	The Lovers, Judgement	Gemini, Fire	East-Above, North to South	Right Foot, Brain
	Meaning: gold							
126	ZTh (זֹת)	407	473 (1123)	27	The Lovers, The World	Gemini, Saturn	East-Above, Center	Right Foot, Left Ear
	Meaning: This; an olive; olive-branch, leaf, tree							

Number of Gate	Hebrew Alphabet Pair	Simple Number Value	Letter Name Value	Tarot Numeral Value	Tarot Card Pair	Astrological Conjunction	Directions in Space	Human Body
127	ChT (חט)	17	837	15	The Chariot, Strength	Cancer, Leo	East-Below, North-Above	Left Foot, Right Kidney (testicle)
			Meaning: To dig, cut out, hollow; to cut, polish, glisten, jewels; failure, sin, sinner; mistake, inadvertance, sin					
128	ChI (חי)	18	438	16	The Chariot, The Hermit	Cancer, Virgo	East-Below, North-Below	Left Foot, Left Kidney (testicle)
			Meaning: Life, living, alive; living creature; initials of Eve and God: ChVH IHVH (חוה יהוה)					
129	ChK (חכ)	28	518 (1238)	17	The Chariot, The Wheel of Fortune	Cancer, Jupiter	East-Below, West	Left Foot, Right Ear
			Meaning: Taste; palate; persuasive word					
130	ChL (חל)	38	492	18	The Chariot, Justice	Cancer, Libra	East-Below, Northwest	Left Foot, Liver
			Meaning: Vinegar; to penetrate; cavities, to perforate; the initials of Eve and Lilith, Adam's two brides: ChVH LILITh (חוה לילית)					
131	ChM (חמ)	48	508 (1068)	19	The Chariot, The Hanged Man	Cancer, Water	East-Below, East to West	Left Foot, Genitals
			Meaning: Khem, a name of Egypt meaning black hot soil; hot, warm, heat, Sun					
132	ChN (חנ)	58	524 (1174)	20	The Chariot, Death	Cancer, Scorpio	East-Below, Southwest	Left Foot, Spleen
			Meaning: Grace, charm, without sin, blemish, attribute of the letter Peh in the *Sepher Yetzirah*; initials of an early title for the Qabalah: ChKMH NSThRH (חכמה נסתרה)—The Secret Wisdom					
133	ChS (חס)	68	538 (1018)	21	The Chariot, Temperance	Cancer, Sagittarius	East-Below, West-Above	Left Foot, Gall
			Meaning: Initials of Eve and Satan: ChVH STNf (חוה שטן); sparing; forbearance; God spare him!					

Number of Gate	Hebrew Alphabet Pair	Simple Number Value	Letter Name Value	Tarot Numeral Value	Tarot Card Pair	Astrological Conjunction	Directions in Space	Human Body
134	ChO (חע)	78	548 (1198)	22	The Chariot, The Devil	Cancer, Capricorn	East-Below, West-Below	Left Foot, Stomach (colon)
	Meaning: Initials of ChMH QVLM (חכמה עולם)—the Sun on High, the Heavenly Sun							
135	ChP (חפ)	88	503	23	The Chariot, The Tower	Cancer, Mars	East-Below, North	Left Foot, Right Nostril
	Meaning: To cover, veil; canopy							
136	ChTz (חצ)	98	522	24	The Chariot, The Star	Cancer, Aquarius	East-Below, South-Above	Left Foot, Bladder
	Meaning: Arrow; arrow of the gods-lightning; the iron head of a spear							
137	ChQ (חק)	108	604 (1324)	25	The Chariot, The Moon	Cancer, Pisces	East-Below, South-Below	Left Foot, Rectum
	Meaning: To draw a circle; limit, law, statute; appointed time; initials of ChKMH QBLH (חכמה קבלה)—the Wisdom of the Qabalah							
138	ChR (חר)	208	928	26	The Chariot, The Sun	Cancer, Sun	East-Below, South	Left Foot, Right Eye
	Meaning: Cave, hollow, cavity, round							
139	ChSh (חש)	308	778 (1438)	27	The Chariot, Judgement	Cancer, Fire	East-Below, North to South	Left Foot, Brain
	Meaning: Feel heavy, feel pain, suffer, anxiety, fear; initials of Eve and Shaitan: ChVH ShTN (חוה שטן)							
140	ChTh (חת)	408	824	28	The Chariot, The World	Cancer, Saturn	East-Below, Center	Left Foot, Left Ear
	Meaning: Broken, fear, alarm, terror, confounded; initials of Eve and the World: ChVH ThBL (חוה תבל)							

Number of Gate	Hebrew Alphabet Pair	Simple Number Value	Letter Name Value	Tarot Numeral Value	Tarot Card Pair	Astrological Conjunction	Directions in Space	Human Body
141	TI (טי)	19	439	17	Strength, The Hermit	Leo, Virgo	North-Above, North-Below	Right Kidney (testicle), Left Kidney (testicle)
	Meaning: Potter's clay, mud, loam							
142	TK (טכ)	29	519 (1239)	18	Strength, The Wheel of Fortune	Leo, Jupiter	North-Above, West	Right Kidney (testicle), Right Ear
	Meaning: To stamp, tread, press, fill up, squeeze on							
143	TL (טל)	39	493	19	Strength, Justice	Leo, Libra	North-Above, Northwest	Right Kidney (testicle), Liver
	Meaning: The two letters whose Zodiacal attributes require a switch of Key VIII and XI in the Tarot: TL (טל) = Leo,Libra = VIII+XI; dew drop; lamb, cover, veil							
144	TM (טמ)	49	509 (1069)	20	Strength, The Hanged Man	Leo, Water	North-Above, East to West	Right Kidney (testicle), Genitals
	Meaning: Unclean; to pollute oneself; to defile; to profane							
145	TN (טנ)	59	525 (1175)	21	Strength, Death	Leo, Scorpio	North-Above, Southwest	Right Kidney (testicle), Spleen
	Meaning: A basket; traveling box							
146	TS (טס)	69	539 (1019)	22	Strength, Temperance	Leo, Sagittarius	North-Above, West-Above	Right Kidney (testicle), Gall
	Meaning: To fly, soar, glisten, glitter							
147	TO (טע)	79	549 (1199)	23	Strength, The Devil	Leo, Capricorn	North-Above, West-Below	Right Kidney (testicle), Stomach (colon)
	Meaning: Idol; to go astray, err							

Number of Gate	Hebrew Alphabet Pair	Simple Number Value	Letter Name Value	Tarot Numeral Value	Tarot Card Pair	Astrological Conjunction	Directions in Space	Human Body
148	TP (פת)	89	504	24	Strength, The Tower	Leo, Mars	North-Above, North	Right Kidney (testicle), Right Nostril
Meaning: Little children; innocence; to be joined, to touch closely								
149	TTz (צת)	99	523	25	Strength, The Star	Leo, Aquarius	North-Above, South-Above	Right Kidney (testicle), Bladder
Meaning: Pretense, excuse, subterfuge, concealment								
150	TQ (קת)	109	605 (1325)	26	Strength, The Moon	Leo, Pisces	North-Above, South-Below	Right Kidney testicle), Rectum
Meaning: Arm; prepare for battle; guard								
151	TR (רת)	209	929	27	Strength, The Sun	Leo, Sun	North-Above, South	Right Kidney (testicle), Right Eye
Meaning: Castle; place for augury								
152	TSh (שת)	309	779 (1439)	28	Strength, Judgement	Leo, Fire	North-Above, North to South	Right Kidney (testicle), Brain
Meaning: To hide, protect, reserve; to be hidden								
153	TTh (תת)	409	825	29	Strength, The World	Leo, Saturn	North-Above, Center	Right Kidney (testicle), Left Ear
Meaning: Serpent								
154	IK (יכ)	30	120 (840)	19	The Hermit, The Wheel of Fortune	Virgo, Jupiter	North-Below, West	Left Kidney (testicle), Right Ear
Meaning: A net; to be firm, stand upright								

Number of Gate	Hebrew Alphabet Pair	Simple Number Value	Letter Name Value	Tarot Numeral Value	Tarot Card Pair	Astrological Conjunction	Directions in Space	Human Body
155	IL (ל')	40	94	20	The Hermit, Justice	Virgo, Libra	North-Below, Northwest	Left Kidney (testicle), Liver
Meaning: To bring forth, beget, to be born, originate; child; initials of Jehovah and Lilith:IHVH LILITh (ה'ל'י); the howl of a monster; lamentation								
156	IM (ם')	50	110 (670)	21	The Hermit, The Hanged Man	Virgo, Water	North-Below, East to West	Left Kidney (testicle), Genitals
Meaning: Sea, ocean, lake								
157	IN (ן')	60	126 (776)	22	The Hermit, Death	Virgo, Scorpio	North-Below, Southwest	Left Kidney (testicle), Spleen
Meaning: Wine; dove; to shake, awaken, stir up								
158	IS (ס')	70	140 (620)	23	The Hermit, Temperance	Virgo, Sagittarius	North-Below, West- Above	Left Kidney (testicle), Gall
Meaning: Foundation, basis, support								
159	IO (ע')	80	150 (800)	24	The Hermit, The Devil	Virgo, Capricorn	North-Below, West-Below	Left Kidney (testicle), Stomach (colon)
Meaning: The hand (I, ') and the eye (O, ע); shovel, spade; Hebrew form of Greek chant: IO (IΩ), meaning "Hail"								
160	IP (פ')	90	105	25	The Hermit, The Tower	Virgo, Mars	North-Below, North	Left Kidney (testicle), Right Nostril
Meaning: very fine; choice; beautiful; distinguished								
161	ITz (צ')	100	124	26	The Hermit, The Star	Virgo, Aquarius	North-Below, South-Above	Left Kidney (testicle), Bladder
Meaning: To go forth, rise, go out; to be sent away; to be released; to take out; lead forth, bring forth								

Number of Gate	Hebrew Alphabet Pair	Simple Number Value	Letter Name Value	Tarot Numeral Value	Tarot Card Pair	Astrological Conjunction	Directions in Space	Human Body
162	IQ (ק׳)	110	206 (926)	27	The Hermit, The Moon	Virgo, Pisces	North-Below, South-Below	Left Kidney (testicle), Rectum
Meaning: To be pious: reverence: obedience, submission to God; initials of God and Qain: IHVH and QIN (קין and יהוה)								
163	IR (יר)	210	530	28	The Hermit, The Sun	Virgo, Sun	North-Below, South	Left Kidney (testicle), Right Eye
Meaning: To fear, be afraid; to be in awe; to tremble for joy; reverencing; holy fear								
164	ISh (יש)	310	380 (1030)	29	The Hermit, Judgement	Virgo, Fire	North-Below, North to South	Left Kidney (testicle), Brain
Meaning: An old man, elder, ancient of days; to be white; uprightness								
165	ITh (ית)	410	426	30	The Hermit, The World	Virgo, Saturn	North-Below, Center	Left Kidney (testicle), Left Ear
Meaning: A nail; a club								
166	KL (כל)	50	174 (894)	21	The Wheel of Fortune, Justice	Jupiter, Libra	West, Northwest	Right Ear, Liver
Meaning: KL (כל) is the middle of the alphabet of 22 letters, as ATh (את) is the first and last; the whole, totality; any, of all kinds, even, one; all, wholly, altogether								
167	KM (כמ)	60	190 (1470)	22	The Wheel of Fortune, The Hanged Man	Jupiter, Water	West, East to West	Right Ear, Genitals
Meaning: How, how many, how much, how long								
168	KN (כנ)	70	206 (1576)	23	The Wheel of Fortune, Death	Jupiter, Scorpio	West, Southwest	Right Ear, Spleen
Meaning: Base, stand, rest, the base of the scales and the scales; social status, position in life; here, for such a purpose; after this; therefore								

Number of Gate	Hebrew Alphabet Pair	Simple Number Value	Letter Name Value	Tarot Numeral Value	Tarot Card Pair	Astrological Conjunction	Directions in Space	Human Body
169	KS (כס)	80	220 (1420)	24	The Wheel of Fortune, Temperance	Jupiter, Sagittarius	West, West-Above	Right Ear, Gall
					Meaning: The throne of God; the body of the celestial chariot; to be covered with light, the Full Moon; cup, vessel, chalice			
170	KO (כע)	90	230 (1600)	25	The Wheel of Fortune, The Devil	Jupiter, Capricorn	West, West-Below	Right Ear, Stomach (colon)
					Meaning: To be dark, ugly, repulsive; an excited serpent			
171	KP (כפ)	100	185 (905)	26	The Wheel of Fortune, The Tower	Jupiter, Mars	West, North	Right Ear, Right Nostril
					Meaning: The letter-name Kaph; the palm of the hand, the lines of the palm of the hand; a hand cupped; something arched, hollow, a cave, vault, scale-pan; the crest over the genitals; Mason's trowel, censer, top branch of palm tree; glove; initials for the Greek terms Kteis and Phallos, the magick weapons of the IX° (OTO)			
172	KTz (כצ)	110	204 (924)	27	The Wheel of Fortune, The Star	Jupiter, Aquarius	West, South-Above	Right Ear, Bladder
					Meaning: How; in what manner; to curl, to shrink			
173	KQ (כק)	120	286 (1726)	28	The Wheel of Fortune, The Moon	Jupiter, Pisces	West, South-Below	Right Ear, Rectum
					Meaning: Initials for KVKB QSMf (כוכב קסמ)—star divination; divining through the stars			
174	KR (כר)	220	610 (1330)	29	The Wheel of Fortune, The Sun	Jupiter, Sun	West, South	Right Ear, Right Eye
					Meaning: Lamb; fattened lamb; a pasture of lambs, meadow, a battering ram; a camel's saddle; the initials of the founder of the Rosicrucian Order as Hebrew: Christian Rosenkreutz			
175	KSh (כש)	320	460 (1830)	30	The Wheel of Fortune, Judgement	Jupiter, Fire	West, North to South	Right Ear, Brain
					Meaning: To knock, strike; move to and fro; shake; to entangle, catch, confound			

Number of Gate	Hebrew Alphabet Pair	Simple Number Value	Letter Name Value	Tarot Numeral Value	Tarot Card Pair	Astrological Conjunction	Directions in Space	Human Body
176	KTh (כת)	420	506 (1226)	31	The Wheel of Fortune, The World	Jupiter, Saturn	West, Center	Right Ear, Left Ear
					Meaning: To pound, crush (olives for oil); to join closely, to come in contact, to powder; image, likeness			
177	LM (למ)	70	164 (724)	23	Justice, The Hanged Man	Libra, Water	Northwest, East to West	Liver, Genitals
					Meaning: The middle of the 27-letter alphabet (LMMf [למםף] 13th, 14th and 15th) to join, arrange; to protect, lead, teach; vanity, nothing; to murmur			
178	LN (לנ)	80	180 (830)	24	Justice, Death	Libra, Scorpio	Northwest, Southwest	Liver, Spleen
					Meaning: Woolen garments; nighttime, overnight			
179	LS (לס)	90	194 (624)	25	Justice, Temperance	Libra, Sagittarius	Northwest, West-Above	Liver, Gall
					Meaning: Cheek, jaw			
180	LO (לע)	100	204 (854)	26	Justice, The Devil	Libra, Capricorn	Northwest, West-Below	Liver, Stomach (colon)
					Meaning: The throat, the tongue; language			
181	LP (לפ)	110	159	27	Justice, The Tower	Libra, Mars	Northwest, North	Liver, Right Nostril
					Meaning: To join, arrange; to cling to, to clasp, embrace; to swathe, bandage			
182	LTz (לצ)	120	178	28	Justice, The Star	Libra, Aquarius	Northwest, South-Above	Liver, Bladder
					Meaning: Scorn, scoffer; frivolous person, bad company; lasciviousnes			

Number of Gate	Hebrew Alphabet Pair	Simple Number Value	Letter Name Value	Tarot Numeral Value	Tarot Card Pair	Astrological Conjunction	Directions in Space	Human Body
183	LQ (לק)	130	260 (980)	29	Justice, The Moon	Libra, Pisces	Northwest, South-Below	Liver, Rectum
	Meaning: To lap, lick; lapping, greedy							
184	LR (לר)	230	584	30	Justice, The Sun	Libra, Sun	Northwest, South	Liver, Right Eye
	Meaning: Below, beneath							
185	LSh (לש)	330	434 (1084)	31	Justice, Judgement	Libra, Fire	Northwest, North to South	Liver, Brain
	Meaning: To be strong, firm; to knead; to knead dough; juice of plant, secretion, foam, spittle							
186	LTh (לת)	430	480	32	Justice, The World	Libra, Saturn	Northwest, Center	Liver Left Eye
	Meaning: That which clings to a person, fate, luck; to join, attach; first and last letter of LILITh (לילית), Adam's first wife							
187	MN (מנ)	90	196 (1406)	25	The Hanged Man, Death	Water, Scorpio	East to West, Southwest	Genitals, Spleen
	Meaning: Number of parts, portion; strings of a musical instrument; going out; receding, departing							
188	MS (מס)	100	210 (1250)	26	The Hanged Man, Temperance	Water, Sagittarius	East to West, West-Above	Genitals, Gall
	Meaning: One who is consumed with desire; one pining away; tribute to be rendered by work; juice; melting, fainting							
189	MO (מע)	110	220 (1430)	27	The Hanged Man, The Devil	Water, Capricorn	East toWest, West-Below	Genitals, Stomach (colon)
	Meaning: Belly, womb, inside, bowels							

Number of Gate	Hebrew Alphabet Pair	Simple Number Value	Letter Name Value	Tarot Numeral Value	Tarot Card Pair	Astrological Conjunction	Directions in Space	Human Body
190	MP (מפ)	120	175 (735)	28	The Hanged Man, The Tower	Water, Mars	East to West, North	Genitals, Right Nostril
	Meaning: Memphis—a city in Egypt, an utterance from the lips; breathing; the bellows of a blacksmith							
191	MTz (מצ)	130	194 (754)	29	The Hanged Man, The Star	Water, Aquarius	East to West, South-Above	Genitals, Bladder
	Meaning: Chaff, husk; to press; to suck, suckle							
192	MQ (מק)	140	276 (1556)	30	.The Hanged Man, The Moon	Water, Pisces	East to West, South-Below	Genitals, Rectum
	Meaning: To soften, to decay; to dissolve; be languid, pine after							
193	MR (מר)	240	600 (1160)	31	The Hanged Man, The Sun	Water, Sun	East to West, South	Genitals, Right Eye
	Meaning: Myrrh; bitter herb; to speak, say; man, lord, master							
194	MSh (מש)	340	450 (1660)	32	The Hanged Man, Judgement	Water, Fire	East to West, North to South	Genitals, Brain
	Meaning: To feel, touch, rub; wash and dry; carrying; handling; dealings; worldly affairs and intercourse; burden, burden of prophecy, substance, essence, reality; to grope, search for							
195	MTh (מת)	440	496 (1056)	33	The Hanged Man, The World	Water, Saturn	East to West, Center	Genitals, Left Ear
	Meaning: Dying, death, corpse; home, place, town; man							
196	NS (נס)	110	226 (1356)	27	Death, Temperance	Scorpio, Sagittarius	Southwest, West-Above	Spleen, Gall
	Meaning: Something lifted up, a token to be seen far; banner, flag, a flag pole; any sign which warns							

Number of Gate	Hebrew Alphabet Pair	Simple Number Value	Letter Name Value	Tarot Numeral Value	Tarot Card Pair	Astrological Conjunction	Directions in Space	Human Body
197	NO (עס)	120	236 (1536)	28	Death, The Devil	Scorpio, Capricorn	Southwest, West-Below	Spleen, Stomach (colon)
Meaning: Shaking, motion, to move to and fro; to vacillate; to wander, to cause to stagger								
198	NP (פס)	130	191 (841)	29	Death, The Tower	Scorpio, Mars	Southwest, North	Spleen, Right Nostril
Meaning: To fan, winnow, sift; to blow, breathe								
199	NTz (צס)	140	210 (960)	30	Death, The Star	Scorpio, Aquarius	Southwest, South-Above	Spleen, Bladder
Meaning: Flower; hawk, blossom								
200	NQ (קס)	150	292 (1662)	31	Death, The Moon	Scorpio, Pisces	Southwest, South-Below	Spleen, Rectum
Meaning: A fissure of a rock; to hollow out, excavate; pure, clear, innocent								
201	NR (רס)	250	616 (1266)	32	Death, The Sun	Scorpio, Sun	Southwest, South	Spleen, Right Eye
Meaning: A lamp, a candle, a light; the soul as a light; initials for two parts of the soul: Neschemah and Ruach (NShMH RVCh, רוח נשמה)—Intuition and intellect								
202	NSh (שס)	350	466 (1766)	33	Death, Judgement	Scorpio, Fire	Southwest, North to South	Spleen, Brain
Meaning: To take up, to lift up; to lift up one's head; to lift up the eyes; to lift up the soul; to lift up oneself; to lift up the voice in praise and song; to pardon sin; to bear, carry; to suffer, bear with; to help, aid, offer gifts								
203	NTh (תס)	450	512 (1162)	34	Death, The World	Scorpio, Saturn	Southwest, Center	Spleen, Left Ear
Meaning: To give; to place, put, to desire, think of; to be given, be intended; to be put on the altar (as offering)								

Number of Gate	Hebrew Alphabet Pair	Simple Number Value	Letter Name Value	Tarot Numeral Value	Tarot Card Pair	Astrological Conjunction	Directions in Space	Human Body
204	SO (סע)	130	250 (1380)	29	Temperance, The Devil	Sagittarius, Capricorn	West-Above, West-Below	Gall, Stomach (colon)
Meaning: Council; company; troop, band, party; escort; traveling company, caravan								
205	SP (סף)	140	205 (685)	30	Temperance, The Tower	Sagittarius, Mars	West-Above, North	Gall, Right Nostril
Meaning: To cut, hollow out; to join; door-sill, border, pavement; bank of a river								
206	STz (סצ)	150	224 (704)	31	Temperance, The Star	Sagittarius, Aquarius	West-Above, South-Above	Gall, Bladder
Meaning: Initials of SPR TzLMf (ספר צלם)—The Book of Picture Images (a Hebrew name for the Tarot)								
207	SQ (סק)	160	306 (1506)	32	Temperance, The Moon	Sagittarius, Pisces	West-Above, South-Below	Gall, Rectum
Meaning: Sack, sack cloth; sack-carrier								
208	SR (סר)	260	630 (1110)	33	Temperance, The Sun	Sagittarius, Sun	West-Above, South	Gall, Right Eye
Meaning: Low-spirited; one whom courage has left								
209	SSh (סש)	360	480 (1610)	34	Temperance, Judgement	Sagittarius, Fire	West-Above, North to South	Gall, Brain
Meaning: Splitting, rending								
210	STh (סת)	460	526 (1006)	35	Temperance, The World	Sagittarius, Saturn	West-Above, Center	Gall, Left Ear
Meaning: Winter; winter-fruits, late-fruits; stone-cutter								

Number of Gate	Hebrew Alphabet Pair	Simple Number Value	Letter Name Value	Tarot Numeral Value	Tarot Card Pair	Astrological Conjunction	Directions in Space	Human Body
211	OP (עפ)	150	215 (865)	31	The Devil, The Tower	Capricorn, Mars	West-Below, North	Stomach (colon), Right Nostril
	Meaning: To fly around; to double, bend, curve; wing; bird							
212	OTz (עצ)	160	234 (884)	32	The Devil, The Star	Capricorn, Aquarius	West-Below, South-Above	Stomach (colon), Bladder
	Meaning: Tree of Life; tree; wood							
213	OQ (עק)	170	316 (1686)	33	The Devil, The Moon	Capricorn, Pisces	West-Below, South-Below	Stomach (colon), Rectum
	Meaning: Trouble, distress							
214	OR (ער)	270	640 (1290)	34	The Devil, The Sun	Capricorn, Sun	West-Below, South	Stomach (colon), Right Eye
	Meaning: Awake: arousal; hater; bird of prey; evil, to lay bare, strip, denude; to stir up, excite to; to protest, contest, object							
215	OSh (עש)	370	490 (1790)	35	The Devil, Judgement	Capricorn, Fire	West-Below, North to South	Stomach (colon), Brain
	Meaning: The constellation the great bear (Ursa Major); to do, work, prepare, to cause to do, order; to become, doing, action; strength, wrought iron; iron ball; crystal ball, glass ball							
216	OTh (עת)	470	436 (1186)	36	The Devil, The World	Capricorn, Saturn	West-Below, Center	Stomach (colon), Left Ear
	Meaning: 24 astronomical hours; the number 24; time; to be curved, crooked, to make suitable, adjust; accumulation of wealth							
217	PTz (פצ)	170	189	33	The Tower, The Star	Mars, Aquarius	North, South-Above	Right Nostril, Bladder
	Meaning: To open the mouth, to split open: to wound, to be branched; board, column, page							

Number of Gate	Hebrew Alphabet Pair	Simple Number Value	Letter Name Value	Tarot Numeral Value	Tarot Card Pair	Astrological Conjunction	Directions in Space	Human Body
218	PQ (פק)	180	271 (991)	34	The Tower, The Moon	Mars, Pisces	North, South-Below	Right Nostril, Rectum
	Meaning: To move to and fro, to go out, to bring to an end; exit, end; escape, to drive a wedge in, force open, make a breach							
219	PR (פר)	280	595	35	The Tower, The Sun	Mars, Sun	North, South	Right Nostril, Right Eye
	Meaning: A bull, young bullock; to be borne swiftly; wild ass, to break in pieces; to make void; to divide							
220	PSh (פש)	380	445 (1095)	36	The Tower, Judgement	Mars, Fire	North, North to South	Right Nostril, Brain
	Meaning: Pride, ferocity; rebelliousness							
221	PTh (פת)	480	491	37	The Tower, The World	Mars, Saturn	North, Center	Right Nostril, Left Ear
	Meaning: Bread, to break bread, a piece of; to cut, divide, break bread; the number two							
222	TzQ (צק)	190	290 (1010)	35	The Star, The Moon	Aquarius, Pisces	South-Above, South-Below	Bladder, Rectum
	Meaning: Affliction, torment, distress; mountain cliff, to be narrow, straightened, compressed; to pour							
223	TzR (צר)	290	614	36	The Star, The Sun	Aquarius, Sun	South-Above, South	Bladder, Right Eye
	Meaning: Stone, rock; knife; create, design, draw, paint, embroider, sculpt							
224	TzSh (צש)	390	464 (1114)	37	The Star, Judgement	Aquarius, Fire	South-Above, North to South	Bladder, Brain
	Meaning: To go forth, finish, to be ended; end, destruction							

Number of Gate	Hebrew Alphabet Pair	Simple Number Value	Letter Name Value	Tarot Numeral Value	Tarot Card Pair	Astrological Conjunction	Directions in Space	Human Body
225	TzTh (צת)	490	510	38	The Star, The World	Aquarius, Saturn	South-Above, Center	Bladder, Left Ear
	Meaning: To listen, to obey, to cause to listen							
226	QR (קר)	300	696 (1416)	37	The Moon, The Sun	Pisces, Sun	South-Below, South	Rectum, Right Eye
	Meaning: To dance, revel, to cry, cackle; to be cold, chilled, carriage							
227	QSh (קש)	400	546 (1916)	38	The Moon, Judgement	Pisces, Fire	South-Below, North to South	Rectum, Brain
	Meaning: To be stiff, hard, erect, strong; to knock, strike, shake, ring, shoot forth							
228	QTh (קת)	500	592 (1312)	39	The Moon, The World	Pisces, Saturn	South-Below, Center	Rectum, Left Ear
	Meaning: Pelican							
229	RSh (רש)	500	870 (1620)	39	The Sun, Judgement	Sun, Fire	South, North to South	Right Eye, Brain
	Meaning: Power, control, authority, to be stamped, crushed; poor, poverty							
230	RTh (רת)	600	916	40	The Sun, The World	Sun, Saturn	South, Center	Right Eye, Left Ear
	Meaning: Compassionate, lenient, indulgent, lax; awe, fear; clemency							
231	ShTh (שת)	700	766 (1416)	41	Judgement, The World	Fire, Saturn	North to South, Center	Brain, Left Ear
	Meaning: Base of altar, foundation, loom; to weave, warp of fabric; to found, establish, start, to come down slowly, flow gently; to be saturated by wine							

THIRD KEY

ARABIC

OVERVIEW

The mysticism surrounding the Arabic alphabet has been claimed by
many commentators to be the source for the symbolism of the Jewish Qabalah. This argument is based on the fact that the term
Qabalah, as we know it, was coined around 1200 CE, a time after the mystical symbolism for the Arabic alphabet was developed. However, as shown
elsewhere in this text, the Hebraic tradition of ascribing symbolic meaning
to their alphabet may have occurred prior to 400 BCE, which would predate
the beginnings of Islam by more than a thousand years.

One interesting pattern found in the development of the Arabic alphabet betrays a Hebraic Qabalistic source for the numbering of the Arabic
alphabet. This is the reordering of the Arabic alphabet by the Eastern
Egyptian method, known as the "Abjad" code. In this preferred method of
ascribing number value to letter, the normal order of the Arabic alphabet
of A, B, T, Th is reordered to form the order of A, B, J, D (hence the name
of this method as Abjad). This order is the same order as the Hebrew
alphabet (Aleph, Beth, Gimel, Daleth), allowing the Arabic phonetic values
to parallel their Hebraic prototype in sound as well as number value.

The Arabic language is worthy of much study and number analysis, for
the metaphors provided blend with those offered by the Qabalahs of
Hebrew, Greek, and Latin. Aleister Crowley, in his own Qabalistic analysis
of *The Book of The Law,* felt that the Arabic Qabalah could be a special key
for interpretation. It should also be remembered that the great esoteric
learning centers of Fez and Damascus influenced the beginnings of the
Rosicrucian movement around 1600 CE. The Western European tradition in
Alchemy, for instance, had its source solely in the Arabic alchemical cor-

pus, which slowly but surely was translated into Latin.

The third key begins with an historical overview of the Arabic alphabet. The first table of this section shows the Arabic alphabet in its original format and the English transliteration that will be used throughout the remainder of the key. In terms of the original format of the 28 letters which compose the alphabet, this table shows both the isolated form of the letter (when the letter is written alone) as well as the three basic cursive forms of initial, medial, and final letters. The cursive, flowing, rope-like quality of written Arabic results in as many as three forms of each letter, depending on whether the letter occurs as the first letter of a word (initial), the middle letter(s) of a word (medial), or the last letter of a word (final).

This is a very difficult alphabet for the beginning student to work with, since discerning where one letter ends and another begins is difficult at first. However, in clearly typeset texts, original Arabic words will have a discernible, yet small, gap between each letter of a word. Practice, with the aid of the phonetic transliteration to guide you, will ultimately result in the correct identification of the letters composing any given word and thus the correct number value. Arabic, like Hebrew, gives a number value to any given word by adding the values of each of its component letters together.

The second table in this chapter details the Western Moroccan number code, based on the normal sequential order of the Arabic alphabet. This should be the lesser of the two codes which you should begin your work with on numbering the Arabic language. However, it should not be ignored.

The third table lays out both the Eastern Abjad order and the the Western Moroccan order. Both the number values for the individual letters themselves as well as the letter name for each of these letters are given. This table is followed by 28 select names for God, whose initials correspond to the 28 letters of the Arabic alphabet. These God names are each given two number values, the Egyptian "Abjad" and the Moroccan "Serial" values. These are cipher values which should be substituted for the normal values of the Arabic alphabet for an additional esoteric set of number values for any given word.

Like the astrological attributes of the *Sepher Yetzirah,* the Arabic alphabet developed a set of cosmological attributes through the Sufi commentaries of Ibn al-Arabi. The next table gives the cosmological symbols for each of the 28 letters, which should be used when analyzing any given sacred word in Arabic. This table divides the cosmological attributes of the Arabic alphabet as follows:

- Ladder of 28 degrees

- Element

- Zodiac

- Planet

- Planetary color

- Days of the week

• Days of the lunar cycle

Next 29 magickal formulas, which occur as chapter (sura) headings in the Quran, are categorized by their corresponding Arabic letter. This table is followed by an interpretation of each of these secret Quranic codes. Finally, a miscellaneous list of alphabet symbols are given, derived from Sufic commentary on the Quran.

This is followed by a listing of the 99 Beautiful Names of God. Their number values are computed by both the Egyptian and Moroccan number codes.

Appended to this section is a discussion of the separate mystical tradition for the Persian alphabet. This alphabet (known as Pahlavi or Farsi) contains four additional letters to the Arabic 28, making a sacred numerical alphabet of 32 characters. Though I can find no direct reference in print to giving a number value to these distinct four additional Persian letters *(Pe, Chim, Zhe,* and *Ghaf)*, I have conjectured a possible set of values, based on the number value of the parallel Arabic letters upon which these four Persian letters were modeled. These four sub-values are given as the first table.

The Persian alphabet is then detailed as follows:

• Original letter form

• Letter name

• Transliteration

• Sequential number value

• Number value (derived from Arabic Abjad code)

• Symbolic meanings (including astrological symbolism)

Now, armed with the two basic number values for the Arabic and Persian alphabet, any symbolism relating to the Sufi tradition can be numbered.

This chapter also contains an addendum relating to the numerical philosophy of Georges Ivanovitch Gurdjieff. Since Gurdjieff, a 20th-century Russian philosopher and religious teacher, often stylized his teachings as derived from esoteric Islamic and Christian traditions, his numerical philosophy has been included here.

Gurdjieff modified the cosmological ladder, or classification system, of Ibn al-Arabi to classify his own eclectic philosophical system. This ladder of numbers divides the cosmos into 11 basic levels. The first table gives the 11 basic divisions, their number values, and corresponding kingdoms for this cosmological ladder of numbers.

This number scale of 11 basic numbers is based on a doubling of the number 3 and begins with the source of all numbers, 1. This range of numbers leads with 1, proceeds to 3, and then continues to expand by a doubling of 3 as 6, 12, 24, 48, 96, 192, 384, 768, and 1536. In more elaborate diagrams, the scale is numbered as far as 12,288. Now these 11 numbers (1, 3, 6, 12, 24, 48, 96, 192, 384, 768, 1536) are also viewed as two sets of ascending and descending numbers centered around 48. In this alternate set, 48 = ±0, 1 = +1, and 1536 = −1. These 11 numbers can then be paired as follows:

The Mirror Image of
Positive and Negative Gurdjieffian Numbers

Normal Scale (1 to 1536)	Alternate ± Scale (+1 to -1)
1 = 1536	+1 = -1
3 = 768	+3 = -3
6 = 384	+6 = -6
12 = 192	+12 = -12
24 = 96	+24 = -24
48 = 48	+0 = -0

The second table allocates the planets and the zodiac to this range of numbers. Gurdjieff did not explicitly give in open writings these astrological correspondences. He did, however, openly disclose the seven days of the week as the range of numbers between 768 (Sunday) and 12 (Saturday). From these correspondences, the seven planets can easily be extrapolated, and from the zodiacal rulership of these planets, the corresponding 12 signs of the zodiac can be deduced.

The third table, the seven notes of the octave, gives the occult range of the octave as two sets of correspondences. The first set shows the primary seven notes of the octave based upon the planetary correspondences which span the number range of 768 to 12. The second set of correspondences shows the higher octave of eight notes which ascends into the Godhead, spanning the number range of 192 to 1.

The fourth table, "The Seven Rays of Creation," gives an alternate cosmological scale of 96 to 1, spanning the orbit of the Moon (the lowest of the seven rays) to the highest ray of Absolute being.

The fifth table, "The Seven Brains of Man," shows the seven centers in man which parallel the seven rays of creation. Here, The Body = 96 = The Moon, while, The Soul = 1 = The Absolute. In this set of correspondences most of humanity operates only at the range of 96 to 12, while the three higher ranges of 6, 3, and 1 are only developed through conscious intentional suffering.

The sixth and seventh tables reduce the division of the ladder of 11 numbers from 7 to 5. The sixth table shows the fourfold body spanning the range of 48 (center of movement) to 6 (center of self), while 3 (the soul) is earned from harmonizing the fourfold body (of 48, 24, 12, and 6). The seventh table shows the corresponding five Western alchemical elements for this number range of 48 to 3, based on the Platonic order of Fire, Air, Water, and Earth crowned by Spirit. These two tables combine to bring out a scale in which the lower end corresponds to the Earth = 48 = physical movement, while the upper end corresponds to the Ether = 3 = the soul.

The eighth table, "The Eleven Levels of Human Consciousness," involves the complete range of 11 basic Gurdjieffian numbers spanning 1536 to 1. The center of the diagram, 48, is the neutral state of slumbering humanity. The highest human consciousness can attain is 3, representing enlightenment. The lowest that human consciousness can descend is 768, representing insanity. The uppermost point and absolute lowest point are beyond human consciousness, and represent God and the Devil. The alternate number range shown in the first table, "The Eleven Levels of Cosmos," should be used in interpreting the 11 levels of consciousness. This alternate range gives to 48 the value of +0 or -0, to 1 the value of +1, and to 1536 the value of -1. By these correspondences, God is +1 and the Devil is -1, while humanity resides in dynamic tension between these two poles of light and darkness as ±0. This brings out the Qabalistic mathematical formula of (+1) + (-1) = 0, reminiscent of Crowley's Thelemic formula of 2 = 0.

The ninth table, "The Table of Fourteen Hydrogens," premises the composite nature of matter as graded by this cosmological ladder of numbers. To the basic scale of 11 numbers, three additional numbers of 3072, 6144, and 12,288 are added. Here soil (and iron) = 3072, dead matter = 6144, and matter in its densest state = 12,288.

By combining part of the elemental allocations of this table of hydrogens with the other cosmological scales of Gurdjieff, the tenth and last table is created, showing the 11 interacting levels of the cosmos as a Cosmic Food Chain. Here the number range is laid out in three separate columns centered around the number 48, where any given number feeds upon two lower octaves, while it in turn serves as food for that which is two octaves above. Thus 48 (vertebrates) feeds upon 192 (plants), but is food for 12 (angels). This is a wonderful evolution of the basic cosmological scales of Hermeticism, showing a marvelous interdependency of that which is Above to that which is Below.

All of the symbols in the above tables should be entered into your number file under the number series 1, 3, 6, 12, 24, 48, 96, 192, 384, 768, 1536, 3072, 6144, and 12,288. Later, when other entries occur at these numbers, you can verify the integrity of Gurdjieff's own use of this number series. All in all, I have found this system very useful in classifying my own various states of consciousness. My research shows that this system dovetails right into the more traditional Western Qabalistic and magickal symbol sets.

The second section of this addendum details the geometric symbol peculiar to the work of Gurdjieff, known as the Enneagram. The Enneagram is a nine-pointed star, whose nine numbered points are connected in a specific pattern of 1, 4, 2, 8, 5, 7, 3, 6, 9. There are many commentaries recently published which give a psychological meaning to these nine points as a linear progression of 1, 2, 3, 4, 5, 6, 7, 8, 9. Indeed, the classic texts on the Enneagram by J. G. Bennett and Irmis B. Popoff dissect the dimensions of the Enneagram in this linear fashion.

However, the analysis offered in this section is based on the esoteric order of 3, 6, 9; 8, 5, 7; and 1, 4, 2. Gurdjieff shows that there are two basic numerical laws governing all of creation, the Law of Threes and the Law of Sevens. The secret order of the Enneagram generates both of these laws as repeating decimal figures, for 1 divided by 7 results in 0.142857142857, while 1 divided by 3 results in 0.333, which can be equated to 3 added to 3 to produce 6, and 3 added to 6 to produce 9. Now, if the Enneagram is viewed as a dance of numbers moving in the order of 1, 4, 2, 8, 5, 7, 3, 6, 9, the esoteric order of the Enneagram can be unlocked.

Utilizing this secret order, this section allocates two separate Western symbol sets to give the true esoteric symbolism behind the Enneagram. The first symbol set is that of Raymond Lull (fully detailed in the 10th Key, Latin). Here Lull's use of nine select Latin letters is paralleled to the nine esoteric points of the Enneagram. The second symbol set allocates the upper nine Sephiroth of the Tree of Life to the nine esoteric points of the Enneagram. Here Malkuth, the tenth and lowest Sephirah, corresponds to the Enneagram as a whole. Both of these systems are clearly shown in four sets of tables, allowing the Enneagram to serve as a symbolic classification system not unlike the Tree of Life, the classic Western mandala.

Again, both of these systems are of my own invention. However, in *The Harmonious Circle,* James Webb gives a variation to the above symbolism based upon the exoteric linear order of the Enneagram, without working out the correspondences in any detail. My own conclusions were drawn independently of Webb's analysis.

This addendum ends with a detailing of the Georgian alphabet. Gurdjieff was fluent in Georgian, and since Georgian possesses its own unique number code, this language may prove to be a primary source for his own number philosophy. As such, the numerical key to this language ends the commentary on Gurdjieff.

Origin

600 CE—Classical Arabic developed out of the older Cufic Arabic script

1200 CE—The creation of Ibn Arabi's astrological system for Arabic paralleling the Hebraic Yetziratic system and the Greek Soma Sophia Alphabet

1300 CE—The introduction of the Hindu cipher symbol "0" to Europe by the Arabic scholar Jeber

Alphabet Code

Classical Arabic is the last living language to be modeled on the Semitic-Hellenistic alphabet spanning the number range 1 to 1000.

The alphabet of 28 characters composing Classical Arabic developed out of Cufic Arabic around 600 CE. Like Hebrew and Greek, Arabic is additional in nature. The individual values of each letter in any given word are added together to produce the number value of the word.

The actual shape of the Arabic alphabet departs radically from the Phonecian proto-alphabet which influenced the shaping of most isosephic languages. Where Greek and Hebrew alphabet characters were modeled on the linear Egyptian hieroglyphs, Arabic resembled the curling of rope or string as well as the swirling of smoke and water. If anything, the alphabet of classical Arabic resembles the curling lines of the Deva-Nagari alphabet of Sanskrit.

Through the Arabic scholar Jeber, the West received a new set of ten symbols (0 through 9) apart from their alphabet to designate the infinite number range. Jeber ultimately obtained these ten numeral symbols from India, but Western tradition refers to them as "Arabic" numerals.

A second inheritance from Arabic is a cursive alphabet, which is the source of the English long-hand script. In the Koranic Arabic alphabet, the letters of any given word are joined to one another by a continuous line of writing. This flowing script inspired the cursive alphabet of medieval Latin, which ultimately developed into the long-hand script of English. Each letter of the Arabic alphabet has three distinct forms: an initial, medial, and final format (whether the letter appears at the beginning, middle, or end of a word). There is also a distinct character for two alphabet letters standing alone.

The three cursive alphabet forms for Arabic are as follows:

Cursive Arabic

Isolated Letter	Trans- literation	——— Cursive Forms ———		
		Final	Medial	Initial
ا	A	ل		
ب	B	ب	ـبـ	بـ
ت	T	ت	ـتـ	تـ
ث	Th	ث	ـثـ	ثـ
ج	J	ـج	ـجـ	جـ
ح	Ḥ	ـح	ـحـ	حـ
خ	Kh	ـخ	ـخـ	خـ
د	D	ـد		
ذ	Dh	ـذ		
ر	R	ـر		
ز	Z	ـز		
س	S	ـس	ـسـ	سـ
ش	Sh	ـش	ـشـ	شـ

Isolated Letter	Trans- literation	Cursive Forms		
		Final	Medial	Initial
ص	Ṣ			
ض	Ḍ			
ط	Ṭ			
ظ	Tz			
ع	O			
غ	Gh			
ف	F			
ق	Q			
ك	K			
ل	L			
م	M			
ن	N			
ه	H			
و	W			
ى	Y			

Conjoined Letter Lam-Alif (LA): لا

Three Long Vowels: Ā   Ū   Ī

Three Short Vowel Marks: A   U   I

Hamza: Ā

There are two basic number codes for Arabic: Western and Eastern. The Western school is known as the Moroccan number code and numbers the Arabic alphabet in its normal sequential order (Alif, Ba, Ta, Tha). This code establishes an order at variance with the normal Semitic-Hellenistic order of A, B, G, and is secondary in Sufic usage.

The Normal Order of the Arabic Alphabet and the Western Moroccan Number Code

Transliteration	Sequential Order	Western Moroccan Number Value
A	1	1
B	2	2
T	3	3
Th	4	4
J	5	5
Ḥ	6	6
Kh	7	7
D	8	8
Dh	9	9
R	10	10
Z	11	20
S	12	30
Sh	13	40
Ṣ	14	50
Ḍ	15	60
Ṭ	16	70
Tz	17	80
O	18	90
Gh	19	100
F	20	200
Q	21	300
K	22	400
L	23	500
M	24	600
N	25	700
H	26	800
W	27	900
Y	28	1000

The Eastern school is known as the Egyptian number code and, betraying its basic Qabalistic source, rearranges the normal order of the Arabic alphabet to parallel the alphabetic order of Hebrew. This code is also known as ABJaD, for its first four letters, Alif, Ba, Jim and Dal, valued at 1, 2, 3, and 4 (paralleling the Hebrew Aleph, Beth, Gimel, and Daleth, also valued at 1, 2, 3, and 4). It is this Abjad code that produces a wealth of numerical symbolism that enhances the Greek-Semitic metaphors for the number system.

As an elaboration of the 27-character Hebrew and Greek alphabets, Arabic offers an additional 28th character. This 28th character receives the number value of 1000, a value that in both Greek and Hebrew is achieved by multiplying the first letter (A) by 1,000 (either by enlargement of the character or by vowel pointing). In the Moroccan system, this omega-like letter representing the grand number 1,000 is Ya (valued at 10 in the Egyptian system), while in the Egyptian system this 28th letter is Ghain (valued at 100 in the Moroccan system). Note that the number series 10, 100, and 1000 is generated by these two letters. Like Hebrew and Greek, the Arabic alphabet has a letter name, or nominal name, for each of the 28 letters. These letter names form a secret or extended number value for each of the 28 letters.

The following table details the number values of the 28 alphabet characters of classical Arabic.

The Secret Order of the Arabic Alphabet
The Eastern Egyptian Code and Its Western Variant

		Number Value			
	Letter	Letter		Nominal	
Letter	Name	Egyptian	Moroccan	Egyptian	Moroccan
A	ĀLF	1	1	111	701
B	BĀ	2	2	3	3
J	JYM	3	5	53	1605
D	DAL	4	8	35	509
H	HĀ	5	800	6	801
W	WAW	6	900	13	1801
Z	ZĀ	7	20	8	21
Ḥ	ḤĀ	8	6	9	7
Ṭ	ṬĀ	9	70	10	71
Y	YĀ	10	1000	11	1001
K	KAF	20	400	101	601
L	LAM	30	500	71	1101

The Secret Order of the Arabic Alphabet
The Eastern Egyptian Code and Its Western Variant (cont'd.)

Letter	Letter Name	Number Value			
		Letter		Nominal	
		Egyptian	Moroccan	Egyptian	Moroccan
M	MYM	40	600	90	2200
N	NWN	50	700	106	2300
S	SYN	60	30	120	1730
O	OYN	70	90	130	1790
F	FĀ	80	200	81	201
Ṣ	ṢAD	90	50	95	59
Q	QAF	100	300	181	501
R	RĀ	200	10	201	11
Sh	ShYN	300	40	360	1740
T	TĀ	400	3	401	4
Th	ThĀ	500	4	501	5
Kh	KhĀ	600	7	601	8
Dh	DhAL	700	9	731	510
Ḍ	ḌAD	800	60	805	69
Tz	TzĀ	900	80	901	81
Gh	GhYN	1000	100	1060	1800
Ā (accent over A)	HMZ	no value	no value	52	1420
LA (conjoined letters of Lam and Alif)		31	501	182	1802

In addition to these four sets of number values, two more sets of values were developed out of 28 names of God in the Quran. These names begin with the 28 letters of the Arabic alphabet. This Sufi code substitutes the number values of these divine names of God for each letter of the alphabet.

These 28 names can be numbered either by the Egyptian or Moroccan number method as shown in the table on the following page.

Alternate Divine Name Number Values
(Alphabetical Initials of God)

| Alphabet | Divine Name | | Number Value | |
	Arabic	Translation	Egyptian	Moroccan
A	ALLH	One God	66	1801
B	BAQY	He who remains	113	1303
J	JAMO	He who assembles	114	696
D	DYAN	Judge	65	1708
H	HADY	Guide	20	1809
W	WLY	Master	46	2400
Z	ZKY	Purifier	37	1420
Ḥ	ḤQ	Truth	108	306
Ṭ	ṬAHR	Holy	215	87
Y	YSYN	Chief	130	2730
K	KAFY	Sufficient	111	1601
L	LṬYF	Benevolent	129	1770
M	MLK	King	90	1500
N	NWR	Light	256	1610
S	SMYO	Hearer	180	1720
O	OLY	Lofty	110	1590
F	FTAḤ	He who opens	489	210
Ṣ	ṢMD	Eternal	134	658
Q	QADR	Powerful	305	319
R	RB	Lord	202	12
Sh	ShFYO	He who accepts	460	1330
T	TWB	He who brings back to righteousness	408	905
Th	ThABT	Stable	903	10
Kh	KhALQ	Creator	731	808
Dh	DhAKR	He who remembers	921	1111
Ḍ	ḌAR	Punisher	1001	71
Tz	TzAHR	Apparent	1106	891
Gh	GhFWR	Indulgent	1286	1210

The Arabic alphabet, like its Hebrew parent, is symbolically rich with magickal associations. Thus each letter of the alphabet can be construed as an element, planet, zodiacal sign, color, day of the week, or lunar month as well as a rung on a cosmic ladder of 28 steps. These cosmological attributes were recorded in the writings of the Sufi Ibn al Arabi in the 13th century and are listed in the following table. Note that the alphabet is ordered in a special manner so that each letter of the alphabet corresponds to the 12 signs of the zodiac as 28 lunar divisions, on a cycle of seven planets and four alternating elements. This is far more sophisticated than the Hebrew Yetziratic separation of three elements from seven planets and twelve zodiacal signs.

Arabic Astrological Symbols (of Ibn al-Arabi)

Alphabet	Ladder of 28 Degrees	Element	Zodiac	Planet	Color Based on Planet	Days of the Week	Days of the Moon
A	First Intellect The Pen	Fire	Aries	Saturn	Black	1st Week Saturday	1 (New Moon)
H	Universal Soul The Tablet	Air	Aries	Sun	Yellow	Sunday	2
O	Universal Nature	Water	Aries-Taurus	Moon	White	Monday	3
Ḥ	Universal Substance	Earth	Taurus	Mars	Red	Tuesday	4
Gh	Universal Body	Fire	Taurus-Gemini	Mercury	Sandal-wood	Wednesday	5
Kh	The Form of God	Air	Gemini	Jupiter	Blue	Thursday	6
Q	The Throne of God	Water	Gemini	Venus	Green	Friday	7 (1/4 Lunar Cycle)
K	The Pedestal of the Throne	Earth	Cancer	Saturn	Black	2nd Week Saturday	8
J	Heaven Around the Zodiac	Fire	Cancer	Sun	Yellow	Sunday	9

Arabic Astrological Symbols (of Ibn al-Arabi—cont'd.)

Alphabet	Ladder of 28 Degrees	Element	Zodiac	Planet	Color Based on Planet	Days of the Week	Days of the Moon
Sh	Sun of Paradise, Fixed Stars	Air	Cancer-Leo	Moon	White	Monday	10
Y	1st Heaven, Saturn, Abraham	Water	Leo	Mars	Red	Tuesday	11
Ḍ	2nd Heaven, Jupiter, Moses	Earth	Leo-Virgo	Mercury	Sandalwood	Wednesday	12
L	3rd Heaven, Mars, Aaron	Fire	Virgo	Jupiter	Blue	Thursday	13
N	4th Heaven, Sun, Enoch, Hermes	Air	Virgo	Venus	Green	Friday	14 (Full Moon) 1/2 Lunar Cycle
R	5th Heaven, Venus, Joseph	Water	Libra	Saturn	Black	3rd Week Saturday	15
T	6th Heaven, Mercury, Jesus	Earth	Libra	Sun	Yellow	Sunday	16
D	7th Heaven, Moon, Adam	Fire	Libra-Scorpio	Moon	White	Monday	17
Ṭ	Ether, Fire, Meteors	Air	Scorpio	Mars	Red	Tuesday	18
Z	Air, Sky	Water	Scorpio-Sagittarius	Mercury	Sandalwood	Wednesday	19
S	Water, Oceans	Earth	Sagittarius	Jupiter	Blue	Thursday	20
Ṣ	Earth	Fire	Sagittarius	Venus	Green	Friday	21 (3/4 Lunar Cycle)

Arabic Astrological Symbols (of Ibn al-Arabi—cont'd.)

Alphabet	Ladder of 28 Degrees	Element	Zodiac	Planet	Color Based on Planet	Days of the Week	Days of the Moon
Tz	Metals, Minerals	Air	Capricorn	Saturn	Black	4th Week Saturday	22
Th	Vegetable	Water	Capricorn	Sun	Yellow	Sunday	23
Dh	Animal	Earth	Capricorn-Aquarius	Moon	White	Monday	24
F	Angels	Fire	Aquarius	Mars	Red	Tuesday	25
B	Genii	Air	Aquarius-Pisces	Mercury	Sandal-wood	Wednesday	26
M	Man	Water	Pisces	Jupiter	Blue	Thursday	27
W	The 28 Degrees of The Ladder	Earth	Pisces	Venus	Green	Friday	28 (No Moon)

Ibn al-Arabi's Ladder of 28 degrees, grading the Arabic alphabet from God to Man, is based on both the Jewish-Qabalistic Tree of Life and the Hellenistic-Gnostic Aeons.

Raymond Lull undoubtedly was exposed to at least the Sufi system of al-Arabi and borrowed from him the use of letters of the alphabet to classify the universe. From Lull's work, the cosmological alphabet graphs of Giorgi, Dee, and Kircher were developed (refer to the addendum under "Latin" for a detailing of these systems).

Beyond the astrological symbols, al-Arabi developed a set of 28 God names for the Arabic alphabet. These 28 appellations were derived from the Quran, the supreme source for all alphanumerical investigations in Arabic.

Within the Quran, 29 secret alphabet codes are found concealed in the beginning of 29 select suras (chapters), each code or formula corresponding to one letter of the alphabet.

The table on the following page delineates the Quranic symbols of both God names and Sura codes for the Arabic alphabet, according to the Abjad or Egyptian order.

Arabic Quranic Symbols

Alphabet (Egyptian Order)	God Name	Sura Magical Formula	Numerical Value of Formula Egyptian	Morroccan
A	Divine Essence (God)	ALM (Sura 2)	71	1101
B	The Subtle	ALM (S. 3)	71	1101
J	The Independent	ALMṢ (S. 7)	161	1151
D	The Evident	ALR (S. 10)	231	511
H	The One Who Calls Forth	ALR (S. 11)	231	511
W	The One Who Possesses Sublime Degrees	ALR (S .12)	231	511
Z	The Living	ALMR (S. 13)	271	1111
Ḥ	The Last	ALR (S. 14)	231	511
Ṭ	The One Who Causes Contraction	ALR (S 15)	231	511
Y	The Lord	KHYOS (S. 19)	195	2340
K	The Grateful	ṬH (S. 20)	14	870
L	The Victorious	ṬSM (S. 26)	109	700
M	The One Who Gathers	ṬS (S. 27)	69	100
N	The Light	ṬSM (S. 28)	109	700
S	The One Who Gives Life	ALM (S. 29)	71	1101
O	The Hidden	ALM (S. 30)	71	1101
F	The Strong	ALM (S. 31)	71	1101
Ṣ	The One Who Slays	ALM (S. 32)	71	1101
Q	The One Who Encompasses All	YS (S. 36)	70	1030
R	The Giver of Forms	Ṣ (S. 38)	90	50
Sh	The Powerful	ḤM (S. 40)	48	606
T	The Reckoner	ḤM (S. 41)	48	606
Th	The One Who Nourishes	ḤM OSQ (S. 42)	278	1026
Kh	The Wise	ḤM (S. 43)	48	606
Dh	The One Who Humbles	ḤM (S. 44)	48	606
Ḍ	The Knowing	ḤM (S. 45)	48	606
Tz	The Precious	ḤM (S. 46)	48	606
Gh	The Manifest	Q (S. 50)	100	300
Hamza		N (S. 68)	50	700

The 29 magickal Sura formulas have no traditional explanation or definition. However, they are acrostic in nature and form the initial letters of 14 secret codes. These 14 secret codes are as follows:

The Fourteen Secret Codes

Code	Translation	Appearance in Quran
ALM	A—Beginning (God) L—End (Gabriel, Messenger Angel) M—Middle (Mohammed, Prophet)	Six times
ALMṢ	A—Beginning L—End M—Middle Ṣ—Parables, Stories, Tradition	Once
ALR	A—Beginning L—End R—Teacher	Five times
ALMR	A—Beginning L—End M—Middle R—Teacher	Once
KHYOṢ	K—The 5 Attributes of God (One Sufficient in Himself) H—He Who Guides Y—Hand as Power of God O—The All Knowing Ṣ—The True One	Once
ṬH	Ṭ—Oh Ḣ—Man	Once
ṬSM	Ṭ—Mount Ṡ—Sinai M—Moses	Twice
ṬS	Ṭ—Mount Ṡ—Sinai	Once
YS	Y—Oh S—Leader of Men (Mohammed)	Once
Ṣ	Ṣ—Righteous, Tradition	Once
ḤM	ḤM as MḤ—Mohammed	Six times
ḤM OSQ	ḤM as MḤ—Mohammed O—The All Knowing S—Leader of Men Q—Spiritual Mountain	Once

The Fourteen Secret Codes (cont'd.)

Code	Translation	Appearance in Quran
Q	Q—The Mountain Qaf which encompasses the whole world; the matter is decided	Once
N	N—The table of God upon which is the pen of God filled with ink from the fish Behemoth	Once

NINETY-NINE NAMES OF GOD

One final Islamic number-letter tradition can be seen in the 99 attributes of God known as the 99 Beautiful Names of Allah. These descriptions of God are derived from the holy verses of the Quran. Each of the 99 appellations represents a power of God which can be contacted by repeatedly chanting that name with a purified heart and mind.

One or more of these God names can be engraved on an amulet to talismanically tap into the powers of the various names.

All 99 names are an extension of the supreme secret 100th name of God which is hidden in the Quran. The Greatest Name is hidden by God so that the faithful may discover this name by reading the entire Quran.

The table that begins on the following page lists all 99 names of God, giving their order, the original Arabic, the pronunciation of the name, the meaning of the divine appellation, the talismanic power of each name, and the number value of the name by both the Egyptian and Moroccan method of numbering Arabic. By the Egyptian code, these 99 names total to 36,613, while by the Moroccan method their total is 182,346.

The Arabic names were derived from three sources: Shems Friedlander's *99 Names of Allah*, E. A. Wallis Budge's *Amulets and Talismans*, and Aleister Crowley's appendix to his *777*.

Ninety-Nine Beautiful Names of God

Order	Arabic	Pronunciation	Meaning	Power	Number Egyptian	Number Moroccan
1	AL RḤMN	Ar-Rahman	The Beneficent	Memory and Awareness	330	1,817
2	AL RḤYM	Ar-Rahim	The Merciful	Friendliness	289	2,117
3	AL MLK	Al-Malik	The King	Respect	121	2,001
4	AL QDWS	Al-Kuddus	The Holy	Freedom from Anxiety	201	1,739
5	AL SLAM	As-Salam	The Peace	Regain Health	162	1,632
6	AL MWMN	Al-Mumin	The Faithful	Freedom from Harm	167	3,301
7	AL MHYMN	Al-Muhaimin	The Protector	Inner Illumination	176	4,201
8	AL OZYZ	Al-Aziz	The Mighty	Independence from Others	125	1,631
9	AL JBAR	Al-Jabbar	The Repairer	Freedom from Compulsion	237	519
10	AL MTKBR	Al-Mutakabbir	The Great	Fertile Intercourse	693	1,516
11	AL KhALQ	Al-Khalik	The Creator	Create Guardian Angel	762	1,309
12	AL BARY	Al-Bari	The Maker	Evolve	213	1,013
13	AL MSWR	Al-Musawwir	The Fashioner	Barren Made Fertile	367	2,061
14	AL GhFAR	Al-Ghaffar	The Forgiver	Forgiven of Sin	1,312	812
15	AL QHAR	Al-Kahhar	The Dominant	Conquer Desire	337	1,612
16	AL WHAB	Al-Wahhab	The Bestower	Appeal to God	45	2,204
17	AL RZAQ	Ar-Razzak	The Provider	Provided with Sustenance	339	832
18	AL FTAH	Al-Fattah	The Opener	Opening of the Heart	520	711
19	AL OLYM	Al-Alim	The Knower	Illuminating of the Heart	181	2,691
20	AL QABḌ	Al-Kabiz	The Restrainer	Freedom from Hunger	934	864

Ninety-Nine Beautiful Names of God (cont'd.)

Order	Arabic	Pronunciation	Meaning	Power	Number Egyptian	Moroccan
21	AL BASṬ	Al-Basit	The Expander	Free of Need from Others	103	604
22	AL KhAFḌ	Al-Khafiz	The Abaser	No Harm from One's Enemy	1,512	769
23	AL RAFO	Ar-Rafi	The Exalter	Honor, Richness, and Merit	382	802
24	AL MOZ	Al-Muizz	The Honorer	Dignity in the Eyes of Others	148	1,211
25	AL MDhL	Al-Muzil	The Destroyer	Protection from Jealousy	801	1,610
26	AL SMYO	As-Sami	The All-Hearing	Granting of One's Desires	211	2,221
27	AL BSYR	Al-Basir	The All-Seeing	Esteem from Others	333	1,563
28	AL ḤKM	Al-Hakim	The Judge	Reveal Secrets	99	1,507
29	AL ODL	Al-Adl	The Just	Obedience from Others	135	1,100
30	AL LTYF	Al-Latif	The Subtle	Desires Fulfilled	160	2,271
31	AL KhBYR	Al-Khabir	The Aware	Freedom from Bad Habits	843	1,520
32	AL ḤLYM	Al-Halim	The Clement	Healthy Crops	119	2,607
33	AL OTzYM	Al-Azim	The Great One	Gain Respect	1,051	2,271
34	AL GhFWR	Al-Ghafur	The Forgiving	Relief of Ailment	1,317	1,711
35	AL ShKWR	Ash-Shakur	The Grateful	Lighten the Heart	557	1,851
36	AL OLY	Al-Ali	The Most High	Raise Faith, Open Destiny, Reach Home	141	2,099
37	AL KBYR	Al-Kabir	The Most Great	Have Esteem	263	1913
38	AL ḤFYTz	Al-Hafiz	The Guardian	Protection	1,029	1,787
39	AL MQYT	Al-Mukit	The Strengthener	Bad Change to Good in a Child	541	1,804
40	AL ḤSYB	Al-Hasib	The Reckoner	Freedom from Fears	103	1,533

Ninety-Nine Beautiful Names of God (cont'd.)

Order	Arabic	Pronunciation	Meaning	Power	Number Egyptian	Number Moroccan
41	AL JLYL	Al-Jalil	The Sublime One	To be Revered	104	2,506
42	AL KRYM	Al-Karim	The Generous One	Esteem in This World and the Next	301	2,511
43	AL RQYB	Ar-Rakib	The Watcher	God's Protection	343	1,813
44	AL MJYB	Al-Mujib	The Responsive	Appeal Answered	86	2,108
45	AL WASO	Al-Wasi	The All-Embracing	Good Earnings	168	1,522
46	AL ḤKYM	Al-Hakim	The Wise	Work Without Difficulty	109	2,507
47	AL WDWD	Al-Wadud	The Loving	Resolving Quarrels	51	2,317
48	AL MJYD	Al-Majid	The Glorious	Gain Glory	88	2,114
49	AL BAOTh	Al-Baith	The Resurrector	Gain the Fear of God	504	597
50	AL ShHYD	Ash-Shahid	The Witness	Obedience of a Child	350	2,349
51	AL ḤQ	Al-Hakk	The Truth	Find What Is Lost	139	807
52	AL WKYL	Al-Wakil	The Advocate	Protection from Fire or Water	97	3,301
53	AL QWY	Al-Kawi	The Strong	Free from Enemy	147	2,701
54	AL MTYN	Al-Matin	The Firm	Troubles Disappear	531	2,804
55	AL WLY	Al-Wali	The Patron	Friend of God	77	2,901
56	AL ḤMYD	Al-Hamid	The Laudable	Love and Praise	93	2,115
57	AL MḤSY	Al-Muhsi	The Counter	No Fear of Judgment Day	179	2,157
58	AL MBDY	Al-Mubdi	The Beginner	Successful Pregnancy	87	2,111
59	AL MOYD	Al-Muid	The Restorer	Return Safely	155	2,199
60	AL MHYY	Al-Muhyi	The Giver of Life	Burden Taken Away	99	3,107

Ninety-Nine Beautiful Names of God (cont'd.)

Order	Arabic	Pronunciation	Meaning	Power	Number Egyptian	Moroccan
61	AL MMYT	Al-Mumit	The Killer	Destroy Enemy	521	2,704
62	AL HY	Al-Hayy	The Living	Long Life	49	1,507
63	AL QYWM	Al-Kaiyum	The Self-Subsisting	Avoid Accidents	187	3,301
64	AL WAJD	Al-Wajid	The Finder	Richness of Heart	44	1,414
65	AL MAJD	Al-Majid	The Noble	Enlightened Heart	79	1,115
66	AL WAHD	Al-Wahid	The Unique	Freedom from Delusion	50	1,416
67	AL AHD	Al-Ahad	The One	Opening of Certain Secrets	44	516
68	AL SMD	As-Samad	The Eternal	Providing One's Needs	165	1,159
69	AL QADR	Al-Kadir	The Powerful	All Desires Fulfilled	336	820
70	AL MQTDR	Al-Muktadir	The Prevailing	Awareness of Truth	775	1,422
71	AL MQDM	Al-Mukaddim	The Expediter	Fearless in Battle	215	2,009
72	AL MWKhR	Al-Mukhir	The Delayer	Love of God and No Other	877	2,018
73	AL AWL	Al-Awwal	The First	To Meet a Traveler	68	1,902
74	AL AKhR	Al-Akhir	The Last	Good Life and Good Death	832	519
75	AL TzAHR	Az-Zahir	The Manifest	To Enter into Divine Light	1,137	1,392
76	AL BATN	Al-Batin	The Hidden	See the Truth	93	1,274
77	AL WALY	Al-Wali	The Governor	Safe Shelter	78	2,902
78	AL MTOALY	Al-Mutaali	The Exalted	Benevolence of God	582	2,695
79	AL BR	Al-Barr	The Righteous	Child Free from Misfortune	233	513
80	AL TWAB	At-Tawwab	The Turner of Hearts	Acceptance of Repentance	440	1,407

Ninety-Nine Beautiful Names of God (cont'd.)

Order	Arabic	Pronunciation	Meaning	Power	Number Egyptian	Number Moroccan
81	AL MNTQM	Al-Muntakim	The Avenger	Victory over Enemies	661	2,704
82	AL OFW	Al-Afuw	The Pardoner	Sins Forgiven	187	1,691
83	AL RWF	Ar-Rauf	The Kind	Blessed by God	317	1,611
84	MALK AL MLK	Malik Ul-Mulk	The Ruler of the Kingdom	Esteem Among People	212	3,502
85	DhWAL JLAL WAL AKRAM	Dhul-Jalal Wal-Ikram	The Lord of Majesty and Bounty	Rich	1,100	4,829
86	AL MQST	Al-Muksit	The Equitable	Free from the Devil	240	1,501
87	AL JAMO	Al-Jami	The Collector	Find That Which Is Lost	145	1,197
88	AL GhNY	Al-Ghani	The Independent	Contentment	1,091	2,301
89	AL MGhNY	Al-Mughni	The Enricher	Self-Sufficient	1,131	2,901
90	AL MANO	Al-Mani	The Preventer	Good Family Life	192	1,892
91	AL DAR	Az-Zarr	The Distresser	Raising of Status	1,032	572
92	AL NAFO	Al-Nafo	The Profiter	Free from Harm	232	1,492
93	AL NWR	An-Nur	The Light	Inner Light	287	2,111
94	AL HADY	Al-Hadi	The Guide	Spiritual Knowledge	51	2,310
95	AL BDYO	Al-Badi	The Incomparable	Troubles Disappear	117	1,601
96	AL BAQY	Al-Baki	The Everlasting	Freedom from Disasters	144	1,804
97	AL WARTh	Al-Warith	The Heir	Long Life	738	1,416
98	AL RShYD	Al-Rashid	The Guide to the Right Path	To Be Guided Aright	545	1,559
99	AL SBWR	As-Sabur	The Patient	Rescue from Difficulty	329	1,463

ADDITIONAL SYMBOLS

The Sufi mystical tradition has ascribed additional minor symbols to each of the 28 alphabet letters. Some of these symbols are based on the actual shape of the letter while others are based on acrostic symbolism. The following list delineates these poetical-mystical interpretations for the alphabet.

A—First letter of "God" (Allah), the pen, the upright body, the staff, the penis, the line of the nose dividing the face, the slender stature of the beloved, the straight line which is the essence of all alphabet letters, the vital upright letter—all other letters are curved by impurity or illness; Alif is also Satan, for it bows before none but God (A being the first letter of "God"); the vowel which opens up the heart; posture of QUAMA (standing upright)

B—First letter of Quran, humility, prostrating the body before God, the nose; intellect

J—Curls of hair; the soul

D—Tresses of hair; nature; posture of RUKU (bowing down)

H—Buildings, structures, last letter of "God" (Allah); creator above his creation

W—The joiner, that which unites God and Creation; the vowel which stimulates the lips of the mouth; intellect above its contemplations

Z—Increase; soul connected to the universe

H—Teacher; nature above its inhabitants

T—The secret path of initiation, mountain, purities, essences; material world

Y—Faithful, fraternal help, the hand offering; plan of God; the vowel which opens up the third eye

K—The hand holding back, cloth garment; structure of the universe

L—Middle, mediator (as the L in "Gabriel"), the lover turned into its own beloved (as the double L in "Allah"), God's pure knowledge of Himself and His own understanding of the illusion of God as a divided self (also as the double L in "Allah"), kneeling in prayer, the double edged sword; the divine commandments

LA—The close embrace of two lovers, as lovers, who are two and one (in embrace) and none (in orgasm), (the Arabic formula of Lam-Alif is 2 = 1 = 0, here L = vagina, A = penis)

M—Reign, waters of the ocean, the 40 gradations of universal wisdom from God to Man back to God, the name Mohammed placed on the heart; the mouth; the created universe; posture of SAJDAH (kneeling in a prone position)

N—Victory, the body with the hands, head and feet cut off, the fish without head or tail; twofold nature of being

S—The last letter of the Quran, combined with the first letter, B, produces the word BS, meaning "enough, sufficient"; relationship between the universe and its structure

O—Eye, source, essence, forgiveness; the interlinking chain or commandments which govern the universe

F—The heart, to split or break the head

S—Sufi, pure, the straight narrow path; connection between God's commandments, the pattern of the universe and created matter

Q—Mount Qaf, the mythical mountain that surrounds the world, the station at the end of the created world; the ordering of all the universe in accordance with God's pattern

R—Ascetic, discipline; unity and the return of the all into one

Sh—The Sun rising above the mountains of the East

T—Complete submission to a master, education, learning

Kh—Selfishness

Dh—Humility, abasement

D—The Arabic people and language

Tz—Unjust

Gh—Dimple

The Persian Alphabet

One other alphabet directly influenced by the Arabic numbering system is the Persian Alphabet of 32 letters (known anciently as Pahlavi and currently as Farsi).

The Persian alphabet used all 28 letters of the Arabic alphabet (retaining the Egyptian number value for each letter), and added to these letters four additional signs.

These four extra letters (known as Pe, Chim, Zhe, and Ghaf) posses no number value of their own. However, since all four are modeled on the Arabic letters which precede each of the four in the normal Persian alphabetical order, these additional Persian letters can be given a number value secondary to their Arabic models:

Four Additional Persian Letter Subvalues

Persian Letter Name	Alphabet Order	Persian Letter	Arabic Model	Number Value
Pe	3	پ	ب	2
Chim	7	چ	ج	3
Zhe	14	ژ	ز	7
Ghaf	26	گ	ک	20

The following table shows the numerical and symbolic values of the 32 letters composing the Persian alphabet:

The Persian Alphabet

Letter	Letter Name	Transliteration	Sequence	Number Value	Symbolic Meaning
ا	alef	A	1	1	Taurus, Sunday, unmarried man
ب	be	B	2	2	Gemini, Monday, seventh lunar month: Rajab
پ	pe	P	3	—	Step, ladder, foot, three grades, by degrees
ت	te	T	4	400	A fold, plait, single sheet of paper, a single-stringed lute
ث	se	Sh	5	500	Garments, threefold, fixed stars
ج	jim	J	6	3	Cancer, Tuesday, sixth lunar month: Jamada, camel, a silk robe embroidered in gold
چ	chim	Ch	7	—	A wheel, orbit, circle, fourfold
ح	he hoti	Ḥ	8	8	Sagittarius, a good man
خ	khe	Kh	9	600	Tuesday, the shoulder
د	dal	D	10	4	Wednesday, Leo, Mercury, a basket, an eagle

The Persian Alphabet (cont'd.)

Letter	Letter Name	Trans-literation	Sequence	Number Value	Symbolic Meaning
ذ	zal	Dz	11	700	To move lightly, swiftly; last month of Arabic year: Zul-Hijjat
ر	re	R	12	200	The Moon, the month Rabiu-Lakhir, guardian
ز	ze	Z	13	7	Saturday, Scorpio, to beget, a glutton
ژ	zhe	Zh	14	—	Ditch, cistern, reservoir, quicksilver
س	sin	S	15	60	Sun, a ringlet, lock, the breast
ش	shin	Sh	16	300	North, dishonor, a man addicted to venery
ص	sad	Ṣ	17	90	The second Arabic month, Safar; to mark as true, genuine; copper, brass
ض	zad	Ẓ	18	800	Vulva, setting upon, filling a bottle
ط	ta	Ṭ	19	9	Capricorn; the Moon's descendent, a man who frequents the society of women (or is given to frequent sexual intercourse)
ظ	za	Ẓh	20	900	The evident, the breasts of an old woman
ع	ain	Ā	21	70	Flowing water; injured by evil eye; eye, sight, vision
غ	ghain	Gh	22	1,000	Nightingale (bird of 1,000 songs), aspect of the square in astrology, cloud covering the skies, thirst
ف	fe	F	23	80	Moon in her ascent, froth (foam) of the sea, beloved object

The Persian Alphabet (cont'd.)

Letter	Letter Name	Trans-literation	Sequence	Number Value	Symbolic Meaning
ﻕ	ghaf	Q	24	100	The mythical mountain Qaf which surrounds the world, mount Caucasus, the Quran, from one end of the world to the other
ﻙ	kaf	K	25	20	Pisces, little, the creative word or power, all, whole, total, universal
ﮒ	ghaf	G	26	—	A crack, fissure, exceeding all bounds, boasting
ﻝ	lam	L	27	30	Aries, night, the planet Saturn, opposite aspect in astrology, ringlet of hair, to or for God's sake, the ragged garment of a dervish, crooked, curved, bent; a feathered arrow
ﻡ	mim	M	28	40	Sunday, first Arabic month Muharram, logic, penis, wine, well, rose-water, goblet
ﻥ	non	N	29	50	Conjunction of stars, ink, sharpest part of sword, fish, vulva, bow, the eyebrow
ﻭ	vav	W	30	6	Friday, Libra, O, ah, alas, woe, color of water, a large cloud, camel stallion, faith in Allah and Muhammad
ﻩ	he havaz	H	31	5	Thursday, Virgo, Venus, take, give, grant
ﻯ	ye	Y	32	10	Jupiter, Aquarius, thou, bowstring notch

ADDENDUM

G. I. GURDJIEFF

The 20th-century Russian religious teacher Georges Ivanovitch Gurdjieff used Ibn al Arabi's ladder of 28 degrees as a model for his own cosmological classification system. Gurdjieff's system utilized 11 basic numbers to measure the entire range of creation. These 11 numbers are 1, 3, 6, 12, 24, 48, 96, 192, 384, 768, and 1536. Stretched upon a vertical line, these 11 numbers span the cosmos from God to inert matter:

Eleven Levels of Cosmos

(+ 1)	1	Absolute (God)
(+ 3)	3	Eternal Unchanging, Time (The Great Heropass) (Celestial Government)
(+ 6)	6	Archangels
(+12)	12	Angels
(+24)	24	Man
(+ 0)	48	Vertebrates
(-24)	96	Invertebrates
(-12)	192	Plants
(- 6)	384	Minerals
(- 3)	768	Metals
(- 1)	1536	Absolute Inert Matter (Devil)

Gurdjieff's cosomological ladder of 11 degrees has at its center the number 48. This number is considered 0, between the negative number series 96, 192, 384, 768, and 1536, and the positive number series of 24, 12, 6, 3, and 1. Man is placed just above this center zone, differing from al-Arabi's placement of Man next to last in the scale of 28.

Gurdjieff utilized this basic number scale to classify a variety of concepts. In accordance with al-Arabi's astrological scale, Gurdjieff classified the seven planets, the seven days of creation, and the twelve signs of the Zodiac by his number scale, as shown on the opposite page.

Astrological Scale, Seven Planets and Twelve Signs

	Seven Planets	Seven Days of the Week	Seven Days of Creation	Twelve Signs Ruled by Seven Planets
1				
3		Beyond the influence of the 7 planets and 12 signs		
6				
12	Saturn	Saturday	7th Day	Capricorn and Aquarius
24	Venus	Friday	6th Day	Taurus and Libra
48	Jupiter	Thursday	5th Day	Sagittarius and Pisces
96	Mercury	Wednesday	4th Day	Gemini and Virgo
192	Mars	Tuesday	3rd Day	Aries and Scorpio
384	Moon	Monday	2nd Day	Cancer
768	Sun	Sunday	1st Day	Leo
1536	The Four Elements (devoid of planetary or Zodiacal qualities)			

Gurdjieff placed at the center of his number scale the harmony of the musical scale of seven notes. These seven notes span the number scale of 1 to 768 in two different ranges. This sevenfold scale also spans the seven rays of creation and the seven brains of man, as follows.

The Seven Notes of the Octave

1		(Do)
3	Interval	(Ti)
6	Interval	(La)
12	Ti	(Sol)
24	La	(Fa)
48	Sol	(Mi)
96	Fa	(Re)
192	Mi	(Do)
384	Re	
768	Do	
1536		

The Seven Rays of Creation

1	—	1st Ray (Absolute)
3	—	2nd Ray (All Worlds)
6	—	3rd Ray (All Suns)
12	—	4th Ray (Our Sun)
24	—	5th Ray (All Planets)
48	—	6th Ray (The Earth)
96	—	7th Ray (The Moon)

The Seven Brains of Man

1	—	The Soul
3	—	Higher Intellectual Center
6	—	Higher Emotional Center
12	—	Intellectual Center
24	—	Emotional Center
48	—	Moving Center, Instinctive Center, Sex Center
96	—	The Body

Gurdjieff was also able to use part of this number scale to classify various divisions of the cosmos. He selected the five numbers 3, 6, 12, 24, and 48 to divide the body of man as well as the five elements, as follows.

The Fourfold Body

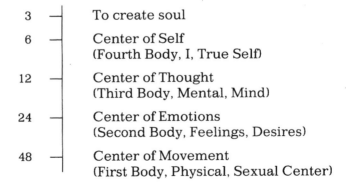

3	—	To create soul
6	—	Center of Self (Fourth Body, I, True Self)
12	—	Center of Thought (Third Body, Mental, Mind)
24	—	Center of Emotions (Second Body, Feelings, Desires)
48	—	Center of Movement (First Body, Physical, Sexual Center)

The Five Elements

3	Ether
6	Fire
12	Air
24	Water
48	Earth

Ultimately this elaborate scale of numbers was utilized by Gurdjieff in his teachings to explain every level of human consciousness. One in this scale represented Heaven, 48 the neutral state of being asleep, and 1536 Hell itself.

This scale of consciousness is as follows.

The Eleven Levels of Human Consciousness

1 — Heaven (Creator)
Not directly accessible to human consciousness, but approached through Level 3

3 — All is One (Unity), enlightenment, seeing God, highest level of lucidity, (center of all solar systems, Center of Heaven), contact with higher intellectual center

6 — Superconsciousness (Psychedelics)
Powers of the Adept (clairaudience, clairvoyance, meditation), contact with higher emotional center

12 — Blissful State (Hashish)
Being in love, prayer, chanting, Head and Heart in Harmony, alcohol intoxication at its purest state

24 — Absorbing, Attentive Activity, stimulants (positive side of cocaine, caffeine, amphetamines), positive dosage of alcohol; the self is lost in pleasurable activities

48 — Neutral State, Normal consciousness for Humanity, receptive, asleep, lack of awareness

96 — Negative emotions, depression, pain, guilt, fear, depressants (too much alcohol, light intoxication of opium, negative side of amphetamines and cocaine)

192 — Suffering extreme body pain divorcing consciousness from the body, heavy opium intoxication, heroin

384 — Loss of hope and direction, despair, anguish loss of ego, meaninglessness, negative effects of psychedelics

768 — All is against One, All is Two, Existential viewpoint, Satanic, seeing Beelzebub, center of Hell, Duality, schizophrenia, nervous breakdown, insanity, deception

1536 — Hell (Beelzebub), not directly accessible to human consciousness, but approached through Level 768

One more Gurdjieffian number table should be detailed. Gurdjieff extended his scale of 11 basic numbers (ranging from 1 to 1536) to a scale of 14. Three additional numbers—3072, 6144, and 12,288—were added to the cosmological scale of 11 to produce what Gurdjieff referred to as the "Table of 14 Hydrogens." These 14 basic hydrogens represent the elemental building blocks of all creation. Using this table Gurdjieff was able to produce another complementary table which detailed the cosmic food chain of all creation.

In this secondary table, the 14 groupings of hydrogen were rearranged upon the ladder of 11 steps to demonstrate that every step of creation feeds upon a lower rung of the ladder and is itself food for a higher rung of the ladder. This one table is a radical departure from the cosmological graphs of al-Arabi, Lull, Giorgi, Dee, and Kircher, whose cosmic symbolic tables do not address this unique symbiotic relationship which Gurdjieff has so aptly detailed. These two Gurdjieffian tables are as follows:

Table of Fourteen Hydrogens

1 —	Hydrogen 1	Carbon
3 —	Hydrogen 3	Nitrogen
6 —	Hydrogen 6	Oxygen
12 —	Hydrogen 12	Carbon, Nitrogen, Oxygen
24 —	Hydrogen 24	Flourine
48 —	Hydrogen 48	Chlorine
96 —	Hydrogen 96	Bromine (rarefied gasses that man cannot breath)
192 —	Hydrogen 192	Iodine (Air, which man can breath)
384 —	Hydrogen 384	Water
768 —	Hydrogen 768	Food
1536 —	Hydrogen 1536	Wood
3072 —	Hydrogen 3072	Iron, soil
6144 —	Hydrogen 6144	Dead matter
12,288 —	Hydrogen 12288	Matter in its densest state

Cosmic Food Chain

What they themselves serve as food for (a higher order)	Ladder of 11 steps	What serves as food for them (a lower order)
	Spirit Absolute 1	Archangels 6
	Eternal Unchanging 3	Angels 12
Spirit Absolute 1	Archangels 6	Man 24
Eternal Unchanging 3	Angels 12	Vertebrates 48
Archangels 6	Man 24	Invertebrates 96
Angels 12	Vertebrates 48	Plants 192
Man 24	Invertebrates 96	Minerals 384
Vertebrates 48	Plants 192	Metals 768
Invertebrates 96	Minerals 384	Inert Matter 1536
Plants 192	Metals 768	Soil 3072
Minerals 384	Inert Matter 1536	Dead Matter 6144
		(matter without spirit)

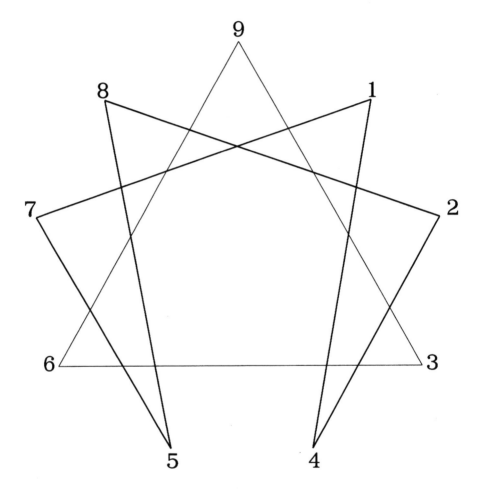

Gurdjieff's Enneagram

Gurdjieff's Enneagram

In addition to the number ladders, Gurdjieff synthesized his whole teachings into one geometrical symbol, which he designated as the Enneagram. The Gurdjieffian Enneagram is based on the nine-pointed star (or ennead) that is at the center of Raymond Lull's Christianized Qabalah.

In Lull's nine-pointed star, every point around the circle is connected to every other point to form a symmetrical star. However, in Gurdjieff's Enneagram (which is supposedly derived from Essene teachings), not all nine points are connected to one another. Rather, a triangle is superimposed upon an irregular six-sided figure, with each of the nine points numbered in successive order, as shown on the following page.

Within this figure two laws are demonstrated, The Law of Three and The Law of Seven.

The Law of Three is demonstrated by the equilateral triangle formed by points 3, 6, and 9. If 3 is divided into 1, the repeating decimal figure of 0.3333 is generated. Three doubles to 6 doubles to 9 to form the equilateral triangle of the Enneagram.

The Law of Seven is demonstrated by the irregular figure formed by points 1, 2, 4, 5, 7, and 8. If 7 is divided into 1 the resultant repeating decimal figure is 0.142857142857. The six numbers 1, 4, 2, 8, 5, 7 are the order of the six points as connected by the lines forming the Enneagram.

The results of these two decimal numbers of 0.33 and 0.142857142857 determine the dance, or motion, of the Enneagram and can be divided into the threefold Renaissance universe of God, angel, and man.

Threefold Enneagram Worlds

Ruler	Points of Enneagram
God	3, 6, 9
Angel	8, 5, 7
Man	1, 4, 2

If the Qabalistic ninefold classification system of Lull is applied to this Enneagram, the correspondences in the following tables are revealed for this mysterious geometrical figure. Both P. D. Ouspensky and Gurdjieff studied Lull's system intently when they first met in St. Petersburg. It was at this point in Gurdjieff's career that the Enneagram was first drawn up as a grand symbol of the Gurdjieffian system of "Work on Oneself." As such, in light of Lull's Qabalah, the rich set of symbols shown in the tables on the following pages can be extracted from the "Dance" of the Enneagram.

The Enneagram Decoded by the Lullian Art

Lull's Threefold Universe

Enneagram Point	Latin Alphabet	Three Worlds	Three Rulers	Man	Astrology	Trinity	Geometry	Three Centers
1	K	Terrestrial (Third World)	Man	Body	Elements	Son	Square	Will
4	I							
2	H							
8	G	Celestial (Second World)	Angels	Soul	Planets	Holy Ghost	Triangle	Memory
5	F							
7	E							
3	D	Supercelestial (First World)	God	Spirit	Zodiac	Father	Circle	Intellect
6	C							
9	B							

The Three Worlds

Enneagram Point	Latin Alphabet	All Three Worlds	Supercelestial (First World)	Celestial (Second World)	Terrestrial (Third World)
1	K	Tools of Arts and Sciences	Angels	Moon	Tools of Arts and Sciences
4	I	Four Elements	Archangels	Mercury	Earth
2	H	Plants	Principalities	Venus	Water
8	G	Sensation	Powers	Sun	Air
5	F	Imagination	Virtures	Mars	Fire
7	E	Man	Dominions	Jupiter	Plants
3	D	Stars	Thrones	Saturn	Animals
6	C	Angels	Cherubim	Zodiac	Imagination
9	B	God	Seraphim	First Cause	Man

The Enneagram Decoded by the Lullian Art (cont'd.)

Enneagram Point	Latin Alphabet	Religion			Science		
		Names of God	Virtue	Vice	Measure	Category	Question
1	K	Glorious	Devotion	Inconsistency	Lesser	Place	In what way
4	I	True	Patience	Falsehood	Equal	Time	Where
2	H	Virtuous	Charity	Anger	Greater	Position	When
8	G	Willful	Hope	Envy	End	Nature	What kind
5	F	Wise	Faith	Bitterness	Middle	Passive	How much
7	E	Powerful	Temperance	Arrogance	Beginning	Active	Why
3	D	Lasting	Strength	Excess	Opposites	Relation	From where
6	C	Great	Prudence	Gluttony	Agreement	Quality	What
9	B	Good	Justice	Avarice	Difference	Quantity	Whether

Hebrew Qabalah Based on Lull's Celestial World

Enneagram Point	Latin Alphabet	Tree of Life	Sephirotic Color	Human Body
1	K	Yesod	Violet	Genitals
4	I	Hod	Orange	Left Leg
2	H	Netzach	Green	Right Leg
8	G	Tiphereth	Yellow	Heart
5	F	Geburah	Red	Left Arm
7	E	Chesed	Blue	Right Arm
3	D	Binah	Black	Left Eye
6	C	Chockmah	Gray	Right Eye
9	B	Kether	White	Crown of Head

The Georgian Alphabet

In addition to the number ladders and Enneagram of Gurdjieff, there exists a language which may hold a key to unlocking the elaborate word symbolism found in his writings. This ancient language, which may be at the heart of Gurdjieff's use of esoteric words within his own writings, is Georgian. The Georgian language was developed around 330 CE by the scholar Mesrob, who devised the 39-letter alphabet upon the pattern of Greek. The Georgian language is closely related to Armenian, the language Gurdjieff used to write most of his work.

The beauty of the Georgian language is that it is isosephic and, as the Greek alphabet numbers from 1 to 1,000, the Georgian numbers from 1 to 10,000, allowing many more word metaphors for the higher range of numbers. These higher-number metaphors may be able to unlock the higher end of numbers which appear in Gurdjieff's "Table of Fourteen Hydrogens."

Two distinct styles of writing developed for the Georgian alphabet:

- The "Khutsuri" or Priestly letters, which were the original form of the alphabet and are square in shape, and

- The "Mkhedruli" or Warrior letters, which were developed around 1000 CE and are cursive in shape.

The Mkhedruli alphabet in its cursive shape resembles Gurdjieff's own secret alphabet that he utilized in the Study House (at the Priere). With the development of this second script, the Georgian alphabet was gradually reduced from 39 to 33 letters.

The following table shows these two separate scripts, as well as their letter names, transliterations, number values, and Greek alphabet models.

Georgian Alphanumeric Code

Khutsuri-Priestly Letters	Mkhedruli-Warrior Letters	Letter Name	Trans-literation	Number Value	Greek Model
௳	Ⴃ	An	A	1	A
Ⴁ	Ⴄ	Ban	B	2	B
Ⴂ	Ⴅ	Gan	G	3	G
Ⴃ	Ⴖ	Don	D	4	D

Georgian Alphanumeric Code (cont'd.)

Khutsuri-Priestly Letters	Mkhedruli-Warrior Letters	Letter Name	Trans-literation	Number Value	Greek Model
Ⴄ	ე	En	E	5	E
Ⴅ	ვ	Vin	V	6	St
Ⴆ	ზ	Zen	Z	7	Z
Ⴡ	ჱ	He	Ey	8	H
Ⴇ	თ	Tan	T	9	Th
Ⴈ	ი	In	I	10	I
Ⴉ	კ	Ḳan	Ḳ	20	K
Ⴊ	ლ	Las	L	30	L
Ⴋ	მ	Man	M	40	M
Ⴌ	ნ	Nar	N	50	N
Ⴢ	ჲ	Hie	Y	60	X
Ⴍ	ო	On	O	70	O
Ⴎ	პ	P̣ar	P̣	80	P
Ⴏ	ჟ	Ẑan	Ẑ	90	Q

Georgian Alphanumeric Code (cont'd.)

Khutsuri-Priestly Letters	Mkhedruli-Warrior Letters	Letter Name	Trans-literation	Number Value	Greek Model
Ჷ	ᲩᲜ	Rae	R	100	R
Ⴊ	Ⴑ	San	S	200	S
Ⴒ	Ⴚ	Ţar	Ţ	300	T
Ⴓ	Ⴅ	Vie	Vi	—	—
Ⴔ	Ⴣ	Un	U	400	U
Ⴕ	Ⴢ	Par	P	500	Ph
Ⴖ	Ⴆ	Kan	K	600	Ch
Ⴗ	Ⴟ	Ĝan	Ĝ	700	—
Ⴘ	Ⴤ	Qar	Q̣	800	—
Ⴙ	Ⴥ	Ŝin	Ŝ	900	—
Ⴛ	⴦	Ĉin	Ĉ	1000	—
Ⴜ	Ⴧ	Can	C	2000	—
Ⴝ	⴨	Jil	J	3000.	—
Ⴞ	⴩	Çil	Ç	4000	—

Georgian Alphanumeric Code (cont'd.)

Khutsuri- Priestly Letters	Mkhedruli- Warrior Letters	Letter Name	Trans- literation	Number Value	Greek Model
5	Ϡ	Ĉar	Ĉ	5000	—
Ⴉ	Ⴚ	Xan	X	6000	—
Ⴊ	Ⴍ	Qar	Q	7000	—
Ⴋ	Ⴞ	Ĵan	Ĵ	8000	—
Ⴌ	Ⴟ	Hae	H	9000	—
Ⴍ	Ⴢ	Hoe	Oy	10,000	Ō
	Ⴔ	Fi	F	—	

FOURTH KEY

SANSKRIT

OVERVIEW

In terms of extending to its limits the esoteric knowledge available to the West, this one key may be the most important contribution to the Western tradition of Qabalistic magick, for this chapter gives, in great detail, for the first time in print, all of the esoteric numbering systems for the Sanskrit alphabet.

When I first began my studies of the Hebrew Qabalah, I was already familiar with both Sanskrit and the Indian chakra system. When I discovered the Qabalistic Tree of Life whose branches are composed of the Hebrew alphabet, I immediately connected this diagram to the chakra symbolism of flower petals decorated with the Sanskrit alphabet letters. With my acquired knowledge of a number value for each of the Hebrew letters, I premised that the Sanskrit letters upon the chakras must also contain a numerical key. But it was not until many more years of hard-earned Qabalistic knowledge that I would be able to unlock this Sanskrit numerical puzzle. The necessary key would be found in the Vedic secret number tradition, whose origins may date back as far as 6000 BCE.

In the history of Western magick there has always been a fascination with the East. The sheer fact that most Eastern languages were undecipherable to all but a few select scholars in the West until the advent of the 20th century makes the East all the more mysterious and compelling. Therefore, when the vast majority of magickal texts written before 1875 containing supposed Eastern occult lore are deeply studied and analyzed, their content is found not to be true Eastern esoteric lore but either a fabrication by the author or Western magickal correspondences wrapped in an Eastern garb.

However, with the creation of the Theosophical movement in 1875, the infusion of authentic Eastern esoteric lore entered into the mainstream of Western occult traditions. The copious magickal writings of Madame Blavatsky in the 19th century, and Aleister Crowley in the 20th, integrated the teachings of the East with those of the West. Both writers were trendsetters and ground breakers, yet both are belittled by modern scholarship that details the exoteric side of these teachings and neglects the esoteric side.

Yet in the copious writings of both Blavatsky and Crowley we are unable to find the correct numerical key to the Sanskrit alphabet. However, 20th-century scholarship has uncovered and translated the texts which contain these codes, without fully appreciating or detailing these keys. In this chapter, such an analysis has finally been accomplished.

The fourth key begins with a short historical overview of the basic elements of the Sanskrit alphabet. The Sanskrit alphabet, which is composed of 50 basic letters (16 vowels and 34 consonants), is laid out to show the original alphabet characters, the transliterations used throughout this key, and the basic symbolic meanings derived from Hindu, Tantrik, and Buddhist esoteric commentaries on the spiritual nature of Sanskrit. This table is followed by a few basic rules which govern the combining of one Sanskrit consonant with another to form a composite character, known as a "conjoined consonant." It is important to be able to clearly discern the letters of a conjoined consonant in order to ascribe the correct number value to any given Sanskrit term.

Next, all the major esoteric systems which imbue number value to Sanskrit are fully tabled out. To help the reader unfamiliar with the Sanskrit alphabet, all of the elaborate tables utilize the English transliterations established at the beginning of the key rather than the original alphabet characters. This is true for all tables of symbolic alphabet correspondences occurring throughout this book. In regards to the transliterations used for Sanskrit here, one point of clarification is required. My own English transliterations differ in part from many standard versions (such as the transliteration used in Arthur A. MacDonnel's *Practical Sanskrit Dictionary*). For each Sanskrit letter I have modeled a distinct English letter (and vowel point), in order to be able to clearly distinguish one letter from another. For a more accurate phonetic rendition, turn to such texts as the above-mentioned dictionary. However, by the convention I have used, no confusion will arise when converting the transliteration back to its original Sanskrit alphabet character.

Again, the method which was used to create this book should be emphasized here. I am not a scholar, nor am I fluent in the many languages used throughout this text. I am self-taught, and my research is directed by inner rather than outer resources. By combining the essential information given in any grammar for a specific language with the secret information found for each alphabet in the body of occult texts East and West, I have been able to discover every major code governing every major esoteric language of the world. Where scholarship must stop, I have been able to advance, guided by my own insight and inspiration, which is the reward of many, many years of persistent study and meditation upon the ancient languages of the world. I am not saying this to brag, inflate my ego, or make an unwarranted claim, but rather to describe the mechanism which produced the mass of tables in this book detailing the secret language of alphabet symbolism.

Since the beginning of my research I have always had a deep love for Sanskrit. Instinctively I knew Sanskrit contained a number key, not unlike Hebrew, that would unlock the rich metaphors with which Sanskrit could add to the number series already defined by Hebrew. After many years of unsuccessful research, the clues offered in two books permitted the complete numerical decipherment of Sanskrit. These two books are *The History of Hindu Mathematics* by B. Datta and *Vedic Mathematics* by Bharati K. Tirthaji, an affiliate of Yogananda. Neither text gave the codes in full, but both did provide the skeletal clues necessary to fully decipher each system. Once I had established the correct numerical attributes, I was able to use this key to unlock the pattern of Sanskrit letters upon the petals of the flowers composing the seven chakras. A complete analysis of the symbolism for these seven chakras can be found in the addendum to this chapter.

The rules which govern the numbering of Sanskrit are so complex that only a brief overview of each code will be given in this introduction. Basically, there are eight separate major esoteric alphanumeric codes for Sanskrit. Each was intended to flesh out a set of metaphors for the infinite number range, using such sophisticated techniques as alphabet letters as digits of numbers, zero as a place value, decimal fractions, and number values for letters as high as 100 quadrillion. Though these numerical ciphers for Sanskrit had a utilitarian application to create a very sophisticated body of scientific mathematical techniques, the core essential purpose of these codes, dating back to the origin of the Vedic hymns, is the ability to give symbolic meanings to abstract numbers.

The first four numerical codes for Sanskrit detailed in this section possess the same sophisticated basis for numbering. In this most elaborate method of all for numbering a language, each consonant or conjoined consonant is a digit of a composite number. Unlike the Western Hellenistic-Semitic tradition of adding the values of the individual letters of a word together, this Sanskrit code utilizes:

- Alphabet letters as digits of a number

- A base ten numbering system

- Zero as a place value for certain letters, and

- A floating decimal point that can be inserted at any point in a word to change the value of that word to a decimal fraction

The four codes detailed in this section are named:

- KaTaPaYa

- ARYaBhaTa II (digital variant)

- KaTaPaYa II (Kerala)

- KaTaPaYa III (Pali)

The most pristine of the four codes is the third code detailed, the Kerala variant of KaTaPaYa. This variant allows the best interface to the metaphors established by Hebrew, Greek, and Arabic. The original code of KaTaPaYa should also be studied, for it is the source of the other three variants. However, the Kerala variant, which I refer to as KaTaPaYa II, is averred by some to be the true Vedic code for Sanskrit, unlocking the hidden lore found in the written verses of the Vedic Hymns. If this is so, the symbolic metaphors found in the decoded Vedas would easily parallel the decoded Torah (Hebrew), New Testament (Greek), and Quran (Arabic).

After these four codes are outlined, examples of all four codes in action are given, followed by a detailed analysis of the numbers 31 and 93 (thrice 31), the two key numbers to Crowley's *Book of the Law.*

Next the code known as ARYaBhaTa is detailed, which is a variant to KaTaPaYa. In KaTaPaYa, the vowels receive no number or place value, but in ARYaBhaTa the combination of a vowel and a consonant determine the number value of a word. Further, in KaTaPaYa, the individual components of a word (consonants) are the digits of a number, but in ARYaBhaTa, the individual components of a word (consonants and their vowels) are added together to obtain the resultant number value of a word.

Note that in this particular code, the values assigned to individual Sanskrit consonants and vowels can be so astronomically high, that one consonant and vowel combination can result in a number value of one hundred quadrillion (18 place values)! Therefore, the ARYaBhaTa code was devised to flesh out the number range to an extent that most other number codes cannot offer. This code can yield metaphors for the enormous symbolic numbers encountered in such Sanskrit religious classics as the Vedas and the Mahabharata.

The ARYaBhaTa code may be the most difficult for the beginner to work with in analyzing Sanskrit words, but every rule necessary to understanding this code is clearly detailed in this chapter. Perseverance will pay off. As an example of how distinctly differently from KaTaPaYa this code generates a number value, let us look at the word *Yoga* in its original Sanskrit form:

- By KaTaPaYa II, YO + Ga = 1(0) + 3 = 13

- By ARYaBhaTa I, YO + Ga = 3,000,000,000,000,000 + 3 = 3,000,000,000,000,003

By KaTaPaYa, we get 13 as the key number for Yoga, but by ARYaBhaTa we get an astounding 3,000,000,000,000,003. One does not supplant the other, but rather the high value afforded by ARYaBhaTa is an extension of the lower value established by KaTaPaYa.

Next in this section, the two addition-based serial order codes are detailed. The first is the Southern Indian system, followed by the Pali variant. In the Southern Indian system, the serial order is set by the consonants, while in the Pali variant the serial order is set by the vowels. It is this Pali variant which influenced the development of the secret number code for Tibetan.

The Sanskrit section then ends with the eighth and last code, the Indian word numerals of Varahamikira. In this system, certain key words in Sanskrit can designate the number values. When these key words are combined, they produce the number value of word as composite digits of a number (not unlike KaTaPaYa).

In all eight of these codes certain words are numbered as examples. These examples should be copied and entered into your number files. Your files can then be expanded by choosing the Sanskrit alphabet code with which you are most comfortable. Then, with the aid of a good dictionary or source book on Sanskrit, and using the rules described in this chapter, your files can be expanded by direct research. If any one code could be recommended, I would suggest basing your research on the Kerala variant of KaTaPaYa.

The Sanskrit key ends with an addendum detailing the esoteric symbolism for the seven chakras. For the first time, the correct numerical values for the seven chakras are fully revealed. The Eastern chakra system premises a series of seven secret centers grouped within the spinal column and brain of the human body. The first or lowest chakra is situated at the base of the spine, while the seventh or highest chakra is located at the crown of the brain.

This system of esoteric physiology was introduced into Western occultism by the Theosophical movement and has been popularized by many writers of Western occult literature since that time. Blavatsky's own version of the chakras, as popularized by C. W. Leadbeater's *Chakras*, displaces the second chakra from its original position at the genitals to that of the spleen. However, with the advent of Arthur Avalon's publication of *The Serpent Power*, the correct allocations of the chakras were introduced into the mainstream of Western occultism.

It should be noted that Crowley's version of the Tarot, *The Book of Thoth*, uses Leadbeater's clairvoyant version of the chakras rather than the esoteric tantrik version which clearly shows the Sanskrit alphabet. Specifically, Key XI, Lust, shows the root chakra within the grail; Key VII, The Chariot, shows the naval chakra at the center of the charioteer's shield; Key XIX, The Sun, shows the heart chakra at the center of the Sun.

This addendum divides the commentary upon the seven chakras into two sections. The first section details the esoteric symbolism for each of the seven chakras in 33 tables, using Eastern and Western esoteric commentaries. The second section unlocks the number values for the 50 petals composing the six lower flowers of the chakra system.

In the first section, dealing with the symbolism of the tantrik chakra system, the 33 tables are first given followed by a commentary on each of the tables. These tables are keyed to each of the seven chakras. Therefore, when studying these tables, follow out all the correspondences for each of the seven centers. In this matter, their unique symbolic natures will become apparent. The tables describe the chakras as follows.

- Order
- Sanskrit Name

- Translation of Name
- Planetary Star (Eastern)
- Alchemical Element (Eastern)
- Position in Human Body (correct location, not blinded attributes)
- Function in Body
- Sense (derived from Tattva)
- Number of Rays or Petals
- Division of Spine into 33 Esoteric Joints (basis for 33° Freemasonry)
- Location in Body (according to Blavatsky)
- Location in Body (according to Leadbeater)
- Location in Body (according to Crowley)
- Location in Body (according to Fortune)
- Seven Worlds (Lokas)
- God-Form
- Goddess-Form
- Vehicle of God and Goddess
- Symbolic Animal
- Tattva (geometric shape)
- Color of Tattva according to element
- Color of Tattva according to Shat-Chakra
- Color of Tattva according to Shiva Sanhita
- Color of Tattva according to Leadbeater
- Color of Tattva according to Pranic
- ·Original Sanskrit Name
- Number Value of Name (according to KaTaPaYa II)
- Letters and Their Number (according to KaTaPaYa II)
- Seed Syllable and Number (according to KaTaPaYa II)
- Western Sevenfold Tree of Life Divisions (according to Crowley)
- Western Sevenfold Tree of Life Divisions (according to Fortune)
- Western Sevenfold Tree of Life Divisions (according to Seven Levels)
- Western Sevenfold Tree of Life Divisions (according to Seven Planetary Sephiroth)

The second section of the addendum, the 50 petal-alphabet letters, gives the correct number values for each of the chakras. In the first table, each of the 50 chakra petals is listed by chakra name, order of the petal (from 1–50), and corresponding Sanskrit letter. The Sanskrit letters are then given their esoteric number values by five different methods:

1. KaTaPaYa Number Values

2. ARYaBhaTa Number Values

3. Southern Indian Serial Number Values

4. Pali Serial Number Values

5. Alphabet Order

The deepest numerical secrets for these chakras are found in the KaTaPaYa number code. A final table shows the correspondence between the normal alphabet order for Sanskrit, and the esoteric order upon the chakras.

ORIGIN

6000–3000 BCE—Vedic Hymns, original source of alphabet code

800 BCE—Recorded hymns

400 CE—Establishment of Vedic number code in print (Katapayadhi)

500 CE—Aryabhata code appears in print

ALPHABET CODE

The Sanskrit Alphabet is composed of 16 vowels and 34 consonants. In terms of its mystical or esoteric development in India, this 50-character alphabet, known as the Deva-Nagari Script (Divine-City or Temple Writing), possesses three classification systems:

- As 50 basic symbols of categories of the universe

- As 50 basic number ciphers

- As 50 basic categories or divisions of the chakra scheme of the human body

As an alphabet of symbolic nature, the 16 vowels and 34 consonants each have a variety of symbolic interpretations. The symbolic interpretations for each specific alphabet character are based on both the graphic shape of the letter itself and special select sacred words which contain the specific letter. The following table shows the 50 letters of the Deva-Nagari script and their symbolic interpretations.

Symbolic Nature of the Sanskrit Alphabet

Sixteen Vowels

Initial	Letter w/Consonant	Transliteration	Symbolic Meaning
अ	—	A (a)	The first of three sounds composing "AUM"; symbolic of Vishnu, Brahma, and Siva. The negative particle, hence absence, negation, beyond comprehension. The concept of going inward, within or in; the life breath; the sound which forms all vocalization of words; 1st Kala (mask)
आ	T	Â	Interjection "yes"; compassion (ah); pain or regret; the concept of nearness, near to, towards from all sides. The reverse of action; the Goddess Lakshmi (Venus); 2nd Kala (hider)
इ	ि	I	Kamadeva (Cupid); desire, anger, compassion; wonder, awe; to go beyond, to obtain, reach; to undertake, learn, study; to approach; (3rd Kala (cool)
ई	ी	Î	Kamadeva (Cupid); dejection, pain, sorrow; perception or consciousness; to pervade, shine; 4th Kala (controller)
उ	ु	U	The second of three sounds composing "AUM"; command, acceptance, interrogation; 5th Kala (seductress)
ऊ	ू	Û	The Moon, calling, compassion, protection; of Shiva; 6th Kala (clear)
ऋ	ृ	Ri	To obtain, acquire, reach, raise towards, meet with; calling, invoking; 7th Kala (wet)
ॠ	ॄ	Rî	Warding off; exorcising; terror, fear; demon; 8th Kala (mixed)
ऌ	ॢ	Li	Clasp, cling to, stick, adhere, hold; 9th Kala (yoni)
ॡ	ॣ	Lî	Rock, sway, tremble, vibrate; 10th Kala (lustful)

Symbolic Nature of the Sanskrit Alphabet (cont'd.)

Sixteen Vowels (cont'd.)

Initial	Letter w/Consonant	Trans-literation	Symbolic Meaning
ए	े	E	Of Brahma (first of triad), creating; 11th Kala (agitator)
ऐ	ै	Ai	Of Siva (second of triad), destroying; 12th Kala (giver)
ओ	ो	O	Of Vishnu (third of triad), preserving; 13th Kala (bright)
औ	ौ	Au	Addressing, naming, calling, invoking; 14th Kala (lover)
अं	ं	Am	Beginning, first, creation; 15th Kala (flame)
अः	ः	Ah	End, last, dissolution; 16th Kala (elixir)

Thirty-Four Consonants

Letter	Transliteration	Symbolic Meaning
क	K	A knot or joint (of the spine); the head, the mind, a word, sound, a king, the soul, God (Brahman); fire, wind, cloud, air, the Sun; Garuda (the king of the birds), a peacock; happiness, joy, pleasure
ख	Kh	A dot (cipher), hole, cavity, hollow, the hollow of the tree, a wound, the apertures of the body; the jewels of the sky (the Sun, Moon, and stars), a planet, meteor, an arrow, the eastern mountain on which the Sun rises; a bird's nest, the flight in the air of the hawk, falcon, and Garuda; the divine woman, the Moon, smoke, darkness, snow, rain dew

Symbolic Nature of the Sanskrit Alphabet (cont'd.)

Thirty-Four Consonants (cont'd.)

Letter	Transliteration	Symbolic Meaning
ग	G	Buddha-nature; going, moving, being; a song, hymn; to have sexual intercourse with
घ	Gh	A bell; striking, killing; destroying; just, indeed, certainly
ङ	Ṅ	From the sea, wave of the ocean, fishhook
च	C	The Moon, a tortoise; to join words together (and), copulation, joining, linking; the one and the other; to move, wave, shake; cane, straw; a basket; a large black bee
छ	Ch	A part, fragment; kundalini bound three and a half times at the base of the spine
ज	J	Birth, living, born from, produced, or caused; being; luster; a battle, conqueror; an imp, poison, a sickle or hook
झ	Jh	Flash of light, sparkle, to happen at once; wind accompanied by rain; beating, jingling, rattling, shaking; roaring of the wind, hurricane, gale; drum, cymbal, metal ornaments; the age of Kali (Kali-Yuga)
ञ	Ñ	The branches of a tree; knowledge, wisdom, teaching; cosmic consciousness
ट	Ṭ	Sword, bow, hatchet, chisel, axe, spade, hoe; to tie, bind; a bird
ठ	Ṭh	Metallic sound; idol, deity, divinity
ड	Ḍ	Mixture, blend, riot, uproar, tumult, bombast, confusion
ढ	Ḍh	A double drum; warrior armed with a shield; a goose
ण	Ṇ	A lake, pool of water, many rivers coming together as one, a thread
त	T	A string, bow string, string of a musical instrument; a sinew, tail; a loom; a spell, magickal incantation, talisman, charm, medicine, remedy, drug

Symbolic Nature of the Sanskrit Alphabet (cont'd.)

Thirty-Four Consonants (cont'd.)

Letter	Transliteration	Symbolic Meaning
थ	Th	A mountain; reverence, auspiciousness, devotion, awe, terror; protection, preservation, the sound of a musical instrument
द	D	A wife; heat, fire, passion; giving, granting, producing, bestowing, imparting; gift, offering, present; divine, the heavens, omen, sign, divination
ध	Dh	Scale, bow; placing, holding; virture; merit (true wealth); Brahman; to seize, hold, grasp; to assume, exhibit; to suffer, undergo; to perform, do; to receive into oneself, admit; to cover, hide, deceive, obscure; to hinder, obstruct; to view, to aim at, to believe, to put faith in; to concentrate, put into focus; the inner self; the real self
न	N	Star, night, Moon; a pearl; the lotus plant, mother, the menstrual cycle; space, empty, vacant, naked; no not, negative
प	P	A leaf (of the Tree of Life), an egg; air, wind; guardian, ruler, protector; the Sun and Moon; the face
फ	Ph	Serpent coiled in a tree, the hood of a serpent; to swell, undulate, expand, bloom; fruit of a tree
ब	B	Deity, God-Head (Brahman); teacher; power, might, a seed, grain, letter of the alphabet; intelligence, the planet Mercury
भ	Bh	The planet Venus, the morning star; the zodiac, the number 27, the revolution of the planets
म	M	Magical formula, word of power, vibration of the seed syllable in the mouth of God which created the universe, Om; the Moon, water, the third eye; time, the cosmos, poison, drug; happiness
य	Y	One who goes or moves, a goer, mover; the animating principle, the true self as the rider of a carriage; day, sky, wind, air; union; the heart; fame

Symbolic Nature of the Sanskrit Alphabet (cont'd.)

Thirty-Four Consonants (cont'd.)

Letter	Transliteration	Symbolic Meaning
र	R	Fire, heat; sexual intercourse, love, desire; rapidity, speed; the color red
ल	L	Waves of the sea; rocking, moving, shaking, vibrating; to adhere, clasp, hold tight; love, pleasure, joy, bliss; to melt, dissolve; to lie with, rest; love play, the goddess Venus as Lakshmi
व	V	Circle, oval, the rim of the universe, the circular sky above; air, wind; the ocean; the arm; residence, dwelling, the world
श	Ṡ	Siva (God of Destruction); sword, weapon of war; destroyer
ष	Sh	Sixfold, the hexagonal cell of a bee; best, excellent; final emancipation
स	S	A snake; seven; the seven chakras, the seven stars of the "Big Dipper," the seven rishis (sages) who watch over our world
ह	H	The sound which ends creation, the last; the exhalation of breath; verily, indeed, certainly; blood or water as a mark of Siva
क्ष	Kṣ	The 34th consonant of the Sanskrit alphabet; the spiral, a coiling, ether, space, a conjunction of Ka + Sh, valued at zero in the Vedic code and treated as a separate letter in the chakra system
ळ	Ĺ	The 35th consonant of the Pali alphabet; the pelvis, the Mulhadhara chakra, Kundalini
:	Ḥ	The Visarga, two dots appearing at end of the word, equivalent to Ha, which receives no number value.
ꣳ	Ṁ	The Anvasika, one dot and crescent appearing above a letter, equivalent to M, which receives no number value
̇	Ṅg	The Anusvara, one dot appearing above a letter, equivalent to Ng, which receives no number value

The 34 consonants can combine into more than 300 combinations. When two or more consonants are combined to form a conjoined consonant sign, they are placed one below the other, or one after the other. They are then read from top to bottom, or left to right. The furthest sign below or to the right is the last consonant of the combination (and will be the basis for numbering that particular conjoined consonant).

The conjoined consonants are typically reduced in size, and usually the vertical downstroke, typical to all letters in Sanskrit, is removed. However the furthest letter to the right always retains this downstroke.

The specific letters forming most conjoined consonants are obvious, but in eight select combinations the letters are modified when conjoined to another:

1. क Ka + त Ta = क्त KTa

2. क Ka + ष Sha = क्ष or क्ष Kṣa
   (This combined consonant is the 34th consonant of the 50-letter chakra scheme, and is the positional zero in the Katapayadhi system.)

3. ज Ja + ञ Ña = ज्ञ JÑa

4. त Ta + त Ta = त्त TTa

5. द Da + ध Dha = द्ध DDha

6. र Ra as last letter of combination is a slanting foot:

   त Ta + र Ra = त्र TRa

7. र Ra as first letter of combination is a hook:

   र Ra + त Ta = र्त RTa

8. श Ṡa in combination with other letters becomes:

   श Ṡa + व Va = श्व ṠVa

With the above guidelines most combined consonants occuring in Sanskrit words will be possible to clearly decipher.

Sanskrit Alphanumerics

The origin of the Sanskrit alphabet number code (the so-called "Vedic Number Code") is obscured by history. The code Katapayadhi, however, is associated by its name to the Vedic hymns, and serves as a key for unlocking the number value of the 50-letter Sanskrit alphabet.

The Vedic hymns may date back as far as 6000 BCE in terms of an oral tradition. However, the recording of these hymns occurred between 1400 and 800 BCE. The actual recording of the Vedic number code Katapayadhi occurred between 300 and 400 CE. It assumed the form of algebraic like notation, which facilitated the memorization of complex mathematical formulae, but the true nature of this code is cryptographic, allowing a secret cipher system for the poetical structure of the Vedas.

This code has gone through four basic permutations, and it is the first and third permutation (the Kerala variant) which reveal the most sublime alpha-number metaphors for Sanskrit. The following table details these four alpha codes for Sanskrit.

The Thirty-Four Sanskrit Consonants

Sanskrit	Trans-literation	KaTa-PaYa	ARYa-BhaTa II	KaTaPaYa II (Kerala Variant)	KaTaPaYa III (Pali Variant)
क	K	1	1	1	1
ट	Ṭ	1	1	1	1
प	P	1	1	1	1
य	Y	1	1	1	1
ख	Kh	2	2	2	2
ठ	Ṭh	2	2	2	2
फ	Ph	2	2	2	2
र	R	2	2	2	2
ग	G	3	3	3	3
ड	Ḍ	3	3	3	3
ब	B	3	3	3	3
ल	L	3	3	3	3
घ	Gh	4	4	4	4
ढ	Ḍh	4	4	4	4
भ	Bh	4	4	4	4
व	V	4	4	4	4
ङ	Ṅ	5	5	5	5
ण	Ṇ	5	5	5	5
म	M	5	5	5	5
श	Ś	5	5	5	—
च	C	6	6	6	6
त	T	6	6	6	6

The Thirty-Four Sanskrit Consonants (cont'd.)

Sanskrit	Trans-literation	KaTa-PaYa	ARYa-BhaTa II	KaTaPaYa II (Kerala Variant)	KaTaPaYa III (Pali Variant)
ष	Sh	6	6	6	—
छ	Ch	7	7	7	7
थ	Th	7	7	7	7
स	S	7	7	7	5
ज	J	8	8	8	8
द	D	8	8	8	8
ह	H	8	8	8	6
झ	Jh	9	9	9	9
ध	Dh	9	9	9	9
ञ	Ñ	0 (place value)	0 (place value)	0 (place value)	0 (place value)
न	N	0 (place value)	0 (place value)	0 (place value)	0 (place value)
क्ष	Kṣ	0 (place value)	0 (place value)	0 (place value)	0 (place value)
ळ	(Ĺ)	—	—	—	7

The Sixteen Sanskrit Vowels

PV = Place Value
NV = No value
IWA = If Written Alone (i.e., without a conjoined consonant)

Sanskrit	Trans-literation	KaTa-PaYa	ARYa-BhaTa II	KaTaPaYa II (Kerala Variant)	KaTaPaYa III (Pali Variant)
अ	A (a)	PV IWA	NV or PV	NV or PV	PV IWA
आ	Â	PV IWA	NV or PV	NV or PV	PV IWA
इ	I	PV IWA	NV or PV	NV or PV	PV IWA
ई	Î	PV IWA	NV or PV	NV or PV	PV IWA
उ	U	PV IWA	NV or PV	NV or PV	PV IWA

The Sixteen Sanskrit Vowels (cont'd.)

Sanskrit	Trans-literation	KaTa-PaYa	ARYa-BhaTa II	KaTaPaYa II (Kerala Variant)	KaTaPaYa III (Pali Variant)
ऊ	Û	PV IWA	NV or PV	NV or PV	PV IWA
ऋ	Ri	PV IWA	NV or PV	NV or PV	PV IWA
ॠ	Rî	PV IWA	NV or PV	NV or PV	PV IWA
ऌ	Li	PV IWA	NV or PV	NV or PV	PV IWA
ॡ	Lî	PV IWA	NV or PV	NV or PV	PV IWA
ए	E	PV IWA	NV or PV	NV or PV	PV IWA
ऐ	Ai	PV IWA	NV or PV	NV or PV	PV IWA
ओ	O	PV IWA	NV or PV	NV or PV	PV IWA
औ	Au	PV IWA	NV or PV	NV or PV	PV IWA
अं	Am	PV IWA	NV or PV	NV or PV	PV IWA
अः	Ah	PV IWA	NV or PV	NV or PV	PV IWA

Note that in all four variants the consonants Ka Ta Pa Ya are each valued at 1. Thus Katapayadhi means the science (Dhi) of equating KaTaPaYa to 1111 as a number code.

The above table of values for the alphabet is used for substituting the number value of a component digit for each letter of the word (usually only consonants). Thus a word of one consonant would be valued as a one-digit number, a word of two consonants would be valued as a two-digit number, and so on. The rules for KaTaPaYaDhi and its three variants are as follows.

FORMATION OF NUMBER

KaTaPaYa:

- Right to left formation of the composite number. The letter denoting the units place value is the letter written first in any given word.

- Consonants conjoined to vowels receive a number value. If a consonant is written alone without a qualifying vowel, it has no value.

- When two or more consonants are conjoined, only the last sounded has numerical value.

- Vowels written alone receive the place value of zero. Vowels qualified by a consonant receive no value.

ARBhaYaTa II (a sophistication of ARBhaYaTa I)

- Left to right formation (resembling the digits of numbers). The letter denoting the units place is always the letter written last.

- Consonants do not need to be conjoined to vowels to receive number value.

- When two or more consonants are conjoined, each consonant is a successive digit of the composite number.

- Vowels have no place or number value.

KaTaPaYa II (Kerala Variant)

- Left to right formation of the composite number. The letter denoting the units place is written last.

- Consonants do not need to be conjoined to vowels to receive number value.

- When two or more consonants are conjoined, only the last consonant has numerical value.

- Vowels have no place or number value (and represent symbolically that which is unnumbered and unsounded)

KaTaPaYa III (Pali Variant)

The rules are the same as those given above for KaTaPaYa I, with the following exceptions:

- Two letters in Sanskrit are not in the Pali script: Ṡ, valued at 5, and Sh, valued at 6. With these removed, the letter S (usually 7) becomes 5, while the letter H (usually 8) becomes 6.

- Pali has a letter not in Sanskrit: Ḷ, valued at 7, because this letter follows H, valued at 6

These four Vedic number codes diverge from the simplicity of the Semitic-Hellenistic additional systems found in the alphabet codes of the West and Middle East. This Far Eastern system represents the actual digits of the number value by the letters which form any word. As a further sophistication, a decimal point can be interjected before or after any digit composing the number value of any given word (transforming a whole number into a fraction).

As an example, the following three Sanskrit words will be numbered in order to illustrate the three sophisticated alpha-number codes for Sanskrit:

YOGa—the name for the spiritual discipline of Yoga

BUDDha—the proper name for Buddha, also "awakened," "enlightened"

AKṣaN—"eye"

- By KTPY I (KaTaPaYa 1)

  YOGa = 31 (Ga = 3, YO = 1)

  BUDDha = 93 (DDha = 9, BU = 3)

AKṣaN = 00 (N = no value, Kṣa = 0, A = 0)

- By ARBY II (ARBhAYaTa 2)

YOGa = 13 (YO = 1, Ga = 3)

BUDDha = 389 (BU = 3, D = 8, Dha = 9)

AKṣaN = 00 (Kṣ = 0, N = 0)

- By KTPY II (KaTaPaYa, Kerala variant)

YOGa = 13 (YO = 1, Ga = 3)

BUDDha = 39 (BU =3 , DDha = 9)

AKṣaN = 00 (Kṣ = 0, N = 0)

- By KTPY III (KaTaPaYa, Pali variant)

Same as KTPY I above

SANSKRIT AND THE 93 CURRENT

The most recondite and precise word-meanings for the Thelemic numbers 31 and 93 found throughout the writings of Aleister Crowley can be found in the Sanskrit language in light of the two number codes Katapayadhi and the Kerala variant of Katapayadhi. The following analysis details the rich metaphors Sanskrit possesses for the 93 current.

31 =

(KTPY II) (Kerala Variant)

GP

1. GOPÎ—Krishna as the watcher of the cowherd; female watcher, cowherdess; goddess of yoga; wife

GY

2. GaNYa—To be counted, calculated

3 GUHYa—To be concealed, hidden; kept secret; mystery; silently

4. AGRiHYa—Inconceivable; beyond (the realm of the senses)

5. AGOHYa—Not be hidden, kept secret

ḌP

6. UḌUPa—Moon

BK

7. BUKKa—Heart

BY

8. BUDhNYa—The depths; dragon of the deep

9. BODhYa—To be understood; to be instructed; to be brought to one's senses

LK

10. LOK—See, perceive, regard; observe, behold, know

11. LOKa—World, sphere, universe; space; division of the universe into heaven and earth; the universe subdivided into three, seven, and ten worlds

12. ALIKa—Forehead

13. ÂLOKa—Seeing, looking; sight, light, luster

14. ULÛKa—Owl

LṬ

15. LÂTa—Woman, belonging to woman

LP

16. LaP—Speech; the mouth (tongue); talk, whisper, murmur; address, converse, teach

17. LIP—Ointment, drug, poison; anoint, smear, pollute

18. LIPI—Writing, handwriting, inscription; written letter or line

19. LEPa—Anointing, smearing; ointment, moral taint, sin

20. LOPa—Transgression, violation

LY

21. LaYa—Extinction, dissolution; absorption, destruction; death, rest, repose; visualizing the chakra system within the body

22. ÂLaYa—Dwelling place, house; seat

23. LeKhYa—To be written down, recorded, written document; book, scroll; drawing; illustration, painting, symbol

24. LeŚYa—Light

25. LOKYa—Lawful, correct, real; bestowing freedom

(KTPY I)

PG

26. PÛGa—Society

YG

27. YÂGa—Sacrifice

28. YUGa—Yoke, pair, double; generation, period of life; cosmic age, world age; race of mankind

29. YOGa—Discipline, exertion, fitness; yoking; team, vehicle; combination, mixture, union; unity of soul and body; concentration

KL

30. KaLÂ—Small part of time; 1/16th of Moon's disk; the 16th secret sexual secretion of the yoni

31. KÂLa—Dark blue, black; the black in the eye (a token of Siva); age, era, time, due season, hour; appointed or right time; fate, death, God of Death

32. KaLÎ—Side of a die marked with one point

33. KÂLÎ—Goddess of Birth and Death as the Black Mother; the color black

34. KILa—Game; playing

35. KULÂ—Tantrik circle of initiates (usually 32 couples); secret circle of initiates

36. KULI—Thunderbolt (of Indra); the Tantrik sexual posture the thunderbolt

PL

37. PaLa—Flesh

38. PÂLa—Watchman, guardian; protector of the earth

39. PaLI—Female guardian

40. AuPaLa—Made of stone

YL

41. VYÂLa—Beast of prey

93 =

(KTPY II) (Kerala Variant)

DhL

43. DhULI—Pollen

(KTPY I)

BDh

43. BÂDhA—Resistance; suffering; tormentor; pain

44. BaNDha—Bond, fettered; posture, position of hands and feet

45. BUDDhI—Understanding; comprehension, perception; mind, intelligence; reason, intellect; meditate upon

46. BODha—Buddha; Mercury; blossoming of flowers; awakening, arousal; consciousness, waking state; dawn

47. BODhI—Enlightenment; the Bodhi tree of knowledge under which the Buddha obtained enlightenment

LDh

48. LaBDha—Obtain, acquire, find, discover, fulfill

49. LaBDhI—Discovery or perception of

50. LUBDha—The star Sirius; the hunter

ARYABHATA NUMBER CODE

ARYaBhaTa, a variant of the code KaTaPaYaDhi, appeared in the 5th century CE. Named after its author, Aryabhata the Elder, this code was primarily used as a mathematical code.

The rules for Aryabhata are as follows.

ARYaBhaTa I (499 CE)

- Only a limited number of vowels are used (9 as opposed to 16).

- Thirty-three consonants are divided into 25 *varga* and 8 *avarga* letters. ("Varga" and "Avarga" are Sanskrit words meaning "normal letter" and "variant letter")

- The letters of any word form the digits of a composite number. This code is digital (positional) rather than additional.

- Vowels determine the place value of the number, consonants the actual number value of any given place value.

- Each of the 9 select vowels (A, I, U, Ri, Li, E, Ai, O, Au) has two place values, varga and avarga. The varga value is used when the vowel is joined to one of the 25 varga consonants (from K to M), while the avarga value is used when the vowel is joined to one of the 8 avarga consonants (from Y to H).

- The 33 varga and avarga consonants receive the following number values.

The Twenty-Five Varga Letters

क K = 1	च C = 6	ट Ṭ = 11	त T = 16	प P = 21
ख Kh = 2	छ Ch = 7	ठ Ṭh = 12	थ Th = 17	फ Ph = 22
ग G = 3	ज J = 8	ड Ḍ = 13	द D = 18	ब B = 23
घ Gh = 4	झ Jh = 9	ढ Ḍh = 14	ध Dh = 19	भ Bh = 24
ङ Ṅ = 5	ञ Ñ = 10	ण Ṇ = 15	न N = 20	म M = 25

The Eight Avarga Letters

य Y = 3	श Ś = 7
र R = 4	ष Sh = 8
ल L = 5	स S = 9
व V = 6	ह H = 10

- The double varga-avarga place values for the nine vowels are as shown in the table on the opposite page.

The Varga-Avarga Place Values

Vowel		When Combined with Varga Consonants	When Combined with Avarga Consonants	Number of Zeroes Added to Consonant	
				Varga	Avarga
अ	A (a)	units place	tens	—	1
इ	I	hundreds	thousands	2	3
उ	U	ten thousands	one hundred thousands	4	5
ऋ	Ri	one millon	ten million	6	7
ॡ	Li	one hundred million	one billion	8	9
ए	E	ten billon	one hundred billion	10	11
ऐ	Ai	one trillion	ten trillion	12	13
ओ	O	one hundred trillion	one quadrillion	14	15
औ	Au	ten quadrillion quadrillion	one hundred quadrillion	16	17

Composite Number

0	0	0,	0	0	0,	0	0	0,	0	0	0,	0	0	0,	0	0	0
(A)	(V)	(A)	(V)	(A)	(V)	(A)	(V)	(A)	(V)	(A)	(V)	(A)	(V)	(A)	(V)	(A)	(V)
Au		O		Ai		E		Li		Ri		U		I		A	

(A) = Avarga, (V) = Varga

- When a vowel stands alone it receives no number or place value.

- When a vowel is conjoined to a consonant, it determines the place value of that consonant. Each vowel has two place values; thus the correct place value is determined by whether the consonant conjoined to a vowel is avarga or varga. As an example, the Sanskrit letters KI and YI will be numbered. The vowel "I" represents both the hundreds place (varga) and the thousands place (avarga). The varga consonant "K" is valued at 1, while the avarga consonant "Y" is 3. Thus "KI" would be numbered as 100 (because "K" is a varga consonant valued at 1 and "I" is the hundreds place when joined to a varga consonant), while "YI" would be numbered as 3,000 (because "Y" is an avarga consonant valued at 3, and "I" is the thousands place when joined to an avarga consonant).

- When two consonants are joined to one vowel, the number value representing both consonants is given the avarga-varga place value of the same vowel. In the word "YKI," the consonants "Y" and "K" (3 + 1) would both be given the place value of "I." Since "Y" is avarga and "K" is varga, "I" as avarga would make "Y" 3000 and "I" as varga would make "K" 100. Thus "YKI" represents the number 3100.

• The following three words numbered by Aryabhata I will help illustrate this complex mathmatical-digital code for the Sanskrit alphabet.

YOGa = 3,000,000,000,000,003. "Y" is an avarga consonant valued at 3, joined to the vowel "O," which as an avarga place value is one quadrillion. Thus "YO" is three quadrillion. "G" is a varga consonant valued at 3, joined to the vowel "A," which as a varga place value is the units place. Thus "Ga" is 3. Combined, YOGa is three quadrillion and three.

BUDDha = 23,037. "B" is a varga consonant valued at 23, joined to the vowel "U," which as a varga place value is the ten thousands place. Thus "BU" is 23,000. "DDha" is composed of two varga consonants, "D" and "Dh," valued at 18 and 19, joined to the vowel "A," which as a varga place value is the units place. Thus D + Dh = 18 + 19 = 37. "BU" conjoined to "DDha" becomes 23,000 + 37 = 23,037.

NIRVANa = 2,115. "N" is a varga consonant valued at 20, joined to the vowel "I," which as a varga place value is the hundreds place. Thus "NI" = 20 x 100 = 2000. "RVA" is composed of two avarga consonants, "R" and "V," valued at 4 and 6, joined to the vowel "A," which as an avarga place value is the tens place. Thus "RVA" = (4 x 10) + (6 x 10) = 40 + 60 = 100. "NA" is a varga consonant valued at 15, joined to the vowel "A," which as a varga place value is the units place. Thus "Na" is 15. Together, "NI" + "RVA"+ "Na" = 2000 + 100 + 15 = 2,115

Note that ARYaBHaTa created a variant of the KaTaPaYaDhi system, which is described above as ARYaBhaTa II.

SERIAL ALPHABET CODES

A third number system, used in volume, chapter, and page numbering of sacred texts, was invented in Southern India (Malabar and Andhra). This system used the serial order of the 34 consonants (Ka through Kṣa) to denote the number values 1 through 34. With the addition of 16 vowels, the number range 1 through 544 was produced. This system is the source for the Tibetan alpha-number code of Thon-mi-Sambhota.

In Pali, a variant of this serial code occurred. By the Pali method, the vowels A through Am represent 1 through 16, while the 34 consonants qualify the number range from 1 through 544. On the opposite page are two tables delineating the alphabet code as both single letters and conjoined consonants and vowels.

Serial Value—Sanskrit Vowels

Letter		S. Indian	Pali
अ	A (a)	0	1
आ	Â	34	2
इ	I	68	3
ई	Î	102	4
उ	U	136	5
ऊ	Û	170	6
ऋ	Ri	204	7
ॠ	Rî	238	8
ऌ	Li	272	9
ॡ	Lî	306	10
ए	E	340	11
ऐ	Ai	374	12
ओ	O	408	13
औ	Au	442	14
अं	Am	476	15
अः	Ah	510	16

Serial Order—Sanskrit Consonants

Letter		S. Indian	Pali	Letter		S. Indian	Pali
क	K	1	0	द	D	18	272
ख	Kh	2	16	ध	Dh	19	288
ग	G	3	32	न	N	20	304
घ	Gh	4	48	प	P	21	320
ङ	Ṅ	5	64	फ	Ph	22	336
च	C	6	80	ब	B	23	352
छ	Ch	7	96	भ	Bh	24	368
ज	J	8	112	म	M	25	384
झ	Jh	9	128	य	Y	26	400
ञ	Ñ	10	144	र	R	27	416
ट	Ṭ	11	160	ल	L	28	432
ठ	Ṭh	12	176	व	V	29	448
ड	Ḍ	13	192	श	Ṡ	30	464
ढ	Ḍh	14	208	ष	Sh	31	480
ण	Ṇ	15	224	स	S	32	496
त	T	16	240	ह	H	33	512
थ	Th	17	256	क्ष	Kṣ	34	528

Southern Indian Serial Alphabet Code

34 Consonants		16 Vowels														
		A	Â	I	Î	U	Û	Ri	Rî	Li	Lî	E	Ai	O	Au	Am	Ah
K	1	35	69	103	137	171	205	239	273	307	341	375	409	443	477	511
Kh	2	36	70	104	138	172	206	240	274	308	342	376	410	444	478	512
G	3	37	71	105	139	173	207	241	275	309	343	377	411	445	479	513
Gh	4	38	72	106	140	174	208	242	276	310	344	378	412	446	480	514
Ṅ	5	39	73	107	141	175	209	243	277	311	345	379	413	447	481	515
C	6	40	74	108	142	176	210	244	278	312	346	380	414	448	482	516
Ch	7	41	75	109	143	177	211	245	279	313	347	381	415	449	483	517
J	8	42	76	110	144	178	212	246	280	314	348	382	416	450	484	518
Jh	9	43	77	111	145	179	213	247	281	315	349	383	417	451	485	519
Ñ	10	44	78	112	146	180	214	248	282	316	350	384	418	452	486	520
Ṭ	11	45	79	113	147	181	215	249	283	317	351	385	419	453	487	521
Ṭh	12	46	80	114	148	182	216	250	284	318	352	386	420	454	488	522
Ḍ	13	47	81	115	149	183	217	251	285	319	353	387	421	455	489	523
Ḍh	14	48	82	116	150	184	218	252	286	320	354	388	422	456	490	524
Ṇ	15	49	83	117	151	185	219	253	287	321	355	389	423	457	491	525
T	16	50	84	118	152	186	220	254	288	322	356	390	424	458	492	526
Th	17	51	85	119	153	187	221	255	289	323	357	391	425	459	493	527
D	18	52	86	120	154	188	222	256	290	324	358	392	426	460	494	528
Dh	19	53	87	121	155	189	223	257	291	325	359	393	427	461	495	529
N	20	54	88	122	156	190	224	258	292	326	360	394	428	462	496	530
P	21	55	89	123	157	191	225	259	293	327	361	395	429	463	497	531
Ph	22	56	90	124	158	192	226	260	294	328	362	396	430	464	498	532
B	23	57	91	125	159	193	227	261	295	329	363	397	431	465	499	533
Bh	24	58	92	126	160	194	228	262	296	330	364	398	432	466	500	534
M	25	59	93	127	161	195	229	263	297	331	365	399	433	467	501	535
Y	26	60	94	128	162	196	230	264	298	332	366	400	434	468	502	536
R	27	61	95	129	163	197	231	265	299	333	367	401	435	469	503	537
L	28	62	96	130	164	198	232	266	300	334	368	402	436	470	504	538
V	29	63	97	131	165	199	233	267	301	335	369	403	437	471	505	539
Ṡ	30	64	98	132	166	200	234	268	302	336	370	404	438	472	506	540
Sh	31	65	99	133	167	201	235	269	303	337	371	405	439	473	507	541
S	32	66	100	134	168	202	236	270	304	338	372	406	440	474	508	542
H	33	67	101	135	169	203	237	271	305	339	373	407	441	475	509	543
Kṣ	34	68	102	136	170	204	238	272	306	340	374	408	442	476	510	544

Pali Serial Alphabet Code

34 Consonants

	16 Vowels															
	A	Â	I	Î	U	Û	Ri	Rî	Li	Lî	E	Ai	O	Au	Am	Ah
K	1	2	3	4	5	6	7	8	9	10	11	12	13	14	15	16
Kh	17	18	19	20	21	22	23	24	25	26	27	28	29	30	31	32
G	33	34	35	36	37	38	39	40	41	42	43	44	45	46	47	48
Gh	49	50	51	52	53	54	55	56	57	58	59	60	61	62	63	64
Ṅ	65	66	67	68	69	70	71	72	73	74	75	76	77	78	79	80
C	81	82	83	84	85	86	87	88	89	90	91	92	93	94	95	96
Ch	97	98	99	100	101	102	103	104	105	106	107	108	109	110	111	112
J	113	114	115	116	117	118	119	120	121	122	123	124	125	126	127	128
Jh	129	130	131	132	133	134	135	136	137	138	139	140	141	142	143	144
Ñ	145	146	147	148	149	150	151	152	153	154	155	156	157	158	159	160
Ṭ	161	162	163	164	165	166	167	168	169	170	171	172	173	174	175	176
Ṭh	177	178	179	180	181	182	183	184	185	186	187	188	189	190	191	192
Ḍ	193	194	195	196	197	198	199	200	201	202	203	204	205	206	207	208
Ḍh	209	210	211	212	213	214	215	216	217	218	219	220	221	222	223	224
Ṇ	225	226	227	228	229	230	231	232	233	234	235	236	237	238	239	240
T	241	242	243	244	245	246	247	248	249	250	251	252	253	254	255	256
Th	257	258	259	260	261	262	263	264	265	266	267	268	269	270	271	272
D	273	274	275	276	277	278	279	280	281	282	283	284	285	286	287	288
Dh	289	290	291	292	293	294	295	296	297	298	299	300	301	302	303	304
N	305	306	307	308	309	310	311	312	313	314	315	316	317	318	319	320
P	321	322	323	324	325	326	327	328	329	330	331	332	333	334	335	336
Ph	337	338	339	340	341	342	343	344	345	346	347	348	349	350	351	352
B	353	354	355	356	357	358	359	360	361	362	363	364	365	366	367	368
Bh	369	370	371	372	373	374	375	376	377	378	379	380	381	382	383	384
M	385	386	387	388	389	390	391	392	393	394	395	396	397	398	399	400
Y	401	402	403	404	405	406	407	408	409	410	411	412	413	414	415	416
R	417	418	419	420	421	422	423	424	425	426	427	428	429	430	431	432
L	433	434	435	436	437	438	439	440	441	442	443	444	445	446	447	448
V	449	450	451	452	453	454	455	456	457	458	459	460	461	462	463	464
Ś	465	466	467	468	469	470	471	472	473	474	475	476	477	478	479	480
Sh	481	482	483	484	485	485	487	488	489	490	491	492	493	494	495	496
S	497	498	499	500	501	502	503	504	505	506	507	508	509	510	511	512
H	513	514	515	516	517	518	519	520	5241	522	523	524	525	526	527	528
Kṣ	529	530	531	532	533	534	535	536	537	538	539	540	541	542	543	544

Poetic Word-Numerals

Beyond the assignment of the alphabet as numbers, the use of word-symbols to describe the numerals 0 through 9 (as well as a select few numbers above 9) was developed around 500 CE. These metaphors would be substituted in the text for a number which allowed a certain amount of poetical leeway in assigning words to numbers.

The earliest record of this system is found in the mathematical writings of Varahamihira, occurring around the same time that both the Katapayadhi and Aryabhata systems were first put into print.

The metaphors for the number series (which resemble the Pythagorean metaphors for number) are as follows.

The Indian Word-Numerals of Varahamihira

Number	Metaphors
0	Void (ŚÛNYa)
	Empty Space of Heaven (ÂKÂŚa, AMBaRa)
	Dot (BINDU)
1	One Piece (RÛPa)
	The Moon (INDU, ŚAŚIN, ŚITARaŚMI, RAŚMI)
	The Earth (BhÛ, MaHÎ)
	Beginning (ÂDI)
	Brahman (PITÂMaHa)
	The Hero (NÂKaYa)
	The Body (TANU)
2	First Pair, Twins (YaMa)
	The Twin Gods (AŚVIN, DaSRa)
	Two Wings (PaKṣa)
	The Two Hands (KaRa)
	The Two Eyes (NaYaNa)
	The Two Arms (BÂHU)
	The Two Ears (KaRNa)
	The Two Ankles (GULPha)
	Husband and Wife (KUṬUMBa)
	Sun and Moon (RaVI CaNDRAu)
3	Sacrificial Fire (AGNI)
	The Three Ramas (of Poetry) (RÂMÂḤ)
	The Three Elements (GUṆa)
	The Three Worlds (TRILOKa)
	Three Times (TRIKÂLa)
	Three Sounds (TRIGaTa)
	Three Eyes of Siva (TRINETRa)
	Male Triplets (SaHODaRÂḤ)

The Indian Word-Numerals of Varahamihira (cont'd.)

Number	Metaphors

Number   Metaphors

4
Four Dice (KRiTa, ÂYa)
The Fourfold Vedas (VEDa, ŚRUTI)
The Four Oceans (ABDhI, JaLaDhI)
The Four Cardinal Points (DIŚ)
The Four Ages of the World (YUGa)
Four Castes (VaRNa)
Four Brothers (BaNDhU)
Four Faces of Brahma (BRaHMÂSYa)
Four Arms of Vishnu (HaRIBaHÛ)
Four Positions of Human Body (IRYa)

5
The Five Elements (BhÛTa)
The Fivefold Breaths (PRÂNa)
The Five Senses (INDRIYa)
The Objects of the Five Senses (ARTha, VIShaYa)
The Five Arrows of Desire (KÂMa, IShU)
The Five Jewels (RaTNa)
The Five Sons of Pandu (PÂNDaVa)
The Five Faces of Shiva (RUDRÂSYa)
The Five Sacrifices (MaHÂYaJÑa)

6
Six Faces of Kumara (KUMÂRaVaDaNa)
Six Months of the Year (MÂSÂRDha)
Six Flavors (RaSa)
Six Seasons (RiTU)
Six Principle Philosophical Systems (DaRŚaNa)
Six Principle Tunes, Modes (RÂGa)
Sixfold Body (KÂYa)
The Auxiliary Teachings of the Vedas (ANGa)
The (Internal) Foes (of Men) (ARI)

7
Seven Notes (Vowels) (SVaRa)
Seven Elements (DhÂTU)
Seven Sciences (DhÎ)
Seven Horses of the Chariot of the Sun (AŚVa)
Seven Mountains (AGa)
Seven Metrical Scales (ChaNDaS)
Seven Sages of the Night Sky (RiShI, MUNI)
Fear (BhaYa)

8
The Elephants Guarding the Eight Directions (GaJa)
Eight Forms of Shiva (MÛRTI)
Eight Supernatural Powers (SIDDhI)
Eight Auspicious Omens (MaNGaLa)
Eight Classes of Snakes (NÂGa, AHI)
Eight Vasu Gods (VaSU)
Octosyllabic Metre (ANUShTUBh)

The Indian Word-Numerals of Varahamihira (cont'd.)

Number	Metaphors
9	Nine Numerals (ANKa)
	Nine Planets (GRaHa)
	Nine Orifices of the Body (ChIDRa)
	Nine Nandas (NaNDa)
	Nine Treasures (of Kubera) (NIDhI)
	The God Brahma (AJa)
10	The Moon and The Cipher (KhENDU)
	The Points of Horizon (DISaH)
	Ten Incarnations of Vishnu (AVaTÂRa)
	Ten Heads of Ravana (RÂVaNaSIRaS)
	Ten Ritual Ceremonies (KaRMaN)
11	Acquirement of Knowledge (LÂBha)
	The Eleven Rudras (RUDRa)
	Shiva, First of the Gods (SIVa)
	Isa, First of the Gods (ÎSa)
12	The Twelve Suns (ARKa)
	The Twelve Sun Gods (ÂDITYa)
13	The Thirteen All Encompassing Gods (VISVa)
	Kama, The Most Famous of Thirteen (KÂMa)
	Thirteen Syllable Meter (ATIJaGaTÎ)
14	The Fourteen Worlds (LOKa)
	The Fourteen Sages (MaNU)
	The Fourteen Indras (INDRA)
15	Fifteen Lunar Days (TIThI)
	Fifteen Solar Days (AHaN)
	One-Half of a Month (PaKṣa)
16	Sixteen Divisions of the Tantrik Lunar Cycle (KaLÂ)
	Sixteen Famous Kings (BhÛPa)
	Sixteen Syllable Meter (AShṬI)
17	Seventeen Syllable Meter (ATYaShṬI)
18	Eighteen Syllable Meter (DhRiTI)
19	Nineteen Syllable Meter (ATIDhRiTI)
20	The Twenty Nails of the Hands and Feet (NaKha)
	Twenty Syllable Meter (KRiTI)
21	Twenty-One Syllable Meter (UTKRiTI)
	Heaven (SVaRGa)
22	Birth (JÂTI)
24	Twenty-Four Teachings of the Jains (JINa)

The Indian Word-Numerals of Varahamihira (cont'd.)

Number   Metaphors

25   Twenty-Five Tattvas (TaTTVa)

26   Twenty-Six Syllable Meter (UTKRiTI)

28   Twenty-Eight Lunar Mansions (NaKṣaTRa)

32   The Thirty-Two Teeth (DaNTa)

33   The Thirty-Three Gods of Heaven (SURa)

40   The Forty Hells (PÂÑCaSIDDhÂNTIKÂ)

49   The Forty-Nine Tones (TÂNa)

These metaphors allow composite numbers (in base 10, with a positional zero) to be formed by combining select word numerals. The order of the numbers are in ascending powers of ten from left to right.

Thus the three numbers 93, 418, and 330 could be written as follows:

93 = Element-Planet, GUNA-GRAHA, 3 + 9(0) = 93

418 = Snake-Moon-Dice, NAGA-RASMI-KRITA, 8 + 1(0) + 4(00) = 418

330 = Void-3 Times-3 Worlds, SUNYA-TRIKALA-TRILOKA,
        0 + 3(0) + 3(00) = 330, or

330 = Etheric Space-The Gods, AKASHA-SURA, 0 + 33(0) = 330

Addendum

The Chakras

The word "chakra" in Sanskrit can be defined as both a blossoming flower and a revolving (potter's) wheel. Both connote a sense of power, either as a circular blossoming forth, or a spiral twist.

In the West these same chakras are referred to as interior stars or precious alchemical metals.

Though in the Eastern tantrik tradition the human body contains seven orthodox chakras, or vortices of energy, within it, there exist literally thousands of such centers. These myriad centers of energy have their counterpart in China as acupuncture points.

Kundalini, the energy latent at the base of the spine, traverses the pathway of the chakras from the first or lowest chakra, Muladhara, to the last or highest chakra, Sahasrara. Kundalini is symbolized by a serpent coiled 3-1/2 times around an upright lingam in the center of the Muladhara chakra. Through tantrik yoga meditational techniques, each of the chakras is pierced by the rising kundalini until the lowest is united with the highest.

This union is symbolized by Shiva (Male) and Shakti (Female) united in sexual intercourse (Shiva being the brow chakra and Shakti being the lowest chakra). This union occurring in the crown chakra produces the state of enlightenment known as Satya (ultimate reality) and Nirvana (absolute existence), the goal of yoga.

Chakra in the original Sanskrit (CaKRa) is valued at 62 by the KaTa-PaYaDhi number system. The equivalent Sanskrit words which total 62 bring to light much of the chakra symbolism discussed above, for 62 is also the value in Sanskrit of:

- TÂRÂ—Star, luminary

- ANTaRa—Inner, within, inward; entrance

- UTTaRa—North, higher, upper, left

- CaNDRa—Shining, bright; tail of a peacock

- CITRa—Rainbow, variegated, many colored

These five meanings describe the chakras as bright inner stars whose colors span the spectrum of the rainbow. A sixth word connects "chakra" directly to Tantra, for "Tantra" is also valued at 62:

- TaNTRa—Magickal system; loom; warp; essence; groundwork

Thus the formula . . .

Chakra = 62 = Tantra

. . . can be obtained by the KaTaPaYaDhi system.

The Symbolism of the Tantrik Chakra System

The following 33 tables illustrate the wealth of symbolism for the tantrik chakra system, both in the East and in the West.

I. The Basic Attributes of the Seven Chakras (Tables 1–5)

Table 1. Order—The order of the seven chakras is listed, where the bottom chakra is the first and the top chakra is the seventh.

Table 2. Sanskrit Name—The common transliterations for the seven chakras are listed here. Refer to table 26 for the original Sanskrit.

Table 3. Translation—English for tables 2 and 26.

Table 4. Planetary Star—The esoteric order of the planets to the seven chakras given here corresponds to both Eastern and Western traditions.
In the West, the planetary order found in the seven Major Arcana cards in the Tarot reveals the proper Western yogic method of arousing kundalini. The seven double letters in Hebrew, when translated to the seven planetary Tarot cards of the Major Arcana, show this esoteric chakra order measured from Key XXI, The World, to Key 1, The Magician, as follows.

Chakra-Planetary-Tarot Esoteric Order

Tarot Major Arcana Order	Hebrew Double Letter	Yogic Planetary Order	Order of Chakra Unfoldment
Key XXI, The World	Th	Saturn	1st
Key XIX, The Sun	R	Sun	4th
Key XVI, The Tower	P	Mars	2nd
Key X, Wheel of Fortune	K	Jupiter	3rd
Key III, The Empress	D	Venus	5th
Key II, The High Priestess	G	Moon	6th
Key I, The Magician	B	Mercury	7th

I. The Basic Attributes of the Seven Chakras (cont'd.)

The planetary order of Saturn, Sun, Mars, Jupiter, Venus, Moon, and Mercury translates to the chakra order of First (lowest), Fourth, Second, Third, Fifth, Sixth, and Seventh.

In this secret Western Tarot order, after visualizing the dormant, bound kundalini in the first chakra at the base of the spine, the fourth chakra (the heart) is opened before the dangerous dynamo of energy located in the second chakra (at the genitals) is unleashed. In other words, the heart of compassion is opened up before the sexual forces are directly tapped. This order protects the beginning student from the disabling martial powers of the Svadhisthana chakra.

This order is paralleled in the Theosophical school of chakra theory, where the sexual second chakra is displaced from the genitals to the spleen and referred to as the spleen chakra.

Table 5. Alchemical Element—The corresponding Western (as well as Eastern) alchemical-planetary associations are given in this table. By these associations, traditional Western alchemical terminology can be paralleled to the seven chakras. Here are three examples:

- Lead changed to gold is kundalini raised from the base of the spine to the heart chakra, from Saturn to the Sun, and is the basis of the Western Tarot chakra order

- The Union of the Sun and the Moon denotes the opening of both the heart (Sun) and third eye (Moon), the union of devotional love and intuitional mind

- The Mercury of the Wise becomes the crown or top chakra, the 1,000-petaled lotus of the Sahasrara, symbolizing enlightment.

I. The Basic Attributes of the Seven Chakras (cont'd.)

1. Order	2. Sanskrit Name	3. Translation	4. Planetary Star	5. Alchemical Element
First	Muladhara	Foundation, Root Entrance	Saturn	Lead
Second	Svadhisthana	Own Place, Dwelling Place of the Self	Mars	Iron
Third	Manipura	Full of Rays; Pointed Stone; City of Jewels	Jupiter	Tin
Fourth	Anahata	Soundless Sound; Unstricken Bell	Sun	Gold
Fifth	Visuddha	Pureness	Venus	Copper
Sixth	Ajna	Guru's Command: Unlimited Power; Beyond Knowledge	Moon	Silver
Seventh	Sahasrara	Thousand-Petaled Flower	Mercury	Quicksilver

II. Eastern Chakra Correlations to the Human Body (Tables 6–10)

Table 6. Position in Body—This table delineates the location of the seven major chakras according to the Eastern tradition. With the transmission of this information to the West, through Theosophy in the late 19th Century, the attribute of Svadhisthana (the genitals) was blinded in all printed teachings.

Table 7. Function in Body—Seven levels of the functions of the human body are listed in this table according to Eastern teachings.

Table 8. Tattvic Senses—The five exoteric and two esoteric Tattvas of Indian tantrik symbolism correspond to the five senses contained by the mind and then by the higher self. These seven senses are correlated to the seven chakras.

Table 9. Number of Rays or Petals—The seven chakras have been given various numerations as to the number of petals which make up each chakra. The orthodox numeration is given here (according to the tantrik text, *Shat-Chakra*). The petals increase in total number as follows:

Blossoming of the Chakra Petals

Chakra	Number of Petals
1st Muladhara	4 petals = 4 petals
2nd Svadhisthana	4 + 6 petals = 10 petals
3rd Manipura	10 + 10 petals = 20 petals
4th Anahata	10 + 12 petals = 32 petals
5th Visuddha	32 + 16 petals = 48 petals
6th Ajna	48+ 2 petals = 50 petals
7th Sahasrara	20 x 50 petals = 1,000 petals

A variant to this orthodox scheme is found in the *Shat-Chakra* as rays emanating from the Tattvas situated in each chakra. These variants are as follows:

II. Eastern Chakra Correlations to the Human Body (cont'd.)

Chakra Petal Variant

Chakra	Number of Rays
1st Muladhara	= 56 Rays
2nd Svadhisthana	= 62 Rays
3rd Manipura	= 52 Rays
4th Anahata	= 54 Rays
5th Visuddha	= 72 Rays
6th Ajna	= 64 Rays
7th Sahasrara	= 360 Rays (Total of first six chakras)

LIṄGa = 33

Table 10. Division of Spine as 33 Esoteric Joints—In Sanskrit symbolic tantrik anatomy, the spinal column is made up of 33 divisions. This may be based on the upright post of Shiva, the Linga, which in Sanskrit is also the number 33:

This chart is an attempt to allocate the spinal column of 33 divisions to the seven chakras. The lowest chakra is the first three vertebrae from the base of the spine. The last three vertebrae at the top of the spine are the fifth, sixth, and seventh chakras.

These positions are derived from Leadbeater's chart, "The Chakras and the Nervous System," appearing in his book, *The Chakras*. His correspondences are shown on the following page.

II. Eastern Chakra Correlations to the Human Body (cont'd.)

Leadbeater's Chakra Correspondences

The Spine and the Six Lower Chakras

Chakra	Location	Spine
Muladhara	Base of Spine	4th Sacral
Svadhisthana	Over the Spleen	1st Lumbar
Manipura	Over the Navel	8th Thoracic
Anahata	Over the Heart	8th Cervical
Visuddha	At the Throat	3rd Cervical
Ajna	On the Brow	1st Cervical

II. Eastern Chakra Correlations to the Human Body (cont'd.)

Chakra	6. Position in Body	7. Function in Body	8. Tattvic Senses	9. Number of Rays or Petals	10. Division of Spine as 33 Esoteric Joints
Muladhara (1st)	Between the Anus and Genitals (Base of Spine)	Eliminative Center	Smell	4	1st, 2nd, 3rd
Svadhisthana (2nd)	Genitals	Generative Center	Taste	6	7th
Manipura (3rd)	Navel (Solar Plexus)	Digestive Center	Sight	10	16th
Anahata (4th)	Center of the Breast (Heart)	Respiratory Center (Circulation of Prana and Blood)	Touch	12	26th
Visuddha (5th)	Throat	Vocalization of Thought	Hearing	16	31st
Ajna (6th)	Forehead, Brow (Between the Eyebrows)	Waking Consciousness (Coordination of the Body)	Mind	2	32nd
Sahasrara (7th)	Crown of the Head	Supercon-sciousness	Higher Self	50 x 20 (1000)	33rd

III. Western Chakra Correlations to the Human Body (Tables 11–14)

Table 11. Blavatsky (Esoteric Instructions)—This table divides the body into six zones surrounded by a seventh Auric Egg. It is derived from H.P. Blavatsky's secret instructions to her esoteric section of Theosophists.

Table 12. Leadbeater (*The Chakras*)—The major Western variant system of allocating the chakras to the human body is listed in this table. The controversial substitution is spleen for genitals, based on a literal translation of the second chakra, "Svadhisthana" as "Other Place," the "Other Place" being spleen (as opposed to genitals).

Table 13. Crowley (*Liber 777*)—The location in the human body of the seven chakras as found in Aleister Crowley's 777 is listed here. Crowley confounds the lingam of the second chakra with the anus of the first chakra (possibly an intended Crowleyan joke) and places in the second chakra the navel of the third chakra.

Table 14. Fortune (*The Mystical Qabalah*)—Dion Fortune's correction of Western Qabalistic-chakra symbolism in light of Eastern tradition is recorded in her book, *The Mystical Qabalah*. This table is in accord with table 6 of the Eastern System.

III. Western Chakra Correlations to the Human Body (cont'd.)

Chakra	11. Blavatsky (Esoteric Instructions)	12. Leadbeater (The Chakras)	13. Crowley (Liber 777)	14. Fortune (The Mystical Qabalah)
Muladhara (1st)	Knees to Feet	Base of the Spine	Lingam and Anus	Perineum, Anus, Function of Excretion
Svadhisthana (2nd)	Thighs to Knees	Over the Spleen	Navel	Generative Organs
Manipura (3rd)	Shoulders and Arms to Thighs	At the Navel	Solar Plexus	Solar Plexus
Anahata (4th)	Throat to Navel	Over the Heart	Heart	Breast
Visuddha (5th)	Head	At the Front of the Throat	Larynx	Larynx
Ajna (6th)	Third Eye or Pineal Gland	In the Space between the Eyebrows	Pineal Gland	Pineal Gland
Sahasrara (7th)	Auric Egg enveloping the Whole Body	On the Top of the Head	Above Head	Above Head

IV. Godforms and Worlds Correlating to the Seven Chakras (Tables 15–19)

Table 15. Seven Lokas (Worlds)—The seven worlds of tantrik tradition correlate to each of the seven chakras as shown in this table. These worlds should be seen as seven spherical planes, each linked to another in ascending order.

Table 16. God-form—This table details the God presiding in each of the seven chakras. The Indian triad of Brahma, Vishnu, and Shiva, form the lower three chakras, while all three united as one form the highest chakra.

Table 17. Shakti (Goddess)—The female counterpart to the God-forms of table 16 are listed here. Coupled to each Goddess is the force which both limits and empowers each chakra.

Table 18. Vehicle—The seven vehicles which each pair of God and Goddess move within each of the seven chakras are listed in this table. The first five are animals, while the last two are the circulation of energy in the body and the power point which is circulated consciously through the body.

Table 19. Characteristic—Each of the seven chakras behaves in a symbolic fashion, the first six being animals while the seventh is the constant light of a lamp.

IV. Godforms and Worlds Correlating to the Seven Chakras (cont'd.)

Chakra	15. Seven Lokas (Worlds)	16. God-form	17. Shakti (Goddess)	18. Vehicle	19. Characteristic
Muladhara (1st)	Bhu (Physical)	Bala Brahma (Child-God)	Dakini (Security)	Elephant with seven Trunks (Airavata)	Ant
Svadhisthana (2nd)	Bhuvar (Astral)	Vishnu (Preserver)	Rakini (Sexuality)	Crocodile	Butterfly
Manipura (3rd)	Svarga (Celestial)	Braddha-Rudra (Elder Shiva)	Lakini (Authority)	Ram	Cobra
Anahata (4th)	Manas (Balance)	Ishana Rudra Shiva (Lord of the Northeast)	Kakini (Devotion)	Deer	Deer
Visuddha (5th)	Jana (Human)	Pancha-Vaktra Shiva (Five-faced Shiva)	Shakini (Knowledge)	Elephant with one Trunk (Gaja)	Peacock
Ajna (6th)	Tapas (Austerity)	Shiva-Shakti (Male & Female in Union)	Hakini (Insight)	Nada (Vessel of Prana)	Swan
Sahasrara (7th)	Satya (True Reality)	Guru (Inner Teacher: Brahma, Vishnu, Shiva)	Maha Shakti (Union)	Bindu (Point, Dot)	The Flame of a Lamp

V. Tattva and Color Correspondences of The Seven Chakras (Tables 20–25)

Table 20. Tattva—The five basic Tattvas are assigned to the five lower chakras and are emblematically present in illustrations of each chakra. Beyond these five basic Tattvas are two esoteric Tattvas, an amalgam of all five Tattvas, and a single dot or point. These seven Tattvas are listed, giving name, element (where appropriate), and symbolic shape.

Table 21. Element (Color)—The traditional colors for the Tattvas in table 20 are shown in this table.

Table 22. Color (Shat-Chakra)—The traditional color for each of the seven Tattvas, as found in the tantrik text Shat-Chakra, is listed in this table. This color should be combined with the tattvic color in table 21 to generate the two basic colors of each chakra.

Table 23. Color (Shiva Sanhita)—An alternate set of colors for the chakras, as listed in the tantrik text Shiva Sanhita, is given in this table.

Table 24. Color (Leadbeater)—The Theosophical color scheme for the seven chakras, as perceived clairvoyantly by C. W. Leadbeater.

Table 25. Color (Pranic)—The seven pranic colors whose vibrations correspond to the seven chakras, according to Theosophical correspondences of H.P. Blavatsky's esoteric-section teachings.

Yet another set of Western color correspondences can be seen in the Golden Dawn color scheme for the seven planets. The following table lists both the King Scale for the seven planets as paths of the Tree of Life and the Queen Scale for the seven planets as Sephiroth of the Tree of Life.

G.D. Chakra Color Scheme

		Color	
Chakra	Planet	(Atziloth-King Scale—Paths)	(Briah-Queen Scale—Sephiroth)
Muladhara	Saturn	Blue-Violet	Black
Svadhisthana	Mars	Red	Red
Manipura	Jupiter	Violet	Blue
Anahata	Sun	Orange	Yellow
Visuddha	Venus	Green	Green
Ajna	Moon	Blue	Violet
Sahasrara	Mercury	Yellow	Orange

V. Tattva and Color Correspondences of The Seven Chakras (cont'd.)

Chakra	20. Tattva	21. Element (Color)	22. Color (Shat-Chakra)	23. Color (Shiva Sanhita)	24. Color (Leadbeater)	25. Color (Pranic)
Muladhara (1st)	Prithivi (Earth-Square)	Yellow	Yellow	Red	Fiery Orange Red	Orange Red
Svadhisthana (2nd)	Apas (Water-Crescent)	White	Light Blue	Vermillion	Glowing, sunlike	Rose
Manipura (3rd)	Tejas (Fire-Triangle)	Red	Flame Red	Golden	Various Reds and Greens	Green
Anahata (4th)	Vayu (Air-Circle)	Blue	Smoky Green	Deep Red	Golden	Yellow
Visuddha (5th)	Akasha (Ether-Oval)	Blue-Violet	Smoky Purple	Brilliant Gold	Silvery, Blue	Light Blue
Ajna (6th)	Maha-Tattva (All Five Tattvas Combined as One)	Rainbow of Five Colors	Camphor White (Translucent Blue)	White	Yellow and Purple	Dark Blue, Blue-Violet
Sahasrara (7th)	Bindu (Point, Dot)	Clear	Rainbow, Variegated	Clear	Violet	Violet

VI. The Number-Alphabet Attributes of the Seven Chakras (Tables 26–29)

Table 26. Original Sanskrit—The original titles for the chakras are rendered in transliterated English in this table. Their meanings can be found in table 3.

Table 27. Number Value (KaTaPaYaDhi)—The number values of the original Sanskrit in table 26 are tabulated in this table according to the numbering system of KaTaPaYaDhi II (Kerala Variant). Note that the seven chakras total to the number 24,191.

Table 28. Letters and Their Number (KaTaPaYaDhi)—The letters composing each of the six lower chakras are delineated in this table along with their appropriate number values by the system of KaTaPaYaDhi II (Kerala Variant). By these number values a specific number can be given to each chakra based on the total numerical value of each set of petals. These values, unique to each chakra, are as follows:

Number Values for Each Flower Chakra by the Letters Upon the Petals

Chakra	Number Value of Petals	Total Sum Value
Muladhara	4 + 5 + 6 + 7	22
Svadhisthana	1 + 2 + 3 + 3 + 4 + 5	18
Manipura	1 + 2 + 3 + 4 + 5 + 6 + 7 + 8 + 9 + (1)0	55
Anahata	1 + 2 + 3 + 4 + 5 + 6 + 7 + 8 + 9 + (1)0 + (1)1 + (1)2	78
Visuddha	16 vowels without number or place value	0
Ajna	8 + 0	8
Sahasara	All 50 letters repeated 20 times in a spiral of 1,000 petals	1,000

VI. The Number-Alphabet Attributes of the Seven Chakras (cont'd.)

For every Sanskrit number value possible for all 50 petals, see the table appearing at the end of this essay on chakras.

Table 29. Seed Syllable and Number—The Sanskrit letter appearing at the center of each chakra is known as the seed syllable and is distinct from the letters composing the petals of each chakra. This table shows both the original Sanskrit and the number value according to KaTaPaYaDhi II (Kerala Variant). The letters can also be terminated in Ng instead of M. For the Anahata chakra, PaM is often substituted for YaM, both of which are valued at 1 by the KaTaPaYaDhi code. Note that the seven seed syllables total to 18 by this code. By this sum value, the total number for both the letters assigned to the petals and center of each chakra is 1181 + 18 or 1199.

Chakra	26. Original Sanskrit	27. Number Value (KaTaPaYaDhi)	28. Letters and Their Number (KaTaPaYaDhi)	29. Seed Syllable and Number
Muladhara (1st)	MŪLÂDhÂRa	5392	V(4) S(5) Sh(6) S(7)	LaM (3)
Svadhisthana (2nd)	SVÂDhiShThÂNa	4920	B(3) Bh(4) M(5) Y(1) R(2) L(3)	VaM (4)
Manipura (3rd)	MAṆIPÛRa	5512	Ḍ(3) Ḍh(4) Ṇ(5) T(6) Th(7) D(8) Dh(9) N(0) P(1) Ph(2)	RaM (2)
Anahata (4th)	ANÂHaTa	86	K(1) Kh(2) G(3) Gh(4) Ṅ(5)	YaM (1)
Visuddha (5th)	VISÛDDha	459	C(6) Ch(7) J(8) Jh(9) Ñ(0) Ṭ(1) Ṭh(2)	HaM (8)
			A, Â, I, Î, U, Û, Ri, Rî Li, Lî, E, Ai, O, Au, Ah, Am (All 16 vowels receive no number or place value)	
Ajna (6th)	ÂJÑÂ	0	H(8) Kṣ(0)	AuM (0)
Sahasrara (7th)	SaHaSRÂRa	7822	(All 50 letters) x 20 = 1000 petals	Ḥ (0)

VII. Tree of Life Correlations to the Seven Chakras (Tables 30–33)

Table 30. Crowley (*Liber 777*)—The Tree of Life parallels to the seven chakras are shown in this table, as detailed by Aleister Crowley's 777. Here Malkuth as the body containing the seven chakras is excluded, the upper nine Sephiroth being the range of the seven chakras.

Table 31. Fortune (*The Mystical Qabalah*)—The Tree of Life parallels to the seven chakras are shown in this table, as detailed by Dion Fortune in *The Mystical Qabalah*. In these attributes, the triad of Tiphereth, Netzach, and Hod is only implied by the other Sephiroth. However, Malkuth is equated to the lowest chakra while Kether is equaled to the highest.

Table 32. Levels of Tree of Life—The Golden Dawn divided the Tree of Life into seven horizontal planes which emcompass all ten Sephiroth as seven levels. Though not equated to the chakras in the Golden Dawn, this system of seven divisions offers the most satisfactory connection between the Tree of Life and the seven chakras.

The parallel between the human body and the chakras is best enhanced by these Qabalistic correspondences, as the following table demonstrates. Note that Daath may be more appropriate for the location of Visuddha on the Tree of Life.

Qabalistic Anatomy and the Chakras

Tree of Life	Qabalistic Parts of Body	Chakra	Chakra Division of The Body
Malkuth	Anus (Feet)	Muladhara	Anus
Yesod	Genitals	Svadhisthana	Genitals
Netzach and Hod	Right and Left Hip (Leg)	Manipura	Solar Plexus
Tiphereth	Heart	Anahata	Heart
Chesed and Geburah	Right and Left Shoulders, Arms	Visuddha	Throat
Chockmah and Binah	Right and Left Eye	Ajna	Third Eye
Kether	Crown of Head	Sahasrara	Crown of Head

VII. Tree of Life Correlations to the Seven Chakras (Tables 30–33)

Table 33. Seven Planets as Seven Planetary Sephiroth—In this last table of correspondences, the platonic order of the seven planets as arranged on the Tree of Life is paralleled to the planetary-star order of table 4. Both the Sephirothic title and planet are listed. Note that Malkuth can be substituted for Binah as the ruling Saturnian Sephiroth for the Muladhara chakra.

Chakra	30. Crowley (*Liber 777*)	31. Fortune (*The Mystical Qabalah*)	32. Levels of Tree of Life	33. Seven Planets as Seven Planetary Sephiroth
Muladhara (1st)	Yesod	Malkuth	Malkuth	Binah (Saturn)
Svadhisthana (2nd)	Hod	Yesod	Yesod	Geburah (Mars)
Manipura (3rd)	Netzach	Geburah	Netzach and Hod	Chesed (Jupiter)
Anahata (4th)	Chesed, Geburah, Tiphereth	Chesed	Tiphereth	Tiphereth (Sun)
Visuddha (5th)	Binah	Binah and Daath	Chesed and Geburah	Netzach (Venus)
Ajna (6th)	Chockmah	Chockmah and Daath	Chockmah and Binah	Yesod (Moon)
Sahasrara (7th)	Kether	Kether	Kether	Hod (Mercury)

THE FIFTY PETAL-ALPHABET LETTERS.

Beyond the number values set out for the chakras in Table 28 (letters and their number), a variety of other values can be established from the many different numbering systems for Sanskirt.

The following table delineates the various number values for each petal of the chakra system.

Chakra Number Pattern for Fifty Petal-Alphabet Letters

			Number Value				
Chakra	Chakra Petal	Sanskrit Letter	Katapa-yadhi	Arya-bhata	S.Indian Serial	Pali Serial	Alphabet Order
Muladhara	1	व V	4	6	29	448	45
Muladhara	2	श S	5	7	30	464	46
Muladhara	3	ष Sh	6	8	31	480	47
Muladhara	4	स S	7	9	32	496	48
Svadhisthana	5	ब B	3	23	23	352	39
Svadhisthana	6	भ Bh	4	24	24	368	40
Svadhisthana	7	म M	5	25	25	384	41
Svadhisthana	8	य Y	1	3	26	400	42
Svadhisthana	9	र R	2	4	27	416	43
Svadhisthana	10	ल L	3	5	28	432	44
Manipura	11	ड D	3	13	13	192	29
Manipura	12	ढ Dh	4	14	14	208	30
Manipura	13	ण N	5	15	15	224	31
Manipura	14	त T	6	16	16	240	32
Manipura	15	थ Th	7	17	17	256	33
Manipura	16	द D	8	18	18	272	34
Manipura	17	ध Dh	9	19	19	288	35
Manipura	18	न N	0	20	20	304	36
Manipura	19	प P	1	21	21	320	37
Manipura	20	फ Ph	2	22	22	336	38
Anahata	21	क K	1	1	1	0	17
Anahata	22	ख Kh	2	2	2	16	18
Anahata	23	ग G	3	3	3	32	19
Anahata	24	घ Gh	4	4	4	48	20
Anahata	25	ङ N	5	5	5	64	21
Anahata	26	च C	6	6	6	80	22
Anahata	27	छ Ch	7	7	7	96	23
Anahata	28	ज J	8	8	8	112	24

Chakra Number Pattern for Fifty Petal-Alphabet Letters (cont'd.)

Chakra	Chakra Petal	Sanskrit Letter		Number Value				Alphabet Order
				Katapa-yadhi	Arya-bhata	S.Indian Serial	Pali Serial	
Anahata	29	झ	Jh	9	9	9	128	25
Anahata	30	ञ	Ñ	0	10	10	144	26
Anahata	31	ट	Ṭ	1	11	11	160	27
Anahata	32	ठ	Ṭh	2	12	12	176	28
Vissudhi	33	अ	A	no value	0	0	1	1
Vissudhi	34	आ	Â	no value	0	34	2	2
Vissudhi	35	इ	I	no value	0	68	3	3
Vissudhi	36	ई	Î	no value	0	102	4	4
Vissudhi	37	उ	U	no value	0	136	5	5
Vissudhi	38	ऊ	Û	no value	0	170	6	6
Vissudhi	39	ऋ	Ri	no value	0	204	7	7
Vissudhi	40	ॠ	Rî	no value	0	238	8	8
Vissudhi	41	ऌ	Li	no value	0	272	9	9
Vissudhi	42	ॡ	Lî	no value	0	306	10	10
Vissudhi	43	ए	E	no value	0	340	11	11
Vissudhi	44	ऐ	Ai	no value	0	374	12	12
Vissudhi	45	ओ	O	no value	0	408	13	13
Vissudhi	46	औ	Au	no value	0	442	14	14
Vissudhi	47	अं	Am	no value	0	476	15	15
Vissudhi	48	अः	Ah	no value	0	510	16	16
Ajna	49	ह	H	8	10	33	512	49
Ajna	50	क्ष	Kṣ	0	—	34	528	50

Note that the normal order of the Sanskrit alphabet naturally groups the six lower chakras, which contain the 50 letters of the alphabet, into the sequential order of the fifth, fourth, third, second, first, and sixth chakra (dividing the alphabet into six groups in descending order of 16–12–10–6–4–2).

Normal Alphabet Order of Sanskrit as a Key to the Chakras

Alphabet	Serial Order	Chakra	Petal Order	
A	1	Visuddha (5th)	33	
Â	2	Visuddha	34	
I	3	Visuddha	35	
Î	4	Visuddha	36	
U	5	Visuddha	37	
Û	6	Visuddha	38	
Ri	7	Visuddha	39	
Rî	8	Visuddha	40	
Li	9	Visuddha	41	16
Lî	10	Visuddha	42	
E	11	Visuddha	43	
Ai	12	Visuddha	44	
O	13	Visuddha	45	
Au	14	Visuddha	46	
Am	15	Visuddha	47	
Ah	16	Visuddha	48	
K	17	Anahata (4th)	21	
Kh	18	Anahata	22	
G	19	Anahata	23	
Gh	20	Anahata	24	
Ṅ	21	Anahata	25	
C	22	Anahata	26	
Ch	23	Anahata	27	12
J	24	Anahata	28	
Jh	25	Anahata	29	
Ñ	26	Anahata	30	
Ṭ	27	Anahata	31	
Ṭh	28	Anahata	32	
Ḍ	29	Manipura (3rd)	11	
Ḍh	30	Manipura	12	
Ṇ	31	Manipura	13	
T	32	Manipura	14	
Th	33	Manipura	15	
D	34	Manipura	16	10
Dh	35	Manipura	17	
N	36	Manipura	18	
P	37	Manipura	19	
Ph	38	Manipura	20	

Normal Alphabet Order of Sanskrit as a Key to the Chakras (cont'd.)

Alphabet	Serial Order	Chakra	Petal Order	
B	39	Svadhisthana (2nd)	5	
Bh	40	Svadhisthana	6	
M	41	Svadhisthana	7	
Y	42	Svadhisthana	8	6
R	43	Svadhisthana	9	
L	44	Svadhisthana	10	
V	45	Muladhara (1st)	1	
Ṡ	46	Muladhara	2	
Sh	47	Muladhara	3	4
S	48	Muladhara	4	
H	49	Ajna (6th)	49	2
Kṣ	50	Ajna	50	

FIFTH KEY

TIBETAN

OVERVIEW

Of the Tibetan number code, next to nothing exists in print in English. I have found no printed sources for the secret number value for Tibetan. My own personal discovery of the code came from studying the existing Tibetan-English language dictionaries. In most Tibetan dictionaries, a number value will be given for each of the 30 consonants composing the Tibetan alphabet. These 30 letters in combination with 5 vowel sounds produce a combination of 150 numbers. This numeration was used in Tibetan as index numbers for multiple-volume sets of books.

Now this same method is utilized in the West, in such religious texts as the Greek New Testament, the Hebraic Torah, and the Arabic Quran. As such, the number values ascribed to the Tibetan letters, when assigned to the letters of any given Tibetan word, and added together produce the correct number value for that word. The pattern for the Tibetan number system is the Pali serial order system for Sanskrit. Blavatsky did not disclose this code in any of her copious writings, but she would have been delighted with this code, since her famous initials H.P.B., as Tibetan, yield 57, the same value as Lama (or spiritual master) in Tibetan.

English	Tibetan	Number Value
H.P.B.	HPB	29 + 13 + 15 = 57
Lama	BLaMa	15 + 26 + 16 = 57

Since the literature upon the esoteric number value for Tibetan is not available in the West, this section can offer only the basics for the correct numbering of Tibetan. The 30 original consonants of the Tibetan alphabet are shown, followed by their transliterations, secret number values, and symbolic meanings. These consonants are followed by the five basic vowels, their number values, their corresponding elements, and Tattvas. Note that the vowel "a" is not marked but is automatically assigned to each consonant or conjoined consonant when no other vowel mark is present.

The rules for numbering Tibetan are given, followed by five Tibetan words, each valued at 51. These five numbered examples are followed by the complete 150 serial combinations of 30 consonants and 5 vowels.

As an addendum to Tibetan, the Eastern Tattva system, which divides the universe into five basic shapes, is fully detailed. These five Eastern elemental shapes are:

- Oval

- Circle

- Triangle

- Crescent

- Square

The tables presented in this section group the philosophy of these five esoteric geometric shapes to six schools of thought:

1. Indian Sankhya philosophy (original Tattva system)

2. Hatha Yoga system (of Breath)

3. Tantrik Yoga system

4. Esoteric Tibetan Buddhist system (most secret refinement of Tattvas)

5. Blavatsky's Theosophical system (conjecturing seven Tattvas)

6. Golden Dawn Masonic System (offshoot of Theosophical system)

The first table presented in this section details the 25 counterchanges of Kapila's Sankhya Tattva system. Here the five basic Tattvas are counterchanged with each of the five Tattvas to produce 25 counterchanges. The Golden Dawn Tattva scheme utilized these 25 counterchanges rather than Blavatsky's 49 esoteric counterchanges for their own Tattva scheme. This table is followed by a discussion of the second school of thought, the Hatha yoga system based on the Vidya Prana (Science of Breath). Twenty-seven separate tables detail the symbolism behind the five basic Tattvas according to the writings of Rama Prasad (which is ultimately the source for Blavatsky's own system).

These tables are followed by a discussion of the third system, the Tantrik chakra-Tattva system. Fourteen separate tables give the symbolism for the Tattvas, as derived from their corresponding chakras. The fourth school of thought is then detailed, the Tibetan Tattva system. This is not the esoteric system developed by Blavatsky, but the true Tibetan Buddhist system, based on the fivefold directional symbolism of all Tibetan mandalas. These corresponding Tattvic directions are as follows:

Tibetan Directional Mandalas and the Five Tibetan Tattvas

Tibetan Tattva	Direction of Mandala	Direction in Space
Dot	Middle	Center
Semi-circular Bow	Right	North
Pyramidal Cone	Above	West
Sphere	Below	East
Cube	Left	South

The esoteric symbolism for the Tibetan Tattvas are described in 32 tables. This system may be the most refined of the six major schools of Tattvic thought. It is for this reason that this commentary on the Tattvas appears as an addendum to Tibetan.

After the Tibetan system is shown, the Theosophical esoteric Tattvas are described. First to be detailed are the sixth and seventh additional Tattvas peculiar to the Theosophical system. These two esoteric shapes are a crescent Moon (containing a radiant Sun) and an egg. Eight separate sets of symbols are given for these additional Tattvas, followed by 12 tables detailing the attributes of the five exoteric Tattvas. In the Theosophical school of thought, two additional Tattvas were conjectured so that the seven chakras could be equated to seven Tattvas. The next table in this section shows six separate sets of symbols for this sevenfold Tattvic system.

Ultimately, these seven Theosophical Tattvas are counterchanged to form seven times seven, or 49, counterchanges. This expands Kapila's 25 counterchanges by an additional 24 symbols, which can classify all of the universe. These 49 counterchanges are laid out in a table which describes each of these Tattvas as a:

- Tattva

- Planet

- Color

- Sanskrit Letter and Number

This table is the most elaborate classification system to evolve out of any of the Tattvic schools of thought.

The Theosophical section is followed by the magickal teachings of the Golden Dawn concerning the Tattvas. The sheer fact that the esoteric instructions of the Golden Dawn contain teachings regarding the Tattvas (derived from the Theosophical sources) refutes any ancient lineage to these teachings prior to 1875 CE, because, except for a reference to the Tattvas in Lytton's 19th-century novel *Zanoni*, the Tattvas are not revealed to the mainstream of Western occultism until the advent of Theosophy.

The Golden Dawn system is given in 39 tables. These magickal equivalents for the five basic Tattvas are followed by two separate discussions

concerning the practical application of the Tattvas in the West. The first
discussion gives the Golden Dawn technique for using the Tattvas as
"astral doorways" in the most rudimentary form. Real work with this system should be supplemented with Regardie's *Golden Dawn* writings. The
second discussion lists in table form for the first time the actual division of
time for the Tattvic tides, which govern the flow of time in any given day.

The addendum ends with a key to all of the major Tattva tables in the
text, giving additional commentary on these tables. The various Tattva systems described in this section each possess their own unique color
schemes and shapes for the individual Tattvas.

Using the correct symbols described in each of these sets of Tattva correspondences, you can construct the following Tattva sets:

- The 25 counterchanges of the Kapila Sankhya system. Each of
  these 25 Tattva counterchanges should be drawn so that the predominant Tattva is larger than the subordinate Tattva counterchange. Thus in "Tejas of Vayu," place a small triangle (Tejas) in a
  large circle (Vayu), while for "Vayu of Tejas," place a small circle
  in a large triangle. You can use any of the color correspondences
  found in any Tattva system given in this section for this specific set
  of 25 Tattvas.

- The Five Tattvas of Rama Prasad. The shape and color for this system are found in the first two tables labeled "Shape" and "Color."

- The Five Tantrik Chakra Tattvas. The shape and color for this system are found in the first table (Shape) and the fifth table (Color).
  A more elaborate design for these five Tattvas is detailed in the
  table "Chakra-Tattva Shapes."

- The Five Tibetan Buddhist Tattvas. The shape and color can be
  found in the first table and second table (Shape and Stupa) and the
  fifth table (Color). Additional information can be found in the table
  "Tibetan Tattva Shapes."

- The Seven Theosophical Tattvas. The shape and color for the first
  five Tattvas are found in the table "The Theosophical Exoteric
  Tattva System." Tables 2 and 3 show the shape (esoteric and exo-
  teric), while tables 10 and 11 show the color (tantrik and esoteric).
  The two additional Tattvas are shown in the table, "The Sixth and
  Seventh Theosophical Esoteric Tattvas." The shape is shown in
  table 1, while the color is shown in table 6. These seven basic
  Tattvas can also be made into an elaborate counterchange of 49
  Tattvas, as shown in the table "The 7x7 Theosophical Counter-
  changes."

- The Five Basic Golden Dawn Tattvas. These are shown in the table
  "Golden Dawn Tattva System." Table 1 shows the basic shape, and
  table 2 shows the basic color. Additional colors are given in tables
  14–17, and table 29 (as metallic colors). Again, as stated in (1) above,
  the five basic Golden Dawn Tattvas can also be executed as the
  more elaborate five-by-five counterchange system of 25 Tattvas.

In order to construct these Tattvas, posterboard or other heavy paper stock should be used. Cut the basic cards out in squares of equal size (these can range in size from 3" x 3" to 12" x12"). Alternate shapes for these Tattva cards could be rectangles, ovals, or circles. Draw the designs first in pencil and then color them with watercolors, acrylics, or any other bright medium. Leave the backgrounds white, or paint them black. The brighter and purer the colors used, the easier to charge the Tattvas in meditation, divination, or astral travel. Additional sets of Tattvas can be constructed which are embellished with one or more symbols from the many tables of attributes found in this section.

Each of the above six Tattva card sets (known as YaNTRa in Sanskrit), once constructed, can be used as follows:

- As a form of meditation, using the correspondences found within each table to guide your meditation

- As a form of divination, the set of Tattva cards can be shuffled, and one then can be randomly drawn and interpreted oracularly by its own corresponding symbols

- As an astral doorway as described in the Golden Dawn system

- As a philosophical system in which any shape or concept in nature is described by studying one or more Tattvas in combination

- As a measure of time using a cycle of Tattvas, in which any given hour of the day can be judged auspicious or inauspicious

- As a ritual and oracle for the Spring Equinox (as shown in the table "Tattva Vernal Equinoctial Oracle."

ORIGIN

799 CE—Revision of older Tibetan "Bon" language by Thon-mi-Sambhota

ALPHABET CODE

Tibet as well as India developed an alphabet which served as both phonetic sound and number value. This alphabet was created in 799 CE by Thon-mi-Sambhota as a revision of the older Tibetan language, the Shamanistic "Bon" language.

In Thon-mi-Sambhota's recension, a new language based on Buddhist ideologies combined the languages Tibetan, Chinese, Nepalese, and Sanskrit into a mystical hybrid. This new language possessed an alphabet of 30 consonants and five vowels. The name of this alphabet was the "Kali" or skull alphabet, because the shapes of the characters were patterned after the cranial sutures of the human skull (this was also the mythical source of the Brahmi script of India).

The number value assigned to Tibetan by Thon-mi-Sambhota was based on the Southern Indian serial order number code for Sanskrit. The following table delineates the number code for the Tibetan alphabet.

Tibetan Alphabet

Alphabet (30 Consonants)	Trans-literation	Number Value	Symbolic Meaning of Letter
ཀ	K	1	Root, beginning, power
ཁ	Kh	2	Face, mouth, front side
ག	G	3	Essence of Buddha; the hidden
ང	Ñ	4	I; matter in constant change; dissolution
ཙ	C	5	Noise, cry, clamour, sound
ཚ	Ch	6	Intelligence, word
ཇ	J	7	Tea, herb
ཉ	Ñ	8	Wisdom, knowledge, the Full Moon, the vagina
ཏ	T	9	Door of admission to all things
ཐ	Th	10	Everything, all, total
ད	D	11	Now, the present moment
ན	N	12	Faith, perseverance
པ	P	13	Pureness, the unity of all
ཕ	Ph	14	Beyond, father, bull, penis
བ	B	15	Prima materia, cow
མ	M	16	Attachment, below, mother, womb
ཙ	Ts	17	Contemplation, meditation
ཚ	Tsh	18	Salt, protection
ཇ	Ds	19	The eternal mother, the beginning of that which has not yet been born
ཝ	W	20	Occult science; subtlety

Tibetan Alphabet (cont'd.)

Alphabet (30 Consonants)	Trans- literation	Number Value	Symbolic Meaning of Letter
ཤ	Sh	21	That which covers the head, the celestial river ganga
ཟ	Z	22	Food and other necessities for life
འ	Ḥ	23	The humming of the ears during meditation
ཡ	Y	24	Above, up, the macrocosm, pair
ར	R	25	Alone, atomic, individual, freedom
ལ	L	26	Mountain pass, summit, ascent of a mountain, a candle
ཤ	Ç	27	Perfect peace, avoidance of misery
ས	S	28	Earth, soil, land, purity of intention, holy vows
ཧ	H	29	Breath, to breathe; delight, ecstasy
ཨ	Ah	30	The last letter, the sound which all speaking depends on; hence the deity, that which was before everything else, the last being the first (note: "A" in almost all the isosephic alphabets begins the alphabet, but in Tibetan is in the mystical position of "Omega" rather than "Alpha," the seed syllable assigned to the lowest Tibetan chakra, the Root Entrance, or secret place.

Tibetan Alphabet (cont'd.)

(Five Vowels)

Location	Letter	Trans-literation	Number	Element	Tattva
Unmarked		a	0	Earth	Prithivi
(Above Letter)	᠗	I	30	Water	Apas
(Below Letter)	᠔	U	60	Fire	Agni
(Above Letter)	⌒	E	90	Air	Vayu
(Above Letter)	⌣	O	120	Ether	Akasa

Unnumbered aspirants

(Above Letter)	•	Ṁ			
(Right Side of Letter)	⁝	Ḣ			

This alphabet code numbers the Tibetan language as follows:

- Words are read from left to right.

- The 30 consonants receive the number values 1 through 30, while the five vowels receive the number values of 0, 30, 60, 90, 120.

- By combining 30 consonants with 5 vowels, the numbers 1 through 150 are designated.

- If two consonants conjoin to make one compound consonant, both values are counted.

- The numerical value of any word is the combined total of each consonant and vowel that compose that word.

As an example of this code, the following five words in Tibetan each number to 51, the number value in Sanskrit (by Katapayadhi) for both "MaYa"—the illusion of this world, and "MRiYU"—death.

1. MThaR—the end of life, at last, finally in conclusion (M = 16, Th = 10, a = 0, R = 25, 16 + 10 + 0 + 25 = 51)

2. LTaGPa—that which is normally concealed; the back part of anything, especially the head (L = 26, T = 9, a = 0, G = 3, P = 13, a = 0; 26 + 9 + 0 + 3 + 13 + 0 = 51)

3. TaLMa—immediately, a moment, an instant, quickly, without delay (T = 9, a = 0, L = 26, M = 16, a = 0; 9 + 0 + 26 + 16 + 0 = 51)

4. RaL—a break in continuity, a rent, cleft, gorge, cliff, abyss (R = 25, a = 0, L = 26; 25 + 0 + 26 = 51)

5. ZaMPa = a bridge to the other side; Z = 22, a = 0, M = 16, P = 13, a = 0; 22 + 0 + 16 + 13 + 0 = 51)

Taken together, the 30 consonants and 5 vowels form the serial order 1 through 150. These alphabet-numerals are often used to number the serial order of volumes of books.

The alphabet code for 1 through 150 is as follows.

Serial Number Code for Tibetan

			Vowels		
		◌	◌	◌	◌
Consonants		**a**	**I**	**U**	**E**	**O**
K	ཀ	1	31	61	91	121
Kh	ཁ	2	32	62	92	122
G	ག	3	33	63	93	123
Ṅ	ང	4	34	64	94	124
C	ཙ	5	35	65	95	125
Ch	ཚ	6	36	66	96	126
J	ཇ	7	37	67	97	127
Ñ	ཉ	8	38	68	98	128
T	ཏ	9	39	69	99	129
Th	ཐ	10	40	70	100	130
D	ད	11	41	71	101	131
N	ན	12	42	72	102	132
P	པ	13	43	73	103	133
Ph	ཕ	14	44	74	104	134
B	བ	15	45	75	105	135
M	མ	16	46	76	106	136
Ts	ཙ	17	47	77	107	137
Tsh	ཚ	18	48	78	108	138
Ds	ཛ	19	49	79	109	139
W	ཝ	20	50	80	110	140
Sh	ཤ	21	51	81	111	141
Z	ཟ	22	52	82	112	142
H	འ	23	53	83	113	143
Y	ཡ	24	54	84	114	144
R	ར	25	55	85	115	145
L	ལ	26	56	86	116	146
Ç	ཤ	27	57	87	117	147
S	ས	28	58	88	118	148
H	ཧ	29	59	89	119	149
Ah	ཨ	30	60	90	120	150

Addendum

The Eastern Tattva System

The division of the physical universe into five distinct shapes known as the five Tattvas emerged out of the Indian philosophical school known as Sankhya philosophy around 700 BCE. At this date, the Indian philosopher Kapila divided the universe into five times five Tattvas or fundamental principles.

Tattva comes from the Vedantic compound of "Tat" and "Tvam," meaning "that" and "thou." Therefore, Tattva came to mean essence or thatness, the real being of anything. "Tat" signified the God-Head, and "Tvam" signified the individual, implying "That (which is the universe) art thou."

The roots of this Tattvic philosophy go back to 2000 BCE, but its ultimate refinement occurs in the Tibetan Buddhist fivefold chakra system of the human body.

The shapes of the five basic Tattvas are oval, circle, triangle, crescent, and square. From these five shapes all forms in the physical universe are generated.

The five basic Sanskrit names for these five Tattva shapes are Akasha, Vayu, Tejas (or Agni), Apas, and Prithivi. They in turn correspond to the Hindu-Tibetan cycle of five elements of Ether, Air, Fire, Water, and Earth. The following table will show these basic correlations.

Five Eastern Tattvas

Tattva Name		Shape	Element
Akasha	Oval	⬤	Ether (or Space)
Vayu	Circle	◯	Air (or Wind)
Tejas	Triangle	△	Fire (or Agni)
Apas	Crescent	☽	Water
Prithivi	Square	☐	Earth

Though these five basic shapes have their origin in Indian philosophy, especially the school of Hatha and Kundalini Yoga, their ultimate synthesis appears in the esoteric teachings of Tibetan Buddhism. Although these five shapes correspond in Indian Tantrik philosophy to the five lower energy centers of the human body, known as the chakras, they also correspond to all five psychic centers of the Tibetan chakra scheme.

In essence, the very nature of the Tibetan fivefold division of the universe is the underpinning pattern of all Tibetan mandalas and conceals the fivefold symbolism of the Tattvas.

This Tattvic school of thought evolved through six basic stages of development, the Tibetan being the fourth in a series of six. These six esoteric Tattvic schools are as follows.

SIX TATTVIC SCHOOLS OF THOUGHT

First School

Kapila's Sankhya philosophical system divides the universe into five basic Tattvic shapes, which counterchanged become five times five, or 25.

↓

Second School

The hatha yoga school of Tattvic philosophy is epitomized in the eighth chapter of the Shivagama, known as "The Science of Breath and the Philosophy of the Tattvas." This school links the energy found in breathing (prana) with the cycle of the five Tattvas.

↓

Third School

The printed Buddhist texts of Indian Tantra describe the seven energy centers of the human body in connection with the five Tattvas.

↓

Fourth School

The Tibetan Buddhist fivefold division of esoteric symbolism utilizes the five basic Tattvas for categorizing the universe.

↓

Fifth School

H. P. Blavatsky's Theosophical Society based in Adyar, India, combines the hatha yoga school of Tattvic thought (epitomized in the writings of Rama Prasad) with the esoteric Tibetan Buddhist tradition.

↓

Sixth School

MacGregor Mathers' magickal Order of the Golden Dawn incorporates the Theosophical Tattva system as the one Eastern component of its magickal classification systems. Mathers finds his inspiration in Bulwer-Lytton's novel, *Zanoni*.

These six schools of thought each developed its own unique set of symbols for the Tattvas. Only when all six systems are detailed and integrated can the real symbolic meanings behind these five Tattvas be seen.

KAPILA'S SANKHYA TATTVA SYSTEM

The first school of thought is Kapila's Sankhya philosophical system. In this system, the origin of both the name and order for the five Tattvas is established. The universe is divided into five sets of five attributes. The middle, or third, set gives the names and order of the Tattvas as Akasha, Vayu, Tejas, Apas, and Prithivi.

Secretly, each of these 25 symbols corresponds to the five times five counterchanges of the Tattvas. Each Tattva combines with each other Tattva, the main Tattva being superimposed over the secondary or counterchanged Tattva.

The Sankhya Tattvic universe unfolds the fivefold division in the following five stages, each under the influence of a Tattva.

1. The five states of consciousness (Akasha)

2. The five senses (Vayu)

3. The five elements (Tejas)

4. The five organs of perception (Apas)

5. The five organs of action (Prithivi)

Each set of five attributes evolves out of and depends upon the previous set of five attributes. These 25 symbols are the original symbol set for the Tattva system.

The table on the opposite page details these 25 Tattvic symbols and pairs each to its appropriate counterchange of Tattvas.

Upon this fives times fivefold division of the universe, all other schools of Tattvic thought must depend for their own symbolic variants. By this system, the Tattvas are a subset of consciousness and not the other way around. They are the third set of correspondences (11–15) and thus correspond to Tejas, since their forms as yantras (or meditational diagrams) are apprehended by sight as colors. They are also the intermediate rank between the intangible (levels of consciousness and the concept of the senses) and the tangible (the organs of senses and actions).

The first of 25 counterchanges, AVYaKTa, is the source and root essence of the other 24 counterchanges. AVYaKTa corresponds to an oval within an oval (or dot within a dot) as Akasha of Akasha. It is the zero symbol of the Tarot, and the void mind of Zen Buddhism. The 24 counterchanges end with the most material of the 25 Tattvas, Prithivi of Prithivi, which appropriately corresponds to the organ of expulsion or excretion (the anus), excrement being an ultimate symbol for created matter.

Out of Kapila's fivefold division of the five perceptual organs evolved the hatha yoga school of Tattvic lore, based on the circulation of prana in the body. The symbolism of this system has been recorded in Rama Prasad's translation of the "Vidya Prana," or "Science of Breath," the eighth chapter to the Indian tantrik text, Shivaguma. This second school of Tattva philosophy is the basis for both the Theosophical and Golden Dawn Tattva systems.

Kapila's Sankhya Tattva System

Fivefold Division	Tattva Counterchanges				
	(Akasha)	(Vayu)	(Tejas)	(Apas)	(Prithivi)
Counsciousness	1. AVYaKTa Unmanifest, unevolved, the void; the no-mind (To be not)	2. BUDDhI The higher intellect; perception, discrimination (To know)	3. AHaṄKÂRa Conceptual sense of self, ego, I (To be)	4. MaNaS The mind, organ of thought (To think)	5. PURUSha The mental body, the animator, spirit (To move)
(Akasha)	Akasha of Akasha	Vayu of Akasha	Tejas of Akasha	Apas of Akasha	Prithivi of Akasha
Senses	6. ŚaBDa Sound	7. SPaRŚa Touch	8. RÛPa Sight (Color)	9. RaSa Taste	10. GaNDha Smell
(Vayu)	Akasha of Vayu	Vayu of Vayu	Tejas of Vayu	Apas of Vayu	Prithivi of Vayu
Elements	11. ÂKÂŚa Ether (Space, Void)	12. VÂYU Air (Wind)	13. TEJaS Fire (Heat)	14. APaS Water (Coolness)	15. PRiThIVÎ Earth (Matter)
(Tejas)	Akasha of Tejas	Vayu of Tejas	Tejas of Tejas	Apas of Tejas	Prithivi of Tejas
Organs of Perception	16. ŚROTRa Ear	17. TVaK Skin	18. AKsU Eye	19. JIHVÂ Tongue	20. GhRÂNa Nose
(Apas)	Akasha of Apas	Vayu of Apas	Tejas of Apas	Apas of Apas	Prithivi of Apas
Organs of Action	21. VÂCh Voice	22. PÂNI Hands	23. PÂDaS Feet	24. UPaSTha Genitalia	25. PÂYUS Anus
(Prithivi)	Akasha of Prithivi	Vayu of Prithivi	Tejas of Prithivi	Apas of Prithivi	Prithivi of Prithivi

Yogic Tattva System

The hatha yoga approach to the Tattvas bases the Tattva shapes on the misty images upon a mirror created by breath flowing from the right (solar) or left (lunar) nostril. These five shapes are in turn the five basic matrices of all created matter. These five shapes are as follows.

Vidya Prana Tattva Shapes

Tattva	Shape
Akasha	Spotted, dot, ear-shaped, oval
Vayu	Circular, spherical
Tejas (Agni)	Triangular, pyramidal
Apas	Semi-lunar, Semi-circular
Prithivi	Quadrangular, cube

The basis for the division of the five Tattvas by prana (or energized breath) is the fivefold division of breath known as the five vayus. Each vayu (or wind) is allocated to a Tattva as follows:

The Five Vayus

Tattva	Five Vayus
Akasha	PRANA VAYU The impulse to inhale, intake of prana
Vayu	VYANA VAYU Circulation, movement, penetration of prana in the body
Tejas	SAMANA VAYU Assimilation of prana in the blood and body, producing heat
Apas	UDANA VAYU Inhalation of prana (through right nostril) inward, upward movement
Prithivi	APANA VAYU Exhalation of prana (through left nostril), downward, outward movement

The tables on the following pages fully detail the fivefold attributes of Rama Prasad's description of the "Vidya Prana Tattva System." Note that in this system the third Tattva of Tejas possesses an alternate title of Agni (the Vedic sacrifical fire, and the interior fire of Kundalini yoga).

Rama Prasad's Yogic Tattva System

Table 1. Shape—The original shapes of the Tattvas are shown here. Note that the attribute of Akasha as spotted, or an ear-shaped oval, is the only attribute that has substantially changed over the evolution of the Tattvas.

Table 2. Color—The original colors are shown here. Note that Akasha, as every color or clear, is the only attribution that is different from modern attributions.

Table 3. Element—These elemental attributions are the basis for all other schools of thought regarding the Tattvas.

Table 4. Planet—Seven planets, rather than five, are assigned to the Tattvas, with two Tattvas receiving double attributions. These two extra attributions are the luminaries, the Sun paired to the heat of Tejas and the Moon paired to the coolness of Apas.

Table 5. Senses—These attributions are taken directly from Kapila's attributions. Color is considered the sense for Tejas as sight.

Tattva	1. Shape	2. Color	3. Element	4. Planet	5. Senses
Akasha	Spotted, ear-shaped oval	Every color, clear	Ether	Mercury	Sound
Vayu	Spherical	Blue	Air	Saturn	Touch
Agni (Tejas)	Triangular	Red	Fire	Mars (and Sun)	Color (Sight)
Apas	Semi-Lunar	White	Water	Venus (and Moon)	Taste
Prithivi	Quadrangular	Yellow	Earth	Jupiter	Smell

Rama Prasad's Yogic Tattva System (cont'd.)

Table 6. Direction—The four directions and center or middle are attributed so that the polarity of East and West is the two lower Tattvas of Apas and Prithivi, while the polarity of North and South is the pair Vayu and Tejas.

Table 7. Quality—The physical composition of space and motion is listed here.

Table 8. Motion—The classification of motion is captured in this table. These attributions are also the basis of the movement found in each of the five lower chakras of the human body.

Table 9. Flow of Energy—This table is an extension of the attributions of motion shown in table 8.

Table 10. Flow of Prana (Breath) from Nostrils—Each Tattva flows out of the nostrils in the exhalation of breath. The length of that exhalation determines which Tattva is predominant. In ancient times, this was measured by a mirror placed under the nostrils. The shape condensed on this mirror also determined what Tattva was predominant.

Tattva	6. Direction	7. Quality	8. Motion	9. Flow of Energy	10. Flow of Prana (Breath) from Nostrils
Akasha	Center	Space	Outward (all directions)	Between every two Tattvas	Upwards (none or one finger)
Vayu	North	Motion	Outward (sixfold directions)	At acute or right angles	Downwards (8 fingers)
Agni (Tejas)	South	Expansion	Upward	Up	Downwards (4 fingers)
Apas	East	Contraction	Downward	Down	Downwards (16 fingers)
Prithivi	West	Cohesive resistance	Movement on a line or wave	Midway	Downwards (12 fingers)

Rama Prasad's Yogic Tattva System (cont'd.)

Table 11. Taste—The tongue can classify taste by the five Tattvas, ranging from bitter to sweet, as shown in this table.

Table 12. Consciousness—Five levels of consciousness are measured by the Tattvas. Normal waking consciousness is in Prithivi while superconsciousness is in Akasha.

Table 13. Action—The effect in the world of each Tattva is listed. Note that Prithivi and Apas form a pair of "that which endures or is transitory," while Tejas and Vayu represent "that which arouses or reduces." Akasha stands alone in still meditation.

Table 14. Fivefold Attributes—The Vidya Prana categorizes each of the five Tattvas by five attributes. For Prithivi, "Nadi" has an alternate attribute of feces to parallel Apas as "urine."

Tattva	11. Taste	12. Consciousness	13. Action	14. Fivefold Attributes
Akasha	Bitter	Pure consciousness	Yoga (Meditation)	Desire to have; Desire to repel; Shame; Fear; Forgetfulness
Vayu	Acid	Beyond waking	Reduction (or killing)	Removing; Walking; Smelling; Contraction; Inflation
Agni (Tejas)	Pungent	Dreamless	Arousing (Harsh)	Hunger; Thirst; Sleep; Light; Drowsiness
Apas	Astringent	Dreaming	Transitory	Male Seed; Female Egg; Fat; Urine; Saliva
Prithivi	Sweet	Waking	Long Lasting	Bone; Muscle; Skin; Hair; Nadi (vessels of prana)

Rama Prasad's Yogic Tattva System (cont'd.)

Table 15. Power—The magickal powers of the yogi or saddhu that each of the Tattvas possess are shown here.

Table 16. Business—The cycles of the Tattvas from Prithivi to Akasha measure the tides within the marketplace. Prithivi and Apas are positive, while Tejas, Vayu, and Akasha are negative.

Table 17. Life—This table shows which Tattvas are sympathetic to human life and which are not. Prithivi is the most beneficial to human life, while Akasha is the least beneficial.

Table 18. Outcome of Battle—This table is used to divine the outcome of a battle beforehand.

Table 19. Wounds in Battle—The Tattvas control the location of wounds to the body inflicted during battle. These locations are listed in this table.

Tattva	15. Power	16. Business	17. Life	18. Outcome of Battle	19. Wounds in Battle
Akasha	Knowledge of Past, Present and Future	Continuous scarcity	Least concerned with life (immaterial)	Death	Head
Vayu	Moving in space, flying like birds	Loss	Not concerned with life	Death	Hands
Agni (Tejas)	Endure burning heat, consume great amounts	Inequality of prices	Neutral to life	Defeat	Thighs
Apas	To be cooled, endure hunger and thirst	Income immediate	Concerned with life	Results equal	Feet
Prithivi	Freedom from disease, lightness of body	Income late	Most concerned with life (Material)	Fight equal	Belly

Rama Prasad's Yogic Tattva System (cont'd.)

Table 20. Sanskrit Letter—Each Tattva is identified by a seed-syllable, which when chanted in concert with meditation upon the Tattva, opens up that Tattva as an astral doorway. The five consonants which form these seed syllables are listed here, and are derived from the chakra alphabet allocation. The one variant to the chakra system is that of Vayu, which shows the letter "P" in this system, but "Y" in the chakra system.

Tables 21. through 24—These four tables are the four separate number values from four separate Sanskrit traditions for the alphabet letters listed in table 20.

Tattva	20. Sanskrit Letter	Number Values			
		21. Katapayadhi	22. Aryabhata	23. S. Indian Serial Order	24. Pali Serial Order
Akasha	H	8	10	33	512
Vayu	P	1	21	21	320
Agni (Tejas)	R	2	4	27	416
Apas	V	4	6	29	448
Prithivi	L	3	5	28	432

Rama Prasad's Yogic Tattva System (cont'd.)

Table 25. Weight (Palas)—Each Tattva exerts a specific weight measured in Palas. Akasha is the lightest while Prithivi is the heaviest.

Table 26. Divination—This table gives symbolic meanings for each of the five Tattvas, when a Tattva is randomly generated for divinatory purposes.

Table 27. Outcome of Year According to Tattvic Tide at Spring Equinox—The yearly divinatory meanings for the dominant Tattva at the moment of the Spring Equinox are listed in this table. Refer to the end of this essay for a discussion of the Tattvic tides.

Tattva	25. Weight (Palas)	26. Divination	27. Outcome of Year According to Tattvic Tide at Spring Equinox
Akasha	10	Death, void	Want of food and comfort
Vayu	20	Travel elsewhere	Confusion, accidents, famine
Agni (Tejas)	30	Metals, minerals, gains and losses	Drought, subversion, epidemics
Apas	40	Benefit, birth, life and death	Plenty of rain, no wants, comfort
Prithivi	50	Auspicious will stay, roots, of the earth	Plenty, prosperity, abundance, enjoyment

Tantrik Chakra Tattva System

Evolving concurrently out of the Kapila-Tattva system with hatha yoga's pranic-Tattva system is the Kundalini chakra-Tattva system. This system first comes into print around 500 CE through Buddhist textbooks on meditation. The system however is much older, having its roots in Tibetan-Siberian shamanism.

This Tattva system divides the human body into seven divisions (known as chakras) along the spinal column. To the first five divisions (or chakras) are allocated the five Tattvas.

The five shapes used in this system to designate the five Tattvas, and the five chakras corresponding to each, are as follows.

Chakra-Tattva Shapes

Tattva	Shape	Chakra
Akasha	Dot in a dot (Symbolizing Akasha of Akasha)	Visuddha (5th)
Vayu	Circle (inscribed with a hexagram)	Anahata (4th)
Tejas	Down-pointing triangle (Each side terminating in a "T")	Manipura (3rd)
Apas	Crescent Moon (On back with horns pointing upward)	Svadhisthana (2nd)
Prithivi	Square (whose center contains a downward pointing triangle whose center is a lingam bound by the 3-1/2 coils of Kundalini	Muladhara (1st)

Each of these five chakras contains a complex set of symbols that can be equated as symbolic expressions of each of the five Tattvas.

This chakra-Tattva correlation is the root principle behind the Tibetan-Tattva system, which may represent the ultimate refinement of the original Sankhya Tattva system.

The tables on the following pages detail the Indian Tantrik chakra symbolism for each of the Tattvas.

Tantrik Chakra Tattva System

Table 1. Shape—This table lists the Tantrik chakra Tattva shapes. Note that Vayu is often represented as a hexagram alone, based on the movement of Vayu into six directions.

Table 2. Chakra—The names of the five lower chakras and their correspondences to the five Tattvas are listed in this table.

Table 3. Planet—The five lesser planets and their correspondences to the five Tattvas are shown here based on the chakra order. These attributes differ from Rama Prasad's system.

Table 4. Metal—The alchemical metal associated with each chakra is listed in this table, based on the planetary order of table 3.

Table 5. Color—The color of both the chakra and its corresponding Tattva is captured in this table.

Table 6. Seed Syllable—The mantra to activate each chakra-Tattva is shown here, with its qualifying terminative of "Ṁ."

Tattva	1. Shape	2. Chakra	3. Planet	4. Metal	5. Color	6. Seed Syllable
Akasha	Oval, dot	Visuddha (5th) (Pure)	Venus	Copper	Clear (Smoky purple)	Ha(Ṁ)
Vayu	Circle (inscribed with a hexagram)	Anahata (4th) (Soundless)	Sun	Gold	Smoky green	Ya(Ṁ)
Tejas	Down pointing equilaterial triangle	Manipura (3rd) (Jeweled City)	Jupiter	Tin	Red	Ra(Ṁ)
Apas	Crescent (with horns pointing upward)	Svadhisthana (2nd) (Seat of Self)	Mars	Brass	White	Va(Ṁ)
Prithivi	Square	Muladhara (1st) (Root Entrance)	Saturn	Lead	Yellow	La(Ṁ)

Tantrik Chakra Tattva System (cont'd.)

Table 7. Body—The zone of the body which each Tattva rules is listed in accordance with Tantrik physiology.

Table 8. Animal (Chakra)—The animals which rule each of the five lower chakras are paired to their Tattvas. Notice that the crocodile, which appears at the foot of the Tarot card, The Fool, in many French Tarot decks, corresponds to the Apas Tattva and the Svadhisthana chakra, which rules the genitals.

Table 9. Animal (Tattva Movement)—Each Tattva can be classified by the movement of certain animals. This table designates five animals whose movement in nature imitates the abstract motion associated to each Tattva.

Table 10. Animal (Slayed by Tattva)—The five animals classified in this table have a weakness symbolized by one of the five Tattvas, which causes their death. As an example, the moth is associated with Tejas, since Tejas is the light of a candle which can lure and kill a moth.

Tattva	7. Body	8. Animal (Chakra)	9. Animal (Tattva movement)	10. Animal (Slain by Tattva)
Akasha	Throat	White elephant	Monkey (in all directions)	Deer (Hearing)
Vayu	Heart	Antelope	Bird (in Air)	Elephant (Touch)
Tejas	Navel	Ram	Serpent (in waves)	Moth (Light)
Apas	Genitals	Crocodile	Frog (in curving leaps)	Fish (Taste)
Prithivi	Anus	Gray elephant	Ant (in a straight line)	Bee (Smell)

Tantrik Chakra Tattva System (cont'd.)

Table 11. God of Chakra—This table lists the five Tantrik male god forms which control the five Tattvas.

Table 12. Goddess of Chakra—The five divine consorts to the gods of the chakra are shown in this table.

Table 13. Vedic God—This table lists the five Vedic god forms for each of the five Tattvas.

Tattva	11. God of Chakra	12. Goddess of Chakra	13. Vedic God
Akasha	Sada Siva (Eternal Destroyer)	Sakini (five-headed)	Disah (Directions of space)
Vayu	Isa (Godhead)	Kakini (four-headed)	Vayu (Wind-God)
Tejas	Rudra (Absorber)	Lakini (three-headed)	Aditya (Sun-God)
Apas	Visnu (Preserver)	Rakini (two-headed)	Varuna (God of Expanse)
Prithivi	Brahma (Creator)	Dakini (one-headed)	Asvins (Horsemen of the Sun)

Table 14. Sanskrit Alphabet—Petals of Flower-Chakras—Each of the five lower chakras, corresponding to the five Tattvas, possesses a different number of flower petals engraved with the letters of the Sanskrit alphabet. This table lists the alphabet division of the Tattvas and their order as blossoming flower petals.

14. Sanskrit Alphabet—Petals of Flower-Chakras

Tattva																
Akasha	16 Petals:	A	Â	I	Î	U	Û	Ri	Rî	Li	Lî	E	Ai	O	Au	Ah	Am
		33	34	35	36	37	38	39	40	41	42	43	44	45	46	47	48
Vayu	12 Petals:	K	Kh	G	Gh	Ṅ	C	Ch	J	Jh	Ñ	Ṭ	Ṭh				
		21	22	23	24	25	26	27	28	29	30	31	32				
Tejas	10 Petals:	Ḍ	Ḍh	Ṇ	T	Th	D	Dh	N	P	Ph						
		11	12	13	14	15	16	17	18	19	20						
Apas	6 Petals:	B	Bh	M	Y	R	L										
		5	6	7	8	9	10										
Prithivi	4 Petals:	V	Ṣ	Sh	S												
		1	2	3	4												

Tibetan Buddhist Tattva System

The fourth school of Tattva philosophy is that of Tibetan Buddhism. It is quite possibly the ultimate rescension of the original Sankhya Tattva system.

The Indian chakra system is compressed from seven to five to encompass the complete human body within the cycle of five Tattvas. These five Tattvas are then placed as five directions of space and the five directions of all basic mandalas.

Ultimately these five Tattvas become the five basic components of the three-dimensional Tibetan stupas. The five basic Tibetan Tattva shapes, their stupa shapes, and the corresponding Indian chakras are as follows.

Tibetan Tattva Shapes

Tattva	Shape	Stupa Form	Chakras
Akasha	Dot	Yod shaped flame	Sahasara (7th) and Ajna (6th)
Vayu	Semi-circular bow	Half circle cup	Visuddha (5th)
Tejas	Triangle	Pyramidal cone	Anahata (4th)
Apas	Disk	Sphere	Manipura (3rd)
Prithivi	Square	Cube	Svadhisthana (2nd) and Muladhara (1st)

Note that Apas and Vayu are interchanged in their symbol shapes:

	Tattva	
Symbol	**India**	**Tibet**
Circle	Vayu	Apas
Half Circle (Crescent)	Apas	Vayu

The Tibetan chakras are referred to as a five-tiered pagoda. In the Indian tradition these chakras represent flowers numbered by their petals totaling to 50 as 4+6+10+12+16+2. But in the Tibetan system the chakras are wheels whose spokes total to 124 as 4+64+8+16+32.

The tables on the following pages delineate the esoteric Tibetan Buddhist Tattva system.

Tibetan Buddhist Tattva System

Table 1. Shape—The shapes for the Tibetan Tattva system are a departure from the Indian tradition. Specifically, Vayu and Apas are counterchanged: Vayu is a circle in India, while in Tibet it is a semi-circular bow. Further, Apas is a crescent in India, while in Tibet it is a disc.

Table 2. Stupa—The Tibetan stupa, an obelisk like construction, is the source for the Tibetan Tattvic shapes. Here the five geometrical divisions of the stupa are paralleled to the five Tattvas.

Table 3. Element—This entry shows two sets of elemental attributes, Indian and Chinese, ordered by the Tibetan Tattvas. Note that by this Tibetan set of correspondences, the Chinese "metal" is equivalent to the Indian "ether" ("Spirit" in Western mysticism).

Table 4. Tibetan Planet—The five Tibetan planets are allocated to the five Tattvas. This system varies from that of Rama Prasad in that Jupiter and Saturn are exchanged.

Table 5. Color—The traditional Buddhist colors for the Tibetan mandalas are equated to the Tattvas.

Table 6. Direction—The symbolic use of directions in Tibetan mandalas is allocated to the Tattvas.

Table 7. Mandala—The position of the mandala to the viewer in light of the directions listed in table 6 are keyed to the Tattvas.

Tattva	1. Shape	2. Stupa	3. Element		4. Tibetan Planet	5. Color	6. Direction	7. Mandala
			India	China				
Akasha	Dot	Yod shaped flame	Ether	Metal	Mercury	Blue (Black)	Center	Middle
Vayu	Semi-circular bow	Half circle cup	Air	Wood	Jupiter	Green	North	Right
Tejas	Triangle, pyramid, cone	Pyramidal cone	Fire	Fire	Mars	Red	West	Above
Apas	Disc, sphere	Sphere	Water	Water	Venus	White	East	Below
Prithivi	Square, cube	Cube	Earth	Earth	Saturn	Yellow	South	Left

Tibetan Buddhist Tattva System (cont'd.)

Table 8. Season—The division of the Tibetan year by the Tattvas is shown in this table. Akasha, being the ever-present moment, embraces all four seasons at once.

Table 9. Time of Day—The division of the day, paralleling the division of the seasons in table 8, is shown in this table.

Table 10. 5 Tiered Pagoda—The Tibetan use of the five-tiered tower to symbolize the human body is shown in this table. This may be the source for Gurdjieff's use of a three-storied factory to describe the human body with its three Gurdjieffian centers.

Table 11. 5 Tibetan Chakras—The Tibetan chakra system reduces the Indian Tantrik scheme of seven interior stars to five chakras. The lower and upper two chakras are each combined into one center of energy. This table parallels the chakra division to the Tattvas.

Table 12. Five Centers of Body—The five divisions of the human body, which are symbolized in the five tiers of the pagoda in table 10, are paralleled in this table to the Tattvas.

Tattva	8. Season	9. Time of Day	10. Five Tiered Pagoda	11. Five Tibetan Chakras	12. Five Centers of Body
Akasha	The ever present moment	Timeless	Top tier (roof)	Sahasara and Ajna	Brain (Crown and Third Eye)
Vayu	Summer	Midnight	Fourth tier	Visuddha	Throat
Tejas	Spring	Sunset	Middle tier (Center of Palace)	Anahata	Heart
Apas	Winter	Sunrise	Second tier	Manipura	Navel
Prithivi	Autumn	Noon	Bottom tier (Door, entrance)	Svadhisthana and Muladhara	Perineum (Genitals, Anus)

Tibetan Buddhist Tattva System (cont'd.)

Table 13. 5 Zones of the Body—The range of influence of each of the five Tibetan chakras is allocated here to the Tattvas.

Table 14. Senses—The five senses are allocated to the Tattvas according to Tibetan Buddhist symbology, which differs from all other schools of thought in this allocation.

Tables 15 through 17.—These three tables show the causes of ignorance for the human race as controlled by the five Tattvas. Each set corresponds to the order of the five senses as set out in table 14.

Tattva	13. Five Zones of Body	14. Senses	15. Five Poisons	16. Stumbling Blocks of the Senses	17. Initial reaction to Tattva
Akasha	Third eye to crown of head	Sight	Fascination (Ignorance)	Visible form	Bewilderment
Vayu	Throat to third eye	Taste	Envy	Habits from past lives	Panic
Tejas	Heart to throat	Smell	Lust	Ideas	Isolation
Apas	Navel to heart	Sound	Rage (Hatred)	Intellectual discrimination	Paranoia
Prithivi	Feet (anus) to navel	Touch	Pride	Emotions	Hollowness

Tibetan Buddhist Tattva System (cont'd.)

Table 18. Animal—Five symbolic animals found in Buddhist mythology epitomize the cycle of the five Tattvas as shown in this table.

Table 19. Buddhist Symbol—Five symbols, common to most Tibetan directional mandalas, are equated to the five Tattvas in this table.

Tables 20 through 22.—These three tables show the Gods and Goddesses of Tibetan Buddhism allocated to the five Tattvas.

Tattva	18. Animal	19. Buddhist Symbol	20. Dhyani (Peaceful) Buddhas	21. Heruka (Terrifying) Buddhas	22. Dakini (Blood-Drinking) Consorts
Akasha	Lion	Wheel	VAIROCANA (Great Symbol) (Blue)	BUDDHA (Wisdom) (Brown)	AKASA-DHATESVARI The Embodiment of The Great Void) (Red)
Vayu	Bird-man	Sacrificial double-headed sword	AMOGHA-SIDDHI (Karmic Results) (Green)	KARMA (Action) (Dark Green)	TARA (Help across to the other side) (Green)
Tejas	Peacock	Open lotus	AMITABHA (Life) (Red)	PADMA (Lotus) (Red-Black)	PANDARAVA-SINI (White-Robed) (Red)
Apas	Elephant	Lightning bolt	AKSOBHYA (Spontaneous Enlightenment) (White)	VAJRA (Lightning Bolt) (Black)	LOCANA (Buddha-Eye) (White)
Prithivi	Horse	Jewel	RATNA-SAMBHAVA (Earth) (Yellow)	RATNA (Jewel) (Tawny)	MAMAKI (My children, mineness) (Yellow)

Tibetan Buddhist Tattva System (cont'd.)

Table 23. Five Buddhist Wisdoms—Five appellations for enlightenment are listed here in the order of the Tattvas.

Table 24. Sheaves (Kosas)—The inner and outer body of man is equated to the cycle of five Tattvas. This table is the basis for the Theosophical sevenfold division of the psychic and physical bodies of man.

Table 25. Chakra Levels of Consciousness—The energy which can be tapped through the Tattvas to each of the five Tibetan chakras is shown in this table.

Table 26. Seed Syllable HUM—The Sanskrit seed syllable which sounds the end of creation (as OM heralds its beginning) can be divided into five parts, each associated with one of the five Tattvas.

Tattva	23. Five Buddhist Wisdoms	24. Five Sheaves (Kosas)	25. Chakra Levels of Consciousness	26. Seed Syllable HUM
Akasha	Way, Path	Universal Conscious-ness (Essence)	Universal Mind (Higher Intellect)	Blue Flame (Bindu-M)
Vayu	All accomplishing	Potential Consciousness	Mantric Sound (Speech)	Green "H" and vowel mark (U)
Tejas	Discriminating	Thought Body (Personality)	Compassion (Intuitive Mind)	Red body of lead "H"
Apas	Mirror-like	Subtle Body (Prana)	Transformation (Assimilation)	White crescent (Part of "M")
Prithivi	Equalizing	Physical Body	Potential Seed (Energy Bound)	Yellow head of lead "H"

Tibetan Buddhist Tattva System (cont'd.)

Table 27. Sanskrit Chakra Mantras—Five select Sanskrit mantras are the seed syllables which can unlock the potential of the five Tattvas, as listed in this table.

Table 28. Tibetan Chakra Mantras—The five corresponding Tibetan seed syllables which can unlock the astral doorways of the five Tattvas are listed in this table.

Table 29. Tibetan Transliteration and Number Value—The correct Tibetan lettering and numbering of table 28 is shown here.

Tattva	27. Sanskrit Chakra Mantras	28. Tibetan Chakra Mantras	29. Tibetan Transliteration and Number Value
Akasha	KhaM	Om	AhOṂ (150)
Vayu	YaM	Hrih	HRIḤ (107)
Tejas	RaM	Hum	ḤHUṂ (112)
Apas	VaM	Tram	TRaṂ (34)
Prithivi	LaM	Ah	AhḤHi (53)

Tibetan Buddhist Tattva System (cont'd.)

Tables 30. and 31.—The Tibetan alphabet can be divided to correspond to the five Tattvas as shown in this table.

Table 32. Spokes of Tibetan Chakra Wheels—The Tibetan chakra scheme of five chakras is often symbolized as five wheels. Here the spokes of each chakra-wheel are shown in light of the Tattvas. Note that the total number of spokes composing this system is 124, the value in Sanskrit of the triad Brahma-Vishnu-Shiva as 25 + 45 + 54.

Tattva	30. Fivefold Division of Thirty Consonants and Number Values	31. Five Vowels and Number Values	32. Spokes of Tibetan Chakra Wheels
Akasha	K, Kh, G, Ñ, C, Ch (1, 2, 3, 4, 5, 6)	O (120)	32
Vayu	J, Ñ, T, Th, D, N (7, 8, 9, 10, 11, 12)	E (90)	16
Tejas	P, Ph, B, M, Ts, Tsh (13, 14, 15, 16, 17, 18)	U (60)	8
Apas	Ds, W, Sh, Z, H, Y (19, 20, 21, 22, 23, 24)	I (30)	64
Prithivi	R, L, Ç, S, H, Ah (25, 26, 27, 28, 29, 30)	A (unmarked) (0)	4

THEOSOPHICAL TATTVA SYSTEM

While the first four schools represent the Eastern Tattva systems, the last two schools of Tattva philosophy evolved in the last hundred years out of the West.

The fifth school representing the first bridging of East and West is Madame Blavatsky's Theosophical Tattva system. Based on Rama Prasad's Vidya Prana Tattva system, Blavatsky combines Western and Eastern strains of thought, a process which would be consummated in the sixth school of Tattvic Philosophy.

The main variation initiated by the Theosophical Tattva system is the premising of two higher Tattvas to correspond to the sixth and seventh Indian chakras.

These two additional Tattvas are titled Anupapadaka and Adi. Their esoteric attributes are as follows.

The Sixth and Seventh Theosophical Esoteric Tattvas

Tattva	1. Esoteric Shape	2. Element	3. Body	4. Chakra	5. Sense	6. Color (Esoteric)	7. Planet	8. Musical Note
ADI (7th) (the first)	Egg	Materia Prima Spirit of Ether Akasa	Auric egg enveloping body, Light of Kundalini	SAHASARA (Crown of head)	All embracing consciousness	Blue (Rainbow)	Jupiter	G
ANUPAPADAKA (6th) (Self-created)	Crescent Moon (containing radiant White Sun)	Spirit (Spiritual Essence, Divine Flame)	Third Eye (Pineal gland) Astral Body	AJNA (forehead)	Spiritual understanding	Yellow	Mercury	E

By this system the total number of counterchanged Tattvas becomes 49 as seven times seven. Each set of seven corresponds to one of the seven layers or sheaths (or kosas) of the Theosophical universe. The following tables delineate the symbolism for the lower five Tattvas.

Theosophical Exoteric Tattva System

Table 1. Element—The five elemental allocations to the Tattvas are shown in this table in conformity with those attributes as recorded by Rama Prasad.

Table 2. Esoteric Shape—The Theosophical system allocates the Eastern Tattva shapes to Western magickal shapes as shown in this table.

Table 3. Exoteric Shape—The common geometrical shapes for the Tattvas, seen as exoteric as opposed to the esoteric attributes of table 2, are listed here.

Table 4. Parts of Body—The Theosophical division of the human body in light of Tattva correspondences ordered by the five lower chakras is listed in this table.

Table 5. Chakra—The Tantrik chakra scheme is paralleled to the five Theosophical Tattvas, in accordance with traditional chakra symbolism.

Table 6. Esoteric Principle—The division of the soul and body in accordance with Theosophical principles are correlated to the five Tattvas.

Theosophical Exoteric Tattva System (cont'd.)

Tattva	1. Element	2. Esoteric Shape	3. Exoteric Shape	4. Parts of Body	5. Chakra	6. Esoteric Principle
Akasha (Alaya)	Ether	Upward pointing triangle	Oval	Head (Heart, throat)	Visuddha (5th)	Higher Manas— higher intellect, Atma—self
Vayu	Air	Downward pointing triangle	Circle	Navel (Stomach, spine)	Anahata (4th)	Lower Manas— higher emotion, Manas—mind
Tejas (Agni)	Fire	Inverted pentagram	Triangle	Shoulder (umbilical cord)	Manipura (3rd)	Kama—desire, Buddhi—intellect
Apas	Water	Two lower points of upright pentagram	Crescent	Knees (Spleen, liver)	Svadhisthana (2nd)	Linga Sarira— astral body, Chittam— thought stuff
Prithivi	Earth	Upright pentagram excluding the two lower points	Square	Feet (root of nose between eyebrows)	Muladhara (1st)	Prana—breath Ahankara—ego

Theosophical Exoteric Tattva System (cont'd.)

Table 7. Planet (Esoteric)—The planetary correspondences to the Tattvas as perceived by Madame Blavatsky are shown in this table.

Table 8. Musical Note—The sound correlations which can activate the five Tattvas are shown in this table according to the Theosophical correlation of sound and color.

Table 9. Rectified Planet—The traditional Theosophical planetary scheme of table 7 is removed of its occult blinds to correspond to the color and sound attributes of tables 11 and 8. This is accomplished by switching Saturn with Venus so that the traditional Western attributions can be correctly allocated to the East, as follows:

The Tattvas as Theosophical Sound and Color

Theosophical Planet		Color	Sound	Tattva
Blinded	Corrected			
Venus	Saturn	Indigo	A	Akasha
Saturn	Venus	Green	F	Vayu
Mars	Mars	Red	C	Tejas
Moon	Moon	Violet	B	Apas
Sun	Sun	Orange	D	Prithivi

Tables 10. and 11.—These tables correlate the two color schemes of the Tantrik and Theosophical traditions to the order of the five Tattvas.

Table 12. Sanskrit Alphabet Consonants—The Theosphical attribution of the Sanskrit alphabet to the five Tattvas is listed in this table. This is not the chakra scheme of alphabet letters, but rather a phonetic correlation of five basic sound groups.

Theosophical Exoteric Tattva System (cont'd.)

Tattva	7. Planet (Esoteric)	8. Musical Note	9. Rectified Planet	Color 10. Tantrik	11. Esoteric	12. Sanskrit Alphabet Consonants
Akasha	Venus	A	Saturn	Black (Colorless)	Indigo (Blue-Violet)	P Ph B Bh M V
Vayu	Saturn	F	Venus	Blue	Green	T Th D Dh N L S
Tejas	Mars	C	Mars	Red	Red	Ṭ Th Ḍ Dh Ṇ R Sh Kṣ (or Ḷ)
Apas	Moon	B	Moon	White	Violet	C Ch J Jh Ñ Y S
Prithivi	Sun	D	Sun	Yellow	Orange	K Kh G Gh Ṅ H

Since the Theosophical Tattva system contains seven Tattvas, the possible counterchanges increase from 25 to 49. Each counterchange is a sevenfold division of seven worlds as well as a letter of the (49-letter) Sanskrit alphabet. The sevenfold world division of the Theosophical Tattvas are as shown on the following page.

Seven Worlds—Seven Tattvas

Table 1. Lower Worlds (Talas)—The seven lower worlds of the Theosophical cosmogony are paralleled to the seven esoteric Tattvas of the Theosophical school, ranging from the outer body of man as Prithivi to the very concept of reincarnation (death and rebirth) as Adi.

Table 2. Higher Worlds (Lokas)—The seven higher worlds of the Theosophical cosmogony are paralleled to the seven esoteric Tattvas, ranging from the world of this earth as Prithivi to the realm of Nirvana as Adi.

Table 3. Kosmos—The seven key terms in Theosophy for the combination of the Higher and Lower worlds found in tables 1 and 2 are listed in this table in their esoteric Tattva order.

Table 4. Chakra—The seven chakras as they relate to the seven Theosophical worlds are ordered here in light of the esoteric Tattva scheme.

Table 5. Planet—The seven planets, corrected in light of switching Saturn with Venus, are correlated to the seven Theosophical worlds and seven esoteric Tattvas.

Table 6. Esoteric Color—The Western alchemical-planetary rainbow scale of seven rays is correctly aligned to the seven Theosophical worlds. These seven colors are the correct Theosophical color correspondences for the seven esoteric Tattvas.

Seven Worlds—Seven Tattvas (cont'd.)

Tattva	1. Lower Worlds (Talas)	2. Higher Worlds (Lokas)	3. Kosmos	4. Chakra	5. Planet	6. Esoteric Color
ADI	Atala (Death and Rebirth)	Satya (Nirvana)	Auric or Prakritic World	Sahasara	Jupiter	Blue
ANUPA-PADAKA	Vitala (Separation of higher from lower)	Tapar (the dwelling place of the Gods and Goddesses)	Alayic World	Ajna	Mercury	Yellow
Akasha	Sutala (Mind struggling with Desire)	Janar (Beyond the physical plane)	Mahatic World	Visuddha	Saturn	Blue-Violet
Vayu	Talatala (lower mind-objective life)	Mahar (between earth and utmost limits of universe)	Fohatic World	Anahata	Venus	Green
Tejas	Rasatala (Desire Body)	Svar (between Sun and Pole Star) Yogis	Jivic World	Manipura	Mars	Red
Apas	Mahatala (Astral shadow or double body)	Bhuvar (between earth and Sun) Wise-men	Astral World	Svadhisthana	Moon	Violet
Prithivi	Patala (Gross Body)	Bhur (Earth) Populus	Objective World	Muladhara	Sun	Orange

Each of these seven worlds possesses seven gradations of divisions of seven sub-worlds. Thus there are a total of seven times seven or 49 worlds corresponding to the 49 Tattva counterchanges. These 49 counterchanges correspond to the Pali serial order and number value of Sanskrit for 16 vowels and 33 consonants as show in the following table.

The 7 x 7 Theosophical Tattva Counterchanges and the Sanskrit Alphabet of 49 Letters

	Auric	Alayic	Mahatic	Fohatic	Jivic	Astral	Objective
Auric							
Tattva	1. Adi of Adi	2. Anupapadaka of Adi	3. Akasha of Adi	4. Vayu of Adi	5. Tejas of Adi	6. Apas of Adi	7. Prithivi of Adi
Planet	Jupiter of Jupiter	Mercury of Jupiter	Saturn of Jupiter	Venus of Jupiter	Mars of Jupiter	Moon of Jupiter	Sun of Jupiter
Color	Blue of Blue	Yellow of Blue	Blue-violet of Blue	Green of Blue	Red of Blue	Violet of Blue	Orange of Blue
Sanskrit	A = 1	Â = 2	I = 3	Î = 4	U = 5	Û = 6	Ri = 7
Alayic							
Tattva	8. Adi of Anupapadaka	9. Anupapadaka Anupapadaka	10. Akasha of Anupapadaka	11. Vayu of Anupapadaka	12. Tejas of Anupapadaka	13. Apas of Anupapadaka	14. Prithivi of Anupapadaka
Planet	Jupiter of Mercury	Mercury of Mercury	Saturn of Mercury	Venus of Mercury	Mars of Mercury	Moon of Mercury	Sun of Mercury
Color	Blue of Yellow	Yellow of Yellow	Blue-Violet of Yellow	Green of Yellow	Red of Yellow	Violet of Yellow	Orange of Yellow
Sanskrit	Rî = 8	Li = 9	Lî = 10	E = 11	Ai = 12	O = 13	Au = 14
Mahatic							
Tattva	15. Adi of Akasha	16. Anupapadaka of Akasha	17. Akasha of Akasha	18. Vayu of Akasha	19. Tejas of Akasha	20. Apas of Akasha	21. Prithivi of Akasha
Planet	Jupiter of Saturn	Mercury of Saturn	Saturn of Saturn	Venus of Saturn	Mars of Saturn	Moon of Saturn	Sun of Saturn
Color	Blue of Blue-Violet	Yellow of Blue-Violet	Blue-Violet of Blue-Violet	Green of Blue-Violet	Red of Blue-Violet	Violet of Blue-Violet	Orange of Blue-Violet
Sanskrit	Ah = 15	Am = 16	K = 0	Kh = 16	G = 32	Gh = 48	Ṅ = 64

The 7 x 7 Theosophical Tattva Counterchanges and the Sanskrit Alphabet of 49 Letters (cont'd.)

		Auric	Alayic	Mahatic	Fohatic	Jivic	Astral	Objective
Fohatic	Tattva	22. Adi of Vayu	23. Anupapa-daka of Vayu	24. Akasha of Vayu	25. Vayu of Vayu	26. Tejas of Vayu	27. Apas of Vayu	28. Prithivi of Vayu
	Planet	Jupiter of Venus	Mercury of Venus	Saturn of Venus	Venus of Venus	Mars of Venus	Moon of Venus	Sun of Venus
	Color	Blue of Green	Yellow of Green	Blue-Violet of Green	Green of Green	Red of Green	Violet of Green	Orange of Green
	Sanskrit	C = 80	Ch = 96	J = 112	Jh = 128	Ñ = 144	T = 160	Th = 176
Jaivic	Tattva	29. Adi of Tejas	30. Anupapa-daka of Tejas	31. Akasha of Tejas	32. Vayu of Tejas	33. Tejas of Tejas	34. Apas of Tejas	35. Prithivi of Tejas
	Planet	Jupiter of Mars	Mercury of Mars	Saturn of Mars	Venus of Mars	Mars of Mars	Moon of Mars	Sun of Mars
	Color	Blue of Red	Yellow of Red	Blue-Violet of Red	Green of Red	Red of Red	Violet of Red	Orange of Red
	Sanskrit	D = 192	Dh = 208	N = 224	T = 240	Th = 256	D = 272	Dh = 288
Astral	Tattva	36. Adi of Apas	37. Anupapa-daka of Apas	38. Akasha of Apas	39. Vayu of Apas	40. Tejas of Apas	41. Apas of Apas	42. Prithivi of Apas
	Planet	Jupiter of Moon	Mercury of Moon	Saturn of Moon	Venus of Moon	Mars of Moon	Moon of Moon	Sun of Moon
	Color	Blue of Violet	Yellow of Violet	Blue-Violet of Violet	Green of Violet	Red of Violet	Violet of Violet	Orange of Violet
	Sanskrit	N = 304	P = 320	Ph = 336	B = 352	Bh = 368	M = 384	Y = 400
Objective	Tattva	43. Adi of Prithivi	44. Anupapa-daka of Prithivi	45. Akahsa of Prithivi	46. Vayu of Prithivi	47. Tejas of Prithivi	48. Apas of Prithivi	49. Prithivi of Prithivi
	Planet	Jupiter of Sun	Mercury of Sun	Saturn of Sun	Venus of Sun	Mars of Sun	Moon of Sun	Sun of Sun
	Color	Blue of Orange	Yellow of Orange	Blue-Violet of Orange	Green of Orange	Red of Orange	Violet of Orange	Orange of Orange
	Sanskrit	R = 416	L = 432	V = 448	Ṡ = 464	Sh = 480	S = 496	H = 512

The Golden Dawn Magickal-Tattva System

The Golden Dawn magickal-Tattva system, which is the final or sixth school of Tattva philosophy, emanated directly out of the Theosophical school and Westernized the symbol set to its ultimate refinement.

The secret magickal instructions of the Golden Dawn, which were undoubtedly the brainchild of S. L. MacGregor Mathers, were based on Western magickal correspondences as classified by the Jewish Qabalah. However one Eastern magickal system was adopted to Mathers' own Qabalistic correspondences: the Tattva system of Rama Prasad. Mathers extracted the basic Indian Tattva attributes from the Theosophical edition of Prasad's *Science of Breath*.

His motivation for an Eastern infusion into his Western system was not Madame Blavatsky, but rather the novelist Edward Bulwer-Lytton. In Lytton's famous Rosicrusian novel *Zanoni,* a poisoning of the main character was neutralized by the magickal visualization of the Apas Tattva. Mathers treasured this novel to such a degree that he derived his own nickname, ZAN, from the main character, Zanoni.

It is on account of Lytton's use of the Tattvas (which must be one of the earliest examples in English literature, if not the first) that Mathers felt compelled to add the Tattva system to his own arsenal of Western magick, which included the Tarot, astrology, geomancy, the Qabalah, and the obscure Enochian system of John Dee. It is intriguing to note that neither Mathers nor Blavatsky included the *I Ching* in their magickal teachings, a deficiency which Aleister Crowley would correct in his own researches.

In any event, the recorded instructions for the Tattvas found in the secret writings of the Golden Dawn are little more than a synopsis of Prasad's Tattva work.

However, Mathers was able to parallel the five Tattvas to the four Western elements (Fire, Water, Air, and Earth) plus Spirit, which linked the East with the West in a more thorough fashion than Blavatsky could with her own Tattva correspondences.

The following tables detail this Golden Dawn Tattva system.

The Golden Dawn Tattva System

Table 1. Shape—The five shapes for the Tattvas, based on Rama Prasad's symbolism, are shown here with the three-dimensional correspondences shown in parentheses.

Table 2. Color—The five orthodox Tattva colors, and their variants in parentheses are shown in light of Golden Dawn color symbolism.

Table 3. Element—The Western equivalents to the Eastern system of elemental Tattva allocations are listed here. The Theosophical Tattva school, of which the Golden Dawn Tattva school represents a refinement, does not overtly table out these elemental correspondences.

Table 4. Planet—The planetary symbolism of the Golden Dawn is correlated to the five Tattvas. In these attributes the symbolism of Rama Prasad is combined with that of Theosophy.

Table 5. Direction as Enochian Watchtowers—The directions and their correspondences to the Enochian Watchtowers as laid out in a Golden Dawn ritual temple are paralleled to the five Tattvas.

Table 6. The Middle Pillar and the Human Body—The Sephiroth which divide the Middle Pillar of the Tree of Life into five divisions are equated here to five zones in the human body in the order of the five Tattvas.

The Golden Dawn Tattva System (cont'd.)

Tattva	1. Shape	2. Color	3. Element	4. Planet	5. Direction as Enochian Watchtowers	6. The Middle Pillar and the Human Body
Akasha	Oval, vesica piscis (egg)	Blue-Violet (black, dark, no color)	Spirit	Saturn	Central Tablet of Union	Kether—Crown of Head
Vayu	Circle (sphere)	Sky Blue (Green)	Air	Jupiter, Venus	Eastern Watchtower of Air	Daath—Throat
Tejas	Upright Triangle (Pyramid)	Red (red-orange)	Fire	Mars	Southern Watchtower of Fire	Tiphereth—Heart
Apas	Crescent with horns upright (Cup)	Silver-White (all colors)	Water	Moon	Western Watchtower of Water	Yesod—Genitals
Prithivi	Square (Cube)	Yellow (Deep yellow)	Earth	Mercury, Sun	Northern Watchtower of Earth	Malkuth—Anus (Feet)

The Golden Dawn Tattva System (cont'd.)

Tables 7. through 9.—These tables show three methods of allocating the Tarot deck to the five Tattvas in light of the Golden Dawn magickal symbology.

Table 10. Pentagrammaton—The fivefold sacred name Jehoshuah is ordered in light of the elemental order of the Tetragrammaton with the letter Shin as Spirit. This name is the combination of the Tetragrammaton with the letter Shin as Spirit.

Table 11. Number Value of Shape—The geometrical shapes in table 1 can be assigned a number value. Akasha as an oval is zero, Vayu as a circular dot is one, Apas as a crescent horn two, Tejas as a triangle is three, while Prithivi as a square is four.

Table 12. Musical Note—The correct sound attributes for the Tattvas in light of Golden Dawn sound and color symbolism are listed here. They are based on the following color-sound-planetary correlations:

Five Tattvas as Golden Dawn Sound and Color

Tattva	Sound	Color	Planet
Tejas	C	Red	Mars
Prithivi	E	Yellow	Sun (Mercury)
Vayu	G#	Blue	Jupiter (Venus)
Akasha	A	Blue-Violet	Saturn
Apas	A#	Violet	Moon

Table 13. Points of Upright Pentagram—The order of Tattvas as a pentagram, based on Tables 3 and 10, is listed in accordance with the pentagram rituals of the Golden Dawn.

The Golden Dawn Tattva System (cont'd.)

Tattva	Tarot 7. Major	8. Minor	9. Deck	10. Pentagrammaton	11. Number value of Shape	12. Musical Note	13. Points of Upright Pentagram
Akasha	Key XXI	Ace	Major Arcana	Shin	0	A	Apex point
Vayu	Key X	King	Swords	Vav	1	G#	Upper Left
Tejas	Key XVI	Knight	Wands	Yod	3	C	Lower Right
Apas	Key II	Queen	Cups	Heh	2	A#	Upper Right
Prithivi	Key I	Page	Pentacles	Heh (Final)	4	E	Lower Left

The Golden Dawn Tattva System (cont'd.)

Tables 14. through 17—These tables detail the four-world Qabalistic color scale unique to Golden Dawn symbolism for the Tree of Life, as applied to the five Tattvas. The allocating of the five Tattvas to five paths of the Tree of Life is derived from Crowley's Liber 777, table 22, for these specific Tattva-color correlations.

Crowley's Tattva-Path Attributions

Tattva	Path on Tree of Life
Akasha	31st path as the alternate attribute Spirit
Vayu	11th path as the attribute Air
Tejas	31st path as the attribute Fire
Apas	23rd path as the attribute Water
Prithivi	32nd path as the alternate attribute Earth

Tables 18. and 19—These two tables of Gods and Goddesses are extracted from Crowley's 777 in light of the path allocations shown above.

Tattva	14. King Scale	15. Queen Scale	Additional Colors 16. Emperor Scale	17. Empress Scale	18. Egyptian God Forms	19. Greek God Forms
Akasha	White merging into Gray	Deep Purple, nearly Black	7 Prismatic colors, Violet on outside	White, Red, Yellow, Blue, Black (Black on outside)	Asar	Iacchus
Vayu	Bright Pale Yellow	Sky Blue	Blue Emerald Green	Emerald flecked Gold	Nu	Zeus
Tejas	Glowing Orange Scarlet	Vermillion	Scarlet flecked Gold	Vermillion flecked Crimson and Emerald	Horus	Hades
Apas	Deep Blue	Sea Green	Deep Olive Green	White flecked Purple	Isis	Poseidon
Prithivi	Citrine, Olive, Russet, Black	Amber	Dark Brown	Black flecked Yellow	Nephthys	Demeter

The Golden Dawn Tattva System (cont'd.)

Table 20. Elemental Hebrew Letter—The Hebrew mantras for the five Tattvas based on table 3 are listed here.

Table 21. Elemental Enochian Letter (Crowley)—The corresponding Enochian mantras for table 20 are worked out, based on Crowley's elemental allocation for the five Enochian letters excluded from the Golden Dawn's "Book of the Concourse of Forces."

Tattva	20. Elemental Hebrew Letter	21. Elemental Enochian Letter (Crowley)
Akasha	O	D
Vayu	A	H
Tejas	Sh	C
Apas	M	Q
Prithivi	Th	X

The Golden Dawn Tattva System (cont'd.)

Table 22. Quadrant of Enochian Watchtower—Each Enochian Watchtower of 156 squares is laid out as the four directions and center of the Golden Dawn elemental order. This table parallels these Enochian attributes to the Tattvas.

Table 23. Letters of Tablet of Union—The Enochian "fifth watchtower" assigned to Spirit is composed of five sets of four letters which can be allocated to the five Tattvas as laid out in this table.

Table 24. Geomancy (as Elements)—The geomantic shapes can be allocated to the four elements and spirit so that these 16 shapes can be subdivided among the five Tattvas, as demonstrated in this table.

Table 25. Kerubic Angels—The four kerubic angels can be premised as five, if the fifth is seen as a synthesis of the four. Here the kerubic order is placed in the Tattvic order, where the fifth kerubic creature (as a sphinx, child or dove) is equated to Akasha.

Table 26. Tree of Life (Elemental)—The five lower Sephiroth form the elemental chain of Spirit, Fire, Water, Air, and Earth (from Tiphereth to Malkuth). Here each of the five lower Sephiroth is paired to one of the five Tattvas.

Table 27. 5 Lower Grades (Golden Dawn)—The five lower Golden Dawn grades which correspond to the elemental chain of table 26 are here paired to the Tattvas.

The Golden Dawn Tattva System (cont'd.)

Tattva	22. Quadrant of Enochian Watchtower	23. Letters of Tablet of Union	24. Geomancy (as Elements)	25. Kerbuic Angels	26. Tree of Life (Elemental)	27. Five Lower Grades (Golden Dawn)
Akasha	Center (two squares)	ehnb	Cauda Draconis, Caput Draconis	Sphinx (Child, Dove)	Tiphereth (Spirit)	Adeptus Minor (5=6)
Vayu	Upper Left (5 x 6 squares)	xCai	Albus, Puella, Tristitia	Angel	Yesod (Air)	Theoricus (2=9)
Tejas	Lower Right (5 x 6 squares)	paam	Puer, Fortuna Major, Acquisitio, Fortuna Minor	Lion	Netzach (Fire)	Philosophus (4=7)
Apas	Upper Right (5 x 6 squares)	aont	Populus, Rubeus, Laetitia, Via	Eagle	Hod (Water)	Practicus (3=8)
Prithivi	Lower Left (5 x 6 squares)	rmTo	Amissio, Conjunctio, Carcer	Ox	Malkuth (Earth)	Zelator (1=10)

The Golden Dawn Tattva System (cont'd.)

Table 28. Five Lower Grades (Crowley's A∴A∴)—Crowley's revision of the grades shown in table 27 is listed in this table.

Table 29. Tree of Life—Two attributes are given in this table, both based on table 26, for the planet and metal corresponding to each of the five lower Sephiroth, paired to the five Tattvas.

Table 30. Magickal Weapon—The five magickal weapons of the pentagram are shown here in accordance with the Sephirotic order of table 26.

Table 31. God-Name—The directional God names of the lesser pentagram ritual are allocated to the Tattvas, based on the directional order of table 5.

Table 32. Hebrew and Number—The Hebrew equivalents and gematria values for table 31 are listed here.

| Tattva | 28. Five Lower Grades (Crowley's A∴A∴) | 29. Tree of Life | | 30. Magickal Weapon | 31. God-Name | 32. Hebrew and Number |
		Planet	Alchemy			
Akasha	Adeptus Minor (5=6)	Sun	Gold	Lamp	Yehoshuah	IHShVH (326)
Vayu	Zelator (2=9)	Moon	Silver	Dagger	Yod He Vav He	IHVH (26)
Tejas	Philosophus (4=7)	Venus	Copper	Wand	Adonai	ADNI (65)
Apas	Practicus (3=8)	Mercury	Quicksilver	Cup	Eheieh	AHIH (21)
Prithivi	Neophyte (1=10)	Earth	Lead	Pentacle	Agla	AGLA (35)

The Golden Dawn Tattva System (cont'd.)

Table 33. Archangels—The four archangels of the lesser pentagram ritual are tabled here in accordance with the Tattva order.

Table 34. Hebrew and Number—The Hebrew equivalents and gematria number values for table 33 are listed here.

Table 35. Parts of the Soul—The Qabalistic division of the soul, based on five zones of the Tree of Life are applied to the Tattvas by their elemental equivalents as follows:

The Five Elemental Tattvas and the Fivefold Soul of the Tree of Life

Five Tattvas	Five Elements	Five Zones of Tree of Life	Five Gradations of the Soul
Akasha	Spirit	Kether	Yechidah
Tejas	Fire	Chockmah	Chiah
Apas	Water	Binah	Neschamah
Vayu	Air	Chesed-Yesod	Ruach
Prithivi	Earth	Malkuth	Nephesch

Table 36. Hebrew and Number—The Hebrew equivalents and gematria values for table 35 are listed here.

Tattva	33. Archangels	34. Hebrew and Number	35. Parts of the Soul	36. Hebrew and Number
Akasha	Adam	ADM (45, 605)	Yechidah (The Divine Self)	IChIDH (37)
Vayu	Raphael	RPAL (311)	Ruach (Vital Breath)	RVCh (214)
Tejas	Michael	MICAL (101)	Chiah (Vital Energy)	ChIH (23)
Apas	Gabriel	GBRIAL (246)	Neschamah (Aspiration)	NShMH (395)
Prithivi	Auriel	AVRIAL (248)	Nephesch (Subtle, Astral Body)	NPSh (430)

The Golden Dawn Tattva System (cont'd.)
Case's Golden Dawn Tarot

Tables 37. through 39.—These three tables detail Paul Foster Case's version of Book T in light of the use of the Tattvas as symbols within a Tarot deck.

Table 37 shows the combination of all five Tattvas appearing in Key VII, The Chariot, of the Major Arcana. Though based on Waite's design of the same card, Case intentionally works all five Tattvas into his own version of this card. The charioteer represents Hermes as the originator of sound, color, and number, the three measures of the Tattva classification system. This card is also the 418 number current of *The Book of the Law*, in light of Crowley's research.

Table 38 shows the parts of the Minor Arcana implements (or pips) which correspond to each of the five Tattvas.

Table 39 shows a partial listing of the five Tattvas as they appear in the cards of the Major Arcana.

Though Case edited out all references to the Enochian system in his version of Golden Dawn magick, he retained the Tattva system in its entirety.

The Golden Dawn Tattva System (cont'd.)
Case's Golden Dawn Tarot

Tattva	37. Key VII—The Chariot	38. Minor Arcana	39. Major Arcana
Akasha	Shield on Chariot	Mouth (Cup), Oval Pummel (Sword), Crown (Penetrated by Ace of Swords)	Crown (Key V), Rim of Crown (Key XVI), Mouth of Trumpet (Key XX), Wreath (Key XXI), Outline of Arms, Body and Chains (Key XV), Seed in Sky (Key XIII)
Vayu	Circle below cup on shield and circle above shield	Rim (Pentacle), Circular Ends and Dividers (Wand), Circular Bottom (Cup)	Wheel (Key X), Sun and Faery Circle (Key XIX), Globe (Key IV), Circle in Crown (Key XI)
Tejas	Diamond in Cup and Wings of Disc	Pentagram (Pentacle), Crystal Heads (Wand), Blade (Sword), Base (Cup)	Triangle on Breast (Key III), Hexagram (Key IX), Bell of Trumpet (Key XX), Arms and Head (Keys IV, XII, XXI), Termination of Lightning Bolt (Key XVI)
Apas	Crescent cup on shield	Calyx and Body of Cup	Moon and Horns of Crown (Key II), Moon Face (Key XVIII), Moons upon Tunic (Key XII), Scales (Key XI), Shoulders (Key VII)
Prithivi	Square chariot body	Shaft of Wand, Stem of Cup, Hilt of Sword	Body of Tower (Keys XVI, XVIII), Cube (Keys II, IV, VII, XV), Table (Key I), Throne (Keys III, V, XI), Coffins (Key XX)

THE ASTRAL DOORWAYS OF THE GOLDEN DAWN TATTVAS

The Golden Dawn Tattva system possesses an esoteric tradition unique to itself: the use of the Tattvas as doorways to other dimensions. This method used the charged imagination to pass through the Tattvas.

Mathers undoubtedly developed this method, which resembles the Renaissance active meditational method known as skrying (popularized by John Dee and Edward Kelley). This method can also be applied to any magickal symbol at large, but the best results come from the use of the Tattvas.

This Tattva active meditational method depends upon the opposite or flashing color that each Tattva possesses. These flashing colors are as follows.

Golden Dawn Tattva Flashing Colors

Tattva	Normal Color	Flashing Color
Akasha	Blue-Violet	Yellow-Orange
Vayu	Blue	Orange
Tejas	Red	Green
Apas	White	Pale Silver-Violet
Prithivi	Yellow	Violet

The procedures for using the Tattvas as astral doorways are as follows.

• A Tattva is selected from the 25 counterchanges.

• The Tattva is placed before the magician.

• The magician stares fixedly at the Tattva for a few minutes while regulating the breath.

• The eyes are then closed. The Tattva will slowly appear before the mind's eye in its flashing or opposite color.

• The magician now wills with the imagination the Tattva to grow larger and larger until it can be passed through as a doorway to the astral world.

• This passage through the imaged Tattva door is likened to an upward ascent, known as rising on the planes.

• Once through this doorway, the magician should encounter the elemental landscape associated with this Tattva. Thus if Prithivi of Apas was selected, a seashore (Earth of Water) or an island should be encountered, relating to the elemental counterchange. (This technique is fully detailed in the esoteric Tattva writings of the Golden Dawn.)

• The visions encountered are fully tested for their veracity. After the journey is ended, the magician returns to his body by descending back to this earthly plane and safely closes off the astral doorway and the magickal operation itself.

TATTVIC TIDES

The cycle of the five Tattvas traditionally marks the 24 hours of each day. Rama Prasad's Tattvic research divulged a cycle of 12 two-hour intervals beginning at sunrise.

Following these clues, the Golden Dawn established a basic cycle of one Tattva, starting with Akasha, for each of these two-hour intervals. These two-hour Tattvic tides are composed of two complete rounds of the five Tattvas plus one extra round of Akasha and Vayu. These 12 basic Tattvic tides each correspond to one of the 12 Zodiacal signs beginning with Aries as sunrise. Their division of the day is as follows.

The Twelve Tattvas and the 24-Hour Day

Time of Day	Tattva	Zodiac
6:00 am–8:00 am	Akasha	Aries
8:00 am–10:00 am	Vayu	Taurus
10:00 am–Noon	Tejas	Gemini
Noon–2:00 pm	Apas	Cancer
2:00 pm–4:00 pm	Prithivi	Leo
4:00 pm–6:00 pm	Akasha	Virgo
6:00 pm–8:00 pm	Vayu	Libra
8:00 pm–10:00 pm	Tejas	Scorpio
10:00 pm–Midnight	Apas	Sagittarius
Midnight–2:00 am	Prithivi	Capricorn
2:00 am–4:00 am	Akasha	Aquarius
4:00 am–6:00 am	Vayu	Pisces

The obvious drawback with this Tattvic cycle is that the five Tattvas cannot be evenly distributed among the 12 divisions of the day.

J. W. Brodie-Innes of the Golden Dawn felt that this cycle could be evenly applied to all the Tattvas of all 25 counterchanges of the Sankhya Kapila Tattva system cycle through each of the 12 two-hour stations. Following this clue, the Golden Dawn historian Francis King has premised that each of these 25 counterchanges lasts exactly four minutes and 48 seconds. This would result in a grand cycle of 300 total Tattva counterchanges for each day.

The following two tables delineate these Tattvic Tides.

Tattva Tide Table (Sunrise at 6:00 am)

Tattva Counterchange	Time Period	Planet (Vidya Prana)	Element (Golden Dawn)
Akasha-Akasha	6:00:00 am–6:04:48	Mercury of Mercury	Spirit of Spirit
Akasha-Vayu	6:04:48–6:09:36	Saturn of Mercury	Air of Spirit
Akasha-Tejas	6:09:36–6:14:24	Mars of Mercury	Fire of Spirit
Akasha-Apas	6:14:24–6:19:12	Venus of Mercury	Water of Spirit
Akasha-Prithivi	6:19:12–6:24:00	Jupiter of Mercury	Earth of Spirit
Vayu-Akasha	6:24:00–6:28:48	Mercury of Saturn	Spirit of Air
Vayu-Vayu	6:28:48–6:33:36	Saturn of Saturn	Air of Air
Vayu-Tejas	6:33:36–6:38:24	Mars of Saturn	Fire of Air
Vayu-Apas	6:38:24–6:43:12	Venus of Saturn	Water of Air
Vayu-Prithivi	6:43:12–6:48:00	Jupiter of Saturn	Earth of Air
Tejas-Akasha	6:48:00–6:52:48	Mercury of Mars	Spirit of Fire
Tejas-Vayu	6:52:48–6:57:36	Saturn of Mars	Air of Fire
Tejas-Tejas	6:57:36–7:02:24	Mars of Mars	Fire of Fire
Tejas-Apas	7:02:24–7:07:12	Venus of Mars	Water of Fire
Tejas-Prithivi	7:07:12–7:12:00	Jupiter of Mars	Earth of Fire
Apas-Akasha	7:12:00–7:16:48	Mercury of Venus	Spirit of Water
Apas-Vayu	7:16:48–7:21:36	Saturn of Venus	Air of Water
Apas-Tejas	7:21:36–7:26:24	Mars of Venus	Fire of Water
Apas-Apas	7:26:24–7:31:12	Venus of Venus	Water of Water
Apas-Prithivi	7:31:12–7:36:00	Jupiter of Venus	Earth of Water
Prithivi-Akasha	7:36:00–7:40:48	Mercury of Jupiter	Spirit of Earth
Prithivi-Vayu	7:40:48–7:45:36	Saturn of Jupiter	Air of Earth
Prithivi-Tejas	7:45:36–7:50:24	Mars of Jupiter	Fire of Earth
Prithivi-Apas	7:50:24–7:55:12	Venus of Jupiter	Water of Earth
Prithivi-Prithivi	7:55:12–8:00:00	Jupiter of Jupiter	Earth of Earth

Zodiacal Cycle for Tattva Tides
(Based on Sunrise at 6:00 am)

Time	Zodiac	Tattva Counterchanges
6:00 am–8:00 am	Aries	1–25
8:00 am–10:00 am	Taurus	26–50
10:00 am–Noon	Gemini	51–75
Noon–2:00 pm	Cancer	76–100
2:00 pm–4:00 pm	Leo	101–125
4:00 pm–6:00 pm	Virgo	126–150
6:00 pm–8:00 pm	Libra	151–175
8:00 pm–10:00 pm	Scorpio	176–200
10:00 pm–Midnight	Sagittarius	201–225
Midnight–2:00 am	Capricorn	226–250
2:00 am–4:00 am	Aquarius	251–275
4:00 am–6:00 am	Pisces	276–300

The two foregoing tables are calculated for sunrise at exactly 6:00 am. For all days when sunrise is not at 6:00 am, these tables can be corrected by adjusting the real time of sunrise with respect to 6:00 am. For example, if sunrise is at 5:43 am, you would subtract 17 minutes from each of the above times.

These tables can be used with the Vidya Prana Tattva system at the Spring Equinox to determine an oracular Tattva counterchange which will govern the next 12 months. Using the above tables, determine the Tattva counterchange which occurs exactly when the Sun enters Aries. Then use the following table to determine if the counterchange is auspicious or inauspicious.

Tattva Vernal Equinoctal Oracle

Tattva	Oracle
Akasha	Want of grain and comfort
Vayu	Confusion, accidents, famine, little rain
Tejas	Famine, subversion or fear of it, fearful epidemics, least possible rain
Apas	Plenty of rain, plenty of grain, no want, great comfort, well-grown fields
Prithivi	Plenty and prosperity, good crops, much comfort and enjoyment

Sixth Key

Chinese

Overview

This is the most formidable chapter in the book since it deals with the most remotely Eastern thought. However, due to the pioneering research of Aleister Crowley, the basic elements of the Chinese cosmology can be successfully integrated into the heart of the Western magickal tradition. Originally my research covering the Eastern traditions for this book did not penetrate into Chinese thought, but stopped at Tibetan. Although my initial studies touched upon Chinese, I was unable to find the correct key for its numbering. In fact, I was unable to discover any printed reference indicating that the characters forming the Chinese language *could* be numbered. However, I intuitively sensed that Chinese calligraphy, by its ordered brush strokes, might possess a number value.

As my work drew near to completion, I was still unable to find an authentic source document detailing a method ascribing number value to Chinese characters. At that point of my research I decided that I would first complete my definitive text on number languages, ending the Eastern section with Tibetan. As I put the finishing touches on the book I came across a translation of the Chinese almanac known as *T'ung Shu*. The 29th section clearly described a Taoist method for numbering Chinese based on the number of brush strokes required for each character.

Overwhelmed by the knowledge that my own intuitions concerning the esoteric makeup of Chinese could now be supported by a traditional text, I postponed the finalization of the book to include one last chapter analyzing in full the Chinese language. The first frustration I met was the fact that this Chinese Taoist method of numbering is intimately connected with the 384 lines which compose the 64 hexagrams of the *I Ching*. I realized that in order to clearly delineate the Taoist method of numbering Chinese, a version of the *I Ching* must be included as a point of reference. The last task I wanted to take on at the end of my research was a rewrite of the *I Ching*, but as I progressed with my dissertation on Chinese, I was forced to come to terms with developing a version of the *I Ching* to include in the text.

I have always been fond of the *I Ching*. As a divinatory tool it is just as supportive and workable as the Tarot. And as a philosophical system, I can think of no greater text to capture the essence of the Taoist philosophy of Yin and Yang. But like so many Westerners who rely on the *I Ching* translations available, being incapable of verifying such translations, I was at a loss to find a way to include the text in my own book. Then I came upon a device which very early in my career I had attempted without success. This device was the distillation of every poetical translation of the *I Ching* to an essential reading, free of any extraneous commentaries. After many months of writing and rewriting I was able to come up with what I felt to be the bottom line of oracular meaning for each of the 64 hexagrams.

After developing a workable rewrite of the *I Ching* to be included in my text, I realized that the beginning reader would need a basic understanding of the elements of Chinese cosmology before the real pattern behind the *I Ching* could be clearly perceived. So I set out a clear explanation of the basic Chinese cosmological divisions of:

- Yin and Yang
- The Five Elements
- The Ten Heavenly Stems
- The Twelve Earthly Roots
- The Sixty-Year Cycle of 5 x 12.

Therefore you will find in this section on Chinese:

- A very extensive commentary on Chinese cosmology
- The pattern behind the 64 hexagrams of the *I Ching*
- An essential reading of the text of the *I Ching*
- The esoteric meanings for the first ten numbers
- The method of numbering Chinese calligraphy and its tie-in to the *I Ching*.

This sixth key begins with one of the most extensive timelines in the book, spanning 8000 BCE to 1876 CE. It should be noted here that much insight can be gained by taking every timeline in this book and combining them into one large timeline. From such a timeline it will instantly be apparent what systems predate any other system. And the oldest of all magickal systems is the Chinese cosmological theories as fully outlined in this text.

The first cosmological concept that is discussed in the main body of this chapter is the concept of Yin and Yang. Yin and Yang represent the ultimate polarity which permeates all things on this physical plane. Yin is traditionally assigned to the feminine, receptive energy, while Yang is assigned to the masculine, penetrating energy. A table entitled "Taoist Yin and Yang" details all of the major pairs or couples of attributes. Innovative to this table is the classification of left to male and right to female. In the Western schools of occult symbolism, the right is invariably masculine, while the left is feminine. Refer, for instance, to the Hebraic table showing the binary symbolism found in the *Zohar*. However the attributes expressed in this table are based on the Chinese compass, which places the South at the top and the North at the bottom. In this orientation of facing South, the left occupies the East (rising Sun), while the right occupies the West (setting Sun). Therefore the increase of light, heralded by sunrise, is left, masculine, and Yang; the decrease of light is conversely heralded by sunset and is right and Yin.

This discussion of Yin and Yang is followed by an analysis of "The Five Elements." The Chinese system of five basic elements composing the makeup of the universe is the oldest magickal elemental tradition. It is obviously the source for the Indian Tattva system, the Platonic solids, and the Western hermetic alchemical elements. The correct correspondences between these four systems is clearly shown in the table entitled "Fivefold Attributes of the World." The basic parallels between Chinese and Western elemental symbolism are as follows:

Five Basic Elements

East	West
Earth	Spirit
Fire	Fire
Wood	Air
Water	Water
Metal	Earth

It should be noted that there are two basic systems within the Chinese fivefold elements. In one system Spirit is equated to Earth; in the other system Spirit is equated to Metal. The Spirit-Earth system is based on the symbolism of the four directions (Spirit = Center), while the Spirit-Metal system is based on the symbolism of the pentagram (Spirit = apex).

In the West, Earth as an element is the most removed from Spirit, usually designating the denseness of matter. But in the East, both Earth and Metal are symbols of the supreme Spirit. This may be due to the fact that the ancient Chinese were spiritually in tune with the earth and lived in harmony with the planet, while the West is out of synch with the earth and sees spirit as antithetical to matter. At another level of symbolism, the Chinese system is evocative of alchemical sensibilities. For the precious metals of Alchemy denote spirit, and the earth whose womb nurtures the growth of these precious metals is also spirit.

In the table entitled "Five Chinese Elements," every basic Taoist classification system derived from this fivefold division is listed. Some of the
symbol sets involved (such as the five poisons) have been rectified from
blinded source documents. All rectifications found in this table are based
on Earth as Spirit. After a listing of these elemental qualities, the relationships between the five elements are shown in a table called "Harmony of
The Five Chinese Elements." Each element, in relation to the other
remaining four elements, is either a parent, a child, an enemy, or a friend.
This table can be used when analyzing any pair of elements. From this
analysis the basic sympathy or antipathy of any one element to another
can easily be determined.

The pentagram, which in some ways is the supreme symbol for Western magick, has its origin in the Chinese elemental system. In the West the
apex of the pentagram is the controlling point for Spirit. In the Chinese
system, this apex is governed by Metal (in its alternate, Spirit). These
attributes are clearly detailed in the table entitled "The Chinese Elemental Pentagram." The Chinese Taoist magickal system utilizes the pentagram in four different ways to invoke:

- Creation

- Destruction

- Love

- Fear

These four methods are described in the table entitled "Four Chinese
Pentagonal Cycles." The discussion of the five elements ends with a com-
parison between the five traditional Western elements, and the twofold
Chinese element division (based on the pentagram or the four directions).

Next the symbolism of the Ten Celestial Stems is discussed. These ten
stems are also the ten basic numbers. As elements, each pair of stems corresponds to one of five elements. This is followed by an analysis of the
Twelve Earthly Branches. In essence these 12 earthly branches are the 12
Chinese yearly Zodiac animals. Although the West divides the year into 12
Zodiacal divisions, the Chinese divide the 12 years into 12 one-year Zodiacal divisions. These two systems are compared in the table entitled "Eastern and Western Zodiacs as Parallel Cycles."

Now these two cycles of 10 stems and 12 branches combine to form one
of the most ancient symbolic classifications of all time: the Chinese sexagenary cycle of two parallel cycles of 6 x 10 stems and 5 x 12 roots. The sexagenary cycle determines the symbolic quality of each year (beginning
with the Chinese New Year).

It is from this system that the ruling Zodiac animal for each New Year
is determined. Each year contains a host of symbolic meanings to determine whether the year is auspicious or inauspicious. All these attributes
are shown in the table entitled "The Sexagenary Cycle." This table ends
the first section of this key, dealing with the elements of Chinese cosmology. Like many other dating systems described in this text, you should

experiment with this table by converting important dates (such as your own birth date) to their respective symbol sets.

The next section of this key deals with the esoteric structure of the *I Ching*. This section begins with a timeline denoting its evolution. Unknown to most Westerners, there are three separate versions of the *I Ching*. The version we are familiar with is the third, most recent version, dating from around 1150 BCE. This timeline is followed by a flowchart entitled "Tree of I Ching," detailing the evolution of the philosophical structure of the *I Ching* from the basic concept of Yin and Yang to the *I Ching* as it exists today.

Next comes a detailed discussion of each of the components which make up the hexagrams of the *I Ching*. The *I Ching* is the oldest surviving oracle, whose correct interpretations have been preserved in writing. It involves the random manipulation of 64 separate symbols. Each symbol is known as a hexagram, made up of six separate lines. Each of the six lines composing a hexagram is either a straight or a broken line. The straight line denotes Yang while the broken line denotes Yin. Thus the hexagrams are symbols of 64 separate combinations of six groupings of Yin and Yang, each hexagram being a unique grouping.

The 64 hexagrams had their origin in an early version of four two-line symbols known as the Ssu Hsiang. These four bigrams are clearly shown in the text, along with their original oracular meanings. My own theory is that the main application of this precursor of the *I Ching* was to obtain oracular advice for the conduct of war. As a war oracle, the four basic bigrams of Ssu Hsiang gave advice to either

- Remain silent and concealed,

- Prepare for an attack,

- Act with force, or

- Withdraw

These bigrams evolved to eight trigrams, which are the basic building blocks for the 64 hexagrams.

In order to clearly understand the symbolism of any hexagram, the hexagram must be broken down into its two component trigrams. Therefore, any hexagram can be defined as the interaction of two trigrams (composing the bottom three and top three lines of a hexagram). As such, a very detailed discussion of every aspect of the trigrams is given next. The trigrams are first analyzed as three levels of symbolism, as the upper, middle, and lower line. Next, the eight basic Chinese names, their meanings, and elements ascribed in nature are listed, followed by an analysis of the true elemental nature of each trigram. Finally, the four basic symbolic methods of ordering the trigrams are fully detailed:

- The Yin and Yang ordering of the trigrams

- The directions the trigrams originally took when positioned in heaven

- The directions the trigrams now take when positioned on earth

- The family structure of eight members (resembling the Tetragrammaton family of the Hebraic Qabalah)

After the discussion of the structure of the trigrams, two tables of symbolic correspondences for each of the eight trigrams are presented. Forty
tables contain the symbolism found in the East, and an additional 40 tables
contain the symbolism found in the West (as pioneered by Crowley). The 40
Eastern trigram tables contain every symbol set found in the Confucian
commentary to the *I Ching*, known as the *Ten Wings*. In addition, every
modern Chinese commentary on the trigrams have been included. These
first 40 tables should be used to determine the authentic, original symbolism for any two trigrams composing a hexagram. When a hexagram is cast
through divination (the required technique is shown later in this section),
the applicable trigrams from these tables should be meditated upon in
depth in order to grasp the hidden, unwritten meaning concealed in the
trigram structure of each hexagram.

After the tabling of the 40 Eastern trigram symbol sets, a discussion of
Crowley's fusion of the *I Ching* with the Hebraic Qabalah is presented. In
the two great 19th-century occult movements, the Theosophical Society
and the Golden Dawn, the symbolism of the *I Ching* was not addressed.
The most Eastern of techniques which both groups utilized was the Indian
Tattva system. Aleister Crowley, however, upon being exposed to James
Legge's translation of the *I Ching*, was able to connect the eight basic trigrams with eight select sephiroth of the Qabalistic Tree of Life. In his bril-
liant fusion of the Tree of Life with the eight trigrams, a link was
established between the elemental-planetary attributes of the Tree of Life
and the trigrams themselves. This linkage permitted any of the 64 hexagrams to be successfully interpreted as Western magickal Qabalistic
equivalents. This unique blending of Eastern and Western thought
extended the occult East conquered by Theosophy from the borders of
Tibet into the heart of China.

Crowley recorded his Qabalistic attributes for the *I Ching* in both his
Liber 777 (1909) and *The Book of Thoth* (1944). It is in *The Book of Thoth* that
we find the most refined set of attributes, which permits a Western interpretation of the *I Ching*. In light of these findings, I developed the 40 trigram tables of the West based mainly on the Qabalistic symbolism detailed
in Crowley's *777*. These tables should also be extensively used when analyzing a specific hexagram, in light of Western magickal correspondences.

The trigram tables are followed by a discussion of the symbolism for
each of the six lines composing the 64 hexagrams. These individual lines
are called *yao* in Chinese. Each yao has its own hierarchical relationship
to every other yao. These relationships are fully detailed in the table entitled "Six Yao (Lines) of the Hexagram."

After the detailing of the yao symbolism, the two trigrams which make
up each hexagram are analyzed in light of four methods for generating a
secondary or subsidiary hexagram. The four basic permutations of the trigram pairs which make up each hexagram are:

- Nuclear

- Reversed

- Overturned

- Changing Lines

Note that these four subsidiary hexagrams are completely worked out for each of the 64 hexagrams in the main body of the *I Ching* text found in this section.

Following this discussion of the four basic hexagram permutations, the format of the *I Ching* text is described. The original text for each hexagram has been reduced to its essential meaning. The analysis of each hexagram contains the following components:

- The hexagram itself

- The serial number, Chinese name, and translation

- The symbolic imagery for the hexagram (usually the two trigrams) found in the original text and commentaries

- The oracular advice found in the original text

- The four permutations of the hexagram (nuclear, reversed, overturned, and changing lines)

- An analysis of the trigram names composing the hexagram (including the Chinese names, meanings, and directions corresponding to heaven and earth)

- An analysis of the symbolic qualities of the trigrams (element, planet, color, and number) derived from the 40 trigram tables of the East

- A parallel analysis to the above based on the 40 trigram tables of the West

After working with this version of the *I Ching* for over three years, I have found that this essential reading is more valuable and more accurate in providing clear, concise oracular advise than any other version. If you have had difficulty in working with other versions of the *I Ching*, you will find that the precision of this version will dispel any vagueness or ambiguities encountered in other translations.

The method of casting a hexagram is given next, under the section "Oracular Language." The most complicated (and oldest) divinatory method for consulting the *I Ching* is the casting of yarrow stalks. This method can be found in most translations of the *I Ching* but has not been detailed here because of its complexity. Rather, I have given in this section two simple methods for casting a hexagram:

- The coin toss method (used by most Western practitioners of this art)

- The magick square of Mercury method (which I have invented rather than derived from other sources)

The coin toss method produces the hexagram one line at a time, from bottom to top. By casting three coins, four possible values are generated for each line: 6, 7, 8, or 9. If 6 or 9 is cast for any of the six lines, a secondary hexagram is also generated, those lines which are 6 or 9 becoming changing lines. If 6 is cast, the line for the primary hexagram is Yin, but in the secondary hexagram becomes Yang. If 9 is cast, the line for the primary hexagram is Yang, but in the secondary hexagram becomes Yin. Each of these changing lines has an additional oracular meaning derived from the Duke of Chou's *Changing Line Commentary*. These attributes will be found at the end of this chapter in the table entitled, "Hexagram Key to Chu-Ko's Spirit Calculation for the Numbers 1–384."

The coin toss method is followed by a rectified hexagram generator. By selecting the appropriate inner and outer trigrams, the exact number of any given hexagram can readily be found. This version of the hexagram generator is unique to my system, for I have rearranged the order of the trigrams bordering this table to correspond to the true Yin and Yang order of the trigrams (which begins with all Yang and ends with all Yin).

Next comes my unique method for generating a hexagram. This method utilizes a Tarot deck and the eight-by-eight Western magick square associated to the planet Mercury. In this method first a Tarot deck is shuffled, then one card is turned at a time from the top of the deck until one card from each of two specific sets of cards turns up: the Ace through 8 of Wands, and Key 0 through Key VII of the Major Arcana. These two groups of cards mark the horizontal and vertical grids of the Mercury square. From their intersection the number on the Mercury square becomes the number of the hexagram cast. I have devised this method for specifically casting a hexagram on each Equinox, which would govern the next six months of the equinoctial cycle; however, it can be used for any ritual purpose desired. Its beauty comes from combining the Tarot, the planetary magick square appropriate to Mercury, and the 64 I Ching hexagrams themselves into an oracular method that bridges the East and the West.

As with the Tattvas, a set of I Ching cards can be developed to be used for both oracular and meditative purposes. Two different sets of I Ching cards can be made for either the eight trigrams or the complete 64 hexagrams.

The trigram cards require two sets of eight cards each. Draw each of the eight basic trigrams on rectangular cards. Be sure to draw the straight or broken lines that compose each trigram in a thick uncolored outline. Then, using the color correspondences for the trigrams (found in the trigram tables), pick one set and color all eight trigrams in that fashion. Next, draw a second set of eight trigram cards and color these trigrams with an alternate set of color correspondences.

You will now have two sets of trigram cards. With these two sets you can combine any two trigrams to form each of the 64 hexagrams. This is perfect for meditational purposes, or you can randomly shuffle each stack of trigram cards, draw the top card from each pile, and, by combining the two, generate a divinatory hexagram.

A more ambitious project can be the production of a complete set of 64 hexagram cards. Using the color correspondences found in the main body of the *I Ching* commentary, you can draw and color a separate card for each hexagram. These, in turn, can be shuffled like a Tarot deck and used for divination.

In addition, you can embellish both the trigram and hexagram cards with any appropriate set of symbols taken directly from the corresponding tables in the text. You can also add the appropriate elemental or planetary sigils for each card.

The *I Ching* section ends with an in-depth analysis of the esoteric structure which orders the sequence of the 64 hexagrams. This detailed analysis is a result of my intensive one-year study of all available translations and commentaries of the *I Ching*. Since my first exposure to the *I Ching*, I have wondered why the hexagrams are arranged in their own peculiar order. During my beginning research there seemed no apparent pattern to their order, from the 1st to the 64th hexagram. However, after distilling the *I Ching* to an essential reading and coming to terms with the rich symbolism of the trigrams which compose each hexagram, I was able to penetrate into the true patterns governing the layout of the hexagrams.

The section entitled "The Pattern Behind the Sequence of 64 Hexagrams" details every underlining structure of the hexagram arrangements, unique to my own study of the *I Ching*. These esoteric patterns are as follows:

- The 64 hexagrams can form 32 successive pairs. Each pair of hexagrams is a mirror image of the other hexagram in terms of Yin and Yang. These 32 pairs can easily be equated to the 32 component divisions of the Qabalistic Tree of Life. The first and second hexagram equal the first path on the Tree of Life, while the 63rd and 64th hexagram equal the 32nd path.

- Twelve select hexagrams denote the circulation of light within the subtle body. These 12 hexagrams show, in progression, every Yin line filling with Yang and then emptying back to all Yin.

- The first, middle, and last hexagrams form by their own composition a balance of Yin and Yang. The beginning hexagrams are all Yang or Yin, the middle hexagrams balance half Yin with half Yang, while the last two hexagrams alternate Yin and Yang in each of their six lines.

- All 64 hexagrams can be rearranged to form a new perfect order in which the first hexagram is all Yin, the last (and 64th) hexagram is all Yang, and the intervening 62 hexagrams show a progression of all Yin changing to all Yang.

- There are eight double-trigram hexagrams. Each of these appears in the order of the first four cardinal points of the compass followed by the four oblique points of the compass. This order can only be determined by the directions of heaven according to Fu-Hsi.

- Similar to the above, there are eight directional hexagrams in which the inner trigram corresponds to the compass point of heaven (Fu-Hsi) and the outer trigram corresponds to the same compass point for earth (King Wen).

- Finally, there exists a secret pattern behind the 64 hexagrams in their normal progression which has yet to be detected by any commentator. This secret order is the ratio of Yin to Yang in a never ending battle, which is only resolved by the last two hexagrams, which fully integrate Yin and Yang.

This detailed analysis of the pattern behind the *I Ching* is followed by the basic Chinese symbolic meanings for the numbers 1 through 10. There are two basic symbolic number maps used in the Chinese system to attribute symbolic meaning to the first ten numbers. The first map is Fu Hsi's Yellow River Map. In this arrangement the first ten numbers are paired to the four cardinal directions and center. From this directional map the first ten numbers can be equated to their corresponding directional elements. This is laid out in a table entitled "Yellow River Number Map," which details the first ten numbers as:

- An element
- A direction
- Heaven or earth
- Odd or even
- White or black

The second number map described is known as Yu's River Writing Map. This map is the origin of the three-by-three planetary magick square associated with Saturn. This nine-celled square arranges the first nine numbers in such a way that any diagonal or straight line of three squares always totals 15. In the original Chinese numbering system, this square of nine cells was allocated to the eight basic compass points and the center. To these directional correspondences, the eight basic trigrams of the *I Ching* are added. From their combination the first nine numbers are given symbolic meaning. The number ten is also conjectured as a subvalue of five. The table entitled "Lo Shu Number Map" gives the symbolic meanings for the nine basic numbers as:

- Direction
- Element
- Trigram (according to both King Wen and Fu Hsi)
- Trigram element
- Good or bad fortune
- Divinatory meaning

Beyond the traditional square of nine cells, this Chinese system conjectures a unique combination for each of the nine basic numbers. This expanded system is referred to as the Lo Shu System of Nine Houses. Each number from one to nine has its own Saturn square in which that specific number resides in the central square. All nine of these houses are detailed in this section showing for each number:

- A direction
- A trigram
- An element
- A planet
- A Zodiacal animal
- A color
- Good or bad fortune
- The number harmonies of each unique square of nine cells

This discussion is followed by a detailed analysis of the number metaphors that correspond to the basic components of the Chinese magick square of nine. Metaphors from Chinese, Sanskrit, Tibetan, Hebrew, Arabic, Greek, Enochian, Latin, and English are given for the number values of 3, 9, 15, and 45.

Originally, Chinese numeral philosophy was based on the first ten whole integers. But within the canon of Taoist thought emerged the philosophical concept of zero. This conception of zero is discussed, followed by three more philosophical systems for the number series. These three systems are:

- The Chinese Ch'an Buddhist metaphor of taming the bull as ten symbolic images for the first ten numbers
- The parallel Japanese Zen Buddhist metaphor of taming an ox as another set of ten symbolic images
- The Japanese Soto Zen numerical doctrine of five circles corresponding to the first five numbers

After weathering through the copious detail concerning the Chinese philosophy of number symbolism, this sixth key ends with a detailing of the actual method of numbering Chinese calligraphy. Its intimate connection with the 384 lines composing the 64 hexagrams necessitated the need to understand the *I Ching* prior to confronting the Taoist method for numbering calligraphy.

This number system is different from any other system you will encounter in this book, for Chinese is unique among the magickal languages in not possessing an established alphabet. All other philosophical numbering systems depend upon a set alphabet whose components can each be given a number value. But in Chinese, the actual brush strokes required to execute any word determines the number value of that word.

In this last section of the Chinese key, the five basic calligraphic styles for Chinese are first discussed. Of the five styles, only two lend themselves easily to the Taoist method for numbering Chinese. These two styles are the Official Style (Li-Shu) and the Regular Style (K'ai-Shu). Both letter Chinese in an elegant straight, square fashion, bound by a canon to determine the order of the strokes as well as their shapes. After a discussion of the different script styles, the two basic methods for numbering Chinese calligraphy are described.

The first method imparts a number value to any given character based on the number of strokes used to execute that character. Thus a character requiring eight strokes would be valued at 8, while a character of 18 strokes would be valued at 18. This is the basis for the construction of the 214 basic radical characters in Chinese, which govern the formation of all other Chinese characters.

The second method is an elaboration of the first, applies to any multiple set of characters, and is especially applicable for any set of three characters. This method first counts the strokes required for each character in a multiple set of characters. If any character is composed of ten or more strokes, only the units place is used as its number value. Each numbered character then becomes a digit of a composite number. The first character is accorded the highest place value, while the last character is accorded the lowest. This method is especially applicable for determining whether any given name is auspicious or inauspicious.

To serve as concrete illustrations for this unique method of numbering a language, the Chinese key meanings for the number range of 1 through 33 are detailed. These examples give the number value, the character in its original composition, the transliteration (in either Mandarin or Cantonese), the method of calculation, and the meaning of the character (literal and symbolic). Note that for the phonetic values I have mixed Cantonese with Mandarin. This is due to my limited knowledge of Chinese. Hopefully further revisions of this text will correct this inconsistency. However, it should be stressed here that the different phonetic values for any Chinese character do not affect its number value. The number value is not determined by the pronunciation of the character but rather by the intrinsic brush strokes which compose the character.

In light of this, the Japanese language can also be successfully numbered by this Taoist method, if only the Japanese Kanji characters are considered. Japanese possesses three basic scripts: Kanji, Hiragana, and Katakana. Only Kanji (taken from the Chinese square script) can be numbered. The other two scripts are phonetic alphabets, which do not readily number. (It should be noted that the Korean use of Chinese calligraphic characters is also susceptible to this Chinese Taoist brush-stroke count.)

Since Japanese Kanji characters can also be numbered, an abundance of Japanese Zen Buddhist terminology is also tabled as numbered examples. This may indeed be the basis in Japanese for giving a set of numerological values for any Japanese name in its original Kanji characters.

It has been rumored that the Japanese family clan of TOYODA, when first entering the automotive industry, found that their initial commercial success was less than anticipated. They therefore consulted a Shinto priest, who determined that the stroke count for the name TOYODA was inauspicious. However, if the last syllable was changed from DA to TA, the resultant name, TOYOTA, would generate an auspicious number. Consequently the clan changed their name within the business world and discovered that this transformed name changed their luck. I have not been able to verify this rumor, but if it is indeed true, then it would offer substantial proof that the Taoist method of numbering Chinese directly applies as well to Japanese.

How is the number value of any given name deemed auspicious or inauspicious? The answer lies in the interconnectiveness between the 384 lines of the *I Ching* hexagrams and this Taoist stroke-count method. When a prospective business is about to begin, many times a Chinese Taoist diviner (Feng Shui) is consulted to determine whether or not the selected name of the business will bring good or bad luck. Usually the diviner would request that the name be composed of three characters to correspond to the standards set by Chu-Ko's spirit-calculation technique. However, this method can apply to any number of characters.

The name given to the diviner is reduced to its essential number value. If the value is greater than 384, multiples of 384 are subtracted from the number until a number between 1 and 384 is reached. Then the diviner consults a book of 384 obscure, metaphorical poems, each poem corresponding to a specific number. If the commentary is positive, the diviner determines that the name is auspicious, but if the poem is negative (or unclear), the diviner determines that the name is inauspicious. If inauspicious, the diviner may help in the modification of the chosen name so that the revised name falls to an auspicious number.

The basis behind these 384 poems is the 64 hexagrams of the *I Ching*. Each hexagram is composed of six lines, making a grand total of 384 lines of Yin or Yang. Therefore these 384 poems are based on the symbolic meaning behind each of the 384 lines of the hexagrams. Around 1000 BCE, the Duke of Chou set down symbolic meanings for each of these 384 lines. His commentary is the true pattern for determining the auspiciousness of any number between 1 and 384.

In this correspondence, the bottom line of the first hexagram corresponds to the number 1, while the top line of the last hexagram corresponds to the number 384. All these correspondences are shown in the last table of this chapter, entitled "Hexagram Key to Chu-Ko's Spirit Calculation for the Numbers 1–384." This table should also be used whenever a changing line is generated when casting an *I Ching* hexagram. Thus ends the largest chapter of this book, possibly the most extensive commentary there is on Chinese magick and mysticism in light of the Western magickal tradition.

Origin

8000 BCE—Earliest stage of Chinese script as the beginnings of pictographs.

4000 BCE—The beginnings of Chinese script as ideograms.

3000 BCE—Taoist tradition relates that Fu-Hsi (the first of the Three August

Ones) invented the written characters of Chinese (with its secret brush stroke count) and/or the eight mystic symbols known as the eight trigrams (the basis of the *I Ching*). Fu-Hsi's magickal creation was inspired by a vision of either a dragon horse or giant tortoise rising out of the Yellow River. Emblazoned upon this mythical animal's back were the essential calligraphic strokes of Chinese and the eight divinatory trigrams (spread out over the eight points of the compass). In this myth, word and number combine as a source of magick and divination.

2637 BCE—The traditional beginning point of the Chinese calendar, commemorating the year in which the First August Emperor Huang-ti invented the 60-day and 60-year calendrical cycle marked by the simultaneous progression of 5 x 12 Earthly Branches and 6 x 10 Heavenly Stems.

This sexagenary system would become the basis for all Taoist almanacs concerned with the divinatory mapping of auspicious and inauspicious days.

2256 BCE—The beginning date found in the first magickal calendar, the Shu Ching, which was during the reign of Emperor Yao.

1750–1112 BCE—Chinese script that has survived from this period (Shang Dynasty) is inscribed on tortoise shell and bone, primarily for imperial divination. Here the idea of magick and written character are inseparable.

1000 BCE—The text of the *I Ching* in its most skeletal form is written down by a group of diviners in order to preserve that which had passed down orally since 3000 BCE. By tradition, in this period King Wen, while imprisoned by the Shang King Diyi, recorded the written commentary for each of the 64 hexagrams.

The Duke of Zhou (Chou) at this period then wrote the commentary for the six lines of each hexagram.

The combination of the writings of King Wen and the Duke of Zhou form the body of the *I Ching*, which must have been established by 500 BCE.

1000 BCE–25 CE—Chinese script evolves from pictographs and ideographs to determinative-phonetic characters. Language completes its structural evolution while calligraphy is established in its final square form, which can be numbered by its stroke count.

The standardizing of the stroke count for each character serves an outer and inner purpose:
- Outwardly, the stroke count will order the 540 basic characters upon which all of Chinese is based.
- Inwardly, the stroke count secretly affixes a number value to every word concept in Chinese.

250 BCE—Earliest surviving version of the Chinese magickal calendar known as the *Shu-Ching*.

221 BCE–65 CE—The stroke value of calligraphy, and the digital place value (without zero) of multiple characters is created by Chu-ko Liang, founder of the Taoist Pole Star Sect (and inventor of Wu-tang Shan, a precursor of T'ai Chi Ch'uan).

Chu-ko Liang's method has been preserved in the 29th section of the almanac *T'ung Shu*, entitled, "The Secret Book of Chu-ko's Spirit Calculation."

During this period, a set of 384 poetic predictions (for the number range 1–384) was recorded as a numerical metaphor guide for the stroke calculation of Chinese.

121 CE—The first great dictionary of Chinese is completed by Xu Shen, entitled *Shuo Wen Jie Zi*. This dictionary categorizes all of its entries by 540 basic characters (called radicals) arranged by the numerical order of their stroke count.

600 CE—Two versions of the *I Ching* appear, written by Li Dingzuo and Kong Yingda.

1000 CE—Derived from earlier version, a canon for the *I Ching* is printed that will become the standard version for 1000 years.

1190 CE—The publication of the Taoist canon known as the *Tao-Tsang*. This work is composed of more than 50,000,000 characters and several thousand diagrams in seven sections. The source for the core of this material dates back to the Shamanistic practices of 2000 BCE.

1290 CE—Kuo Shou Ching combines all existing magickal almanacs into a system of divination known as the *Sou-Shi-Shuh*. This work is eventually refined into the *Ta-Tung*, or "Official Almanac," the model for the popular *T'ung Shu*.

1644 CE—The Ching Dynasty Imperial Dictionary, *Kang Xi Zi Dian*, reduces the standard of 540 numbered radicals to 214 radicals, which today still exists as the standard measure of radicals for both Chinese and Japanese.

1680 CE—Jesuit missionaries in China encounter for the first time the text of the *I Ching*. The book was deeply studied for a time until the Vatican discouraged any further research.

1700 CE—Gottfried von Leibniz, after learning the Chinese concept of Yin and Yang, realized that his own binary mathematical system had already been envisioned by the Chinese Taoist master of the *I Ching*.

1854–5 CE—James Legge first completed his translation of the *I Ching* during this period. It was subsequently published in 1882.

1876 CE—The first English translation of the I Ching is printed in Shanghai. It was translated by the Reverend Canon McClatchie.

ALPHABET CODE

THE CONCEPT OF YIN AND YANG

The Chinese approach to a philosophical or poetic interpretation of the number series is twofold. The first method can be summed up in the philosophical discourse on mystical Chinese number theory known as the *I Ching*, based on the binary code of Yin and Yang. The second method is the stroke count inherent in any given Chinese character, which allows a number value to be given to any word concept.

At the heart of all number classifications in Chinese is the Taoist concept of Yin and Yang (– and +). This concept of female and male polarity is infused in all art and mysticism, and is the basis for the eight trigrams of Fu-Hsi and the 64 hexagrams of King Wen. Originally the designation of Yin and Yang was used to classify the two sides of a mountain. The Yin side was the shady northern side of a mountain while the Yang side was the southern sunny side. These terms later became a general classification of anything dark or light.

The Chinese dualistic view of the universe allows any object in nature to be categorized as Yin, Yang, or a combination of both (Tao or Li). Many subtle puns in poetry and painting depend upon this Yin-Yang classification. This binary system is also the basis for the Hebrew Qabalistic system outlined in the *Zohar*, where the universe is classified by left and right (Geburah and Chesed on the Tree of Life). Zero and One, or One and Two, divide the universe into dynamic interacting pairs or couples of Yin and Yang, which can be outlined as follows.

Taoist Yin and Yang

Yin	Yang
Female	Male
Right Hand (as West, Moon, Sunset)	Left Hand (as East, Sun, Sunrise)
The Setting Sun (as Right when facing South)	The Rising Sun (as Left when facing South)
Black	White
Blue	Red
Green	Red
Silver	Gold
Dark	Bright
Obscured	Clear
Retreat	Advance

Taoist Yin and Yang (cont'd.)

Yin	Yang
Pull in, Grab	Push out, Punch
Receptive	Penetrating
Abyss	Celestial
Yielding	Firm
North	South
Winter	Summer
Night	Day
Midnight	Noon
Moon	Sun
Earth	Heaven, Sky
Square	Circle, Oval
Horizontal Lines	Vertical Lines
Curving, Swirling Lines	Straight Lines
Clouds, Mist, Water	Sun
Vagina	Penis
Foreskin	Clitoris
Clay (Bronze)	Jade (Congealed semen of the dragon)
The river that flows beneath	Bridge
Receptive Vase	Swelling Mushroom
Hollow Horn of Rhinoceros	Horns of a Deer
Geomantic Lines of Earth	Constellations of Sky
Peach	Red Feng Bird
Peacock	Flying Dragon
Ebb of the Tide	Flow of the Tide
Convoluted stones full of holes and hollows	Stars of the Night Sky
Waning of the Moon	Waxing of the Moon
Valley	Mountain
Downpour of Rain on Earth	Cloudburst and Lightning in Heaven
Zero	One
Two	One
Two	Three
Even	Odd
Front (of Body)	Back (of Body)
Inside (of Body)	Outside (of Body)

The Five Elements

Out of this binary classification developed an elementary theory of five basic components to all physical manifestations. These five Chinese elements are the basis for the five Indian Tattvas of the East and the Five Platonic solids of the West. The origin of these five basic elements is attributed to Fu-Hsi (3000 BCE). These three fivefold elemental systems and their Western magickal equivalents are as follows.

Fivefold Elements of the World

Chinese	Indian Tattvas	Platonic Solids	Western Hermetic Alchemical
Water	Apas	Icosahedron	Water
Fire	Agni	Pyramid	Fire
Wood	Vayu	Octahedron	Air
Metal	Prithivi	Cube	Earth
Earth	Akasa	Dodecahedron	Spirit

The Chinese developed a detailed fivefold cosmology based on these five elements, and it ultimately structured the very nature of their pentatonic musical scale. The basic attributes for these five Chinese elements are as given in the following 22 tables.

Five Chinese Elements

Table 1. Planet—The cycle of five Chinese elements are intimately connected to the five lesser planets (minus the luminaries). This connection is such that each of these five planets are referred to by their elemental title as follows:

Elemental Titles of the Five Chinese Planets

Planet	Elemental Title
Jupiter	Wood Star
Mars	Fire Star
Saturn	Earth Star
Venus	Metal Star
Mercury	Water Star

Table 2. Direction—The five elements are allocated to the four directions and the Center, the Center being Spirit as the element Earth. In Chinese Taoist symbolism, the Earth is the supreme symbol for Spirit, which is antithetical to Western religious symbolism.

Table 3. Season—Each direction in table 2 is allocated to a division of the year as listed in this table.

Table 4. Color—The five shades of the Chinese elemental rainbow are listed here. Note their similarity to the essential colors for the five Tattvas.

Table 5. Virtue—The five basic virtues associated with the five elements are tabled here in their traditional order.

Element	1. Planet	2. Direction	3. Season	4. Color	5. Virtue
Wood	Jupiter	East	Spring	Green (Blue)	Benevolence
Fire	Mars	South	Summer	Red	Propriety
Earth	Saturn	Center	Last 18 Days of Year	Yellow	Faith
Metal	Venus	West	Autumn	White	Righteousness
Water	Mercury	North	Winter	Black (Blue)	Wisdom

Five Chinese Elements (cont'd)

Table 6. Symbolic Animal—The five basic animal symbols from Chinese martial arts tradition are here allocated to the five elements. An alternate set of attributes for each of the five elements is as follows.

Alternate Chinese Elemental Animals

Element	Animal
Wood	Dragon
Fire	Phoenix
Earth	Ox, Buffalo
Metal	Tiger
Water	Snake, Tortoise

Table 7. Climate—The equivalent climate for the seasons in table 3 is shown here.

Table 8. Emperor—The rulership of five Chinese emperors is tabled here in light of their planetary-elemental associations.

Table 9. Orifice of the Head—The orifices of the head are correlated to the five divisions of the elements in this table. By extension, the five senses can also be correlated as follows.

The Five Senses and the Five Chinese Elements

Element	Sense
Wood	Hearing
Fire	Sight
Earth	Touch
Metal	Smell
Water	Taste

Table 10. Musical Note—The five traditional notes of the pentatonic scale are listed here in their elemental order. This scale of C-D-E-G-A, when directly paralleled to the five elements, produces the elemental order of Earth, Metal, Wood, Fire, Water.

Element	6. Symbolic Animal	7. Climate	8. Emperor	9. Orifice of Head	10. Musical Note
Wood	Tiger	Windy	Fu-Hsi	Ears	E—Kyo
Fire	Dragon	Hot	Shen Nung	Eyes	G—Chi
Earth	Bear	Humid	Huang-Ti	Mouth	C—Kung
Metal	Eagle	Dry	Shoa-Hao	Nose	D—Shang
Water	Monkey	Cold	Chuan-hsu	Tongue	A—Yu

Five Chinese Elements (cont'd)

Table 11. Sound—The five sounds which correlate to the five orifices of the head (table 9) are listed here.

Table 12. Odor—The five odors essential to each of the five elements are listed here.

Table 13. Flavor—The five flavors derived from the five odors (table 12) are listed here in their elemental order.

Table 14. Emotion—The five emotions which are the opposites of the five virtues (table 5) are listed here in their elemental order.

Table 15. Number—The ten numbers knows as the Ten Celestial Stems are tabled here in their five corresponding elemental pairs.

Element	11. Sound	12. Odor	13. Flavor	14. Emotion	15. Number
Wood	Shouting	Rancid	Sour	Anger	1, 2
Fire	Laughing	Scorched	Bitter	Joy	3, 4
Earth	Singing	Fragrant	Sweet	Sympathy	5, 6
Metal	Weeping	Rotten	Pungent	Grief	7, 8
Water	Groaning	Putrid	Salt	Fear	9, 10

Five Chinese Elements (cont'd)

Table 16. Magic Square—The Chinese magick square of nine cells, which is the Square of Saturn in the West, is allocated to the five elements by the directions of the square itself. This table parallels the nine numbers of the square to the five elements.

Table 17. Masonic—The five implements of Chinese Masonry (which are parallel in Western Freemasonry) are listed here in their elemental order.

Table 18. Astrology—The division of the night sky into five major aspects is shown here in light of the elemental order. These symbols are an addition to the planetary attributes of table 1. Together, these two tables form the following astrological hierarchy.

Astrological Hierarchy of Chinese Elements

Celestial Order	Elemental Order
Stars (Zodiac)	Wood
Saturn	Earth
Jupiter	Wood
Mars	Fire
Sun	Fire
Venus	Metal
Mercury	Water
Moon	Water
28 Lunar Mansions	Metal
Earth	Earth

Table 19. Poison—Five poisonous animals used in both Taoist magickal and martial arts symbolism are listed here in accordance with the five elements, as allocated to the five points of the pentagram. The pentagonal correspondences are as follows.

The Chinese Pentagram of Five Poisons

Point of Pentagram	Poison
Lower Right	Centipede
Lower Left	Viper
Upper Left	Scorpion
Apex	Toad
Upper Right	Spider (Lizard)

Element	16. Magick Square	17. Masonic	18. Astrology	19. Poison
Wood	3, 8	Compass	Stars (Zodiac)	Centipede
Fire	2, 7	Ruler	Sun	Viper
Earth	5	Plumb-line	Earth	Scorpion
Metal	4, 9	Square	28 Lunar Mansions	Toad
Water	1, 6	Scale	Moon	Spider (Lizard)

Five Chinese Elements (cont'd)

Table 20. Animal—The five armors or coatings of the animal kingdom are tabled in light of their elemental order.

Table 21. Parts of Body—The five major systems of the human body are allocated to their elemental correspondences in this table.

Table 22. Organ of Human Body—The ten basic Chinese internal organs of the human body are paralleled to their five elemental qualities in this table. This table should be contrasted to tables 21 and 9 for a complete elemental overview of Chinese Taoist physiology.

Element	20. Animal	21. Parts of Body	22. Organ of Human Body
Wood	Feathered	Muscles	Liver (Gall Bladder)
Fire	Hairless	Nerves	Heart (Small Intestine)
Earth	Hairy	Skeleton	Spleen (Stomach)
Metal	Armored	Skin	Lung (Large Intestine)
Water	Scaled	Blood	Kidney (Bladder)

Harmony of the Five Chinese Elements

Element	Parent (Source for Element)	Child (Product of Element)	Enemy (Opposition)	Friend (Sympathy)
Wood	Water	Fire	Metal	Earth
Fire	Wood	Earth	Water	Metal
Earth	Fire	Metal	Wood	Water
Metal	Earth	Water	Fire	Wood
Water	Metal	Wood	Earth	Fire

These five Chinese elements are allocated to the five points of the upright pentagram, just as the Western magickal elemental system is also pentagonal in nature. The five points of the Chinese pentagram and their Western equivalents are shown on the following page.

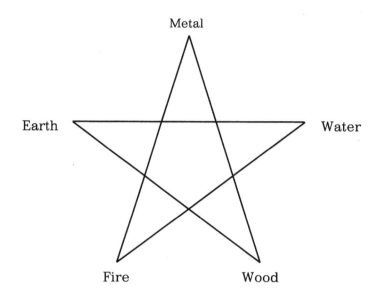

The Chinese Elemental Pentagram

Chinese Element	Point of Pentagram	Western Equivalent of Pentagram
Wood	Lower Right	Fire
Fire	Lower Left	Earth
Earth	Upper Left	Air
Metal	Apex	Spirit
Water	Upper Right	Water

Four magickal cycles can be traced around this pentagram: Creation and Destruction, and Love and Fear. The four cycles are formed by starting with the apex point of Metal and tracing the elements by the lines of the pentagram or the circle surrounding the five points of the pentagram.

Four Chinese Pentagonal Cycles

Cycle	Shape	Elemental Order				
Creation	Circular (Clockwise)	Metal	Water	Wood	Fire	Earth
Destruction	Pentagonal (Banishing)	Metal	Wood	Earth	Water	Fire
Love	Circular (Counterclockwise)	Metal	Earth	Fire	Wood	Water
Fear	Pentagonal (Invoking)	Metal	Fire	Water	Earth	Wood

In the Chinese series of five elements, the equivalent position of Spirit is twofold in its allocation.

In the pentagonal arrangement, Metal occupies the apex of the pentagram and is therefore Spirit. In the directional arrangement, Earth occupies the center of the four directions and is therefore Spirit.

The below table shows Eastern and Western elemental equivalents.

The Five Eastern Elements and Their Western Equivalents

Western Elements Equivalents	Eastern Elements	
	Chinese Pentagram	Chinese Directions
Spirit	Metal	Earth
Fire	Fire	Fire
Water	Water	Water
Air	Wood (Wind)	Wood (Wind)
Earth	Earth	Metal

Yellow Earth as Spirit is found in the West in the Golden Dawn alchemical symbolism of Sulfur, Mercury, and Salt. Salt is Earth and is represented by a yellow Greek Theta (Θ). Traditionally this symbol is the body of the triad Spirit, Soul, and Body (as Mercury, Sulfur, and Salt), but in the secret symbols of the Golden Dawn rituals Salt is in the apex position of this alchemical triad, and Spirit.

These five elements are also the source for the sexagenary system of Huang-ti (2637 BCE), for these five elements in their progression produce ten heavenly stems and twelve earthly branches.

The Ten Heavenly Stems

The ten heavenly stems are the five elements (ordered by the four directions) as five pairs of symbols. These twice five attributes are also governed by the five Chinese planets. These ten stems (or roots) each possess a character name, direction in space, planet in the sky, element in nature, and a symbolic meaning in the cycle of ten (or 60) (see table on opposite page).

The Symbolism of the Ten Celestial Stems

Stem Number	Name	Meaning	Direction	Yin-Yang	Planetary	Element	Symbolic Meaning in Cycle of Ten (60)
1	Chia	Helmet, Armor, Shell of a Tortoise	East	Yang	Jupiter Wood Star	Fir Tree (Trees)	Sprouting
2	Yia	Germination, Movement	East	Yin	Jupiter Wood Star	Bamboo (Timber)	Tendril, Twig, Spread of Growth
3	Ping	Fire, House on Fire, Calamity	South	Yang	Mars Fire Star	Torch Flame (Lightning)	Bloom
4	Ting	Nail, to Nail	South	Yin	Mars Fire Star	Lamplight (Burning Material)	Lush Vegetation, Maturity
5	Wu	Crescent Sword, to Attack, Swordplay	Center	Yang-Yin	Saturn Earth Star	Mountains (Land)	Exuberance; Overabundance
6	Ki	Threads of a Loom	Center	Yin-Yang	Saturn Earth Star	Level Ground (Earthware)	Hibernation, Order of Things
7	King	Two Hands Grasping a Pestle, Milling (Pounding) of Rice	West	Yang	Venus Metal Star	Weapon (Metal, Ore)	Harvest, Fullness
8	Hsin	Chastisement	West	Yin	Venus Metal Star	Cauldron (Metal Items)	Restoration, Ripened Fruit
9	Jen	Bear a Burden	North	Yang	Mercury Water Star	Large Wave (Salt Sea)	Height of Function; Pregnancy
10	Kwei	Sacrificial Wine Falling on an Offering of Grass	North	Yin	Mercury Water Star	Unruffled Stream (Free Water)	Seed Planted for New Harvest

The Twelve Earthly Branches

Counterpoised to the ten heavenly stems are the twelve earthly branches (which combine to 22 as 10 + 12, paralleling the division of the Hebrew alphabet as outlined in the *Sepher Yetzirah*).

The twelve earthly branches pertain to the division of the twelve Chinese Zodiacal years. Each of the twelve earthly branches is a two-hour station in the day, a compass point, part of the body, a character name, a symbolic image, an inner symbolic meaning as a cycle of twelve (or 60), and a Zodiacal animal.

The Symbolism of the Twelve Earthly Branches

Branch Number	Name	Meaning	Action	Hour of Day	Compass Point	Body
1	Tzu	Child	Begin	11 PM–1 AM	N	Gall Bladder
2	Chou	Cord	End	1 AM–3 AM	NNE	Liver
3	Yin	Revere	Create	3 AM–5 AM	ENE	Lung
4	Mao	A Period of Time	Partition	5 AM–7 AM	E	Large Intestine
5	Chen	Vibration	Occupy	7 AM–9 AM	ESE	Stomach
6	Szu	End	Equalize	9 AM–11 AM	SSE	Spleen-Pancreas
7	Wu	Oppose	Limit	11 AM–1 PM	S	Heart
8	Wei	Not Yet	Govern	1 PM–3 PM	SSW	Small Intestine
9	Shen	Expand	Tame	3 PM–5 PM	WSW	Bladder
10	Yu	Ripe	Dare	5 PM–7 PM	W	Kidney
11	Shu	Guard	Complete	7 PM–9 PM	WNW	Heart Constrictor
12	Hai	Kernel	Accept	9 PM-11 PM	NNW	Triple Heater

The Symbolism of the Twelve Earthly Branches (cont'd.)

Branch Number	Name	Zodiacal Animal	Personality	Yin or Yang	Symbolic Image	Symbolic Meaning as Cycle of Twelve (or 60)
1	Tzu	Rat	Alluring	Yang	Yang Stirring Underground	Regeneration
2	Chou	Ox	Enduring	Yin	Hand Half Opened	Untying a Knot
3	Yin	Tiger	Ferocious	Yang	Wriggling Earthworm	Awakening of Life
4	Mao	Rabbit	Gentle	Yin	Opening a Gate	Plants breaking through the soil
5	Chen	Dragon	Occult	Yang	Thunderstorm	Planting a seed
6	Szu	Snake	Intuitive	Yin	Serpent	Supremacy of Yang
7	Wu	Horse	Sensual	Yang	Yin in Hidden Growth	Yin reasserting Herself
8	Wei	Sheep (Goat)	Sensitive	Yin	Tree in Full Bloom	Taste of Fruit
9	Shen	Monkey	Curious	Yang	Clasped Hands	Yin growing Strong
10	Yu	Cock	Aware	Yin	Wine-press	Completion
11	Shu	Dog	Dependable	Yang	Yang Withdrawing Underground	Exhaustion
12	Hai	Pig	Practical	Yin	Yang in touch with Yin	Root

It should be noted that each of the 12 Zodiacal animals do not comprise a month, but rather a year, as a Zodiacal cycle.

However there exists an esoteric correspondence of Eastern and Western Zodiacal symbols grounded in the four Eastern symbols of Tiger, Snake, Horse, and Goat. In the West, these four symbols would be Leo, Scorpio, Sagittarius, and Capricorn. By the equivalence of Eastern "Dog" with Western "Aries," these four symbols of East and West are paired together.

Eastern and Western Zodiacs as Parallel Cycles

Chinese Yearly		Western Monthly	
	(approximate)		
Symbolic Animal	Year	Month	Symbolic Animal
Dog	1982	April	Ram (Aries)
Pig	1983	May	Bull (Taurus)
Rat	1984	June	Twins (Gemini)
Ox	1985	July	Crab (Cancer)
Tiger	1986	August	Lion (Leo)
Rabbit	1987	Sept.	Virgin (Virgo)
Dragon	1988	October	Scales (Libra)
Snake	1989	November	Scorpion (Scorpio) (Snake, Eagle)
Horse	1990	December	Centaur (Sagittarius)
Goat (Sheep)	1991	January	Goat-Fish (Capricorn)
Monkey	1992	February	Water-Pails (Aquarius) (Man)
Cock	1993	March	Fish (Pisces)

THE CYCLE OF TEN AND TWELVE

Both the Ten Celestial Stems and the Twelve Earthly Branches emanate out of the cyclical order of the five basic Chinese elements. The five, ten, and twelve symbolic components combine as follows:

The Fivefold Elemental Pattern of the Ten Stems and Twelve Branches

Five Elements	Ten Stems	Twelve Branches
1. Wood	1. Chia	1. Tzu
	2. Yi	2. Chou
2. Fire	3. Ping	3. Yin
	4. Ting	4. Mao
3. Earth	5. Wu	5. Chen
	6. Ki	6. Szu
4. Metal	7. Keng	7. Wu
	8. Hsin	8. Wei
5. Water	9. Jen	9. Shen
	10. Kwei	10. Yu
		11. Shu
		12. Hai

THE SEXAGENARY CYCLE.

For the sexagenary cycle, the ten stems are repeated ten times and paired to five cycles of the twelve branches. This measure of 60 years denotes, by the conjunction of one stem and one branch, 60 divinatory meanings for each of the 60 years. The following 10-page table delineates the 60-year cycle during the founding of the Theosophical Society, the Golden Dawn, and the A.˙.A.˙., as well as the reception of *The Book of the Law,* to illustrate the 60 divinatory meanings.

The Sexagenary Cycle
And Its Divinatory Meanings for the Years 1864 to 1923 CE and 1984 to 2043 CE

Year	Number	Stem-Branch	Name	Element	Astrology	Harmony	Direction	Symbol	Sexagenary Image
1864 (1984)	1	(1) Chia	Armor	Wood	Jupiter	Yang	E	Fir Tree	Sprouting
		(1) Tzu	Child	Wood	Rat		N	Yang stirring underground	Regeneration
1865 (1985)	2	(2) Yi	Germination	Wood	Jupiter	Yang	E	Bamboo	Tangled growth
		(2) Chou	Cord	Wood	Ox		NNE	Hand half opened	Untying a knot
1866 (1986)	3	(3) Ping	Fire (calamity)	Fire	Mars	Yang	S	Torch flame	Blooming
		(3) Yin	Revere	Fire	Tiger		ENE	Wriggling earthworm	Awakening of life
1867 (1987)	4	(4) Ting	Nail	Fire	Mars	Yang	S	Lamplight	Maturity
		(4) Mao	Time	Fire	Rabbit		E	Opening a gate	Plants breaking through the soil
1868 (1988)	5	(5) Wu	Sword	Earth	Saturn	Yin-Yang	Center	Mountains	Overabundance
		(5) Chen	Vibration	Earth	Dragon		ESE	Thunderstorm	Planting a seed
1869 (1989)	6	(6) Ki	Threads of a loom	Earth	Saturn	Yin-Yang	Center	Level ground	Order of things
		(6) Szu	End	Earth	Snake		SSE	Serpent	Supremacy of Yang

The Sexagenary Cycle (cont'd).
And Its Divinatory Meanings for the Years 1864 to 1923 CE and 1984 to 2043 CE

Year	Number	Stem-Branch	Name	Element	Astrology	Harmony	Direction	Symbol	Sexagenary Image
1870 (1990)	7	(7) Keng	Two hands grasping a pestle	Metal	Venus	Yin	W	Weapon	Harvest
		(7) Wu	Oppose	Metal	Horse		S	Yin hidden in growth	Yin reasserting herself
1871 (1991)	8	(8) Hsin	Chatisement	Metal	Venus	Yin	W	Cauldron	Restoration
		(8) Wei	Not yet	Metal	Sheep		SSW	Tree in full bloom	Taste of fruit
1872 (1992)	9	(9) Jen	Endure	Water	Mercury	Yin	N	A large wave	Pregnancy
		(9) Shen	Expand	Water	Monkey		WSW	Clasped hands	Yin growing strong
1873 (1993)	10	(10) Kwei	Offering to the Gods	Water	Mercury	Yin	N	Unruffled stream	Seed planted for new harvest
		(10) Yu	Ripe	Water	Cock		W	Winepress	Completion
1874 (1994)	11	(1) Chia	Armor	Wood	Jupiter	Parent	E	Fir Tree	Sprouting
		(11) Shu	Guard	Water	Dog		WNW	Yang withdrawing underground	Exhaustion
1875 (1995)	12	(2) Yi	Germination	Wood	Jupiter	Parent	E	Bamboo	Twig
		(12) Hai	Kernel	Water	Pig		NNW	Yang in touch with Yin	Root

The Sexagenary Cycle (cont'd).
And Its Divinatory Meanings for the Years 1864 to 1923 CE and 1984 to 2043 CE

Year	Number	Stem-Branch	Name	Element	Astrology	Harmony	Direction	Symbol	Sexagenary Image
1876 (1996)	13	(3) Ping	House on fire	Fire	Mars	Parent	S	Torch flame	Bloom
		(1) Tzu	Child	Wood	Rat		N	Yang stirring underground	Regeneration
1877 (1997)	14	(4) Ting	Nail	Fire	Mars	Parent	S	Lamplight	Maturity
		(2) Chou	Cord	Wood	Ox		NNE	Hand half opened	Untying a knot
1878 (1998)	15	(5) Wu	Sword	Earth	Saturn	Parent	Center	Mountains	Exuberance
		(3) Yin	Revere	Fire	Tiger		ENE	Wriggling earthworm	Awakening of life
1879 (1999)	16	(6) Ki	Threads of a loom	Earth	Saturn	Parent	Center	Level ground	Hibernation
		(4) Mao	A period of time	Fire	Rabbit		E	Opening of a gate	Plants breaking through soil
1880 (2000)	17	(7) Keng	Milling of rice	Metal	Venus	Parent	W	Weapon	Harvest
		(5) Chen	Vibration	Earth	Dragon		ESE	Thunderstorm	Planting a seed
1881 (2001)	18	(8) Hsin	Chastisement	Metal	Venus	Parent	W	Cauldron	Restoration
		(6) Szu	End	Earth	Snake		SSE	Serpent	Supremacy of Yang

The Sexagenary Cycle (cont'd).
And Its Divinatory Meanings for the Years 1864 to 1923 CE and 1984 to 2043 CE

Year	Number	Stem-Branch	Name	Element	Astrology	Harmony	Direction	Symbol	Sexagenary Image
1882 (2002)	19	(9) Jen	Bear a Burden	Water	Mercury	Parent	N	Large wave	Pregnancy
		(7) Wu	Oppose	Metal	Horse		S	Yin hidden in growth	Yin reasserting herself
1883 (2003)	20	(10) Kwei	Offering	Water	Mercury	Parent	N	Unruffled stream	Seed planted for harvest
		(8) Wei	Not yet	Metal	Sheep		SSW	Tree in full bloom	Taste of fruit
1884 (2004)	21	(1) Chia	Armor	Wood	Jupiter	Enemy	E	Fir Tree	Sprouting
		(9) Shen	Expand	Water	Monkey		WSW	Clasped hands	Yin growing strong
1885 (2005)	22	(2) Yi	Germination	Wood	Jupiter	Enemy	E	Bamboo	Spread of growth
		(10) Yu	Ripe	Water	Cock		W	Winepress	Completion
1886 (2006)	23	(3) Ping	Calamity	Fire	Mars	Enemy	S	Torch flame	Bloom
		(11) Shu	Guard	Water	Dog		WNW	Yang withdrawing underground	Exhaustion
1887 (2007)	24	(4) Ting	Nail	Fire	Mars	Enemy	S	Lamplight	Lush vegetation
		(12) Hai	Kernel	Water	Pig		NNW	Yang in touch with Yin	Root

The Sexagenary Cycle (cont'd).
And Its Divinatory Meanings for the Years 1864 to 1923 CE and 1984 to 2043 CE

Year	Number	Stem-Branch	Name	Element	Astrology	Harmony	Direction	Symbol	Sexagenary Image
1888 (2008)	25	(5) Wu / (1) Tzu	Sword / Child	Earth / Wood	Saturn / Rat	Enemy	Center / N	Mountain / Yang stirring underground	Exuberance / Regeneration
1889 (2009)	26	(6) Ki / (2) Chou	Threads of a loom / Cord	Earth / Wood	Saturn / Ox	Enemy	Center / NNE	Level ground / Hand half opened	Order of things / Untying a knot
1890 (2010)	27	(7) Keng / (3) Yin	Milling (of rice) / Revere	Metal / Fire	Venus / Tiger	Enemy	W / ENE	Weapon / Earthworm	Harvest / Awakening of life
1891 (2011)	28	(8) Hsin / (4) Mao	Chastisement / Time	Metal / Fire	Venus / Rabbit	Enemy	W / E	Cauldron / Opening a gate	Ripe fruit / Plants breaking through soil
1892 (2012)	29	(9) Jen / (5) Chen	Endure / Vibration	Water / Earth	Mercury / Dragon	Enemy	N / ESE	Large wave / Thunderstorm	Pregnancy / Planting a seed
1893 (2013)	30	(10) Kwei / (6) Szu	Sacrificial Wine / End	Water / Earth	Mercury / Snake	Enemy	N / SSE	Unruffled stream / Serpent	Seed for new harvest / Supremacy of Yang

The Sexagenary Cycle (cont'd).
And Its Divinatory Meanings for the Years 1864 to 1923 CE and 1984 to 2043 CE

Year	Number	Stem-Branch	Name	Element	Astrology	Harmony	Direction	Symbol	Sexagenary Image
1894 (2014)	31	(1) Chia	Armor	Wood	Jupiter Horse	Enemy	E	Fir Tree	Sprouting
		(7) Wu	Oppose	Metal			S	Yin hidden in growth	Yin reasserting herself
1895 (2015)	32	(2)Yi	Movement	Wood	Jupiter	Enemy	E	Bamboo	Spread of growth
		(8) Wei	Not yet	Metal	Sheep		SSW	Tree in full bloom	Taste of fruit
1896 (2016)	33	(3) Ping	Calamity	Fire	Mars Monkey	Enemy	S	Torch Flame	Bloom
		(9) Shen	Expand	Water			WSW	Clasped hands	Yin growing strong
1897 (2017)	34	(4) Ting	To nail	Fire	Mars Cock	Enemy	S	Lamplight	Lush vegetation
		(10) Yu	Ripe	Water			W	Winepress	Completion
1898 (2018)	35	(5) Wu	Attack	Earth	Saturn Dog	Child	Center	Mountains	Exuberance
		(11) Shu	Guard	Water			WNW	Yang withdrawing underground	Exhaustion
1899 (2019)	36	(6) Ki	Threads of a Loom	Earth	Saturn	Child	Center	Level ground	Hibernation
		(12) Hai	Kernel	Water	Pig		NNW	Yang touching Yin	Root

The Sexagenary Cycle (cont'd).
And Its Divinatory Meanings for the Years 1864 to 1923 CE and 1984 to 2043 CE

Year	Number	Stem-Branch	Name	Element	Astrology	Harmony	Direction	Symbol	Sexagenary Image
1900 (2020)	37	(7) Keng	Milling of rice	Metal	Venus	Friend	W	Weapon	Fullness
		(1) Tzu	Child	Wood	Rat		N	Yang stirring underground	Regeneration
1901 (2021)	38	(8) Hsin	Chastisement	Metal	Venus	Friend	W	Cauldron	Restoration
		(2) Chou	Cord	Wood	Ox		NNE	Hand half opened	Untying a knot
1902 (2022)	39	(9) Jen	Endure	Water	Mercury	Friend	N	Large wave	Pregnancy
		(3) Yin	Revere	Fire	Tiger		ENE	Wriggling earthworm	Awakening of life
1903 (2023)	40	(10) Kwei	Sacrifice	Water	Mercury	Friend	N	Unruffled stream	Seed for new harvest
		(4) Mao	A period of time	Fire	Rabbit		E	Opening a gate	Plants breaking through soil
1904 (2024)	41	(1) Chia	Shell of a Tortoise	Wood	Jupiter	Friend	E	Fir Tree	Sprouting
		(5) Chen	Vibration	Earth	Dragon		ESE	Thunderstorm	Planting a seed
1905 (2025)	42	(2) Yi	Movement	Wood	Jupiter	Friend	E	Bamboo	Twig, tendril
		(6) Szu	End	Earth	Snake		SSE	Serpent	Supremacy of Yang

The Sexagenary Cycle (cont'd).
And Its Divinatory Meanings for the Years 1864 to 1923 CE and 1984 to 2043 CE

Year	Number	Stem-Branch	Name	Element	Astrology	Harmony	Direction	Symbol	Sexagenary Image
1906 (2026)	43	(3) Ping	Calamity	Fire	Mars	Friend	S	Torch flame	Bloom
		(7) Wu	Oppose	Metal	Horse		S	Yin hidden in growth	Yin reasserting herself
1907 (2027)	44	(4) Ting	Nail	Fire	Mars	Friend	S	Lamplight	Maturity
		(8) Wei	Not yet	Metal	Sheep		SSW	Tree in full bloom	Taste of fruit
1908 (2028)	45	(5) Wu	Attack	Earth	Saturn	Friend	Center	Mountains	Overabundance
		(9) Shen	Expand	Water	Monkey		WSW	Clasped hands	Yin growing strong
1909 (2029)	46	(6) Ki	Threads of a loom	Earth	Saturn	Friend	Center	Level ground	Order of things
		(10) Yu	Ripe	Water	Cock	Child	W	Winepress	Completion
1910 (2030)	47	(7) Keng	Two hands grasping a pestle	Metal	Venus	Child	W	Weapon	Fullness
		(11) Shu	Guard	Water	Dog		WNW	Yang withdrawing underground	Exhaustion
1911 (2031)	48	(8) Hsin	Chastisement	Metal	Venus	Child	W	Cauldron	Restoration
		(12) Hai	Kernel	Water	Pig		NNW	Yang in touch with Yin	Root

The Sexagenary Cycle (cont'd).
And Its Divinatory Meanings for the Years 1864 to 1923 CE and 1984 to 2043 CE

Year	Number	Stem-Branch	Name	Element	Astrology	Harmony	Direction	Symbol	Sexagenary Image
1912 (2032)	49	(9) Jen	Endure	Water	Mercury	Child	N	Large wave	Height of function
		(1) Tzu	Child	Wood	Rat		N	Yang stirring underground	Regeneration
1913 (2033)	50	(10) Kwei	Offering	Water	Mercury	Child	N	Unruffled stream	Seed for new harvest
		(2) Chou	Cord	Wood	Ox		NNE	Hand half opened	Untying a knot
1914 (2034)	51	(1) Chia	Helmet	Wood	Jupiter	Child	E	Fir Tree	Sprouting
		(3) Yin	Revere	Fire	Tiger		ENE	Wriggling earthworm	Awakening of life
1915 (2035)	52	(2) Yi	Movement	Wood	Jupiter	Child	E	Bamboo	Spread of growth
		(4) Mao	A period of time	Fire	Rabbit		E	Opening a gate	Plants breaking through soil
1916 (2036)	53	(3) Ping	Fire	Fire	Mars	Child	S	Torch flame	Bloom
		(5) Chen	Vibration	Earth	Dragon		ESE	Thunderstorm	Planting a seed
1917 (2037)	54	(4) Ting	To nail	Fire	Mars	Child	S	Lamplight	Lush vegetation
		(6) Szu	End	Earth	Snake		SSE	Serpent	Supremacy of Yang

The Sexagenary Cycle (cont'd).
And Its Divinatory Meanings for the Years 1864 to 1923 CE and 1984 to 2043 CE

Year	Number	Stem-Branch	Name	Element	Astrology	Harmony	Direction	Symbol	Sexagenary Image
1918 (2038)	55	(5) Wu	Attack	Earth	Saturn	Child	Center	Mountains Yin hidden in growth	Overabundance Yin reasserting herself
		(7) Wu	Oppose	Metal	Horse		S		
1919 (2039)	56	(6) Ki	Threads of a loom	Earth	Saturn	Child	Center	Level ground	Hibernation
		(8) Wei	Not yet	Metal	Sheep (Goat)		SSW	Tree in full bloom	Taste of fruit
1920 (2040)	57	(7) Keng	Milling of rice	Metal	Venus	Child	W	Weapon	Harvest
		(9) Shen	Expand	Water	Monkey		WSW	Clasped hands	Yin growing strong
1921 (2041)	58	(8) Shin	Chastisement	Metal	Venus	Child	W	Cauldron	Ripened fruit
		(10) Yu	Ripe	Water	Cock		W	Winepress	Completion
1922 (2042)	59	(9) Jen	Endure	Water	Mercury	Yin	N	Large wave Yang withdrawing	Pregnancy
		(11) Shu	Guard	Water	Dog		WNW		Exhaustion
1923 (2043)	60	(10) Kwei	Offering	Water	Mercury	Yin	N	Unruffled stream	Seed for new harvest
		(12) Hai	Kernel	Water	Pig		NNW	Yang touching Yin	Root

The *I Ching*

The most important and well-known Chinese system of philosophical numbers is the *I Ching*, or Book of Changes. The *I Ching* is composed of 64 unique divinatory symbols (known as hexagrams) which can advise mankind on all levels of activity, both spiritual and material.

The text of the *I Ching* itself dates back to 1000 BCE, but the essential building blocks of the 64 hexagrams, known as the eight trigrams, may date back as far as 3000 BCE.

The Taoist Yin-Yang classification system, which has been discussed earlier, is the basis for the symbolism employed in the *I Ching*. Yang is represented by a long, straight horizontal line, while Yin is represented by two short, broken horizontal lines.

From these two basic principles, 4 two-line symbols (known as Greater and Lesser Yin and Yang) are generated, followed by 8 three-line symbols (known as Trigrams) and 64 six-line symbols (known as Hexagrams).

THE EVOLUTION OF THE *I CHING*

Prior to 3000 BCE—Man observed in nature the interaction of Yin and Yang. Yin is identified with the broken, wavy lines of nature while Yang is identified with the solid, straight lines. Out of this primitive binary system evolved the four symbols known as "Ssu Hsiang," the first four combinations of Yin and Yang.

2953 BCE—Fu-Hsi is given the mythic stature of the creator of the eight basic trigrams which form in their combinations the 64 hexagrams of the *I Ching*. These eight symbols were first seen engraved on the shell of a giant tortoise who was rising out of the Yellow Sea. These eight trigrams grouped perfectly on the back of the tortoise to mark the eight compass points. Fu-Hsi is the inventor of the trigrams, equivalent to Thoth-Hermes as the inventor of number, color, and alphabet.

2205 BCE—The prototype of the *I Ching* is invented, known as the "Lien Shan." This is the first attempt to combine Fu-Hsi's eight trigrams to form 64 permutations. The trigram chosen to lead this series is "Tui," Lake, made up of two Yang lines crowned by a Yin line. This text is now lost, the material used to record it perishing with time.

1766 BCE—The second prototype of the *I Ching* is invented, known as the "Kuei Tsang." The first trigram to lead this order of 64 hexagrams is "K'un," Earth, made up of three Yin lines.

The *I Ching* that we know took the exact opposite tack and led the 64 hexagram permutations with "Ch'ien," Heaven, made up of three Yang lines.

The "Kuei Tsang" was recorded at a time when the proto-Chinese writing we know today was inscribed on bone and tortoise shell. As such, the "Kuei Tsang" has not survived.

1150 BCE—King Wen preserves in writing the system of 64 hexagrams leading with the trigram, Ch'ien. This text is known as the *I Ching*, or *Chou I*, since its invention heralded the Chou dynasty, which lasted from 1150 to 249 BCE.

1100 BCE—King Wen's invention of the *I Ching* is further elaborated upon by his son, Duke Chou, to become the paramount Chinese text used for 3000 years of divination.

King Wen detailed the order of hexagrams, their name and number, and wrote the basic text composed of an oracular poem detailing the image constructed by the composite trigrams of each hexagram and a basic divinatory judgment for each hexagram.

Duke Chou expanded this oracular poem for each hexagram to incorporate a symbolic image for each of the six lines composing the 64 hexagrams, a total of 384 oracular images. Out of these images developed the concept of a changing line and the ability to generate a second hexagram from the one first cast.

1150–249 BCE—During the Chou Dynasty, the great magickal-mathematical constructs were developed. The beginnings of Indian Buddhism (around 500 BCE) would ultimately impact and change the Chou and Confucian meanings first established for the *I Ching*.

500 BCE—Confucius, as a result of his deep study of all existing commentaries on the *I Ching* of his time, distilled the very essence of symbolic interpretation for the philosophical-mathematical framework of the *I Ching* into the *I Ching* commentary known as the "Chuan," or "Ten Wings."

This text became an integral part of all future complete publications of the *I Ching*, and survives to this day.

215 BCE—Chin Shih-Huang's overthrow of the Chou dynasty (to establish the Chin Dynasty), as a way of breaking from the past, ordered the destruction of all books in the hope of unifying the country under one language.

The one book spared from the conflagration is the *I Ching*, since it was the advice of this exact text that enabled Chin to overthrow the Chou Dynasty.

From the above timeline, the evolution of the *I Ching* can be seen as naturally growing out of a germinal conception of Yin and Yang. This blossoming of thought, continuing through many generations of research, expanded the concept of 2 to 4 to 8 to 64.

This tree, whose roots are in the Yin-Yang and branches in the detailed philosophical musings of the Chou Dynasty, can be outlined as shown on the following page.

TREE OF *I CHING*

Yin/Yang
↓
Four symbols (Greater and Lesser Yin and Yang)
↓
Eight Trigrams
(ordered first by Fu-Hsi with Ch'ien as South and K'un as North)
↓
64 Hexagrams leading with Tui (Lake), in the "Lien Shan"
↓
64 Hexagrams leading with K'un (Earth), in the "Kuei Tsang"
↓
Eight Trigrams of Fu-Hsi rearranged
by King Wen with "Li" as South and "K'an" as North
↓
64 Hexagrams leading with Ch'ien (Heaven)
in the *Chou I,* or *I Ching* as 64 oracular poems
↓
The 384 line oracular commentary for
the six lines of each *I Ching* hexagram
↓
The copious magickal diagrams for the *Chou I* order of the 64 hexagrams
↓
The ultimate philosophical commentary
on the structure of the *I Ching*, the "Ten Wings" of Confucius
↓
The *I Ching* as it exists today

SSU HSIANG, OR THE FOUR SYMBOLS

In order to understand the 64 hexagrams of the *I Ching*, one must first understand the two basic number systems from which they have evolved, that is the four symbols and the eight symbols.

The four symbols, known as Ssu Hsiang, are the first prototype of the hexagrams. The four symbols are four bigrams of Yin and Yang in their four possible pairings. Out of these four symbols, Fu-Hsi constructed the eight trigrams.

The four symbols are made up of straight horizontal lines for Yang and broken horizontal lines for Yin. The four symbols are four two-line symbols known as Greater Yin, Lesser Yang, Greater Yang, and Lesser Yin. The four forms are as shown on the next page.

The Four Symbols

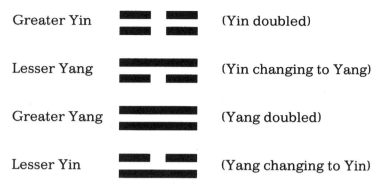

Greater Yin		(Yin doubled)
Lesser Yang		(Yin changing to Yang)
Greater Yang		(Yang doubled)
Lesser Yin		(Yang changing to Yin)

The top line of each of the four symbols determines Yin or Yang. For the trigrams, it will be the bottom line that determines the gender.

These four symbols, forming a miniature fourfold *I Ching*, developed a set of oracular symbols. These symbols may predate 3000 BCE.

Oracular Meanings for "Ssu Hsiang"

	Greater Yin	Lesser Yang	Greater Yang	Lesser Yin
Yin Yang Cycle	Yin	Yin to Yang	Yang	Yang to Yin
Quality	Cold	Light	Hot	Dark
Tai-Chi, Two Fishes	Black fish	White eye on black head	White fish	Black eye on white head
Direction	North	East	South	West
Phase of Sun	Winter	Spring	Summer	Fall
Phase of Moon	New Moon	First Quarter	Full Moon	Last Quarter
Heaven	Moon	Fixed Stars (Zodiac)	Sun	Planets
Earth	Emperor	Prince	Ruler (King)	Duke
Head	Ears	Nose	Eyes	Mouth
Oracular Advice	Remain silent and concealed	Prepare for attack	Act with force	Withdraw
Trigrams Generated	Ken and K'un	Sun and K'an	Ch'ien and Tui	Li and Chen

THE EIGHT TRIGRAMS OF FU-HSI

Out of the concept of the four symbols evolved the eight trigrams of Fu-Hsi, the real building blocks of the *I Ching*.

The trigrams are eight in number. As Yin and Yang form one horizontal level of symbols, and the four symbols form two horizontal levels of symbols, the eight trigrams form three horizontal levels of Yin and Yang.

The real poetic beauty and oracular power of these eight trigrams results from the multiplicity of meanings which have evolved out of thousands of years of commentaries in the East and Aleister Crowley's recent transplanting of the *I Ching* into the Western magickal tradition.

Each line of a trigram (or hexagram) is referred to as "yao" (line = yao):

Trigram Yao Symbolism

Three Lines of Trigram	Yao	Macro- cosm	Micro- cosm	Rank	Attributes of Inner Trigram	Attributes of Outer Trigram
▬▬▬	Upper	Heaven	Child	Third	Light	Yielding
▬▬ ▬▬	Middle	Humanity	Mother	Second	Will	Love
▬▬▬	Lower	Earth	Father	First	Firm	Dark

The trigrams are always viewed from the bottom up. The lower yao is the foundation and is considered the point of strength. The upper yao is the roof of the house and is considered the point of weakness, and the middle yao, being the walls of the house, determines the strength of the link between roof and foundation.

The eight trigrams, their names, and meanings are shown on the opposite page.

The Eight Basic Trigrams

Trigram	Name	Meaning	Element
	Ch'ien	Creative	Sky
	Tui	Joyful	Lake
	Li	Clinging	Fire
	Chen	Arousing	Thunder
	Sun	Gentle	Wood (Wind)
	K'an	Keeping Still	Water
	Ken	Abysmal	Mountain
	K'un	Receptive	Earth

The elemental associations to the trigrams may at first seem obtuse in comparison to Western correspondences. The eight symbols are all taken from nature.

Two of the trigrams form the polarity of Heaven and Earth:

Ch'ien (Heaven) and K'un (Earth)

Four of the trigrams are the four elements known to the West:

Li (Fire), Tui (Water)
Sun (Wind as Air), and Ken (Mountain as Earth)

Two of the trigrams are additional symbols for Fire and Water:

Chen is Fire as Thunder
(while Li is Fire as Lightning)
K'an is Water as Mist and Fog
(where Tui is Water as Rivers and Lakes)

Because Li and Tui have alternates, Li is grouped with K'an in a subset to the above, as Sun and Moon, a parallel to Heaven and Earth, and Fire and Water:

Li (Sun) and K'an (Moon)

In the above trigram pairings, "Sun," known as Wood, is given the elemental attribute of Air. This is derived from its alternate title, "Wind." "Sun" is both Wood (as in Tree) and Wind, since the wind moves the branches of the tree. A breeze can easily be detected rippling through the trees of a forest. Hence the symbolic equivalents of Wood = Wind = Air.

Sun can be fuel to fire as wood, or enflame that fire as wind. As a trigram, Sun shows two Yang lines in the middle and upper yao (suggesting Heaven) with the lower yao as Yin (suggesting the whirling winds of the sky).

THE ORDER OF THE TRIGRAMS

The eight trigrams possess four main symbolic orders:

1. The position of Yin or Yang in the three yao of the trigrams

2. The direction the trigrams originally taken when positioned in the heavens

3. The direction of the trigrams as they appear now on earth

4. The family structure, the Tetragrammaton of the Qabalah doubled

These four symbolic orders are detailed as follows.

1. The position of Yin or Yang in the three yao of the trigrams

The first and possibly the oldest manner of ordering the trigrams is based on the number of yao that are Yin or Yang.

The first of the eight is pure Yang and the last of the eight is pure Yin. Between these two poles are arranged the remaining six measured by both the amount of Yang or Yin yao, and their position in relation to the three levels of yao. This order and its justification are shown on the next page.

The Yin and Yang Ordering of Trigrams

Order	Trigram		Yin/Yang	Description
1		Ch'ien	Yang-Yang-Yang	The first movement of energy is completely active, without reservation.
2		Tui	Yang-Yang-Yin	The first appearance of Yin, from above in the weakest yao.
3		Li	Yang-Yin-Yang	Yin is able to move to the middle yao, but Yang outnumbers Yin.
4		Chen	Yang-Yin-Yin	Yin is able to outnumber Yang; Yang can only hold the lower yao, which is the strongest. (Note that the lower yao always determines whether the trigram is essentially Yin or Yang. The first four trigrams are Yang, the last four are Yin.)
5		Sun	Yin-Yang-Yang	The first appearance of Yin in the lower (ruling) yao occurs when the middle and upper yao are Yang, outnumbering Yin (Sun parallels Chen).
6		K'an	Yin-Yang-Yin	Yin now gains control of upper and lower yao, but cannot control its center (K'an parallels Li).
7		Ken	Yin-Yin-Yang	Now all but the upper yao is Yin. Yin predominates at the foundation and overthrows the roof (Ken parallels Tui).
8		K'un	Yin-Yin-Yin	Yin which has been introduced in the second trigram and is apparent from then on wins out, with all three yao Yin (K'un parallels Ch'ien).

The 80 tables used to describe the trigrams in this text are all ordered in this fashion, starting with all Yang and ending with all Yin, as will the magick square hexagram generator (which is not used in most translations of the *I Ching*). Aleister Crowley, the first commentator to successfully link the Eastern *I Ching* with the Western Qabalah, was aware of this trigram order and utilized it in the Trigram Appendix to his book *Liber 777*.

2. The direction the trigrams originally taken when positioned in the heavens

The directions the trigrams take in the night sky of the heaven was first envisioned by Fu-Hsi 5,000 years ago. Referred to as the Pre-Heaven Arrangement, the trigrams are arranged on a South-North axis, with South as Ch'ien and North as K'un. This arrangement is as follows.

Fu-Hsi's Heavenly Trigram Compass

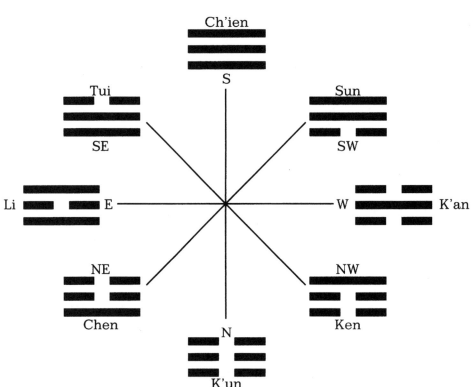

Fu-Hsi's directional compass is based on the Chinese concept of South being at the top of the map. This brings out the following directional correspondences for the trigrams.

- The South is the Sun at midday, the most vital point for Yang and, as such, Ch'ien.

The opposite pole, of North and K'un, corresponds to midnight, the point when Yin is most active. This is in harmony with the original definitions for Yin and Yang, where Yin is the northern side of a mountain and Yang is the southern side.

• Standing in the center of Fu-Hsi's directions and facing the South, the left hand becomes East and the rising Sun. The right hand is the opposite of Li and becomes West and the setting Sun, as K'an (the Moon and night). Li as the rising Sun is composed of two outer Yang and one inner Yin (light emerging out of dark). K'an as the setting Sun (and Moon) is composed of two outer Yin and one inner Yang (dark concealing light).

• The diagonal directionals are placed by the predominate yao of Yang or Yin. Southeast and Southwest are two Yang and one Yin each, since they border all Yang in the South. Northeast and Northwest are two Yin and one Yang each, since they border Yin in the North. They are also arranged so that the complete left side (the Yang side) of the diagram possesses Yang in the lower (ruling) yao, while the complete right side (the Yin side) possesses Yin in the lower (ruling) yao. All Chinese martial arts schools of discipline manuever on this eightfold arrangement of Fu-Hsi.

• The eight directions are also the basis for the family division described below. Father and Mother are South and North while East and West are the Middle Daughter and Son. The axis Southwest and Northeast are Older Daughter and Son, while the axis Southeast and Northwest are the Younger Daughter and Son. These attributes are not brought out by King Wen's directional arrangements.

3. The direction of the trigrams as they appear now on earth

The directions the trigrams take after descending to Earth were envisioned by King Wen 3,000 years ago. Referred to as the Later Heaven Arrangement, the South-North axis becomes Li and K'an (Sun and Moon), which in Fu-Hsi's arrangement is the East-West coordinate.

With King Wen's revision, the positions of all eight trigrams are altered. The symmetry of Yin and Yang found in Fu-Hsi's is displaced, with Sun and Moon replacing Heaven and Earth as the poles of the Universe.

As Fu-Hsi's directions are used to divine that which is of Heaven, King Wen's arrangement foretells the fortunes of men in worldly affairs (especially gambling, when aligned with the Chinese magick square of Saturn).

The Later Heaven Arrangement is shown on the following page.

King Wen's Earthly Trigram Compass

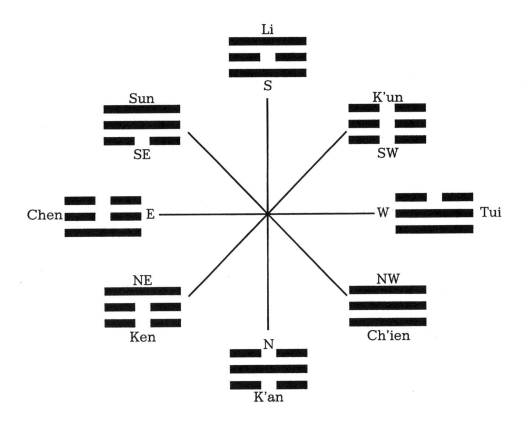

All modern commentators focus upon King Wen's variation, yet Fu-Hsi's arrangement is the real structure of the order for the 64 hexagrams. The following can be deduced from this variant:

- The quadrant West is composed of the lead trigram of three versions of the *I Ching*:

The West

Direction	Trigram	Version	Order
West	Tui	Lien Shan	First
Southwest	K'un	Kuei Tsang	Second
Northwest	Ch'ien	Chou I (*I Ching*)	Third

- Only the South-North axis contains polar opposites, the Sun (Li) in the South and the Moon (K'an) in the North. This is in accord with the *I Ching*, since the calligraphic stroke for "I Ching" is the Sun above the Moon, while the last two hexagrams of the *I Ching* (the 63rd and 64th) are composed of these two trigrams Sun above Moon and Moon above Sun.

- As the South is the Sun (Li), the East is the fire of the Sun (Chen). As the North is the Moon (K'an), the West is the water of the Moon (Tui).

- As the Northwest is the Sky (Ch'ien), its opposite, the Southeast is the wind of the Sky (Sun). As the Southwest is the Earth (K'un), its opposite, the Northeast, is the mountains of the Earth (Ken).

4. The family structure, the Tetragrammaton of the Qabalah doubled

The fourth basic structure for the *I Ching* is the eightfold family structure based on Yin and Yang. This family structure is, as it were, the Western esoteric family unit of the Hebraic Tetragrammaton doubled upon itself to form the ogdoadic Chinese family.

This double fourfold family pattern is composed of four males and four females, structured upon the appearance of Yang or Yin as Father, Mother, three sons, and three daughters:

The Ogdoadic Family

Trigram	Family Member		Yin-Yang
	Ch'ien	Father	All Yang
	K'un	Mother	All Yin
	Chen	Eldest Son	Yang couples with Yin in the first yao.
	K'an	Middle Son	Yang couples with Yin in the second yao.
	Ken	Youngest Son	Yang couples with Yin in the third yao.
	Sun	Eldest Daughter	Yin couples with Yang in the first yao.
	Li	Middle Daughter	Yin couples with Yang in the second yao.
	Tui	Youngest Daughter	Yin couples with Yang in the third yao.

The trigrams for Father and Mother are sexed by the appearance of either all Yang (father) or all Yin (mother). The children, however, are sexed by the least amount of either Yang lines (sons) or Yin lines (daughters).

Thus the three sons are always composed of two Yin lines and one Yang line. The position of the one Yang line in the trigram determines the rank of the son (since Yang = male). The bottom yao is the position of the eldest son, the middle yao is the middle son, and the top yao is the youngest son. The same pattern governs the three daughters, who are always composed of two Yang lines and one Yin line. The position of the one Yin line determines the rank of the daughter (since Yin = female). Like the sons, the bottom yao is the eldest daughter, the middle yao is the middle daughter, and the upper yao is the youngest daughter.

The following table illustrates this principle of least amount of Yin or Yang.

Rank of Son and Daughter of Ogdoad

Trigram Line	Rank	Appearance of Yang Line (Son)	Apperance of Yin Line (Daughter)
Top	Third	Youngest Son	Youngest Daughter
Middle	Second	Middle Son	Middle Daughter
Bottom	First	Eldest Son	Eldest Daughter

If the ogdoad family attributes are laid upon the eight directions of the compass as Fu-Hsi allocated in his heavenly arrangement, the following family order is generated:

- The Father and Mother become the South-North axis. Father is the Sun at noon in the South; Mother is the Moon at midnight in the North. The Father is in the front, while the Mother is in the rear.

- The youngest daughter and youngest son become the Southeast-Northwest axis. The youngest daughter is in the position of front-left, while the youngest son is in the position of rear-right.

- The middle daughter and middle son become the East-West axis. The middle daughter is the rising Sun at dawn in the East, while the middle son is the setting Sun in the West. The middle daughter is left; the middle son is right.

- The Eldest daughter and Eldest son are the Southwest-Northeast axis. The Eldest daughter is in the position of front-right, while the Eldest Son is in the position of rear-left.

These four axes of the eight directions can be categorized as shown on the opposite page.

Fu-Hsi's Directional Ogdoad Family

| | | Direction | | |
| | | Compass | Martial | |
Family Member	Trigram	Point	Arts Stance	Time of Day
Middle Daughter	Li	E	Left	Sunrise
Youngest Daughter	Tui	SE	Left-Front	Morning
Father	Ch'ien	S	Front	Noon
Eldest Daughter	Sun	SW	Front-Right	Afternoon
Middle Son	K'an	W	Right	Sunset
Eldest Son	Ken	NW	Right-Rear	Evening
Mother	K'un	N	Rear	Midnight
Youngest Son	Chen	NE	Rear-Left	Predawn

Beyond the above four divisions of Yin and Yang, heavenly winds, earthly directions, and family structure, a lore of equal complexity to that of the Hebrew and Arabic Qabalahs developed concerning the symbols for the eight trigrams both in the East and in the West.

The giants of the East who contributed to the development of these symbols are Fu-Hsi, King Wen, and Confucius. In the West, the one leading light in discovering the correlation of the eight trigrams to the Hebrew Tree of Life (and therefore the Qabalah) is Aleister Crowley.

In the East, the distillation of the Trigrammaton symbol system can be found in the appendices to the *I Ching* known as the "Ten Wings" and attributed to Confucius. This work represents a distillation of the Chinese mystery school of mathematician-philosophers who worked between the inception of the *I Ching* (1150 BCE) and the time of Confucius (500 BCE).

In order to truly understand the symbolism behind the 64 hexagrams, the symbol set for the eight trigrams that make up each of the 64 hexagrams must be clearly understood. The following 80 trigram tables, 40 from the East and 40 from the West, delineate every nuance of symbolism that has evolved for the trigrams since Fu-Hsi's discovery in 2953 BCE up to Crowley's last word on the subject in 1944 CE (found in the appendices of his *Book of Thoth*), encompassing 4,897 years of esoteric symbolism for the trigrams.

THE FORTY TRIGRAM TABLES OF THE EAST

These 40 tables (as well as the 40 tables of the West) are ordered by the preponderance of Yang or Yin, starting with Ch'ien and ending with K'un. These 80 eightfold tables can be seen as a Chinese equivalent to Crowley's 183 tables composing *Liber 777*, which classifies the symbols of the world on a 33-fold division of the Tree of Life.

LIBER TRIGRAMMATON
VEL LIBER 888
(80 TRIGRAM TABLES FOR THE EAST AND THE WEST)

The Forty Trigram Tables of the East

Table 0. Trigram Name—The table marked Zero is the Chinese name for each trigram, first by the Wade-Giles system and second in the modern Pin-Yin.

Table 1. Name (Translation)—The traditional name for the trigram and alternate translations.

Table 2. Element in Nature—The elemental symbol which will be the basis for the allocation of the 64 hexagrams to Taoist images in nature.

Trigram	0. Name	1. Name (Translation)	2. Element in Nature
	Ch'ien (Qian)	Creative (strong, rulership)	Sky
	Tui (Dui)	Joyful (pleasure, pleasing)	Lake (sea, marsh)
	Li (Li)	Clinging (bright, warm)	Fire (lightning, the Sun)
	Chen (Zhen)	Arousing (motion, stimulating)	Thunder (Thunderstorm)
	Sun (Sun)	Gentle (penetration, dispersion)	Wind, Wood
	K'an (Kan)	Abysmal (perilous, moist)	Water (the Moon, clouds, streams, springs
	Ken (Yin/Gen)	Keeping Still (blocking, standstill)	Mountain (hills)
	K'un (Kun)	Receptive (store up, shelter, obedient)	Earth

The Forty Trigram Tables of the East (cont'd.)

Table 3. The Five Chinese Elements—The elemental variants which are derived from the "Lo Map" (the magick square of nine squares).

Table 4. Chinese Pentagonal Planets—The corresponding Chinese planets to the Lo Map trigram number symbolism.

Table 5. Chinese Zodiac—The Twelve Earthly Branches which correspond to the double fivefold elements of the Ten Stems.

Table 6. Liang Yi Yin-Yang Map—The basis for the order of these tables, first shown as a combination of Yang and Yin and then as a symbol name.

Trigram	3. Chinese Element	4. Chinese Planet	5. Chinese Zodiac	6. Liang Yi Yin-Yang Map
☰	Metal	Venus	Horse	Three Yang (three continuous lines)
☱	Metal	Venus	Sheep (Goat)	Two Yang/one Yin (deficient top)
☲	Fire	Mars	Tiger and Rabbit	Yang-Yin-Yang (empty middle)
☳	Wood (Wind)	Jupiter	Rat	One Yang/two Yin (upturned cup)
☴	Wood (Wind)	Jupiter	Ox	One Yin/two Yang (broken bottom)
☵	Water	Mercury	Monkey, Dog, Cock, and Pig	Yin-Yang-Yin (full middle)
☶	Earth	Saturn	Dragon	Two Yin/one Yang (overturned cup)
☷	Earth	Saturn	Snake	Three Yin (three broken lines)

The Forty Trigram Tables of the East (cont'd.)

Table 7. Family—Caste—The trigrams both as the nuclear family and as the caste system of Chinese society.

Table 8. Four Symbols (Ssu Hsiang)—The trigrams seen only as the bottom two lines.

Trigram	7. Family (Caste)	8. Four Symbols (Ssu Hsiang)
	Father (King, Ruler) Great Yang	Greater Yang
	Youngest Daughter (sorceress) Third Female Third coupling of Yang with Yin	Greater Yang
	Middle Daughter (women) Second Female Second coupling of Yang with Yin	Lesser Yin
	Oldest Son (young men) First Male First coupling of Yin with Yang	Lesser Yin
	Oldest Daughter (merchants) First Female First coupling of Yang with Yin	Lesser Yang
	Middle Son (thieves) Second Male Second coupling of Yin with Yang	Lesser Yang
	Youngest Son (officials) Third Male Third coupling of Yin with Yang	Greater Yin
	Mother (People, multitude) Great Yin	Greater Yin

The Forty Trigram Tables of the East (cont'd.)

Table 9. Four Symbols as Eight Parts—The four two-line symbols which combine to form the eight trigrams.

Table 10. Fu-Hsi Yin-Yang—Fu-Hsi's classification of the trigrams by the bottom yao only.

Table 11. King Wen Yin-Yang—King Wen's classification based on the least apperance of Yin or Yang (unless all Yin or all Yang).

Trigram	9. Four Symbols as Eight Parts	10. Fu-Hsi Yin-Yang	11. King Wen Yin-Yang
	Greater Yang and Greater Yang	Yang	Yang
	Greater Yang and Lesser Yin	Yang	Yin
	Lesser Yin and Lesser Yang	Yang	Yin
	Lesser Yin and Greater Yin	Yang	Yang
	Lesser Yang and Greater Yang	Yin	Yin
	Lesser Yang and Lesser Yin	Yin	Yang
	Greater Yin and Lesser Yang	Yin	Yang
	Greater Yin and Greater Yin	Yin	Yin

The Forty Trigram Tables of the East (cont'd.)

Table 12. Fu-Hsi's Eight Directions—These eight directions are the measure of the heavens by the eight winds and are known as the Heavenly, Pre-Heaven, or Abstract System.

Table 13. Fu-Hsi's Seasons—Time of year measured by Fu-Hsi's directions.

Table 14. Fu-Hsi's Time of Day—Time of day measured by Fu-Hsi's directions.

Trigram	12. Fu Hsi's Eight Directions	13. Fu Hsi's Seasons	14. Fu Hsi's Time of Day
	South (front)	Summer	10:30 AM–1:30 PM (noon, midday)
	Southeast (front-left)	Spring changing to Summer	7:30 AM–10:30 AM (9 AM, morning)
	East (left)	Spring	4:30 AM–7:30 AM (6 AM, dawn)
	Northeast (rear-left))	Winter changing to Spring	1:30 AM–4:30 AM (3 AM, early morning)
	Southwest (front-right)	Summer changing to Fall	1:30 PM–4:30 PM (3 PM, afternoon)
	West (right)	Fall	4:30 PM–7:30 PM (6 PM, sunset)
	Northwest (rear-right)	Fall changing to Winter	7:30 PM–10:30 PM (9 PM, evening)
	North (rear)	Winter	10:30 PM–1:30 AM (12 PM, midnight)

The Forty Trigram Tables of the East (cont'd.)

Table 15. King Wen's Eight Directions—These eight directions are the measure of the earth by the four quarters and eight directions and are known as the Earthly, Later Heaven, or Temporal System.

Table 16. King Wen's Seasons—Time of year measured by King Wen's directions.

Table 17. King Wen's Time of Day—Time of day measured by King Wen's eight directions.

Trigram	15. King Wen's Eight Directions	16. King Wen's Seasons	17. King Wen's Time of Day
	Northwest (rear-right)	Fall changing to Winter	7:30 PM–10:30 PM (9 PM, early night)
	West (right)	Fall	4:30 PM–7:30 PM (6 PM, sunset)
	South (front)	Summer	10:30 AM–1:30 PM (noon,.midday)
	East (left)	Spring	4:30 AM–7:30 AM (6 AM, dawn)
	Southeast (front-left)	Spring changing to Summer	7:30 PM–10:30 AM (9 AM, morning)
	North (rear)	Winter	10:30 PM–1:30 AM' (12 PM, midnight)
	Northeast (rear-left)	Winter changing to Spring	1:30 AM–4:30 AM (3 AM, early morning)
	Southwest (front-right)	Summer changing to Fall	1:30 PM–4:30 PM (3 PM, afternoon)

The Forty Trigram Tables of the East (cont'd.)

Table 18. Numerical Order—The order of the trigrams, where Ch'ien is first and K'un is last.

Table 19. Pre-Heaven Lo Map—the trigrams arranged on the Saturn square as the Heavenly directions of Fu-Hsi, and their oracular significance.

Table 20. Later Heaven Lo Map—the traditional arrangement of the trigrams on the Saturn square according to King Wen, and their oracular significance. Here the three trigrams made of two Yin and one Yang are the three lucky trigrams.

Trigram	18. Numerical Order	19. Pre-Heaven Lo Map	20. Later Heaven Lo Map
	1	9 (bad luck)	6 (rejection)
	2	4 (repentance)	7 (calamity)
	3	3 (good fortune which may turn bad)	9 (bad luck)
	4	8 (good fortune)	3 (good fortune which may) turn bad)
	5	2 (error)	4 (repentance)
	6	7 (calamity)	1 (good luck)
	7	6 (rejection)	8 (good fortune)
	8	1 (good luck)	2 (error)

The Forty Trigram Tables of the East (cont'd.)

Table 21. Nine House Astrology—The fivefold Chinese planets as numbers on the Lo Map (according to King Wen).

Table 22. Fingers—The eight lesser fingers of the two hands as the eight trigrams, where the left hand equals East, Sun, and Yang, while the right hand equals West, Moon , and Yin.

Table 23. Lunar Cycle—The Moon measured by the cycle of Yin and Yang (Yang = Full Moon , Yin = no Moon).

Trigram	21. Nine House Astrology	22. Fingers	23. Lunar Cycle
	Six White Metal Star (rejection)	Left little finger	Full
	Seven Blue Metal Star (catastrophe)	Left ring finger	From First Quarter to Full
	Nine Yellow-Orange Fire Star (bad luck)	Left middle finger	First Quarter
	Three Red-Orange Wood Star (good luck)	Left index finger	From New to First Quarter
	Four Jade Green Wood Star (regret)	Right index finger	From Full to Last Quarter
	One Crimson Water Star (lucky)	Right middle finger	Last Quarter
	Eight Yellow Earth Star (fortune)	Right ring finger	From Last Quarter to New
	Two Black Earth Star (error)	Right little finger	New

The Forty Trigram Tables of the East (cont'd.)

Table 24. Tai Chi Symbol—The two fishes or Yin/Yang symbol, dissected into eight pie-shaped slices and allocated to the eight trigrams (Yang = white, Yin = black).

Table 25. Color (Elemental)—The classic Taoist colors for the eight trigrams derived from the eight elements in nature.

Table 26. Alternate Colors—Variations to the classic symbols in table 25.

Trigram	24. Tai Chi Symbol	25. Color (Elemental)	20. Alternate Colors
	All white (the body of the white fish)	White	Midnight Blue, Deep Red
	More white than black (head of the white fish)	Deep Blue (Indigo)	Gold, White
	The black eye (in the middle of the white fish)	Yellow-Orange	Buff, Purple, Red
	More black than white (tail of the black fish)	Red-Orange	Blue, Green
	More white than black (tail of the white fish)	Green	Blue, White
	The white eye (in the middle of the black fish)	Crimson (Red-Violet)	Black
	More black than white (head of the black fish)	Bright Yellow	Brown, Green, Black
	All black (the body of the black fish)	Black	Yellow, Variegated Colors

The Forty Trigram Tables of the East (cont'd.)

Table 27. Family Trait—Family traits derived from the Family Ogdoadic order.

Table 28. Personality—Eight personalities derived from the general nature of the trigrams.

Table 29. Quality—Personality trait derived from the name of the trigram

Trigram	27. Family Trait	28. Personality	29. Quality
	Firmness, rulership	Warm-hearted, benevolent	Leadership
	Joyous, cheerful, pleasing	Gentle, affable	Laughter
	Brilliant, radiant, warm	Optimistic, open-minded	Intuition
	Moving, arousing	Unlucky	Surprise
	Gentle, penetrating, dispersing	Cool, heartless	Empathy
	Dangerous, abysmal, moist,	Clever, deceitful	Rebelliousness
	Still, silent, standstill	Fair, objective	Honesty
	Receptive, obedient, sheltering	Warm-hearted, benevolent	Devotion

The Forty Trigram Tables of the East (cont'd.)

Table 30. Power—Taoist forces that can be tapped in each of the eight trigrams.

Table 31. Action—Oracular advice for each trigram on how to act in any given situation.

Table 32. All Living Creatures—The trigrams as eight ways humanity interacts.

Trigram	30. Power	31. Action	32. All Living Creatures
	Courage	Act with strength	Battle one another
	Sexual desire	Break free	Are given joy with one another
	Clarity	Shine within	Perceive one another
	Determination	Rush forward	Come forth into being
	Concentration	Kneel down to	Are brought to completion
	Cunning	Stand over an abyss	Toil for one another
	Stillness	Restrain oneself	Are brought to perfection
	Endurance	Yield	Serve one another

The Forty Trigram Tables of the East (cont'd.)

Table 33. The Tao—The eight ways the Tao manifests in nature.

Table 34. The Four Pairings—The four elemental pairings of the eight trigrams in nature.

Trigram	33. The Tao	34. The Four Pairings
	The Tao struggles	Heaven with Earth determines direction, North and South pole
	The Tao rejoices	Lake unites with mountain
	The Tao is manifested to one another	Fire does not combat water
	The Tao comes forth into action	Thunder arouses wind
	The Tao is balanced and in full power	Wind arouses thunder
	The Tao withdraws and rests	Water does not combat fire
	The Tao completes its work	Mountain unites with lake
	Great service is done to the Tao	Earth with Heaven determines direction, North and South pole

The Forty Trigram Tables of the East (cont'd.)

Table 35. Animals—Traditional Taoist art symbols for the eight tri-grams as animals.

Table 36. Human Body—The eightfold Taoist division of the body.

Trigram	35. Animals	36. Human Body
☰	Horse (tiger, lion)	Head (lingam, bones)
☱	Sheep (goat, deer, birds, monkey)	Mouth and tongue (throat, teeth, lungs)
☲	Pheasant (phoenix, shellfish, tortoise, oyster)	Eyes (large belly, blood, heart)
☳	Dragon (snake, eagle, swallow, cricket)	Feet (liver, gall bladder)
☴	Cock (fowl, unicorn, crane)	Thighs (high forehead, receding hairline, legs, nervous system)
☵	Pig (fox, bat, rat)	Ears (urinary tract, kidneys, sex organs)
☶	Dog (mouse, bull leopard)	Hands, fingers
☷	Ox (cow, mare, ant, cat)	Belly (yoni)

The Forty Trigram Tables of the East (cont'd.)

Table 37. Trees, Plants, Flowers, Herbs—Traditional Taoist art symbols for the eight trigrams as vegetation; also food that contains the essence of the eight trigrams.

Table 38. Locations—The eight trigrams as the measure of land and dwellings by the Feng Shu geomancer's compass.

Trigram	35. Trees, Plants, Flowers, Herbs	38. Locations
☰	Chrysanthemum, fresh fruits, herbs, teas, grains	Temple, shrine, mountain retreat, the study of a house
☱	Gardenia, magnolia, lake plants, rice	Lakes, valleys, marshes, the bedroom of a house
☲	Maple, pepper, watermelon, tomatoes, peanuts, dried fruits	Lighthouse, lighted streets of a city at night, the patio (or front porch) of a house
☳	Green vegetables, young green bamboo, evergreen, peach, plum	Forests, buildings, the living room of a house
☴	Lily, poppy, grass, trees	Forest glades, libraries, the hallways of a house
☵	Lotus, reed, swamp plants	Rivers, wells, waterfalls, the bathroom of a house
☶	Mushroom, mango, banana, avocado	Castles, palaces, paths, gates, graves, the dining room of a house
☷	Ginger, yam, potato, beet, bulb flowers, taro	Fields, farms, bottom of the sea, the kitchen of a house

The Forty Trigram Tables of the East (cont'd.)

Table 39. Climate—Taoist art symbolism of weather for the eight trigrams.

Table 40. Additional Symbols—Symbols for the most part found at the end of the "Ten Wings."

Trigram	39. Climate	40. Additional Symbols
	Clear, crisp and cold	Circle, jade, metal, cold, ice, cogwheel, clock, machine
	Rain, mist and fog	Concubine, reflection, magick, decay, picking fruits, stringed instruments, sword, salt
	Clear, dry and warm	Helmet, spear, armor, hollow tree, spiral, drought
	Thunderstorms and storms clearing	Great highway, decision, vehemence, a messenger, a message, speed, swiftness
	Windiness and tornadoes	Plumbline, carpenter's square, long, lofty, indecision leading to decision, business
	Dark, rainy and cold	Channels, ditches, hidden, concealed, wheel, thief, crooked road, strong tree, danger
	Cloudiness and mild temperature	Bypath, small rock, gateway, guardian, bridge, gnarled tree trunk, seeds
	Cloudy	Square cloth, cauldron, parsimony, turning lathe, large wagon, handle, support, multitude, black soil

CROWLEY'S MAGICKAL *I CHING*

The one man responsible for bringing the *I Ching* into the arsenal of Western magick is Aleister Crowley. Neither the 19th century Theosophical Society nor the Golden Dawn utilized the symbolism of the *I Ching*. The most Eastern of magickal practices engaged in by these organizations was the Tattva system of India (as popularized by Rama Prasad).

Crowley's own exposure to the *I Ching* came between 1895 and 1900, through James Legge's translation in Max Muller's Sacred Books of the East Series. On account of Crowley's own magickal training in regards to the Western Qabalah, he was able to penetrate into the very heart of the *I Ching* which is the trigrams, and to correctly align these eight trigrams to the Qabalistic Tree of Life. Thus he successively integrated the eight trigrams with eight select Sephiroth on the Tree of Life, linking the eight trigrams with both the Western fourfold elemental symbolism and the astrological planetary cycle.

Crowley developed three distinct sets of Western magickal attributions, two of which were recorded in *Liber 777* (1908) and a third, revised set included in *The Book of Thoth* (1944). The table on the following page details his three distinct systems.

Crowley's Western Equivalents for the Eight Trigrams

The Trigrams		From Liber 777		From Book of Thoth
		Yetziratic	Planetary	Tree of Life
☰	Ch'ien	Lingam	Sun	Saturn (Daath)
☱	Tui	Water	Venus	Jupiter (Chesed)
☲	Li	Sun	Jupiter	Sun (Tiphereth)
☳	Chen	Fire	Mars	Mars (Geburah)
☴	Sun	Air	Mercury	Mercury (Hod)
☵	K'an	Moon	Saturn	Moon (Yesod)
☶	Ken	Earth	Earth	Venus (Netzach)
☷	K'un	Yoni	Moon	Earth (Malkuth)

The ultimate classification Crowley developed for the trigrams was derived from the planetary attributes of the ten Sephiroth of the Tree of Life, as recorded in diagram 3 of appendix B in *The Book of Thoth*.

He placed the trigram Ch'ien (Heaven) above in Daath's position (representing the invisible point) of the Supernal triad. Counterpoised to Ch'ien, he then placed the trigram K'un (Earth) below in Malkuth's position (representing Daath fallen into the material world as the suspended pendant Earth). Ch'ien became Saturn (as Binah in the position of Daath) and K'un became Earth as the four elements.

Crowley then placed the pair of trigrams Li and K'an, representing the Sun and Moon, as Tiphereth and Yesod (which correspond to the Sun and Moon as Hebraic-planetary attributes).

He then had four remaining trigrams to place as the four elements. Crowley interpreted the remaining four Chinese trigrams as Fire, Water, Air, and Earth, which he attributed to Chesed, Geburah, Netzach, and Hod on the Tree of Life, as follows.

The Four Elemental Trigrams on the Tree of Life

Trigram	Chinese Elemental	Western Element	Tree of Life	Planet
Chen	Thunder	Fire	Geburah	Mars
Tui	Water	Water	Chesed	Jupiter
Sun	Wood (Wind)	Air	Hod	Mercury
Ken	Earth	Earth	Netzach	Venus

Thus Crowley was able to correctly link the eight trigrams of the East to the eight Western concepts of Heaven, Earth (world), Sun, Moon, Fire, Water, Air, and Earth (element). His complete Qabalistic correspondences to the Chinese concept are as follows.

Crowley's Chinese Cosmos

Number	Chinese Attribute	Tree of Life Parallel	Planetary Correspondences
0	Tao	Ain Soph Aur	Void
1	Tao-Teh	Kether	Primum Mobile
2	Yang	Chockmah	Zodical Belt
3	Yin	Binah	Saturn
11 (33)	Ch'ien	Daath	Saturn (Lingam)
4	Tui	Chesed	Jupiter
5	Chen	Geburah	Mars
6	Li	Tiphereth	Sun
7	Ken	Netzach	Venus
8	Sun	Hod	Mercury
9	K'an	Yesod	Moon
10	K'un	Malkuth	Four Elements (Yoni)

By applying the Yetziratic table found in 777 and the planetary revision found in *The Book of Thoth*, 40 tables can be created for the parallel Western trigram symbolism that Crowley envisioned in his writings.

These 40 tables are numbered 41 to 80, and are seen as an extension rather than a replacement of the Eastern symbol set.

The planetary table found in 777 has been excluded as the basic ordering for these Western tables, since Crowley's recension found in *The Book of Thoth* is the ultimate in Qabalistic harmony to the *I Ching*.

The Forty Trigram Tables of the West

Table 41. Element and Planet *(777)*—Crowley's original research into the *I Ching* as found in *Liber 777*. The planets are erroneous in that he revised these attributes later in his life.

Table 42. Planet *(Book of Thoth)*—Crowley's revision of the trigrams to planets as found in *The Book of Thoth*. These attributes are the basis for the Western trigram tables.

Table 43. Tree of Life—The positions on the Tree of Life corresponding to Crowley's revised planetary attributes. In this system, "Daath" is equivalent to "Binah" as Saturn. It is derived from placing a hexagram on the Tree of Life whose center is Tiphereth and apex point is Daath as Binah displaced.

Trigram	41. Element and Planet (777)	42. Planet (Book of Thoth)	43. Tree of Life
	Lingam (Sun)	Saturn	Daath (knowledge)
	Water (Venus)	Jupiter	Chesed (mercy)
	Sun (Jupiter)	Sun	Tiphereth (beauty)
	Fire (Mars)	Mars	Geburah (severity)
	Air (Mercury)	Mercury	Hod (splendor)
	Moon (Saturn)	Moon	Yesod (foundation)
	Earth (Earth)	Venus	Netzach (victory)
	Yoni (Moon)	Earth (four elements)	Malkuth (kingdom)

The Forty Trigram Tables of the West (cont'd.)

Table 44. Zodiac—The trigrams as the 12 signs of the Zodiac in light of their ruling planets.

Table 45. Geomancy—The 16 geomantic shapes which form eight corresponding pairs to the Zodiacal attributes of table 44.

Table 46. Alchemical (Planetary)—The traditional planetary correspondences of alchemical metals where lead is Saturn and gold is the Sun.

Trigram	44. Zodiac	45. Geomancy	46. Alchemical (Planetary)
	Capricorn and Aquarius	Carcer and Tristitia	Lead
	Sagittarius and Pisces	Acquisitio and Laetitia	Tin
	Leo	Fortuna Major and Fortuna Minor	Gold
	Aries and Scorpio	Puer and Rubeus	Iron
	Gemini and Virgo	Albus and Conjunctio	Quicksilver
	Cancer	Populus and Via	Silver
	Taurus and Libra	Amissio and Puella	Copper
	Elementals (Tarot: Pages); Devoid of Zodiacal qualties	Caput Draconis and Cauda Draconis	Fire, Water, Air, Earth

The Forty Trigram Tables of the West (cont'd.)

Table 47. Alchemical (Qabalistic)—The alchemical metal variants found in the Qabalistic text, *The Purifying Fire*.

Table 48. Alchemical (Barrett)—The alchemical elemental qualities found under the number 8 in Barrett's *The Magus*.

Table 49. Tattvas—The Golden Dawn-Theosophical system of the Tattvas as found in the writings of Rama Prasad.

Trigram	47. Alchemical (Qabalistic)	48. Alchemical (Barrett)	49. Tattvas
	Sulfur (Tin)	The heat of Air	Akasa-Akasa (Linga)
	Silver	The moisture of Water	Apas Tattva
	Iron	The heat of Fire	Pingala Nadi (right Solar current)
	Gold	The dryness of Fire	Agni Tattva (Tejas)
	Tin (Brass)	The moisture of Air	Vayu Tattva
	Lead (Mercury)	The coldness of Water	Ida Nadi (left Lunar current)
	Copper (Hermaphroditical Brass)	The dryness of Earth	Prithivi Tattva
	Mercury Philosophorum (Medicinia Metallorum)	The coldness of Earth	Prithivi-Prithivi (Yoni)

The Forty Trigram Tables of the West (cont'd.)

Table 50. Chakras—The seven chakras, or interior wheels, of the human body classified by their traditional Hindu planetary attributes.

Table 51. Hebrew (Elemental)—The corresponding Hebrew letters to table 41, the elemental attributes found in Crowley's *777*.

Table 52. Hebrew (Planetary)—The corresponding Hebrew letters to table 42, the Sephirotic planetary attributes.

Trigram	50. Chakras	51. Hebrew (Elemental)	52. Hebrew (Planetary)
	Kundalini, the serpent force within the spine	פ (P) (Linga)	א (A) (Spirit)
	Third chakra— Manipura	מ (M) (Water)	כ (K) (Jupiter)
	Fourth chakra— Anahata	ר (R) (Sun)	ר (R) (Sun)
	Second chakra— Svadhisthana	ש (Sh) (Fire)	פ (P) (Mars)
	Seventh chakra— Sahasara	א (A) (Air)	ב (B) (Mercury)
	Sixth chakra— Ajna	ג (G) (Moon)	ג (G) (Moon)
	Fifth chakra— Visuddha	ת (Th) (Earth)	ד (D) (Venus)
	First chakra— Muladhara	כ (K) (Yoni)	ת (Th) (Earth)

The Forty Trigram Tables of the West (cont'd.)

Table 53. English Alphabet (Serial)—The elemental attributes of Crowley applied to the serial order of the English alphabet.

Table 54. English Alphabet *(Liber Trigrammaton)*—The trigram allocation to the English alphabet found in Crowley's *Liber Trigrammaton*.

Table 55. Number Hebrew and Tarot (Elemental)—The number values for the Hebrew attributes found in table 51, when calculated as Hebrew numerals and Tarot keys (Crowley-Golden Dawn order).

Table 56. Number Hebrew and Tarot (Planetary)—The number values for the Hebrew attributes found in table 52, when calculated as Hebrew numerals and Tarot keys (Crowley-Golden Dawn order).

Trigram	53. English Alphabet (Serial)	54. English Alphabet (Liber Tri-grammaton)	55. Number Hebrew and Tarot (Elemental)	56. Number Hebrew and Tarot (Planetary)
	I (Linga)	N	80 (16)	1 (0)
	X (Water)	Q	40 (12)	20 (10)
	T (Sun)	R	200 (19)	200 (19)
	W (Fire)	D	300 (20)	80 (16)
	Y (Air)	E	1 (0)	2 (1)
	S (Moon)	K	3 (2)	3 (2)
	Z (Earth)	V	400 (21)	4 (3)
	V (Yoni)	U	20 (10)	400 (21)

The Forty Trigram Tables of the West (cont'd.)

Table 57. Number (Serial Order)—The number values for the English alphabet found in table 53 (A = 1, Z = 26).

Table 58. Number *(Liber Trigrammaton)*—The number values for the English alphabet found in table 54 (I = 1, U = 26).

Table 59. Sephirotic Number—Qabalistic number assigned to the planets found in table 42. These numbers are also the number correspondences for the planetary, magick squares.

Table 60. Binary Code—The three lines composing the trigrams as binary code. The bottom yao is the lead number. Yin is zero and Yang is one. These eight numbers total to 444.

Trigram	57. Number (Serial Order)	58. Number (Liber Tri-grammaton)	59. Sephirotic Number	60. Binary Code
	9	19	11 (or 33)	111
	24	22	4	110
	20	21	6	101
	23	25	5	100
	25	20	8	011
	19	24	9	010
	26	23	7	001
	22	26	10	000

The Forty Trigram Tables of the West (cont'd.)

Table 61. Color (Elemental)—The traditional Western elemental colors for table 41.

Tables 62–65. The Four Sephirotic Color Scales—The four Qabalistic Worlds of the Tree of Life as the color symbolism found in the Golden Dawn. Table 62 is Atziloth, the highest and innermost world, while table 65 is Assiah, the lowest and outermost world.

Trigram	61. Color (Elemental)	Sephirotic Color Scales	
		62. Atziloth	63. Briah
	White	Lavender	Gray-white
	Blue	Deep Violet	Blue
	Gold	Clear Pink Rose	Golden Yellow
	Red	Orange	Scarlet-Red
	Yellow	Violet-Purple	Orange
	Silver	Indigo	Violet
	Black	Amber	Emerald
	Red	Yellow	Russet, Olive, Citrine, Black

The Forty Trigram Tables of the West (cont'd.)

Tables 64–65. The Four Sephirotic Color Scales (continued)—The four Qabalistic Worlds of the Tree of Life as the color symbolism found in the Golden Dawn. Table 64 is Yetzirah, while table 65 is Assiah.

Table 66. Magickal Weapons—Eight select magickal weapons found in 777 that correspond to the eight trigrams, based on table 42.

Trigram	Sephirotic Color Scales		66. Magickal Weapons
	64. Yetzirah	65. Assiah	
☰	Deep Violet	Gray flecked Gold	Lamp (outer robe, cup)
☱	Deep Purple	Deep Azure flecked Yellow	Wand
☲	Rich Salmon	Gold Amber	Lamen (rose cross)
☳	Bright Scarlet	Red flecked Black	Sword
☴	Red Russet	Yellow-Brown flecked White	Book of Names and Spells (Apron)
☵	Very Dark Purple	Citrine flecked Azure	Perfumes (sandals)
☶	Bright Yellow-Green	Olive flecked Gold	Girdle
☷	Four elemental colors flecked Gold	Black rayed Yellow	Magical Circle, triangle (Pantacle)

The Forty Trigram Tables of the West (cont'd.)

Table 67. Magickal Formulae—Eight Thelemic magickal formulae for the eight trigrams, revised from *777*, based on table 42.

Table 68. Magickal Powers—Eight Western magickal abilities of the magus based on the general Chinese meanings of the trigrams.

Table 69. Egyptian Gods—Eight select Egyptian Gods for the trigrams, and their variants, based largely on *777*, on the pattern of table 42.

Trigram	67. Magickal Formulae	68. MagickalPowers	69. EgyptianGods
	TO MEGA THERION	To Will	Asar (Hadit)
	IHVH	The Power of the Sex force	Amoun (Isis)
	IAO	To Know	Ra (Hrumachis)
	ALHIM	To Dare	Horus (Nephthys)
	ABRAHA-DABRA	The Power of Words	Thoth (Anubis)
	ALIM	The Power of the Elemental (demonic) Plane	Shu (Typhon)
	AGAPE	To Be Silent	Hathoor
	BABALON	The Power of Invisibility	Osiris (Nu)

The Forty Trigram Tables of the West (cont'd.)

Table 70. Greek Gods—Eight select Greek Gods for the trigrams from *777*, on the pattern of table 42.

Table 71. Archangels—The archangelic choirs of the World of Assiah, found in *777*, on the pattern of table 42. The archangelic network for the Enochian magickal workings.

Table 72. Human Body—The Western equivalents to the human body for the trigrams, from *777*, on the pattern of table 42.

Trigram	70. Greek Gods	71. Archangels	72. Human Body
	Iacchus	TzPQIAL (צפקיאל) (Tzophqiel)	Organ of Intelligence
	Poseidon	TzDQIAL (צדקיאל) (Tzadqiel)	Digestive System
	Apollo	RPAL (רפאל) (Raphael)	Circulatory System
	Ares	KMAL (כמאל) (Kamael)	Muscular System
	Hermes	MIKAL (מיכאל) (Michael)	Cerebral and Nervous System
	Hecate	GBRIAL (גבריאל) (Gabriel)	Lymphatic System
	Aphrodite	HANIAL (האניאל) (Haniel)	Genital System
	Persephone	SNDLPVN (סנדלפון) (Sandalphon)	Excretory System

The Forty Trigram Tables of the West (cont'd.)

Table 73. Precious Stones—Eight magickal gems for the eight trigrams, from *777*, on the pattern of table 42.

Table 74. Animals—Eight animals (real and imaginary) symbolizing the eight trigrams, from *777*, on the pattern of table 42.

Table 75. Drugs—The magickal herbal correspondences for the eight trigrams, revised from *777*, and based both on elemental and planetary attributes.

Trigram	73. Precious Stones	74. Animals	75. Drugs
	Pearl	Crowned Sphinx with Sword	Jimson Weed (Stramonium)
	Amethyst	Unicorn	Opium
	Topaz	Phoenix	Coffee
	Ruby	Basilisk	Tobacco (Cocaine)
	Opal	Jackal	Peyote (Mescaline)
	Quartz	Elephant	Ginseng (Aphrodisiacs)
	Emerald	Lynx	Cannabis Indica
	Rock Crystal	Crocodile	Alcohol

The Forty Trigram Tables of the West (cont'd.)

Table 76. Tarot (Elemental)—Crowley's Tarot card elemental correspondences for the eight trigrams, based on table 41.

Table 77. Tarot (Planetary)—Crowley's Tarot card planetary correspondences for the eight trigrams based on table 42.

Table 78. Enochian (Dee)—Eight Enochian letters based on Dee's original Qabalistic order for Enochian, ordered by Crowley's elemental attributes of the trigrams found in table 41.

Trigram	76. Tarot (Elemental)	77. Tarot (Planetary)	78. Enochian (Dee)
	XVI—The Tower	XXI—The World	P (Ω) Mals
	XII—The Hanged Man	X—The Wheel of Fortune	M (Ɛ) Tal
	XIX—The Sun	XIX—The Sun	S (⌐l) Fam
	XX—Judgement	XVI—The Tower	T (/) Gisa
	0—The Fool	I—The Magician	A (ϟ) Un
	II—The High Priestess	II—The High Priestess	G (ḅ) Ged
	XXI—The World (or The four Aces)	III—The Empress	U (ᕁ) Vau
	X—The Wheel of Fortune	The four Aces	K (l3) Veh

The Forty Trigram Tables of the West (cont'd.)

Table 79. Enochian (Golden Dawn)—Eight pairs of Enochian letters based on the Golden Dawn's geomantic attributes for Enochian, ordered by table 45.

Table 80. Demons—The demonic order of the Hebrew Qliphoth, based on the inverted Tree of Life.

Trigram	79. Enochian (Golden Dawn)	80. Demons
☰	U (ā) Vau and M (Ɛ) Tal	SAThARIAL (סאתאריאל) (The Obscure One)
☱	I (Ղ) Gon and R (Ɛ) Don	GOShKLH (געשכלה) (The Smiter)
☲	G (Ն) Ged and Z (P) Ceph	ThGRIRVN (תגרירון) (The Imprisoner)
☳	B (V) Pe and N (Ɔ) Drun	GVLChB (גולחב) (The Burning One)
☴	E (ᒣ) Graph and S (ᒣ) Fam	SMAL (סמאל) (The Poisoner)
☵	P (Ո) Mals and L (C) Ur	GMLIAL (גמליאל) (The Obscene One)
☶	A (ꭓ) Un and O (Ļ) Med	ORB ZRQ (ערב זרק) (The Black Raven of Death)
☷	T (/) Gisa and F (ⵋ) Orth	LILITh (לילית) (The White Owl of Night)

THE SIX YAO AND TWO TRIGRAMS.

The eight trigrams of Fu-Hsi ultimately combined into the 64 hexagrams of King Wen to form the *I Ching* (around 1150 BCE).

These 64 hexagrams are made up of two component elements: six yao and two trigrams.

Six Yao

The six yao (lines) which make up the 64 hexagrams each possess a complex set of attributes, adding to the oracular and symbolic imagery of the *I Ching*. These six yao are viewed from the bottom to the top of each hexagram, the bottom line being the first and the top line being the last (and sixth). The top line is the Sky and Foundation; the top line is the Sky and Roof.

The following table details the intricate symbolism for each of the six yao of the 64 hexagrams.

Six Yao (Lines) of the Hexagram

Yao	Yin and Yang Good	Bad	Cheng Wei	Three Kingdoms	Three Pairs of Kingdoms	Element	Space and Time	Humanity
Sixth	Yin	Yang	Dark	Heaven	Upper Heaven	Water	Future	Sage (Hermit)
Fifth	Yang	Yin	Light	Heaven	Upper Man	Metal	Present	King (Ruler)
Fourth	Yin	Yang	Dark	Man	Upper Earth	Earth	Past	Minister
Third	Yang	Yin	Light	Man	Lower Heaven	Earth	Height	Official
Second	Yin	Yang	Dark	Earth	Lower Man	Fire	Width	Scholar
First	Yang	Yin	Light	Earth	Lower Earth	Wood	Depth	Worker (all people)

Six Yao (Lines) of the Hexagram (cont'd.)

Yao	Body	Head	Human Qualities		Time	Oracular Meanings Action	Divination
Sixth	Head and Neck	Forehead	Wisdom (Insight)	Future	Future	Withdraw and Be on Guard	Outcome (Success)
Fifth	Shoulders, Arms, Chest	Eyes	Authority (Will)	Present	Future	Act with Strength	Success (Achievements)
Fourth	Abdomen (Stomach)	Ears	Society (Communication)	Past	Present	Move with Caution	Fortune (Fears)
Third	Waist, Genitals, Thighs	Nose	Individuality	Future	Present	Withdraw and Be on Guard	Conflict (Misfortune)
Second	Legs and Calves	Cheeks	Desires (Aspirations)	Present	Past	Act with Strength	Goal (Praise)
First	Feet and Ankles	Jaws	Instincts (Intuitions)	Past	Past	Move with Caution	Beginning (Dangers)

Two Trigrams

The two trigrams which pair up to form each of the 64 hexagrams can be rearranged in four basic ways which further defines the symbolic layout of each hexagram: Nuclear, Reversed, Overturned, and Changing Line.

The first three yao of each hexagram form the lower or inner trigram while the last three yao form the upper or outer trigram.

"Above" and "below" are the traditional Western designations for these two trigrams, but the Western connotation of these spatial directions reverses the Chinese intent. Therefore, "inner" and "outer" trigrams have been chosen for the trigram commentary on the 64 hexagrams. The meanings for the inner trigrams should always be read first, while the meanings for the outer trigrams should be qualified in light of the lower or inner trigrams:

Yao 4, 5, 6—Outer—Above—Upper—Second—Effect

Yao 1, 2, 3—Inner—Below—Lower—First—Cause

The four basic permutations for the trigram pairs are as follows.

1. **Nuclear Trigrams:** In their interaction, the four inner yao of each hexagram (yao 2, 3, 4, 5) form a nuclear hexagram. Yao 2, 3, and 4 form the inner trigram of the nuclear hexagram, while yao 3, 4, and 5 form the outer trigram.

Original Hexagram		Nuclear Hexagram	
Yao 6 ⎫		Yao 5 ⎫	
Yao 5 ⎬ Outer Trigram		Yao 4 ⎬ Outer Trigram	
Yao 4 ⎭		Yao 3 ⎭	
Yao 3 ⎫		Yao 4 ⎫	
Yao 2 ⎬ Inner Trigram		Yao 3 ⎬ Inner Trigram	
Yao 1 ⎭		Yao 2 ⎭	

2. **Reversed Trigrams:** The inner trigram becomes the outer trigram and the outer trigram becomes the inner trigram. Yao 4, 5, and 6 form the reversed inner trigram, while yao 1, 2, and 3 form the reversed outer trigram.

Original Hexagram		Reversed Hexagram	
Yao 6 ⎫		Yao 3 ⎫	
Yao 5 ⎬ Outer Trigram		Yao 2 ⎬ Outer Trigram	
Yao 4 ⎭		Yao 1 ⎭	
Yao 3 ⎫		Yao 6 ⎫	
Yao 2 ⎬ Inner Trigram		Yao 5 ⎬ Inner Trigram	
Yao 1 ⎭		Yao 4 ⎭	

3. **Overturned Trigrams:** The first yao of the hexagram becomes the sixth yao of the overturned hexagram, while the sixth yao of the original becomes the first of the overturned. Thus the hexagram is turned upside down.

Original Hexagram   **Overturned Hexagram**

Yao 6 ⎤   Yao 1 ⎤
Yao 5 ⎬ Outer Trigram   Yao 2 ⎬ Outer Trigram
Yao 4 ⎦   Yao 3 ⎦

Yao 3 ⎤   Yao 4 ⎤
Yao 2 ⎬ Inner Trigram   Yao 5 ⎬ Inner Trigram
Yao 1 ⎦   Yao 6 ⎦

4. **Changing Line:** This is the traditional oracular generation of a new hexagram. A Yin yao in the original hexagram becomes a Yang yao in the new Changing Line hexagram, and a Yang yao becomes a Yin yao.

Original Hexagram		**Changing Line Hexagram**
6 Yao if Yang	becomes	Yin in new 6 Yao
5 Yao if Yang	becomes	Yin in new 5 Yao
4 Yao if Yang	becomes	Yin in new 4 Yao
3 Yao if Yang	becomes	Yin in new 3 Yao
2 Yao if Yang	becomes	Yin in new 2 Yao
1 Yao if Yang	becomes	Yin in new 1 Yao
6 Yao if Yin	becomes	Yang in new 6 Yao
5 Yao if Yin	becomes	Yang in new 5 Yao
4 Yao if Yin	becomes	Yang in new 4 Yao
3 Yao if Yin	becomes	Yang in new 3 Yao
2 Yao if Yin	becomes	Yang in new 2 Yao
1 Yao if Yin	becomes	Yang in new 1 Yao

FORMAT OF THE *I CHING*

The following tables describing the 64 hexagrams of the *I Ching* reflect all four permutations for each of the 64 hexagrams. The tables are formated as follows:

- Each hexagram is shown with proper name, number and translation.

- The divinatory text is split into Image and Oracle, reducing the text of each hexagram to the essential description of the hexagram as a symbol in nature, and the oracular advice derived from such symbolic imagery.

- The actual commentary for each line of each hexagram, developed by King Wen's son the Duke of Chou, has been excluded from the *I Ching* divinatory text. However it is included later in this key to serve as a cipher for Taoist calligraphic stroke count.

- The four basic methods of permutation (Nuclear, Reversed, Overturned, Changing Line) are applied to each hexagram and the four basic hexagrams generated are named and numbered.

- The trigrams which compose each hexagram are named and commented upon. Each hexagram is reviewed according to both Eastern and Western trigram tables, as already delineated in the text:

    —The names and meanings of the trigrams are derived from Trigram Tables 0, 1, and 31.

    —The directions for the trigrams are taken from Trigram Table 12 (Heaven) and Table 15 (Earth).

    — The Eastern element is from Trigram Table 2, the Eastern planet is from Trigram Tables 3 and 4, the Eastern color is from Trigram Table 25, and the Eastern number is from Trigram Table 19 (Pre-Heaven) and Table 20 (Later Heaven), corresponding to the directional pair listed above.

    —The Western element is from Trigram Table 41, the Western planet is from Trigram Table 42, the Western color is from Trigram Table 63 (Briah), and the Western number is from Trigram Table 59, corresponding to the Tree of Life rather than a direction in space.

THE TEXT OF THE *I CHING*

1. **Ch'ien** (Qian)—The Creative
(Heaven, Origin, Strength)

Divination

Image: Mounting six dragons as a stairway to heaven (two in deep sea, two on land, two in the sky); The Secret King, who towers above five lower rulers; two heavens, the heaven of the sky, and of the Gods

Oracle: Continual persistence in seeking only one's true will, excluding all other activity, results in success; rapid advance through six correct decisions at the right moment; inner strength; unrestricted energy; primal power; the beginning of any undertaking

Nuclear: 1. Ch'ien (Creative)

Reversed: 1. Ch'ien (Creative)

Overturned: 1. Ch'ien (Creative)

Changing Line: 2. K'un (Receptive)

Trigram	Name	Meaning	Direction Heaven	Earth
Outer	Ch'ien (Creative)	Act with strength (strong rulership)	S	NW
Inner	Ch'ien (Creative)	Act with strength (strong rulership)	S	NW

Eastern

Trigram	Element	Planet	Color	Number
Outer	Sky	Venus (Metal Star)	White	9 (6)
Inner	Sky	Venus (Metal Star)	White	9 (6)

Western

Trigram	Element	Planet	Color	Sephirah
Outer	Lingam	Saturn (Daath)	Gray-White	11 (or 33)
Inner	Lingam	Saturn (Daath)	Gray-White	11 (or 33)

2. **K'un** (Kun)—The Receptive
Earth, Quiet Submission, Great Success)

Divination

Image: A mare as yin, calm, receptive; 11 mouths to feed and the ancient ones who support all; two earths, the earth of the world and the middle kingdom

Oracle: To assent, yield, comply with, withdraw, retreat, become inactive; follow rather than lead to find guidance; a vision, goal, objective, divine inspiration, genius; quiet, efficient, patient work reaches the goal

Nuclear: 2. K'un (Receptive)

Reversed: 2. K'un (Receptive)

Overturned: 2. K'un (Receptive)

Changing Line: 1. Ch'ien (Creative)

| | | | Direction | |
Trigram	Name	Meaning	Heaven	Earth
Outer	K'un (Receptive)	To yield (accept)	N	SW
Inner	K'un (Receptive)	To yield (accept)	N	SW

Eastern

Trigram	Element	Planet	Color	Number
Outer	Earth	Saturn (Earth Star)	Black	1 (2)
Inner	Earth	Saturn (Earth Star)	Black	1 (2)

Western

Trigram	Element	Planet	Color	Sephirah
Outer	Yoni	Earth (Malkuth)	Russet, Olive, Citrine, Black	10
Inner	Yoni	Earth (Malkuth)	Russet, Olive, Citrine, Black	10

3. **Chun** (Tun)—Difficulty at the Beginning
(Danger, gather support to advance)

Divination

Image: Thunder and rain fill the air; heavenly dragon descends to the abyss; the child between the woman above and the man below

Oracle: Nothing should be done alone, rather regroup one's army, gather friends, helpers and supporters which one can guide; keep going despite all difficulties

Nuclear: 23. Po (Splitting Apart)

Reversed: 40. Hsieh (Deliverance)

Overturned: 4. Meng (Youthful Folly)

Changing Line: 50. Ting (The Cauldron)

Trigram	Name	Meaning	Direction Heaven	Earth
Outer	K'an (Abysmal)	Stand over an abyss	W	N
Inner	Chen (Arousing)	Rush forward	NE	E

Eastern

Trigram	Element	Planet	Color	Number
Outer	Water (Moon, Clouds)	Mercury (Water Star)	Crimson	7 (1)
Inner	Thunder	Jupiter (Wood Star)	Red-Orange	8 (3)

Western

Trigram	Element	Planet	Color	Sephirah
Outer	Moon	Moon (Yesod)	Violet	9
Inner	Fire	Mars (Geburah)	Scarlet-Red	5

4. **Meng** (Meng)—Youthful Folly
(Rebellious Youth, Young [Green] Shoot)

Divination

Image: An inexperienced youth stopping at the edge of the abyss (pit) (Chinese symbol of the fool, which parallels the Tarot key entitled "The Fool"); spring at the foot of a mountain; fog obscuring the mountain peak

Oracle: To be blind to the pitfalls of the world; knowledge can only be internalized gradually; consult the oracle only once (trust the first casting)

Nuclear: 24. Fu (Return)

Reversed: 39. Chien (Obstruction)

Overturned: 3. Chun (Difficulty at the Beginning)

Changing Line: 49. Ko (Revolution)

Trigram	Name	Meaning	Direction Heaven	Earth
Outer	Ken (Keeping Still)	Restrain oneself	NW	NE
Inner	K'an (Abysmal)	Stand over an abyss	W	N

Eastern

Trigram	Element	Planet	Color	Number
Outer	Mountain	Saturn (Earth Star)	Bright Yellow	6 (8)
Inner	Clouds, Water	Mercury (Water Star)	Crimson	7 (1)

Western

Trigram	Element	Planet	Color	Sephirah
Outer	Earth	Venus (Netzach)	Emerald	7
Inner	Moon	Moon (Yesod)	Violet	9

5. **Hsu** (Wu)—Waiting
(Nourishment, Sincerity, Patience)

Divination

Image: The clouds of heaven which will nourish as rain in its own time; fog rising from earth to heaven; a man holding on to the tail of a flying dragon

Oracle: Strength in the face of danger must wait patiently for the right moment to attack; to endure to the end; to boldly step across the abyss (great river) at the right moment

Nuclear: 38. K'uei (Opposition)

Reversed: 6. Sung (Conflict)

Overturned: 6. Sung (Conflict)

Changing Line: 35. Chin (Progress)

Trigram	Name	Meaning	Direction Heaven	Earth
Outer	K'an (Abysmal)	Stand over an abyss	W	N
Inner	Ch'ien (Creative)	Strong action	S	NW

Eastern

Trigram	Element	Planet	Color	Number
Outer	Clouds	Mercury (Water Star)	Crimson	7 (1)
Inner	Sky	Venus (Metal Star)	White	9 (6)

Western

Trigram	Element	Planet	Color	Sephirah
Outer	Moon	Moon (Yesod)	Violet	9
Inner	Lingam	Saturn (Daath)	Gray-White	11 (or 33)

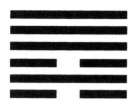

6. **Sung** (Song)—Conflict
(Strife, Opposition, Contention)

Divination

Image: Heaven above separates from the abysmal deep causing contention, argument, battle, quarrel, lawsuit; an eagle swooping from the sky to catch its prey; an omen in the clouds of the sky; a tiger sleeping at the foot of a mountain

Oracle: Two opposing parties and a mediator, the need for an impartial judge; dangerous enterprises should not begin in times of strife

Nuclear: 37. Chia Jen (The Clan)

Reversed: 5. Hsu (Waiting)

Overturned: 5. Hsu (Waiting)

Changing Line: 36. Ming I (Darkening of the Light)

Trigram	Name	Meaning	Direction Heaven	Earth
Outer	Ch'ien (Creative)	Act with strength	S	NW
Inner	K'an (Abysmal)	Stand over an abyss	W	N

Eastern

Trigram	Element	Planet	Color	Number
Outer	Sky	Venus (Metal Star)	White	9 (6)
Inner	Clouds	Mercury (Water Star)	Crimson	7 (1)

Western

Trigram	Element	Planet	Color	Sephirah
Outer	Lingam	Saturn (Daath)	Gray-White	11 (or 33)
Inner	Moon	Moon (Yesod)	Violet	9

7. **Shih** (Shi)—The Army
(Experience of Age, Multitude, the People)

Divination

Image: General leading five men, invisible power stored within; horse soaring to heaven; stored water in the middle of the earth as in a well

Oracle: Discipline needed to slowly advance and meet the enemy; Rebellion inside, obedience outside; hidden revolution within the masses

Nuclear: 24. Fu (Return)

Reversed: 8. Pi (Holding Together)

Overturned: 8. Pi (Holding Together)

Changing Line: 13. Tung Jen (Fellowship with Men)

			Direction	
Trigram	Name	Meaning	Heaven	Earth
Outer	K'un (Receptive)	Yield (Obey)	N	SW
Inner	K'an (Abysmal)	Stand over an abyss	W	N

Eastern

Trigram	Element	Planet	Color	Number
Outer	Earth	Saturn (Earth Star)	Black	1 (2)
Inner	Clouds (Water)	Mercury (Water Star)	Crimson	7 (1)

Western

Trigram	Element	Planet	Color	Sephirah
Outer	Yoni	Earth (Malkuth)	Russet, Olive, Citrine, Black	10
Inner	Moon	Moon (Yesod)	Violet	9

8. **Pi** (Bi)—Holding Together
(Union, Loyalty, Help, Alliance)

Divination

Image: The rivers of the earth flow as one into the ocean; The land is flooded with water; A Full Moon is above the earth; Ursa Major and Minor circling the pole star (emperor)

Oracle: Cooperation as one is required against an enemy, do not ally yourself with strangers; all yield to the emperor; cast the oracle again for reassurance; to arrive late is unlucky

Nuclear: 23. Po (Splitting Apart)

Reversed: 7. Shih (The Army)

Overturned: 7. Shih (The Army)

Changing Line: 14. Ta Yu (Possesion in Great Measure)

Trigram	Name	Meaning	Direction Heaven	Earth
Outer	K'an (Abysmal)	Stand over an abyss	W	N
Inner	K'un (Receptive)	Yield (Obey)	N	SW

Eastern

Trigram	Element	Planet	Color	Number
Outer	Clouds (Water)	Mercury (Water Star)	Crimson	7 (1)
Inner	Earth	Saturn (Earth Star)	Black	1 (2)

Western

Trigram	Element	Planet	Color	Sephirah
Outer	Moon	Moon (Yesod)	Violet	9
Inner	Yoni	Earth (Malkuth)	Russet, Olive, Citrine, Black	10

9. **Hsiao Ch'u** (Xiaoxu)—The Taming Power of the Small
(Small Restraint)

Divination

Image: Rain clouds dispersing before a storm; a mountain climber conquering a mountain; a great sword of power concealed in its scabbard; a weak minister (fourth yao) controlling five strong warriors

Oracle: Gentleness keeping strength in check; the subordinate kneeling to the superior

Nuclear: 38. K'uei (Opposition)

Reversed: 44. Kou (Coming to Meet)

Overturned: 10. Lu (Treading)

Changing Line: 16. Yu (Enthusiasm)

Trigram	Name	Meaning	Direction Heaven	Earth
Outer	Sun (Gentle)	Kneel down to	SW	SE
Inner	Ch'ien (Strong)	Act with strength	S	NW

Eastern

Trigram	Element	Planet	Color	Number
Outer	Wood (Wind)	Jupiter (Wood Star)	Green	2 (4)
Inner	Sky	Venus (Metal Star)	White	9 (6)

Western

Trigram	Element	Planet	Color	Sephirah
Outer	Air	Mercury (Hod)	Orange	8
Inner	Lingam	Saturn (Daath)	Gray-White	11 (or 33)

10. **Lu** (Lu)—Treading
(Proper conduct)

Divination

Image: Sky above water below; treading upon the tail of a tiger; an umbrella; the vagina (Yin in the third yao) of a nude woman (five Yang yao)

Oracle: Treading one's right path in life; the strong treading on the weak; facing one's difficulties with success; to advance unharmed against a powerful opponent

Nuclear: 37. Chia Jen (The Family)

Reversed: 43. Kuai (Break Through)

Overturned: 9. Hsiao Ch'u (The Taming Power of the Small)

Changing Line: 15. Ch'ien (Modesty)

			Direction	
Trigram	**Name**	**Meaning**	**Heaven**	**Earth**
Outer	Ch'ien (Strong)	Act with strength	S	NW
Inner	Tui (Joyful)	Break free	SE	W

Eastern

Trigram	**Element**	**Planet**	**Color**	**Number**
Outer	Sky	Venus (Metal Star)	White	9 (6)
Inner	Lake (Sea)	Venus (Metal Star)	Deep Blue	4 (7)

Western

Trigram	**Element**	**Planet**	**Color**	**Sephirah**
Outer	Lingam	Saturn (Daath)	Gray-White	11 (or 33)
Inner	Water	Jupiter (Chesed)	Blue	4

11. **T'ai** (Tai)—Peace
(Harmony, Union, Blending)

Divination

Image: Yin is above moving downward; Yang is below moving upward, blending in harmony; Heaven seems to be on Earth, resulting in Spring; sexual posture: woman above, man below

Oracle: The small departs, the great approaches; the superior favors the inferior; light conquers dark; outside is dark, inside is light; small goes forward, great draw back; that which is above is that which is below

Nuclear: 54. Kuei Mei (Marrying Maiden)

Reversed: 12. Pi (Standstill)

Overturned: 12. Pi (Standstill)

Changing Line: 12. Pi (Standstill)

Trigram	Name	Meaning	Direction Heaven	Earth
Outer	K'un (Receptive)	Yield	N	SW
Inner	Ch'ien (Creative)	Act with strength	S	NW

Eastern

Trigram	Element	Planet	Color	Number
Outer	Earth	Saturn (Earth Star)	Black	1 (2)
Inner	Sky	Venus (Metal Star)	White	9 (6)

Western

Trigram	Element	Planet	Color	Sephirah
Outer	Yoni	Earth (Malkuth)	Russet, Olive, Citrine, Black	10
Inner	Lingam	Saturn (Daath)	Gray-White	11 (or 33)

12. **P'i** (Bi)—Standstill
(Opposition, Separation, Conflict)

Divination

Image: Yang is above moving downward, yin is below moving upward blocked in opposition; Heaven recedes into the sky, Earth descends to the deep, resulting in Autumn; sexual posture: man above, woman below

Oracle: The small approaches; the inferior rise, the superior fall; dark conquers light; inside is dark, outside is light; great goes forward, small draws back; that which is above has no relation to that which is below

Nuclear: 53. Chien (Development)

Reversed: 11. T'ai (Peace)

Overturned: 11. T'ai (Peace)

Changing Line: 11. T'ai (Peace)

Trigram	Name	Meaning	Direction Heaven	Earth
Outer	Ch'ien (Creative)	Act with strength	S	NW
Inner	K'un (Receptive)	Yield	N	SW

Eastern

Trigram	Element	Planet	Color	Number
Outer	Sky	Venus (Metal Star)	White	9 (6)
Inner	Earth	Saturn (Earth Star)	Black	1 (2)

Western

Trigram	Element	Planet	Color	Sephirah
Outer	Lingam	Saturn (Daath)	Gray-White	11 (or 33)
Inner	Yoni	Earth (Malkuth)	Russet, Olive, Citrine, Black	10

13. **T'ung Jen** (Tong Ren)—Fellowship with Men

Divination

Image: Unity of clan (five Yang lines) guided by an enlightened leader (Yin in second yao) to meet an opponent; flame rising to heaven; an arrow shot at a mountain peak

Oracle: Clarity within, strength without; union with others of like mind (lodge, secret society, clan, army)

Nuclear: 44. Kou (Coming to Meet)

Reversed: 14. Ta Yu (Possession in Great Measure)

Overturned: 14. Ta Yu (Possession in Great Measure)

Changing Line: 7. Shih (The Army)

Trigram	Name	Meaning	Direction Heaven	Earth
Outer	Ch'ien (Creative)	Act with strength	S	NW
Inner	Li (Clinging)	Shine within	E	S

Eastern

Trigram	Element	Planet	Color	Number
Outer	Sky	Venus (Metal Star)	White	9 (6)
Inner	Fire (Sun)	Mars (Fire Star)	Yellow-Orange	3 (9)

Western

Trigram	Element	Planet	Color	Sephirah
Outer	Lingam	Saturn (Daath)	Gray-White	11 (or 33)
Inner	Sun	Sun (Tiphereth)	Golden Yellow	6

14. **Ta Yu** (Da You) Possession in Great Measure

Divination

Image: Supreme wealth and success to a high ranking official (Yin in fifth yao) who possesses unselfish modesty; Sun shining at noon to the South (midheaven)

Oracle: Great wealth and resources enabling great accomplishments; the community as a whole striving for the common good; strength within, clarity without

Nuclear: 43. Kuai (Break Through)

Reversed: 13. T'ung Jen (Fellowship with Men)

Overturned: 13. T'ung Jen (Fellowship with Men

Changing Line: 8. Pi (Holding Together)

Trigram	Name	Meaning	Direction Heaven	Earth
Outer	Li (Clinging)	Shine within	E	S
Inner	Ch'ien (Creative)	Act with strength	S	NW

Eastern

Trigram	Element	Planet	Color	Number
Outer	Fire (Sun)	Mars (Fire Star)	Yellow-Orange	3 (9)
Inner	Sky	Venus (Metal Star)	White	9 (6)

Western

Trigram	Element	Planet	Color	Sephirah
Outer	Sun	Sun (Tiphereth)	Golden Yellow	6
Inner	Lingam	Saturn (Daath)	Gray-White	11 (or 33)

15. **Ch'ien** (Qian)—Modesty (Humility, Patience)

Divination

Image: The inferor (third yao) rises through modesty (silent behavior); treasure hidden in the depths of a mountain; mountains leveled and valleys filled; the penis (Yang in third yao) of a nude man (five Yin lines) (compare with Hexagram 10)

Oracle: To endure work to completion without boasting; superior and inferior are made equal (leveled); the need to be thorough; aiming at more than can be accomplished

Nuclear: 40. Hsieh (Deliverance)

Reversed: 23. Po (Splitting Apart)

Overturned: 16. Yu (Enthusiasm)

Changing Line: 10. Lu (Treading)

| | | | Direction | |
| | | | Heaven | Earth |
Trigram	Name	Meaning		
Outer	K'un (Receptive)	Yield	N	SW
Inner	Ken (Keeping Still)	Restrain oneself	NW	NE

Eastern

Trigram	Element	Planet	Color	Number
Outer	Earth	Saturn (Earth Star)	Black	1 (2)
Inner	Mountain	Saturn (Earth Star)	Bright Yellow	6 (8)

Western

Trigram	Element	Planet	Color	Sephirah
Outer	Yoni	Earth (Malkuth)	Russet, Olive, Citrine, Black	10
Inner	Earth	Venus (Netzach)	Emerald	7

16. **Yu** (Yu)—Enthusiasm
(Devotion, Joy)

Divination

Image: A leading official (Yang in fourth yao) met with enthusiasm by his inferiors (five Yin lines); twin mountain ranges; thunder coming out of the earth; moving along the line of least resistance (fourth yao)

Oracle: To appoint officers and set armies in motion; new beginning; music as joy to the heart

Nuclear: 39. Chien (Obstruction)

Reversed: 24. Fu (Return)

Overturned: 15. Ch'ien (Modesty)

Changing Line: 9. Hsiao Ch'u (Taming Power of the Small)

Trigram	Name	Meaning	Direction Heaven	Earth
Outer	Chen (Arousing)	Rush forward	NE	E
Inner	K'un (Receptive)	Yield	N	SW

Eastern

Trigram	Element	Planet	Color	Number
Outer	Thunder	Jupiter (Wood Star)	Red-Orange	8 (3)
Inner	Earth	Saturn (Earth Star)	Black	1 (2)

Western

Trigram	Element	Planet	Color	Sephirah
Outer	Fire	Mars (Geburah)	Scarlet-Red	5
Inner	Yoni	Earth (Malkuth)	Russet, Olive, Citrine, Black	10

17. **Sui** (Sui)—Following
(The Quest, Search)

Divination

Image: An older man arousing a younger woman and inducing her to follow him through pleasure; thunder in the center of the lake; ocean calm on the surface but thunderous within

Oracle: To obtain one's quest; to do what is blameless with persistence, resulting in success; to adopt any situation to one's favor; in order to rule, one must first serve

Nuclear: 53. Chien (Development)

Reversed: 54. Kuei Mei (Marrying Maiden)

Overturned: 18. Ku (Work on What has Been Spoiled)

Changing Line: 18. Ku (Work on What has Been Spoiled)

Trigram	Name	Meaning	Direction Heaven	Earth
Outer	Tui (Joyful)	Break free	SE	W
Inner	Chen (Arousing)	Rush forward	NE	E

Eastern

Trigram	Element	Planet	Color	Number
Outer	Lake	Venus (Metal Star)	Deep Blue	4 (7)
Inner	Thunder	Jupiter (Wood Star)	Red-Orange	8 (3)

Western

Trigram	Element	Planet	Color	Sephirah
Outer	Water	Jupiter (Chesed)	Blue	4
Inner	Fire	Mars (Geburah)	Scarlet-Red	5

18. **Ku** (Gu)—Work on What has Been Spoiled
(Arrest of Decay, Renovation)

Divination

Image: A wing blowing on a mountain and eroding all vegetation

Oracle: That which is spoiled is made good through effort; do not recoil from danger or hard work; a strong leader removes stagnation by arousing public opinion and speaking to the hearts of men; three days planning and review are required before and after the completion of a venture; indifference meets rigid inertia, resulting in stagnation

Nuclear: 54. Kuei Mei (Marrying Maiden)

Reversed: 53. Chien (Development)

Overturned: 17. Sui (Following)

Changing Line: 17. Sui (Following)

Trigram	Name	Meaning	Direction Heaven	Earth
Outer	Ken (Keeping Still)	Restrain oneself	NW	NE
Inner	Sun (Gentle)	Kneel down to	SW	SE

Eastern

Trigram	Element	Planet	Color	Number
Outer	Mountain	Saturn (Earth Star)	Bright Yellow	6 (8)
Inner	Wind	Jupiter (Wood Star)	Green	2 (4)

Western

Trigram	Element	Planet	Color	Sephirah
Outer	Earth	Venus (Netzach)	Emerald	7
Inner	Air	Mercury (Hod)	Orange	8

19. **Lin** (Lin) Approach
(Approach of Authority)

Divination
   Image: Viewing a valley from the height of a mountain; the shoreline borders above a lake; light illuminating the dark recesses; the approach of a master to his waiting disciples
   Oracle: To approach, draw near to the goal; expend extra energy when the time is ripe; the sage who guides all of humanity; an inferior rises from below to lead by charismatic influence

Nuclear: 24. Fu (Return)

Reversed: 45. Ts'ui (Gathering Together)

Overturned: 20. Kuan (Contemplation)

Changing Line: 33. Tun (Retreat)

			Direction	
Trigram	**Name**	**Meaning**	**Heaven**	**Earth**
Outer	K'un (Receptive)	Yield	N	SW
Inner	Tui (Joyful)	Break free	SE	W

Eastern

Trigram	**Element**	**Planet**	**Color**	**Number**
Outer	Earth	Saturn (Earth Star)	Black	1 (2)
Inner	Lake	Venus (Metal Star)	Deep Blue	4 (7)

Western

Trigram	**Element**	**Planet**	**Color**	**Sephirah**
Outer	Yoni	Earth (Malkuth)	Russet, Olive, Citrine, Black	10
Inner	Water	Jupiter (Chesed)	Blue	4

20. **Kuan** (Guan)—Contemplation
(View)

Divination

Image: A ruler contemplating the laws of heaven; a watchtower on a mountain; the wind that blows over the earth bending the grass by its power; the wind moving over the eight directions of earth (King Wen's directions)

Oracle: To continue to observe rather than to act; to acquire the right frame of mind before any new venture; tapping the spiritual power hidden within

Nuclear: 23. Po (Splitting Apart)

Reversed: 46. Sheng (Pushing Upward)

Overturned: 19. Lin (Approach)

Changing Line: 34. Ta Chuang (The Power of the Great)

Trigram	Name	Meaning	Direction Heaven	Earth
Outer	Sun (Gentle)	Kneel down to	SW	SE
Inner	K'un (Receptive)	To yield (accept)	N	SW

Eastern

Trigram	Element	Planet	Color	Number
Outer	Wood (Wind)	Jupiter (Wood Star)	Green	3 (4)
Inner	Earth	Saturn (Earth Star)	Black	1 (2)

Western

Trigram	Element	Planet	Color	Sephirah
Outer	Air	Mercury (Hod)	Orange	8
Inner	Yoni	Earth (Malkuth)	Russet, Olive, Citrine, Black	10

21. **Shih Ho** (He Shi)—Biting Through

Divination

Image: Open mouth biting through obstruction (Yang in fourth yao); thunder and lightning removing obstacles in nature; clarity of lightning (clear judgment) and terror of thunder (just penalty); phoenix rising out of the flames unscathed

Oracle: Deliberate obstruction which must be opposed vigorously; corrective punishment as reform; yielding to a higher authority

Nuclear: 39. Chien (Obstruction)

Reversed: 55. Feng (Abundance)

Overturned: 22. Pi (Grace)

Changing Line: 48. Ching (The Well)

			Direction	
Trigram	**Name**	**Meaning**	**Heaven**	**Earth**
Outer	Li (Clinging)	Shine within	E	S
Inner	Chen (Arousing)	Rush forward	NE	E

Eastern

Trigram	**Element**	**Planet**	**Color**	**Number**
Outer	Fire (Sun)	Mars (Fire Star)	Yellow-Orange	3 (9)
Inner	Thunder	Jupiter (Wood Star)	Red-Orange	8 (3)

Western

Trigram	**Element**	**Planet**	**Color**	**Sephirah**
Outer	Sun	Sun (Tiphereth)	Golden-Yellow	6
Inner	Fire	Mars (Geburah)	Scarlet-Red	5

22. **Pi** (Pen)—Grace
(Ornament, Beauty)

Divination

Image: Fire at the foot of a mountain illuminating its heights; clarity within, quiet without

Oracle: Art as pure contemplation of beauty of nature; apprehension of rarefied thoughts which exalt; by beauty of form and grace the inferior can advance; simple and direct judgment in matters of lesser importance

Nuclear: 40. Hsieh (Deliverance)

Reversed: 56. Lu (The Wanderer)

Overturned: 21. Shih Ho (Biting Through)

Changing Line: 47. K'un (Oppression)

Trigram	Name	Meaning	Direction Heaven	Earth
Outer	Ken (Keeping Still)	Restrain oneself	NW	NE
Inner	Li (Clinging)	Shine within	E	S

Eastern

Trigram	Element	Planet	Color	Number
Outer	Mountain	Saturn (Earth Star)	Bright Yellow	6 (8)
Inner	Fire (Sun)	Mars (Fire Star)	Yellow-Orange	3 (9)

Western

Trigram	Element	Planet	Color	Sephirah
Outer	Earth	Venus (Netzach)	Emerald	7
Inner	Sun	Sun (Tiphereth)	Golden-Yellow	6

23. **Po** (Bao)—Splitting Apart
(Peeling, Breaking Apart)

Divination

Image: Yin moves upward to displace Yang in the sixth yao; the shattered roof of a collapsed house; a man falling from the height of a house (tower) that has collapsed; a steep mountain on a narrow base toppling over the earth; the summer solstice heralding the approach of darkness

Oracle: Stay put, for it is not the time for any venture; endure the bad times and remain quiet; the inferior (by undermining gradually) overthrows the superior

Nuclear: 2. K'un (Receptive)

Reversed: 15. Ch'ien (Modesty)

Overturned: 24. Fu (Return)

Changing Line: 43. Kuai (Break Through)

Trigram	Name	Meaning	Direction Heaven	Earth
Outer	Ken (Keeping Still)	Restrain oneself	NW	SE
Inner	K'un (Receptive)	Yield	N	SW

Eastern

Trigram	Element	Planet	Color	Number
Outer	Mountain	Saturn (Earth Star)	Bright Yellow	6 (8)
Inner	Earth	Saturn (Earth Star)	Black	1 (2)

Western

Trigram	Element	Planet	Color	Sephirah
Outer	Earth	Venus (Netzach)	Emerald	7
Inner	Yoni	Earth (Malkuth)	Russet, Olive, Citrine, Black	10

24. **Fu** (Fu)—Return
(The Turning Point)

Divination

Image: The winter solstice heralding that the time of darkness is past; thunder within the earth (gold hidden in the earth); the first Yang will drive out the five Yin; seventh stage as return of the first; six (great darkness) is increased by one to produce seven (the new young light)

Oracle: The discarding of the old and the embracing of the new; rest gives way to movement; return of friends; allowing energy to renew itself by rest; the situation will get better and better

Nuclear: 2. K'un (Receptive)

Reversed: 16. Yu (Enthusiasm)

Overturned: 23. Po (Splitting Apart)

Changing Line: 44. Kou (Coming to Meet)

			Direction	
Trigram	Name	Meaning	Heaven	Earth
Outer	Kun (Receptive)	Yield	N	SW
Inner	Chen (Arousing)	Rush forward	NE	E

Eastern

Trigram	Element	Planet	Color	Number
Outer	Earth	Saturn (Earth Star)	Black	1 (2)
Inner	Thunder	Jupiter (Wood Star)	Red-Orange	8 (3)

Western

Trigram	Element	Planet	Color	Sephirah
Outer	Yoni	Earth (Malkuth)	Russet, Olive, Citrine, Black	10
Inner	Fire	Mars (Geburah)	Scarlet-Red	5

25. **Wu Wang** (Wu Wang)—Innocence
(Unassuaged of Purpose)

Divination

Image: A precious jewel hidden in the center of a stone; thunder in the sky

Oracle: Be as you are and all will be in accord; innocence brings success free from all expectations; by following one's right path, the unexpected can occur; earthly activity in alignment with heavenly activity; if something is impossible (out of accord with one's true nature), do not attempt it

Nuclear: 53. Chien (Development)

Reversed: 34. Ta Chuang (The Power of the Great)

Overturned: 26. Ta Ch'u (The Taming Power of the Great)

Changing Line: 46. Sheng (Pushing Upward)

Trigram	Name	Meaning	Direction Heaven	Earth
Outer	Ch'ien (Creative)	Act with strength	S	NW
Inner	Chen (Arousing)	Rush forward	NE	E

Eastern

Trigram	Element	Planet	Color	Number
Outer	Sky	Venus (Metal Star)	White	9 (6)
Inner	Thunder	Jupiter (Wood Star)	Red-Orange	8 (3)

Western

Trigram	Element	Planet	Color	Sephirah
Outer	Lingam	Saturn (Daath)	Gray-White	11 (or 33)
Inner	Fire	Mars (Geburah)	Scarlet-Red	5

26. **Ta Ch'u** (Da Xu)—The Taming Power of the Great (Great Accumulation)

Divination

Image: The minister and his prince restrain an army; dragon hidden in a mountain; hidden knowledge (treasure) concealed in a mountain

Oracle: The active is tamed by the inactive; hold firmly to creative power when it comes; a strong personality is required to store up creative power; after much discipline a new venture can begin; the words of the past as a great storehouse for the present

Nuclear: 54. Kuei Mei (Marrying Maiden)

Reversed: 33. Tun (Retreat)

Overturned: 25. Wu Wang (Innocence)

Changing Line: 45. Ts'ui (Gathering Together)

Trigram	Name	Meaning	Direction Heaven	Earth
Outer	Ken (Keeping Still)	Restrain oneself	NE	E
Inner	Ch'ien (Creative)	Act with strength	S	NW

Eastern

Trigram	Element	Planet	Color	Number
Outer	Mountain	Saturn (Earth Star)	Bright Yellow	6 (8)
Inner	Sky	Venus (Metal Star)	White	9 (6)

Western

Trigram	Element	Planet	Color	Sephirah
Outer	Earth	Venus (Netzach)	Emerald	7
Inner	Lingam	Saturn (Daath)	Gray-White	11 (or 33)

27. I (Yi)—Corners of the Mouth
(Providing Nourishment)

Divination

Image: Thunder at the foot of the mountain; picture image of an open mouth (Yang at first and sixth yao being the lips)

Oracle: To care for yourself and the deserving people around you; to be concerned with the nourishment of others as much as oneself; nourish the superior to take care of the inferior; through inner tranquility be careful of one's words (movement from within to without) and be temperate in eating and drinking (movement from without to within); your extravagance will be your undoing

Nuclear: 2. K'un (Receptive)

Reversed: 62. Hsiao Kuo (Preponderance of the Small)

Overturned: 27. I (Corners of the Mouth)

Changing Line: 28. Ta Kuo (Preponderance of the Great)

| | | | Direction | |
Trigram	Name	Meaning	Heaven	Earth
Outer	Ken (Keeping Still)	Restrain oneself	NW	NE
Inner	Chen (Arousing)	Rush forward	NE	E

Eastern

Trigram	Element	Planet	Color	Number
Outer	Mountain	Saturn (Earth Star)	Bright Yellow	6 (8)
Inner	Thunder	Jupiter (Wood Star)	Red-Orange	8 (3)

Western

Trigram	Element	Planet	Color	Sephirah
Outer	Earth	Venus (Netzach)	Emerald	7
Inner	Fire	Mars (Geburah)	Scarlet-Red	5

28. **Ta Kuo** (Da Guo)—Preponderance of the Great

Divination
Image: A ridgepole (thick in the middle and thin on the ends) which cannot support the weight of a roof; strong on the inside, weak on the outside; lake rises over treetops

Oracle: Find a way out as quickly as possible and act on it immediately; nothing can be accomplished by force; stand firm even though alone, be joyous even when overwhelmed; to be overburdened, requiring new action; great carefulness

Nuclear: 1. Ch'ien (Creative)

Reversed: 61. Chung Fú (Inner Truth)

Overturned: 28. Ta Kuo (Preponderance of the Great)

Changing Line: 27. I (Corners of the Mouth)

			Direction	
Trigram	Name	Meaning	Heaven	Earth
Outer	Tui (Joyful)	Break free	SE	W
Inner	Sun (Gentle)	Kneel down to	SW	SE

Eastern
Trigram	Element	Planet	Color	Number
Outer	Lake	Venus (Metal Star)	Deep Blue	4 (7)
Inner	Wind (Wood)	Jupiter (Wood Star)	Green	2 (4)

Western
Trigram	Element	Planet	Color	Sephirah
Outer	Water	Jupiter (Chesed)	Blue	4
Inner	Air	Mercury (Hod)	Orange	8

29. **K'an** (Kan)—The Abysmal
(The Pit)

Divination

Image: Water pours down from heaven forming all rivers, lakes, and oceans of the earth; a Yang line is plunged between two Yin lines (water channeled into a ravine); Moon above in sky, moonlight reflected below in water; light enclosed in dark (heart enclosed in body)

Oracle: One must be sincere (have faith) when confronted with difficulties; danger will return; to use a dangerous situation to protect yourself; endurance, consistency, and repetition in work will bring success; endure to the end; to rise out of an abyss by finding the right path

Nuclear: 27. I (Corners of the Mouth)

Reversed: 29. K'an (Abysmal)

Overturned: 29. K'an (Abysmal)

Changing Line: 30. Li (Clinging)

Trigram	Name	Meaning	Direction Heaven	Earth
Outer	K'an (Abysmal)	Stand over an abyss	W	N
Inner	K'an (Abysmal)	Stand over an abyss	W	N

Eastern

Trigram	Element	Planet	Color	Number
Outer	Water (Moon)	Mercury (Water Star)	Crimson	7 (1)
Inner	Water (Moon)	Mercury (Water Star)	Crimson	7 (1)

Western

Trigram	Element	Planet	Color	Sephirah
Outer	Moon	Moon (Yesod)	Violet	9
Inner	Moon	Moon (Yesod)	Violet	9

30. **Li** (Li)—The Clinging
(Fire)

Divination

Image: Sun lighting the day, Moon lighting the night; fire flames up from the earth; two light lines (Yang) cling to a central dark (line), and by its diminishment produce light; fire clings to wood in order to burn and illuminate; the two lights in nature: Sun and Moon at their appropriate stations in heaven

Oracle: To find one's place in the world; to be aware of one's dependency on others in order to survive; two cycles of the Sun (two days); a second sunrise follows a first to continue illuminating the world; to set a path and follow it and no other; attachment to

Nuclear: 28. Ta Kuo (Preponderance of the Great)

Reversed: 30. Li (Clinging)

Overturned: 30. Li (Clinging)

Changing Line: 29. K'an (Abysmal)

Trigram	Name	Meaning	Direction Heaven	Earth
Outer	Li (Clinging)	Shine within	E	S
Inner	Li (Clinging)	Shine within	E	S

Eastern

Trigram	Element	Planet	Color	Number
Outer	Fire (Sun)	Mars (Fire Star)	Yellow-Orange	3 (9)
Inner	Fire (Sun)	Mars (Fire Star)	Yellow-Orange	3 (9)

Western

Trigram	Element	Planet	Color	Sephirah
Outer	Sun	Sun (Tiphereth)	Golden Yellow	6
Inner	Sun	Sun (Tiphereth)	Golden Yellow	6

31. **Hsien** (Xian)—Influence
(Wooing, Courtship)

Divination

Image: Weak above, strong below; a mountain with a lake on its summit

Oracle: Courtship, the man subordinate to the woman and influencing her by keeping still; mutual attraction; keeping still within while experiencing joy without (not being attached to the pleasure experienced); keeping the mind humble, free, open to advice and new direction; unexpected help will come from above; utmost sincerity which influences all

Nuclear: 44. Kou (Coming to Meet)

Reversed: 41. Sun (Decrease)

Overturned: 32. Heng (Duration)

Changing Line: 41. Sun (Decrease)

Trigram	Name	Meaning	Direction Heaven	Earth
Outer	Tui (Joyful)	Break free	SE	W
Inner	Ken (Keeping Still)	Restrain oneself	NW	NE

Eastern

Trigram	Element	Planet	Color	Number
Outer	Lake	Venus (Metal Star)	Deep Blue	4 (7)
Inner	Mountain	Saturn (Earth Star)	Bright Yellow	6 (8)

Western

Trigram	Element	Planet	Color	Sephirah
Outer	Water	Jupiter (Chesed)	Blue	4
Inner	Earth	Venus (Netzach)	Emerald	7

32. **Heng** (Heng)—Duration
(Marriage)

Divination

Image: Strong above, weak below; wind moving clouds filled with rain and thunder; gentleness within, movement without

Oracle: Marriage, the woman subordinate to the man; enduring union of opposites; exhalation following inhalation; duration; renewal; do not change your guiding star; to keep abreast of the times and adapt to its changes without giving up one's goal; keeping to the path

Nuclear: 43. Kuai (Break Through)

Reversed: 42. I (Increase)

Overturned: 31. Hsien (Influence)

Changing Line: 42. I (Increase)

Trigram	Name	Meaning	Direction Heaven	Earth
Outer	Chen (Arousing)	Rush forward	NE	E
Inner	Sun (Gentle)	Kneel down to	SW	SE

Eastern

Trigram	Element	Planet	Color	Number
Outer	Thunder	Jupiter (Wood Star)	Red-Orange	8 (3)
Inner	Wind (Wood)	Jupiter (Wood Star)	Green	2 (4)

Western

Trigram	Element	Planet	Color	Sephirah
Outer	Fire	Mars (Geburah)	Scarlet	5
Inner	Air	Mercury (Hod)	Orange	8

33. **Tun** (Tun)—Retreat
(Withdrawal)

Divination
Image: Mountain under heaven (to go far beyond the mountain in sight); power of dark (Yin) in ascent, light (Yang) withdrawing to safety; the superior keeping the inferior from encroaching; mountain reaching to heaven but heaven receding to infinity

Oracle: Withdrawal as natural rather than willed; retreat (not flight) in order not to exhaust one's forces; success depends on carrying out a retreat correctly, avoiding a life or death struggle; to retreat from an inferior and by withdrawal placing the inferior at a standstill; to prepare a counterattack while retreating; to retreat and then offer resistance

Nuclear: 44. Kou (Coming to Meet)

Reversed: 26. Ta Ch'u (The Taming Power of the Great)

Overturned: 34. Ta Chuang (The Power of the Great)

Changing Line: 19. Lin (Approach)

Trigram	Name	Meaning	Direction Heaven	Earth
Outer	Ch'ien (Creative)	Act with strength	S	NW
Inner	Ken (Keeping Still)	Restrain oneself	NW	NE

Eastern

Trigram	Element	Planet	Color	Number
Outer	Sky	Venus (Metal Star)	White	9 (6)
Inner	Mountain	Saturn (Earth Star)	Bright Yellow	6 (8)

Western

Trigram	Element	Planet	Color	Sephirah
Outer	Lingam	Saturn (Daath)	Gray-white	11 (or 33)
Inner	Earth	Venus (Netzach)	Emerald	7

34. **Ta Chuang** (Da Zhuang)—The Power of the Great

Divination

Image: Light (Yang) in ascendancy, dark (Yin) in retreat; charging ram breaking through his pen; the weak retreating to the background, the strong coming to the foreground

Oracle: Powerful upward motion of strength resulting in illuminating fire; inner worth mounting with great strength and manifesting in the world as power; true power which does not degenerate into sheer force or brute strength; danger in acting too quickly because of one's enormous strength; to act in accord with what is right when power is given to you

Nuclear: 43. Kuai (Break Through)

Reversed: 25. Wu Wang (Innocence)

Overturned: 33. Tun (Retreat)

Changing Line: 20. Kuan (Contemplation)

			Direction	
Trigram	**Name**	**Meaning**	**Heaven**	**Earth**
Outer	Chen (Arousing)	Rush forward	NE	E
Inner	Ch'ien (Creative)	Act with strength	S	NW

Eastern

Trigram	**Element**	**Planet**	**Color**	**Number**
Outer	Thunder	Jupiter (Wood Star)	Red-Orange	8 (3)
Inner	Sky	Venus (Metal Star)	White	9 (6)

Western

Trigram	**Element**	**Planet**	**Color**	**Sephirah**
Outer	Fire	Mars (Geburah)	Scarlet-Red	5
Inner	Lingam	Saturn (Daath)	Gray-White	11 (or 33)

35. **Chin** (Jin)—Progress
(Advancement)

Divination

Image: Sun rises over earth; light dispelling dark; three times (K'un) in a single day (Li); a powerful prince (Li) having audience with the King three times (K'un) in one day; a ruler (Li) is offered a great number of horses (K'un); a leader with great clarity leading his devoted subjects

Oracle: Rapid, easy progress; to motivate by reward; an opportunity presents itself to obtain one's heartfelt goal; to enhance one's outlook by rising above previous convictions with great clarity; wait to be awarded advancement, not to attempt it on one's own initiative

Nuclear: 39. Chien (Obstruction)

Reversed: 36. Ming I (Darkening of the Light)

Overturned: 36. Ming I (Darkening of the Light)

Changing Line: 5. Hsu (Waiting)

Trigram	Name	Meaning	Direction Heaven	Earth
Outer	Li (Clinging)	Shine within	E	S
Inner	K'un (Receptive)	Yield	N	SW

Eastern

Trigram	Element	Planet	Color	Number
Outer	Fire (Sun)	Mars (Fire Star)	Yellow-Orange	3 (9)
Inner	Earth	Saturn (Earth Star)	Black	1 (2)

Western

Trigram	Element	Planet	Color	Sephirah
Outer	Sun	Sun (Tiphereth)	Yellow	6
Inner	Yoni	Earth (Malkuth)	Russet, Olive, Citrine, Black	10

36. **Ming I** (Ming Yi)—Darkening of the Light

Divination

Image: Sun sets below earth; dark displacing light; the wounding of the light; a gold coin (Li) broken in two (K'un); a pheasant (phoenix) who after a short flight must land back upon the earth; an evil man in position of authority does harm to the wise

Oracle: Persevere in the face of adversity; do not allow oneself to be shaken in one's beliefs, or swept away by the concerns of the present; maintain one's inner clarity while outwardly offering no resistance; all adversaries will be conquered if one conceals one's power and persevering will

Nuclear: 40. Hsieh (Deliverance)

Reversed: 35. Chin (Progress)

Overturned: 35. Chin (Progress)

Changing Line: 6. Sung (Conflict)

Trigram	Name	Meaning	Direction Heaven	Earth
Outer	K'un (Receptive)	To yield (accept)	N	SW
Inner	Li (Clinging)	Shine within	E	S

Eastern

Trigram	Element	Planet	Color	Number
Outer	Earth	Saturn (Earth Star)	Black	1 (2)
Inner	Fire (Sun)	Mars (Fire Star)	Yellow-Orange	3 (9)

Western

Trigram	Element	Planet	Color	Sephirah
Outer	Yoni	Earth (Malkuth)	Russet, Olive, Citrine, Black	10
Inner	Sun	Sun (Tiphereth)	Yellow	6

37. **Chia Jen** (Jia Ren)—The Family
(Clan, Gathering)

Divination

Image: Strong leader rules the different members of the clan; father and son, husband and wife, elder and younger brother; wind emanating out of fire (the Sun); heat creating movement; an omen (Li) is seen in the clouds (Sun); to kneel down to the head of the clan

Oracle: To find happiness in one's station (position, rank) in life; faithfulness to duty, loyalty, and deference; love, chaste conduct, and correct behavior; woman in control within the home, man in control without the home; influence working from within to without; strong leadership required to rule a clan

Nuclear: 64. Wei Chi (Before Completion)

Reversed: 50. Ting (The Cauldron)

Overturned: 38. K'uei (Opposition)

Changing Line: 40. Hsieh (Deliverance)

			Direction	
Trigram	Name	Meaning	Heaven	Earth
Outer	Sun (Gentle)	Kneel down to	SW	SE
Inner	Li (Clinging)	Shine within	E	S

Eastern

Trigram	Element	Planet	Color	Number
Outer	Wind	Jupiter (Wood Star)	Green	2 (4)
Inner	Fire (Sun)	Mars (Fire Star)	Yellow-Orange	3 (9)

Western

Trigram	Element	Planet	Color	Sephirah
Outer	Air	Mercury (Hod)	Orange	8
Inner	Sun	Sun (Tiphereth)	Golden-Yellow	6

38. **K'uei** (Kui)—Opposition
(Complementary Alliance of Opposites, Enemies)

Divination

Image: Fire separating from water; fire flames upward and away, water seeps downward and within; the Sun rising out of the ocean at dawn; fire and water not comingling but maintaining their essential natures of fire above and water below

Oracle: When two are in opposition, only lesser undertakings can be accomplished; opposition does not preclude agreement; to have different roles but the same goal; harmonious rulership divides, resulting in the inability to rule cohesively until the two powers are reunited; the polarity which maintains the structure of the Universe

Nuclear: 63. Chi Chi (After Completion)

Reversed: 49. Ko (Revolution)

Overturned: 37. Chia Jen (The Family)

Changing Line: 39. Chien (Obstruction)

			Direction	
Trigram	Name	Meaning	Heaven	Earth
Outer	Li (Clinging)	Shine within	E	S
Inner	Tui (Joyful)	Break free	SE	W

Eastern

Trigram	Element	Planet	Color	Number
Outer	Fire (Sun)	Mars (Fire Star)	Yellow-Orange	3 (9)
Inner	Lake	Venus (Metal Star)	Deep Blue	4 (7)

Western

Trigram	Element	Planet	Color	Sephirah
Outer	Sun	Sun (Tiphereth)	Golden Yellow	6
Inner	Water	Jupiter (Chesed)	Blue	4

39. **Chien** (Cu)—Obstruction
(Obstacle, Danger)

Divination

Image: Bottomless pit before, inaccessible mountain behind; Moon rising over a mountain; lake on a mountain; fog (mist) obscuring the mountain's peak; the silence (Ken) of the night (K'an)

Oracle: To face the abyss; danger must not be met head on but must be retreated from until one has the power to cross the abyss; to turn to wise counsel to find a way out; difficulties which force one to turn inward for strength and guidance; to use an adverse situation as a tool for inner development; northeast does not further (do not advance), southwest furthers (do retreat) (King Wen's directions)

Nuclear: 64. Wei Chi (Before Completion)

Reversed: 4. Meng (Youthful Folly)

Overturned: 40. Hsieh (Deliverance)

Changing Line: 38. K'uei (Opposition)

Trigram	Name	Meaning	Direction Heaven	Earth
Outer	K'an (Abysmal)	Stand over an abyss	W	N
Inner	Ken (Keeping Still)	Restrain oneself	NW	NE

Eastern

Trigram	Element	Planet	Color	Number
Outer	Water (Moon)	Mercury (Water Star)	Crimson	7 (1)
Inner	Mountain	Saturn (Earth Star)	Bright Yellow	6 (8)

Western

Trigram	Element	Planet	Color	Sephirah
Outer	Moon	Moon (Yesod)	Violet	9
Inner	Earth	Venus (Netzach)	Emerald	7

40. **Hsieh** (Jie)—Deliverance
(Escape)

Divination

Image: Rain pouring out of storm clouds; the Moon and thunder; thunderstorm which clears the air; to rush forward across the abyss; water cleansing everything

Oracle: To cross the abyss; unraveling a knot; movement takes one out of danger; to be released from prison; sudden change in circumstances allows dangers (problems) which have been avoided to be met head on; all preparations should already be accomplished—if not, hasten to accomplish them; do not push forward farther than necessary to overcome one's obstacles

Nuclear: 63. Chi Chi (After Completion)

Reversed: 3. Chun (Difficulty at Beginning)

Overturned: 39. Chien (Obstruction)

Changing Line: 37. Chia Jen (The Family)

			Direction	
Trigram	Name	Meaning	Heaven	Earth
Outer	Chen (Arousing)	Rush forward	NE	E
Inner	K'an (Abysmal)	Stand over an abyss	W	N

Eastern

Trigram	Element	Planet	Color	Number
Outer	Thunder	Jupiter (Wood Star)	Red-Orange	8 (3)
Inner	Water (Moon)	Mercury (Water Star)	Crimson	7 (1)

Western

Trigram	Element	Planet	Color	Sephirah
Outer	Fire	Mars (Geburah)	Scarlet-Red	5
Inner	Moon	Moon (Yesod)	Violet	9

41. **Sun** (Sun)—Decrease

Divination

Image: Lake evaporating at the foot of a mountain and becoming clouds; water underground, drilling for a well; decrease of the lower in favor of the upper; the foundations of a house weakened, while the walls are precariously strengthened

Oracle: Time to accept poverty and not try to conceal it; to reduce your level of involvement, to seek a subordinate position for the time being; to tap the inner when the outer is depleted; inner strength through simplicity; passions curbed by higher instincts; anger decreased by keeping still; do not expect results the first time, but persevere until successful

Nuclear: 24. Fu (Return)

Reversed: 31. Hsien (Influence)

Overturned: 42. I (Increase)

Changing Line: 31. Hsien (Influence)

			Direction	
Trigram	Name	Meaning	Heaven	Earth
Outer	Ken (Keeping Still)	Restrain oneself	NW	NE
Inner	Tui (Joyful)	Break free	SE	W

Eastern

Trigram	Element	Planet	Color	Number
Outer	Mountain	Saturn (Earth Star)	Bright Yellow	6 (8)
Inner	Lake	Venus (Metal Star)	Deep Blue	4 (7)

Western

Trigram	Element	Planet	Color	Sephirah
Outer	Earth	Venus (Netzach)	Emerald	7
Inner	Water	Jupiter (Chesed)	Blue	4

42. I (Yi)—Increase

Divination

Image: Wind and thunder increasing in their interaction in the sky; thunder below clouds of the sky; a sacrifice in the higher allowing an increase in the lower

Oracle: To imitate the good in others and rid evil in oneself; the powerful bending down and helping the weak rise; to seize the moment and advance beyond any previous gain

Nuclear: 23. Po (Splitting Apart)

Reversed: 32. Heng (Duration)

Overturned: 41. Sun (Decrease)

Changing Line: 32. Heng (Duration)

Trigram	Name	Meaning	Direction Heaven	Earth
Outer	Sun (Gentle)	Kneel down to	SW	SE
Inner	Chen (Arousing)	Rush forward	NE	E

Eastern

Trigram	Element	Planet	Color	Number
Outer	Wind (Wood)	Jupiter (Wood Star)	Green	2 (4)
Inner	Thunder	Jupiter (Wood Star)	Red-Orange	8 (3)

Western

Trigram	Element	Planet	Color	Sephirah
Outer	Air	Mercury (Hod)	Orange	8
Inner	Fire	Mars (Geburah)	Scarlet-Red	5

43. **Kuai** (Kui)—Break Through
(Resoluteness)

Divination

Image: A lake rising up to heaven; a cloudburst, a river flooding; a dam bursting; a sword (the first five yao) cutting through a serpent (sixth yao); the strong dominate, the weak recede

Oracle: To purge all weakness in oneself; to break through all resistance; a bursting forth of great pent up tension; an outcome other than expected; a warning allowing flight from danger; a weak line of defense offering attack; the rule of the inferior over the superior is about to end

Nuclear: 1. Ch'ien (Creative)

Reversed: 10. Lu (Treading)

Overturned: 44. Kou (Coming to Meet)

Changing Line: 23. Po (Splitting Apart)

Trigram	Name	Meaning	Direction Heaven	Earth
Outer	Tui (Joyful)	Break free	SE	W
Inner	Ch'ien (Strong)	Act with strength	S	NW

Eastern

Trigram	Element	Planet	Color	Number
Outer	Lake	Venus (Metal Star)	Deep Blue	4 (7)
Inner	Sky	Venus (Metal Star)	White	9 (6)

Western

Trigram	Element	Planet	Color	Sephirah
Outer	Water	Jupiter (Chesed)	Blue	4
Inner	Lingam	Saturn (Daath)	Gray-White	11 (or 33)

44. **Kou** (Gou)—Coming to Meet

Divination

Image: Earth meets heaven; wind blowing under heaven; the wind measuring the eight directions of heaven (Fu-Hsi's directions); the road of initiation that is at first the hardest (first yao) but soon becomes easier to traverse because of the master guiding the pupil (second to sixth yao)

Oracle: A dangerous, unpredictable situation forces one not to act; the female actively seeks the male; do not marry the bold, powerful woman; avoid subjugation by being on one's own; after the dark has been dispelled by the light, it returns from within and below

Nuclear: 1. Ch'ien (Creative)

Reversed: 9. Hsiao Ch'u (The Taming Power of the Small)

Overturned: 43. Kuai (Break Through)

Changing Line: 24. Fu (Return)

Trigram	Name	Meaning	Direction Heaven	Earth
Outer	Ch'ien (Strong)	Act with strength	S	NW
Inner	Sun (Gentle)	Kneel down to	SW	SE

Eastern

Trigram	Element	Planet	Color	Number
Outer	Sky	Venus (Metal Star)	White	9 (6)
Inner	Wind (Wood)	Jupiter (Wood Star)	Green	2 (4)

Western

Trigram	Element	Planet	Color	Sephirah
Outer	Lingam	Saturn (Daath)	Gray-White	11 (or 33)
Inner	Air	Mercury (Hod)	Orange	8

45. **Ts'ui** (Cai)—Gathering Together
(Massing)

Divination

Image: A lake collects water over the earth; the king approaches the gateway of his temple; a carp swims up the waterfall to heaven; carp's tail (first to third yao), carp's body (fourth and fifth yao), carp's open mouth (sixth yao)

Oracle: To arm (prepare) oneself to gather together a large group composed of different inclinations; to group together; collect; to amass friends and family to overcome one's opponent; a family gathers around the grand patriarch

Nuclear: 53. Chien (Development)

Reversed: 19. Lin (Approach)

Overturned: 46. Sheng (Pushing Upward)

Changing Line: 26. Ta Ch'u (The Taming Power of the Great)

Trigram	Name	Meaning	Direction Heaven	Earth
Outer	Tui (Joyful)	Break free	SE	W
Inner	K'un (Receptive)	Yield	N	SW

Eastern

Trigram	Element	Planet	Color	Number
Outer	Lake	Venus (Metal Star)	Deep Blue	4 (7)
Inner	Earth	Saturn (Earth Star)	Black	1 (2)

Western

Trigram	Element	Planet	Color	Sephirah
Outer	Water	Jupiter (Chesed)	Blue	4
Inner	Yoni	Earth (Malkuth)	Russet, Olive, Citrine, Black	10

46. **Sheng** (Sheng)—Pushing Upward
(Ascending)

Divination

Image: A tree pushing upward through the soil at the top of a mountain; to remove the dust from a mirror; the carp descending from heaven to earth, mate to the carp of hexagram 45; carp's open mouth grasping tail of its mate (first yao), carp's body (second and third yao), carp's tail (fourth to sixth yao)

Oracle: The will to push upward, to advance to the Sun in the South; to work at a higher level than before; to seek help from someone in a higher position; to adapt to obstacles by moving around them, rather than opposing them

Nuclear: 54. Kuei Mei (Marrying Maiden)

Reversed: 20. Kuan (Comtemplation)

Overturned: 45. Ts'ui (Gathering Together)

Changing Line: 25. Wu Wang (Innocence)

Trigram	Name	Meaning	Direction Heaven	Earth
Outer	K'un (Receptive)	To yield (accept)	N	SW
Inner	Sun (Gentle)	Kneel down to	SW	SE

Eastern

Trigram	Element	Planet	Color	Number
Outer	Earth	Saturn (Earth Star)	Black	1 (2)
Inner	Wind (Wood)	Jupiter (Wood Star)	Green	2 (4)

Western

Trigram	Element	Planet	Color	Sephirah
Outer	Yoni	Earth (Malkuth)	Russet, Olive, Citrine, Black	10
Inner	Air	Mercury (Hod)	Orange	8

47. **K'un** (Kun)—Oppression
(Exhaustion)

Divination

Image: No water in the lake; water seeps below and escapes from the lake above; to pour water into a reservoir and revive the fish within

Oracle: To meet one's obstacles with enthusiasm, thereby turning adversity to one's advantage; to surround and exhaust the enemy; it is time to remain silent, since no one will believe what one says; do not let oneself be broken by exhaustion, but bend under its weight in order to jump back at the right moment; to follow one's own will and instincts in time of oppression and exhaustion

Nuclear: 37. Chia Jen (The Family)

Reversed: 60. Chieh (Limitation)

Overturned: 48. Ching (The Well)

Changing Line: 22. Pi (Grace)

Trigram	Name	Meaning	Direction Heaven	Earth
Outer	Tui (Joyful)	Break free	SE	W
Inner	K'an (Abysmal)	Stand over an abyss	W	N

Eastern

Trigram	Element	Planet	Color	Number
Outer	Lake	Venus (Metal Star)	Deep Blue	4 (7)
Inner	Water (Moon)	Mercury (Water Star)	Crimson	7 (1)

Western

Trigram	Element	Planet	Color	Sephirah
Outer	Water	Jupiter (Chesed)	Blue	4
Inner	Moon	Moon (Yesod)	Violet	9

48. **Ching** (Jing)—The Well

Divination

Image: The roots of plants and trees lifting water out of the earth; a bucket upon a pole descends into the well to bring up water: the bucket (sixth and fourth yao), the water in the bucket (fifth yao), the water of the well (third and second yao), the bottom of the well (first yao)

Oracle: That which cannot change but gives subsistence to all; that which is constant, dependable; the ruler encouraging his people to perform well; to be rescued from a dangerous situation by a rope

Nuclear: 38. K'uei (Opposition)

Reversed: 59. Huan (Dispersion)

Overturned: 47. K'un (Oppression)

Changing Line: 21. Shih Ho (Biting Through)

Trigram	Name	Meaning	Direction Heaven	Earth
Outer	K'an (Abysmal)	Stand over an abyss	W	N
Inner	Sun (Gentle)	Kneel down	SW	SE

Eastern

Trigram	Element	Planet	Color	Number
Outer	Water (Moon)	Mercury (Water Star)	Crimson	7 (1)
Inner	Wind (Wood)	Jupiter (Wood Star)	Green	2 (4)

Western

Trigram	Element	Planet	Color	Sephirah
Outer	Moon	Moon (Yesod)	Violet	9
Inner	Air	Mercury (Hod)	Orange	8

49. Ko (Ge)—Revolution
(Change)

Divination

Image: Leopard changing its pelt to that of a tiger; the Sun setting in the ocean; fire below water bringing it to a boil; water suppresses fire; young daughter contends with middle daughter

Oracle: Radical change brought about right now will remove all regret; to be aware of the right moment for upheaval; the time is right for one's words to be believed

Nuclear: 44. Kou (Coming to Meet)

Reversed: 38. K'uei (Opposition)

Overturned: 50. Ting (The Cauldron)

Changing Line: 4. Meng (Youthful Folly)

Trigram	Name	Meaning	Direction Heaven	Earth
Outer	Tui (Joyful)	Break free	SE	W
Inner	Li (Clinging)	Shine within	E	S

Eastern

Trigram	Element	Planet	Color	Number
Outer	Lake	Venus (Metal Star)	Deep Blue	4 (7)
Inner	Fire (Sun)	Mars (Fire Star)	Yellow-Orange	3 (9)

Western

Trigram	Element	Planet	Color	Sephirah
Outer	Water	Jupiter (Chesed)	Blue	4
Inner	Sun	Sun (Tiphereth)	Golden Yellow	6

50. **Ting** (Ding)—The Cauldron

Divination

Image: A bronze cauldron containing fire; the sacrificial three-legged vessel known as the Ting: three feet (first yao), body of the cauldron (second to fourth yao), two handles (ears) of the cauldron (fifth yao), carrying pole placed between two handles (sixth yao); fire kindled by wood and wind cooking food to sustain the clan

Oracle: To be adaptable, flexible, dextrous; to have one's life in harmony with one's true destiny (will); a new regime comes into power; to sacrifice earthly values for the divine

Nuclear: 43. Kuai (Break Through)

Reversed: 37. Chia Jen (The Family)

Overturned: 49. Ko (Revolution)

Changing Line: 3. Chun (Difficulty at the Beginning)

Trigram	Name	Meaning	Direction Heaven	Earth
Outer	Li (Clinging)	Shine within	E	S
Inner	Sun (Gentle)	Kneel down to	SW	SE

Eastern

Trigram	Element	Planet	Color	Number
Outer	Fire (Sun)	Mars (Fire Star)	Yellow-Orange	3 (9)
Inner	Wood (Wind)	Jupiter (Wood Star)	Green	2 (4)

Western

Trigram	Element	Planet	Color	Sephirah
Outer	Sun	Sun (Tiphereth)	Golden Yellow	6
Inner	Air	Mercury (Hod)	Orange	8

51. **Chen** (Zhen)—The Arousing
(Shock, Thunder)

Divination

Image: Shock upon shock, thunder upon thunder; shower of thunderbolts spreading 100 miles; the eldest son seizing rulership with great zeal; fiery upward movement which inspires terror

Oracle: The shock resulting from the inner manifestation of Spirit; to come to grips with one's innermost fears in order to guard against any terrors from without; inner strength which deflects all outer shocks

Nuclear: 39. Chien (Obstruction)

Reversed: 51. Chen (The Arousing)

Overturned: 52. Ken (Keeping Still)

Changing Line: 57. Sun (The Gentle)

Trigram	Name	Meaning	Direction Heaven	Earth
Outer	Chen (Arousing)	Rush forward	NE	E
Inner	Chen (Arousing)	Rush forward	NE	E

Eastern

Trigram	Element	Planet	Color	Number
Outer	Thunder	Jupiter (Wood Star)	Red-Orange	8 (3)
Inner	Thunder	Jupiter (Wood Star)	Red-Orange	8 (3)

Western

Trigram	Element	Planet	Color	Sephirah
Outer	Fire	Mars (Geburah)	Scarlet-Red	5
Inner	Fire	Mars (Geburah)	Scarlet-Red	5

52. **Ken** (Yin)—Keeping Still
(Mountain, Peace)

Divination

Image: Male principle striving upward, female principle pressing downward; a mountain range, mountain upon mountain; a lookout upon a high mountain

Oracle: To come to rest after a long journey in order to begin a new journey; to see beyond the struggles of everyday life; do not allow your thoughts to wander beyond the goal; to be passed over by one's enemies; to remain undetected and escape harm

Nuclear: 40. Hsieh (Deliverance)

Reversed: 52. Ken (Keeping Still)

Overturned: 51. Chen (Arousing)

Changing Line: 58. Tui (The Joyous)

Trigram	Name	Meaning	Direction Heaven	Earth
Outer	Ken (Keeping Still)	Restrain oneself	NW	NE
Inner	Ken (Keeping Still)	Restrain oneself	NW	NE

Eastern

Trigram	Element	Planet	Color	Number
Outer	Mountain	Saturn (Earth Star)	Bright Yellow	6 (8)
Inner	Mountain	Saturn (Earth Star)	Bright Yellow	6 (8)

Western

Trigram	Element	Planet	Color	Sephirah
Outer	Earth	Venus (Netzach)	Emerald	7
Inner	Earth	Venus (Netzach)	Emerald	7

53. **Chien** (Jian)—Development
(Gradual Progress)

Divination

Image: A tree growing on top of a mountain; the vantage point of the highest peak; a watchtower; a jar containing medicine is placed on the earth; to climb a ladder stretched between heaven and earth

Oracle: Calm within, forceful penetration without; the gradual development of a relationship leading to a successful marriage; gradual advance in a difficult battle; the perseverance needed to traverse a long path; the gradual progress of natural growth which proceeds step by step

Nuclear: 64. Wei Chi (Before Completion)

Reversed: 18. Ku (Work on What Has Been Spoiled)

Overturned: 54. Kuei Mei (Marrying Maiden)

Changing Line: 54. Kuei Mei (Marrying Maiden)

Trigram	Name	Meaning	Direction Heaven	Earth
Outer	Sun (Gentle)	Kneel down to	SW	SE
Inner	Ken (Keeping Still)	Restrain oneself	NW	NE

Eastern

Trigram	Element	Planet	Color	Number
Outer	Wind	Jupiter (Wood Star)	Green	2 (4)
Inner	Mountain	Saturn (Earth Star)	Bright Yellow	6 (8)

Western

Trigram	Element	Planet	Color	Sephirah
Outer	Air	Mercury (Hod)	Orange	8
Inner	Earth	Venus (Netzach)	Emerald	7

54. **Kuei Mei** (Gui Mei)—The Marrying Maiden

Divination

Image: Thunder rippling the shimmering waters of a lake; a young girl under the guidance of an older man; entrance of the wife into the husband's house; the eldest son leads and marries the youngest daughter

Oracle: The time is not right for any new undertaking; it is not time to advance boldly into battle; do not initiate, but follow; tact, caution, and reserve are required in order not to be distracted from one's path

Nuclear: 63. Chi Chi (After Completion)

Reversed: 17. Sui (Following)

Overturned: 53. Chien (Development))

Changing Line: 53. Chien (Development)

Trigram	Name	Meaning	Direction Heaven	Earth
Outer	Chen (Arousing)	Rush forward	NE	E
Inner	Tui (Joyful)	Break free	SE	W

Eastern

Trigram	Element	Planet	Color	Number
Outer	Thunder	Jupiter (Wood Star)	Red-Orange	8 (3)
Inner	Lake	Venus (Metal Star)	Deep Blue	4 (7)

Western

Trigram	Element	Planet	Color	Sephirah
Outer	Fire	Mars (Geburah)	Scarlet Red	5
Inner	Water	Jupiter (Chesed)	Blue	4

55. **Feng** (Feng)—Abundance
(Fullness)

Divination

Image: Light (fire) from the Sun; thunder and lightning in the heavens; Sun rising to its zenith at noon; bamboo on fire; clarity within, advancement without

Oracle: To forcefully take full advantage of the moment, fully aware of all obstacles ahead; abundance resulting from advancement, which eventually must come to an end; the clear and even application of laws and punishments; to lead with great clarity

Nuclear: 28. Ta Kuo (Preponderance of the Great)

Reversed: 21. Shih Ho (Biting Through)

Overturned: 56. Lu (The Wanderer)

Changing Line: 59. Huan (Dispersion)

Trigram	Name	Meaning	Direction Heaven	Earth
Outer	Chen (Arousing)	Rush forward	NE	E
Inner	Li (Clinging)	Shine within	E	S

Eastern

Trigram	Element	Planet	Color	Number
Outer	Thunder	Jupiter (Wood Star)	Red-Orange	8 (3)
Inner	Fire (Sun)	Mars (Fire Star)	Yellow-Orange	3 (9)

Western

Trigram	Element	Planet	Color	Sephirah
Outer	Fire	Mars (Geburah)	Scarlet-Red	5
Inner	Sun	Sun (Tiphereth)	Golden Yellow	6

56. **Lu** (Lu)—The Wanderer

Divination

Image: Fire ascending to heaven, mountain bearing down to earth; grass on fire on top of a mountain, burning out quickly; three guiding stars in the night sky

Oracle: To wander in strange lands; to be cautious and reserved when among strangers; to avoid pitfalls and evil in exploring new territory; to quickly pass over lawsuits and penalties

Nuclear: 28. Ta Kuo (Preponderance of the Great)

Reversed: 22. Pi (Grace)

Overturned: 55. Feng (Abundance)

Changing Line: 60. Chieh (Limitation)

Trigram	Name	Meaning	Direction Heaven	Earth
Outer	Li (Clinging)	Shine within	E	S
Inner	Ken (Keeping Still)	Restrain oneself	NW	NE

Eastern

Trigram	Element	Planet	Color	Number
Outer	Fire (Sun)	Mars (Fire Star)	Yellow-Orange	3 (9)
Inner	Mountain	Saturn (Earth Star)	Bright Yellow	6 (8)

Western

Trigram	Element	Planet	Color	Sephirah
Outer	Sun	Sun (Tiphereth)	Golden Yellow	6
Inner	Earth	Venus (Netzach)	Emerald Green	7

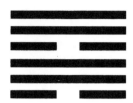

57. **Sun** (Sun)—The Gentle
(Penetrating Wind)

Divination

Image: The gentle, penetrating flow of wind dispersing all clouds in the sky; wind fills the sails of a boat; the roots of a tree penetrating the soil; the eight winds of the heavens; wind blown bamboo bending under the force of the gale

Oracle: A gradual gain which can be enhanced by associating oneself with a person in a position of power; a gradual, lasting influence on others; gradual, continual work not readily detected by others; small success

Nuclear: 38. K'uei (Opposition)

Reversed: 57. Sun (The Gentle)

Overturned: 58. Tui (The Joyous)

Changing Line: 51. Chen (Arousing)

Trigram	Name	Meaning	Direction Heaven	Earth
Outer	Sun (Gentle)	Kneel down to	SW	SE
Inner	Sun (Gentle)	Kneel down to	SW	SE

Eastern

Trigram	Element	Planet	Color	Number
Outer	Wind (Wood)	Jupiter (Wood Star)	Green	2 (4)
Inner	Wind (Wood)	Jupiter (Wood Star)	Green	2 (4)

Western

Trigram	Element	Planet	Color	Sephirah
Outer	Air	Mercury (Hod)	Orange	8
Inner	Air	Mercury (Hod)	Orange	8

58. **Tui** (Dui)—The Joyous
(Lake)

Divination

Image: Two lakes joined together; a river emanates from a lake; a system of pools linked by many streams

Oracle: To win an argument through friendly persuasion; to join with friends for a discussion, new enterprise, or entertainment; inner joy, gentleness of spirit; to share knowledge in order to revitalize it

Nuclear: 37. Chia Jen (The Family)

Reversed: 58. Tui (The Joyous)

Overturned: 57. Sun (The Gentle)

Changing Line: 52. Ken (Keeping Still)

			Direction	
Trigram	Name	Meaning	Heaven	Earth
Outer	Tui (Joyful)	Break free	SE	W
Inner	Tui (Joyful)	Break free	SE	W

Eastern

Trigram	Element	Planet	Color	Number
Outer	Lake	Venus (Metal Star)	Deep Blue	4 (7)
Inner	Lake	Venus (Metal Star)	Deep Blue	4 (7)

Western

Trigram	Element	Planet	Color	Sephirah
Outer	Water	Jupiter (Chesed)	Blue	4
Inner	Water	Jupiter (Chesed)	Blue	4

59. **Huan** (Huan)—Dispersion
(Dissolution)

Divination

Image: The king approaching his temple; wind blowing over the water turns to fog; a boat follows the currents of a stream; a wind-blown sky; foam and mist rising from the waters; a temple deep in the mountains hidden in the fog; warm wind of spring dissolving the winter ice upon the lake

Oracle: To disperse or dissolve the weaker element in oneself; to dissolve the ice upon the lake of winter; religious ecstasy, awe, reverence opened through ritual; to dissolve the ego through the crucible of repeated ritual; to gently break up all that is holding one back

Nuclear: 27. I (Corners of the Mouth)

Reversed: 48. Ching (The Well)

Overturned: 60. Chieh (Limitation)

Changing Line: 55. Feng (Abundance)

			Direction	
Trigram	**Name**	**Meaning**	**Heaven**	**Earth**
Outer	Sun (Gentle)	Kneel down to	SW	SE
Inner	K'an (Abysmal)	Stand over an abyss	W	N

Eastern

Trigram	**Element**	**Planet**	**Color**	**Number**
Outer	Wind (Wood)	Jupiter (Wood Star)	Green	2 (4)
Inner	Water (Moon)	Mercury (Water Star)	Crimson	7 (1)

Western

Trigram	**Element**	**Planet**	**Color**	**Sephirah**
Outer	Air	Mercury (Hod)	Orange	8
Inner	Moon	Moon (Yesod)	Violet	9

60. **Chieh** (Ji)—Limitation

Divination

Image: The joints (third, fourth, and sixth yao) which divide the bamboo stalk (first, second, and fifth yao); the shore of an ocean, the bank of river; the edge of a lake that can contain no more water and sets the boundary

Oracle: To limit one's economy or actions in order to gain greater control of one's life; to be sparing, fix limits, know one's boundaries; to restrain but not become inflexible; the creation of number and measure, which sets the limits of the universe

Nuclear: 27. I (The Corners of the Mouth)

Reversed: 47. K'un (Oppression)

Overturned: 59. Huan (Dissolution)

Changing Line: 56. Lu (The Wanderer)

Trigram	Name	Meaning	Direction Heaven	Earth
Outer	K'an (Abysmal)	Stand over an abyss	W	N
Inner	Tui (Joyful)	Break free	SE	W

Eastern

Trigram	Element	Planet	Color	Number
Outer	Water (Moon)	Mercury (Water Star)	Crimson	7 (1)
Inner	Lake	Venus (Metal Star)	Deep Blue	4 (7)

Western

Trigram	Element	Planet	Color	Sephirah
Outer	Moon	Moon (Yesod)	Violet	9
Inner	Water	Jupiter (Chesed)	Blue	4

61. **Chung Fu** (Zhong fu)—Inner Truth
(Innermost Sincerity)

Divination

Image: A round coin with a square hole in the center; the bamboo: hard without, hollow within; the wind moving water by penetrating it; an egg: its shell (first and sixth yao), its white (second and fifth yao), its yolk (third and fourth yao); a flying crane with a letter in its mouth; two strong armies electing not to fight at their borders

Oracle: To examine any accusation to its core in order to truly discern between good and evil; to influence a pig or fish (the most difficult animals to influence); to be receptive to one's opponent's viewpoint and thereby win them over to one's own cause; the superior is lenient to the inferior, the inferior is faithful to the superior; to be active without, calm within; to be open in the center, allowing the light to come inside

Nuclear: 27. I (Corners of the Mouth)

Reversed: 28. Ta Kuo (Preponderance of the Great)

Overturned: 61. Chung Fu (Inner Truth)

Changing Line: 62. Hsiao Ku (Preponderance of the Small)

Trigram	Name	Meaning	Direction Heaven	Earth
Outer	Sun (Gentle)	Kneel down to	SW	SE
Inner	Tui (Joyful)	Break free	SE	W

Eastern

Trigram	Element	Planet	Color	Number
Outer	Wind (Wood)	Jupiter (Wood Star)	Green	2 (4)
Inner	Lake	Venus (Metal Star)	Deep Blue	4 (7)

Western

Trigram	Element	Planet	Color	Sephirah
Outer	Air	Mercury (Hod)	Orange	8
Inner	Water	Jupiter (Chesed)	Blue	4

62. **Hsiao Kua** (Zrao Guo)—Preponderance of the Small

Divination

Image: The two wings of a bird in flight (first, second, fifth, and sixth yao); two armies meeting strong at their frontlines, but weak within; iron wrapped with cotton; the soft concealing the hard; thunder at the top of a mountain; the flames of the sacrifice rising from a tripod; a watchman on a gate

Oracle: Attempt the small, avoid the great; to maintain a role of authority beyond one's abilities through extreme prudence; the strong within influencing the weak without; do not strive upward but wait for a message; light in the center while darkness is all around

Nuclear: 28. Ta Kuo (Preponderance of the Great)

Reversed: 27. I (Corners of the Mouth)

Overturned: 62. Hsiao Kuo (Preponderance of the Small)

Changing Line: 61. Chung Fu (Inner Truth)

Trigram	Name	Meaning	Direction Heaven	Earth
Outer	Chen (Arousing)	Rush forward	NE	E
Inner	Ken (Keeping Still)	Restrain oneself	NW	NE

Eastern

Trigram	Element	Planet	Color	Number
Outer	Thunder	Jupiter (Wood Star)	Red-Orange	8 (3)
Inner	Mountain	Saturn (Earth Star)	Bright Yellow	6 (8)

Western

Trigram	Element	Planet	Color	Sephirah
Outer	Fire	Mars (Geburah)	Scarlet-Red	5
Inner	Earth	Venus (Netzach)	Emerald	7

63. **Chi Chi** (Ji Ji)—After Completion
(Finished)

Divination

Image: Day turning to night; the Moon above, the Sun below; woman above man; water over fire; the Moon crowning the Sun; Sun-Moon-Sun-Moon; water in a kettle heating over a fire; a boat approaches the shore; bright within, dark without; strong and weak in their proper places (Yang in first, third, and fifth yao; Yin in second, fourth, and sixth yao); autumnal equinox

Oracle: The time is at hand to end one's undertakings, which requires utmost care in order to properly complete; if one does not fully concentrate after 99 per cent of one's work is done, the results aimed at will be spoiled; the great effort required to transfrom 99 per cent into 100 per cent; to take all precautions against misfortunes before completing any matter

Nuclear: 64. Wei Chi (Before Completion)

Reversed: 64. Wei Chi (Before Completion)

Overturned: 64. Wei Chi (Before Completion)

Changing Line: 64. Wei Chi (Before Completion)

Trigram	Name	Meaning	Direction Heaven	Earth
Outer	K'an (Abysmal)	Stand over an abyss	W	N
Inner	Li (Clinging)	Shine within	E	S

Eastern

Trigram	Element	Planet	Color	Number
Outer	Water (Moon)	Mercury (Water Star)	Crimson	7 (1)
Inner	Fire (Sun)	Mars (Fire Star)	Yellow-Orange	3 (9)

Western

Trigram	Element	Planet	Color	Sephirah
Outer	Moon	Moon (Yesod)	Violet	9
Inner	Sun	Sun (Tiphereth)	Golden Yellow	6

64. **Wei Chi** (Wei Ji)—Before Completion
(Unfinished)

Divination

Image: Night turning to day; the Sun above, the Moon below; man above woman; fire over water; to empty the lake to find the pearl; the Sun crowning the Moon; Moon-Sun-Moon-Sun; a fox warily crossing over thin ice; fire flaming upward, water rushing downward; strong in the weak points and weak in the strong points; bright without, dark within; vernal equinox

Oracle: To emerge out of stagnation with renewed enthusiasm to finish the task at hand; to ford the river with great deliberation, aware of the rocks within the river; transition from chaos to order is not over yet, but incomplete success

Nuclear: 63. Chi Chi (After Completion)

Reversed: 63. Chi Chi (After Completion)

Overturned: 63. Chi Chi (After Completion)

Changing Line: 63. Chi Chi (After Completion)

Trigram	Name	Meaning	Direction Heaven	Earth
Outer	Li (Clinging)	Shine within	E	S
Inner	K'an (Abysmal)	Stand over an abyss	W	N

Eastern

Trigram	Element	Planet	Color	Number
Outer	Fire (Sun)	Mars (Fire Star)	Yellow-Orange	3 (9)
Inner	Water (Moon)	Mercury (Water Star)	Crimson	7 (1)

Western

Trigram	Element	Planet	Color	Sephirah
Outer	Sun	Sun (Tiphereth)	Golden Yellow	6
Inner	Moon	Moon (Yesod)	Violet	9

ORACULAR LANGUAGE

The revision of the divinatory text for the *I Ching,* as it appears above, should be used in conjunction with a standard *I Ching* translation, but the essential reduction and comment is thorough enough to serve as a basic primer for oracular use.

There are two traditional oracular methods for casting the hexagrams of the *I Ching*: the yarrow-stalk method and the coin-toss method.

The elaborate yarrow-stalk count can be found in most translations of the *I Ching*. However, the method demonstrated here will be the coin toss.

The Coin-Toss Method

The Coin-Toss Method involves the casting of three coins six times to form the six yao of the hexagram, beginning with the first or bottom yao.

The heads and tails of each coin represent the numbers two and three. Heads represents Yang and the number three, while tails represents Yin and the number two.

If one or three of the coins is Yang, the yao line generated is Yang. If one or three of the coins is Yin, the yao line generated is Yin. However, when all three coins are either Yang or Yin, that specific yao is a changing line that will generate a second hexagram in which the corresponding yao is the opposite of Yang or Yin.

Each of four possible coin-toss totals corresponds to a trigram, one of the four symbols, a cardinal direction, and a changing or stationary line:

Coin Toss Symbols

Coin Toss	Yin/Yang	Changing Line	Trigram	Four Symbol	Direction (Fu Hsi)
9	3 + 3 + 3 (three Yang)	Yang to Yin	Ch'ien	Old Yang	S
8	3 + 2 + 3 (Yang-Yin-Yang)	Yin (Stationary)	Li	Young Yin	E
7	2 + 3 + 2 (Yin-Yang-Yin)	Yang (Stationary)	K'an	Young Yang	W
6	2 + 2 + 2 (three Yin)	Yin to Yang	K'un	Old Yin	N

To recapitulate, the rules for the Coin-Toss Method are:

• Toss three coins six times, once for each line of the hexagram, starting with the bottom (first) line and working up to the top (last) line.

• Count heads as three, tails as two.

• The total will be six, seven, eight, or nine.

- If the total is seven, an unchanging Yang line is cast.

- If the total is eight, an unchanging Yin line is cast.

- If the total is six, a changing Yin line is cast. This line will be Yin in the present hexagram, but Yang in the secondary (future) hexagram.

- If the total is nine, a changing Yang line is cast. This line will be Yang in the present hexagram, but Yin in the secondary (future) hexagram.

- If in all six tosses of the three coins only the totals seven or eight come up, only one hexagram will be generated

- However, if the totals six or nine occur within the six coin tosses, that specific line generates a second hexagram. For every line that is six (or Yin), the second (changing line) hexagram line will be Yang. And for every line which is nine (or Yang), the second hexagram line will be Yin. Also, each six or nine line in the original hexagram has an additional divinatory meaning (see below).

- In this second hexagram, any line which is seven or eight (stationary) in the original remains stationary:

Original Hexagram		Changing Line Hexagram
If 6 (Yin)	then	Yang
If 9 (Yang)	then	Yin
If 8 (Yin)	then	Yin
If 7 (Yang)	then	Yang

- The new or Changing Line hexagram is usually viewed in divination as the near future (what is about to occur), or a resolution to the problem stated in the first hexagram cast.

Each of the six yao which are either six or nine, and generate a changing line, possesses additional oracular symbols known as the *Duke of Chou's Changing Line Commentary*. When a six or nine is cast in the original hexagram, refer to Chou's commentary (on pages 561–579) for the additional divinatory meanings for that specific line of the original hexagram. The oracular text of the original hexagram must be modified by the divinatory meanings associated with each changing line. The oracular images for each of the 384 lines that compose the 64 hexagrams can be found later in this chapter in the table titled "Hexagram Key to Chu-Ko's Spirit Calculation for the Numbers 1 to 384."

The following table based on the Liang Yi trigram order will enable the quick identification of a hexagram cast by viewing the hexagram as an inner and outer trigram.

Liang Yi, Hexagram Generator

Outer Trigram

11	19	36	24	46	7	15	2
26	41	22	27	18	4	52	23
5	60	63	3	48	29	39	8
9	61	37	42	57	59	53	20
34	54	55	51	32	40	62	16
14	38	30	21	50	64	56	35
43	58	49	17	28	47	31	45
1	10	13	25	44	6	33	12

Inner Trigram

The Divinatory Magick Square of Eight

A second method that involves the Tarot deck and the magick square for Mercury can be used for casting a hexagram:

- A complete deck of Tarot cards is shuffled and cut.
- One card is turned at a time until one card from each of two specific sets of cards turns up: the Ace through eight of Wands, and Key 0 through Key VII of the Major Arcana (The Fool through The Chariot).
- The first appearance of the selected Wand card is put aside, as is the first appearance of the selected Major Arcana card.
- As soon as the appropriate Wand card (Ace through Eight) and Major Arcana card (Key 0 through VII) appear, the hexagram has been cast and no further cards are drawn.
- The Wand and Major Arcana card drawn are the horizontal and vertical axis of the Mercury square. From their intersection, the number of the Mercury square that is selected is the number of the hexagram cast.
- If a changing line is desired, two hexagrams are cast and the lines which are different in these two hexagrams become the changing lines.
- The Mercury magick square correctly gridded by the Tarot cards for generating an *I Ching* hexagram is as follows.

Mercury Square Hexagram Generator

		Major Arcana							
		Key 0	Key I	Key II	Key III	Key IV	Key V	Key VI	Key VII
Wands	Ace	8	58	59	5	4	62	63	1
	2	49	15	14	52	53	11	10	56
	3	41	23	22	44	48	19	18	45
	4	32	34	38	29	25	35	39	28
	5	40	26	27	37	36	30	31	33
	6	17	47	46	20	21	43	42	24
	7	9	55	54	12	13	51	50	16
	8	64	2	3	61	60	6	7	57

The Major Arcana cards of Key 0 through VII are used to correspond to the first eight Hebrew letter-numerals, symbolizing the number progression of the eight trigrams.

The Wand cards of Ace through Eight of Wands are used to symbolize the divining rods or yarrow stalks cast to generate the oracular image.

The Mercury Square is used to combine the *I Ching* order with the Western Mercurial arrangement of the 32 symmetrical pairs of numbers, each totaling 65.

The Pattern Behind the Sequence of 64 Hexagrams

King Wen's *I Ching* possesses many levels of interpretation for this sequencing of the 64 hexagrams. The four basic permutations (of Nuclear, Reversed, Overturned, and Changing Line) form, in their combination, one basic progression of the 64 hexagrams as 32 mirror-image pairs: the underlying pattern to the order of the *I Ching* is 32 pairs of mirror images based on the six yao as Yin or Yang.

If the *I Ching* is viewed in light of the four basic hexagram permutations ordering 32 pairs of hexagrams, the permutation which predominates is the Overturned Hexagram that turns the six yao of each hexagram upside down. In all, 29 of the 32 pairs are Overturned permutations of each other.

However, the first pair (Hexagrams 1 and 2) is generated by the Changing Line permutation, while the only appearance of the Nuclear Trigram permutation appears in the 32nd and last pair (Hexagrams 63 and 64). This last pair of hexagrams is also the only pair that can be permutated by all four basic methods.

As to the permutation of Reversed Trigrams, in every appearance of this permutation, the permutation of Overturned can also be applied. However, in the sixth pair (Hexagrams 11 and 12), the third permutation of Changing Line as well as Reversed and Overturned governs the pairing of the hexagrams.

In addition to the four basic hexagram permutations, these 32 pairs can be viewed as six yao of Yin and Yang mirror images. The first pair shows Yang in all six yao in Hexagram 1, mirrored by Yin in all six yao of Hexagram 2. The last pair shows Yang in yao one, three, and five for Hexagram 63, while Yin is in yao one, three, and five for Hexagram 64.

This Yin-Yang mirror imaging is very complex but is intentionally employed in the original ordering of the hexagrams for the *I Ching* (or Chou I) by King Wen.

Since the 64 hexagrams are ordered as 32 pairs, a very obvious parallel can be drawn between these 32 pairs and the 32 Paths of the Western Tree of Life, further uniting Eastern and Western magickal symbolism in the *I Ching*.

The method upon which this ordering is based links the first two hexagrams with the first Path on the Tree of Life and the last two hexagrams with the 32nd Path.

The following three tables delineate these three symbol sets for the 32 hexagram pairs: (1) as four basic permutations, (2) as Yin and Yang, and (3) as the 32 Paths of the Tree of Life.

The Permutations Which Generate
the Thirty-Two Pairs of Hexagrams

Hexagram Pair	Order	Permutation
1 & 2	1st	Changing Line
3 & 4	2nd	Overturned
5 & 6	3rd	Reversed, Overturned
7 & 8	4th	Reversed, Overturned
9 & 10	5th	Overturned
11 & 12	6th	Reversed, Overturned, Changing Line
13 & 14	7th	Reversed, Overturned
15 & 16	8th	Overturned
17 & 18	9th	Overturned, Changing Line
19 & 20	10th	Overturned
21 & 22	11th	Overturned
23 & 24	12th	Overturned
25 & 26	13th	Overturned
27 & 28	14th	Changing Line
29 & 30	15th	Changing Line
31 & 32	16th	Overturned
33 & 34	17th	Overturned
35 & 36	18th	Reversed, Overturned
37 & 38	19th	Overturned
39 & 40	20th	Overturned
41 & 42	21st	Overturned
43 & 44	22nd	Overturned
45 & 46	23rd	Overturned
47 & 48	24th	Overturned
49 & 50	25th	Overturned
51 & 52	26th	Overturned
53 & 54	27th	Overturned, Changing Line
55 & 56	28th	Overturned
57 & 58	29th	Overturned
59 & 60	30th	Overturned
61 & 62	31st	Overturned
63 & 64	32nd	Nuclear, Reversed, Overturned and Changing Line

Thirty-two Hexagram Pairs as Yin and Yang

Hexagram	Yin/Yang Mirror Image
1 & 2	1 has all Yang; 2 has all Yin
3 & 4	3 has Yang in yao 1, 5; 4 has Yang in yao 2, 6
5 & 6	5 has Yin in yao 4, 6; 6 has Yin in yao 1, 3
7 & 8	7 has Yang in yao 2; 8 has Yang in yao 5
9 & 10	9 has Yin in yao 4; 10 has Yin in yao 3
11 & 12	11 has Yang in inner trigram, Yin in outer; 12 has Yin in inner trigram, Yang in outer
13 & 14	13 has Yin in yao 2; 14 has Yin in yao 5
15 & 16	15 has Yang in yao 3; 16 has Yang in yao 4
17 & 18	17 has Yang in yao 1, 4, 5; 18 has Yin in yao 1, 4, 5
19 & 20	19 has Yang in yao 1, 2; 20 has Yang in yao 5, 6
21 & 22	21 has Yang in yao 1, 4, 6; 22 has Yang in yao 1, 3, 6
23 & 24	23 has Yang in yao 6; 24 has Yang in yao 1
25 & 26	25 has Yin in yao 2, 3; 26 has Yin in yao 4, 5
27 & 28	27 has Yang in yao 1, 6; 28 has Yin in yao 1, 6
29 & 30	29 has Yang in yao 2, 5; 30 has Yin in yao 2, 5
31 & 32	31 has Yang in yao 3, 4, 5; 32 has Yang in yao 2, 3, 4
33 & 34	33 has Yin in yao 1, 2; 34 has Yin in yao 5, 6
35 & 36	35 has Yang in yao 4, 6; 36 has Yang in yao 1, 3
37 & 38	37 has Yin in yao 2, 4; 38 has Yin in yao 3, 5
39 & 40	39 has Yang in yao 3, 5; 40 has Yang in yao 2, 4
41 & 42	41 has Yin in yao 3, 4, 5; 42 has Yin in yao 2, 3, 4
43 & 44	43 has Yin in yao 6; 44 has Yin in yao 1
45 & 46	45 has Yang in yao 5, 6; 46 has Yang in yao 2, 3
47 & 48	47 has Yang in yao 2, 4, 5; 48 has Yang in yao 2, 4, 6
49 & 50	49 has Yin in yao 2, 6; 50 has Yin in yao 1, 5
51 & 52	51 has Yang in yao 1, 4; 52 has Yin in yao 3, 6
53 & 54	53 has Yang in yao 3, 5, 6; 54 has Yin in yao 3, 5, 6
55 & 56	55 has Yang in yao 1, 3, 4; 56 has Yang in yao 3, 4, 6
57 & 58	57 has Yin in yao 1, 4; 58 has Yin in yao 3, 6
59 & 60	59 has Yang in yao 2, 5, 6; 60 has Yang in yao 1, 2, 5
61 & 62	61 has Yin in yao 3, 4; 62 has Yang in yao 3, 4
63 & 64	63 has Yang in yao 1, 3, 5; 64 has Yin in yao 1, 3, 5

Thirty-Two Pairs of Hexagrams as the
Thirty-Two Paths of the Tree of Life

Hexagram Pair	Path of Tree of Life Number	Name	Zodiacal Quality
1 & 2	1	Kether	Primum Mobile
3 & 4	2	Chockmah	Zodiacal Belt
5 & 6	3	Binah	Saturn
7 & 8	4	Chesed	Jupiter
9 & 10	5	Geburah	Mars
11 & 12	6	Tiphereth	Sun
13 & 14	7	Netzach	Venus
15 & 16	8	Hod	Mercury
17 & 18	9	Yesod	Moon
19 & 20	10	Malkuth	The Four Elements
21 & 22	11	Aleph	Air (Spirit)
23 & 24	12	Beth	Mercury
25 & 26	13	Gimel	Moon
27 & 28	14	Daleth	Venus
29 & 30	15	Heh	Aries
31 & 32	16	Vav	Taurus
33 & 34	17	Zain	Gemini
35 & 36	18	Cheth	Cancer
37 & 38	19	Teth	Leo
39 & 40	20	Yod	Virgo
41 & 42	21	Kaph	Jupiter
43 & 44	22	Lamed	Libra
45 & 46	23	Mem	Water
47 & 48	24	Nun	Scorpio
49 & 50	25	Samekh	Sagittarius
51 & 52	26	Ayin	Capricorn
53 & 54	27	Peh	Mars
55 & 56	28	Tzaddi	Aquarius
57 & 58	29	Qoph	Pisces
59 & 60	30	Resh	Sun
61 & 62	31	Shin	Fire (Spirit)
63 & 64	32	Tav	Saturn (Earth)

ADDITIONAL ESOTERIC PATTERNS OF THE *I CHING*

Beyond the 32 hexagram pairs, the *I Ching* possesses in its complex ordering many subsets of symbols involving selected hexagrams as they appear in the serial order of the 64 hexagrams. Six of these subsets are as follows.

1. Twelve-Hexagram Cycle

Twelve select hexagrams were used to describe the movement upward of Yang from the first yao to the sixth, and then Yang's recession back into Yin beginning with the first yao. The cycle is then Yin to Yang to Yin, showing that strength can never last forever but will always be obscured by the return of the weak. These 12 hexagrams also describe the circulation of light or energy (Chi) through the body by Taoist meditation techniques. This circulation starts at the back of the body at the base of the spine and moves upward over the top of the head and then down the front of the body in an oval motion.

Since there are 12 select hexagrams, each represents an earthly branch. The first select hexagram (the 24th, Fu) corresponds to the first earthly branch (Tze) and Zodiacal sign (Rat).

This cycle of 12 divides the year as well into 12 stations of light and dark beginning with the 30 days after the winter solstice. This point corresponds roughly to the Western Zodiacal sign of Capricorn. Therefore the Western Zodiacal cycle from Capricorn to Sagittarius roughly corresponds to these 12 hexagrams.

The table on the following pages shows the Taoist cycle of 12 hexagrams with the corresponding symbols of Earthly Branch, Chinese and Western Zodiac, Taoist circulation system, the cycle of life, and the cycle of Yin and Yang.

The Taoist Circulation of Light in the Subtle Body of Man and the Twelve-Hexagram Cycle of Yin and Yang

Order	Twelve Hexagrams	Twelve Earthly Branches	Chinese Zodiac Signs	Taoist Circulation System	Cycle of Life	Cycle of Yin and Yang	Western Zodiac
1st	24. Fu Return	Tze (Child)	Rat	Chi enters at the lowest gate at the base of the spine	Return from death, renewal, reincarnation, the beginning of birth, coitus	Yang enters at the first yao	Capricorn
2nd	19. Lin Approach	Chu (Cord)	Ox	Chi moves up the back to the level of the Lowest Cauldron	First three months' growth of fetus	Yang moves upward to the first two yao	Aquarius
3rd	11. T'ai Peace	Yin (Revere)	Tiger	Chi moves up the back to the level of the Middle Cauldron	Fourth and fifth month of fetus	Yang dominates the lower trigram of three yao	Pisces
4th	34. Ta Chung The Power of the Great	Mao (Time)	Rabbit	Chi passes through the Middle Gate of the back	Fifth through ninth month of fetus (full growth)	Yang outnumbers Yin and encroaches from below	Aries

The Taoist Circulation of Light in the Subtle Body of Man and the Twelve-Hexagram Cycle of Yin and Yang (cont'd.)

Order	Twelve Hexagrams	Twelve Earthly Branches	Chinese Zodiac Signs	Taoist Circulation System	Cycle of Life	Cycle of Yin and Yang	Western Zodiac
5th	43. Kuai Break Through	Chen (Vibration)	Dragon	Chi moves up the back to the level of the Heart	The moment of birth, breakthrough	All but the last or highest place has been changed to Yang	Taurus
6th	1. Ch'ien The Creative	Ssu (End)	Snake	Chi enters the Jade Gate of the Head	From the moment of birth to full growth	All Yang (Light)	Gemini
7th	44. Kou Coming to Meet	Wu (Oppose)	Horse	Chi circulates to the top of the Head	End of youth and beginning of adulthood	Yin enters at the first yao	Cancer
8th	33. Tun Retreat	Wei (Not yet)	Sheep (Goat)	Chi moves over the head from the back to the front of the body and enters the Top Cauldron—Shen	Old age causing retreat of vital energy and restraint	Yin moves upward and gaint the first two yao	Leo

The Taoist Circulation of Light in the Subtle Body of Man and the Twelve-Hexagram Cycle of Yin and Yang (cont'd.)

Order	Twelve Hexagrams	Twelve Earthly Branches	Chinese Zodiac Signs	Taoist Circulation System	Cycle of Life	Cycle of Yin and Yang	Western Zodiac
9th	12. P'i Standstill	Shen (Expand)	Monkey	Chi descends into the fire of the Heart	Death becoming the focus of one's attention, stagnation replacing growth	Yin dominates the lower, Yang dominates the upper	Virgo
10th	20. Kuan Contemplation	Yu (Ripe)	Cock	Chi descends into the Middle Cauldron—Ch'i	Contemplation of one's life; preparing for death	Yin outnumbers Yang and enters above from below	Libra
11th	23. Po Splitting Apart	Shu (Guard)	Dog	Chi descends into the Lowest Cauldron—Ching	The moment of death, last hour of life on earth	All but the last or highest place has been changed to Yin	Scorpio
12th	2. K'un The Receptive	Hai (Kernel)	Pig (Boar)	Chi descends to the perineum between the genitals and anus	Death winning over life; the afterlife and potential of rebirth	All Yin (Dark)	Sagittarius

2. IAO Order

The Greek triliteral name for God, the Gnostic Trigrammaton IAO (IAΩ), is composed of the middle, first, and last vowel of the Greek alphabet. This first, middle, and last symbolism is also a basic pattern for King Wen's *I Ching* order: the hexagrams possess an IAO order which epitomizes the polarity of Yin and Yang and its tension.

Eight trigrams form the beginning, middle, and end of King Wen's *I Ching* order.

The beginning of this hexagram order (A of IAO) is formed by the first two hexagrams, Ch'ien and K'un. This pair is the ultimate Yang and Yin of the system, the only two pure hexagrams of Yang or Yin. Their interaction (as lovers) forms the other 62 hexagrams, Ch'ien being extreme Yang and K'un being extreme Yin. In Fu-Hsi's order they are the head and tail of the universe, the poles of South and North.

The middle of this hexagram order (the I of IAO) is formed by two pairs of hexagrams, the 11th and 12th, and the 29th and 30th. The 11th and 12th, T'ai and Pi, represent the first comingling of the trigrams of Heaven (Ch'ien) and Earth (K'un). In the 11th hexagram (Tai), Earth is in Heaven and Heaven is in Earth. In the 12th hexagram (Pi), Earth is in Earth and Heaven is in Heaven.

The second pair of trigrams that also occupy the middle further define the polairty of Yin and Yang, Earth and Heaven, as the Moon and Sun. The 29th hexagram, Kan, is composed of the double trigram K'an (The Moon), while the 30th hexagram, Li, is composed of the double trigram Li (The Sun). This middle pair of hexagrams shows Yin first dominating Yang (the 29th hexagram K'an as four Yin and two Yang yao) and then Yang dominating Yin (the 30th hexagram Li as four Yang and two Yin yao). In King Wen's order, these two hexagrams (K'an and Li) are the North and South Pole, while Fu-Hsi saw K'an as West and Li as East.

The end of this hexagram order (the O of IAO) is formed by the last two hexagrams, Chi Chi (the 63rd) and Wei Chi (the 64th).

Chi Chi (the 63rd and second to last hexagram) symbolizes: (1) Ch'ien as first, third, and fifth yao and K'un as the second, fourth, and sixth yao; (2) Li (Sun) below and K'an (Moon) above; (3) Yin and Yang in perfect proportion; (4) Yin and Yang in their auspicious places; (5) the four directions of the compass as light and then darkness; and (6) after completion, that which comes after the end of a cycle.

Wei Chi (the 64th and last hexagram) symbolizes: (1) Ch'ien as the second, fourth, and sixth yao and K'un as the first, third, and fifth yao; (2) Li (Sun) above and K'un (Moon) below; (3) Yin and Yang in perfect proportion; (4) Yin and Yang in their inauspicious places; (5) the four directions of the compass as darkness and then light; and (6) before completion, that which comes just before the end of a cycle.

In these last two hexagrams, the tension developed by the polarities of heaven and earth, Sun and Moon, above and below, East and West, North and South, and Yang and Yin resolve themselves in the proper intermingling of Yin and Yang for the six lines and two trigrams composing each of the 64 hexagrams.

The eight-trigram IAO cycle and its symbolic correspondences are shown in the table on the opposite page.

IAO Sequence of Eight Trigrams

Hexagrams	Trigrams		IAO Order	Fu-Hsi		King Wen		Yin/Yang Ratio	Yao Position + = Good, – = Bad					
	Inner	Outer		Inner	Outer	Inner	Outer		1st	2nd	3rd	4th	5th	6th
1 Ch'ien	Ch'ien	Ch'ien	First (A)	S	S	NW	NW	0:6	+	–	+	–	+	–
2 K'un	K'un	K'un	First (A)	N	N	SW	SW	6:0	–	+	–	+	–	+
11 T'ai	Ch'ien	K'un	Middle (I)	S	N	NW	SW	3:3	+	–	+	+	–	+
12 Pi	K'un	Ch'ien	Middle (I)	N	S	SW	NW	3:3	–	+	–	–	+	–

IAO Sequence of Eight Trigrams (cont'd.)

Hexagrams	Trigrams Inner	Outer	IAO Order	Fu-Hsi Inner	Outer	King Wen Inner	Outer	Yin/Yang Ratio	Yao Position + = Good, - = Bad 1st	2nd	3rd	4th	5th	6th
29 K'an	K'an	K'an	Middle (I)	W	W	N	N	2:4	-	-	-	+	+	+
30 Li	Li	Li	Middle (I)	E	E	S	S	4:2	+	+	+	-	-	-
63 Chi Chi	Li	K'an	Last (O)	E	W	S	N	3:3	+	+	+	+	+	+
64 Wei Chi	K'an	Li	Last (O)	W	E	N	S	3:3	-	-	-	-	-	-

3. Circular Arrangement of Shao Yung

All 64 hexagrams can be arranged to show this same Taoist circulation of Yin and Yang. The most famous of Taoist arrangements to capture this motion is the circular arrangement of Shao Yung.

This circular arrangement places the first hexagram, Ch'ien (composed of all Yang), at the top point of the circle (which is South), and the second hexagram, K'un (composed of all Yin), opposite Ch'ien at the bottom of the circle (North). Between these two poles the remaining 62 hexagrams are arranged to show a balanced distribution of Yin and Yang between the South and North pole.

However, a secret order further refines Shao Yung's Taoist order by showing the 64 hexagrams as Yin ascending from the bottom yao of Earth to the top yao of Heaven as all Yang. This filling the dark by the light is based on the sequence of the eight trigrams as Yin moving upward to Yang as follows.

The Trigrams as Dark Ascending to Light

Eight Trigrams		Circulation of Light	Nature
	K'un	All Yin and No Yang	Earth
	Chen	Yang enters by the first Yao	Fire
	K'an	Yang moves to the Middle	Moon
	Ken	Yang rises to the Top	Mountain
	Tui	Yang controls the first two Yao	Water
	Li	Yang gains Top by losing Middle	Sun
	Sun	Yang moves up to conquer the Middle and Top but loses its Base	Wind
	Ch'ien	Yang fills all three Yao	Heaven

If the foregoing sequencing of the eight trigrams is applied to the 64 hexagrams at large, the following order of Yin changing to Yang can be overlaid on the magick square for Mercury.

Earth Ascending to Heaven
Yin Changing to Yang, Ordering the Sixty-Four Hexagrams

1	2	3	4	5	6	7	8
2. K'un	24. Fu	7. Shih	15. Chi'en	16. Yu	8. Pi	23. Po	19. Lin

9	10	11	12	13	14	15	16
36. Ming I	51. Chen	3. Chun	27. I	46. Sheng	40. Hsieh	29. K'an	4. Meng

17	18	19	20	21	22	23	24
62. Hsiao Kuo	39. Chien	52. Ken	45. Ts'ui	35. Chin	20. Kuan	11. T'ai	54. Kuei Mei

25	26	27	28	29	30	31	32
60. Chieh	41. Sun	55. Feng	63. Chi Chi	22. Pi	17. Sui	21. Shih Ho	42. I

33	34	35	36	37	38	39	40
32. Heng	48. Ching	18. Ku	47. K'un	64. Wei Chi	59. Huan	31. Hsien	56. Lu

41	42	43	44	45	46	47	48
53. Chien	12. P'i	34. Ta Chuang	5. Hsu	26. Ta Ch'u	58. Tui	38. K'uei	61. Chung Fu

49	50	51	52	53	54	55	56
49. Ko	30. Li	37. Chia Jen	25. Wu Wang	28. Ta Kuo	50. Ting	57. Sun	6. Sung

57	58	59	60	61	62	63	64
33. Tun	43. Kuai	14. Ta Yu	9. Hsiao Ch'u	10. Lu	13. T'ung Jen	44. Kou	1. Ch'ien

Regarding the table on the preceding page, the upper left corner is the first hexagram while the lower right is the 64th or last. The diagonal right-sloping line formed by the sequence of the 1st, 10th, 19th, 28th, 37th, 46th, 55th, and 64th hexagrams corroborates the Chou I order of King Wen's *I Ching*.

The first and last (64th) hexagrams correspond to King Wen's first and second hexagram, while the middle of this diagnoal line, the 28th and 37th, correspond to King Wen's last two hexagrams (the 63rd and 64th):

First, Middle, and Last Hexagrams

Hexagram	South-North Pole	King Wen's Arrangement	Earth Ascending to Heaven Square Arrangement
Ch'ien	Fu-Hsi's Eight	First (1st)	Last (64th)
K'un	Directions	Two (2nd)	First (1st)
Chi Chi	King Wen's Eight	Last (63rd)	Middle (28th)
Wei Chi	Directions	Two (64th)	Two (37th)

The last two hexagrams of King Wen's order for the *I Ching* conceal in their trigram order the very ideograms which compose the Chinese name *I Ching*. The 63rd and 64th hexagrams are each made up of the trigrams Li and K'an, the Sun and Moon, while the eight caligraphic strokes for *I Ching* are also the Sun and Moon; the Sun placed above the Moon.

The Name *I Ching*

Calligraphy	*I Ching* Title Stroke Count	Trans-literation	Meaning	Hexagram 63. Chi Chi	64. Wei Chi
彐	4	I (Yi)	Sun	Inner Trigram	Outer Trigram
刕	4	Ching (King)	Moon	Outer Trigram	Inner Trigram

The recurring four hexagrams on this diagonal are the four elemental double hexagrams (whose upper and lower trigrams are the same), as shown in the table at the top of the following page.

The Four Elemental Hexagrams

Hexagram	King Wen Sequence	Earth Ascending to Heaven Sequence	Element in Nature (777)
Chen	51	10th	Fire
Ken	52	19th	Earth
Tui	58	46th	Water
Sun	57	55th	Air

Two of the double hexagrams are excluded from this right-sloping diagonal line: K'an, the Moon, the 29th hexagram, and Li, the Sun, the 30th hexagram. These two hexagrams are located instead on the left-sloping diagonal line as the 50th and 15th in the sequence.

Their two substitutes on the right diagonal are Chi Chi and Wei Chi, which are each composed of both Sun and Moon trigrams as follows.

Sun and Moon Hexagrams

Missing Double Trigram	Trigram Outer	Inner	King Wen Order	Yin/Yang Sequence	Substitute Hexagram	Trigram Outer	Inner	King Wen Order	Yin/Yang Sequence
K'an	K'an	K'an	29th	15th	Wei Chi	Li	K'an	64th	37th
Li	Li	Li	30th	50th	Chi Chi	K'an	Li	63rd	28th

Again, the association of Sun and Moon describes the calligraphic strokes for *I Ching* (Sun-Moon).

The two central hexagrams on the left diagonal line (the 29th and 36th in sequence) are each composed of three Yin and three Yang lines. They are mirror images of each other (changing line hexagrams) in that the first, fourth, and sixth lines and the second, third, and fifth lines change to Yin and Yang. Both symbolize the 62 hexagrams stretched between all Yin and all Yang and are an attempt to reconcile Yin and Yang in a balanced arrangement that can be epitomized by Chi Chi and Wei Chi, King Wen's last two hexagrams (the middle two hexagrams of the right-sloping diagonal).

The Equalizing of Yin and Yang

Hexagram		King Wen Order	Yin/ Yang Sequence	Yin Yao	Yang Yao	Preponderance of Yin	Preponderance of Yang
	Pi	22	29th	2, 5, 6	1, 3, 4	Outer Trigram	Inner Trigram
	K'un	47	36th	1, 3, 4	2, 5 ,6	Inner Trigram	Outer Trigram

The remaining four trigrams are composed of uneven amounts of Yin and Yang in the ratio of 4:2 and 2:4; those contending ratios will be shown later in this section as the secret underlying tension that holds together the very framework of King Wen's *I Ching*. These four hexagrams and their ratio of Yin and Yang lines are shown on the following page.

The 4:2 Ratio of Yin and Yang

Hexagram		King Wen Order	Yin/Yang Sequence	Yin Yao	Yang Yao	Yin and Yang Predominating	Ratio of Yin to Yang
Lin		19	8th	3,4,5,6	1,2	Yin Above	4:2
Kuan		20	22nd	1,2,3,4	5,6	Yin Below	4:2
Ta Chuang		34	43rd	5,6	1,2,3,4	Yang Below	2:4
Tun		33	57th	1,2	3,4,5,6	Yang Above	2:4

If this magick square is turned upside down, the order then reveals Yang in all six yao draining to all Yin, light returning to dark.

4. Duplication of Trigrams

Eight select hexagrams appear in the cycle of 64 which are made up of one trigram duplicated above and below. The trigrams appear in the unique order of Ch'ien, K'un, K'an, Li, Chen, Ken, Sun, and Tui.

This order of appearance of eight trigrams corresponds to the compass points of Fu-Hsi. The four cardinal points appear first, then the four oblique points of the compass, as follows.

Eight Double-Trigram Hexagrams

Hexagram	Fu-Hsi Compass Point	Yin/Yang Configuration	Governing Trigram
1. Ch'ien Creative	S	All Yang	Ch'ien
2. K'un Receptive	N	All Yin	K'un
29. K'an Abysmal	W	Yang in Yao 2 and 5	K'an
30. Li Clinging	E	Yin in Yao 2 and 5	Li
51. Chen Arousing	NW	Yang in Yao 1 and 4	Chen
52. Ken Keeping Still	NE	Yang in Yao 3 and 6	Ken
57. Sun Gentle	SW	Yin in Yao 1 and 4	Sun
58. Tui Joyous	SE	Yin in Yao 3 and 6	Tui

When the order of the hexagrams is studied as to when all eight trigrams appear, by the 17th hexagram all eight trigrams have appeared in the outer trigram, while by the 18th hexagram all eight trigrams have appeared in the inner trigram.

5. Eight Directional Hexagrams

The trigram's dual directional attributes of Fu-Hsi and King Wen are concealed in a sequence of eight directional hexagrams, whose inner trigrams are in Fu-Hsi's order, while the outer trigrams are in King Wen's order.

These eight select hexagrams govern the eight compass points, Fu-Hsi's Pre-Heaven sequence forming the foundation trigram upon which King Wen's Later-Heaven sequence is placed. This order then shows a progression from the Pre-Heaven to the Later-Heaven directional arrangement.

The sequence of these eight hexagrams forms two concentric circles, with the inner circle as the eight inner trigrams and the outer circle as the eight outer trigrams. These are placed on eight directional spokes as follows.

The Eight Directional Hexagrams

Direction	Hexagram		Inner (Fu-Hsi) Pre-Heaven	Trigrams Outer (King Wen) Later-Heaven
S		14. Ta Yu (Possession in Great Measure)	Ch'ien	Li
N		8. Pi (Holding Together)	K'un	K'an
SW		46. Sheng (Pushing Upward)	Sun	K'un
NW		33. Tun (Retreat)	Ken	Ch'ien

The Eight Directional Hexagrams (cont'd.)

Direction	Hexagram		Inner (Fu-Hsi) Pre-Heaven	Trigrams Outer (King Wen) Later-Heaven
E		55. Feng (Abundance)	Li	Chen
W		47. K'un (Oppression)	K'an	Tui
SE		61. Chung Fu (Inner Truth)	Tui	Sun
NE		27. I (Corners of the Mouth)	Chen	Ken

6. The Battle of Yin and Yang

If the 64 hexagrams are measured by the occurrence of Yin and Yang in the six composite lines of each hexagram, the ultimate pattern behind the ordering of the 64 hexagrams can be discerned. Yin and Yang occur three times each in 20 hexagrams. A total of 15 hexagrams have four Yang and two Yin, while another 15 have two Yang and four Yin. There are 6 hexagrams with five Yang and one Yin while a parallel 6 have one Yang and six Yin. Finally, one occurrence of six Yang and one occurrence of six Yin round out the 64 hexagrams.

The 64 hexagrams, when ordered by the occurrence of Yin and Yang in the first 12 hexagrams, open up to a pattern which, though convoluted, can be mapped out.

In the first 12 hexagrams, Yin and Yang occur in alternating pairs as shown on the following page.

The Ratios of Yin and Yang

Number of Hexagram	Number of Lines	
	Yin	Yang
1	0	6
2	6	0
3	4	2
4	4	2
5	2	4
6	2	4
7	5	1
8	5	1
9	1	5
10	1	5
11	3	3
12	3	3

This pattern of zero-six, six-zero, four-two, two-four, five-one, one-five, and three-three measures the ebb and flow of the ordering for the 64 hexagrams (see table on next page).

This secret order when analyzed reveals that:

- The first two hexagrams, 1 and 2, are the only occurrences of pure Yang and pure Yin without any blending. Six Yang come first followed by six Yin.

- The first two hexagrams of purely Yang or Yin are counterbalanced by the 11th and 12th hexagrams, which are the first two appearances of equal portions of Yin and Yang.

- The last two hexagrams reinforce the position of the 11th and 12th, for the 63rd and 64th hexagrams end the cycle by combining three Yin and three Yang lines in equal portion.

- The first six pairs of numbers descend in the seven orders of Yin and Yang. Then, starting with 13 and 14, the numbers rise from three Yin and three Yang (found in the 11th and 12th hexagrams) to one Yin and five Yang, to the 15th and 16th hexagram with five Yin and one Yang (a mirror of the 13th and 14th).

- After this initial rise, the appearance of three Yin and three Yang (with the 17th and 18th hexagram) occurs again. This is to intersperse balance at times of great ascent (as well as descent). This will occur throughout the 64 hexagrams with the 63rd and 64th hexagram ending in perfect balance.

- The 19th and 20th hexagrams quickly rise to the number harmony of four Yin and two Yang, which will be the highest point on this graph throughout the remaining hexagrams.

The Yin and Yang of the Six Yao
The Secret Order of the *I Ching*

Number of Yao		Hexagram
Yin	**Yang**	
0	6	1
6	0	2
4	2	3 4 — 19 20 — 27 — 29
2	4	5 6 — 25 26 — 28 — 30
5	1	7 8 — 15 16 — 23 24
1	5	9 10 — 13 14
3	3	11 12 — 17 18 — 21 22 — 31 32
0	6	
6	0	
4	2	35 36 — 39 40 — 45 46 — 51 52 — 62
2	4	33 34 — 37 38 — 49 50 — 57 58 — 61
5	1	
1	5	43 44
3	3	41 42 — 47 48 — 53 54 55 56 — 59 60 — 63 64

- The 21st and 22nd hexagrams form the three-three balance that Yang and Yin seek to maintain throughout these 64 changes and is the low point of this graph (as six Yang, no Yin is the high point).

- The 23rd and 24th hexagrams now appear to end the sixth occurrence of five Yin and one Yang. The cycle of 19—20, 21—22, and 23—24 is paralleled in 39—40, 41—42, and 43—44 (the last of five 5 Yin and one Yang): 19–20 and 39–40 are both four Yin and two Yang, while 21–22 and 41–42 are both three Yin and three Yang. As five Yin and one Yang end on the 23rd and 24th hexagrams, one Yin and five Yang end on the 43rd and 44th hexagrams.

- Now from the pairing of the 25th and 26th hexagrams to the 61st and 62nd hexagrams, two Yin and four Yang quarrel with four Yin and two Yang, with three Yin and Yang interceding throughout the battle to even things out.

- The 27th and 28th hexagrams are the first two singular hexagrams since the 1st and 2nd. The 27th is four Yin and two Yang, while the 28th is two Yin and four Yang. These singular hexagrams battle again in the 29th and 30th, where 29th = 27th, and 28th = 30th.

- The 31st and 32nd hexagrams bring the battle to a point of rest with three Yin and three Yang in equal portions.

- Then the Yin/Yang battle of two-four, four-two, two-four, four-two occurs again with the 33rd, 34th, 35th, 36th, 37th, 38th, 39th, and 40th hexagrams.

- The 41st and 42nd hexagrams parallel the 31st and 32nd hexagrams in that they represent the second break from the battle of four Yin and two Yang with four Yang and two Yin.

- The appearance of the 43rd and 44th hexagrams represent one Yin and five Yang and end the cycle of 9th-10th, 13th-14th, and 43rd-44th. The 13th and 14th hexagrams (also one Yin and five Yang) were the first hexagrams on the graph to ascend from the descent begun with 1st-2nd and ending with 11th-12th. This pair of 43rd-44th hexagrams is the only occurrence since the 25th hexagram of another pair of Yin and Yang other than four-two, two-four, or three-three.

- The 45th and 46th hexagrams represent an ascent as high as the hexagrams can go (four Yin and two Yang), followed by the 47th and 48th hexagrams again equaling the six lines out to three Yin and three Yang.

- The 49th-50th and 51st-52nd resume the contention of two Yin-four Yang with four Yang-two Yin.

- This is followed by the only occurence of the same Yin and Yang count four times in a row, being three Yin and three Yang in the 53rd, 54th, 55th, and 56th hexagrams. Note that in the last 12 hexagrams, and equal balance of Yin and Yang occurs eight times.

- This is followed by the 57th and 58th, the last pair of hexagrams with two Yin and four Yang (the first after the initial 12 being the 25th and 26th).

- The 59th and 60th bring matters back to peace, with three Yin and three Yang, followed by the last quarrel of two-four and four-two.

- The 61st hexagram is the last singular instance of two Yin and four Yang, while the 62nd hexagram is the last singular instance of four Yin and two Yang, suggesting that four Yin and two Yang have won out over four Yang and two Yin.

- The hexagrams now end in harmony with the 63rd and 64th restoring peace as three Yin and three Yang.

THE NINE NUMBERS AND THE CHINESE MAGICK SQUARE OF NINE

Two magickal diagrams appearing in the "Ten Wings" of the *I Ching* are the source for Chinese numerology for the first nine numbers (1 through 9) and the cipher (0) as the number ten. These two diagrams are described as "River" maps, and in their flow of numbers combine the eight basic trigrams of the *I Ching* with the nine basic numbers and zero as ten. The first diagram is the Yellow River Map (Ho T'u) of Fu-Hsi, while the second is the Writing from the River Lo (Lo Shu) of Master Yu.

These two magickal river diagrams were first seen in vision emblazoned upon the backs of two mythic animals. Fu-Hsi beheld in a vision the Yellow River Map as interconnecting dots upon the back of a mythic Dragon-Horse rising from the Yellow River (around 2900 BCE). Master Yu beheld the Lo Shu Map in a vision as a magick square of nine cells marked on the shell of a mythic Striped Turtle rising from the Lo River (around 2000 BCE). Both mythic animals also bore upon their backs the eight trigrams in, respectively, Fu-Hsi's and King Wen's directional arrangements.

Yellow River Map

Fu-Hsi's Yellow River Map shows the cycle of the number series 1 through 10 as five elemental pairs of odd and even. The five elements are spread to the five directions, and the pattern behind this diagram can be seen as a directional-elemental cross:

	S Fire	
E Wood	Center Earth	W Metal
	Water N	

To this four-directional cross are added the ten numbers as five pairs of odd-even numbers forming Fu-Hsi's Yellow River Map:

(Note that 5 is in the center surrounded by 10.)

The 10 numbers are arranged in such a way that the total value of 15 is produced in four ways by a southeast-northwest diagonal:

$$8 + 7 = 15$$

$$3 + 2 + (5) + 1 + 4 = 15$$

$$10 + 5 = 15$$

$$6 + 9 = 15$$

This sum value of 15 is also the basis for the arrangement of the second river diagram, Lo Shu. Note that the four extreme points of the Yellow River map contain the four coin values for casting a hexagram: six, seven, eight, and nine. Six is Yin changing to Yang, seven is Yang, eight is Yin, and nine is Yang changing to Yin.

The complete set of attributes for the ten numbers described by Fu-Hsi's river map is shown in the table on the opposite page.

Yellow River Number Map

Number	Element	Direction	Heaven and Earth	Odd and Even	White and Black
1	Water	N	Heaven	Odd	White
2	Fire	S	Earth	Even	Black
3	Wood	E	Heaven	Odd	White
4	Metal	W	Earth	Even	Black
5	Earth	Center	Heaven	Odd	White
6	Water	N	Earth	Even	Black
7	Fire	S	Heaven	Odd	White
8	Wood	E	Earth	Even	Black
9	Metal	W	Heaven	Odd	White
10	Earth	Center	Earth	Even	Black

The main difference between Fu-Hsi's Yellow River Map and Yu's Lo River Map is the omission of the number 10 in the center of Yu's revised Lo River Map.

The Chinese calligraphic numeral name for ten is "Shr," formed by the crossing of two lines (+), suggesting the shape of the Yellow River Map.

This character is affixed to all numeral names beyond ten which have a positional zero (such as 20, 30, 40, etc.) As such, this 10 is equivalent to zero as a positional value, and the 10 in the center of Fu-Hsi's Yellow River Map should be viewed in this light. Fu-Hsi's numeral map can therefore show the first nine numbers and the cipher zero.

River Writing Map

The second arrangement of numbers known as Yu's Lo Shu (or River Writing Map) is the Eastern source for the Western hermetic-alchemical tradition of planetary squares. This River Map of Yu is known in the West as the planetary magickal square for Saturn. The nine numbers are arranged in such a way that any line of three numbers totals to 15 (the diagonal value of Fu-Hs's arrangement):

4	9	2
3	5	7
8	1	6

It is assumed by this diagram that 10 as 0 is also in the central square, which as zero does not affect the summations of 15.

These nine numbers are each in turn a direction in space, modeled after Fu-Hsi's directional map, with South above and North below. The directions to this square are as follows:

SE	S	SW
E	Center	W
NE	N	NW

This is the source for King Wen's allocation of the eight trigrams to the eight compass points (as Fu-Hsi's river map is his own source for his heavenly directional arrangment of the eight trigrams). As such, the eight trigrams can be allocated to the eight border squares, while the center is Yin and Yang combined in harmony.

Sun	Li	K'un
Chen	Yin and Yang	Tui
Ken	K'an	Chien

This nine-number system has two sets of trigram attributes. The first set is based on King Wen's Later Heaven (or Terrestrial) arrangement and is the set of allocations found in the "Ten Wings" of the *I Ching*. A second secret set is based on Fu-Hsi's Pre-Heaven (or Celestial) arrangement.

King Wen's attributions apply to numbers when used in speculation of worldly matters, especially gambling. Fu-Hsi's attributions apply to numbers when measuring the heavenly bodies or divining the ways of the Gods.

Fu-Hsi's own Pre-Heaven directions offer a secret alternate trigram order as follows:

Tui	Ch'ien	Sun
Li	Yin and Yang	K'an
Chen	K'un	Ken

However, all Lo Shu allocations are based on King Wen's directional trigrams.

Out of these three allocations of number, direction, and trigram evolved the basis for all Chinese numerological attributions for the numbers 1 through 9.

In terms of good and bad luck (auspicious and inauspicious numbers), the directional coordinates of Northeast and Southwest determine whether a number is lucky or unlucky.

The Northeast corner of the magick square (composed of N, NE, E) symbolizes good luck, the center of the square average luck, and the remaining southwesterly squares (SE, S, SW, W, NW) bad luck.

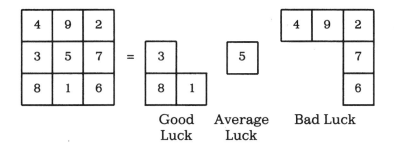

Good   Average   Bad Luck
Luck   Luck

The complete allocations for the nine numbers according to Yu's writing of the River Map are given on the following page.

Lo Shu Number Map

Number	Direction	Element	Trigram (King Wen)	Trigram Element	Luck	Divinatory Meaning	Alternate Trigram (Fu-Hsi)
1	N	Water	K'an	Water	Chi—Lucky	Difficulties at beginning; opposition; advance is blocked	K'un
2	SW	Earth	K'un	Earth	Chiu—Error	To base one's present position on past accomplishments; Creativity may not be tapped	Sun
3	E	Wood	Chen	Thunder	Hsiang—Good Luck	Advance is possible; to take the initiative; progress	Li
4	SE	Wood	Sun	Wind (Wood)	Lin—Regret	To concentrate; to direct one's progress; to travel	Tui
5 (10 as 0)	Center	All	Tao-Teh (Tai Chi)	Yin and Yang	P'ing—Average	Goal reached; peace, rest; accord; internalization	Tai Chi symbol
6	NW	Metal	Ch'ien	Heaven	Hui—Rejection	To attack with strength; to meet your opposition; to advance through one's ambition	Ken
7	W	Metal	Tui	Lake	Tsai—Catastophe	To find joy in one's accomplishments; to reap the benefit of one's efforts	K'an
8	NE	Earth	Ken	Mountain (Earth)	Hsiu—Fortune	A winding down of one's efforts; Reaching completion; ending one project and starting another	Chen
9	S	Fire	Li	Fire	Hsiung—Bad Luck	To end what one begins; to bring into manifestation what one visualizes; to have one's accomplishments visible to all	Ch'ien

Ultimately this nine-celled magick square of nine numbers known as Lo Shu is expanded into nine separate houses of nine squares, known as the Lo Shu System of Nine Houses.

Each house, or magick square, corresponds to one of the eight directions and its center. The number in the central square of each house corresponds to that number in the original Lo Shu square of nine. In essence, each of the nine numbers possesses its own unique magick square of nine squares, whose summations are in harmony with that specific number. The nine-house system is as follows:

Lo Shu System of Nine Houses

SE

3	8	1
2	4	6
7	9	5

S

8	4	6
7	9	2
3	5	1

SW

1	6	8
9	2	4
5	7	3

E

2	7	9
1	3	5
6	8	4

Center

4	9	2
3	5	7
8	1	6

W

6	2	4
5	7	9
1	3	8

NE

7	3	5
6	8	1
2	4	9

N

9	5	7
8	1	3
4	6	2

NW

5	1	3
4	6	8
9	2	7

Each of these nine houses is governed by the number within the central square. The eight variant squares around the central ninth, each correspond to a trigram and its varied symbolic attributes. The symbolism for each of these nine numeral houses are as follows.

Number: 1
  House of North

9	5	7
8	1	3
4	6	2

Trigram: K'an ☵

Element: Water

Planet: Mercury

Zodiac: Monkey, Cock, Dog, Pig

Color: Crimson (Red Violet)

Luck: Chi (Lucky)

Number Harmonies:

  Border Squares

   $S + N = 5 + 6 = 11 = 1 + 1 = 2$

   $E + W = 8 + 3 = 11 = 1 + 1 = 2$

   $SE + NW = 9 + 2 = 11 = 1 + 1 = 2$

   $NE + SW = 4 + 7 = 11 = 1 + 1 = 2$

  Center

   1 in Center is 1/2 of 2

Number: 2

House of Southwest

1	6	8
9	2	4
5	7	3

Trigram: K'un ☷

Element: Earth

Planet: Saturn

Zodiac: Snake

Color: Black

Luck: Chui (Error)

Number Harmonies:

Border Squares

$S + N = 6 + 7 = 13 = 1 + 3 = 4$

$E + W = 9 + 4 = 13 = 1 + 3 = 4$

$SE + NW = 1 + 3 = 4$

$NE + SW = 8 + 5 = 13 = 1 + 3 = 4$

Center

2 in Center is 1/2 of 4

Number: 3
House of East

2	7	9
1	3	5
6	8	4

Trigram: Chen ☳

Element: Wood (Wind)

Planet: Jupiter

Zodiac: Rat

Color: Red-Orange

Luck: Hsiang (Good Luck)

Number Harmonies:

Border Squares

S + N = 7 + 8 = 15 = 1 + 5 = 6

E + W = 1 + 5 = 6

SE + NW = 2 + 4 = 6

NE + SW = 6 + 9 = 15 = 1 + 5 = 6

Center

3 in Center is 1/2 of 6

Number: 4

House of Southeast

3	8	1
2	4	6
7	9	5

Trigram: Sun ☴

Element: Wood (Wind)

Planet: Jupiter

Zodiac: Ox

Color: Jade Green

Luck: Lin (Regret)

Number Harmonies:

  Border Squares

   $S + N = 8 + 9 = 17 = 1 + 7 = 8$

   $E + W = 2 + 6 = 8$

   $SE + NW = 3 + 5 = 8$

   $NE + SW = 7 + 1 = 8$

  Center

   4 in Center is 1/2 of 8

Number: 5 (also 10 and 0)
House of the Center

4	9	2
3	5	7
8	1	6

Trigram: All eight trigrams as directional diagram "Pa Kua"

Element: Yin and Yang (the building blocks of all five elements)

Planet: Earth as the center of the universe

Zodiac: The Sun in the center of the Zodiacal belt as the heart in the human body

Color: The Rainbow and Gray (White and Black mixture)

Luck: P'ing (Average, a balance between good and bad)

Number Harmonies:

Border Squares

$S + N = 9 + 1 = 10$

$E + W = 3 + 7 = 10$

$SE + NW = 4 + 6 = 10$

$NE + SW = 8 + 2 = 10$

Center

5 in Center is 1/2 of 10

(Note: In Yellow River Map, 10 is a substitute for 5 in the center. 10 is also 0.)

Number: 6

House of Northwest

5	1	3
4	6	8
9	2	7

Trigram: Ch'ien

Element: Metal

Planet: Venus

Zodiac: Horse

Color: White

Luck: Hui (Rejection)

Number Harmonies:

Border Squares

S + N = 1 + 2 = 12 (as 1 + 2)

E + W = 4 + 8 = 12

SE + NW = 5 + 7 = 12

NE + SW = 9 + 3 = 12

Center

6 in Center is 1/2 of 12

(where 12 = 1 + 2 = 3,
6 in center is twice 3)

Number: 7
    House of West

6	2	4
5	7	9
1	3	8

Trigram: Tui ☱

Element: Metal

Planet: Venus

Zodiac: Sheep (Goat)

Color: Deep Blue (Indigo)

Luck: Tsai (Catastrophe)

Number Harmonies:

    Border Squares

        S + N = 2 + 3 = 5 (as 1 + 4)

        E + W = 5 + 9 = 14

        SE + NW = 6 + 8 = 14

        NE + SW = 1 + 4 = 14

    Center

        7 in Center is 1/2 of 14 (14 = 1 + 4 = 5)

Number: 8

House of Northeast

7	3	5
6	8	1
2	4	9

Trigram: Ken ☶

Element: Earth

Planet: Saturn

Zodiac: Dragon

Color: Bright Yellow

Luck: Hsiu (Fortune)

Number Harmonies:

Border Squares

S + N = 3 + 4 = 7 (as 1 + 6)

E + W = 6 + 1 = 16 (as 1 + 6)

SE + NW = 7 + 9 = 16

NE + SW = 2 + 5 = 7 (as 1 + 6)

Center

8 in Center is 1/2 of 16 (16 = 1 + 6 = 7)

Number: 9
   House of South

8	4	6
7	9	2
3	5	1

Trigram: Li   ☲

Element: Fire

Planet: Mars

Zodiac: Tiger and Rabbit

Color: Yellow-Orange

Luck: Hsiung (Bad Luck)

Number Harmonies:

   Border Squares

      S + N = 4 + 5 = 9

      E + W = 7 + 2 = 9

      SE + NW = 8 + 1 = 9 (as 1 + 8 = 18)

      NE + SW = 3 + 6 = 9

   Center

      9 in center is equal to its borders

      (and 1/2 of 18)

By their trigram allocations, any of the 64 hexagrams can generate two Lo Shu number squares corresponding to the inner and outer trigrams.

As an example, the last hexagram, Wei Chi is made up of the two trigrams K'an and Li . These two trigrams correspond to the Lo Sho numbers of 9 (K'an) and 1 (Li). Thus the 64th heagram Wei Chi can be seen as the numbers 9 and 1.

These squares can also be used to determine the divinatory nature of any date in two ways:

1. To find any date, refer only to the last digit of the date (1904 = 4). This number refers to the corresponding Lo Shu Directional House. In the case of the last digit of the date being zero, use the directional house for 5 (whose alternate number values are 10 and 0).

2. A more complicated system uses the method of reduction found in the bordering squares of each house. Add the digits of a date together, reducing it to 1 through 9 (1904 = 1 + 9 + 0 + 4 = 14 = 1 + 4 = 5). In the case of 10, reduce the number to 1 (as 1 + 0 = 1). The resultant number corresponds to the particular Lo Shu directional house.

These two methods work especially well with the sexegenany cycle of 10 stems and 12 branches. Thus 1904 CE is the 41st combination of Chia-Chen in the cycle of 60.

By the first method, 41 = 1, 1904 CE would thus indicate the first directional house.

By the second method, 41 = 4 + 1=5, 1904 CE would thus indicate the fifth directional house.

Chinese Magick Squares East and West

The basic nine-cell Chinese magick square contains in its construction a fixed series of four numbers: 3, 9, 15, and 45. The first number (3) is the number of squares of any given side. The second number (9) is the total number of cells composing the square. The third number (15) is the sum total for every row, column, and diagonal of three squares. The fourth number (45) is the total sum of the nine numbers on the nine cells of the square.

These four basic number values that govern the construction of the Chinese magick square can be deciphered when paralleled to the word-metaphors that total to these four numbers. The following table will provide the key phrases from the nine number-language traditions, both East and West, in which this square of nine numbers appears.

The following tables detail a fourfold symbolism for the magick square of nine cells:

- The nine numbers as a matrix for all words, colors, and planets

- A sigil of the planet Saturn as king or ruler of the other planets

- A sigil for the Godhead

- The path upon which man can become God, the path being the spine marked with the interior alchemical planets

Key to Chinese Magick Square of Nine

4	9	2
3	5	7
8	1	6

Number of squares on each side = 3

Total number of squares = 9

Sum of each row, column, or diagonal = 15

Total sum of all nine numbers = 45

Key to Chinese Magick Square of Nine

Language	Number Value of Number Metaphors			
	3	9	15	45
Chinese	DA (3 strokes)—Large, big, great, macrocosm (man outstretched as a pentagram) SHANG (3 stroke)—Above SYA (3 stroke)—Below	HSING (9 strokes)—The five planets, the stars	CHI KUNG (1 + 5 = 15)—The circulation of breath in the body as vital energy PO (15 strokes)—The animal soul, vital energy, unconscious	SHU MU (4 + 5 = 45)—The numbers, the numbers 1-9
Sanskrit (KaTaPaYaDhi)	Ba—Enlightenment, spirit, Mercury, Buddha-nature UDU—Stars NaGa—serpent, Kundalini	DhI—Thought, intellect, religious meditation, prayer, hymn; knowledge and understanding ADhI—Above, upwards, within ABDhI—Deep, below	YaMa—Saturn (traditional planet ruling square of nine) ÂKaSa—Ruling Tattva, ether, spirit, clear space, sky SYAMa—Black, blue, dark, dark gray	VaRNa—Letter, sound, color, word SVaRNa—Gold NIRVaNa—Cessation of finite existence; absolute existence, supreme bliss
Tibetan	Ga—Essence, Buddha, hidden	Ta—The door of admission to all things	NaD—Air, ether, vapor	LÑa Ba—Flash of light

Key to Chinese Magick Square of Nine (cont'd.)

Language	Number Value of Number Metaphors			
	3	9	15	45
Hebrew	AB—Father, originator, source, master, to go, flow out BA—To come back, return to the source	GV—The interior of the body, middle, back, spine T—The coiled serpent, secret of all spiritual activities	IH—Jah, God, Creator of number and alphabet, One absolute, Father (I), Mother (H) HVD—Glory, splendor (Mercury) HDV—India, the East	ADM—Adam, Man, Humanity AMD—The Fool AChD—One heart, one mind
Arabic (Eastern Code)	AB—Father, to move BA—To bring back down, to draw energy down from above	T—Secret knowledge, concealed wisdom BJD—Root, source, basis, essence JW—Sky, air,	HWD—The Jews, to return to one's duty HWA—Eve HY—She	ADM—Adam, mankind AMD-End, period, span DAM—To persevere, endure, remain; that which perpetually continues
Greek	AB—Father, as in ABBA—The father, and ABRAHAM—Abraham	AGE—Come on, lead, go to	DIA—Dis, Zeus, Godhead ThEA—Goddess GAIA—Goddess of Earth	ThHKH—Scabbard, sheath, receptacle BELH—Fiery darts

Key to Chinese Magick Square of Nine (cont'd.)

Language	Number Value of Number Metaphors			
	3	9	15	45
Enochian (Dee's Code)	L—The, One first God as the first AB—Daughters of Light	Q—Thy	IAD—God	MAD—The same your God EM—Nine I EL—Is one
Latin (Cabala Simplex)	C—The 3rd letter of Latin Cabala Simplex, Roman numeral 100, the kteis, the Moon	I—The 9th letter of Latin Cabala Simplex, Roman Numeral 1, the phallus, the sun	XV—Roman Numeral for last two letters of: LVX—"Light" in Latin	DEUS—God HOMO—Man, Humanity
English (Serial Order)	AB—AlphaBet	AH (AL II:66) HA (AL III:75) I (AL II:4) (Numeral for The Magician)	If (AL I:40) Face (AL III:52) 0 (Numeral for The Fool)	He, She (AL I:16) Gods (AL I:49) Dogs (AL II:27) Pit (AL II:27) A babe, an egg (AL II:40)

THE CHINESE CONCEPT OF ZERO AND THE 10 NUMBERS

At the very heart of Chinese Taoism is the mystical concept of the cipher as the Void or Ultimate Nothingness from which Yin and Yang emerge. This Chinese concept of Zero is referred to philosophically as Tao, Wu-Nien, and Wu-Wei.

- Tao—The Tao, literally, the way or path, is named variously as formless, nameless, the cause of all motion, the maker of all form. Out of the Tao emerges "Teh," the strength, vitality, and virtue of all living beings. Tao as Zero is the source of "Teh" as One. Teh further divides into Yin and Yang, the feminine and the masculine as Two.

$$TAO = 0$$
$$\downarrow$$
$$TEH = 1$$
$$\downarrow$$
$$YIN + YANG = 2$$

The Tao is that which is beyond all forms, thoughts and conceptions.

- Wu-Nien—The Buddhist concept of No-Thought, or No-Mind. As No Mind, Wu-Nien is the idea of an emptying of the lesser or outer self to reveal the true self, characterized as No-Thought; i.e., beyond ordinary thought.
  Here the concept of Zero is that which is beyond normal perception.

- Wu-Wei—The Buddhist concept of Non-Action. Wu-Wei represents the action experienced at the time of enlightenment (Satori), in which all previous action comes to No-Action. It is also action based on will rather than thought.
  Here the concept of Zero is that which is beyond all acting and actions.

All Three concepts of Tao, Wu-Nien, and Wu-Wei parallel the Hebrew Qabalistic concept of the Void as the Hebrew word AIN. Crowley discovered this correspondence in relating the Chinese cosmology to the Tree of Life.

The wedding of this Taoist cipher to the nine numbers of the Chinese magick square produces the number 10, and the number range 1 through 10 emanating out of zero, in which 10 represents a return to zero.

Both Chinese Chan Buddhism and Japanese Zen Buddhism developed a magickal series of ten illustrations each depicting in symbolism of the numbers 1 through 10, known as the "Ten Bulls" or the "Ten Ox-Herding Pictures."

Originally these illustrations may have comprised only a series of eight, but the ultimate form for both the Chinese and Japanese series consists of ten illustrations. The following two tables detail the Chinese and Japanese symbolism for the numbers 1 through 10.

The Ten Bulls of Ch'an Buddhism

Number	Image	Additional Symbols	Poem	Commentary
1	Cowherder (Self) holds out a green branch to attract the attention of the bull, who is running in an open field	Dark clouds conceal the Sun; bull is completely black	Attracting the bull	Attention (Awareness of Self
2	Bull is bridled by cowherder and lead by the nose	Sun and Moon absent from sky; bull is all black except for muzzle	Leading (Goading) the bull	Beginning of discipline
3	Bull on leash obediently follows cowherder	Sun and Moon concealed by mist in sky; Head and horns of bull are white, body is black	Whitening of the head (first transformation)	Perfecting the intellect
4	Bridle of bull is fastened to a willow tree	Sun in sky above willow tree; Front half of bull is white, back half is black	Tying the bull	Being bound to the law of karma
5	Bull follows behind cowherder obediently without bridle or ox-goad	Two rivers flow as one; Only the hind legs of the bull remain black	Leading the bull (without bridle)	Essence leads personality
6	The cowherder plays upon the flute to lull the bull into sleep	Mountain peak protrudes through fog; Only tail and rear end of bull remain black	Charming the bull	The taming of the outer by the inner

The Ten Bulls of Ch'an Buddhism (cont'd.)

Number	Image	Additional Symbols	Poem	Commentary
7	The bull roams free and drinks from a river at the bottom of a mountain while the cowherder sits in deep meditation	Sun in fog above two mountains; bull is all white	Freeing the bull	The inner free from the constraints of the outer
8	Cowherder and bull are one in heaven	Sun and Pole star in heaven; White bull in clouds (Earth disappeared)	Transmuting (transcending) the bull	The inner and the outer are one
9	Cowherder stands before an abyss, bull has fallen into the pit	Pole star, Sun and Big Dipper in sky; Mountain concealed by mist	Disappearance of the bull	The inner is all
10	Bull and cowherder are gone, beginning and end are joined in a circle	White circle being the zero symbol	The Infinite	Neither self (outer) nor not-self (inner)

The Ten Ox Herding Pictures of Zen Buddhism

Number	Image	Additional Symbols	Poem	Commentary
1	The ox herder with bridle and goad walks upon distant paths under a willow tree	Distant paths and rivers upon unknown mountain	Seeking (search for) the ox	Lost in the world and forgetting one's true nature
2	The ox herder runs after footprints under the cover of the clouds in the sky	Footprints along the riverbank under trees in remote mountains	Finding the tracks (discovering the footprints)	Not upon the path, but perceiving the path
3	The ox herder finds the ox hidden in the willow trees by a river	Ox hidden in the willow tree exposing only the hind end and tail	Perceiving the ox (first glimpse)	Entering the gate, first steps on the path
4	The ox herder bridles a charging ox	Ox runs to the heights of the mountain and the depths of the ravine	Catching the ox	The need for discipline
5	Ox herder leads ox down path with bridle and goad	Ox walks upon the path	Taming the ox	Persevering to the end, allowing no room for doubt
6	Ox herder rides atop ox while playing his flute	Clouds above in sky, ox beneath upon the path	Riding the ox home	To only be able to push onward upon the path to end the struggle for discipline
7	Ox herder, abandoning bridle and goad, sits at home alone; ox resting and concealed	Moon emerges from the clouds and illuminates the path below	The ox transcended (forgotten)	All is one, not two

The Ten Ox Herding Pictures of Zen Buddhism (cont'd.)

Number	Image	Additional Symbols	Poem	Commentary
8	The circle of heaven, ox and ox herder merge into the void	Circle whose beginning is joined to its end	Both ox and Self transcended	The mind freed from all limitations
9	The flowing river returns to its source	A river flows before the willow, the sky is filled with strewn leaves and flowers and a flying bird	Returning to the source	To observe all in silence to reflect all clearly while being nonattached
10	The ox herder with a wine bottle on his staff meets the Buddha in the marketplace	Mountain above, two men meet on a path, footprints unheeded	In the world (entering the marketplace with helping hands)	To be in the marketplace, dusty with the road without, clear as a diamond within

In the Chinese version of "The Ten Bulls," the tenth image is a white circle. This connects 10 with 0, a concept which occurs in Chinese numerical calculations, for the character for 10 (+) is also used as the place value of zero, when following another number.

For the Japanese "Ten Ox Herding Pictures," the eighth image is a white circle. This may be a reference to an earlier version which was comprised of only eight illustrations, ending with the circle (the 10th image in the Chinese version).

The addition of 9 and 10 to the Japanese version extends the imagery beyond Satori (symbolized by the circle). As 8 is Satori, 9 is the Buddhist reincarnation cycle and 10 is the Buddhist doctrine of Bodhisattva— the conscious choice to reincarnate into the world as a guide or helper for the still deluded human race rather than be absorbed into the Void (which is Zero).

One other Japanese Buddhist numerical system of symbolic images denoting spiritual awakening is the Soto Zen doctrine of five circles (derived from the school of Ts'ao Shan).

This system uses the numbers 1 through 5 as five different circles, each showing in its shape a stage of both individual spiritual development and the relationship of teacher and student. Like the Chinese Taoist symbol of the two fishes (T'ai Chi), the two basic circles are black and white, black being the most advanced stage. The table on the following page details the symbolism of the five circles.

The Soto Zen Numerical Doctrine of Five Circles

Number	Symbol	Circle	Image	Master/Disciple	Five Ranks of Attainment
1		Large black circle eclipses small white circle	Dark overshadowing light	Master looks down upon Disciple	First awareness of the higher self
2		Large white circle eclipses small black circle	Light overshadowing dark	Disciple identifies as servant of Master	The higher self overshadows temporal personality
3		Black point in center of white circle	Dewdrop on the shining sea	Disciple realizes he is only peripheral to the Master	The higher self as the hub of all mundane activity, the upcoming of the real world
4		White circle	All light	Disciple realizes he is within his Master	The black spot of not-seeing disappears with the light of illumination
5		Black circle	All dark	The Disciple becomes the Master, the Master becomes the Disciple	Non-action, no-mind, non-duality as a result of oneness with the universe

THE TAOIST CALLIGRAPHIC STROKE COUNT

The ultimate Chinese numerical system is alphanumeric in basis, for like the other languages studied in these keys, every word in Chinese can be reduced to a relevant numerical value.

This specific system of numbering a language is completely different in technique from that of any other isopsephic language, for it is based on the actual strokes of the pen that make up any word, verse, poem, or book.

The number of strokes required to execute any given character is uniform, based on a standardized sampling of character strokes known as the "214 Radicals." These 214 radical characters are the basic building blocks for all other written characters. These basic characters are grouped by the number of strokes required to execute a specific character, ranging from 1 to 17 strokes.

All Chinese dictionaries are ordered on the basis of stroke count. Indexes usually group all entries by the strokes required to execute each entry. This is such a basic concept that its esoteric application has escaped notice. Yet by the very application of the number of strokes required to execute any given character, the correct number value can be determined. The phonetic variations for the various Chinese characters do not affect the number value of any given calligraphic character, but the different styles in which a character can be written greatly affect the number value.

Chinese calligraphy has five basic variations in the style of writing script.

Seal Style (Chuan Shu)

The first script for Chinese, inscribed upon tortoise shell and animal bone, was ultimately used on all official seals—therefore the title Seal Style. This script can be distinguished from all other scripts by its use of curves, half circles, and full circles in the formation of ideograms. It is also the most hieroglyphic of all the Chinese styles. Surviving examples of this script date back to around 1800 BCE. It cannot be numbered by stroke count.

Official Style (Li-Shu)

This style was invented by Ch'eng Mao (around 246 BCE) as a replacement to the Seal Style. It became the official government script of the Chin Dynasty (hence the title Official Style). This is a very elegant square style of writing, replacing the curves of the Seal Script with straight, angular lines. The square nature of the alphabet and its ordered execution of lines is the source for the numbering of any given character by its composite strokes. This idea would find full fruition in the K'ai Shu or Regular Style.

Regular Style (K'ai-Shu)

The elegant and elongated court script of the Official Style became more bony and compact with the invention of the Regular Style. The creator is unknown, but it appeared between 200 BCE and 200 CE. This rigid script is the source of the modern square style of printed Chinese. It is the most typical style of executing Chinese and the most accessible style for accurately numbering Chinese.

Running Style (Hsing-Shu)

The fourth major Chinese script appeared around 300 CE as a freer, more spontaneous script. This cursive style was formed by the running hand of the scribe, hence the name Running Style. The curving flow of lines imbued the Taoist concept of Yin into a script which had become Yang by its square shape. This curving Running Style blurs the precise numerical calculations afforded by the Regular Style. However, each flowing stroke required to execute any given character became standardized after centuries of usage.

Grass Style (Ts'ao-Shu)

The fifth style is based on the Hsing-Shu style and first appeared around 400 CE. It is the most fluid and therefore Taoist-like script in its force, rapidity, and circularness. This style is considered the roughest and most uncultivated, hence the name Grass Style. This script in its resemblance to the flowing motion of coils of incense smoke or rippling, flowing water is the source for the Japanese flowing script epitomized in the art of Zen Buddhism. The Grass Style defies the numeration found in the K'ai-Shu script, but it is a style which allows for words to be secretly worked into artwork which depicts flowing water, smoke, or clouds. Like the Running Style, the order in which any given character would be spontaneously brushed out became standardized by the faithful copying of ancient examples of this script.

From the description of the five basic calligraphic styles, we can see that only the Official or Regular Style can be accurately numbered. To further complicate matters, there is a tendency in Modern Mandarin Chinese to simplify the stroke count of many characters, thereby distorting their true number value. It is therefore imperative when numbering Chinese to work with pre-revolutionary dictionaries, such as Fenn's *Five Thousand Dictionary,* or Wieger's *Chinese Characters,* which illustrate the more elaborate strokes for Chinese characters.

If one character alone is being numbered, the stroke count is the only concern in calculating its number value. But if more than one character occurs, such as a phrase, sentence, or verse, a more elaborate Taoist technique must be used in order to properly number this grouping. This technique is referred to as Chu-Ko's Spirit Calculation. In it, the stroke value of multiple characters is calculated as digital place values (without zero). Chu-Ko Liang was the founder of the Taoist Pole Star Sect (around 221 BCE), and his "Secret Book of Chu-Ko's Spirit Calculation" is preserved in the 29th section of the almanac *T'ung Shu.*

The essence of his numbering method which can be applied to any multiple set of characters is as follows.

- When more than one character appears in a phrase or verse that is being numbered, each character becomes the digit of a number.

- The first character has the highest positional value, while the last character has the lowest positional value (the units place)

- Thus, in a three-character phrase, the first character is the 100's place, the second is the 10's place, and the third and last is the unit's place.

- Each character is reduced to a one digit number if its intrinsic stroke count numbers beyond nine.

- If a character is composed of 10 or more strokes, only the units place is used as its number value.

- Thus a character whose stroke count is 13 becomes the number 3 as a composite digital number.

- The exception to this rule occurs when the stroke count is 10, 20 ,or 30 strokes. In this case only, the one digit number becomes 1 rather than 0.

A few examples of this elaborate method of numbering will help illustrate the Taoist technique.

Examples of Taoist Spirit Calculation

Characters	Stroke Count	Resultant Number	Meaning
Ming Wang Sying 冥 王 星 (10)　(4)　(9)	10 = 1, 4, 9	149	Pluto, King of Underworld Star
Tu Jung Hwang 土 中 黄 (3)　(4)　(11)	3, 4, 11 = 1	341	Earth, center and yellow (three symbols of spirit)
Yu Huang Da Di 玉 皇 大帝 (5)　(9)　(3) (9)	5, 9, 3, 9	5,939	The Jade Emperor (The Supreme Deity of Taoism)

Thus by employing both the simple stroke-count technique (derived from the concept of 214 radicals) and the more elaborate digital-positional multiple-character technique (derived from Chu-Ko's Spirit Calculation), the infinite number range can be fleshed out in meaning by the infinite combinations of the Chinese Regular Style calligraphic characters.

The basic Chinese calligraphic metaphors for the number range 0 to 33 are detailed in the following table.

Key Chinese Stroke Count Characters for the Number Range 0–33

Number	Character	Transliteration	Method of Calculation	Meaning
0	+	Shr	As a place value in numerals	The numeral name for ten (Shr) is used as a place value of zero for digits of composite numbers beyond ten
1	|	Yi	One Stroke	The number one as a horizontal line; the older form for "ten" was a vertical stroke in contrast to this horizontal stroke
2	<	Ren	Two Strokes	Man (Male, Yang)
3	夊	Nyu	Three Strokes	Woman (Female, Yin)
4	申	Jung	Four Strokes	Center, middle; as direction in human body: heart; as direction in world: China, the Middle Kingdom; as a hieroglyph: arrow piercing the center of the target
5	玉	Yu	Five Strokes	The precious stone jade (congealed dragon's semen found deep in the earth); the royal stone; the gem which partakes of three worlds, but is found between man and earth

Key Chinese Stroke Count Characters
for the Number Range 0–33 (cont'd.)

Number	Character	Transliteration	Method of Calculation	Meaning
6	字	Zi	Six Strokes	Word, written character, picture symbol (hieroglyph: child under a roof)
7	巫	Wu	Seven Strokes	Shaman, magician, wizard, witch; magick, divination, sorcery; (hieroglyph: two men climbing the world tree from earth to heaven)
8	金	Jing	Eight Strokes	Gold (good luck as eight) any precious metal; (hieroglyph: layers of metal concealed under the earth)
9	星	Hsing	Nine Strokes	Star, planet, the five Chinese elemental planets of Saturn, Jupiter, Mars, Venus, and Mercury
10	神	Shen	Ten Strokes	The Gods of the Heavens; the spirit (of vital energy) which ascends to the head; the illuminating fire of the mind
11	書	Shu	Eleven Strokes	Book; letter; to write, compose

Key Chinese Stroke Count Characters for the Number Range 0–33 (cont'd.)

Number	Character	Transliteration	Method of Calculation	Meaning
12		Dao	12 Strokes	The path, the way; the Tao, root of Taoism; the middle road
13		Ji	13 Strokes	The ultimate; universal energy; the vital energy of the universe; the Chi or Ki of martial arts
14		Jui	14 Strokes	Talisman; auspicious; good luck; jade amulet
15		Po	15 Strokes	Spirit; physical vigor; animal soul
16		Ch'ang	16 Strokes	The gate of heaven; light of dawn rising in the East; light of Sun through opened gates
17		Tai Chi	17 Strokes as 4 + 13 strokes	The great ultimate; the monad which contains the dyad emanating out of nothingness (Wu)

Key Chinese Stroke Count Characters for the Number Range 0–33 (cont'd.)

Number	Character	Transliteration	Method of Calculation	Meaning
18		Ku Wu	18 Strokes as 10 + 8 strokes and positional as (10 = 1) + (8)	To investigate the nature of things
19		Hwai	19 Strokes	Bad, evil; Inauspicious
20		Tang	20 Strokes	A secret lodge; to meet in secret; a dark house
21		Dao Jyao	As a positional number (12 = 2) + (11 = 1)	Taoism; The teaching of the Way
22		Ch'an	22 Strokes	The interior energy of the body (Chi) transmuted in a spiral direction as energy emanating from the body in clockwise and counterclockwise spirals; to bind up, wrap up the body in a spiral form like a silk cocoon
23		Yin Yang	23 Strokes as 11 + 12 strokes	Yin (the first even, 2) and Yang (the first odd, 3) as 23 strokes; 23 as Yin and Yang combined as 2 + 3 = 5

Key Chinese Stroke Count Characters
for the Number Range 0–33 (cont'd.)

Number	Character	Transliteration	Method of Calculation	Meaning
24	木火金林土	Mu Hwo Jing Shwei Tu	24 Strokes as 4 + 4 + 8 + 5 + 3 strokes	The five elements as the pentagonal Wood, Fire, Metal, Water, Earth (where Metal = Spirit). These 24 strokes group as 888 as (Wood + Fire) + (Metal) + (Water + Earth) = (4 + 4) + (8) + (5 + 3)
25	人生	Ren Sheng	Positional number as (2) + (5)	The Life of Man
26	玉皇大帝	Yu Huang Da Di	26 Strokes as 5 + 9 + 3 + 9 strokes	The Jade Emperor, the supreme deity of Taoism
27	達麻摩	Ta Mo	27 Strokes as 13 + 14 strokes	Ta Mo, the Indian Buddhist founder of Chinese Buddhism
28	萬物	Wan Wu	Positional number as (12 = 2) + (8)	10,000 things; all forms of life; the multiplicity of nature
29	雙魚	Shuang Yu	29 Strokes as 18 + 11 strokes	The two fishes; the Tai Chi or Yin Yang symbol

Key Chinese Stroke Count Characters
for the Number Range 0–33 (cont'd.)

Number	Character	Transliteration	Method of Calculation	Meaning
30		Ts'uan	30 Strokes	Chinese hearth; the cover, the cauldron, and the wood and the fire below
31		Ta Ma	Positional number as (3) + (11 = 1)	Tall hemp (cannabis sativa)
32		Kwan Yin	32 Strokes as 23 + 9 strokes	Goddess of Mercy
33		Shang Sya	Positional number as 3 + 3 strokes	Heaven and Earth, Above and Below, On and Beneath

The square Chinese Regular Style script is the basis for two other languages: Korean and Japanese. The same Taoist method of numbering Chinese can be applied equally to these two languages, for their phonetic variances do not affect the instrinsic number value of the Chinese characters used in each language.

Japanese Buddhist terminology is an extremely rich area of metaphor for the number series. The following table details the calligraphic number metaphors in Japanese for select numbers, supplementing the Chinese examples for the number range 0 through 33.

Additional Stroke Count Metaphors of Japanese Zen Buddhist Terminology for the Number Range 0–33

Number	Character	Transliteration	Method of Calculation	Meaning
2		Ni	Two Strokes	Duality, Buddhist Yin-Yang
3		Ni Ichi	Three Strokes as 2 + 1 strokes	Duality (arising out of) unity
3		Ko	Three Strokes	The self
4		Shin	Four Strokes	Heart, mind, center
4		Kyo	Four Strokes	Evil, bad, unlucky
4		Gen	Four Strokes	Phantom, illusion, vision
5		Sei	Five Strokes	World, age, reign

Additional Stroke Count Metaphors of Japanese Zen Buddhist Terminology for the Number Range 0–33 (cont'd.)

Number	Character	Transliteration	Method of Calculation	Meaning
5	主	Sho	Five Strokes	Birth, origin, to be born
5	囚	Shu	Five Strokes	Prisoner, convict; to be imprisoned, continued
6	回	Kai	Six Strokes	Time; turning wheel, wheel within wheels
6	人心	Jin Shin	Six Strokes as 2 + 4 strokes	The soul (essence) of man
7	身	Shin	Seven Strokes	Body
7	坊	Bo	Seven Strokes	Buddhist priest; residence of priest
7	佛	Butsu	Seven Strokes	Buddha

Additional Stroke Count Metaphors of Japanese Zen Buddhist Terminology for the Number Range 0–33 (cont'd.)

Number	Character	Transliteration	Method of Calculation	Meaning
10	悟	Satori	Ten Strokes	Comprehend, become enlightened; Zen Buddhist meditational awakening (Sa = Heart, Tori = 5 + Mouth)
12	更生	Ko Sei	12 Strokes as 7 + 5 strokes	Rebirth; reborn; reincarnation; (Ko = repeat, Sei = essence)
12	無	Mu	12 Strokes	Zen conception of nothingness or no-thing; be not
13	禅	Zen	13 Strokes	Zen Buddhism; as Chinese Ch'an Buddhism
13	僧	So	13 Strokes	Buddhist monk, priest
13	坐禅	Za-Zen	Positional number as (10 = 1) + (13 = 3)	Zen Buddhist meditation posture; sitting in meditation
13	成仏	Jo Butsu	13 Strokes as 6 + 7 strokes	Becoming Buddha

Additional Stroke Count Metaphors of Japanese Zen Buddhist Terminology for the Number Range 0–33 (cont'd.)

Number	Character	Transliteration	Method of Calculation	Meaning
14	心按	Ko-An	14 Strokes as 4 + 10 strokes	Zen puzzle to help rid the mind of rational thought during meditation
14	一心	Ichi Shin	Positional number as (1) + (4)	The mind is one; One mind; One-pointed mind
14	二申一夛	Ni Yu Ichi Yu	14 Strokes as 2 + 5 + 1 + 6 strokes	Duality arises from unity
20	釆畢誓	Sakya	20 Strokes	Sakyamuni, the Buddha as the Great Teacher; to let go, explain, teach
22	圍木冒	En So	22 Strokes as 13 + 9 strokes	Zen circle in Zen caligraphy; the infinite as a circle; first joined to last
23	釆青乄申	Sei Shin	23 Strokes as 14 + 9 strokes	Essence of mind, soul, divinity
23	心脇藏	Shin Zo	23 Strokes as 4 + 19 strokes	The heart of the body

Additional Stroke Count Metaphors of Japanese Zen
Buddhist Terminology for the Number Range 0–33 (cont'd.)

Number	Character	Transliteration	Method of Calculation	Meaning
23	武士道	Bu Shi Do	23 Strokes as 8 + 3 + 12 strokes	The Way of the Warrior (Samurai)
23	坐禅	Za Zen	23 Strokes as 10 + 13 strokes	The Zen posture of meditation
24	人心	Jin Shin	Positional number as (2) + (4)	The Soul of Man
24	幽霊	Yu Rei	24 Strokes as 9 + 15 strokes	Dark spirit; ghost
24	無心	Mu Shin	Positional number as (12 = 2) + (4)	Zen concept of no-mind
24	禅堂	Zen Do	24 Strokes as 13 + 11	Zen meditation hall
26	達磨	Daru Ma	Positional number as (12 = 2) + (16 = 6)	Daruma, name for the Buddha (Dalrul = path, way, to reach, obtain; Ma = tall, as in hemp, polish, refine)
26	禅僧	Zen So	26 Strokes as 13 + 13 strokes	Zen priest, Zen monk

Additional Stroke Count Metaphors of Japanese Zen Buddhist Terminology for the Number Range 0–33 (cont'd.)

Number	Character	Transliteration	Method of Calculation	Meaning
31	禪堂	Zen Do	Positional number as (13 = 3) + (11 = 1)	Zen meditation hall
33	阿弥爾陀	A Mi Da	33 Strokes as 8 + 17 + 8 strokes	Amitabha or Amida, the Buddha of compassion
33	小丁田日	Ko Zo	Positional number as (3) + (13 = 3)	Novitiate; young Buddhist monk
33	禪僧	Zen So	Positional number as (13 = 3) + (13 = 3)	Zen Buddhist priest
888	阿弥爾陀	A Mi Da	Positional number as 8 + (17 = 8) + 8, where 17 reduces to 1 + 7 = 8, rather than to 7	Amida Buddha, the Buddha of Compassion as Thoth-Jesus

In the last example offered for Japanese, "Amida" is numbered as 888 rather than 887. This number variant is conjectured on the 9 x 9 Chinese magick square whose numbers appearing as diagonals and centers are based on what is known in Western Occultism as *Theosophical reduction*. By this method, any composite number can be reduced to a one-digit number by repeated summations of the individual digits forming the composite number.

In Chu-Ko's Spirit Calculation reduction, only the last digit of a composite number is counted, but by Theosophical reduction each digit of the number is added together until one digit is obtained.

In the case of the Japanese word A-Mi-Da, Mi is formed by 17 strokes. By Chu-Ko's method 17 becomes 7, but by Theosophical reduction 17 becomes 1 + 7, which totals to 8.

One other variant to Chu-Ko's method can be deduced from Fu-Hsi's Yellow River Map. In this diagram, the number 10 can be construed as zero. From this concept of ten as zero, a rule can be conjectured which would allow any stroke count ending in zero to be valued as zero rather than one in the composite digital number. This variant would permit word metaphors for the higher number range of 40, 50, 60, 70, 80, 90, 100, 200, 300, . . . etc.

However, it should be stated that neither these two variations of Theosophical reduction and a positional zero nor the application of stroke-count numbering for the Japanese language are explicitly contained in the Taoist writings of Chu-Ko Liang.

Chu-Ko Liang's original method of calligraphic calculations as outlined in the *T'ung Shu* was oracular in nature. The consultant of the oracle would provide a three-character name to be deemed auspicious or inauspicious. This inquiry would be especially appropriate for the name of a store or business.

The three-character name would be reduced to a three-digit number by Chu-Ko's rules, outlined above. If the resultant number totaled less than 385, no further calculation was required. But if the total number exceeded 384, the number would be reduced by subtracting multiples of 384 until a number 1 through 384 was reached.

After the necessary number was obtained, a book of 384 oracular poems was consulted to determine if the number obtained was auspicious or inauspicious. What is the pattern behind these poems and why was 384 selected?

The answer is found in the *I Ching*, for these 384 poems are based on the 384 lines of Yin and Yang that make up the 64 hexagrams of the *I Ching*. The true key to each of the auspicious and inauspicious meanings for the number range of 1 through 384 is the commentary on the lines by Duke Chou.

Thus after reducing the three selected characters to a number between 1 and 384, the corresponding hexagram line for that specific number is read in light of its oracular symbol. From this symbol, the selected characters can be deemed auspicious or inauspicious.

The following table details each of the oracular meanings for the 384 lines that compose the 64 hexagrams.

Hexagram Key to Chu-Ko's Spirit Calculation for the Numbers 1–384

Number	Hexagram	Yao	Yin/Yang Harmony	Duke Chou Symbol
1	1. Ch'ien (Creative)	1 Yang	Good	Hidden Dragon
2		2 Yang	Poor	Dragon in Field
3		3 Yang	Good	To be active day and night
4		4 Yang	Poor	Dragon's wavering flight over abyss
5		5 Yang	Good	Dragon flying over heaven
6		6 Yang	Poor	Flying dragon falling from the heights
7	2. K'un (Receptive)	1 Yin	Poor	Frost of winter heralds ice
8		2 Yin	Good	Square, straight, great pure will without purpose
9		3 Yin	Poor	Hidden, bring to end what one has begun
10		4 Yin	Good	A sack tied at its mouth
11		5 Yin	Poor	Yellow inner garment brings good luck
12		6 Yin	Good	Fighting dragons with black and yellow blood
13	3. Chun (Difficulty at the Beginning)	1 Yang	Good	Hesitation and hindrance
14		2 Yin	Good	Difficulties accumulate, horse and cart separate
15		3 Yin	Poor	To venture in a strange forest without a guide
16		4 Yin	Good	The need to unite that which is falling apart
17		5 Yang	Good	Difficulties bring blessings
18		6 Yin	Good	Separation causes grief
19	4. Meng (Youthful Folly)	1 Yin	Poor	Discipline removes fetters
20		2 Yang	Poor	To tolerate the shortcomings of others
21		3 Yin	Poor	Do not imitate that which you are not
22		4 Yin	Good	Clinging to illusions brings humiliation
23		5 Yin	Poor	Inexperience brings good fortune
24		6 Yang	Poor	Punishing folly does not bring good fortune

Hexagram Key to Chu-Ko's Spirit Calculation for the Numbers 1–384 (cont'd.)

Number	Hexagram	Yao	Yin/Yang Harmony	Duke Chou Symbol
25	5. Hsu (Waiting)	1 Yang	Good	Waiting in the open field
26		2 Yang	Poor	Waiting in sand by the river
27		3 Yang	Good	Waiting in the mud of the river
28		4 Yin	Good	Waiting in blood; escape from the pit
29		5 Yang	Good	Waiting while eating and drinking
30		6 Yin	Good	One falls into the pit, while three strangers arrive
31	6. Sung (Conflict)	1 Yin	Poor	Do not pursue the issue
32		2 Yang	Poor	Retreat brings no disgrace
33		3 Yin	Poor	Seek not fame nor great works
34		4 Yang	Poor	Turn back and change instead of fighting
35		5 Yang	Good	To influence an arbitrator guarantees success
36		6 Yang	Poor	A reward will be taken away three times
37	7. Shih (Army)	1 Yin	Poor	Order is necessary
38		2 Yang	Poor	The center of the army is rewarded three times
39		3 Yin	Poor	Casualties of war
40		4 Yin	Good	Retreat is necessary
41		5 Yin	Poor	Leadership is necessary
42		6 Yin	Good	Victory of war
43	8. Pi (Holding Together)	1 Yin	Poor	Hold on with truth and loyalty; good fortune from without
44		2 Yin	Good	Inward loyalty brings good fortune
45		3 Yin	Poor	Loyalty to the wrong people
46		4 Yin	Good	Outward loyalty brings good fortune
47		5 Yang	Good	Trap three but let the fourth go; Do not be forever cautious
48		6 Yin	Good	No beginning point for loyalty resulting in misfortune

Hexagram Key to Chu-Ko's Spirit Calculation for the Numbers 1–384 (cont'd.)

Number	Hexagram	Yao	Yin/Yang Harmony	Duke Chou Symbol
49	9. Hsiao Ch'u (The Taming Power of the Small)	1 Yang	Good	Return to one's true path
50		2 Yang	Poor	To allow oneself to be drawn into returning
51		3 Yang	Good	The spokes break off the wheels of the wagon
52		4 Yin	Good	Sincerity dispells blood and fear
53		5 Yang	Good	Sincerity and loyalty brings wealth in your neighborhood
54		6 Yang	Poor	Rain and the (approach of) the Full Moon demand rest
55	10. Lu (Treading)	1 Yang	Good	Simple conduct brings progress
56		2 Yang	Poor	A hermit traverses a smooth and level path to good fortune
57		3 Yin	Poor	To tread on the tail of a tiger and be bitten
58		4 Yang	Poor	To tread on the tail of a tiger with caution and succeed
59		5 Yang	Good	To go ahead aware of all dangers
60		6 Yang	Poor	To succeed now from preparation in the past
61	11. T'ai (Peace)	1 Yang	Good	Good time for work which will attract helpers
62		2 Yang	Poor	To walk the middle path
63		3 Yang	Good	To remain in the face of danger
64		4 Yin	Good	To be on equal terms with others without secrets
65		5 Yin	Poor	To generously appease one's contenders
66		6 Yin	Good	The wall falls into the moat; Do not attack now.
67	12. P'i (Standstill)	1 Yin	Poor	To pull another into retirement
68		2 Yin	Good	To endure a standstill brings success
69		3 Yin	Poor	To bear one's inner shame
70		4 Yang	Poor	To remain blameless by acting at the command of the highest
71		5 Yang	Good	To ensure success by many enterprises
72		6 Yang	Poor	Standstill turns to good fortune

Hexagram Key to Chu-Ko's Spirit Calculation for the Numbers 1–384 (cont'd.)

Number	Hexagram	Yao	Yin/Yang Harmony	Duke Chou Symbol
73	13. T'ung Jen (Fellowship with Men)	1 Yang	Good	To meet at the gate with others
74		2 Yin	Good	To meet with members of the clan
75		3 Yang	Good	To secretly prepare for battle for a period of three years
76		4 Yang	Poor	To mount the wall but not be able to attack
77		5 Yang	Good	To joyfully meet after great struggles
78		6 Yang	Poor	To meet in the open
79	14. Ta Yu (Possession in Great Measure)	1 Yang	Good	Do not have realtionships with harmful things
80		2 Yang	Poor	To be able to undertake something
81		3 Yang	Good	Only a prince can offer all to the Sun of Heaven
82		4 Yang	Poor	To act different from others and escape blame
83		5 Yin	Poor	To unobtrusively offer one's truth to others
84		6 Yang	Poor	To do nothing that does not further
85	15. Ch'ien (Modesty)	1 Yin	Poor	To succeed by being modest about one's modesty
86		2 Yin	Good	To naturally express one's modesty
87		3 Yang	Good	Modesty and merit can carry work to its conclusion
88		4 Yin	Good	Modesty furthers movement and action
89		5 Yin	Poor	Do not boast but attack with energy
90		6 Yin	Good	It is time to set the army marching to chastise one's own country
91	16. Yu (Enthusiasm)	1 Yin	Poor	To show one's enthusiasm brings misfortune
92		2 Yin	Good	To be firm as a rock until inappropriate
93		3 Yin	Poor	Hesitation or need for acknowledgement brings misfortune
94		4 Yang	Poor	Do not doubt and succeed
95		5 Yin	Poor	To persist even when near death
96		6 Yin	Good	To be able to change after one's enthusiasm is deluded

Hexagram Key to Chu-Ko's Spirit Calculation for the Numbers 1–384 (cont'd.)

Number	Hexagram	Yao	Yin/Yang Harmony	Duke Chou Symbol
97	17. Sui (Following)	1 Yang	Good	Time to outwardly act with the force of support from others
98		2 Yin	Good	To sacrifice the strong man for the little boy
99		3 Yin	Poor	To sacrifice the little boy for the strong man
100		4 Yang	Poor	To follow brings success, to persevere on one's own brings misfortune
101		5 Yang	Good	To sincerely follow a good leader
102		6 Yin	Good	To meet with a loyal follower and be brought back to one's group
103	18. Ku (Decay)	1 Yin	Poor	Son corrects father's errors; Danger changes to good fortune
104		2 Yang	Poor	Son cannot correct mother's errors, do not be too persevering
105		3 Yang	Good	Son quickly corrects father's errors; No regret, no blame
106		4 Yin	Good	Son tolerates father's errors, continuing humiliation
107		5 Yin	Poor	Son corrects father's errors and is praised
108		6 Yang	Poor	To set one's goals higher than this world of kings and princes
109	19. Lin (Approach)	1 Yang	Good	To draw one's friends together
110		2 Yang	Poor	To lead a joint venture
111		3 Yin	Poor	One's approach is easy, if thoroughly thought out
112		4 Yin	Good	Ascent to leadership
113		5 Yin	Poor	The wise approach of a prince
114		6 Yin	Good	An honest and open approach brings great fortune
115	20. Kuan (Contempla-tion)	1 Yin	Poor	To view from a great distance
116		2 Yin	Good	To view through a crack of the door
117		3 Yin	Poor	To contemplate between advance and retreat
118		4 Yin	Good	To contemplate the light of the kingdom
119		5 Yang	Good	Contemplation of outer life
120		6 Yang	Poor	Contemplation of inner life

Hexagram Key to Chu-Ko's Spirit Calculation for the Numbers 1–384 (cont'd.)

Number	Hexagram	Yao	Yin/Yang Harmony	Duke Chou Symbol
121	21. Shih Ho	1 Yang	Good	Feet fastened in stocks, toes cut off
122	(Biting	2 Yin	Good	To greedily bite through tender meat
123	Through)	3 Yin	Poor	To bite through poisoned meat and stop eating
124		4 Yang	Poor	To bite through dried meat and discover a metal arrow
125		5 Yin	Poor	To bite through dried meat and discover a piece of yellow gold
126		6 Yang	Poor	Neck fastened in stocks, ears cut off
127	22. Pi	1 Yang	Good	Grace in walking manifested through the toes
128	(Grace)	2 Yin	Good	Gracefulness of a flowing beard
129		3 Yang	Good	Gracefulness of an oiled body
130		4 Yin	Good	White rider upon a white winged horse
131		5 Yin	Poor	To be humbled by lack of funds but through sincerity to win in the end
132		6 Yang	Poor	Simple grace without blame
133	23. Po	1 Yin	Poor	The splitting apart of the legs of a bed
134	(Splitting	2 Yin	Good	The splitting apart of the bed itself
135	Apart)	3 Yin	Poor	To split from companions without blame
136		4 Yin	Good	Splitting apart of bed and occupant
137		5 Yin	Poor	To gain favor in the court through its subordinates
138		6 Yang	Poor	Superior receives a carriage, inferior is split apart
139	24. Fu	1 Yang	Good	To return from a short distance
140	(Return)	2 Yin	Good	To return quietly
141		3 Yin	Poor	The danger of repeatedly returning
142		4 Yin	Good	To return alone amidst others
143		5 Yin	Poor	To return with dignity
144		6 Yin	Good	To miss the chance to return, and be unable to wage war for ten years

Hexagram Key to Chu-Ko's Spirit Calculation for the Numbers 1–384 (cont'd.)

Number	Hexagram	Yao	Yin/Yang Harmony	Duke Chou Symbol
145	25. Wu Wang (Unexpected)	1 Yang	Good	Unexpected fortune
146		2 Yin	Good	No expectations bring success to any undertaking
147		3 Yin	Poor	Undeserved misfortune
148		4 Yang	Poor	Continue striving in spite of the obstacles
149		5 Yang	Good	Error not caused by you will pass
150		6 Yang	Poor	Unexpected misfortune
151	26. Ta Ch'u (The Taming Power of the Great)	1 Yang	Good	Stop, for danger is at hand
152		2 Yang	Poor	The axles of the wagon are stolen
153		3 Yang	Good	A horse, aware of danger, following others to safety
154		4 Yin	Good	Restraining the horns of a young bull
155		5 Yin	Poor	The unmenacing tusks of a gelded boar
156		6 Yang	Poor	The way to heaven is obtained
157	27. I (Corners of the Mouth)	1 Yang	Good	To be envious after letting go of one's magick
158		2 Yin	Good	Reliance on superiors brings misfortune
159		3 Yin	Poor	Deviating from the source, do not act for ten years
160		4 Yin	Good	To gain support from above on account of one's spies
161		5 Yin	Poor	To turn away from the path to gain strength to continue one's journey
162		6 Yang	Poor	To be connected to the source, aware of all dangers, and able to complete one's journey

Hexagram Key to Chu-Ko's Spirit Calculation for the Numbers 1–384 (cont'd.)

Number	Hexagram	Yao	Yin/Yang Harmony	Duke Chou Symbol
163	28. Ta Kuo (Preponderance of the Great)	1 Yin	Poor	To set a heavy object down cautiously
164		2 Yang	Poor	An older man is regenerated by a younger woman and sprouts at the root
165		3 Yang	Good	The ridgepole holding the roof sags to the breaking point
166		4 Yang	Poor	The ridgepole is braced, supporting the roof
167		5 Yang	Good	An older woman is regenerated by a younger man and blooms as a flower
168		6 Yin	Good	Passing through water over one's head
169	29. K'an (The Abysmal Water)	1 Yin	Poor	Falling into the pit of the abyss
170		2 Yang	Poor	The danger of the abyss prohibits large undertakings
171		3 Yin	Poor	The abyss is before and behind, requiring one to wait and pause before advancing
172		4 Yin	Good	To simply pass wine and rice through a window
173		5 Yang	Good	The abyss filled only to the rim and not overflowing
174		6 Yin	Good	Imprisoned and bound, for three years one does not find the way
175	30. Li (The Clinging Fire)	1 Yang	Good	The crisscrossing of paths
176		2 Yin	Good	Good fortune as a yellowish golden light
177		3 Yang	Good	To frolic or lament with the setting of the Sun
178		4 Yang	Poor	To suddenly flame up, die down and be consumed
179		5 Yin	Poor	The tears of old age herald good fortune
180		6 Yang	Poor	To kill the leader and capture the followers

Hexagram Key to Chu-Ko's Spirit Calculation for the Numbers 1–384 (cont'd.)

Number	Hexagram	Yao	Yin/Yang Harmony	Duke Chou Symbol
181	31. Hsien (Influence)	1 Yin	Poor	The intention to move is shown in the toes
182		2 Yin	Good	Staying brings misfortune, tarrying brings good fortune
183		3 Yang	Good	Hold back ready to follow, rather than on one's present course
184		4 Yang	Poor	One's mind must not be agitated in order to lead
185		5 Yang	Good	One's influence is as strong as the back of the neck
186		6 Yin	Good	To influence through talking
187	32. Heng (Duration)	1 Yin	Poor	Do not hastily seek anything enduring
188		2 Yang	Poor	The disappearance of remorse
189		3 Yang	Good	Without enduring character one meets disgrace
190		4 Yang	Poor	No game to hunt in the field
191		5 Yin	Poor	To be unchanging is good for a woman, bad for a man
192		6 Yin	Good	Continual restlessness brings misfortune
193	33. Tun (Retreat)	1 Yin	Poor	Danger by being at the tail of the retreat
194		2 Yin	Good	To hold fast so that no one can break free
195		3 Yang	Good	The dangers and fears of a retreat which must halt
196		4 Yang	Poor	Voluntary retreat benefits the superior but is the downfall of the inferior
197		5 Yang	Good	Friendly retreat at the right moment
198		6 Yang	Poor	Cheerful retreat serves only to further
199	34. Ta Chung (The Power of the Great)	1 Yang	Good	Power in advancing will bring misfortune
200		2 Yang	Poor	To persist will result in success
201		3 Yang	Good	A goat is entangled by its horns in a hedge
202		4 Yang	Poor	An entangled goat is freed from a hedge
203		5 Yin	Poor	To lose a charging goat with ease
204		6 Yin	Good	A goat butts against a hedge, unable to advance or retreat

Hexagram Key to Chu-Ko's Spirit Calculation for the Numbers 1–384 (cont'd.)

Number	Hexagram	Yao	Yin/Yang Harmony	Duke Chou Symbol
205	35. Chin (Progress)	1 Yin	Poor	Remain calm if not met with confidence at first
206		2 Yin	Good	In sorrow persist to the end, giving honor to one's ancestors
207		3 Yin	Poor	All is in balance
208		4 Yang	Poor	To continue to amass wealth will bring misfortune
209		5 Yin	Poor	Do not let loss or gain affect one's heart
210		6 Yang	Poor	To advance by attack is permissible only against one's own people
211	36. Ming I (Darkening of the Light)	1 Yang	Good	The light is darkened during flight
212		2 Yin	Good	Wounded by the darkening of the light, advance is made with the strength of a horse
213		3 Yang	Good	The leader is captured while hunting in the South on account of the darkening of the light
214		4 Yin	Good	To go through the very heart of the darkening of the light and leave through the gate
215		5 Yin	Poor	To not be able to leave but persevere instead during the darkening of the light
216		6 Yin	Good	Darkness first climbs to heaven then falls to earth
217	37. Chia Jen (The Clan)	1 Yang	Good	Withdraw back into the family and all remorse will disappear
218		2 Yin	Good	Do not follow your whims, but rather your duty
219		3 Yang	Good	At this point too much severity is preferable to too much play
220		4 Yin	Good	She is the treasure of the clan (house)
221		5 Yang	Good	Do not fear the approach of the King, he will bring good fortune
222		6 Yang	Poor	Work which commands respect will bring good fortune

Hexagram Key to Chu-Ko's Spirit Calculation for the Numbers 1–384 (cont'd.)

Number	Hexagram	Yao	Yin/Yang Harmony	Duke Chou Symbol
223	38. K'uei (Opposition)	1 Yang	Good	Do not seek after one's lost horse, for it shall return on its own accord
224		2 Yang	Poor	To meet one's lord on a narrow street
225		3 Yin	Poor	Bad beginning but good end
226		4 Yang	Poor	Finding an ally in the middle of dangerous opposition
227		5 Yin	Poor	A friend is revealed who was at first not recognized
228		6 Yang	Poor	Companions who were at first enemies are now allies
229	39. Chien (Obstruction)	1 Yin	Poor	Going will be obstructed, coming will be praised
230		2 Yin	Good	Obstacle upon obstacle will appear, not the result of one's own actions
231		3 Yang	Good	Going forward one is blocked and must come back
232		4 Yin	Good	Union cannot be achieved by going but rather by coming
233		5 Yang	Good	An ally is revealed amidst one's greatest obstruction
234		6 Yin	Good	Departure will be blocked; arrival will be rewarded with good fortune
235	40. Hsieh (Deliverance)	1 Yin	Poor	To break through all obstructions without blame
236		2 Yang	Poor	The hunt kills three foxes in the field and receives a yellow arrow
237		3 Yin	Poor	Do not carry upon your back that which your carriage can carry
238		4 Yang	Poor	At the time of deliverance free oneself of the inferior to attract the superior
239		5 Yin	Poor	Only the superior can deliver oneself, bringing no blame from the inferior
240		6 Yin	Good	A hawk on a high wall is shot with the prince's arrow

Hexagram Key to Chu-Ko's Spirit Calculation for the Numbers 1–384 (cont'd.)

Number	Hexagram	Yao	Yin/Yang Harmony	Duke Chou Symbol
241	41. Sun (Decrease)	1 Yang	Good	One can quickly finish the task, if such completion will not decrease the work of others
242		2 Yang	Poor	One can increase others in service without a decrease to self
243		3 Yin	Poor	A journey of three is reduced to two; a journey of one is increased to two
244		4 Yin	Good	Decrease of one's faults, increases one's comrades
245		5 Yin	Poor	Ten oracles will not deny one's increase coming from someone else
246		6 Yang	Poor	If one can increase oneself without depriving others, the understanding will be successful
247	42. I (Increase)	1 Yang	Good	It will further to accomplish great deeds
248		2 Yin	Good	The king presents one before God, increase and good fortune
249		3 Yin	Poor	By keeping to the middle path, one's lot is increased during misfortune
250		4 Yin	Good	One's impartiality is needed in the money affairs of the prince
251		5 Yang	Good	A kind heart will be rewarded without petition on account of one's virture
252		6 Yang	Poor	An unsteady heart causes someone to strike, resulting in misfortune
253	43. Kuai (Break Through)	1 Yang	Good	If one is not prepared or equal to the task when rushing to battle, a mistake will be made
254		2 Yang	Poor	If one is on guard day and night, one has nothing to fear
255		3 Yang	Good	Be true to oneself when falsely judged by the friends one keeps
256		4 Yang	Poor	One really does not want the independence one has and secretly desires to be led
257		5 Yang	Good	When weeding out obstruction, walk resolutely down the middle
258		6 Yin	Good	If one is not thorough, misfortune will come

Hexagram Key to Chu-Ko's Spirit Calculation for the Numbers 1–384 (cont'd.)

Number	Hexagram	Yao	Harmony	Yin/Yang Duke Chou Symbol
259	44. Kou (Coming to Meet)	1 Yin	Poor	A weakness must be checked, else misfortune will eventually come
260		2 Yang	Poor	One must contain the weak element, else all will be spoiled
261		3 Yang	Good	One must be mindful of the danger, else a great mistake will be made
262		4 Yang	Poor	That which was contained escapes creating danger
263		5 Yang	Good	That which was hidden drops down from heaven
264		6 Yang	Poor	To meet with others aggressively now will only bring blame
265	45. Ts'ui (Gathering Together)	1 Yin	Poor	Being sincere from beginning to end will allow one to call out for help without blame
266		2 Yin	Good	Allow oneself to be drawn by another, and if one is sincere bring a small offering
267		3 Yin	Poor	Allying oneself with others only to commiserate will bring no good
268		4 Yang	Poor	To gather together brings great fortune
269		5 Yang	Good	One's position in the gap must stimulate all others into the work
270		6 Yin	Good	Lamenting over the inability to come together may ultimately bring about the alliance
271	46. Sheng (Pushing Upward)	1 Yin	Poor	Pushing upward at the beginning of the ascent meets with success
272		2 Yang	Poor	When attempting to ascend, a small offering given sincerely meets with success
273		3 Yang	Good	One ascends to an empty city
274		4 Yin	Good	One's ascent is met with gifts from the King
275		5 Yin	Poor	Ascent which has been taken step by step meets with success
276		6 Yin	Good	Ascending to the top, one meets with darkness which must be conquered with unceasing will

Hexagram Key to Chu-Ko's Spirit Calculation for the Numbers 1–384 (cont'd.)

Number	Hexagram	Yao	Yin/Yang Harmony	Duke Chou Symbol
277	47. K'un (Oppression)	1 Yin	Poor	When all resources are exhausted one must depend exclusively on one's will
278		2 Yang	Poor	To set forth brings misfortune; to offer sacrifice brings fortune
279		3 Yin	Poor	To permit oneself to be oppressed now will obscure what one really has
280		4 Yang	Poor	To reach the end by humiliating means is permitted
281		5 Yang	Good	When oppressed from above and below one must make sacrifices to advance
282		6 Yin	Good	Even though bound at the feet, an effort to escape brings release
283	48. Ching (The Well)	1 Yin	Poor	The mud of an old well cannot quench one's thirst
284		2 Yang	Poor	Fish caught in a container escape when the container breaks
285		3 Yang	Good	Although the well is now clean, no one will draw from it
286		4 Yin	Good	The well must be repaired before drawing from it
287		5 Yang	Good	The well provides cold, clear water for all to drink
288		6 Yin	Good	The well can be drawn from again and again
289	49. Ko (Revolution)	1 Yang	Good	To hide oneself in activities which will attract little attention
290		2 Yin	Good	When the right time comes, revolution should be undertaken
291		3 Yang	Good	Do not initiate any change until it has been considered three times
292		4 Yang	Poor	The belief by many will allow the change of the government
293		5 Yang	Good	One is changed into a tiger whose force is beyond the prediction of the oracle
294		6 Yin	Good	To leave and hide brings misfortune; to stay and fight like a panther brings fortune

Hexagram Key to Chu-Ko's Spirit Calculation for the Numbers 1–384 (cont'd.)

Number	Hexagram	Yao	Yin/Yang Harmony	Duke Chou Symbol
295	50. Ting (The Cauldron)	1 Yin	Poor	To turn over the cauldron before using it to clean out that which would block
296		2 Yang	Poor	Food in one's cauldron brings envy but not harm
297		3 Yang	Good	The handles of the cauldron do not allow the cauldron to be used
298		4 Yang	Poor	The legs of the cauldron break, bringing misfortune by spilling over on one's guests
299		5 Yin	Poor	The golden rings of the cauldron permit easy use
300		6 Yang	Poor	The jade rings of the cauldron brings great fortune
301	51. Chen (The Arousing)	1 Yang	Good	The shock of fear turns to laughter
302		2 Yin	Good	Only by not pursuing what one has just lost can the lost object be recovered
303		3 Yin	Poor	Let the shock of change spur one into action rather than despair
304		4 Yang	Poor	Shock stops all action
305		5 Yin	Poor	Shock awakens one to the tasks which still must be done
306		6 Yin	Good	Ruin and misfortune which have affected others may not yet reach oneself
307	52. Ken (Keeping Still)	1 Yin	Poor	To remain still at this moment brings no blame
308		2 Yin	Good	By remaining still one cannot rescue the person one is following
309		3 Yang	Good	To remain still will suffocate the desires of the heart
310		4 Yin	Good	To keep the heart still brings no blame
311		5 Yin	Poor	To keep quiet will allow self composure and an ordering of thoughts
312		6 Yang	Poor	The noble effort to remain still when one does not desire to brings good fortune

Hexagram Key to Chu-Ko's Spirit Calculation for the Numbers 1–384 (cont'd.)

Number	Hexagram	Yao	Yin/Yang Harmony	Duke Chou Symbol
313	53. Chien (Development)	1 Yin	Poor	The wild goose slowly drawing near to the shore in its long flight
314		2 Yin	Good	The wild goose flies safely near the cliff over the ocean
315		3 Yang	Good	The wild goose flies off course over a plateau which it cannot conquer
316		4 Yin	Good	The wild goose flies near a tree hoping to land on a branch
317		5 Yang	Good	The wild goose flies to the top of the summit without hindrance
318		6 Yang	Poor	The wild goose flies to the heights of the clouds
319	54. Kuei Mei (The Marrying Maiden)	1 Yang	Good	To undertake brings good fortune
320		2 Yang	Poor	To persevere alone furthers
321		3 Yin	Poor	To win by being subservient to another
322		4 Yang	Poor	That which should be rewarded will come in its due course
323		5 Yin	Poor	The near Full Moon brings good fortune
324		6 Yin	Good	No act at the present will further the goal
325	55. Feng (Abundance)	1 Yang	Good	A man seeking his destined ruler will meet with recognition
326		2 Yin	Good	What one seeks can only be obtained through truth
327		3 Yang	Good	Though being hindered to rule, there is no blame
328		4 Yang	Poor	One meets one's ruler who is of like kind
329		5 Yin	Poor	Blessing and fame draw near
330		6 Yin	Good	To obtain one's goal will cause the present inhabitants to abandon their castle

Hexagram Key to Chu-Ko's Spirit Calculation for the Numbers 1–384 (cont'd.)

Number	Hexagram	Yao	Yin/Yang Harmony	Duke Chou Symbol
331	56. Lu	1 Yin	Poor	Do not bog oneself down with trivial matters
332	(The Wanderer)	2 Yin	Good	To travel with one's property intact
333		3 Yang	Good	The inn to which one has wandered burns down, bringing danger
334		4 Yang	Poor	To be forced to protect one's property in a new environment
335		5 Yin	Poor	To shoot a pheasant with one arrow
336		6 Yang	Poor	The misfortunes of others visits oneself
337	57. Sun	1 Yin	Poor	To persevere as a warrior when advancing or retreating
338	(The Gentle)	2 Yang	Poor	To unveil the hidden with the aid of priests and magicians
339		3 Yang	Good	To repeatedly push brings misfortune
340		4 Yin	Good	Three kinds of game are caught during the hunt
341		5 Yang	Good	Good fortune occurs before and after the change
342		6 Yang	Poor	To deeply understand the situation brings loss and misfortune
343	58. Tui	1 Yang	Good	Joy resulting from contentedness
344	(The Joyous)	2 Yang	Poor	Joy which is sincere
345		3 Yin	Poor	The joy which comes brings misfortune
346		4 Yang	Poor	After mistakes are corrected joy comes
347		5 Yang	Good	To help that which is falling apart will bring misfortune on oneself
348		6 Yin	Good	Joy which is seductive

Hexagram Key to Chu-Ko's Spirit Calculation for the Numbers 1–384 (cont'd.)

Number	Hexagram	Yao	Yin/Yang Harmony	Duke Chou Symbol
349	59. Huan (Dispersion)	1 Yin	Poor	Help is brought with the strength of a horse
350		2 Yang	Poor	After dissolution, one runs to that which offers support
351		3 Yin	Poor	To sacrifice the self in order to gain the goal
352		4 Yin	Good	Good fortune comes about from severing the bond to the group
353		5 Yang	Good	To disperse the group which you rule with sweat, and escape the crisis at hand
354		6 Yang	Poor	To depart from the group like the dissolution of blood
355	60. Chieh (Limitation)	1 Yang	Good	Not passing through the door brings no blame
356		2 Yang	Poor	Not leaving through the courtyard brings misfortune
357		3 Yin	Poor	To know no limitation will eventually cause lament
358		4 Yin	Good	Limitations are contended resulting in success
359		5 Yang	Good	Limitation brings good fortune, going out engenders esteem
360		6 Yin	Good	To persevere in the light of limitations will result in misfortune
361	61. Chung Fu (Inner Truth)	1 Yang	Good	Being prepared and well informed of all intrigues brings success
362		2 Yang	Poor	To share what one has with others
363		3 Yin	Poor	To share the joys and sorrows of life with one's comrades
364		4 Yin	Good	The lead horse temporarily goes astray, the Full Moon peeks out
365		5 Yang	Good	To possess truth which links all together
366		6 Yang	Poor	A crow attempts to fly to heaven

Hexagram Key to Chu-Ko's Spirit Calculation for the Numbers 1–384 (cont'd.)

Number	Hexagram	Yao	Yin/Yang Harmony	Duke Chou Symbol
367	62. Hsiao Kuo (Preponderance of the Small)	1 Yin	Poor	A bird in flight meets with misfortune
368		2 Yin	Good	To not meet one's appointment but to meet with another instead
369		3 Yang	Good	Someone may strike from behind if one is not careful
370		4 Yang	Poor	To not act and thereby be passed by, escaping harm
371		5 Yin	Poor	Dense clouds which give no rain
372		6 Yin	Good	To be passed by, bringing misfortune
373	63. Chi Chi (After Completion)	1 Yang	Good	To brake the wheels, correcting one's course
374		2 Yin	Good	To not run after what is lost and thereby recover it in seven days
375		3 Yang	Good	To not use inferior help to accomplish that which must be waged for a long time
376		4 Yin	Good	The finest clothes can be turned to rags
377		5 Yang	Good	That which is offered with the most sincerity engenders the greatest happiness
378		6 Yin	Good	To get in over one's head becomes dangerous
379	64. Wei Chi (Before Completion)	1 Yin	Poor	To be humiliated by getting one's tail in the water
380		2 Yang	Poor	To correct one's course brings good fortune
381		3 Yin	Poor	To attack before completion brings misfortune
382		4 Yang	Poor	To persevere and struggle at this moment can bring completion
383		5 Yin	Poor	The light of the superior man is true before completion is accomplished
384		6 Yang	Poor	To not be overexuberant before completion

The preceding tables can be used for spirit calculation oracles as well as *I Ching* oracles when changing lines are encountered in casting a hexagram.

In light of the *I Ching,* one other method can be used in conjunction with the concept of stroke count. By using two characters and reducing each to the number range 1 through 9, a hexagram can be generated in which the stroke count of the first character corresponds to the inner trigram while the second character corresponds to the outer trigram. The Lo Shu Number Map is used to determine which trigram is which number. If 5 is calculated as a stroke count, another character must be selected.

Ultimately, the Taoist stroke-count technique can wed the elaborate Yin-Yang cosmology of the *I Ching* with the numbering of the Chinese language and create an oracular method which enhances both.

ANNOTATED ESSENTIAL BIBLIOGRAPHY

This listing of reference material is an attempt to capture the essential texts utilized in the formation of *The Key of It All*. Literally hundreds of texts have been read, reread, digested, and internalized to bring about the all-emcompassing scope of this book. However, only the primary sources which were at hand at the time of the actual writing of the *The Key of It All* have been incorporated into this bibliography.

In all subject matters covered in this book, my understanding and insight have stemmed from my own self-taught regime of instruction. My grasp of the myriad of languages employed within this book is dependent upon the many and varied books which are documented in this bibliography. All phonetic renditions of foreign languages have been extracted directly from the source books used in this text, and in the case of such languages as Chinese, many different systems have been combined in the body of the text. Possibly future revisions of this book can correct this unavoidable inconsistency.

Because I have been able to approach this subject from the vantage point of an occult researcher rather than an academic scholar, I have been able to advance the traditional correspondences of esoteric schools beyond the range of any books in print. For, truly, a purely academic approach to the art of gematria would result in disproving that a valid correspondence can exist between word and number. I have therefore tailored my book to every earnest student on the path of Qabalistic knowledge, supplying him or her with the map and compass necessary to explore an otherwise uncharted universe.

This bibliography is arranged topically to correspond to the major trends found in the book itself. Some references can fall under more than one topic.

0. Overview

Numbers and Symbols

Blavatsky, Helena Petrovna. "Occult Systems: Alphabets and Numerals," in *Collected Writings*, vol. XIV. Wheaton, IL: The Theosophical Publishing House, 1985.

A good overview showing the Theosophical viewpoint concerning the mystical use of sacred alphabets as numbers. Much of Blavatsky's writings address the Qabalistic use of alphabet-numbers.

Bond, Bligh, and Thomas Lea. *Gematria: A Preliminary Investigation of the Cabala*. London: R.I.L.K.O., 1977.

One of the most important 20th-century studies on gematria, dealing chiefly with the Greek Qabalah.

Case, Paul Foster. *The Magical Language*. Los Angeles: B.O.T.A., privately printed.

These writings by Paul Foster Case are the highwater mark of Masonic-Qabalistic research concerning gematria. Deals with the Hebrew, Greek, and Latin Qabalahs.

Higgins, Frank C. *Ancient Freemasonry*. New York: Pyramid Book Company, 1923.

Primary source for the Qabalistic research of Paul Foster Case. Appeared first as articles in the magazine *Azoth* during the period when Case was editor for this magazine.

Higgins, Godfrey. *Anacalypsis, an Attempt to Draw Aside the Veil of the Saitic Isis; or, an Inquiry into the Origin of Languages, Nations and Religions*. London: Longman, Rees, et.al., 1836.

An early sourcebook for all subsequent research concerning the occult origins of language and number.

Kozminsky, Isidore. *Numbers, Their Meaning and Magic*. 1912. Reprint. New York: Samuel Weiser, Inc., 1972.

An admixture of real Qabalistic knowledge with pseudo-Qabalistic numerology. Typical of the times.

MacKenzie, Kenneth. *The Royal Masonic Cyclopedia*. 1877. Reprint. Wellingborough, Northamptonshire: The Aquarian Press, 1987.

Contains many articles of Qabalistic-Masonic alphabet ciphers. A sourcebook for the teachings of the Masonic order, the Hermetic Order of the Golden Dawn.

Mathers, S. L. MacGregor. *The Kabbalah Unveiled.* 1926. Reprint. New York: Samuel Weiser, Inc., 1974.

The introduction to this text, by Mathers, is the most lucid and concise article ever written in English on gematria and the Qabalah at large.

Mitchell, John. *City of Revelations.* London: Garnstone Press, 1972.

A modern extension of the primary field work of Bond and Lea.

Sepherial. *The Kabala of Numbers.* Philadelphia: David McKay Company, n.d.

A perfect specimen of pseudo-Qabalistic research.

Skinner, J. Ralston. *Key to the Hebrew-Egyptian Mystery in the Source of Measures Originating the British Inch and the Ancient Cubit.* 1875. Reprint. Savage, MN: Wizards Bookshelf, 1972.

The classic text in which measurements in inches and cubits are equated to the Hebrew and Greek number-letter symbolism.

Stirling, William. *The Canon: An Exposition of the Pagan Mystery Perpetuated in the Cabala as the Rule of All the Arts.* 1897. Reprint. London: Garnstone Press, 1974.

A wonderful study of the symbolic use of alphabets as numbers, greatly influencing the studies of Bond and Lea.

Westcott, W. Wynn. *Numbers: Their Occult Power and Mystic Virtues.* 1890. Reprint. New York: Allied Publication, n.d.

An excellent example of a standard reference available to students of the Golden Dawn regarding the symbolic meaning of certain numbers.

ORIGIN OF ALPHABET NUMERALS FROM A SCIENTIFIC VIEWPOINT

Andrews, W. S. *Magic Squares and Cubes.* New York: Dover Publications, 1960.

Contains a historical overview regarding the development of magic squares.

Bell, E. T. *The Development of Mathematics.* New York: McGraw Hill, 1945.

The standard reference in the field for early number systems. The Greek and Babylonian alphanumeric systems are outlined, as well as the Sanskrit Aryabhata code.

Brunes, Tons. *The Secrets of Ancient Geometry and Its Use*. Copenhagen: International Science Publishers, 1967.

This work would just as easily be entered under the previous section, for it bridges the scholar's and occultist's viewpoints.

Cajori, Florian. *A History of Mathematical Notations*. Chicago: Open Court Publishing Co., 1928.

Discusses the less obscure alphanumeric systems such as Hebrew and Greek.

Diringer, David. *The Alphabet: A Key to the History of Mankind*. New York: Philosophical Library, 1948.

Focuses only on the Hellenistic-Semitic alphanumeric systems.

Ifrah, Georges. *From One to Zero: A Universal History of Numbers*. New York: Viking Penguin, 1985.

The most thorough non-occultist approach to the alphanumeric tradition. Does not address the codes found in the Sanskrit, Tibetan, or Chinese esoteric traditions.

Jensen, Hans. *Sign, Symbol and Script: An Account of Man's Efforts to Write*. London: George Allen & Unwin, 1970.

A far-reaching account of many of the esoteric alphanumeric codes. Discusses both the Runes and Ogham, as well as Hebrew, Greek, Arabic, and Georgian.

Neugebauer, O. *The Exact Sciences in Antiquity*. New York: Dover Publications, 1969.

Much information on Babylonian and Hellenistic astronomy and mathematics.

Van der Waerden, B. L. *Science Awakening*. Groningen, Netherlands: Wolters Noordhoff Publishing, n.d.

A mathematician's discussion of Egyptian, Babylonian, and Hellenistic systems, including an essential overview of Pythagorean mathematics.

The Book of the Law

Achad, Frater (George Stansfield Jones). *The Anatomy of the Body of God*. New York: Samuel Weiser, Inc., 1969.

Includes the Tree of Life as both an ever-expanding and a three-dimensional model. Throws light on some obscure passages of *The Book of the Law*.

——————. *The Egyptian Revival*. New York: Samuel Weiser, Inc., 1973.

Connects the Egyptian deities of *The Book of the Law* with the revived public interest in things Egyptian during the discovery of King Tut's tomb.

——————. *Liber 31 and Other Related Essays*. San Francisco: Level Press, 1974.

The major Qabalistic proofs of *The Book of the Law* by the magickal child, Frater Achad.

——————. *Q.B.L., or The Bride's Reception*. New York: Samuel Weiser, Inc., 1969.

Contains early extracts from Achad's magickal diaries before his revelation as the magickal child. The basis for Achad's reversal of the Tree of Life is also found in this book, which severed him from Crowley for the remainder of his life

——————. *XXXI Hymns to the Star Goddess*. Montreal: 93 Publishing, 1974.

The essence of Achad's vision concerning *The Book of the Law* in a poetical format.

Crowley, Aleister. *The Book of Lies*. New York: Samuel Weiser, Inc., 1978.

A set of cryptic Qabalistic poems, many that interpret passages from *The Book of the Law*. The book which caused Crowley's rapid advancement in the O.T.O.

——————. *The Book of the Law*. New York: Samuel Weiser, Inc., 1976.

This version is the last publication of *The Book of the Law* by Crowley (1938). Contains the original holographic version of the text.

——————. *The Book of the Law*. Quebec: 93 Publishing, 1975.

An attempt to reset the typed version of *The Book of the Law* in light of the original holographic version. Manuscript and typescript are side by side for easy comparison. The puzzle in Chapter II, verse 76, is correct in format only in this published version.

——————. *The Commentaries of AL*. Edited by Marcelo Motta. New York: Samuel Weiser, Inc., 1975.

The most incomplete version of Crowley's commentaries on *The Book of the Law*.

—————————. *The Equinox,* I:1-10 and III:1. New York: Samuel Weiser, Inc., 1978 and 1974.

These eleven magazines put out by Crowley on the equinoxes from 1909 to 1919 serve as the best source for understanding the magickal symbolism contained in *The Book of the Law.* This series is indispensible for the study of Crowleyanity.

—————————. *The Equinox of the Gods.* Great Britain: privately printed by the O.T.O., 1936.

Crowley's final word on *The Book of the Law.* Contains a facsimile of the original manuscript, hidden in the back cover of the book.

—————————. *The Law is for All.* Edited by Israel Regardie. St. Paul, MN: Llewellyn Publications, 1975.

The old and new commentaries by Crowley concerning The Book of the Law; more reliable than Motta's version.

—————————. *Liber Aleph, or The Book of Wisdom or Folly.* San Francisco: Level Press, 1974.

A series of Qabalistic letters to the magickal child, Frater Achad

—————————. *Magical and Philosophical Commentaries on The Book of the Law.* Edited by John Symmonds and Kenneth Grant. Montreal: 93 Publishing, 1974.

The best published collection of Crowley's commentaries; includes *The Commentary called D, by 666,* found nowhere else.

—————————. *Magick.* Edited by John Symonds and Kenneth Grant. New York: Samuel Weiser, Inc., 1974.

Crowley's best dissertation on the subject of magick, including many references to *The Book of the Law.*

—————————. Θελημα: The Holy Books of Thelema. Edited by Hymenaeus Alpha and others. New York: Samuel Weiser, Inc., 1983.

A compendium of Crowley's Holy Books. Contains a detailed analysis of the verses found on the Stele of Revealing.

—————————. *The Secret Rituals of the O.T.O.* Edited by Francis King. London: C. W. Daniel Company, 1973.

The complete rituals of the German Masonic group as revised by Aleister Crowley in light of The Book of the Law. King's introduction documents the lack of a true lineage to the O.T.O. since the death of Karl Germer in 1962.

Freemasonry, Magick, Rosicrucianism, and Theosophy

Allen, Paul M., ed. *A Christian Rosenkreutz Anthology*. Blauvelt, NY: Rudolf Steiner Publications, 1974.

The most exhaustive anthology to date of Rosicrucian literature and art.

Barrett, Francis. *The Magus: A Complete System of Occult Philosophy*. Secaucus, NJ: The Citadel Press, 1967.

A glimpse of English magick from the beginning of the 19th century.

Blanchard, Charles A. *Revised Knight Templarism Illustrated*. Chicago: Ezra A. Cook, 1947.

A complete detailing of the six Templar degress found in Freemasonry. Though an exposé of Freemasonry, the information offered is a testament to the beauty of the rituals.

Blavatsky, H. P. *Collected Writings*. 14 volumes. Wheaton, IL: The Theosophical Publishing House, Wheaton, IL: 1977.

The Theosophical equivalent to Crowley's *Equinox* series: the complete writings of Blavatsky.

——————. ed. *Five Years of Theosophy*. Los Angeles: The Theosophy Company, 1980.

Gems collected from the first five years of *The Theosophist*.

——————. *Isis Unveiled*. Wheaton, IL: The Theosophical Publishing House, 1972.

Blavatsky's first attempt to synthesize science with theology, the same aim as Crowley's *Equinox* series.

——————. *The Secret Doctrine*. Wheaton, IL: The Theosophical Publishing House, 1978.

Blavatsky's final word on the origin of both the universe and mankind.

——————. *Theosophical Glossary*. Los Angeles: The Theosophy Company, 1973.

A contributor to this compendium of Theosophical terms was Wynn Westcott, one of the three founders of the Golden Dawn.

Case, Paul Foster. *The True and Invisible Rosicrucian Order*. York Beach, ME: Samuel Weiser, Inc., 1985.

The Masonic grades of the Golden Dawn in light of their Hebraic-Tarot symbolism. Case was the Imperator of the Chicago Thoth-Hermes Golden Dawn Temple in the early 1920s.

Colquhoun, Ithell. *Sword of Wisdom*. New York: G. P. Putnam's Sons, 1975.

A compelling study of the origins of the Golden Dawn, which links the magickal basis of the order to the genius of S.L. MacGregor Mathers.

Crowley, Aleister: *Book 4*. Dallas, TX: Sangreal Foundation, 1972.

The simplest and most straightforward statement concerning the theory and practice of modern Golden Dawn derivative magick.

——————, ed. *The Book of the Goetia, or The Lesser Key of Solomon the King*. Mokelumne Hill, CA: Health Research, 1976.

The classic text on demonic invocation, probably translated by Mathers rather than Crowley.

Duncan, Malcolm C. *Duncan's Masonic Ritual and Monitor*. 3rd ed. New York: David McKay Company, Inc., n.d.

A good illustrated exposition of the first three degrees of the Ancient York Rite comprising the Blue Lodge of Freemasonry.

Hall, Manly P. *Codex Rosae Crucis*. Los Angeles: The Philosophical Research Society, Inc., 1974.

A valuable collection of Rosicrucian manuscripts and commentary.

——————. *An Encyclopedia Outline of Masonic, Hermetic, Qabbalistic and Rosicrucian Symbolical Philosophy*. The Golden Anniversary Edition. Los Angeles: The Philosophical Research Society, Inc., 1977.

This all encompassing work is an important addition to any library. Though brief in his entries, Manly P. Hall's scope of interest in the occult was encyclopedic.

Harper, George Mills. *Yeats's Golden Dawn: The Influence of the Hermetic Order of the Golden Dawn on the Life and Art of W. B. Yeats*. Wellingborough, Northamptonshire: The Aquarian Press, 1987.

Primary source material concerning the Golden Dawn, not found in other published studies. Contains much information about the alleged forgery of the cipher manuscript.

Howe, Ellic. *The Magicians of the Golden Dawn*. New York: Samuel Weiser, Inc., 1978.

A fascinating study of the Golden Dawn, showing its origins to be in the hands of Dr. Wynn Westcott and S. L. MacGregor Mathers. Though not written from an occultist's viewpoint, there is much pertinent magickal information.

King, Francis. *Sexuality, Magic and Perversion*. Secaucus, NJ: The Citadel Press, 1974.

A great book, for its title if nothing else. A must for every occultist's bookshelf.

Levi, Eliphas. *Transcendental Magick: Its Doctrine and Ritual*. New York: Samuel Weiser, Inc., 1974.

Eliphas Levi's most thorough exposition on magick. A study of mid-19th-century ritual magick.

Mackenzie, Kenneth. *The Royal Masonic Cyclopædia*. Wellingborough, Northamptonshire: The Aquarian Press, 1987.

The most esoteric of the 19th-century Masonic encyclopedias; a sourcebook for Golden Dawn teachings.

Mackey, Albert G., and Charles T. McClenachan. *Encyclopædia of Freemasonry*. Revised edition. Chicago: Masonic History Company, 1927.

An extensive Masonic encyclopedia, containing clues to the real password, or lost word, of the third degree.

——————. *Manual of the Lodge*. New York: Clark and Maynard, 1870.

In combination with Duncan's *Ritual of Freemasonry,* a key to understanding the true significance of the first three degrees of Freemasonry.

Mathers, S. L. MacGregor. *The Book of the Sacred Magic of Abra-melin the Mage*. 1897. Reprint. New York: Causeway, 1974.

A Qabalistic ritual for obtaining the knowledge and conversation of one's Holy Guardian Angel. Crowley in working with this material turned all the letters appearing in the magickal squares into Enochian.

——————. *The Key of Solomon the King*. 1888. Reprint. New York: Samuel Weiser, Inc., 1976.

The classic magickal text for invocation and command of the demonic and angelic planes. Contains the magick square of SATOR AREPO TENET OPERA ROTAS as the second pentacle of Saturn.

McIntosh, Christopher. *Eliphas Levi and the French Occult Revival*. London: Rider and Company, 1975.

An adequate biography of Eliphas Levi, dealing with all aspects of his life.

——————. *The Rosy Cross Unveiled*. Wellingborough, Northamptonshire: The Aquarian Press, 1980.

A very thorough investigation of the Rosicrucian phenomenon. The best introductory overview to the subject.

McLean, Adam. *The Magical Calendar*. Edinburgh: Magnum Opus Hermetic Sourceworks, 1980.

All of McLean's *Magnum Opus Hermetic Sourceworks* series are worth having: lucid translations of major hermetic treatises, unavailable elsewhere. This particular work translates the complete magickal calendar attributed to Tycho Brahe.

Regardie, Israel. *The Golden Dawn*. 1940. Reprint. St. Paul, MN: Llewellyn Publications, 1970.

This compendium of Golden Dawn material, largely derived from Crowley's early *Equinox* series, remains the most accurate rendition of the core of Golden Dawn magical techniques.

—————. *The Complete Golden Dawn System of Magic*. Phoenix, AZ: Falcon Press, 1984.

This revised anthology of Golden Dawn teachings contains much new information based on earlier material than that used for Regardie's first version of this book. However the essential tables in the main body of the text must be corrected by swapping the attributes of King with Prince (the revised Golden Dawn Court Card titles).

Ryan, Charles J. *H. P. Blavatsky and the Theosophical Movement*. Pasadena, CA: Theosophical University Press, 1975.

A sympathetic and orthodox view of Madame Blavatsky's life. Contains reference to Blavatsky and the Boulak Museum of Cairo.

Symonds, John. *The Lady with the Magic Eyes: Madame Blavatsky— Medium and Magician*. New York: Thomas Yoseloff, 1960.

An unorthodox view of H.P.B. Like Crowley, Blavatsky is dealt with in an unsympathetic manner. However, much material is unique to this book, since Symonds had direct access to original Theosophical material.

Torrens, R. G. *The Secret Rituals of the Golden Dawn*. Wellingborough, Northamptonshire: The Aquarian Press, 1973.

Another rendition of the Golden Dawn rituals, based on manuscript material prior to Regardie's source.

Waite, A. E. *The Brotherhood of the Rosy Cross*. London: Rider and Son, Ltd., 1924.

Waite's best attempt at describing the Rosicrucian movement. Contains a reproduction of one page of the Golden Dawn cipher manuscript, printed upside down in the text.

——————. *The Real History of the Rosicrucians*. London: George Redway, 1887.

Waite's first attempt at a history of the Rosicrucians. Includes a contemporary view of the 19th-century Rosicrucian movement in England.

Walker, D. P. *Spiritual and Demonic Magic from Ficino to Campanella*. London: University of Notre Dame Press, 1975.

A historian's viewpoint of Renaissance magick written by a colleague of Francis Yates.

Webb, James. *The Occult Underground*. La Salle, IL: Open Court Publishing Co., 1974.

The best overview of 19th-century magick from a non-magickal viewpoint. Highly recommended.

——————. *The Occult Establishment*. La Salle, IL: Open Court Publishing Co.,1976.

Companion to *The Occult Underground*, this volume spans the 20th century.

1. Key One

Cuneiform

King, L. W. *Babylonian Religion and Mythology*. London: Kegan Paul, Trench, Trubner & Co., 1899.

An excellent overview of the Babylonian hierarchy of the Gods.

Lenormant, Francois. *Chaldean Magic: Its Origin and Development*. London: S. Bagster and Sons, 1877.

Early sourcebook for the magickal use of Cuneiform.

Mercer, Samuel A. B. *A Sumero-Babylonian Sign List*. New York: AMS Press, Inc., 1966.

Includes an Assyrian sign list, as well as thorough tables cataloging examples of numerals, weights, and measures.

Pinches, T G., and J. N. Strassmaier. *Late Babylonian Astronomical and Related Texts*. Providence, RI: Brown University Press, 1955.

Many examples of Cuneiform as number. A compilation of Cuneiform tablets without translation.

Prince, J. Dyneley. *Assyrian Primer: An Inductive Method of Learning Cuneiform Characters*. New York: AMS Press, Inc., 1966.

A sound introduction to Cuneiform.

Rawlinson, George. *The Five Great Monarchies of the Ancient Eastern World*. New York: Stokes and Allen, 1870.

Complete description of the dimensions for the temple at Borsippa known as the Tower of Babel.

Sayce, A. H. *Astronomy and Astrology of the Babylonians*. San Diego: Wizards Bookshelf, 1981.

The best compilation of esoteric Cuneiform tablets, including a word-for-word transliteration and translation as well as the original Cunieform.

Simon, ed. *The Necronomicon*. New York: Schlangekraft, Inc., 1977.

Contains reference to the Babylonian correspondences of planetary god names as Cuneiform numerals.

Sollberger, Edmond. *The Babylonian Legend of the Flood*. London: British Museum, 1971.

Information concerning the Gilgamesh saga. Examples of original Cuneiform tablets.

Walker, C. B. F. *Cuneiform*. Berkeley: University of California Press, 1987.

A very readable introduction to Cuneiform.

II. Key Two

Hebrew

Crowley, Aleister. *Sepher Sephiroth*, in *The Equinox* I.8. New York: Samuel Weiser, Inc., 1978.

The first attempt in English to compile a number dictionary derived from Hebrew gematria.

Gesenius, Wiliam. *Hebrew and Chaldee Lexicon to the Old Testament Scriptures*. Edited by S. P. Tregelles. Grand Rapids, MI: Wm. B. Eerdmans Publishing Company,1978.

The best dictionary for biblical Hebrew. Indispensable for all Hebrew gematria research.

Jastrow, Marcus. *A Dictionary of the Targumim, the Talmud Babli and Yerushalmi, and the Midrashic Literature.* New York: Judaica Press, 1975.

Important companion volume for Gesenius' Hebrew Lexicon in regards to gematria research.

Landman, Isaac, ed. *The Universal Jewish Encyclopedia.* New York: Universal Jewish Encyclopedia, Inc., 1940.

Important information can be found under the entry for gematria.

Marks, John H., and Virgil M. Rogers. *A Beginner's Handbook to Biblical Hebrew.* New York: Abingdon Press, 1958.

An excellent introduction to biblical Hebrew.

Munk, Rabbi Michael L. *The Wisdom in the Hebrew Alphabet.* Brooklyn, NY: Mesorah Publications, Ltd., 1983.

An exhaustive collection of traditional Qabalistic symbolism for the Hebrew alphabet.

Roth, Cecil. *Encyclopedia Judaica.* New York: MacMillan Co., 1972.

Articles concerning the Qabalah and gematria are rich in information not found elsewhere. A very detailed history of gematria is contained in the article on the subject.

Singer, Isidore. *The Jewish Encyclopedia.* New York: Ktav Publishing House, 1964.

The best in Jewish encyclopedias, disclosing much unique information regarding the Qabalah and gematria. The rules for numbering vowel points can be found in the fifth volume under the article on gematria.

Wigram, George V. *The Englishman's Hebrew and Chaldee Concordance.* London: Samuel Bagster and Sons, Ltd., 1963.

The best cross-reference in Hebrew to the Old Testament.

SEPHER YETZIRAH

Book of Formation: The Letters of Our Father Abraham. Los Angeles: Work of the Chariot, 1970.

This unique version of the *Sepher Yetzirah* includes an original version in Rock Hebrew as well as Square Hebrew. Many tables and illustrations.

Friedman, Irving. *The Book of Creation.* New York: Samuel Weiser, Inc., 1977.

A modern rendition of the *Sepher Yetzirah* with commentary.

Kalisch, Isidor. *Sepher Yezirah: A Book on Creation, or The Jewish Metaphysics of Remote Antiquity.* New York: L. H. Frank & Co., 1877.

The most accurate version of the *Sepher Yetzirah.* Includes original text.

Mordell, Phineas. *The Origin of Letters and Numerals According to the Sefer Yetzirah.* New York: Samuel Weiser, Inc., 1975.

An attempt to reduce the original text to 10 Paths instead of 32 Paths of Wisdom.

Stenring, Knut. *The Book of Formation.* 1923. Reprint. New York: Ktav Publishing House, Inc., 1970.

This translation includes an introduction by Waite. Appendices to text detail a Qabalistic-astrological system different from that of the Golden Dawn.

Suares, Carlo. *The Sepher Yetsira, Including the Original Astrology According to the Qabalah and Its Zodiac.* Boulder, CO: Shambhala Publications, Boulder, 1976.

An original interpretation of the *Sepher Yetzirah* based on the hieroglyphic attributes of every Hebrew letter appearing in the original version of the Hebrew text.

Westcott, W. Wynn. *Sepher Yetzirah: The Book of Formation and the Thirty Two Paths of Wisdom.* New York: Samuel Weiser, Inc., N.Y., 1975.

A new translation, supposedly from the original Hebrew but most likely from Latin.

TREE OF LIFE

Crowley, Aleister. *777: Second Revision, a Reprint of 777 with Much Additional Matter by the Late Aleister Crowley.* San Francisco: Level Press,privately printed c. 1969.

The best reference work of Crowley for both the literal Qabalah and the symbolic correspondences for the 32 Paths of Wisdom which form the Qabalistic Tree of Life.

Fortune, Dion. *The Mystical Qabalah.* London: Ernest Benn, Ltd., 1966.

A restatement of both Mathers' and Crowley's research regarding the 32 Paths of the Tree of Life.

Knight, Gareth. *A Practical Guide to Qabalistic Symbolism.* London: Helios Book Service, 1965.

The most comprehensive discussion of the 32 Paths of the Tree of Life in light of the Tarot.

Papus. *The Qabalah*. Wellingborough, Northamptomshire: Thorsons Publishers, Ltd., 1983.

The best insight into the late 19th-century French school of Qabalistic symbolism.

Regardie, Israel. *A Garden of Pomegranates*. St. Paul, MN: Llewellyn Publications, 1970.

A good supplement to Crowley's and Fortune's works on the Tree of Life.

QABALAH

Bischoff, Dr. Erich. *The Kabbala*. c. 1910. Reprint. York Beach, ME: Samuel Weiser, Inc., 1985.

First published in Germany, this small essay as a series of questions and answers is the best introduction to the Qabalah.

Blau, Joseph Leon. *The Christian Interpretation of the Cabala in the Renaissance*. New York: Columbia University Press, 1944.

A good overview of the Renaissance link between the modern Qabalah of the Golden Dawn and the Jewish Qabalah of the Middle Ages.

Kaplan, Aryeh, trans. *The Bahir*. New York: Samuel Weiser, Inc., 1979.

An important translation of an ancient Qabalistic text dating back to the first century CE.

Scholem, Gershom. *Major Trends in Jewish Mysticism*. New York: Schocken Books, 1967.

The standard reference work for the Hebrew Qabalah from an historian's viewpoint.

—————. *On the Kabbalah and Its Symbolism*. New York: Schocken Books, 1969.

Should be read in conjunction with *Major Trends in Jewish Mysticism*.

Sperling, Harry, trans. *The Zohar*. 5 volumes. London: The Soncino Press, 1956.

The best English translation of the *Zohar*, the most important book in the corpus of Hebrew Qabalistic literature.

Waite, Arthur Edward. *The Holy Kabbalah*. New York: University Books, n.d.

The most extensive discussion of the Qabalah from a Christian Renaissance viewpoint.

III. Key Three

Arabic, Persian, and Georgian

Ali, A. Yusuf, trans. *The Holy Qur'an*. United States: McGregor and Werner, 1946.

Much information on alphabet symbolism in the annotations to the text.

Aronson, Howard I. *Georgian: A Reading Grammar*. Columbus, OH: Slavica Publishers, Inc., 1982.

One of the few English introductions to Georgian.

Bakhtiar, Laleh. *Sufi: Expressions of the Mystic Quest*. New York: Avon Books, 1976.

Chapters dealing with the science of letters, mystical poetry, and sacred geometry.

Burckhardt, Titus. *Mystical Astrology According to Ibn 'Arabi*. Gloucetershire: Beshara Publications, 1977.

The astrological attributions of the Arabic alphabet.

Chisti, Shaykh Hakim Moinuddin. *The Book of Sufi Healing*. New York: Inner Traditions International, Ltd., 1985.

Sections dealing with Arabic and Persian number mysticism.

Friedlander, Shems. *Ninety-Nine Names of Allah*. New York: Harper & Row, 1978.

A beautiful rendition of the 99 names of God, including a description of the powers inherent in each name.

Penrice, John. *A Dictionary and Glossary of the Kur-an*. London: Curzon Press, Ltd., 1976.

A very mystical dictionary concerning Koranic Arabic.

Scott, Charles T. *Persian and Arabic Riddles*. Bloomington: Indiana University Press, 1965.

Shows the use of the secret number language in Persian and Arabic poetry.

Shah, Idries. *The Sufis*. London: The Octagon Press, 1984.

Shah through his own scholarship has repeatedly demonstrated the Sufi adage that the path of the scholar is not that of enlightenment. Contains chapters on alphabet-number symbolism.

Steingass, F. *Persian-English Dictionary*. London: Routledge and Kegan Paul, Ltd., 1977.

The best Persian-English dictionary, containing much mystical lore.

Gurdjieff's Enneagram and Step Diagram

Bennett, J. G. *Enneagram Studies*. York Beach, ME: Samuel Weiser, Inc., 1983.

A very thorough exposition of the pattern behind the nine points of the enneagram.

Da Silva, Andrew J. *Do from the Octave of Man Number Four*. New York: Borderline Press, 1985.

A discussion of both the enneagram and the octave as Gurdjieffian symbols.

Ouspensky, P. D. *In Search of the Miraculous*. New York: Harcourt Brace Jovanovich, 1977.

Includes a record of all of Gurdjieff's early teachings regarding both the enneagram and the step diagram.

Popoff, Irmis B. *The Enneagrama of the Man of Unity*. New York: Samuel Weiser, Inc. 1978.

A profusely illustrated study of the enneagram.

Speeth, Kathleen Riordan. *The Gurdjieff Work*. New York: Pocket Books, 1978.

A simplified approach to the symbolism of the Gurdjieffian Work. A workable introduction for the beginner.

Tereshchenko, Nicolas. *A Look at Fourth Way Work*. Edinburgh: Hermetic Research Series, 1983.

A discussion of the esoteric aspects of Gurdjieff, including references to both the enneagram and the step diagram.

Walker, Kenneth. *Gurdjieff: A Study of His Teachings*. London: Unwin Paperbacks, 1979.

A very lucid discussion of Gurdjieff's teachings, including reference to the number symbolism.

IV. Key Four

Sanskrit

Apte, V. S. *The Student's Sanskrit-English Dictionary*. Delhi: Motilal Banarsidass, 1973.

Many magickal definitions for the Sanskrit alphabet.

Buhler, G. *Indian Paleography*. Calcutta: Indian Studies, Past and Present, 1962.

The sixth chapter deals with Numeral Notation systems.

Datta, Bibbutibhusan. *History of Hindu Mathematics: A Source Book*. Bombay: Asia Publishing House, 1962.

The most complete study of the Sanskrit alphabet as a numeric system.

Leidecker, Kurt F. *Sanskrit: Essentials of Grammar and Language*. New York: The Anchorite Press, 1934.

The best introductory overview of the Sanskrit Language.

MacDonnell, Arthur Anthony. *A Practical Sanskrit Dictionary*. London: Oxford University Press, 1965.

The standard reference work in the field.

——————. *A Vedic Reader for Students*. Madras: Oxford University Press, 1972.

A good sourcebook for annotated Sanskrit passages from the Vedas.

Tirthaji, Bharati Krsna. *Vedic Mathematics*. Delhi: Motilal Banarsidass, 1971.

A discussion of the Ka-Ta-Pa-Ya-Dhi code as the key to the Vedas by an acquaintance of Yogananda.

Tyberg, Judith M. *The Language of the Gods: Sanskrit Keys to India's Wisdom*. Los Angeles: East-West Cultural Centre, 1976.

A marvelous overview of the great Sanskrit classics in the original. Discusses in depth both the chakra and Tattva systems.

Chakras

Johari, Harish. *Chakras*. Vermont: Destiny Books, 1987.

Contains information on the chakras found nowhere else, such as animal movements and hand mudras.

Leadbeater, C. W. *The Chakras*. Wheaton, IL: The Theosophical Publishing House, 1977.

The classic Theosophical text on the chakras. Displaces the second chakra from the genitals to the spleen out of prudishness. The psychic illustrations for the chakras are used throughout Crowley's *Book of Thoth*.

Mookerjee, Ajit. *Tantra Art: Its Philosophy and Physics*. Ravi Kumar, 1983.

The most beautiful compilation of Tantrik art in English. Many references to both the chakra and Tattva systems.

——————. *Tantra Asana: A Way to Self-Realization*. New Delhi: Ravi Kumar, 1971.

Companion piece to *Tantra Art*. A must for the study of the Tantrik path.

Motoyama, Hiroshi. *Theories of the Chakras: Bridge to Higher Consciousness*. Wheaton, IL: The Theosophical Publishing House, 1984.

A modern Theosophical study of the chakras, correcting the errors found in Leadbeater's classic. Also contains modern scientific measurements of the chakra system.

Rawson, Philip. *The Art of Tantra*. Greenwich, CT: New York Graphic Society, Ltd., 1973.

An in-depth study of the philosophy of Tantra as portrayed in meditational Tantrik art. Much information on the chakra system

Woodroffe, Sir John. *The Serpent Power*. Madras: Ganesh & Co., 1964.

The authoritative text on the Tantrik chakra system. Still used in modern research such as Motoyama.

27 [Sri Lokanath]. "Twenty Seven." *Sothis Magazine* 2.2, 1977.

This article gives the names of 15 of the 16 Kalas (magickal secretions of the yoni), the 16th being the elixir Amrita.

V. KEY FIVE

TIBETAN

Buck, Stuart H. *Tibetan-English Dictionary with Supplement*. Washington, D.C.: The Catholic University of America Press, 1960.

A good introductory dictionary to Tibetan.

Chogyam, Ngakpa. *Rainbow of Liberated Energy*. Longmead, Shaftesbury, Dorset: Element Books, 1986.

A discussion of the Tibetan alphabet in light of color and elemental symbolism.

Das, Sarat Chandra. *A Tibetan-English Dictionary with Sanskrit Synonyms*. Berkeley: Shambhala Booksellers, 1974.

The most complete Tibetan-English dictionary, replete with mystical terminology.

Evans-Wentz, W. Y. *Tibetan Yoga and Secret Doctrines*. London: Oxford University Press, 1967.

Contains esoteric symbolism of the Tibetan alphabet.

TATTVA

Abbott, John. *The Keys of Power: A Study of Indian Ritual and Belief*. Secaucus, NJ: University Books, 1974.

A comprehensive study of magic in Indian thought, including references to the Tattva system.

Blavatsky, H. P. *Collected Writings,* vol. XII (1889-1890). Wheaton, IL: The Theosophical Publishing House, 1980.

Includes the instructions to the esoteric school, which details the Theosophical Tattva system.

Crowley, Aleister. *The Equinox* I:4. New York: Samuel Weiser, Inc., 1978.

Contains Crowley's essays on both the Tattva and chakra systems, found in part IV of "The Temple of Solomon the King."

Gilbert, R. A., ed. *The Sorcerer and His Apprentice*. Wellingborough, Northamptonshire: The Aquarian Press, 1983.

Contains essays by both S. L. MacGregor Mathers and J. W. Brodie-Innes on the Tattva system.

Govinda, Lama Anagarika. *Foundations of Tibetan Mysticism*. New York: Samuel Weiser, Inc., 1974.

The sourcebook for the Tibetan Tattva system based upon the mandala of the five Dhyani-Buddhas.

―――――. *Psycho-Cosmic Symbolism of the Buddhist Stupa*. Emeryville, CA: Dharma Publishing, 1976.

The link between the five Tibetan Tattvas and the Buddhist Stupa.

Kanga, D. D., ed. *Where Theosophy and Science Meet.* Madras: Adyar Library Association, 1938.

Contains a Theosophical correlation of the five Tattvas to the Sanskrit alphabet of 49 letters.

King, Francis, ed. *Astral Projection, Ritual Magic and Alchemy.* New York: Samuel Weiser, Inc., 1975.

Contains rare essays by Mathers on Tattva astral projection.

——————. *Tantra for Westerners.* New York: Destiny Books, 1986.

Discusses the Tattvas, as well as the chakras, from both an Eastern and a Western viewpoint. Gives Tattvic tide tables.

Prasad, Rama. *The Science of Breath and the Philosophy of the Tattvas.* New York: Theosophical Publishing Society, 1894.

The basis for both the Theosophical and Golden Dawn versions of the Tattva system. Includes a translation of the eighth chapter of the *Shivagama,* devoted entirely to Tattva lore.

VI. Key Six

Chinese

Fenn, C. H. *The Five Thousand Dictionary.* Harvard University Press, Cambridge, 1979.

The standard reference work in the field: 5,000 basic characters in Chinese. Not Mandarin, but Wade Romanization.

Legeza, Laszlo, and Philip Rawson. *Tao: The Eastern Philosophy of Time and Change.* London: Avon Books, 1973.

A good overview of Taoist philosophy epitomized in Taoist art.

——————. *Tao Magic: The Chinese Art of the Occult.* New York: Pantheon Books, 1975.

Includes many examples of magickal Chinese caligraphy.

Palmer, Martin, ed. *T'ung Shu: The Ancient Chinese Almanac.* Boston: Shambhala, 1986.

Section 29 details Chu-ko's spirit calculation, which gives number to Chinese characters by their intrinsic stroke count.

Wieger, L. *Chinese Characters: Their Origin, Etymology, History, Classification, and Signification*. New York: Dover Publications, Inc., 1965.

This book imbues a magick into the very characters of Chinese.

Wolff, Diane. *Chinese for Beginners*. New York: Barnes and Noble Books, 1985.

A sound introduction to modern Chinese.

Yee, Chiang. *Chinese Calligraphy: An Introduction to Its Aesthetic and Technique*. Cambridge: Harvard University Press, 1973.

A beautiful book offering examples of every major style of Chinese calligraphy

I CHING

Crowley, Aleister. *Shih Yi*. Monthelema, Oceanside, CA: H. Parsons Smith, 1971.

This is Crowley's versification of the *I Ching* and is one of the most relevent divinatory texts for the *I Ching*. Both Crowley's *Liber 777* and *Book of Thoth* contain additional information on the *I Ching*.

Govinda, Lama Anagarika. *The Inner Structure of the I Ching*. San Francisco: Wheelwright Press, 1981.

Extensive diagrams on the Tibetan Buddhist and Chinese Taoist esoterica concerning the *I Ching*.

Jou, Tsung Hwa. *The Tao of I Ching, Way to Divination*. Taiwan: Tai Chi Foundation, 1984.

An important translation and commentary of the *I Ching*, including much information appearing in no other translation. Used extensively in the version of the *I Ching* appearing in Key 6 of this book.

Legge, James. *I Ching: Book of Changes*. 1882. Reprint. New York: Bantam Books, 1969.

Crowley's own source for the oracular meaning of the *I Ching*.

Palmer, Martin, with Kwok Man Ho and Joanne O'Brien. *The Fortune Teller's I Ching*. New York: Ballantine, 1986.

A new translation based on the Imperial edition of 1715 CE.

Trosper, Barry R., and Gin-Hua Leo. *I Ching: The Illustrated Primer*. San Jose, CA: KGI Publications, 1986.

A sumptuous version of the *I Ching*, giving much oracular advice for each of the 64 hexagrams.

Whincup, Greg. *Rediscovering the I Ching*. Garden City, NY: Doubleday & Company, Inc., 1986.

A scholarly new translation of the *I Ching,* reducing the *I Ching* to its essential original commentary.

Wilhelm, Richard, and Cary F. Baynes. *I Ching or Book of Changes*. Princeton, NJ: Princeton University Press, 1967.

Though often unjustly criticized by modern researchers, this one version of the *I Ching* is the most important translation in understanding the real pattern behind the *I Ching*. Used throughout the version of the *I Ching* found in Key 6 of this book.

Taoist Cosmology and Cosmogony

Carus, Paul. *Chinese Astrology: Early Chinese Occultism*. La Salle, IL: Open Court, 1974.

Contains much information regarding the ten heavenly stems, the twelve earthly branches, the eight trigrams, the sixty-year cycle, and the five basic Chinese elements. Originally published in 1907 as *Chinese Thought*.

Chang, Stephen T. *The Great Tao*. San Francisco: Tao Publishing, 1985.

A textbook dealing with all aspects of Taoist magick, though at times the Taoist symbol sets described are at variance from their traditional allocations.

Crowley, Aleister, trans. *The Tao Teh King: Being the Equinox, Vol. III, No. 8*. Kings Beach, CA: Thelema Publications, 1976.

The best versification of Lao Tzu's *Tao Teh King,* replete with footnotes connecting Chinese Taoism to Thelemic Qabalah. Crowley's mathematical formula of $0 = 2$ is described in light of the Taoist void (0), which contains in potential both yin and yang (2).

Legeza, Laszlo. *Tao Magic: The Chinese Art of the Occult*. New York: Pantheon Books, 1975.

A sourcebook for examples of Taoist calligraphic script.

Lip, Evelyn. *Feng Shui: A Layman's Guide to Chinese Geomancy*. Union City, CA: Heian International, Inc., 1987.

A very thorough introduction to Chinese geomancy, including tables delineating the Taoist attributes of the elements, the eight trigrams, the ten heavenly stems, and the twelve earthly branches.

Po-Tuan, Chang. *The Inner Teachings of Taoism*. Trans. Thomas Cleary. Boston: Shambhala, 1986.

A systematic overview of the basic elements found in the symbolic language of Taoist alchemy.

Rawson, Philip, and Laszlo Legeza. *Tao: The Eastern Philosophy of Time and Change*. New York: Avon Books, 1973.

An insightful analysis of Chinese Taoist art in light of the symbolism of Yin and Yang.

Walters, Derek. *Chinese Astrology*. Wellingborough, Northamptonshire: The Aquarian Press, 1987.

The most thorough delineation of every aspect of Chinese Taoist astrology, including the symbolism of the nine-celled magick square.

Wilhelm, Richard, and C. G. Jung. *The Secret of the Golden Flower*. New York: Harcourt, Brace and World, Inc., 1962.

An esoteric treatise dealing with the circulation of Chi in Taoist internal Alchemy.

JAPANESE

Dykstra, Andrew. *Kanji 1–2–3*. Los Altos, CA: William Kaufmann, Inc., 1983.

A good introduction to the stroke count of traditional Japanese calligraphy. Dykstra's viewpoint borders on the mystical.

Hall, Manly Palmer. *First Principles of Philosophy*. Los Angeles: Philosophical Research Society, Inc., 1942.

Contains the Chinese Ch'an Buddhist version of the Ten Bulls, with illustrations.

Kapleau, Philip. *The Three Pillars of Zen: Teaching, Practice, Enlightenment*. New York: Beacon Press, 1967.

Contains a version of the Zen Buddhist Ten Oxherding Pictures with illustrations and commentary.

Koop, Albert, and Hogitaro Inada. *Japanese Names and How to Read Them*. 1923. Reprint. London: Routledge and Kegan Paul, 1961.

The most esoteric of Japanese-English dictionaries. Includes a chapter on symbolic numerical categories ranging from 2 through 100. The typesetting of this dictionary, first published in 1923, is superb.

O'Neill, P. G. *Essential Kanji*. Japan: Weatherhill, 1985.

An easy to use Japanese-English dictionary of 2,000 basic Japanese characters. The stroke count of each character is clearly delineated.

Reps, Paul. *Zen Flesh, Zen Bones.* Japan: Charles E. Tuttle Co., 1965.

The one book to have concerning Zen Buddhism. Contains the Japanese Ten Bulls by Kakuan, with illustrations, as well as 101 Zen stories, The Gateless Gate, and Centering.

Sakade, Florence. *A Guide to Reading and Writing Japanese.* Japan: Charles E. Tuttle Co., 1984.

A good companion volume to O'Neill's *Essential Kanji*.

Sogen, Omori, and Terayama Katsujo. *Zen and the Art of Calligraphy*. London: Routledge and Kegan Paul, 1983.

A good overview of Zen calligraphy, which is derived from the Chinese Taoist Ts'ao-Shu or Grass Style script, a script which defies the numbering of a character by its stroke count.

Wood, Ernest. *Zen Dictionary*. New York: Philosophical Library, 1962.

The best dictionary of its kind. Contains a description of the Soto Zen Doctrine of Five Circles.

c	k	a	l	M
i	8	8	☿	a
g	8	1	8	g
a	8	8	8	i
M	n	a	i	c

INDEX